Researching Interactive Communication Behavior

A Sourcebook of Methods and Measures

SAGE was founded in 1965 by Sara Miller McCune to support the dissemination of usable knowledge by publishing innovative and high-quality research and teaching content. Today, we publish over 900 journals, including those of more than 400 learned societies, more than 800 new books per year, and a growing range of library products including archives, data, case studies, reports, and video. SAGE remains majority-owned by our founder, and after Sara's lifetime will become owned by a charitable trust that secures our continued independence.

Los Angeles | London | New Delhi | Singapore | Washington DC

Researching Interactive Communication Behavior

A Sourcebook of Methods and Measures

C. Arthur VanLear
University of Connecticut

Daniel J. Canary
University of Utah

Los Angeles | London | New Delhi
Singapore | Washington DC

Los Angeles | London | New Delhi
Singapore | Washington DC

FOR INFORMATION:

SAGE Publications, Inc.
2455 Teller Road
Thousand Oaks, California 91320
E-mail: order@sagepub.com

SAGE Publications Ltd.
1 Oliver's Yard
55 City Road
London EC1Y 1SP
United Kingdom

SAGE Publications India Pvt. Ltd.
B 1/I 1 Mohan Cooperative Industrial Area
Mathura Road, New Delhi 110 044
India

SAGE Publications Asia-Pacific Pte. Ltd.
3 Church Street
#10-04 Samsung Hub
Singapore 049483

Printed in the United States of America

ISBN 978-1-4833-0320-4

Acquisitions Editor: Matthew Byrnie
eLearning Editor: Gabrielle Piccininni
Editorial Assistant: Janae Masnovi
Production Editor: Libby Larson
Copy Editor: Jim Kelly
Typesetter: C&M Digitals (P) Ltd.
Proofreader: Jennifer Grubba
Indexer: Will Ragsdale
Cover Designer: Glenn Vogel
Marketing Manager: Ashlee Blunk

This book is printed on acid-free paper.

16 17 18 19 20 10 9 8 7 6 5 4 3 2 1

CONTENTS

PREFACE

THE PURPOSE of this anthology is to present, in one sourcebook, discussions of various issues and methods that are necessary to anyone interested in observing communication behaviors, observational research, and actual interaction. Interaction behaviors constitute a necessary and vital feature of communicative processes, wherein people engage one another using messages, directly perceive those messages, and interpret the meaning of those messages. Interaction behaviors constitute the linchpin for linking people to one another through communication processes. In other words, systematic observations of interaction behavior are fundamental to building a science of communication.

Moreover, systematic observation of interaction behavior greatly benefits researchers who connect communication to related factors, such as relationship stability and satisfaction, gaining compliance, health outcomes, and a host of other factors. To qualify as an "interaction behavioral measure," a measure must be based on direct observation of behavior as it actually occurs—not as self-reports of recalled behavior or any other method that does not record actual interaction. Of course, the codes or scalar values that are actually analyzed represent only the significant features of behaviors as constructed by a researcher using a measurement or category system. However, those codes or values are reliably linked directly to the stimulus properties of the behaviors as they occur during interaction. Although a researcher may use alternative methods (e.g., experimentation, survey) in conjunction with or to complement observational research of communication, this sourcebook focuses solely on the observation of communication behaviors.

This sourcebook addresses a number of conceptual issues related to interaction behaviors and research; it also strives to help researchers "hit the ground running" in designing and conducting observational research. The sourcebook will help both experienced and new researchers translate observed behaviors into usable information to facilitate the most appropriate and useful data analysis techniques available today.

In addition, people teaching observational analysis and methods that require actual interaction should find this sourcebook invaluable. Obviously, researchers planning studies of communication processes will find the book a resource for planning those studies. Such studies can build on the work of other scholars working with the variables these observational systems represent. However, the audience for this book is not limited to communication scholars and students. The methods and observational systems covered have broad applicability, and they have been extensively used by researchers from a variety of disciplines studying individual differences in behavior, social and personal relationships, group dynamics, and other domains of behavior.

Beyond using this book to help develop theory, other reasons warrant the use of observations of interaction behavior. One reason involves how observations by researchers can capture processes that fly below the cognitive radar of participants. Markman and Notarius (1987) stated, "Perhaps the most salient factor mandating observational research is the inability of interactants to describe the ongoing behavioral process, that is, contemporary patterns of interaction" (p. 331). Because they are not computers, people are severely handicapped at recalling their own interaction; for instance, people cannot provide accurate accounts of their own or their partners' communication (Sillars, Roberts, Leonard, & Dunn, 2000), and they certainly cannot provide faithful descriptions of interaction sequences composed of dozens or hundreds of interlocking behaviors. Furthermore, people process and react to certain "spontaneous behaviors" through preattunements that may never reach conscious awareness (Buck & VanLear, 2002). Only researchers using observational methods can systematically depict interaction processes.

Importantly, the vast majority of researchers concur that observations of actual interaction can help explain and predict the quality of people's personal relationships. For instance, Gottman, Markman, and Notarius (1977) found that distressed (dissatisfied, unstable) couples differed from nondistressed couples in their communication behavior. For example, distressed couples were more likely than nondistressed couples to express feelings about problem, mind-read, agree, and disagree; all of these behaviors involved negative emotion. In addition, nondistressed partners used more agreement with neutral affect than did their distressed counterparts. We also know that interparental conflicts affect children in various ways. For example, destructive parental conflict has been closely linked to children's psychological adjustment (e.g., McCoy, George, Cummings, & Davis, 2013). Even when perceptions of behavior produce the effect, it is of little use to tell people, "Be perceived as supportive," or "Be seen as immediate," or "Don't be so domineering," without providing a description of the behavioral features that can be associated with these constructs.

Finally, observed interaction behaviors have been connected to people's physical and mental health (see Denes, Afifi, & Hesse, this volume). For example, the use of negative conflict messages, especially when coupled with loud and fast vocalics, leads to cardiovascular problems, negative hormonal adaptations, and immunological lapses (e.g., Kiecolt-Glaser, McGuire, Robles, & Glaser, 2002). It is essential to continue observations of couple communication, as people are interested to know how their communication behaviors link to health outcomes.

This book is divided into three parts. The first part comprises reviews of behavioral systems within four selected domains. The authors review a variety of behavioral measures and coding systems used to study conflict, family interaction, nonverbal communication, and physiological behaviors and measures. The second part highlights in-depth treatments of specific methods, measurements, and/or category systems of both verbal and nonverbal behaviors. The third part addresses general issues or concerns that cut across domains and measures. These include coding, reliability and validity, and the analysis and modeling of behavioral interaction as a jointly coordinated mutually adaptive process.

We first thank all of the authors for agreeing to share their expertise and for making good on their agreements. We especially appreciate their timeliness, responsiveness, and understanding as we coordinated the initial and revised versions of their chapters during the editorial process. As the reader will see, all contributors present informative and insightful chapters regarding observational research of interaction. We also acknowledge our respective departments and universities—the departments of communication at the University of Connecticut and the University of Utah—for their support of this project. Finally, Arthur thanks his wife, Tessa Dragon VanLear, for her understanding and forbearance as he gave this book the attention it required; likewise, Dan thanks his wife, Heather, for reminding him of what is important.

Last, we extend our thanks to the people at SAGE for making this anthology come alive. Matt Burney acquisitioned the book, made important suggestions regarding its content, and helped us move through the prepublication process. Others at SAGE include Ashe Blank (marketing manager), Jim Kelly (copyeditor), Libby Larson (production editor), Janae Masnovi (editorial assistant), and Jillian Oelsen (senior marketing associate).

We hope that readers will find this sourcebook helpful for understanding observational research and useful as a springboard for conducting their own observational studies.

C. Arthur VanLear (University of Connecticut)

Daniel J. Canary (University of Utah)

References

Buck, R., & VanLear, C. A. (2002). Verbal and nonverbal communication: Distinguishing symbolic, spontaneous, and pseudo-spontaneous nonverbal behavior. *Journal of Communication, 52* (3), 522–541.

Gottman, J., Markman, J., & Notarius, C., (1977). The topography of marital conflict: A sequential analysis of verbal and nonverbal behavior. *Journal of Marriage and the Family, 39*, 461-477

Kiecolt-Glaser, J. K., McGuire, L., Robles, T., & Glaser, R. (2002). Psychoneuroimmunology: Psychological influences on immune function and health. *Journal of Consulting and Clinical Psychology, 70*, 537–547.

Markman, H. J., & Notarius, C. I. (1987). Coding and marital family interaction: Current status. In T. Jacob (Ed.), *Family interaction and psychology* (pp. 329–390). New York: Plenum.

McCoy, K. P., George, M.R.W., Cummings, E. M., & Davies, P. T. (2013). Constructive and destructive marital conflict, parenting, and children's school and social adjustment. *Social Development, 22*, 641–662.

Sillars, A. L., Roberts, L. J., Leonard, K. E., & Dun, T. (2000). Cognition during marital conflict: The relationship of thought and talk. *Journal of Social and Personal Relationships, 17*, 479–502.

ACKNOWLEDGMENTS

The editors would like to thank the following reviewers:

Connie Bullis, The University of Utah

Susan L. Kline, Ohio State University

Gwen M. Wittenbaum, Michigan State University

Alesia Woszidlo, University of Kansas

Joseph B. Walther, Michigan State University

PART 1

Reviews of Behavioral Measures in
Selected Domains of Study:
Contexts and Modes of Behavior

1

■

OBSERVING RELATIONAL CONFLICT

DANIEL J. CANARY

Introduction

Since the publication of Rausch, Barry, Hertel, and Swain's (1974) observations of marital conflict, scholarly research on relational conflict has increased exponentially. As Gottman (1994) stated, "Nearly all the research on marital interaction has involved the observation of conflict resolution" (p. 66). In the past 40 years, researchers have elaborated what constitutes conflict; how conflict emerges, develops, and ends; factors that affect conflict processes; individual and relational differences in the management of conflict; dimensions and content of various typologies of conflict behavior; individual and relational outcomes of conflict communication behaviors; effects of conflict on people's mental and physical health; effects of marital conflict on child adjustment; patterns of conflict strategies and tactics; and other relevant processes.

The purpose of this chapter is to address three broad concerns relevant to how researchers observe conflict communication. These concerns involve how researchers view conflict interaction, how participants' experiences might not align with researchers' observations, and how researchers investigate relational conflict patterns. Such issues are not necessarily unique to conflict researchers, but they nonetheless remain critically important to observing conflict interaction. These three concerns are elaborated in the following subsections: (a) units of analysis, (b) review of three observational coding systems, (c) comparing codes, (d) conflict behavioral dimensions, (e) procedures linked to conflict observation, (f) participant experiences versus researcher observation, (g) selection of topics for discussion, (h) locating conflict patterns, (i) questions about conflict patterns, and (j) the

demand-withdraw pattern. Following this material, the reader will find a brief set of conclusions that emerge from the literature on these topics.

This chapter, however, omits discussion of other issues regarding conflict that are a "given" at this point in the game, are presented elsewhere, do not involve romantic relationships, are theoretical more than methodological, and are not centered on conflict communication processes. In addition, this chapter excludes the task of reviewing or even referencing several conflict coding systems; inclusive analyses of conflict observation systems can be found elsewhere (e.g., Filsinger, 1983; Heyman, 2001; Humbad, Donnellan, Klump, & Burt, 2011; Kerig & Baucom, 2004; Margolin et al., 1998). The first section discusses issues one likely encounters when coding conflict communication.

Issues in Coding Conflict Interaction

The Unit of Analysis

A critical issue for studies of interaction research concerns the unit of analysis (Sillars & Overall, this volume). Units of analysis represent one's conceptual understanding regarding where one can find the best information regarding communication (Heyman, 2001). Accordingly, units of analysis reflect one's perspective regarding the nature, function, and scope of conflict interaction. One's selection of the unit of analysis constitutes a critical first step in conducting interpersonal conflict processes.

Researchers tend to select one of three types of units. *Time* is one type of unit of analysis.

Interpersonal conflict researchers tend to select very brief periods of time for observation (e.g., 15 seconds to 1 minute) (e.g., Sillars, Roberts, Leonard, & Dun, 2000). Although small units of time allow the application of codes in precise ways, time as a unit of analysis requires a researcher to punctuate conflict interaction according to predetermined durations, regardless of whether more or less time would help gain insights about conflict communication.

Other researchers rely on the thought unit for coding. The *thought unit* is the "smallest semantic unit" (Notarius, Markman, & Gottman, 1983, p. 119), for example, one-word responses, independent clauses, and even short nonverbal behaviors that convey an idea (e.g., "ugh" can mean "no"). Thought turns clearly portray shifts in ideas and arguments, which can assist researchers who examine how partners develop ideas with each other (Canary, Brossmann, Brossmann, & Weger, 1995). Yet thought turns vary in their inclusiveness across studies; for example, extensive development of one idea might entail one thought or a set of different subordinate thoughts. One way to constrain how much data one partner provides is to code for both time and thoughts. However, Bakeman and Gottman (1986) argued that duration of time is implied when coding behaviors.

Third, researchers can rely on *speaker turns* as their unit of analysis. That is, switches in who holds the communication floor determine one's unit of observation. Although speaker turns appear clear and reliable, they remain vulnerable to within- and between-partner variability. For example, it is not uncommon for one person to talk more than does his or her partner. In such cases, the loquacious person could be elaborating quite a bit on one idea in long speaker turns, whereas the less verbal partner might offer only a couple of sentences in short speaker turns, yet both persons' speaker turns would be seen as equal.

One important decision concerns whether microanalytic units of observation or macroscopic units offer the better choice to observe interpersonal conflict. Naturally, data analyses depend on and are constrained by one's unit of analysis (e.g., coding every 30 seconds vs. paragraphs of speaker turns; Floyd, O'Farrell, & Goldberg, 1987). Analysis of microanalytic conflict communication yields very precise results regarding specific behaviors. Researchers often build macro-level measures from micro-level units; that is, they decide to observe communication as it emerges in small units (e.g., at the tactical level, such as problem description, solution proposal, positive metacommunication, among many others) and then compile these small tactical units into relevant and more inclusive strategies (integrative behaviors, withdrawal, etc.). Naturally, one cannot deconstruct macro-level codes into micro-level behaviors, because the more specific information simply is not there.

Additionally, researchers have constructed rating systems. One clear advantage of rating systems versus coding systems is that rating systems require much less time for rater training (Floyd et al., 1987). Moreover, rating systems tend to provide mezzo-level data (i.e., ratings of data are more abstract than are codes of the same data).

Three Popular Conflict Coding Systems

As indicated, specific microanalytic codes researchers use to categorize conflict communication systematically operationalize conflict behaviors (see Sillars & Overall, this volume). Over 20 conflict coding systems exist (Woodin, 2011). To provide the reader a concrete grasp of conflict coding systems, in this subsection I summarize three popular coding systems. For other schemes and in-depth analyses of codes, see Kerig and Baucom (2004), Filsinger (1983), and Sillars and Overall (this volume).

First, Rausch et al. (1974) pioneered observational conflict research and derived a coding scheme that contained cognitive acts, affiliative acts, and coercive acts. *Cognitive acts* include the following behaviors: opening the issue or probe, seeking information, suggesting a course of action, agreeing with the other's statement, and others. *Affiliative acts* involve using humor; accepting the other person's plans, actions, ideas, motives, or feelings; seeking reassurance; introducing a compromise; and so on. Finally, *coercive acts* include using power to force the other person to agree, rejecting the other, demanding compensation, disparaging the other, and the like.

Second, the most widely used conflict coding system is the Marital Interaction Coding System (MICS) (Weiss, 1993). Heyman, Eddy, Weiss, and Vivian (1995) conducted a factor analysis of the MICS-IV codes, using archived interactions from 995 couples. Four factors defined the specific codes from the MICS: Hostility, Humor, Constructive Problem Discussion, and Responsibility Discussion. *Hostility* involves a priori blame (with a hostile voice), put-down, criticize, negative mind reading, disagree, and disapprove. *Humor* involves both humor and smile, laugh, and potentially joking disagreement. *Responsibility Discussion* includes accept responsibility, deny responsibility, approval of partner behavior, and women's (but not men's) negative mind read. *Constructive Problem Discussion* comprises problem description, question, positive solution, and disagree. Of the 26 MICS behaviors that were factor-analyzed, a dozen did not load above .30 with any of these factors (e.g., complaining did not load on Hostility).

Heyman et al. (1995) argued that the four-factor solution of the MICS codes provides a standard for future research using the MICS, "in hopes of the results [bringing] an end to the confusion of how to combine MICS codes into categories" (p. 214). Yet 15 years after Heyman et al.'s advice, Larkin, Frazer, and Wheat (2011) examined conflict behaviors using four a priori categories from the MICS. They combined conflict codes in this way: *positive verbal tactics* involved agree, approval, accept responsibility, assent, compromise, and positive solution; *positive nonverbal tactics* were laugh and attention; *negative verbal tactics* were complain, disagree, negative solution, command, and put down; and *negative nonverbal tactics* involved turn off and not tracking.

Third, another widely used coding system is the Couples Interaction Scoring System (CISS) (Gottman, Markman, & Notarius, 1977; Notarius al., 1983), which contains eight summary codes: (a) problem information or feelings about a problem (e.g., "The problem is we don't make enough money"; "That makes me sad"); (b) mindreading-attributing thoughts, feelings, motives, attitudes, or actions to spouse (e.g., "You always get mad in those situations"); (c) proposing a solution (e.g., "Let's take out a loan"); (d) communication talk (e.g., "We're getting off the issue"); (e) agreement (e.g., "Yeah, you're right"); (f) disagreement (e.g., "No," "Yes, but . . .," "No, because it's too late"); (g) summarizing other (e.g., "You're basically suggesting a vacation"); and (h) summarizing self (e.g., "I told you I'm not going") (Notarius et al., 1983, p. 465).

Gottman et al. (1977) used the above eight CISS summary codes to contrast five highly distressed to five nondistressed couples. They also coded positive and negative affect as witnessed in the face, voice, and body. The speaker turn was their unit of analysis. Each turn involving positive affect was coded, and each turn involving negative affect was coded. Of the CISS codes, problem information, proposing a solution, mindreading with positive affect, and agreement were counted as positive; mindreading with negative affect and disagreement were negative codes; and communication talk, summarizing other, and summarizing self were coded as neutral. For multivariate coding, the authors included each of eight codes that represented positive, neutral, or negative affect.

Comparing Codes

From the above, one might rightly ascertain that conflict coding systems share some conceptual similarities but differ in several behaviors and levels of abstraction. Consider the relatively simple act of coding disagreement, a rather common conflict behavior. Rausch et al.'s (1974) coding scheme places disagreement as a cognitive act, "denying the validity of other's argument with or without the use of counterarguments" used for "cognitively oriented rational arguments" (p. 223). No negativity is indicated. The MICS-IV, however, places disagreement under the category of "hostility," combining disagreement with other negative behaviors. Last, the CISS treats disagreement as one of eight higher ordered summary codes, containing various subcategories of disagreement. Using this straightforward example, two implications emerge. First, one can see that the fundamental function of disagreement remains unclear. Disagreement is treated as a lower ordered code in the MICS, a higher ordered code in the CISS, and a stand-alone code in Rausch et al.'s scheme. In other words, research on "disagreement" as a scientific construct is unclear; perspectives on the construct of disagreement are conceptually inconsistent. Such inconsistency should be expected because the *meaning* underlying a code can vary both between coding systems as well as within coding systems; that is, codes are "polysemic" (Sillars & Canary, 2013). Thus, how researchers view their codes as theoretical constructs makes all the difference when interpreting findings. Second, as anticipated, none of the coding systems is comprehensive in its use of conflict codes. That is, no single coding scheme captures all conflict behaviors as they are treated in other coding systems. Emphasizing a set of specific behaviors will of necessity omit other behaviors. These two implications are not necessarily bad. According to Gottman (1994), "There is no final observation system for understanding marital interaction. Instead, each observational system highlights one facet of a many-sided diamond; each system, by itself, represents only a caricature of the richness that is there" (p. 9).

Yet researchers seldom use more than one conflict coding system, nor do they elaborate on the facet of the diamond they view. As an exception, Floyd et al. (1987) compared the MICS with the Communication Skills Test (CST). They predicted that differences between the two coding systems would yield inconsistent findings. Floyd et al. found strong support for their prediction. None of the correlations between the MICS and the CST was significant when controlling for family-wise error. In addition, associations differed for positive and negative summary codes. Remarkably,

the MICS results suggest that spouses tended to reciprocate rates of positive communication behavior but did not reciprocate rates of negative communication behaviors. In contrast, the CST results suggested that spouses tended to reciprocate negative, but not positive, communication behaviors. (Floyd et al., p. 427)

Such differences imply that, when needed, researchers should provide some elaboration on their choices of coding systems.

To illustrate how coding systems can differ, two coding systems are compared here in their application to a small slice of interaction (Gottman & Krokoff, 1989). This exercise indicates that differences in findings due to differences in coding systems can emerge, which can be problematic when they lead to different conclusions about conflict. Consider the conflict interaction below (from Canary, Cupach, & Messman, 1995, p. 39), which was coded using the MICS-IV at the University of Oregon's Oregon Marital Studies Program under the direction of Robert Weiss. I also coded this exchange using Sillars's (1986) Verbal Tactics Coding Scheme (VTCS).

Turn	Message	MICS-IV	VTCS
1.1	W: Sometimes we argue about what to watch on TV.	PI	DES
1.2	W: But it's not like we have a full fight.	DR	EV
2.0	M: Yeah, but you get mad when I flip the channels.	MN	CR
3.0	W: Yeah, but that's rude, 'cuz when you're in the middle of watching a show . . .	DP/TA	CR
4.0	M: (interrupting) Yeah, but we're not watching a show, we're just messing around.	PI	DEN
5.0	W: But that, that's rude!	CR	CR
6.1	M: Oh, "it's rude" (sarcastically).	PU	HJ
6.2	You should just say that instead of yelling.	PS	HI
6.3	That's YOUR problem.	DR	DR
	W: Laughs	SL	UC
6.4	M: You gotta just TALK, and not yell!	NS	HI

In this excerpt, and using the MICS-IV, the wife begins the interaction (Turn 1) with a *problem description internal* (PI) and then qualifies that description with a *denial of responsibility* (DR). The husband responds (Turn 2) with a *mindread-negative* (MN), attributing negative thoughts to the partner. In Turn 3, the wife disapproves in a neutral voice until the husband interrupts in Turn 4 with a problem description that differs from the wife's problem description in Turn 1. Next, the wife criticizes the husband in Turn 5, in response to which he sarcastically *puts down* (PU) the wife (Turn 6.1), offers a *positive solution* (PS) (Turn 6.2), but then denies his role in the conflict with a deny responsibility (DR) (Turn 6.3). At that time, the wife laughs in a neutral tone (coded as a *smile/laugh* [SL]). Finally, the husband presents a *negative solution* (NS) (Turn 6.4).

Sillars's (1986) VTCS reveals a slightly but significantly different picture. In Turn 1, the wife offers a *descriptive statement* (DES) that she follows with an *evasive remark* (EV). The husband responds with a *personal criticism* (CR), and the wife reciprocates (Turns 2 and 3). In Turn 4, the husband uses *direct denial* (DEN) of any real problem. The wife presents a personal criticism (Turn 5), to which the husband responds with a *hostile joke* (HJ) (Turn 6.1), a *hostile imperative* (HI) (Turn 6.2), and a *denial of responsibility* (Turn 6.3), while the wife offers an *uncodable* (UC) behavior. The husband concludes Turn 6 with another hostile imperative.

Two implications emerge from this exercise. First, both systems portray this interaction as generally negative. For example, the final portion of this excerpt (Turns 5 and 6) reveals that both coding systems would treat Turn 5 as a criticism, Turn 6.1 as a form of hostility, and Turn 6.4 as a type of negative command or solution. Second, however, Sillars's (1986) codes reveal a more negative interaction than do Weiss's (1993) MICS-IV codes. According to Sillars's codes, Turns 2 to 6 all contain direct and negative behaviors (i.e., personal criticism, personal criticism, direct denial, personal criticism, hostile joke, hostile imperative, denial of responsibility, and then hostile imperative). From the MICS-IV, a more positive conversation appears in Turns 1 to 6 (i.e., neutral problem description, denial of responsibility, mindread-negative, neutral disapproval, problem description, criticism, put-down, problem-solution, deny responsibility, positive solution, deny responsibility, and negative solution). In this small segment of conversation one can detect how coding systems can complement each other but simultaneously present different specific portrayals of interaction. To solve for differences and to help ensure inclusiveness, researchers might use two or more coding systems (Gottman, 1994) and/or note the subtle but significant differences between coding systems that might affect the results.

Dimensions of Conflict

Operational definitions of conflict frequently vary according to dimensions that researchers use to distinguish conflict communication. That is, observed conflict behaviors reflect one or more dimensional properties. In this way, one might assess conflict behaviors as points on dimensions instead of inferring the meaning of the conflict codes that are not tied to particular dimensions. Linking conflict communication to dimensional properties can be done a priori or through data reduction techniques (e.g., factor analysis).

Consider the use of two popular dimensions. The first dimension concerns the *valence of the behavior*, that is, how the conflict behavior counts as a cooperative or competitive act (Sillars & Canary, 2013). The revelation of negative emotions, such as anger and hostility, often marks a negative tactic. For instance, a compliment said with negative affect is probably sarcasm, and a solution proposal stated in a loud voice could be a command. The second dimension involves the *directness of the behavior*, that is, whether the conflict behavior reflects confrontation or avoidance (Sillars & Canary, 2013). Rausch et al. (1974) referred to the directness-indirectness dimension as engagement-avoidance. Naturally, other researchers have presented similar two-dimensional models of conflict (e.g., Sillars & Overall, this volume; van de Vliert & Euwema, 1994), and they applied different terms to the two dimensions of directness and valence or used one of these dimensions with alternative dimensions (e.g., intensity).

Conceptually, dimensions provide direction for a priori classification of conflict tactics. For example, crossing the two dimensions of valence and directness reveals four macro-level approaches, or strategies, for managing conflict (Sillars, Canary, &

Tafoya, 2004). Using van de Vliert and Euwema's terms, these strategies are *negotiating* (positive and direct), *direct fighting* (negative and direct), *non-confrontation* (positive and indirect), and *indirect fighting* (negative and indirect). Sillars et al. (2004) (revised by Sillars & Canary, 2013) categorized 74 different conflict tactics from four observational coding schemes, including the three presented above plus Sillars's (1986) VTCS. These 74 tactics were readily sorted according to their valence and directness (Sillars et al., 2004). And Sillars et al.'s chapter helped refine an observational rating system in which conflict tactics rely on the two dimensions of *direct-indirect* and *nice-nasty* (valence) properties (or the Direct/Indirect, Nice/Nasty Conflict Rating System II; Gustafson & Canary, 2006).

Another way to select conflict codes involves data reduction techniques. Woodin (2011) conducted a meta-analysis of 64 studies, involving over 5,000 participants and 21 different observational coding schemes. Her primary purpose was to assess the link between conflict tactics and relational satisfaction. Woodin adopted a two-dimensional model that involved valence and intensity, as the intensity of a behavior can alter the course of conflict (Sillars et al., 2004). In brief, Woodin's meta-analysis largely supported a two-dimensional model and explained the emergence of five higher ordered conflict categories: hostility, withdrawal, distress, problem solving, and intimacy. She viewed *hostility* as involving hard negative emotions, unconstructive communication behaviors, and attacking or dominating behaviors. *Withdrawal* refers to avoidant behaviors and detachment from the discussion. *Distress* includes soft negative emotions, displays of vulnerability, and expressions of distress or hurt that do not attack the partner. *Problem solving* contains constructive communication behaviors and neutral emotions. Last, *intimacy* references positive affect and communicative behaviors, messages of closeness, and statements of understanding the partner. In addition, Woodin found moderate effects on marital satisfaction for the following strategies: hostility (negative), distress (negative), intimacy (positive), and problem solving (positive). Finally, interesting effects emerged for sex differences; for example, sex differences in withdrawal interacted with duration of conflict, such that men tended to withdraw as the conflict continued over time.

In a similar vein, Birnbaum, Mikulincer, and Austerlitz (2013) used graduate students to rate conflict interactions on two dimensions: (a) stress-anxiety and (b) warmth-supportiveness. *Stress-anxiety* behaviors involved five adjectives: *stressed, anxious, upset, aroused,* and *hurt.* They operationalized *warmth-supportiveness* with nine adjectives: *supportive, warm, hostile* (reverse scored [RS]), *sarcastic* (RS), *arrogant* (RS), *rejecting* (RS), *understanding, emotionally detached* (RS), and *cold* (RS). The adjectives *hostile, sarcastic, rejecting,* and *cold* represent hostile tactics; *emotionally detached* and *cold* reference a withdraw approach. However, reversing the coding of hostile and cold behaviors (as Birnbaum et al. did) does not necessarily reveal the enactment of positive conflict behaviors; such reversing would only indicate a lack of hostility and withdrawal.

In brief, researchers possess a variety of coding systems that help in observing conflict communication. Naturally, these systems differ; and codes using the same terms can differ, given their polysemous meaning. The implication here is that variation between and within codes limits coherence of findings, especially at the microscopic level, unless researchers discuss these differences and how they might affect their results.

Participant Experiences

Another issue concerns the extent to which scholars presume that a tight connection exists between participants' coded interaction and their experience of their interaction. Indeed, researchers have found little correspondence between participants' coded behavior and participants' self-reported experience of the same conversation (Sillars et al., 2000). This issue becomes central in tying objectively coded behavior to conflict outcomes, because bias works against accuracy. As Humbad et al. (2011) indicated, "individuals interpret their partner's actions through either a generally positive or a generally negative perceptual filter, more or less regardless of the partner's objective behaviors" (p. 759). Although Humbad et al.'s claim is rather absolute, it does underscore that relational conflict emerges and develops within participants' connections between what they actually do and what they subjectively think.

Participants' *field of vision* is external to them (Storms, 1973); that is, people cannot see themselves interacting with their partners. They might see their own hands and own feet move and hear their own voices, but that is about the extent of their field of vision. However, people can readily see their *partners'* interaction behavior. So although people can see their partners wince, they cannot see their own wincing. Simultaneously, people's *field of experience* resides internal to them; naturally, participants' thoughts and feelings affect their interpretations of their experiences (Storms, 1973). Especially during conflict, people must connect these two experiences,

and they simply cannot explain with any accuracy how their specific behaviors connect to their own cognitive and emotional processes.

A question arises whether the actual conflict behaviors or participant-recalled experiences of conflict episodes more accurately predict conflict outcomes, such as relational satisfaction. If actual conflict behaviors are more powerful, then they deserve prominence (which is the case now). If participant perceptions of conflict are more powerful in predicting outcomes and diverge from actual interaction, then one might question the need to examine participants' actual conflict behavior (which is a time-consuming and expensive venture). Regardless of the answer to this question, observations of actual interactions solve for problems arising because of social actors' poor field of vision. For instance, Sillars et al. (2000) dealt with the degree to which people's experience is concordant or discordant with objectively coded interactions. In their study, participants watched 20-second segments of their conflict interactions and related their perceptions of their internal states and behaviors of self and partner. Sillars et al. found very little overlap between one person's interpretations of interaction behavior and the partner's recollections and interpretations (only 1% to 3%). Instead of reaching consensus on the issues at hand and how communication links to each person's objectives, communication behaviors were driven by individuals' own experiences of the event, largely separated from the objectives, perceptions, and interaction behaviors of their partners (Sillars et al., 2000). As a result of people's inability to process much sensory data, they must focus on particular stimuli and overlook a lot. Two people in an interaction typically pay attention to different perceptual data points they each believe are salient and essential. During conflict, people's selectivity increases, and they experience greater emotional intensity. Moreover, increased intensity raises selectivity of data and personal bias (Sillars et al., 2000). In short, relatively objective coders cannot assess memories and perceptions of partners, as they appear to be largely dissimilar to the participants' actual interaction. However, coders can identify actual conflict tactics that can lead to outcomes grounded in behavioral reality and nonintuitive findings.

Selecting Topics

In prototypical formats, conflict interaction research has relied largely on three methods for inducing conflict: experimental, researcher based, and participant generated. Here, analysis entertains the simple matter of which topic(s) participants discuss. As expected, the selection of topics to discuss matters.

First, consider an experimental approach. Heyman (2001) offered eight suggestions for future observational couple interaction research. His fifth suggestion was to use experimental treatment groups to increase the validity of claims regarding conflictual versus nonconflictual interactions. That suggestion can be assessed in light of other methods of eliciting conflict. Consider the simple but vital task of presenting participants with discussion topics.

For example, Johnson (2002) found that feature characteristics of conflict vary by the type of topic—whether it is a *public* (e.g., political) or a *private* (relational) issue. For instance, she found that arguments are less enjoyable and more ego involving when participants are discussing private issues about the relationship than public issues. Similarly, Bates and Samp (2011) found that participants more likely perceived that a conflict was resolved when the topic was nonrelational, as opposed to relational. Finally, Eldridge, Jones, Andrew, Sevier, and Atkins (2007) discovered that participants engaged in more demand-withdraw communication regarding relational issues compared with personal issues (and this was especially true for wife demand–husband withdraw). This finding suggests that demand-withdraw patterns are most salient and potentially harmful to couples who discuss the relationship itself.

One way to manipulate topics experimentally relies on a revealed difference paradigm. Here, the idea is to prompt conflict by presenting the husband and the wife with different scenarios, with each person receiving information that biases the scenarios in favor of his or her sex. For example, Olson and Ryder (1970) created the Inventory of Marital Conflicts, which requires that partners respond to 18 vignettes; 12 of the vignettes were biased toward the sex of the husband or the wife, to make it appear that the opposite sex was to blame for each issue so as to promote conflict interaction. Six neutral items were also created, with two neutral items beginning the scenarios and one concluding the scenarios, which help mask the induction to participants.

Second, the researcher generates the conflict topics. Topics are based on specific research questions, previous research, a similar subsample, and/or the intuition of the researcher given his or her clinical or other experience. Lists of topic issues are presented to participants to discuss. The hope is that one of the issues is relevant to the couple. For instance, Gottman (1979) presented participants with 6 potential conflict topics to discuss (e.g.,

finances, caring for the children). Canary et al. (1995) asked participants to discuss 8 topics. Zietlow and Sillars (1988) presented participants with 10 topics to discuss. This method of generating conflict topics appears to be successful, in part because interaction data born from this method can yield a number of reactions from participants.

Third, participants can generate discussion topics for themselves. Using this method, researchers ask participants to complete a brief survey before the interaction and to nominate two to five issues each person indicates is a problem. Often, participants also rate the importance of the issues and select which issue(s) to discuss. One advantage of self-generated topics concerns *representative validity*, or evidence that the participants in the study engage in discussion of conflict topics that are relevant to them.

Finally, one can combine researcher-generated and participant-generated topics. Manusov (2002) combined methods to generate conflict topics. She described her selection of topics accordingly:

> When the couples arrived at the research laboratory, either the wife or husband was selected and assigned to the role of confederate, using random selection counterbalanced by sex. The confederate was asked to choose three topics for discussion: one that was neutral, one that was positive, and one that was negative for the couple. They were given a list of possible topics (for example, what was happening at work, something current in their relationship, what their children were doing, money/finances, sports), but they could choose anything to discuss that they wished. . . . The order of the positive and negative topics was randomly assigned and counterbalanced to be sure that the order did not affect the likelihood of writing down the behaviors and offering attributions for them. (pp. 21–22)

Conflict Patterns

Locating Conflict Patterns

Researchers often want to explore how conflict tactics and strategies emerge and are developed. If communication is a process, than associating the frequency of different conflict behaviors with other variables would poorly represent process and, in fact, might lead to a very static and incorrect view of conflict communication processes. Three ways of obtaining conflict communication patterns appear in the literature.

First, some researchers argue that frequencies already provide one way to observe conflict patterns. They refer to the use of such frequencies as "base rate" patterns, which provide very global information regarding patterns. As van den Broucke, Vertommen, and Vandereycken (1995) argued, "If [frequency] base rates are approximately the same for the two partners, one could say that the couple's interaction is reciprocal on a long-term basis (i.e., for the total duration of the discussion)" (p. 11). Also, Warner (1992) held that base rates indicate interaction rhythms or *cyclicity*. For example, Vincent, Weiss, and Birchler (1975) explored tactics that nondistressed and distressed partners used in pleasant versus unpleasant activities. They found that distressed couples reported more frequent conflict over a 5-day period (*M* for distressed couples = 3.4, *M* for nondistressed couples = 1.0), more engagement of displeasing behaviors (*M* for distressed couples = 41.3, *M* for nondistressed couples = 13.6), and fewer pleasing behaviors (*M* for distressed couples = 131.6, *M* for nondistressed couples = 259.6). Moreover, Vincent et al. found that distressed couples engaged in more negative tactics and fewer positive statements to their spouses than to strangers. Nondistressed partners relied more on positive statements and less on negative statements to their spouses than they did to strangers.

Base rate–based conflict communication presents data from an overall, abstract level of meaning. However, such data do not provide information about conflict communication processes, that is, communication as it unfolds in actual interaction. The claim that base rates can reflect reciprocation of behavior is at best indirectly supported and tentatively interpreted until act-to-act reciprocation of conflict behavior is observed. Likewise, base rates do not represent how social actors cycle back and forth in their conflict communication. Stated differently, no conflict patterns are adequately measured with base-rate frequencies.

Second, some researchers use correlations to find conflict patterns. For example, Newton, Kielcolt-Glaser, Glaser, and Malarkey (1995) correlated newlywed partners' conflict behaviors of engagement (e.g., criticize, disagreement), withdrawal (e.g., disengage, no eye contact), and humor-distraction (e.g., joking, off-topic comments). They found couple intercorrelations of .61, .31, and .53 involving engagement, withdrawal, and humor-distraction, respectively. Van den Broucke et al. (1995) compared husband-wife correlations among eating disorder couples, in which the wife or female partner suffered from anorexia or bulimia nervosa; maritally distressed couples, defined as those seeking couple therapy or those scoring very low on an index of marital satisfaction; and maritally nondistressed couples. Van den Broucke et al. reported that maritally distressed couples' reciprocity for negative behaviors was stronger (i.e., correlations were stronger) than eating disorder and maritally nondistressed couples' correlations. Using two-tailed tests when examining act-to-act contingencies, the authors reported that none of the three types of marriages contained a significant degree of negative or positive reciprocity. Yet if Van den Broucke et al. had predicted that distressed couples more often reciprocate negative affect, their data suggest that they would have found a significant score for reciprocation of negative behavior (their z score of 1.79 was significant [$p < .05$]).

A third and often used option for locating conflict patterns regards the location of patterns that involve lag 1 or act-to-act sequences (see also VanLear, this volume). These appear superior to the previous two options in depicting conflict patterns. Importantly, the lag 1 unit of analysis constitutes the basis for most conflict observational research, with researchers often requiring that each sequence type represent at least 5% of all potential sequences (Gottman, 1979). Moreover, using sequential analyses offers much more information than do base rates or correlations (see also VanLear, this volume). For instance, Margolin and Wampold (1981) found that act-to-act sequences explained significantly more variance in relational quality indicators than that accounted for by frequencies alone: 8% for marital satisfaction, 15% for desired areas of change, 8% for spouses' pleasing behaviors, and 15% for displeasing spousal behavior.

Analyzing sequences entails relatively simple logic: Cross-tabulating one person's response to his or her partner's reveals interdependency to the extent that the observed responses differ from those expected by statistical chance alone. Rausch et al. (1974) illustrated how partners variously responded to each other in four role-played "improvisations" using six conflict categories:

1. *cognitive acts*, which are neutral behaviors, suggestions, and rational statements;

2. *resolving acts*, which include behaviors aimed at reducing tensions and at reaching a satisfactory outcome;

3. *reconciling acts*, which attempt to bring partners together on an emotional level;

4. *appealing acts*, which include attempts to get the partner to grant one's needs and wants;

5. _rejecting acts_, which reveal a "cold or nasty" disavowal of the partner or the partner's ideas; and

6. _coercive or personal attacks_, which aim to force compliance through use of power, guilt, or ridicule of one's partner (p. 115).

Rausch et al. found that married partners largely reciprocated their spouses' conflict messages. For example, cognitive responses followed cognitive responses over 60% of the time, resolving responses followed resolving tactics over 20% of the time, and coercion followed coercion 19% of the time. Some messages were reciprocated along more general lines; that is, specific positive messages or negative messages followed other kinds of specific positive or negative messages (e.g., coercion followed rejection 30.5% of the time). In addition, Rausch and colleagues found some sex-role asymmetry in conflict tactics. Mostly in unhappy marriages, wives used more coercive and appealing tactics, whereas husbands relied more on reconciling and resolution-minded tactics (pp. 138–174).

Using sequential analyses, Notarius et al. (1983) reported that reciprocation of negative behaviors strongly predicted whether a couple was dissatisfied (vs. satisfied). However, the reciprocation of positive conflict tactics did not differentiate satisfied from dissatisfied partners. Surprisingly, dissatisfied partners were likely to enact quid pro quo positivity. Satisfied partners, however, enacted positive base-rate behaviors more frequently. Notarius et al. explained that interaction patterns in dissatisfied couples are more predictable, which would involve more quid pro quo positive as well as negative sequences. They indicated that patterns in satisfied couples rely less on the partners' previous messages and more on the general positive affect of the marriage. In this vein, satisfied partners remain positive throughout a conflict interaction without being prompted to do so by each other.

When one tests for lag 1 patterns (i.e., one person's immediate response to the partner's preceding behavior), the significance tests of chi-square approximate those of the z test used in lag sequential analysis (Allison & Liker, 1982). Such tests are clear and simple, though the tendency now is to use more sophisticated statistical techniques (VanLear, this volume; Warner, 1992). For instance, using log-linear transitional probabilities, Sillars (1980) reported that roommates reciprocated each other's avoidance messages 73% of the time, distributive (competitive) behaviors 44% of the time, and integrative (cooperative) messages 53% of the time.

Questions About Conflict Patterns

Although observations of patterns appear quite straightforward, several scholars have questioned their construct utility. One indictment is that act-to-act sequences cannot adequately portray the distributive or integrative structures of conflict as they unfold in real time. That is, conflict communication is complex and cannot be represented in first-ordered structures (Sillars & Weisberg, 1987, p. 153). Alberts and Driscoll (1992) disliked act-to-act analyses because they do not clearly show how such sequences "link together to form sequences that become either disintegrative or integrative" (p. 395).

A second reason for not accepting act-to-act analyses likely stems from conceptual ambiguity surrounding the term _pattern_. For some people, patterns refer to reenactment of the same behaviors over a period of time (e.g., across weeks). In this case, the occurrence of lag 1 sequences within a 15-minute conversation underestimates the prevalence of partners' patterned interaction and changes in patterns that require longer durations to unfold. As Revenstorf, Hahlweg, Schindler, and Vogel (1984) stated, "contingencies cannot depict a meaningful interaction" (p. 170). Additionally, some readers want to learn more about the nature of _stationarity_, or the manifestation of patterns across conflict episodes (Sillars & Wilmot, 1994). Stated differently, act-to-act lag 1 sequences of conflict tactics in a 15-minute interaction may not represent complex patterns of interaction that occur after participants' involvement in the study ends.

A third reason why patterns are questionable concerns how some researchers combine two or more lag 1 sequences to present a chain of sequences, which might be tied to marital satisfaction and/or stability. Consider the following hypothetical combinations (using the MICS): _appealing to fairness_ → _accepting blame_ 20% of the time and _accepting blame_ → _introducing a compromise_ 30% of the time. Although each of these patterns occurs systematically, one cannot simply combine them to claim that appealing to fairness leads to compromise through accepting blame. Such a claim requires sophisticated statistics (VanLear, this volume). In fact, it is entirely possible that appealing to fairness contains an insignificant amount of moderated or mediated variance when predicting introducing compromise. Conclusions about longer sequences and patterns of behavior must extend beyond lag 1 sequences.

The Demand-Withdraw Pattern

The demand-withdraw pattern dominates research on conflict patterns (e.g., Caughlin & Vangelisti, 2006). Malis and Roloff (2006) defined the demand-withdraw pattern as "a communication pattern in which one person demands, complains, nags, or criticizes, while the other person withdraws or tries to avoid the issue" (pp. 199–200; see also Caughlin & Vangelisti, 2006; Christensen & Heavey, 1990). Kluwer, Heesink, and van de Vliert (2000) argued that *demand* provides a "general term for 'pursuing' tactics," including requesting change, demanding change, nagging, blaming, accusing, and criticizing; *withdrawal* involves "distancing" behaviors, such as physical withdrawal, becoming silent, defending, and avoiding a discussion (p. 265). Eldridge et al. (2007) used similar terms, including demanding behavior of other, criticizing, making demands, and nagging; they depicted withdrawal as avoiding, withdrawing, and becoming silent (p. 218). These definitions lead to some redundancy in codes used across studies. Codes cited more than once for demand include demanding, complaining, criticizing, accusing, and nagging tactics. Codes cited more than once as withdraw tactics include withdrawing, avoiding, and becoming silent.

Researchers have consistently found that the demand-withdraw pattern is negatively associated with marital satisfaction (Birditt, Brown, Orbuch, & McIlvane, 2010). Nevertheless, Siffert and Schwartz (2011) found that other participant actions during interaction more powerfully predicted subjective well-being than did demand-withdraw behaviors. Naturally, researchers' conceptual and operational definitions point to various views of demand and withdraw behaviors. In addition, operational definitions provide guidelines for future researchers to follow. For example, Caughlin and Vangelisti (2000) relied on Heavey, Layne, and Christensen's (1993) categories, which relied on Christensen and Heavey's (1990) codes.

Two critical issues regarding the demand-withdraw pattern for this chapter concern variance in its content and in levels of abstraction. In terms of content, researchers appear to agree on the use of some codes (as noted above), and this commonality provides focus to the findings. Still, important variance separates these operationalizations. For example, Christensen and Heavey (1990) operationally defined demand-withdraw with four subscales: father demand, mother demand, father withdraw, and mother withdraw. Heavey, Layne, and Christensen (1993) identified demands as involving *discussion* (e.g., attempts to discuss issue, engaged), *blames* (e.g., blames, criticizes), and *pressures for change* (e.g., requests, demands). Those authors identified withdraw as *avoidance* (e.g., changing topics, diverting attention) and *withdraw* (e.g., withdraws, refuses to discuss topic). Yet Papp, Cummings, and Goeke-Morey (2009) were more inclusive of various conflict tactics. They operationalized demanding behavior in subcategories of pursuit and personal insult. *Pursuit* refers to chasing the partner and not allowing the issue or the partner to leave. *Personal insult* includes direct and negative tactics, such as making accusations, insulting the partner, blaming, rejecting, and the use of sarcasm. Papp et al. measured withdrawal tactics with three subcategories. *Defensiveness* involves attempts to escape blame, refuse responsibility, excuse self, and reciprocate partner criticism, among other behaviors. Next, *change topic* concerns attempts to change the topic and avoid interaction. Finally, *withdraw* includes attempts to create distance from the interaction partner; these include stonewalling, leaving the scene, avoiding eye contact, and so forth.

Three implications arise regarding observations of the demand-withdraw pattern. First, differences in behavioral codes limit generalizations regarding the demand-withdraw pattern. What one researcher identifies as the demand-withdraw pattern will not necessarily correspond to what a different researcher identifies. Because variation exists in researcher codes used to operationalize demand and withdraw communication, one cannot be confident regarding either the content or the scope of these behaviors. Second, more inclusive demand-withdraw measures subsume communicative behaviors used in conflict studies not examining demand-withdraw. For instance, making accusations, blaming, rejecting, and so forth, have also been used to operationalize *direct fighting* and *avoidance conflict* strategies (Sillars & Canary, 2013). That is, direct fighting tactics (Table 1) cannot be axiomatically tied to demand behaviors, nor are they functionally equivalent. And the same can be said for various avoidance tactics revealed in the literature; they do not conceptually correspond with withdraw behavior. In this light, inclusive measures of demand and withdraw do not isolate findings that accrue to the demand-withdraw pattern. Research shows that alternative patterns similarly affect relational quality (e.g., attack-defend; Ting-Toomey, 1983). Third, inclusive operationalizations of the demand-withdraw pattern can obscure the search for other conflict patterns. That is, continued inclusive operational definitions of the demand-withdraw pattern might prevent advancement of knowledge regarding other patterns and functions of conflict (e.g., complaint/counter-complaint reflects personal hostility, without seeing the second complaint as some form of withdraw) (e.g., Gottman, 1979; Rausch et al., 1974; Ting-Toomey 1983).

Conclusions

Observational research on conflict interaction enables researchers to identify how various conflict communication associates with important outcomes, such as marital satisfaction and individual well-being. These explorations have yielded theoretical advances and research findings to increase our understanding of the nature, function, and scope of interpersonal conflict. At this point, I want to offer a set of brief conclusions derived mostly from the review presented in this chapter.

First, the idea that a comprehensive conflict coding system can be created must be dismissed. In various ways, researchers have presented inclusive and exhaustive conflict typologies. Sometimes, conflict behaviors are factor-analyzed to create higher order factors that represent and bring structure to specific conflict tactics. At other times, researchers rely on dimensional properties to decide how specific conflict behaviors should be treated. Naturally, researchers find different factors of conflict behaviors, or they decide to use different conflict behavioral codes, or they use the same names that differ in their operational definitions (e.g., negative tactics in one study loosely relate to negative tactics in another study).

One impact of this simple observation concerns how scholars and students might think that conflict dimensions or factors remain similar across studies. They do not. Also, researchers have different aims, which often lead to the selection of different conflict typologies or parts of the same typology (e.g., MICS). Accordingly, one should not presume that "conflict behaviors" in one study converge with conflict behaviors in a different study. The point is not to minimize attempts to use the most comprehensive and/or appropriate coding system one can find. The implication is that differences between or among conflict coding systems prevent quick summaries or general inferences about the findings. Different conflict codes might resemble different features of a diamond, as Gottman suggested. Still, researchers should discuss where important coding differences exist, and researchers and readers should realize that studies contain differences in coding systems that could lead to differences in interpretation of conflict tactics and strategies.

Although various typologies of conflict behaviors exist, they sometimes have considerable overlap. Moreover, dimensions often use elements of valence and directness, which can add coherence to the various facets of the conflict communication diamond. A third way researchers can provide a sense of coherence regards providing a definition or theoretical approach, which could inform the reader how the researcher(s) view the content of conflict.

Second, selecting a coding system depends on the specific research problems being addressed as well as the theoretical point of view one adopts (Heyman, 2001). Even the adoption of the unit of analysis requires that the researcher have an explicit theoretical perspective on what slice of behavior constitutes an instance of conflict communication (Heyman, 2001). Units of analysis and coding systems can also be theory based, or else the conceptual foundation(s) of a study remains oblique. Correspondence between conceptual and operational definitions lies in the way researchers theoretically observe "actual interaction."

Moreover, one's findings are reliable only to the extent that consistent application of the behavioral codes occurs, and findings remain valid to the extent that coders adopt the conceptual perspective of the researcher or work with the researcher to redefine categories and/or their enactment. As several scholars have noted, teaching people how to code communication requires weeks of work. As a general rule, 40 hours of training are required to code 1 hour of interaction, and hours are needed to code a 12-minute conversation (Margolin et al., 1998). One might hope that once coders are trained and obtain reliability, the training stage is complete. However, such is not the case. As Margolin et al. (1998) stated, "Coder training is a continuous process with initial training generally taking place over the course of several meetings and maintenance training sessions continuing throughout the entire coding period" (p. 205).

Third, the examination of conflict communication patterns should be revived. Knowledge about the unfolding of communication patterns remains rudimentary. Such patterns include attack-defend, proposal-counterproposal, metacommunication-metacommunication, and others (e.g., Gottman, 1979; Ting-Toomey, 1983). Students and scholars of communication and related disciplines have heard little about these patterns because follow-up research on them is sparse. In addition, the lion's share of research regarding patterns is held by the current fascination with the demand-withdraw pattern.

Further examinations of the demand-withdraw pattern will, no doubt, occur. Now, however, differences in the conceptualization and operationalization of the demand-withdraw pattern might handicap researchers, who often do not acknowledge differences in operationalizations of what constitutes a demand and what constitutes a withdrawal. Syntheses and generalizations regarding the demand-withdraw pattern should be tempered by behavioral differences that exist across many studies of conflict interaction.

Also, researchers have examined various patterns, relying on lag 1 sequences. Presuming that base-rate data represent patterns, the reality is that base rates provide at best only an indirect and imprecise method to find conflict patterns. This observation also applies to studies in which correlational analyses tie each person's conflict. Also, lag 1 analysis provides a small view of interchanges between partners. Yet it remains quite popular among researchers who study conflict interaction. Clearly, a need exists for more theoretical models that can help researchers observe movements of conflict communication beyond a simple exchange (see VanLear, this volume).

Finally, research now reveals that conflict communication combines with prorelational and positive factors to affect relational satisfaction and stability. That is, direct and positive conflict works in tandem with such factors as relational maintenance strategies, social support behaviors, playfulness, enthusiasm, responsiveness and love, and others (Canary & Lakey, 2013). Examining how conflict communication combines with other prorelationship behaviors to affect outcomes hinges on how one might observe such factors (especially when partners engage in negative tactics). Unfortunately, observational research is unusual in communication journals. Levine (2013, p. 71) noted that surveys, lab experiments, and content analysis constitute the most common data-gathering techniques for interpersonal communication researchers. Regardless, combining observations of conflict interaction with alternative prorelational constructs will deliver much more information regarding the nature and function of conflict communication in relational contexts.

References

Alberts, J. K., & Driscoll, G. (1992). Containment versus escalation: The trajectory of couples' conversational complaints. *Western Journal of Communication*, *56*, 394–412.

Allison, P. D., & Liker, J. K. (1982). Analyzing sequential categorical data on dyadic interaction. *Psychological Bulletin*, *91*, 393–403.

Bakeman, R., & Gottman, J. M. (1986). *Observing interaction: An introduction to sequential analysis*. New York: Cambridge University Press.

Bates, C. E., & Samp, J. A. (2011). Examining the effects of planning and empathic accuracy on communication in relational and nonrelational conflict interactions. *Communication Studies*, *62*, 207–223.

Birditt, K. W., Brown, E., Orbuch, T. L., & McIlvane, J. M. (2010). Marital conflict behaviors and implications for divorce over 16 years. *Journal of Marriage and Family*, *72*, 1188–1204.

Birnbaum, G. E., Mikulincer, M., & Austerlitz, M. (2013). A fiery conflict: Attachment orientations and the effects of relational conflict on sexual motivation. *Personal Relationships*, *20*, 294–310.

Canary, D. J., Brossmann, J. E., Brossmann, B. G., & Weger, H. (1995). Toward a theory of minimally rational argument: Analyses of episode-specific effects of argument structures. *Communication Monographs*, *62*, 183–212.

Canary, D. J., Cupach, W. R., & Messman, S. J. (1995). *Relationship conflict*. Thousand Oaks, CA: Sage.

Canary, D. J., & Lakey, S. (2013). *Strategic conflict*. New York: Routledge.

Caughlin, J. P., & Vangelisti, A. L. (2000). An individual difference explanation of why married couples engage in the demand/withdraw pattern of conflict. *Journal of Social and Personal Relationships*, *17*, 523–551.

Caughlin, J. P., & Vangelisti, A. L. (2006). Conflict in dating and romantic relationships. In J. Oetzel & S. Ting-Toomey (Eds.), *The SAGE handbook of conflict communication* (pp. 129–157). Thousand Oaks, CA: Sage.

Christensen, A., & Heavey, C. L. (1990). Gender and social structure in the demand/withdraw pattern of marital conflict. *Journal of Personality and Social Psychology*, *59*, 73–81.

Eldridge, K. A., Jones, J., Andrew, C., Sevier, M., & Atkins, D. C. (2007). Demand-withdraw communication in severely distressed, moderately distressed, and nondistressed couples: Rigidity and polarity during relationship and personal problem discussions. *Journal of Family Psychology*, *21*, 218–226.

Filsinger, E. E. (Ed.). (1983). *Marriage and family assessment: A sourcebook for family therapy*. Beverly Hills, CA: Sage

Floyd, F. J., O'Farrell, T. J., & Goldberg, M. (1987). Comparison of marital observational measures: The Marital Interaction Coding System and the Communication Skills Test. *Journal of Consulting and Clinical Psychology*, *55*, 423–429

Gottman, J. M. (1979). *Marital interaction: Experimental investigations*. San Diego, CA: Academic Press.

Gottman, J. M. (1994). *What predicts divorce? The relationship between marital processes and marital outcomes*. Hillsdale, NJ: Lawrence Erlbaum.

Gottman, J. M., & Krokoff, L. J. (1989). Marital interaction and satisfaction: A longitudinal view. *Journal of Consulting and Clinical Psychology*, *57*, 47–52.

Gottman, J., Markman, J., & Notarius, C. (1977). The topography of marital conflict: A sequential analysis of verbal and nonverbal behavior. *Journal of Marriage and the Family, 39,* 461–477.

Gustafson, D. A., & Canary, D. J., with Farinelli, L., Eden, J., & Johnson, S. L. (2006). *Direct/Indirect, Nice/Nasty (DINN) Conflict Rating System II.* Unpublished coding manual for rating conflict interactions, Arizona State University, Tempe.

Heavey, C. L., Layne, C., & Christensen, A. (1993). Gender and conflict structure in marital interaction: A replication and extension. *Journal of Consulting and Clinical Psychology, 61,* 16–27.

Heyman, R. E. (2001). Observation of couple conflicts: Clinical assessment applications, stubborn truths, and shaky foundations. *Psychological Assessment, 13,* 5–35.

Heyman R. E., Eddy J. M., Weiss, R. L., & Vivian D. (1995). Factor analysis of the Marital Interaction Coding System. *Journal of Family Psychology, 9,* 209–215.

Humbad, M. N., Donnellan, M. B., Klump, K. L., & Burt, S. A. (2011). Development of the brief romantic relationship interaction coding scheme. *Journal of Family Psychology, 25,* 759–769.

Johnson, A., J. (2002). Beliefs about arguing: A comparison of public issue and personal issue arguments. *Communication Reports, 15,* 99–111.

Kerig, P. K., & Baucom, D. H. (2004). *Couple observational coding systems.* Mahwah, NJ: Lawrence Erlbaum.

Kluwer, E. S., Heesink, J.A.M., & van de Vliert, E. (2000). The division of labor in close relationships: An asymmetrical conflict issue. *Personal Relationships, 7,* 263–282.

Larkin, K. T., Frazer, N. L., & Wheat, A. (2011). Responses to interpersonal conflict among young adult men and women: Influence of cohesion and flexibility of family of origin. *Personal Relationships, 18,* 657–667.

Levine, T. R. (2013). Quantitative communication research: Review, trends, and critique. *Review of Communication Research, 1,* 69–84.

Malis, R. S., & Roloff, M. E. (2006). Demand/withdraw patterns in serial arguments: Implications for well-being. *Human Communication Research, 32,* 198–216.

Manusov, V. (2002). Thought and action: Connecting attributions to behaviors in married couples' interactions. In P. Noller & J. A. Feeney (Eds.), *Understanding marriage: Developments in the study of couple interaction* (pp. 14–31). New York: Cambridge University Press.

Margolin, G., Oliver, P. H., Gordis, E. B., Garcia O'Hearn, H., Medina, A. M., Ghosh, C. M., & Morland, L. (1998). The nuts and bolts of behavioral observation of marital and family interaction. *Clinical Child and Family Psychology Review, 1,* 195–212.

Margolin, G., & Wampold, B. E. (1981). Sequential analysis of conflict and accord in distressed and nondistressed marital partners. *Journal of Consulting and Clinical Psychology, 49,* 554–576.

Newton, T. L. Kielcolt-Glaser, J. K., Glaser, R., & Malarkey, W. B. (1995). Conflict and withdrawal during marital interaction: The roles of hostility and defensiveness. *Personality and Social Psychology Bulletin, 21,* 512–524.

Notarius, C., Markman, H., & Gottman, J. (1983). The Couples Interaction Scoring System: Clinical applications. In E. E. Filsinger (Ed.), *A sourcebook of marriage and family assessment.* Beverly Hills, CA: Sage.

Olson, D. H., & Ryder, R. G. (1970). Inventory of Marital Conflicts (IMC): An experimental interaction procedure. *Journal of Marriage and the Family, 32,* 443–448.

Papp, L. M., Cummings, E. M., & Goeke-Morey, M. C. (2009). For richer, for poorer: Money as a topic of marital conflict in the home. *Family Relations, 58,* 91–103.

Rausch, H. L., Barry, W. A., Hertel, R. K., & Swain, M. A. (1974). *Communication, conflict, and marriage.* San Francisco, CA: Jossey-Bass.

Revenstorf, D., Hahlweg, K., Schindler, L., & Vogel, B. (1984). Interaction analysis of marital conflict. In K. Hahlweg & N. S. Jacobson (Eds.), *Marital interaction: Analysis and modification* (pp. 159–181). New York: Guilford.

Siffert, A., & Schwarz, B. (2011). Spouses' demand and withdrawal during marital conflict and their well-being. *Journal of Social and Personal Relationships, 28,* 262–277.

Sillars, A., & Canary, D. J. (2013). Conflict and relational quality in families. In A. L. Vangelisti (Ed.), *Routledge handbook of family communication* (2nd ed., pp. 338–357). New York: Routledge.

Sillars, A., Canary, D. J., & Tafoya, M. (2004). Communication, conflict, and the quality of family relationships. In A. L. Vangelisti (Ed.), *Handbook of family communication* (pp. 413–446). Mahwah, NJ: Lawrence Erlbaum.

Sillars, A. L. (1980). The sequential and distributional structure of conflict interactions as a function of attributions concerning the locus of responsibility and stability of conflicts. In D. Nimmo (Ed.), *Communication Yearbook 4* (pp. 217–235). New Brunswick, NJ: Transaction.

Sillars, A. L., Roberts, L. J., Leonard, K. E., & Dun, T. (2000). Cognition during marital conflict: The relationship of thought and talk. *Journal of Social and Personal Relationships, 17,* 479–502.

Sillars, A. L., & Weisberg, J. (1987). Conflict as a social skill. In M. E. Roloff & G. R. Miller (Eds.), *Interpersonal processes: New directions in communication research* (pp. 140–171). Newbury Park, CA: Sage.

Sillars, A. L., & Wilmot, W. W. (1994). Communication strategies in conflict and mediation. In J. Wiemann & J. A. Daly (Eds.), *Communicating strategically: Strategies in interpersonal communication* (pp. 163–190). Hillsdale, NJ: Lawrence Erlbaum.

Storms, M. (1973). Videotape and the attribution process: Reversing actors' and observers' points of view. *Journal of Personality and Social Psychology, 27,* 165–175.

Ting-Toomey, S. (1983). Coding conversations between intimates: A validation study of the Intimate Negotiation System (INCS). *Communication Quarterly, 31,* 68–77.

van de Vliert, E., & Euwema, M. C. (1994). Agreeableness and activeness as components of conflict behaviors. *Journal of Personality and Social Psychology, 66,* 674–687.

van den Broucke, S., Vertommen, H., & Vandereycken, W. (1995). Construction and validation of a Marital Intimacy Questionnaire. *Family Relations, 44,* 285–290.

Vincent, J. P., Weiss, R. L., & Birchler, G. R. (1975). A behavioral analysis of problem-solving in married and stranger dyads. *Behavior Therapy, 6,* 475–487.

Warner, R. M. (1992). Cyclicity of vocal activity increases during conversation: Support for a nonlinear systems model of dyadic social interaction. *Behavioral Science, 37,* 128–138.

Weiss, R. L. (1993). *Marital Interaction Coding System–IV (MICS-IV).* Unpublished coding manual.

Woodin, E. M. (2011). A two-dimensional approach to relationship conflict: Meta-analytic findings. *Journal of Family Psychology, 25,* 325–335.

Zietlow, P. H., & Sillars, A. L. (1988). Life-stage differences in communication during marital conflicts. *Journal of Social and Personal Relationships, 5,* 223–245.

2

■

OBSERVING FAMILY COMMUNICATION

HEATHER E. CANARY

The family constitutes a rich context for observing communication behavior. The context is rich not only in terms of the variety of communication behaviors occurring in families but also in terms of the pervasiveness and influence of families across the life span. Indeed, scholars across multiple disciplines observe family communication to better understand a number of relevant phenomena, including problem behavior (e.g., Garcia, Shaw, Winslow, & Yaggi, 2000), substance use (e.g., Jacob, Haber, Leonard, & Rushe, 2000; Metzger et al., 2013), conflict behaviors (e.g., Caughlin & Malis, 2004; Howe, Rinaldi, Jennings, & Petrakos, 2002), and a variety of health and well-being outcomes for family members (e.g., Cline et al., 2006; Fiese, Winter, & Botti, 2011).

Several reasons warrant the use of observational methods in family communication studies. One reason is that people often behave differently than what they report either in surveys or in interviews (Kerig, 2001). Another reason is that, similar to other contexts, observing the interactional enactment of multiple family relationships in situ can provide insights into the complexities of family systems that cannot be revealed by self- or other reports (Kerig, 2001). A number of other benefits and limitations of observational research are described by Sillars and Overall (this volume), which apply to family systems as well as other relational systems.

In this chapter I discuss several issues related to the observational study of family communication. First, I review the theoretical underpinnings of many observational studies and coding systems. Second, I briefly discuss differences between whole-system studies and studies of particular subsystems within families. Third, I describe two representative observational systems and other methods of observing family communication. The observational systems described with some detail provide one example of a macro-coding system, involving researcher ratings of global characteristics of family interactions, and one example of a micro-coding system, involving recording individual communication behaviors as they occur throughout interactions. Fourth, I briefly review common topics for observational research of family interactions. The chapter concludes with suggestions for future observational research of family communication.

Theoretical Foundations

Systems theory is represented in much observational research of family communication. This general perspective is reflected in relational communication theory (see Rogers & Cummings, this volume) and the Circumplex Model (Olson, 2000), as well as in studies focusing on the co-influence across family subsystems. For example, scholars draw on the interdependence principle of systems theory when they study the effect of marital conflict on parent-child interactions and child outcomes (i.e., *interparental conflict*) (e.g., Cummings & Davies, 2010; Gordis & Margolin, 2001; Katz & Woodin, 2002). This theoretical perspective is quite appropriate for observational studies of family communication because investigators can code at both the micro level, such as discrete messages or behaviors, as well as at the macro level, such as overall ratings of warmth or contentiousness displayed within family systems. Some coding systems, such as the Iowa Family Interaction Rating Scales (IFIRS), involve rating subsystem interactions and then making global ratings of the overall system. The systems perspective theoretically supports such analyses of symbolic interaction.

Two theories emerging specifically from the communication discipline, communication accommodation theory (CAT) and family communication patterns theory (FCPT), hold potential for framing observational research but have not been used to their full potential up to this date. Briefly, CAT includes constructs for explaining "how and why people shift their communication to or from those with whom they interact" (Harwood, Soliz, & Lin, 2006, p. 22). CAT constructs and propositions involve four encoding strategies: (a) approximation strategies, (b) interpretability strategies, (c) discourse management, and (d) interpersonal control. *Approximation strategies* accommodate to another person's speech style and communication behaviors, such as when children mimic their parents (Harwood et al., 2006). *Interpretability strategies* accommodate to the other person's ability to understand, such as when parents use simple words to talk with their young children (Harwood et al., 2006). *Discourse management strategies* accommodate to the other person's conversational needs by adjusting topics or other aspects of the conversation as a whole, such as children asking grandparents about things that happened in the past (Harwood et al., 2006). Finally, *interpersonal control* involves strategies to direct the course of a conversation or relationship, such as by interrupting the other person (Harwood et al., 2006). These constructs lend themselves quite naturally to coding observed behavior, and yet little CAT empirical research has involved observation of actual interaction. One study, conducted by Montepare, Steinberg, and Rosenberg (1992), used CAT to study conversations between young adults and their parents and grandparents. Consistent with CAT, the results revealed that participants' vocal qualities changed when they talked with their grandparents compared with their parents. This indicates how different familial roles and attitudes toward intergenerational relationships are differentially reflected through communication behaviors. More recently, Harwood et al. (2006) called for additional observational studies grounded in CAT to identify communication patterns within families or identify when specific strategies are used and to what ends.

Family Communication Patterns theory (FCPT) constitutes a third theory that holds promise for observational research. This theory posits that families develop communication patterns along two dimensions: (a) conversation orientation and (b) conformity orientation (Koerner & Fitzpatrick, 2006). *Conversation orientation* refers to "the degree to which families create a climate in which all family members are encouraged to participate in unrestrained interaction about a wide array of topics" (Koerner & Fitzpatrick, 2006, p. 54). *Conformity orientation* refers to "the degree to which family communication stresses a climate of homogeneity of attitudes, values, and beliefs" (Koerner & Fitzpatrick, 2006, p. 55). One reason its observational potential has not been realized, perhaps, is that the primary instrument developed to examine FCPT constructs is a survey measure. However, two studies have demonstrated the value of observational research for applying and refining FCPT in family interaction contexts. Koerner and Cvancara (2002) used conformity orientation as the independent variable and then coded observed family-level conflict conversations. That study provided a more nuanced understanding of the influence of conformity orientation on micro-level family interactions than would be provided with survey data. In another study, Buijzen and Valkenburg (2008) observed parent-child interactions in a toy store and then administered the Family Communication Patterns Scale to participants. In this context of parent-child communication about purchases, the investigators found no significant associations between FCPT variables and child influence, child coercive behavior, or parent-initiated communication about purchases. Results from these two studies in different family situations indicate that we do not yet know how people enact FCPT constructs in actual family interactions and how different orientations influence everyday communication.

These three theories illustrate how theories offer foundations for observing family communication. Many other theories represented in observational research cannot be discussed here, simply because of space constraints. Importantly, scholars acknowledge that theory plays an important role in providing results from observations that are more than descriptive (Kerig, 2001). By engaging theory in observational research, investigators contribute to the body of knowledge about family systems with nuanced data and explanations. The following section discusses observations of family systems and subsystems, and it illustrates a few nuanced findings.

Systems and Subsystems

Families as a context of communication are challenging to study. They become even more challenging when research goals include needs to record and code observations of the entire system in one interactional event and, especially, across times and contexts. Many researchers have conducted whole-system observational studies successfully, however, so we know it can be done. For instance, a multidisciplinary team of researchers from the University of California, Los Angeles, conducted naturalistic observations of families in their homes with videotape (Repetti, Wang, & Sears, 2013). Additionally, studies of family mealtimes, which are described in more detail below, involve all (or most) family members as observed participants. Coding systems have been developed, either for specific contexts or for general use across contexts, which allow coding of multiple participants. For example, Vuchinich (1987) observed family mealtimes by coding conflict-initiating, conflict-extending, and conflict-stopping behaviors and who performed those behaviors. By including all, or most, members in a routine interaction event, such as eating dinner, Vuchinich offered insight into dynamics across family roles.

Other investigators who focus on the whole system analyze behavior of particular subsystems separately and then analyze associations among those subsystem observations. For instance, Garcia et al. (2000) coded observations of mother-child interactions and then separately coded observations of sibling interaction. Their goal was to examine the combined effect of destructive parenting and sibling conflict on behavior outcomes for young boys. The results support an additive risk model, which is a systems-based theory of child development. Several child development studies have used similar methods to study parent-child and sibling interactions separately and then analyze their links with phenomena of interest.

One area of research that has contributed significant explanations concerning the interdependence of relationships within family systems is that of interparental conflict, described above. Although some research within this area has used survey data, investigators have made important advances with observational methods. For example, Katz and Woodin (2002) observed interparental conversations about a contentious topic, and then they observed coparenting in a lab context immediately after the parental conversation. They then followed those two interactions by observing child participants playing with peers. The results revealed that the combination of hostility and detachment in marital interactions was significantly associated with children's negative affect and noncompliance in peer interactions. Studies such as this demonstrate the importance of capturing family interactions across subsystems to increase our understanding of child behavior inside and outside the family system.

Many observational studies of family communication do not attempt to observe the entire system. Rather, they focus on just one subsystem, such as parent-child, siblings, or marital couples. Because the majority of observational research of marital couples concerns conflict (Feeney & Noller, 2013), and three chapters in this volume discuss marital couple interactions (i.e., D. J. Canary; Rogers & Cummings; Sillars & Overall), I refer the reader to those chapters for information regarding observing marital couple interaction. Parent-child interactions have garnered attention in two main age cohorts: toddlers or preschoolers and adolescents. This additional attention probably arises because these two stages represent dramatic developmental changes within children and dramatic differences within family systems that adjust to those changes. Many child development studies of parents and toddlers or preschoolers have observed interactions in home situations, either with audio or video recordings. For example, Huang, Teti, Caughy, Feldstein, and Genevro (2007) observed mothers and toddlers in their home environments. They developed their own coding system for observations of mother-toddler conflict because the children were for the most part preverbal, and existing coding systems were designed for verbal behaviors. Their results indicated that the toddlers were much less defiant than the "terrible twos" label leads people to believe (Canary & Canary, 2013). Consistent with many other observational studies, Huang et al. (2007) examined associations between coded interaction behavior and variables measured using survey methods. The results indicate that a variety of factors, including knowledge of child development, poverty, and child temperament, are associated with maternal conflict behaviors.

Parent-adolescent interactions are also frequently studied, with much of this research also focusing on conflict. However, some interesting studies of parent-adolescent conversations focus on important topics for today's youth, such as cigarette smoking (Metzger et al., 2013) and sexuality (Pluhar & Kuriloff, 2004). Although these topics may lead to conflict, the studies have focused more broadly on how conversations about such topics reveal relationship qualities between parents and adolescents and how such conversations associate with later behavior. Caughlin and Malis (2004) provided an interesting twist in family observational research by studying the demand-withdraw pattern of conflict interaction between parents and adolescents. This pattern was originally identified in marital couples and typically is studied in romantic dyads. As with married couples, results reveal significant associations between the demand-withdraw pattern and relationship satisfaction for both parents and adolescents. Specifically, parent and adolescent relationship satisfaction self-reports were inversely associated with the demand-withdraw pattern of interaction, which was measured by both self-reports and observational methods.

Siblings are also frequently observed. These studies typically focus on conflict (e.g., Garcia et al., 2000; Howe et al., 2002), which is understandable considering the pervasiveness of sibling conflict across the life span (Canary & Canary, 2013). One study of note illustrates a theoretically grounded nonconflict observational study of sibling communication, although it included more than one subsystem. Howe and Rinaldi (2004) observed mother-child interactions and then observed sibling caretaking interactions in a laboratory setting for the purpose of examining emotional socialization of young children across family interaction contexts and how that manifests in sibling interactions.

At this point, it would be helpful to briefly describe some representative coding systems used in observational family communication research. Also, the following section includes alternative methods for conducting observational studies of family communication and issues to consider when choosing a method.

Methods for Observing Family Communication

Numerous coding systems are represented in family research, and it would be impossible to discuss all of them. Researchers tend to use their own codes that are suited to the particular focus of their research projects rather than relying on more general coding systems (Kerig, 2001). Many times this is warranted, as when studying mealtime interactions (e.g., Patton, Dolan, Smith, Brown, & Powers, 2013) or parent interactions with preverbal toddlers (e.g., Huang et al., 2007). However, Kerig (2001) argued that a body of knowledge concerning focal behavior is inhibited by not using established, validated coding systems in multiple studies for multiple purposes. Two coding systems that various researchers have used are described

below, one general family coding system and one for the specific context of mealtime interactions.

Iowa Family Interaction Rating Scale (IFIRS)

The IFIRS is in its fifth edition, reflecting revisions made over several years (Melby et al., 1998). This macro-coding system includes 60 scales, mostly using ratings on a scale ranging from 1 to 9, or "not at all characteristic" to "mainly characteristic." Coders rate participants on the overall interaction rather than coding each verbal message or interaction turn. Researchers choose which scales are appropriate for their particular study designs. The IFIRS consists of 11 individual characteristic scales (e.g., Sadness), 22 dyadic interaction scales (e.g., Verbal Attack), 2 dyadic relationship scales (e.g., Relationship Quality), 1 group interaction scale (Group Enjoyment), 14 parenting scales (e.g., Consistent Discipline), 5 individual problem-solving scales (e.g., Solution Quantity), and 5 group problem-solving scales (e.g., Problem Difficulty). Table 2.1 lists the categories and scales within each category.

Many researchers have used the IFIRS in multiple contexts (for a review, see Melby & Conger, 2001). For

Table 2.1 Iowa Family Interaction Rating Scales

Individual Characteristics Scales	Dyadic Interaction Scales
Physically Attractive	Hostility
Humor/Laugh	Verbal Attack
Sadness	Physical Attack
Anxiety	Contempt
Whine/Complain	Angry Coercion
Externalized Negative	Escalate Hostile
Positive Mood	Reciprocate Hostile
Indulgent/Permissive	Dominance
Defiance	Lecture/Moralize
Compliance	Interrogation
Rater Response	Denial
Physical Movement[a]	Warmth/Support
Facial Movement[a]	Endearment
Internalized Negative[a]	Physical Affection
Escalate Hostile[a]	Escalate Warmth/Support
Escalate Positive[a]	Reciprocate Warmth/Support
Intellectual Skills[a]	Assertiveness
	Listener Responsiveness

Dyadic Relationship Scales	Communication
Silence/Pause	Prosocial
Relationship Quality	Antisocial
	Avoidant
Group Interaction Scales	Verbally Involved[a]
Group Enjoyment	Body Toward[a]
Group Disorganization[a]	Body Away[a]
Parenting Scales	*Individual Problem-Solving*
Neglecting/Distancing	Solution Quantity
Quality Time	Solution Quality
Parental Influence	Effective Process
Child Monitoring	Disruptive Process
Inconsistent Discipline	Negotiation/Compromise
Consistent Discipline	
Harsh Discipline	*Group Problem-Solving*
Positive Reinforcement	Family Enjoyment
Inductive Reasoning	Agreement on Problem Description
Encourages Independence	Agreement on Solution
Easily Coerced	Implementation Commitment
Intrusive	Problem Difficulty
Sensitive/Child Centered	
Stimulates Cognitive Development	

Source: Melby and Conger (2001).

a. Scales used in first to fourth editions only and defined in fifth edition appendix.

instance, Dunn et al. (2011) used the IFIRS to conduct a study of verbal, nonverbal, and emotional components of family communication about cancer. They used six IFIRS scales to code observations of mother-child conversations about the child's cancer (Positive Mood, Sadness, Warmth/Support, Hostility, Child-Centeredness, and Neglect/Distancing). Their pilot study indicated the feasibility and acceptability of observing parent-child interactions for this population (families of children with cancer). Results also confirmed construct validity of the IFIRS scales used. Williamson, Bradbury, Trail, and Karney (2011) used

the IFIRS to study low-income, ethnically diverse couples, a population underrepresented in family communication research. They found that the results for their sample were similar to results in White, middle-class samples. Also, the results of that study revealed a three-factor structure (negative, positive, and effective communication) that coincides with previous IFIRS studies as well as to factors identified in other interaction coding systems typically used for dyadic research.

The ABC Mealtime Coding System

Some family interaction contexts are better coded by accounting for the unique aspects of the context, such as mealtimes. Mealtimes represent a particularly rich context for observing family interactions because they are "densely packed events" (Fiese, Foley, & Spagnola, 2006, p. 77) in which family roles are enacted, food is consumed, and interaction patterns are reinforced all within approximately 20 minutes. Research consistently demonstrates that positive mealtime interactions are associated with positive outcomes for family members, particularly children (Fiese et al., 2006). Furthermore, scholars across disciplines and time have demonstrated the pervasiveness of family mealtimes, in various forms, across cultural and socioeconomic categories (Larson, Branscomb, & Wiley, 2006). Although researchers have used several coding schemes, the ABC Mealtime Coding System (Fiese, Botti, & Greenberg, 2007) provides an example of a micro-coding system, as opposed to a macro-coding system, represented by the IFIRS. ABC-trained coders record each time a particular behavior occurs, including the category for the behavior, who displayed it, and how long the behavior lasted. In this way, each individual interaction behavior is coded, and analyses can be standardized across samples that have different interaction times, because percentages of total interaction time are computed for each behavior category. The ABC system uses five categories for behavior: (a) *action-oriented behavior*, which includes instances when participants' attention is diverted away from the meal; (b) *behavior control behavior*, which is intended to somehow affect another person's behavior; (c) *meal-oriented communication*, which pertains directly to the food or other meal routine aspects; (d) *positive communication*, which includes friendly joking or sharing information; and (e) *critical communication*, which includes disapproving or other harsh statements about another participant (Fiese et al., 2011). Table 2.2 lists examples of these behaviors, adapted from the ABC coding manual (Fiese et al., 2007).

Table 2.2 ABC Mealtime Coding System Behaviors

Action behaviors	Standing up and leaving the meal to
	Answer the phone/door
	Turn on/off appliance (i.e., TV)
	Get something needed for the meal (e.g., utensils)
	Put utensils/dishes, food, or people elsewhere
	Speak to someone away from the meal
	Use the bathroom
	Play with something near the meal (not facing meal)
	Go somewhere else either in or away from the home
	Conduct any other action that takes place away from meal
Behavior control behaviors	Direct commands to cease or change behavior
Communication behaviors	
Mealtime communication	Discussion of the food at the meal
	All task-oriented or routine-oriented comments
	Discussion of mealtime routine-related issues
	Any discussion pertaining to the camera recording meal
Critical communication	Critical statements in response to another's behavior or person
	Disapproving statements regarding a person with a harsh tone
Positive communication	Comments, questions, or conversations about how one (or many) are feeling, what they are doing, either at time of meal or in some other time period
	Comments, questions, or conversations about information that may be unrelated to family members' feelings or actions (e.g., news, facts, politics)
	Life/family events
	Emotive actions, such as crying or pouting
	Joking or teasing, use of nicknames and inside jokes
	Comments/actions that are in response to others' behavior but without the intent to control

Source: Fiese, B. H., Botti, J. C., & Greenberg, S. (2007). ABC Coding Manual. Used by permission of the first author.

Note: For the full coding manual, contact Dr. Barbara H. Fiese, University of Illinois at Urbana-Champaign, Department of Human and Community Development, 1016B Doris Kelley Christopher Hall, MC-081, 904 W. Nevada, Urbana, IL 61801 (e-mail: bhfiese@illinois.edu).

Fiese et al. (2011) used this coding system to analyze mealtime interactions in families of children with asthma. The results point to important associations between the type of mealtime interactions families engaged in and asthma symptom severity for children. Families who were more engaged with one another during the meal and shared more information about their daily lives tended to have children whose asthma symptoms were less severe and who adhered to medical regimens better. Conversely, action behaviors and critical communication behaviors were negatively associated with symptom severity. Fiese et al. reported a number of additional findings important for overall child health and well-being. Many such studies have focused on various health outcomes and using different coding methods. I review a few of these in the section concerning common topics for observational family communication studies.

To compare mealtime interactions across different races and ethnicities, Kong et al. (2013) used the ABC Mealtime Coding System to analyze Hispanic, African American, and non-Hispanic White families. Although some racial and ethnic differences were found, families were similar in how long meals lasted and in their overall engagement in more action-oriented behaviors than in other coded behaviors. With increased interest in associations between family interactions and health outcomes for members, the results of these two studies indicate a need for continued observational research of families across specific family populations.

Other Observational Methods

Although the majority of observational studies of family communication have used quantitative coding systems, involving assigning numeric scores and using statistical analyses of results (Feeney & Noller, 213), researchers use other methods as well. Qualitative methods constitute another methodological option for observing family communication. Qualitative methodologies focus on relaying participant experiences in nonnumeric forms (Feeney & Noller, 2013). When researchers use interpretive theoretical frameworks, such as symbolic interactionism or phenomenology, qualitative methods might be as or more appropriate to the study's goal(s). Recent research describes how qualitative methods have been used to provide rich description of family conversations in different contexts. For instance, Pluhar and Kuriloff (2004) used qualitative coding methods in their study of conversations between mothers and their adolescent daughters about sex and birth control. Paugh and Izquierdo (2009) also relied on qualitative methods to analyze family mealtime interactions. Orrell-Valente et al. (2007) used qualitative methods first to develop a new coding system of family mealtime interaction and then used that coding system to analyze participants' mealtime interactions.

Many observational studies use multiple methods to analyze both processes and responses to or perceptions of those processes. Such multi-method studies are often quite powerful in explaining associations between internal participant states, such as attitudes, emotions, and interpretations, and external processes, such as verbal and nonverbal behaviors. For example, a project of the Center for the Everyday Lives of Families (CELF) at the University of California, Los Angeles, included videotaping family members in their homes from early in the morning, when they were getting ready for work and school, continuing when they returned home from work and school, and concluding after children went to bed at night. In addition to videotaping everyday family interactions on several different days (including weekdays and weekends), the project also included interviews with all family members to elicit their perceptions about a variety of topics related to their family lives, questionnaires, sampling of stress hormones, mapping and

photographing the homes, and tracking families' uses of space (Paugh & Izquierdo, 2009; Repetti et al., 2013).

Interviews have been used in qualitative observational studies, reflecting a more interpretive methodological commitment to eliciting participant narrative explanations and responses to their family interactions (e.g., Pluhar & Kuriloff, 2004). Other studies adopted survey instruments to measure variables of interest and to analyze associations between interaction features and those variables. For example, Caughlin and Malis (2004) analyzed parent-adolescent conflict interactions and used a survey measure of relational satisfaction to assess associations between conflict interaction patterns and levels of parent-adolescent relational satisfaction. Other studies have used longitudinal designs to observe interactions at one time and then followed up at a later time to assess outcomes, such as risky behavior (e.g., Metzger et al., 2013) or developmental characteristics (e.g., Garcia et al., 2000). Such longitudinal designs are particularly powerful for demonstrating the influence of family interactions on family member outcomes.

Settings and Samples

The methods discussed above raise important issues concerning observational settings and samples included in observational studies. The IFIRS was developed using interactions within a laboratory, but it has subsequently been used in homes. This coding system is designed to be used with video recordings of interactions, so wherever such recording could be possible would likely be suitable for using the IFIRS. Many observational studies, using a variety of coding methods, occur in researcher labs because of logistical difficulties getting observers and/or recording equipment into family homes at the right time. A concern exists about how representative laboratory interactions are when they involve an assigned topic, are being observed, and transpire within a given time limit (e.g., 15 minutes). However, researchers note that family members will not be able to significantly change their behavior just because they want to, and those who do not know how to enact constructive interaction behaviors will not be able to "fake" those behaviors just because they are being observed (Kerig, 2001). Nevertheless, researchers can better observe some family interactions in the home, such as mealtime interactions.

Sampling raises another concern for observational research, and for any family research for that matter. An overabundance exists of family communication research among White, middle-class families. Some researchers use coding systems, such as the IFIRS and the ABC Mealtime Coding System, across ethnically, racially, and socioeconomically diverse samples. Such studies of demographically diverse families provide exemplars of using coding systems to capture ways in which families across ethnic, racial, and socioeconomic groups interact similarly or differently in particular contexts (e.g., Kong et al., 2013; Williamson et al., 2011). Additionally, child ages within sample families are an important consideration (Kerig, 2001). Not all coding systems are appropriate for the ages or developmental stages of focal family members. For example, Huang et al. (2007) investigated mother-toddler conflict in a large, diverse sample (378 dyads) but could not identify appropriate coding systems in prior research that would enable the researchers to capture characteristics of mother-child interactions for both verbal and preverbal children. Accordingly, their first task was to use existing conflict coding systems as a foundation to construct their own coding system that could be used for all ages represented in their sample. With these methodological considerations in mind, in the following section I briefly review common topics of observational family communication studies and how observational methods have resulted in unique insights about family interactions.

What Are We Observing?

Mealtimes

Researchers have been studying mealtime interactions with observational methods for several decades. Indeed, so many studies have been conducted now of family mealtime interactions that all of them cannot possibly be reviewed in this section. One reason for the focus on mealtime is the routine, naturalistic character of this interactional event. Most families develop mealtime routines that reflect broader family dynamics (Fiese et al., 2011). I briefly describe three mealtime studies here as examples of different methodological approaches to studying family mealtimes.

In one of the earlier studies of family mealtime interactions, Vuchinich (1987) posited that mealtimes are an excellent context for identifying spontaneous family conflict. His study focused on nondistressed families representing several socioeconomic groups in multiple regions of the United States and included both White and Black families. Using talk turn as the unit of analysis, coders coded each occurrence of verbally expressed

opposition (although nonverbal expression may have accompanied verbal oppositional expressions). These oppositional talk turns combined to make conflict episodes. By focusing on identifiable conflict episodes during mealtimes, Vuchinich was able to identify how participants in different family roles initiated, extended, and stopped conflict. Coding each talk turn also facilitated analyses of what types of communication behaviors extended and stopped conflict.

Paugh and Izquierdo (2009) used mealtimes as a way to identify parent-child conflicts over health issues, eating, and values in an ethnically diverse sample of middle-class families. Using both interview and video-recorded data of five families from the larger CELF study previously described, Paugh and Izquierdo used qualitative, interpretive methods to identify ways in which parents' ideas about health and nutrition contradicted their everyday mealtime behaviors and interactions. The results of their study also indicate the prevalence of negotiations between parents and children during mealtime interactions.

Relatedly, Orrell-Valente et al. (2007) observed mealtimes in families of kindergartners as representative of children's socialization of eating. Observers wrote detailed narratives describing family interactions they observed, and then those narratives were coded to identify associations between family interactions and children's behavior problems (Orrell-Valente et al., 2007). They developed their own coding system to code for mealtime structure variables (e.g., location, television viewing) and mealtime process variables (e.g., parental strategies to influence children's eating). Overall, the results indicate that parents attempted to get their kindergarten children to eat more during meals than they might have otherwise and that children complied more with positive influence strategies (e.g., praise) than with negative influence strategies (e.g., threats). The researchers noted that an important future direction of mealtime studies is to obtain children's perceptions of such interactions.

Researchers frequently study mealtime interactions as they relate to children with special health concerns, such as asthma (Fiese et al., 2011), type 1 diabetes (Patton et al., 2013), and cystic fibrosis (Mitchell, Powers, Byars, Dickstein, & Stark, 2004). Overall, the results of these studies indicate links between family mealtime interaction features and health-related behaviors and outcomes. However, Patton et al. (2013) did not find significant associations between ineffective parent mealtime behaviors and focal diabetes variables or problematic child mealtime behaviors and those variables. Accordingly, one cannot make generalizations about the impact of mealtime interactions across different health conditions. Readers are encouraged to see primary sources for more information that might contribute to future observational research of the mealtime interaction–health connection.

Risky Behaviors

Researchers recognize the importance of parent-adolescent interactions for child behavioral outcomes, including risky behavior. Simply encouraging parents to talk with their adolescent children about such topics as cigarette smoking, alcohol consumption, drug use, sexual intercourse, and sexuality is not effective in itself. Rather, it is important to consider the relational context, family system, and differences between constructive and destructive interaction behaviors. For example, Metzger et al. (2013) used a study-specific coding scheme, Family Talk About Smoking, which is a global rating scale similar to the IFIRS, to analyze interaction features when parents and adolescents discussed cigarette smoking. They found that when parents initiated smoking discussions and adolescents engaged in active secrecy about their smoking behaviors, adolescents were more likely to increase their smoking behavior 2 years later. Clearly, a global, simple message of "talk to your child" does not explain such outcomes. Somewhat in line with Metzger et al.'s findings, Richmond, Mermelstein, and Wakschlag (2013), using the IFIRS, found that better general communication styles for mothers and fathers predicted a decline in negative affect for teen smokers. Importantly, this longitudinal, multimethod study also revealed that negative affect at baseline predicted smoking behavior in adolescents 24 months later.

Not surprisingly, sexuality and sexual behavior constitute another sensitive topic area for parents and adolescents. Observing actual interactions about these topics, particularly when paired with data about participant perceptions or attitudes, reveals important information that can inform interventions designed to improve parent-adolescent communication about sexuality. For instance, Whalen, Henker, Hollingshead, and Burgess (1996) used a study-specific rating system to observe parent-adolescent conversations about AIDS and also collected survey data about AIDS knowledge and attitudes. They found interesting sex differences in parent-adolescent interactions, pointing to important nuances in how teens respond to such conversations. For example, ratings of mutuality and supportiveness were higher for parent-daughter dyads, whereas sons displayed more withdrawal during interactions than did daughters.

Focusing only on mother-daughter dyads, Pluhar and Kuriloff (2004) used qualitative coding and interview methods to study conversations about sex and sexuality. The researchers observed mothers and daughters discussing sex topics and then interviewed each participant individually about what she thought after viewing the videotaped interaction. Grounded in phenomenology, the analysis revealed that the meanings participants assigned to their conversations were linked much more to affective and stylistic dimensions than to the content of the conversations. The affective dimension included the level of comfort participants had when talking about sex topics, perceptions of empathy from the other, anger, and silence during the conversations. The stylistic dimension included distinctions between didactic conversations controlled by mothers and interactive conversations mutually controlled. The results of the study also reveal the importance of storytelling in mother-daughter conversations about sex and sexuality, with many mothers conveying warnings for their daughters to not follow in their footsteps. Overall, this study is an example of alternative forms of observational research by involving participants in assigning meaning to interactions.

Conflict

Conflict is another common context for observational studies of family communication. Such studies include interparental conflict, parent-child conflict, and sibling conflict. As discussed previously, observational studies of family mealtime interactions also frequently focus on conflict at the whole-family level. Observing conflicts between family members is particularly important because participants often do not recall or perceive such interactions similarly (Sillars, Koerner, & Fitzpatrick, 2005; Sillars, Smith, & Koerner, 2010).

Much observational research of conflict interactions between mothers and young children and among siblings focuses on associations between conflict interactions and child development factors, such as problem behaviors, emotional development, and relationship development (e.g., Garcia et al., 2000; Howe et al., 2002; Huang et al., 2007; Laible & Thompson, 2002). For example, the results of Howe et al.'s (2002) study indicate different strategies young siblings use to manage conflicts with one another during play interactions, the role of birth order in those strategies, and how their sibling conflict strategies, including resolution strategies, are associated with children's social understandings. Similarly, Laible and Thompson (2002) found that mothers' use of conflict-mitigating strategies, such as compromise and bargaining, and justification strategies, such as clarifications and reasoning, when their children were 2.5 years old were associated with several positive child characteristics 6 months later. These positive outcomes included children's emotional understanding, sociomoral competence, and prosocial perceptions of relationships. Huang et al. (2007) observed interactions between mothers and their 16- to 18-month-old children. The results indicated that mothers' preference for constructive responses, such as distraction, reasoning, or negotiation, and simple oppositional responses, such as saying "no," were positively associated with children's adaptive responses (e.g., obeying or negotiating) but were negatively tied to overt oppositional responses (e.g., saying "no," throwing temper tantrums). These studies, and others in this line of research, have contributed substantially to understandings of the role of family conflict in child development and socialization.

Other studies focus on parent-adolescent conflict (e.g., Caughlin & Malis, 2004; Sillars et al., 2005, 2010) and marital conflict (see Canary, this volume). These observational studies often investigate associations between conflict interaction behaviors or patterns with relationship characteristics, such as satisfaction (Caughlin & Malis, 2004; Sillars et al., 2005) and attributions (Sillars et al., 2010). For example, when presented with a replay of their videotaped conversations, parents in Sillars et al.'s (2010) study overattributed negative thoughts to their adolescent children, and adolescents overattributed controlling thoughts to their parents. Although much value lies in observational studies of parent-adolescent conflict, fewer studies of parent-adolescent conflict use observational methods than do studies of parents with young children. Conflict is a deep and broad topic, and it is not possible to adequately cover it in this section. For an overview of family conflict research, including a summary of much observational research, see Canary and Canary (2013).

Health and Disability

The broad area of health and disability constitutes the final common topic for observing family interactions. This area has experienced a huge increase in research attention in the past couple of decades as health communication has developed into a large subfield within the discipline of communication and as interdisciplinary teams conduct large-scale, funded studies. Although many health and disability contexts are represented within this research area, I briefly review select studies in contexts of cancer, other health conditions, disability and development, and family-provider interactions.

Cancer. Cancer is not an individual experience. Rather, cancer is a family experience (Beach, 2009). Beach (2009) provided perhaps one of the most complete observational studies of family interactions in the context of cancer in his conversation analysis of audio-recorded family telephone conversations about a mother's diagnosis, treatment, and ultimate death. This book-length study reveals how members of one family conversationally managed bad news, uncertainty, emotional highs and lows, spirituality, and hope as they shared the cancer journey.

Other studies of family cancer are less ambitious and more narrowly focused on single interaction events. For example, Cline et al. (2006) observed mother-child interactions when children were in a clinic to undergo painful cancer treatments. The researchers developed a study-specific coding system for parent-child communication in the cancer treatment context. Using four behavior types (normalizing, invalidating, supportive, and distancing), the investigators coded parent communication across different types of treatment appointments. They found important associations between parent communication patterns and different types of treatment appointments as well as between parent communication patterns and children's perceptions of pain during treatment. For instance, children who received invalidating messages from their mothers reported more pain and distress than children whose mothers used other types of communication. Dunn et al. (2011) also observed parent-child interactions in the context of childhood cancer, but their study was conducted in a laboratory setting rather than examination or treatment rooms and involved discussion about the children's cancer rather than interactions during actual cancer treatment. This study provided foundational information about the feasibility of observing such family conversations within this population by assessing participation and completion rates. Participation was similar to, although slightly lower than, in other observational studies of family communication in the presence of child health problems. The results also indicate the applicability of the IFIRS in the family cancer context by assessing associations among positive and negative codes and confirming construct validity of the six IFIRS codes used in the study.

Other health conditions. Many other health conditions of family members are represented in observational communication research. For example, mealtime studies, discussed above, often focus on specific health conditions such as asthma, diabetes, cystic fibrosis, and obesity. However, studies of family communication in such health contexts are not limited to mealtime interactions. For instance, Seiffge-Krenke (2002) found significant differences between communication of fathers and their diabetic adolescent children and communication of fathers and nondiabetic adolescents. The researchers used a coding scheme developed specifically for the study, identifying 19 strategies of communication behaviors displayed by fathers in a planning task conversation with their children. Overall, compared with fathers of healthy children, fathers of diabetic adolescents made fewer suggestions, developed fewer contributions, offered fewer alternatives, responded less frequently to their children's requests, agreed with their children less often, and interrupted their children less frequently. The investigators concluded that fathers of diabetic adolescents were generally passive in the planning conversations and did not tend to promote their children's independence by supporting children's contributions to the planning task. Interestingly, these results contradict fathers' self-reports of their levels of involvement with non-health-related issues with their adolescent children. This study, then, provides another example of the importance of observational research across a variety of family contexts.

Disability and development. Researchers interested in disability and developmental issues within family members also investigate family interactions to gain insight into how family communication might influence disabilities or developmental issues and vice versa. Alston and St. James-Roberts (2005) provided one example of a study looking for associations between family communication and child development. The study team observed in-home interactions between mothers and infants to analyze connections between home environments and diagnoses of language development delays. They observed 75 minutes of unstructured play time in participant homes, making notes about mother-child interactions and then assigning global ratings at the end of the observation for maternal sensitivity, maternal intrusiveness, and maternal expressed affect. They found that mothers of children diagnosed as at risk for language and communication difficulty displayed less sensitivity and less positive enjoyment, were more intrusive, and overall had twice as much noninteractive time with their infants than mothers of children not at risk.

Researchers are also interested in how the presence of disability in families might influence interactions. For example, Edwards, Barkley, Laneri, Fletcher, and Metevia (2001) observed parent-adolescent interactions in families with and without teens who had been diagnosed with attention-deficit/hyperactivity disorder (ADHD) and oppositional defiant disorder (ODD). They used the Conflict Rating Scale (Heavey, Layne, & Christensen, 1993) to assign global ratings of participant communication behavior on 15 behavioral dimensions (10 negative and 5 positive). Findings from that study support previous research, in that discussions between parents and teens with ADHD/ODD diagnoses were more negative and less positive than those in the comparison group. However, the results also indicate that the degree of self-reported parental hostility further contributed to levels of parent-adolescent conflict. Both of these exemplar studies indicate the important influence of family interactions on the development and well-being of family members.

Family-provider interactions. Families intersect with multiple social systems, and health care constitutes one of those systems. Recent studies have analyzed family-provider interactions to provide insights into the co-influence of family and other systems (Canary & Cantú, 2012). For example, Dillard, Shen, Laxova, and Farrell (2008) observed conversations between genetic counselors and parents whose infants were being screened for cystic fibrosis. The results of this exploratory study identified five factors within that context that have potential to downgrade parents' abilities to comprehend and retain genetic risk information: (a) copresence, (b) disruptions, (c) variations in parents' knowledge, (d) counselors' behavioral scripts, and (e) emotional interference (p. 242). Wolff and Roter (2012) studied the opposite end of the life span spectrum using the Roter Interaction Analysis System (RIAS) and additional measures for visit duration, patient verbal activity, and ratio of patient-centered communication. The researchers analyzed patient-provider interactions when older patients were and were not accompanied by family members, including comparing findings for patients in good mental health with those in patients in poor mental health. Results indicate that the quality of patient-provider communication was significantly lower when patients with poor mental health were accompanied by family members or companions than when they were not accompanied, including shorter visits and less patient-centered communication.

Studies of family-provider interactions often use the RIAS (Roter, 1999; Roter & Larson, 2002). This coding system focuses on characteristics of messages exchanged in medical interactions using 38 codes of communication behaviors. It is a micro-coding system, coding at "the smallest unit of spoken expression to which a meaningful code can be assigned" (Roter & Larson, 2002, p. 247). This level of coding allows analysis of verbal dominance during interactions and comparisons of types of communication across interactions, as demonstrated in Wolff and Roter's study described above. Table 2.3 presents the broad functional and communication categories of the RIAS.

To address increasing attention to how family characteristics and organizational systems influence provider-family member interactions, my colleagues and I recently developed an interaction coding system called the Resource-Based Interaction Coding System (R-BICS; Canary, Bullis, Cummings, & Kinney, 2014; Canary, Cummings, Bullis, & Kinney, 2013). This coding system was developed in the context of cancer risk conversations between trained interventionists and people at increased risk for cancer because of their family histories. Drawing on constructs of structurating activity theory (Canary, 2010), the R-BICS includes codes for elements of family systems and health-related systems to identify how participants use elements of involved systems as resources that shape their cross-system conversations, health decisions, and health behaviors. It is a micro-coding system, recording each code occurrence in interactions. Future development and research will determine the feasibility of using the R-BICS across contexts of families and health care providers to provide insights into the co-influence of family and professional systems on interactional outcomes such as health behaviors and knowledge. Table 2.4 presents the broad categories of the R-BICS in its current stage of development.

Future Directions for Observing Family Communication

This brief overview of observational research of family communication indicates the enormous potential of such studies. Much insight has been gained by using observational methods. At the same time, much remains to be learned about the complex and pervasive influence of family dynamics on members over the life span. Accordingly, below I describe a few recommendations for future observational research of family communication.

Blurred Boundaries

The nature of families is changing in contemporary society. The notion of "nuclear" and "extended" families is not clear-cut. The first challenge for family researchers is to determine who will "count" as family members in their studies. Although this issue is not unique to observational studies, ways researchers address this issue in study designs and recruitment are consequential methodologically, theoretically, and practically. Most coding systems (see examples in Tables 2.1 to 2.4) do not inherently rely on traditional

Table 2.3 Roter Interaction Analysis System Categories

Functional Grouping	Communication Behavior Categories
Patient education and counseling	Biomedical information-giving Psychosocial information-giving Biomedical counseling Psychosocial counseling
Data gathering	Open-ended questions: medical Open-ended questions: psychosocial Closed-ended questions: medical Closed-ended questions: psychosocial
Building a relationship	Social talk Positive talk Negative talk
Activating and partnering	Participatory facilitators Procedural talk

Source: Roter and Larson (2001).

Table 2.4 Resource-Based Interaction Coding System

Theoretical Category	Involved Activity System	Constitutive Codes
Community	Family	Substantial conversations Brief or nonexistent conversations Family health experiences and stories Family relationships
Division of labor	Family	Family role—caretaker, teacher, role model
Mediating resources—material	CPT	Questionnaire information, written information, materials
	Family	Health insurance, money Other material resources or barriers Time and work schedule, transportation
	PH	Diagnosis, screening, treatment
Mediating resources—symbolic	CPT	Cancer information Dissemination Risk awareness—agreement or acknowledgment Risk awareness—resistance or rejection Ruler to the end
Rules	CPT	Interview interaction rules 　a. Checking participant understanding 　b. Inviting additional questions 　c. Logistics of interview 　d. Suggestive prompt Practice rules 　a. General preventive practices 　b. Screening guidelines
	Family	Health and sickness practices Healthy and good living Philosophy for healthy lifestyle
Subject	Family	Expressing intentions Expressing lack of knowledge General health Identity Knowledgeability and perceptions Personal barriers to screening or treatment 　a. Emotional barriers 　b. Health barriers
Intersections of family and medical systems	CPT-family-PH	Effective or positive intersections Missed or negative intersections
	Family-CPT	Effective or positive intersections through CPT mediating resources Effective or positive intersections through CPT provider Effective or positive intersections through rules Ineffective or negative intersections through CPT mediating resources

(Continued)

Table 2.4 (Continued)

Theoretical Category	Involved Activity System	Constitutive Codes
	Family–PH	Ineffective or negative intersections through CPT rules
		Effective or positive intersections through PH provider
		Effective or positive intersections through PH mediating resources Ineffective or negative intersections through PH provider
Intersections of family and other activity systems	Family-insurance Friends Work	Insurance system rules

Source: Author.

Note: CPT = cancer prevention and treatment; PH = primary health care.

family membership to guide coding. Accordingly, opportunities exist to expand observations of family interactions to apply existing coding systems and theoretical frameworks to a variety of family types and structures. In addition to including multigenerational households as family units, much more attention needs to be paid to observations of single-parent families and families with same-sex partners (Kerig, 2001). These are just a few examples of how much remains to be learned about interactions in families with a variety of memberships and structures.

Methodological Challenges

One methodological challenge in observational research is accounting for the role of time in family relationships and communication (Vangelisti, 2006). Many observational studies use small interaction sequences, such as in 5- or 15-minute segments, and derive relationship characteristics from those segments. Although scholars have argued that such interactions are likely representative of overall interactions in families (e.g., Kerig, 2001), a challenge remains to consider how developmental changes, daily events, and family events influence (or not) interaction patterns within families. Longitudinal designs help meet this challenge. Although longitudinal studies hold challenges not present in cross-sectional studies, such as participants' not completing all portions of the study, the many benefits of taking time into account warrant taking on the extra challenges. Such benefits include being able to link results of Time 1 observations and/or self-reports to later behavior and/or self-reports of focal phenomena. A few studies reviewed

above, investigating parent-child interactions in contexts of conflict and risky behavior, have demonstrated the value of taking longitudinal approaches to understanding the influence of interactions over time. Much more remains to be understood about how time influences family interactions.

Another methodological challenge is to recognize the limitations of observational designs. Observational studies have reported results that do not comport with self-report results of the same phenomena (e.g., Caughlin & Malis, 2004; Dailey, 2006). Such inconsistencies between survey and observational data indicate the need to consider that the two methods might tap different relational dimensions (Dailey, 2006) or that dimensions with similar labels might mean something different to a participant filling out a self-report than to a theorist constructing an operationalization on the basis of behavior. As mentioned earlier in this chapter, many studies include multiple methods in order to build this consideration into study design.

Another methodological challenge for observational research has been the length of time it takes to code observational data. For example, Howe et al. (2002) reported that coding 40 sibling play sessions of 15 minutes each took longer than 12 months. Melby and Conger (2001) noted that using the IFIRS takes approximately 3.5 hours to code one 15-minute family interaction. However, recent technological advances are helping reduce this time burden. For example, Roter and Larson (2002) noted that coders using the RIAS can complete coding of an interaction session in only about 2 times the interaction time. As analysis technology continues to develop for coding video- and audio-recorded interactions, this challenge to observational research is likely to become less of a deterrent.

Rules and Resources

Finally, future observational research of family communication would contribute to our understanding of family systems by accounting for family rules and resources that are both medium for and outcomes of interactions (Canary & Cantú, 2012). Vangelisti (2006) noted that few family communication theories explicitly account for relational or cultural context variables in explaining family communication processes. Recent application of structurating activity theory to the family context, and family member–health care professional interactions specifically (with the R-BICS, discussed above), will contribute to addressing such variables in family communication research. Harwood et al. (2006) also noted that future observational research grounded in CAT should account for the role of family identity, which can be viewed as a resource for family actions and interactions.

Conclusion

The goal of this chapter was to provide an overview of theoretical foundations, methodological issues, topics, and future suggestions for observational research of family communication. Previous research clearly demonstrates that family interactions are consequential for our human experience. Much remains to be learned about the complexities of family life. Observational studies will contribute to this body of knowledge when grounded in theory and designed well. Opportunities abound for scholars interested in family interaction processes across different contexts and life stages and within different family structures.

References

Alston, E., & St. James-Roberts, I. (2005). Home environments of 10-month-old infants selected by the WILSTAAR screen for pre-language difficulties. *International Journal of Language & Communication Disorder, 40,* 123–136.

Beach, W. A. (2009). *A natural history of family cancer: Interactional resources for managing illness.* Cresskill, NJ: Hampton.

Buijzen, M., & Valkenburg, P. M. (2008). Observing purchase-related parent-child communication in retail environments: A developmental and socialization perspective. *Human Communication Research, 34,* 50–69.

Canary, H. E. (2010). Structurating activity theory: An integrative approach to policy knowledge. *Communication Theory, 20,* 21–49.

Canary, H. E., Bullis, C. A., Cummings, J., & Kinney, A. Y. (2014, February). *The Resource-Based Interaction Coding System (R-BICS): Development and application in a colorectal cancer screening intervention program.* Paper presented at the annual convention of the Western States Communication Association, Anaheim, CA.

Canary, H. E., & Canary, D. J. (2013). *Family conflict.* Cambridge, UK: Polity.

Canary, H. E., & Cantú, E. (2012). Making decisions about children's disabilities: Mediation and structuration in cross-system meetings. *Western Journal of Communication, 76,* 270–297.

Canary, H. E., Cummings, J., Bullis, C., & Kinney, A. Y. (2013, November). *Counselor-client conversations in a colorectal cancer screening intervention: An analysis of intersecting activity systems.* Paper presented at the annual convention of the National Communication Association, Washington, DC.

Caughlin, J. P., & Malis, R. S. (2004). Demand/withdraw communication between parents and adolescents as a correlate of relational satisfaction. *Communication Reports, 17,* 59–71.

Cline, R. J., Harper, F. W., Penner, L. A., Peterson, A. M., Taub, J. W., & Albrecht, T. L. (2006). Parent communication and child pain and distress during painful pediatric cancer treatments. *Social Science & Medicine, 63,* 883–898.

Cummings, E. M., & Davies, P. T. (2010). *Marital conflict and children: An emotional security perspective.* New York: Guilford.

Dailey, R. M. (2006). Confirmation in parent-adolescent relationships and adolescent openness: Toward extending confirmation theory. *Communication Monographs, 73,* 434–458.

Dillard, J. P., Shen, L., Laxova, A., & Farrell, P. (2008). Potential threats to the effective communication of genetic risk information: The case of cystic fibrosis. *Health Communication, 23,* 234–244.

Dunn, M. J., Rodriguez, E. M., Miller, K. S., Gerhardt, C. A., Vannatta, K., Saylor, M., . . . Compas, B. E. (2011). Direct observation of mother-child communication in pediatric cancer: Assessment of verbal and non-verbal behavior and emotion. *Journal of Pediatric Psychology, 36,* 464–475.

Edwards, G., Barkley, R. A., Laneri, M., Fletcher, K., & Metevia, L. (2001). Parent-adolescent conflict in teenagers with ADHD and ODD. *Journal of Abnormal Child Psychology, 29,* 557–572.

Feeney, J. A., & Noller, P. (2013). Perspectives on studying family communication: Multiple methods and multiple sources. In A. L. Vangelisti (Ed.), *The Routledge handbook of family communication* (2nd ed., pp. 29–45). New York: Routledge.

Fiese, B. H., Botti, J. C., & Greenberg, S. (2007). *ABC family mealtime coding manual.* Urbana-Champaign: University of Illinois.

Fiese, B. H., Foley, K. P., & Spagnola, M. (2006). Routine and ritual elements in family mealtimes: Contexts for child well-being and family identity. *New Directions for Child and Adolescent Development, 111*, 67–89.

Fiese, B. H., Winter, M. A., & Botti, J. C. (2011). The ABCs of family mealtimes: Observational lessons for promoting healthy outcomes for children with persistent asthma. *Child Development, 82*, 133–145.

Garcia, M. M., Shaw, D. S., Winslow, E. B., & Yaggi, K. E. (2000). Destructive sibling conflict and the development of conduct problems in young boys. *Developmental Psychology, 36*, 44–53.

Gordis, E. B., & Margolin, G. (2001). The Family Coding System: Studying the relation between marital conflict and family interaction. In P. K. Kerig & K. M. Lindahl (Eds.), *Family observational coding systems: Resources for systemic research* (pp. 111–125). Mahwah, NJ: Lawrence Erlbaum.

Harwood, J., Soliz, J., & Lin, M. (2006). Communication accommodation theory: An intergroup approach to family relationships. In D. O. Braithwaite & L. Baxter (Eds.), *Engaging theories in family communication: Multiple perspectives* (pp. 19–34). Thousand Oaks, CA: Sage.

Heavey, C. L., Layne, C., & Christensen, A. (1993). Gender and conflict structure in marital interaction: A replication and extension. *Journal of Consulting and Clinical Psychology, 61*, 16–27.

Howe, N., & Rinaldi, C. M. (2004). "You be the big sister": Maternal-preschooler internal state discourse, perspective-taking, and sibling caretaking. *Infant and Child Development, 13*, 217–234.

Howe, N., Rinaldi, C. M., Jennings, M., & Petrakos, H. (2002). "No! The lambs can stay out because they got cozies": Constructive and destructive sibling conflict, pretend play, and social understanding. *Child Development, 73*, 1460–1473.

Huang, K., Teti, D. M., Caughy, M. O., Feldstein, S., & Genevro, J. (2007). Mother-child conflict interaction in the toddler years: Behavior patterns and correlates. *Journal of Child and Family Studies, 16*, 219–241.

Jacob, T., Haber, J. R., Leonard, K. E., & Rushe, R. (2000). Home interactions of high and low antisocial male alcoholics and their families. *Journal of Studies on Alcohol, 61*, 72–80.

Katz, L. F., & Woodin, E. M. (2002). Hostility, hostile detachment, and conflict engagement in marriages: Effects on child and family functioning. *Child Development, 73*, 636–652.

Kerig, P. K. (2001). Introduction and overview: Conceptual issues in family observational research. In P. K. Kerig, & K. M. Lindahl (Eds.), *Family observational coding systems: Resources for systemic research* (pp. 1–22). Mahwah, NJ: Lawrence Erlbaum.

Koerner, A. F., & Cvancara, K. E. (2002). The influence of conformity orientation on communication patterns in family conversations. *Journal of Family Communication, 2*, 133–152.

Koerner, A. F., & Fitzpatrick, M. A. (2006). Family communication patterns theory: A social cognitive approach. In D. O. Braithwaite & L. A. Baxter, *Engaging theories in family communication: Multiple perspectives* (pp. 50–65). Thousand Oaks, CA: Sage.

Kong, A., Jones, B. L., Fiese, B. H., Schiffler, L. A., Odoms-Young, A., Kim, Y., . . . Fitzgibbon, M. L. (2013). Parent-child mealtime interactions in racially/ethnically diverse families with preschool-age children. *Eating Behaviors, 14*, 451–455.

Laible, D. J., & Thompson, R. A. (2002). Mother-child conflict in the toddler years: Lessons in emotion, morality, and relationships. *Child Development, 73*, 1187–1203.

Larson, R. W., Branscomb, K. R., & Wiley, A. R. (2006). Forms and functions of family mealtimes: Multidisciplinary perspectives. *New Directions for Child and Adolescent Development, 111*, 1–15.

Melby, J. N., & Conger, R. D. (2001). The Iowa Family Interaction Rating Scales: Instrument summary. In P. K. Kerig & K. M. Lindahl (Eds.), *Family observational coding systems: Resources for systemic research* (pp. 33–58). Mahwah, NJ: Lawrence Erlbaum.

Melby, J. N., Conger, R. D., Book, R., Rueter, M., Lucy, L., Repinski, D., et al. (1998). *The Iowa Family Interaction Rating Scales* (5th ed.). Ames: Iowa State University, Institute for Social and Behavioral Research.

Metzger, A., Wakschlag, L. S., Anderson, R., Darfler, A., Price, J., Flores, Z., & Mermelstein, R. (2013). Information management strategies within conversations about cigarette smoking: Parenting correlates and longitudinal associations with teen smoking. *Developmental Psychology, 49*, 1565–1578.

Mitchell, M. J., Powers, S. W., Byars, K. C., Dickstein, S., & Stark, L. J. (2004). Family functioning in young children with cystic fibrosis: Observations of interactions at mealtime. *Developmental and Behavioral Pediatrics, 25*, 335–346.

Montepare, J. M., Steinberg, J., & Rosenberg, B. (1992). Characteristics of vocal communication between young adults and their parents and grandparents. *Communication Research, 19*, 479–492.

Olson, D. H. (2000). Circumplex Model of Marital and Family Systems. *Journal of Family Therapy, 22*, 144–167.

Orrell-Valente, J. K., Hill, L. G., Brechwald, W. A., Dodge, K. A., Pettit, G. S., & Bates, J. E. (2007). "Just three more bites": An observational analysis of parents' socialization of children's eating at mealtime. *Appetite, 48*, 37–45.

Patton, S. R., Dolan, L. M., Smith, L. B., Brown, M. B., & Powers, S. W. (2013). Examining mealtime behaviors in families of young children with type 1 diabetes on intensive insulin therapy. *Eating Behaviors, 14*, 464–467.

Paugh, A., & Izquierdo, C. (2009). Why is this a battle every night? Negotiating food and eating in American dinnertime interaction. *Journal of Linguistic Anthropology, 19*, 185–204.

Pluhar, E. I., & Kuriloff, P. (2004). What really matters in family communication about sexuality? A qualitative analysis of affect and style among African American mothers and adolescent daughters. *Sex Education, 4,* 303–321.

Repetti, R. L., Wang, S., & Sears, M. S. (2013). Using direct observational methods to study the real lives of families: Advantages, complexities, and conceptual and practical considerations. In J. G. Grzywacz & E. Demerouti (Eds.), *New frontiers in work and family research* (pp. 191–210). New York: Routledge.

Richmond, M. J., Mermelstein, R. J., & Wakschlag, L. S. (2013). Direct observations of parenting and real-time negative affect among adolescent smokers and nonsmokers. *Journal of Clinical Child & Adolescent Psychology, 42,* 617–628.

Roter, D., & Larson, S. (2002). The Roter Interaction Analysis System (RIAS): Utility and flexibility for analysis of medical interactions. *Patient Education & Counseling, 46,* 243–251.

Roter, D. L. (1999). *Roter Interaction Analysis System (RIAS): Coding manual.* Unpublished manual, Department of Health Policy and Management, Johns Hopkins School of Public Health, Baltimore.

Roter, D. L., & Larson, S. (2001). The relationship between residents' and attending physicians' communication during primary care visits: An illustrative use of the Roter Interaction Analysis System. *Health Communication, 13,* 33–48.

Seiffge-Krenke, I. (2002). "Come on, say something, Dad!": Communication and coping in fathers of diabetic adolescents. *Journal of Pediatric Psychology, 27,* 439–450.

Sillars, A., Koerner, A., & Fitzpatrick, M. A. (2005). Communication and understanding in parent-adolescent relationships. *Human Communication Research, 31,* 102–128.

Sillars, A., Smith, T., & Koerner, A. (2010). Misattributions contributing to empathic (in)accuracy during parent-adolescent conflict discussions. *Journal of Social and Personal Relationships, 27,* 727–747.

Vangelisti, A. L. (2006). Foreword: Variations and challenges. In D. O. Braithwaite & L. A. Baxter (Eds.), *Engaging theories in family communication: Multiple perspectives* (pp. xi–xviii). Thousand Oaks, CA: Sage.

Vuchinich, S. (1987). Starting and stopping spontaneous family conflicts. *Journal of Marriage and Family, 49,* 591–601.

Whalen, C. K., Henker, B., Hollingshead, J., & Burgess, S. (1996). Parent-adolescent dialogues about AIDS. *Journal of Family Psychology, 10,* 343–357.

Williamson, H. C., Bradbury, T. N., Trail, T. E., & Karney, B. R. (2011). Factor analysis of the Iowa Family Interaction Rating Scales. *Journal of Family Psychology, 25,* 993–999.

Wolff, J. L., & Roter, D. L. (2012). Older adults' mental function and patient-centered care: Does the presence of a family companion help or hinder communication? *Journal of General Internal Medicine, 27,* 661–668.

3

■

ANALYZING VIDEO AND AUDIO NONVERBAL DYNAMICS

Kinesics, Proxemics, Haptics, and Vocalics

JUDEE K. BURGOON, NORAH E. DUNBAR, AND AARON ELKINS

Among the most remarkable abilities we humans possess is our ability to transact interpersonal communication—not only to sense, decode, and interpret the countless signals being given by other humans but also to track that torrent of signals, millisecond by millisecond, to synthesize those signals into coherent wholes, to adapt to them on the fly, and to create sensible and seemingly seamless responses. But how do we know that what we receive matches the meaning another intends to send, especially when the signal palette is ever changing? And how can we determine the fidelity of our perceptual apparatuses, decoding systems, and interpretive inferences? Those questions are the subject of this chapter.

In what follows, we first discuss the importance of researching nonverbal interaction as a dyadic and dynamic system. We then offer practical suggestions for conducting observational studies and experiments, walking through the stages of planning and executing such studies. We conclude by discussing issues in the statistical analysis of dynamic dyadic data.

Characteristics of Nonverbal Behavior in Interpersonal Interaction

Interpersonal communication is generally defined as a dynamic and interdependent exchange of signs and symbols between two or more people. On the surface, this seems to be a very straightforward definition. But when applied to nonverbal communication, it carries some significant implications for how the process should be studied to achieve high-fidelity observation and measurement.

First, whereas the verbal code is digital in form, the nonverbal signal system is composed of both analogic signs and digital symbols. Digital codes are discrete, finite elements with arbitrary meanings that can be found in a dictionary. Nonverbal digital symbols, like verbal symbols, are socially derived signals that obey lexical, syntactic, and semantic rules with culture- and context-bound meanings (Buck & VanLear, 2002; Burgoon, Guerrero, & Floyd, 2010). Analogic signals are naturally arising, continuous, and infinite signals with biologically derived, universal meanings. (VanLear and Withers in this volume provide a somewhat different conceptualization of "analogic communication" than ours.) Voice pitch and conversational distance are examples. For some research purposes, the distinction between biological and social, analogic and digital, signals may not matter. But just a few examples should reveal that the measurement of these signals is more complicated than parsing words, phrases, and sentences in the verbal system.

Smiles can be "authentic" or "false." The former are known as Duchenne smiles; these universal, naturally arising, and spontaneous expressions associated with joy and happiness have a quick onset and offset and activate muscles around the mouth and eyes (Ekman, Davidson, & Friesen, 1990). The "fake" smile, a deliberate, learned expression with a slower onset and offset and longer duration than the Duchenne smile, may activate only muscles around the mouth (Schmidt, Ambadar, Cohn, & Reed, 2006). In the deception research arena, these two types of smiles are thought by some to distinguish truth from deception (Ekman et al., 1990). In the clinical realm, they may distinguish between genuine positive affect and masked psychological discomfort. Measurement of a smile must thus take the subtle distinctions into account, something that is difficult for naked observation but can be done with instrumentation.

Gaze is another example. When does a gaze start and stop? As a continuous behavior, the point at which it morphs from direct eye contact into averted gaze is not easily defined operationally. For this reason, this finely graded analogic signal is often reduced to the cruder dichotomous categories of "looking toward" and "looking away." This conversion of analogic nonverbal signals to digital ones, though facilitative of human observation and perhaps consonant with what the human brain does to make sense of these signals, can lead to mistaken assumptions about their origins and meaning. Looking toward someone may be a primitive information-gathering behavior to size up whether the person is friend or foe rather than a social signal of liking. It may be that analogic signals only become social ones when reduced to a few discrete categories.

A third example is the voice. "Observing" vocal signals can be even more problematic. Often acoustic signals are collected at an extremely high sampling rate (e.g., over 48,000 Hz, which is 48,000 wave oscillations per second) and must be downsampled significantly to correspond to the temporal size of other nonverbal units of analysis. Even with down-sampling, no standard definition exists of what constitutes a loud or soft amplitude, a fast or slow tempo, for example. Instruments can measure acoustic signals at a highly fine grained level, but human perception of necessity reduces the signal stream to a much more restrictive gradient.

In short, a first decision for researchers is whether to conceptualize and measure nonverbal signals as analogic or digital. Analogic signals lend themselves to objective recording with equipment, whereas digital signals lend themselves to more subjective human perception and observation.

Second, nonverbal signals form a system of inextricably intertwined behaviors that are interrelated not only to one another but also to the verbal stream to form an integrated system of meaning (McNeill, 1985). The same semantic intent leads, during the computational stage of constructing messages, to the integrated assembly of words, gestures, facial and head expressions, voice, and other nonverbal signals. Poyatos (1997) described the multimodal combination of language, voice (paralanguage), and kinesics as the basic triple structure of communication. This view that verbal and nonverbal signals are interdependent and complementary in forming meaningful expressions is widely shared by nonverbal scholars (e.g., Burgoon et al., 2010; Knapp, Hall, & Horgan, 2013) and has significant implications for how to study nonverbal expressions (Quek et al., 2002). Studying individual channels (e.g., visual, auditory, tactile) or codes (e.g., kinesics, vocalics, haptics, proxemics) separately, without considering the other coextensive nonverbal signals, linguistic features, and verbal content, suffers from the same deficiencies of decontextualizing any aspect of communication. It risks misunderstanding what communicative function a given nonverbal signal is performing (e.g., is direct eye contact a sign of attraction, an invitation to talk, a threat stare, or a means of gathering information?) as well as misattributing causes and effects of the signals (see Burgoon, Guerrero, & White, 2013). This is why so many nonverbal researchers advocate studying aggregations of nonverbal signals and identifying the verbal context in which they are embedded.

Third, nonverbal behaviors during human interaction reflect not only the sender's intent but also the actions of the receiver; they are the product of mutual influence. For example, during interviewing, what the sender says and does partly conveys the sender's ideas, current mood state, personality, and so forth, but is also influenced by the nonverbal and verbal behavior of the interviewer and the interaction style they jointly create. For this reason, taking a dyadic approach—that is, using the dyad rather than the individual as the unit of analysis—might provide a more complete and accurate depiction of the communication event. Knowing, for instance, that an interviewer uses an adversarial questioning style may lead to a different characterization of an interviewee's gestures and facial expressions than would occur in the absence of that contextual information.

Finally, whereas some nonverbal behaviors are fairly static during a communication episode, most are dynamic. Even fairly unchanging nonverbal signals such as seated interaction distance may still vary over the course of an episode, and most signals are highly changeable. Taking a single sample of a behavior at one point in time may not be at all representative of that behavior and also ignores the trajectories of behavior over time. A longitudinal perspective is therefore preferred over a cross-sectional one. Observations of nonverbal behavior must begin with a decision of whether the unit of analysis will be event-based (e.g., topic, turn at talk) or time-based and, if the latter, how fine grained the measurement will be (e.g., minutes, seconds, milliseconds). Although the capacity exists to capture data at a highly granular level—high-definition near-infrared cameras can record at 250 frames per second (fps)—Burgoon and Baesler (1991) advised selecting a measurement window to match the phenomenological experience of interactants so as to better mirror the "reality" of the participants. If humans basically recognize 4 different conversational distances, measuring 20 such distances becomes overkill. Measurement that is too microscopic may produce a high noise-to-signal ratio. However, as noted with regard to acoustic signals, a highly molecular analysis recorded with instrumentation can be down-sampled to a more molar one; large temporal units of analysis cannot be decomposed later into finer units, which argues for erring on the side of more granular measurement initially.

In sum, the character of nonverbal behaviors poses several critical questions for researchers that should be answered at the outset: (a) Are the behaviors of interest better *conceptualized* as analogic or digital? (b) Are they better *measured* as analogic or digital signals? (c) What functions do they serve? (d) Are they subject to mutual influence and therefore better measured and analyzed dyadically? (e) Are the temporal fluctuations in their presentation sufficiently stable to justify a static measurement approach or should a longitudinal approach be adopted? (f) How small or large should the units of analysis be? (g) Should behaviors be measured objectively or subjectively? (h) Should observation be conducted by humans or machines?

Apart from these guiding questions, a number of logistical decisions must be made. We turn next to these, drawing on our own collective experiences with human and machine measurement of nonverbal behavior.

Steps in Designing and Conducting a Nonverbal Observational Study

When designing an observational study, several logistical factors should be considered before initiating the observations. Begin with theoretical questions of interest and decide what exactly you need to capture before you set up your observation space. We strongly recommend recording what you are observing rather than simply doing live coding, for two main reasons. First, kinesic and vocalic behaviors are fleeting, and because multiple codes can be present simultaneously, it is difficult to catch them all as they are happening without missing any. Live coding also makes it difficult to demonstrate the reliability of your coding, and your codes cannot be verified later.

Second, although this process might begin with one set of questions, new research questions can emerge during the process of collecting the data. If you record the observations, they can be reanalyzed with a new coding scheme in the future. For example, we collected nearly 250 interactions between professional interviewers and undergraduate students who had cheated on a task for a deception detection study (Dunbar et al., 2015). As we were watching the interactions over the course of our 3 months of data collection, we noticed that the interpersonal synchrony of the dyads was diminishing over the course of the interactions. We wondered if the synchrony of the dyad could be used to differentiate between truthtellers and deceivers, which, to our knowledge, had never been investigated before. We formulated a new coding scheme and tested that question using a secondary analysis of the data in two separate studies using both manual (Dunbar, Jensen, Tower, & Burgoon, 2014) and automated coding processes (Yu et al., 2015). Having the recordings available allowed post hoc investigations of new insights.[1]

Facilities and Arrangements

The first task is to plan your design, locale, and instrumentation before the study begins. There are a number of factors to consider so that you capture all the data you need for your later analyses. For example:

1. Will the recording be in a laboratory or a natural field environment? If you have access to a laboratory, that provides you with more control over your environment and can ensure the proper placement of your recording equipment. Recording people in their natural environments, such as children in their classrooms or families at home, can encourage more natural behavior but makes the placement of recording equipment and furniture a challenge.

2. What kinesics are you trying to capture? If you want to examine minute facial expressions, then you will need close-ups of the face. Where will the cameras be placed: so that they

are visible (and potentially intrusive) to the subjects, or can you zoom in on what you need from a distance? If you are capturing gestures, do participants have the space to gesture freely, or are they constrained by the furniture in which they are sitting? If you are studying proxemics, are they standing or sitting? Do they have the freedom to move around?

3. What type of furniture is used? This may seem like a trivial issue, and it may be tempting to just grab the available furniture from a nearby office space. But the furniture can have a major impact on the kinesics you can observe. Are the chairs movable or stationary? If they are movable, it will be more difficult to ensure that participants stay in the camera frame, and it may diminish the audio recording as they move away from microphones. However, stationary seating limits the ability to capture proxemic adjustments. Even the types of chairs can have an impact, because chairs with high armrests can encourage a sideways lean and reduce gesturing.

4. Are you examining individuals or dyads as the focus of your recording? If you are recording individuals, you can position the cameras and microphones near each individual, but if you are recording a dyad, you must consider how you will capture both individuals. Will they be seated together on a couch? It is likely that when they turn to speak to each other, you will capture profile views of their faces. If they are seated across from each other, you can capture the frontal view of their faces, but they will be unable to touch each other. For example, in the cheating study mentioned earlier, we had two cameras positioned so that we could record the face of each participant and a third camera that recorded the whole dyad (see layout in Figure 3.1). Then, to make life easier for our coders, who were examining interactional synchrony, we took the images from Camera 1 and Camera 2 and used video-editing software (Adobe Premiere in this case) to combine them into a split-screen effect (see Figure 3.2).

Creating a floor plan and a flowchart can also help determine in advance where participants will initially report (if coming to a laboratory) and what stations they will progress through as they complete consent forms and any presurveys, complete experimental tasks, complete postexperimental surveys, and undergo debriefing. A similar flowchart is needed for

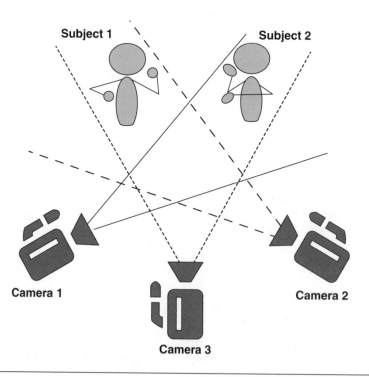

Figure 3.1 Sample camera setup from the Dunbar et al. (2015) cheating study.

Figure 3.2 Split screen of frontal view of subject and interviewer for coding purposes.

Source: Author.

studies conducted in field settings so that every activity has a place. These floor plans and flowcharts facilitate planning staffing needs, deciding where recording equipment will be placed, calculating how long each interaction will take, anticipating any interferences from other activities and noises, and prohibiting participants from overhearing other sessions or interacting with one another.

Selecting Recording Equipment

Once you have determined the design and layout of your investigation, you must determine the recording equipment you will need. The proliferation of video and audio recording equipment in recent years has made observational analysis much more affordable and available than ever before. What used to be a major equipment investment can now be had for a few hundred dollars at your local big box store. We will not discuss particular types of equipment or brands, because the technology changes too rapidly, but there are some things to consider:

1. What level of quality does your recording require? If you need high-definition video or high-quality audio recordings, bear in mind that they require significant storage capability. It is preferable to capture at the highest quality possible; you can always down-sample recordings for analysis, but you can never improve the quality of the source recordings later. Also, combining signals from numerous channels of cameras and microphones will require postprocessing ensuring that the video and audio channels are synchronized. If you are using open-source materials rather than those you capture yourself, you may need to investigate whether the quality is high enough for your use. One pitfall when using open-source materials is that they are often compressed to reduce file size for sharing and streaming on the Internet. These compression algorithms (e.g., MP3) remove audio information that humans are less sensitive to hearing and introduce artifacts and lower fidelity.

2. Will the placement of the equipment affect the quality of the recording? As was discussed earlier with regard to the layout of the observation space, where you place the cameras can affect whether you get profile or frontal views of your participants and also whether you are able to capture full-body versus head and face views. Similarly, microphones should accommodate movement of the subjects and capture the richest signal possible. Both cameras and microphones should be placed so that they are as unobtrusive as possible but still provide you the quality images you need.

3. Are the recordings compatible with your analysis software? A plethora of tools and codices are available, and some planning ahead could save hours of work in your postprocessing. Think about what software you will be using for your later analyses and ensure that your recordings can be captured in the format you

require. As an experimenter, you may not have control over the capture format. In this case, capture at the highest quality available and convert the files to the compatible format prior to analysis. High quality is important because some conversions result in signal degradation. We have had the unfortunate experience of finding code incompatibilities between our and a collaborator's recording equipment, necessitating many hours of rerendering videos for both research labs to analyze.

4. During the recording, are there outside factors that will interfere with your recording? Selecting the appropriate microphone for the environment can greatly improve overall quality. If you are recording speech, consider a microphone that is unidirectional and focuses its recording on a small area or person. For recording groups or an entire room, an omnidirectional microphone can record a larger area but will pick up much more ambient noise. The quality of the microphone matters. Despite the availability of inexpensive microphones integrated into laptops and webcams, these microphones often introduce noise, interference, and filtering technologies that degrade the signal. In general, microphones that are advertised for singers, broadcasters, and podcasters can provide significantly better results when recording human speech.

5. The synchronization of audio and video should be considered before data collection. The best-case scenario would be if the camera accepts an external microphone and ensures that the audio and video are synchronized during recording. If the camera has a built-in microphone, resist the temptation to rely on it for recording audio, as such microphones typically introduce a lot of environmental noise. If you record audio and video separately, you will need to first start the camera and audio recording and introduce a simultaneous audio and visual cue (similar to the clapboards used in movie productions) that can be used to manually synchronize the recordings later using video-editing software.

Measurement

The topic of measuring nonverbal behavior can, and has, filled many chapters and handbooks. Here we touch on only a few major considerations. Early nonverbal observational research almost exclusively relied on *manual coding*, in which researchers would identify verbal or nonverbal cues a priori and then train coders to record those cues, often using a pen-and-paper approach. Kendon (1970) and Condon (Condon, 1980; Condon & Sander, 1974) illustrated the laborious nature of manual coding. Guerrero and Andersen described a process in which teams of coders worked together to time interactions and mark on tally sheets where touch occurred while watching live interactions (Andersen & Guerrero, 2004; Guerrero & Andersen, 1994). Behaviors were coded for each member of a dyad separately, and then sequential analyses were used to examine the synchronization of those behaviors (Bakeman & Gottman, 1997). Julien (2005) described a procedure in which ratings of individual partners could be transformed into "units of contingency" so that changes in immediacy levels can be used to evaluate the degree of synchrony within the dyad.

Another method of manual coding is often referred to as the gestalt method, in which raters perceive the level of some global construct (e.g., involvement, nervousness, pleasantness or smoothness of interaction) and make holistic judgments (Baesler & Burgoon, 1988; Burgoon & Baesler, 1991). For example, Dunbar et al. (2014), in addition to instructing coders to examine synchrony using various body regions, asked coders to make ratings of "global synchrony" at different time points in an interaction.

More recently, researchers have adopted the use of *behavioral observation tools*, which help coders by time-stamping behaviors as they are recorded and allowing them to select behaviors to code with a key stroke rather than manual notes. Early research using these tools often required researchers to create their own systems, such as the "push-button" system described by LaFrance and Ickes (1981). These are semiautomated methods such as the interactive video coding program called MacMax (Grammer, Kruck, & Magnusson, 1998), the immediacy behaviors rating system called SOCNIC (Julien, Brault, Chartrand, & Begin, 2000) and the C# Behavioral Annotation System (C-BAS), a computer application to aid researchers in coding events on video or audio tracks (Dunbar et al., 2014; Meservy, 2010).

Finally, recent advances in computer vision analysis allow the use of multimodal sensors to capture movement automatically and track the synchrony between the behavior streams of two people (Yu et al., 2015). Early research on the use of multimodal sensors often required the use of physical instrumentation such as an apparatus worn on the head to automatically measure head movements (Hadar, Steiner, & Clifford Rose, 1985) or sensors worn on the body to measure physiology (Levenson & Gottman, 1983), but recent research can use noncontact and unobtrusive methods of analyzing video recordings using facial and body tracking software (Jensen, Meservy, Burgoon, & Nunamaker, 2010).

Automated analyses contain several advantages. First, sensors can restrict movement, so using noncontact sensors and remote collection means that interactions can be recorded for later or even real-time analyses without undue pressure on the participants. Second, automated analyses are faster and less labor intensive than human coding. If automated analyses can obtain similar degrees of reliability and validity as humans, laborious coding by humans can be minimized. Third, signal-processing approaches are being developed whereby audio or visual tracks from each person are recorded and processed automatically by computer programs that can examine not just individual behavior but also dyad similarity or overlaps in behavior (Grammer et al., 1998; Schmidt, Morr, Fitzpatrick, & Richardson, 2012; Sun, Lichtenauer, Valstar, Nijholt, & Pantic, 2011). Because these analyses are still new, more testing is needed to know if automated analyses can truly replace or may only augment human coders. Finally, open-source databases are being created that other researchers can use to develop their own methods of analyzing human behavior. The MHI-Mimicry database (http://mahnob-db.eu/mimicry/) is an example.

Recording and Data Preparation

The audiovisual recording of interaction would seem to be rather straightforward. But there are a few pitfalls to be avoided. One is synchronization of all the recordings. If multiple data streams are to be fused into some composite later, it is critically important that all recordings start at the same millisecond. Even very minor discrepancies can make for erroneous combination of signals and conclusions about the degree of correspondence that was present among behaviors. Consider, for instance, video collected at 60 fps. Two different video feeds could be off by only 1 second, but their data will appear to be off by 60 frames and may mask the real correlation between the two feeds. Lining up all the different sensor data, some or all of which are recorded at different time scales (e.g., a 30-fps visible-spectrum camera, a 250-fps near-infrared camera, and a 48-kHz audio signal) requires very precise synchronization. A standard method in commercial recording has been to use a clapboard that introduces a loud audio signal in all recordings. This becomes the point of synchronization. Other recent event recording systems may offer alternative techniques for lining up and integrating data on a second-by-second or millisecond-by-millisecond basis.

The synchronization process becomes especially critical when using newer generation event-recording tools for video and audio recordings. Software tools such as Noldus Observer XT (http://www.noldus .com/human-behavior-research/products/the-observer-xt), C-BAS (Meservy, 2010), ELAN, and Mangold's Interact (http://www.mangold-interna tional.com/software/interact/what-is-interact.html) allow trained human coders to control video and audio with computer software while making moment-to-moment codings on their keyboards by pressing keys (for frequency counts) or holding down keys (for durations). These behavioral observation software suites also include routines for calculating reliabilities and have multiple options for creating templates to map keys to behaviors being coded, for adjusting recordings for the slight lapses that occur between the observation and the key press, and so forth.

Another consideration is how many behaviors to have coders observe at a time and how long the coding sessions should last. Presuming that one has at least two coders so that interrater reliabilities can be calculated, the number of behaviors any coder should rate or record at a time depends on how reliably the behavior can be observed, how gross or subtle the behavior itself is (e.g., counting blinks is much more difficult than counting postural shifts), how much observation of one behavior inadvertently affects observation of another behavior (e.g., watching lip adaptors interferes with tracking head movements), how rapidly the signal is changing, and whether the observation requires a subjective or objective assessment. That said, two to three behaviors and no more than 3 hours of coding in one sitting are probably optimal for maintaining high-quality observations.

It should be noted that some human (manual) observations can be replaced by automated methods. For example, computer imaging techniques for recording head, eye, face, posture, and limb movements automatically now exist. In addition to identifying raw features such as the head, face, and hands, these imaging tools track locations in pixels, velocities in fps, and behavioral trajectories by calculating the x, y, and z axes of features in the two-dimensional and three-dimensional video images. Higher order features such as expansiveness of gestures can also be computed from the same data points (see, e.g., Meservy et al., 2005).

Analysis

Before submitting audio or video for analysis, the recordings must first be preprocessed and cleaned. Despite the availability of automated tools for analysis, all audio and video should first be listened to or watched to identify any anomalies or recording errors. For example, if the volume was incorrect or a microphone was misplaced, the audio file may be muffled or unusable. Or, in the case of video, if the camera was not positioned correctly or recording stopped in the middle of a session, the data may be unusable as well. Once all of these errors are identified, they must be removed and the audio and video files trimmed into a usable set.

When analyzing audio and video, the recordings need to be converted to the appropriate format. For audio, it is a best practice and increases compatibility with most vocal analysis software to first convert the audio into a fixed and lossless format, such as a pulse-code modulation (PCM) .wav file (for reference, CD recordings contain 44.1-kHz PCM audio with 16 bits of resolution) and normalize the audio volume to improve comparability among recordings. With video, most automated tools perform their own conversion of the video and depend on video codecs installed on the computer to process the video. For example, H.264, a popular video compression format used by Blu-ray videos, can be decoded by a computer using an installed codec such as DivX or an open-source tool such as FFmpeg (Tomar, 2006).

The next decision that must be made before submitting the recordings for analysis is what unit of analysis to use. This is currently a very difficult problem in computational analysis of emotion and affect. For example, should you process each phoneme, word, vowel, sentence, utterance, or phrase, or the entire conversation? Particularly in speech, the decision can have an impact on the analysis. The vocal pitch of a participant can be strongly influenced by outliers and noise. At present, the best approach for traditional statistical analysis is to segment the recordings by shorter segments such as phrases or sentences and use longitudinal analysis to model the vocal or video speech features over time (see, e.g., Elkins & Derrick, 2013). One approach being investigated is to use multiple segment sizes (e.g., words, sentences, and utterances) in one analysis hierarchically (Schuller et al., 2008). The results are promising but are currently confined to machine learning methods, which means they offer impressive predictive power but nearly no theoretical insight into the behavior.

After segmenting the audio and video into temporal units, they are now ready for processing using vocalic and computer vision tools. For audio, you can use tools such as Praat (Boersma, 2002) or OpenSMILE (Eyben, Wöllmer, & Schuller, 2010)

to extract features from each audio segment. These features include measurements such as average vocal pitch, median volume, standard deviation of voice quality or shimmer, and many other features. Typically, these tools apply functionals (e.g., Mean, SD, Max, Min, Range, regression slope) to measurements such as pitch, volume, and vocal quality to provide many representations of the dynamics and variation during each unit of speech. The term *functional* can be understood as a descriptive statistic applied to each audio segment. After processing, the features can be used with traditional statistical packages for analysis.

The computer vision tools for analyzing kinesic and proxemic behaviors are improving greatly but are still not as accessible as those for audio. Automatically analyzing the face and body from video requires extensive computational resources. Most automated tools follow this type of procedure: First, images for each frame of the video are extracted (most videos are recorded at least 30 fps), identify a face or feature from each image and extract that part of the image, apply an image-tracking algorithm to identify points on the image to identify specific body parts (e.g., nose, eyes), and finally extract the image information from each body part.

After extracting the image of the body part, there is currently no standard for how to proceed with automatically classifying emotions or facial expressions. Current methods for facial analysis are typically based on Facial Action Units or AUs (Ekman & Friesen, 1978), which correspond to muscle activations that occur when smiling, laughing, or afraid. There are commercial tools that provide basic emotional and gesture feature extraction on the basis of AUs (examples include FaceReader by Noldus and Emotient's FACET). Because the field of computer vision is advancing quickly, commercial tools often trail behind the state-of-the-art methods being actively researched and developed by computer vision scientists (for an example of a recent approach with available tracking code, see Xiong & de la Torre, 2013), which include more sophisticated classification of emotion and robust tracking when lighting or environment conditions are not perfect. When using any computer vision tool, always include a validation study to verify the results of the software before starting analysis.

Dyadic analysis. We have noted that it is often advisable to study nonverbal behaviors at the dyadic level so that the interdependency of actions within the dyad is considered in any statistical analyses that are performed (Kenny, Kashy, & Cook, 2006;

Sabatelli, Buck, & Kenny, 1986). For example, imagine that you are studying the effects of humor and laughter in the classroom on students' satisfaction with their professors. You set up your cameras in several classrooms and record professors teaching, with the intent to correlate the frequency of laughter and humor used by the professors with surveys of student satisfaction. After diligently coding laughter and humor, you find that two professors both use the same amount, but Professor A's students are much more satisfied than those of Professor B. Assuming that humor is a relevant cause of satisfaction, your data leave you without an explanation for why humor works better for one professor than another. If you examined both the student behavior and the professor behavior in a dyadic fashion, you could perhaps see a pattern emerging, such as laughter occurring in response to student complaints versus when illustrating confusing points in lectures. Examining the sequential behavior of the dyads allows a richer understanding of the behaviors in the classroom that lead to the desired outcomes.

We can recommend two sources for understanding the observation of dyads. Bakeman and Gottman's (1997) book *Observing Interaction: An Introduction to Sequential Analysis* walks readers through the process of developing a coding scheme, offers a primer on recording behavioral sequences, and discusses the intricacies of sequential data analysis. Kenny et al.'s (2006) book *Dyadic Data Analysis* offers a guide to analyzing dyadic data without violating the assumptions of independence.

Conclusion

In this chapter, we have attempted to cover best practices and practical suggestions for conducting behavioral observation of dynamic nonverbal behaviors (leaving the issue of statistical analysis strategies to other chapters in this sourcebook). We have drawn our recommendations from the writings and advice of other experienced nonverbal researchers as well as from our own collective experience conducting such research. The methods and tools now available for conducting such research have made remarkable strides over the past few decades, to the point of making this kind of research far less daunting for novices and seasoned researchers alike. As a consequence, research has ignited enthusiastic attention from a broad array of fields that heretofore had not discovered this exciting research frontier. The synergy is evident in the burgeoning amount of research going beyond subjective perceptions to analyzing actual nonverbal kinesic,

proxemic, and vocalic behavior. It is hoped that the material presented here will spur other researchers to join this enterprise and catalyze multidisciplinary collaborations that further advance our understanding of human communication.

References

Andersen, P. A., & Guerrero, L. K. (2004). Measuring live tactile interaction: The body chart coding approach. In V. Manusov (Ed.), *The sourcebook of nonverbal measures: Going beyond words* (pp. 83–93). Mahwah, NJ: Lawrence Erlbaum.

Baesler, E. J., & Burgoon, J. K. (1988). Measurement and reliability of nonverbal behavior and percepts. *Journal of Nonverbal Behavior, 11*, 205–233.

Bakeman, R., & Gottman, J. M. (1997). *Observing interaction: An introduction to sequential analysis*. Cambridge, UK: Cambridge University Press.

Boersma, P. (2002). Praat, a system for doing phonetics by computer. *Glot International, 5*, 341–345.

Buck, R., & VanLear, C. A. (2002). Verbal and nonverbal communication: Distinguishing symbolic, spontaneous, and pseudo-spontaneous nonverbal behavior. *Journal of Communication, 52*, 522–541.

Burgoon, J. K., & Baesler, E. J. (1991). Choosing between micro and macro nonverbal measurement: Application to selected vocalic and kinesic indices. *Journal of Nonverbal Behavior, 15*, 57–78.

Burgoon, J. K., Guerrero, L. K., & Floyd, K. (2010). *Nonverbal communication*. Boston: Allyn & Bacon.

Burgoon, J. K., Guerrero, L. K., & White, C. H. (2013). The codes and functions of nonverbal communication. In C. Müller, A. Cienki, E. Fricke, S. H. Ladewig, D. McNeill, & S. Tessendorf (Eds.), *Body – language – communication: An international handbook on multimodality in human interaction* (pp. 609–626). Berlin, Germany: de Gruyter Mouton.

Condon, W. S. (1980). The relation of interactional synchrony to cognitive and emotional processes. In M. R. Key (Ed.), *The relationship of verbal and nonverbal communication* (pp. 49–65). Berlin, Germany: Walter de Gruyter.

Condon, W. S., & Sander, L. W. (1974). Neonate movement is synchronized with adult speech: Interactional participation and language acquisition. *Science, 183*, 99–101.

Dunbar, N. E., Jensen, M. J., Kelley, K. M. Robertson, K. J., Bernard, D. R., Adame, B., & Burgoon, J. K. (2015). Effects of veracity, modality and sanctioning on credibility assessment during mediated and unmediated interviews. *Communication Research, 42*, 649–674.

Dunbar, N. E., Jensen, M. L., Tower, D. C., & Burgoon, J. K. (2014). Synchronization of nonverbal behaviors in detecting mediated and non-mediated deception. *Journal of Nonverbal Behavior, 38*, 355–376.

Elkins, A. C., & Derrick, D. C. (2013). The sound of trust: Voice as a measurement of trust during interactions with embodied conversational agents. *Group Decision and Negotiation, 22,* 897–913.

Ekman, P., Davidson, R. J., & Friesen, W. V. (1990). The Duchenne smile: Emotional expression and brain physiology: II. *Journal of Personality and Social Psychology, 58,* 342.

Ekman, P., & Friesen, W. V. (1978). *Facial action coding system: A technique for the measurement of facial movement.* Palo Alto, CA: Consulting Psychologists Press.

Eyben, F., Wöllmer, M., & Schuller, B. (2010). OpenSMILE: the Munich versatile and fast open-source audio feature extractor. In *Proceedings of the 9th ACM International Conference on Multimedia, MM* (pp. 1459–1462).

Grammer, K., Kruck, K. B., & Magnusson, M. S. (1998). The courtship dance: Patterns of nonverbal synchronization in opposite sex encounters. *Journal of Nonverbal Behavior, 22,* 3–29.

Guerrero, L. K., & Andersen, P. A. (1994). Patterns of matching and initiation: Touch avoidance across romantic relationship stages. *Journal of Nonverbal Behavior, 18,* 137–153.

Hadar, U., Steiner, T., & Clifford Rose, F. (1985). Head movement during listening turns in conversation. *Journal of Nonverbal Behavior, 9,* 214–228.

Jensen, M. L., Meservy, T. O., Burgoon, J. K., & Nunamaker, J. F. (2010). Automatic, multimodal evaluation of human interaction. *Group Decision and Negotiation, 19,* 367–389.

Julien, D. (2005). A procedure to measure interactional synchrony in the context of satisfied and dissatisfied couples' communication. In V. Manusov (Ed.), *The sourcebook of nonverbal measures: Going beyond words* (pp. 199–208). Mahwah, NJ: Lawrence Erlbaum.

Julien, D., Brault, M., Chartrand, E., & Begin, J. (2000). Immediacy behaviors and synchrony in satisfied and dissatisfied couples. *Canadian Journal of Behavioural Science, 32,* 84–90.

Kendon, A. (1970). Movement coordination in social interaction: Some examples described. *Acta Psychologica, Amsterdam, 32,* 101–125.

Kenny, D. A., Kashy, D. A., & Cook, W. L. (2006). *Dyadic data analysis.* New York: Guilford.

Knapp, M., Hall, J., & Horgan, T. (2013). *Nonverbal communication in human interaction.* Boston: Cengage Learning.

LaFrance, M., & Ickes, W. (1981). Posture mirroring and interactional involvement: Sex and sex typing effects. *Journal of Nonverbal Behavior, 5,* 139–154.

Levenson, R. W., & Gottman, J. M. (1983). Marital interaction: Physiological linkage and affective exchange. *Journal of Personality and Social Psychology, 45,* 587–597.

McNeill, D. (1985). So you think gestures are nonverbal? *Psychological Review, 92,* 350.

Meservy, T. (2010, May). *Enhancing tools for coding human behavior: C-BAS.* Final report to the Center for Identification Technology Research.

Meservy, T. O., Jensen, M. L., Kruse, J., Twitchell, D. P., Tschepenakis, G., Burgoon, J. K., . . . Nunamaker, J. F. (2005). Deception detection through automatic, unobtrusive analysis of nonverbal behavior. *IEEE Intelligent Systems, 20,* 36–43.

Poyatos, F. (1997). The reality of multichannel verbal-nonverbal communication in simultaneous and consecutive interpretation. *Benjamins Translation Library, 17,* 249–282.

Quek, F., McNeill, D., Bryll, R., Duncan, S., Ma, X. F., Kirbas, C., & Ansari, R. (2002). Multimodal human discourse: Gesture and speech. *ACM Transactions on Computer-Human Interaction (TOCHI), 9,* 171–193.

Sabatelli, R. M., Buck, R., & Kenny, D. A. (1986). A social relations analysis of nonverbal communication accuracy in married couples. *Journal of Personality, 54,* 513–527.

Schmidt, K. L., Ambadar, Z., Cohn, J. F., & Reed, L. I. (2006). Movement differences between deliberate and spontaneous facial expressions: Zygomaticus major action in smiling. *Journal of Nonverbal Behavior, 30,* 37–52.

Schmidt, R. C., Morr, S., Fitzpatrick, P., & Richardson, M. J. (2012). Measuring the dynamics of interactional synchrony. *Journal of Nonverbal Behavior, 36,* 263–279.

Schuller, B., Wimmer, M., Mosenlechner, L., Kern, C., Arsic, D., & Rigoll, G. (2008). Brute-forcing hierarchical functionals for paralinguistics: A waste of feature space? In *IEEE International Conference on Speech and Signal Processing* (pp. 4501–4504).

Sun, X., Lichtenauer, J., Valstar, M., Nijholt, A., & Pantic, M. (2011). A multimodal database for mimicry analysis. *Affective Computing and Intelligent Interaction, 6974,* 367–376.

Tomar, S. (2006). Converting video formats with FFmpeg. *Linux Journal, 2006*(146), 10.

Xiong, X., & de la Torre, F. (2013). Supervised descent method and its application to face alignment. In *IEEE Conference on Computer Vision and Pattern Recognition (CVPR).* Retrieved July 9, 2015, from https://courses.cs.washington.edu/courses/cse590v/13au/intraface.pdf

Yu, X., Zhang, S., Yan, Z., Yang, F., Huang, J., Dunbar, N. E., Jensen, M. L. Burgoon, J. K., . . . Metaxas, D. M. (2015). Is interactional dissynchrony a clue to deception? Insights from automated analysis of nonverbal visual cues. *IEEE Transactions on Systems, Man, and Cybernetics, 45,* 506–520.

Endnote

1. We had permission from our institutional review board to keep the recordings from the first study for future analysis, which made the second and third studies possible. Some institutional review boards require that recordings be destroyed after some period of time, which precludes future analyses.

4

■

PHYSIOLOGICAL OUTCOMES OF COMMUNICATION BEHAVIOR

AMANDA DENES, TAMARA D. AFIFI, AND COLIN HESSE

Communication scholars have begun building an impressive body of research examining the interdependence of communication behaviors and physiological outcomes. This work includes links to physiological outcomes measured through saliva (Afifi, Granger, Denes, Joseph, & Aldeis, 2011; Afifi, Granger, Joseph, Denes, & Aldeis, 2013) and blood (Floyd, Boren, Hannawa, Hesse, McEwan, & Veksler, 2009; Floyd, Hesse, & Haynes, 2007; Floyd, Mikkelson, Hesse, & Pauley, 2007). Much of this research has explored the influence of communication (i.e., message behaviors) on physiological stress (e.g., Afifi et al., 2011, 2013) and other factors such as affectionate communication (Floyd, Pauley, & Hesse, 2010) that might influence the association between stress and physiology. Much of this research explores changes in physiology across various time points, though several studies have also focused on more dynamic measures of physiological response, such as heart rate and skin conductance (e.g., Diao & Sundar, 2004; Ivory & Kalyanaraman, 2007; Sundar & Kalyanaraman, 2004; Turner-McGrievy, Kalyanaraman, & Campbell, 2013).

Research exploring the physiological correlates of communication challenges scholars to consider the effects of communication on individuals' bodies. Such approaches allow communication scholars to investigate health outcomes in new and unique ways and capture potentially overlooked effects. For example, individuals might claim that they are not stressed on self-report measures, but physiological measurements of stress might tell a different story. Exploring the physiology of communication allows researchers to uncover such "hidden" patterns and

more completely understand both the ways that physiology influences communication and the effects of communication on physiology.

In this chapter, we present an overview of physiological research in communication with a focus on physiological stress responses. We begin with a brief history of key systems of study, followed by an explanation of practical issues regarding data collection and analysis. The chapter concludes with a review of several studies exploring communication and physiology and future directions for physiological research in communication.

History and Background

Communication scholars have long been interested in associations between communication behavior and physiological outcomes (e.g., Beatty, McCroskey, & Heisel, 1998). Beatty, McCroskey, and Valencic (2001) proposed the "communibiological" paradigm to understand the profound connection between biology and social behavior. This paradigm broadly states "that communication is driven by inborn, neurobiological processes" (Beatty et al., 2001, p. 3). The communibiological paradigm emerged from psychobiological research and early communication research and offers several central propositions (for a full discussion, see Beatty, McCroskey, & Pence, 2009): (a) "all mental processes involved in social interaction are reducible to brain activity," (b) "communicator traits and temperament characteristics represent individual differences in neurobiological functioning," (c) "individual differences in the neurobiological systems underlying communicator traits are principally (but not completely) inherited," and (d) "dimensions of situations have only negligible direct effects on behavior" (pp. 5–12). In other words, the communibiological paradigm argues for the centrality of neurobiological processes in communicative behavior. Although the communibiological paradigm focused heavily on individual differences and static measures, new advances are paving the way for research focused on dynamic factors of psychobiology. Such advances are mentioned throughout this chapter.

The communibiological paradigm has not always been well received, because of assumptions of biological determinism. Rather than viewing biology as having a unidirectional influence on human behavior, researchers today view it as bidirectional. For example, people's genes influence how they communicate in a given situation, and their communication patterns influence their physiological stress responses, including the ability for genes to express themselves over time (see Floyd & Afifi, 2011, for further elaboration). What was particularly important about Beatty and McCroskey's work, however, was their emphasis on biology and the need for researchers to study its influential role in communication. The call to understand the role of physiology in communication interactions has been addressed by many communication scholars in the past decade. A plethora of research investigating communication and physiology uses an evolutionary psychology paradigm (e.g., Floyd et al., 2010; Hesse et al., 2013). The evolutionary psychology paradigm focuses on the role of evolution in human thinking and subsequent behavior and is often linked to psychophysiology (e.g., Floyd & Cole, 2009; Taylor, 2012). Taken together, evolution and psychophysiology suggest that

> particular behaviors, emotions, or cognitions generated in response to perceived environmental threats might have been retained through selection pressures for the viability or fertility advantages they entail, but it is often *through their corresponding physiological experiences* that those advantages are conferred. (Floyd & Cole, 2009, p. 24)

Although these paradigms underlie many physiological studies in the field of communication, scholars often use both communication and psychological theories to explore physiological response systems and test specific pathways derived from various theories and constructs. These include affection exchange theory, relational uncertainty,

and self-regulation theory, among others (Afifi et al., 2011; Crowley, 2014; Priem & Solomon, 2011). Although we will discuss examples of such studies in greater detail in this chapter, we provide a brief overview of two of the major systems that are commonly investigated in communication research: the *neuroendocrine system* and the *cardiovascular system* (defined in detail next). Because these are the two most commonly researched systems, they serve as the basis of this chapter. However, it is important to note that research continues to emerge investigating other important biological systems and their relationships to communication behavior (e.g., the brain and nervous system, the immune system; Floyd & Afifi, 2011).

The Neuroendocrine System

The neuroendocrine system is composed of the nervous system and endocrine system and the interaction of these two systems. Both systems consist of neuroendocrine cells that release hormones and send messages to other cells in the body. Researchers often investigate the neuroendocrine system in studies involving stress. Stress entails psychological and biological reactions to a threat that exceeds people's perceptions of their resources for managing it (Lazarus & Folkman, 1984). This threat could be something acute, such as an exam, or something chronic, such as growing up in poverty, in a violent neighborhood, or in a conflict-ridden household. The brain constitutes the central location where people decipher whether something is stressful. The brain also sends messages to the endocrine system (which consists of glands that produce hormones that regulate various bodily functions) and other systems in the body. The *hypothalamic-pituitary-adrenocortical (HPA) axis* and the *locus coeruleus–norepinephrine/ sympathetic nervous system (LC-NE/SNS)* are two of the primary biological stress response systems of interest to researchers. These systems interact with each other in reaction to stressful stimuli. Consequently, we examine them both in this chapter. When an individual perceives that a threat is real and stressful, the hypothalamus is activated, which signals to the rest of the body that it is stressed, triggering the release of a host of hormones and other biological stress markers. In particular, the activation of the hypothalamus triggers the activation of the pituitary gland and the adrenal glands. The "fight or flight" response refers to the activation of the SNS and a sudden release of hormones. It is a more rapid and short-lived stress response, whereas the HPA axis is studied when investigating long-term stress

(Gordis, Granger, Susman, & Trickett, 2006). The HPA axis has been called a "defeat action," or a passive response (e.g., inaction, avoidant coping, emotional distress) due to the perceived lack of control over a situation (Lundberg & Frankenhaeuser, 1980).

Historically, most research on the psychobiology of the stress response focused on the HPA axis (Shirtcliff, Granger, Booth, & Johnson, 2005). The HPA axis is a primary part of the neuroendocrine system and refers to the interactions among several endocrine glands. More specifically, the HPA axis consists of a series of feedback loops among the hypothalamus (which regulates a number of bodily functions and is responsible for hormone production), the pituitary gland (which produces hormones that control several important endocrine glands), and the adrenal glands (which also produce hormones with a number of functions). When a threat is detected, the hypothalamus triggers the release of the *corticotropin-releasing hormone (CRH)*. CRH stimulates the pituitary gland to release the *adrenocorticotropic hormone (ACTH)*. The ACTH then triggers the adrenal glands to produce the steroid hormone *cortisol* (Lundberg & Frankenhaeuser, 1980). Because cortisol is secreted into individuals' systems when they experience stressors, it is sometimes called the "stress hormone." Chronically high and chronically low cortisol levels are associated with psychological problems such as anxiety and depression, whereas moderate levels indicate adaptive functioning (Gordis et al., 2006).

Among all the stress hormones studied by social scientists, cortisol receives the most attention and is believed to be a reliable indicator of acute and chronic stress. The release of cortisol is a necessary and healthy response to stress, and activation of the hormone is the body's way of combating an impending threat. Salivary cortisol increases after an acute threat, typically peaking approximately 10 to 15 minutes after stress and recovering 30 minutes after stress (Gordis et al., 2006). These patterns allow the body to adjust to the stressor and return to a state of homeostasis (Miller, Chen, & Zhou, 2007). As a result, researchers often examine both the "reaction" to the stress and the "recovery" from it.

In addition to the acute response, the response of the HPA axis involves diurnal (or daily) variation. Cortisol tends to be highest approximately 30 minutes after waking. Researchers call this tendency for cortisol to rise after waking the *cortisol awakening response (CAR)*. Cortisol then declines slowly throughout the day and reaches its lowest point at approximately midnight, at which time it begins to rise again (Edwards, Evans, & Clow, 2001). Environmental stress might affect both the acute functioning of the HPA axis and the diurnal variability of the axis (e.g., DeSantis et al., 2007). Different types of stress can lead to alternative effects on these responses. Acute or more moderate stress might exacerbate the diurnal variability of cortisol, whereas more severe and chronic stress can lead to a blunting of the diurnal variability and the CAR (Stetler & Miller, 2005). In other words, stress can interfere with the natural patterns of cortisol by causing either more extreme daily fluctuations or little to no stress response at all, depending on the type of stress experienced.

Cortisol is considered *dysregulated* (i.e., the HPA axis fails to react or overreacts) when it is too high (i.e., hypercortisolism), too low (i.e., hypocortisolism), or is otherwise irregular or atypical (McEwen, 1998). According to McEwen (1998), the body has a natural homeostasis or ability to return to stability after it responds physiologically to a stressor. When people are exposed to multiple, chronic stressors (e.g., poverty, violence, chronic conflict, unemployment, racism, gangs), the result is prolonged activation of their HPA axes to manage the stressors. This prolonged activation of the HPA axis can burden it, producing "wear and tear" on the body, or allostatic load (McEwen, 1998). There are four primary ways that allostatic load can reveal itself (McEwen, 1998). First, chronic hypercortisolism can occur when people are chronically trying to manage too many stressors at the same time. Second, people also tend to adapt better to stressors and become less aroused after they experience the same stressors repeatedly. When individuals are unable to adapt to the same stressors over time, however, hypercortisolism can result. Third, dysregulated recovery or the inability to recover from a stressful situation can occur when people remain physiologically aroused longer than the rest of the population. Finally, hyporeactivity occurs when people do not become aroused at all or when cortisol arousal is muted. As a result, researchers examine people's baseline cortisol levels, as well as their reactions to stressors and their ability to recover from these stressors.

Understanding how and why the HPA axis becomes dysregulated is important primarily because it provides a pathway to health. For instance, research on allostatic load suggests that chronic stress affects individuals' cortisol levels, which makes them more susceptible to diseases, such as cardiovascular disease, obesity, and diabetes, over long periods of time (see McEwen, 1998; Miller et al., 2007). Dysregulated cortisol levels can also negatively affect people's interpersonal relationships (Afifi et al., 2011). When people are stressed psychologically and physiologically, it can negatively affect their closeness and satisfaction with their relationships.

The fast-acting stress response of the SNS is the basis of what researchers call the fight-or-flight response. The hypothalamus activates the adrenal medulla when a threat is detected, which is part of the *autonomic nervous system (ANS)*. The ANS helps regulate stress in the body. The adrenal medulla secretes the hormone *epinephrine* (or adrenaline), which activates the SNS and reduces the parasympathetic nervous system. Although the HPA axis is often viewed as the "defeat" reaction to stress, the SNS is often viewed as a "defense reaction" (i.e., an individual must decide how to deal with a stressor, such as either fighting or fleeing) that is fueled by novel and challenging situations (Hellhammer, Wust, & Kudielka, 2009), as well as controllable stressors (Henry, 1992). This defense reaction occurs almost immediately and can be measured in physiological stress responses such as increases in heart rate, sweating, blood pressure, and galvanic skin response. These fast-moving physiological responses may be particularly relevant to studying the dynamics of human interaction. Once the threat has passed, the parasympathetic part of the nervous system takes over and restores the body's homeostasis.

Other biosocial markers can also be used to measure activation of the SNS. For example, salivary α-amylase (sAA) is an enzyme that can be collected through saliva. The SNS triggers the release of sAA and has attracted considerable attention recently. Alpha-amylase is an enzyme that helps digest food by breaking down bacteria in the oral cavity (Scannapieco, Torres, & Levine, 1993). The SNS secretes sAA through the salivary glands, reflecting stress-induced changes in the ANS (Chatterton, Vogelsong, Lu, Ellman, & Hudgens, 1996; Nater, Rohleder, Schultz, Ehlert, & Kirschbaum, 2007). When people experience stressful situations, the salivary glands release sAA immediately, and its response is relatively short lived (Afifi et al., 2011, 2013; Gordis et al., 2006). A growing amount of evidence shows that sAA does respond to physical and psychological stress, as well as arousal and anxiety (Nater & Rohleder, 2009).

Measuring Cortisol and sAA

Today, many biosocial markers (e.g., cortisol and sAA) can be tested noninvasively through saliva. A variety of methods can also be used to collect saliva, and the method researchers choose depends on the type and number of biosocial

markers to be tested, the ability of the participants to provide saliva samples, and the desired ease of collection. Two of the most common data collection methods for biosocial markers with the use of saliva include the passive drool method and the use of absorbencies such as Salivettes (see Granger et al., 2007, for a review). The passive drool method involves participants thinking of their favorite foods and gathering saliva in their mouths. They then passively drool into a straw that is inserted into a small vial. The Salivette method involves inserting a one-inch swab underneath the tongue for two or three minutes until it is saturated with saliva. The passive drool method allows researchers to collect a greater volume of saliva compared with the Salivette. If a researcher wanted to test for multiple hormones, the passive drool method might be preferred over the Salivette. The Salivette, however, is quicker and easier to collect, less messy, and less obtrusive than the passive drool method. Social scientists can learn to assay their own saliva for various hormones through "spit camps" at Salimetrics, LLC (State College, PA) and other testing facilities, but this requires access to laboratory equipment and the purchasing of assay kits to test for particular hormones. Because of a lack of access to the appropriate equipment, many social scientists send their samples to outside laboratories to be assayed for hormones. This typically requires an internal or external grant to cover the costs of the assays. Portable devices are also currently being tested that can gather and assay cortisol and other hormones instantaneously, providing instant feedback about stress and health electronically. Such devices could change the landscape of research on stress, health, and human relationships and may be especially valuable for capturing dynamic changes in hormones.

Additional Hormones of Interest

The endocrine system contains multiple glands, but social scientists have focused most of their attention on the pituitary and adrenal glands and the gonads (which produce reproductive cells; see Floyd & Afifi, 2011). The pituitary gland produces eight hormones (see Floyd & Afifi, 2011). One of the most studied of these hormones is *oxytocin*, which facilitates uterine contractions and the letdown reflex in pregnancy and birth (Campbell, 2010; Carter, 2003; Hiller, 2004). Oxytocin also releases neuropeptides into mothers' bodies through touching and being emotionally connected with their infants, which helps foster attachment with their babies, better psychological well-being, calmness, and pleasure (Hiller, 2004). Researchers sometimes call oxytocin the "prosocial hormone" because it facilitates pair bonding and social skills across a wide array of relationships (Feldman, Gordon, & Zagoory-Sharon, 2011; Neumann, 2008).

The adrenal glands also produce small amounts of sex hormones. The male sex hormones are called *androgens* and the female sex hormones are called *estrogens* (Rainey, Carr, Sasano, Suzuki, & Mason, 2002). A third class of "female" sex hormones includes *progesterone*. The gonads, however, are responsible for generating the vast majority of these sex hormones. Although people typically label these sex hormones as "male" or "female" because of the masculine and feminine sex characteristics they produce, they occur in both males and females in varying degrees. Female gonads are referred to as ovaries and produce estrogens and progesterone. Male gonads are called testes and produce androgens, with the most common androgen being testosterone (see Floyd & Afifi, 2011). Testosterone is produced in the testes of men and the ovaries of women, but it is produced in much greater amounts in men. It produces male sex characteristics and regulates sperm production, and it is also associated with competition and dominance in men and women (see Floyd & Afifi, 2011). Within the field of communication, oxytocin and testosterone are theorized to influence postsex disclosures (Denes, 2012; Denes & Afifi, 2014). For example, Denes (2012) suggested that the hormone oxytocin, which is released during sexual activity, may influence patterns of "pillow talk." She further suggested that the reason men disclose less positive feelings than women during pillow talk might be men's higher levels of testosterone, which have been found to dampen the effects of oxytocin (Denes, 2012; Taylor et al., 2002). Denes and colleagues are currently investigating the effects of testosterone on postsex communication by measuring individuals' testosterone levels through saliva samples.

Measurement of other hormones. Whereas some hormones can be collected reliably with saliva, other hormones (e.g., oxytocin, vasopressin, prolactin) are difficult to collect through saliva and continue to be collected through blood samples or urine samples. *Venipuncture* (i.e., puncturing veins) is often required to collect blood samples, and extra precautions are necessary to handle, analyze, and ship blood (Floyd & Afifi, 2011). For example, some researchers have tested oxytocin with saliva, but that method remains highly contested. Most researchers continue to suggest that oxytocin can be tested reliably only with blood (Horvat-Gordon, Granger, Schwartz, Nelson, & Kivlighan, 2005). Nevertheless, even as we write this chapter, improvements in assays for hormones through saliva are being made. By the time this chapter is published, it might be possible to reliably test for oxytocin with saliva. Another example of a controversial test with saliva concerns inflammation. Assays can test for inflammation or cytokines in saliva, but many researchers believe that those tests might really be measuring the inflammation in the oral cavity rather than inflammation in other parts of the body, because of their modest correlations with serum levels (e.g., Minetto et al., 2005). Consequently, saliva assays for inflammation may not measure what some social scientists believe they are measuring. Because the measurement of various factors using hormones continues to develop, researchers should review the most recent literature on the hormones of interest and determine the most reliable way of tapping into those physiological systems.

The Cardiovascular System

Researchers also investigate how stress affects the cardiovascular system. The stress responses in the SNS can negatively affect the cardiovascular system, which primarily includes the heart, blood, and blood vessels (Engler & Engler, 1995). Cardiovascular disease is partially the result of increases in stress due to the overactivation of the adrenal glands (Engler & Engler, 1995). The fight-or-flight response floods the body with epinephrine and cortisol (as mentioned previously). When this influx of stress hormones occurs, it can result in an increased heart rate, more rapid blood flow, heavier breathing, increased fat in the bloodstream, and greater chances of clotting of the blood (which can produce heart attacks and strokes) (Esch, Stefano, Fricchione, & Benson, 2002). Researchers often measure one or many of these physiological responses in combination to assess stress and changes in the cardiovascular system. Blood pressure often indicates stress. The more rapid blood flow raises blood pressure, which researchers often use as one measure of stress in the cardiovascular system (Floyd & Afifi, 2011). High blood pressure is also referred to as *hypertension*.

Stress can also lead to poor health habits, which can foster heart disease. Stressed individuals tend to eat unhealthy foods to feel better. A significant amount of research has been devoted to understanding obesity in the United States and how it is linked to a host of diseases, including diabetes and heart disease. A high-fat, high-sugar diet, particularly when it is combined with a sedentary lifestyle, can contribute to high cholesterol and high blood pressure (Esch et al., 2002). Communication scholars often examine how communication patterns contribute to unhealthy behaviors and health outcomes. Interpersonal scholars often focus on communicative behaviors within relationships that moderate stress levels. For example, Floyd, Mikkelson, Hesse, et al. (2007) found that participants who wrote about their affection for important people in their lives over a three-day period had significant declines in their total cholesterol levels compared with a control group, who experienced increases or no change in cholesterol levels. In another study, Floyd et al. (2009) conducted a study of kissing and cholesterol. Fifty-two healthy adults in married or cohabitating relationships were randomly assigned to an experimental group in which they were asked to kiss their partners more often or a control group in which they were given no such instructions over six weeks. Participants in the kissing condition reported better perceived stress, better relationship satisfaction, and lower serum cholesterol levels. This research, and a host of other research, demonstrates that people's communicative behaviors can improve or magnify their stress levels.

Measuring Blood Pressure and Cholesterol

Blood pressure is the pressure of blood circulating along blood vessel walls. Measurements of blood pressure attend to two specific indices. *Systolic blood pressure* is the pressure or force when blood flows out of the heart or the heart contracts, and *diastolic blood pressure* is the period of time when the heart refills with blood after it has contracted or when it is resting (Caro, 1978). Diagnostic measurement is often done manually with a sphygmomanometer or blood pressure meter, wherein a cuff placed around the arm inflates to restrict blood flow and measures the pressures surrounding the moments when blood begins to flow and flows freely as the pressure in the cuff is released (Bailey & Bauer, 1993). There are also many commercial devices available to measure blood pressure, which are often small and portable. Other systems, such as Biopac, also offer researchers the opportunity to explore dynamic changes in heart rate and skin conductance. Such studies involve placing electrodermal electrodes on individuals' skin and connecting the electrodes to an amplifier, which then records data continuously during the course of the experiment.

Although heart rate and skin conductance offer opportunities to explore dynamic measures, cholesterol does not change quite as quickly. Cholesterol is typically measured through saliva or blood. In communication studies, it is typically measured before and after a series of communicative behaviors have occurred to show changes in cholesterol. One interaction may not be enough to change one's cholesterol, but a series of communicative exchanges have been shown to have an effect on cholesterol (e.g., Floyd, Mikkelson, Hesse, & Pauley, 2007; Floyd et al., 2009).

Considerations When Designing Studies Using Physiological Measurements

Conceptualization

We must start with the understanding that communication researchers normally assess measures such as cortisol or blood pressure to operationalize constructs such as stress (e.g., Floyd, Hesse, et al., 2007). For example, communication researchers are not necessarily interested in blood pressure itself, but are interested in related physiological wellness, arousal, or stress. Of course, researchers need to maintain a clear rationale, whether based on theory or previous research, between a given construct and a physiological measure. Scholars must weigh the differences in expense and difficulty against the differences in validity and utility of the data. There is a wide range of physiological variables that encompass a wide range of costs and degree of difficulty for collection. For example, blood pressure is a fairly inexpensive measurement of stress arousal, whereas cortisol adds several thousand dollars to the budget of a given study.

Validity and Reliability

Psychophysiological measures are somewhat unique in terms of the questions of validity and reliability. In most measures, the idea of validity is to assess the correlation among a given variable, the conceptualization of that variable, and the operationalization of that variable. For example, researchers measuring affection must show empirical support for both their definition and measurement of affection. Psychophysiological measures, on the other hand, are directly observable and thus have less error between the conceptualization and operationalization of the measure. Less error leads to greater levels of measurement power, with smaller sample sizes necessary to examine questions of statistical significance (e.g., Kurup & Kurup, 2003).

Whether researchers rely on one measurement or multiple measurements also affects reliability. For example, Smith and Uchino (2008) discussed the difference between a single physiological measure and an index such as cardiac output, with which the researcher combines the elements of stroke volume and heart rate. That combination leads to a less reliable variable than if the two components were reviewed separately. When determining reliability, researchers could achieve similar results if they assessed, for instance, total cholesterol on two separate occasions from the same person. Overall, psychophysiological measures, if assessed correctly, can be quite strong in terms of validity and reliability. It is important to note, though, that several pitfalls can occur throughout the conceptualization, data collection, and data analysis procedures. These pitfalls, if not addressed, can lead to problematic results for the researcher concerning both reliability and validity.

Steps in Data Collection

Collecting physiological data can be a stressful proposition, as stringent requirements dictate techniques, equipment, and participant controls. These requirements change with every variable, and in this chapter we outline some of the specific protocols in a later section. For now, we focus on a few specific points that can alter the validity or reliability of the measures.

First, it is important to use equipment that has been previously validated for data collection. For example, collecting saliva samples might require the use of Salivettes or Cryovials, while collecting cardiovascular data might require the use of a monitor such as a Dinamap or a W. A. Baum aneroid sphygmomanometer (e.g., Floyd, Hesse, & Haynes, 2007). A few companies can provide assistance in ensuring the use of proper equipment, even holding classes for researchers who desire to learn more about the collection techniques.

Many universities also have strict biosafety requirements for lab spaces where researchers collect physiological data. For example, if researchers collect saliva samples, they may be required to have a sink accessible, appropriate cleaning products, biohazard waste baskets, gloves, and lab jackets for research assistants. The lab requirements for collecting blood samples are often stricter. Researchers may need to take their university's blood-borne pathogens training seminar and have the lab inspected by their biosafety officer before collection. Such labs require many of the same elements as a saliva collection lab, with additional cleaning supplies and safety regulations if using sharps (such as needles). Blood collection labs additionally need floors that can be cleaned with bleach products. Although some saliva collection labs may contain carpets or an interaction space, the specifications for blood collection are often stricter. Researchers studying communication behavior in the lab must be careful to design a lab space that adheres to biosafety standards while fostering a natural environment. For example, if interaction partners are meant to have a conversation replicating real-life interactions, a sterile lab space with biohazard signs can influence ecological validity. Researchers should work closely with biosafety officers to design a lab space that meets multiple needs. For example, biosafety officers might approve of smaller or less brightly colored biosafety signs or furniture that can be sufficiently cleaned while also giving the impression of a living room context.

Researchers also must educate themselves about necessary participant controls for data collection. Participants being tested for cholesterol, for example, must fast for at least 12 hours prior to the collection (Emberson, Whincup, Walker, Thomas, & Alberti, 2002). Other potential instructions include avoiding caffeinated beverages, strenuous physical activity, alcoholic beverages, or sexual activity for some period of time before data collection. Participants are often excluded if they are taking any medications that influence their hormone levels, such as steroids. Participants must obey all instructions to obtain valid data.

Finally, the technique of collection can affect both the validity and reliability of the data. We strongly suggest that research personnel undergo rigorous training before data collection. For example, to prepare for one study using cholesterol as a measurement, all personnel were trained in using the same procedure for procuring a drop of blood. This included (a) using a hand warmer on the participant, (b) using an alcohol swab to clean the area, (c) using the same participant finger and the same general area of the finger for collection, (d) cutting the finger against the grain to ensure a better drop of blood (and avoiding a cut that resembled a paper cut), (e) wiping away the first drop of blood that appeared, (f) drawing a few microliters of blood from the finger while not touching the skin of the finger, and (g) cleaning and putting a bandage on the finger. Because several individuals were involved in data collection, this type of strict protocol was set to achieve a more valid data set (Floyd et al., 2009). Note that with some types of variables, the use of a trained professional is required, such as a phlebotomist, nurse, or neurologist.

In general, research involving physiological data enjoys strong benefits of reliability and validity. For most measures a researcher might use, a wealth of previous research highlighting both the validity and reliability of that measure exists. However, that empirical support is built on a specific procedure of conceptualization, collection, and analysis that requires researcher education and training before proceeding with a specific study.

Major Findings of Research

Although this review is far from exhaustive, we focus on two categories of physiological measures that have been widely used with questions of communication: neuroendocrinological outcomes and cardiovascular outcomes.

Neuroendocrinological Outcomes

The bulk of neuroendocrinological research in communication uses cortisol (linked to stress and emotional arousal) and oxytocin (linked to emotional bonding and attachment) as key variables of interest (though other work also explores ACTH, produced in response to stress; epinephrine, more commonly known as adrenaline; and norepinephrine, which helps the body increase heart rate and oxygen supply) in relation to communication (e.g., Malarkey, Kiecolt-Glaser, & Pearl, 1994). Floyd and Riforgiate (2008), for example, hypothesized a relationship between expressed affection in a spousal relationship and individual diurnal cortisol variation. Their results supported that hypothesis, with a significant linear relationship between spouses' levels of expressed affection and participants' diurnal cortisol variation, as well as waking cortisol levels (Floyd & Riforgiate, 2008).

Moreover, researchers have linked communication both before and during stressful encounters to cortisol levels (e.g., Afifi et al., 2011; Kiecolt-Glaser et al., 1996, 1997; Meuwly et al., 2012). For example, Afifi et al. (2011) investigated the relationship between parents' communication and adult children's physiological stress and anxiety responses as measured through cortisol and sAA. They found that children whose parents disclosed more information about parental conflict issues experienced increases in their sAA levels, a possible indicator of anxiety. Floyd, Mikkelson, Tafoya, et al. (2007) also investigated cortisol responses by bringing participants into the lab and running them through a series of stress-inducing activities. The researchers then split participants into three groups. The two control groups were instructed to sit quietly or think about a loved one for 20 minutes, while the experimental group was instructed to write an affectionate letter to a loved one. Individuals in the experimental group experienced reductions in cortisol levels at a quicker rate than individuals in either of the two control groups. Subsequent studies have extended these links to include elements of relational uncertainty and hurtful interactions (Priem & Solomon, 2011).

Researchers have also used the measurement of oxytocin as a way to measure bonding and closeness in close relationships. This research has linked levels of oxytocin to nonverbal displays of romantic love such as Duchenne smiles (smiles that include the contraction of the muscles around the eyes) and head nods (Gonzaga, Turner, Keltner, Campos, & Altemus, 2006). Floyd et al. (2010) measured participant trait affection (how much affection an individual generally gives) and state affection (how much affection an individual gave in the past week) prior to a lab appointment. During the appointment, participants engaged in a series of stressful activities, including a cold pressor test, a Stroop color word test, a mental math exercise, and viewing a video of couples engaging in conflict. Both state and trait affection predicted increases in oxytocin during the stressful activities, supporting the stress-buffering qualities of affectionate communication (Floyd et al., 2010). In another study, researchers took married couples through a four-week intervention on how to communicate social support through nonverbal signs such as touch and massage. Couples who went through the intervention experienced significant increases in oxytocin levels (Holt-Lunstad, Birmingham, & Light, 2008). Several additional studies have found relationships between levels of oxytocin and positive communication between parents and children (e.g., Gordon, Zagoory-Sharon, Leckman, & Feldman, 2010; Strathearn, Fonagy, Amico, & Montague, 2009).

Cardiovascular Outcomes

Some of the initial forays into physiological research in the context of interpersonal communication examined cardiovascular measures such as heart rate and blood pressure. Two main topics concern the communication of conflict and the communication of intimacy. For conflict, examples include the impressive number of studies by Gottman's team at the University of Washington using cardiovascular arousal (measured by heart rate and blood pressure, among other variables) as an indicator of competent conflict communication (Gottman, 1994), as well as the work of scholars such as Morell and Apple (1990), who found links between negative affect for wives during conflict events and systolic blood pressure. Communication scholars have extended that work to include links to individuals who take roles of avoiders and initiators during conflict events (Denton, Burleson, Hobbs, Von Stein, & Rodriguez, 2001).

Multiple studies have also examined relationships between cardiovascular health and the communication of intimacy. Nonverbal actions such as hugs and other signs of warm touch in romantic couples have been linked to lower blood pressure and heart rate (Holt-Lunstad et al., 2008; Light, Grewen, & Amico, 2005). Individual trait expressed affection (defined as a general tendency to communicate affection to others) is related to resting diastolic and systolic blood pressure (Floyd, Hesse, & Haynes, 2007), whereas levels of verbal and supportive affectionate communication in an individual's most affectionate relationship are inversely related to resting heart rate (Floyd, Mikkelson, Tafoya, et al., 2007).

As mentioned above, systems such as Biopac offer researchers the opportunity to explore dynamic changes in heart rate and skin conductance. For example, Ivory and Kalyanaraman (2007) found that individuals playing more technologically advanced games experienced greater increases in arousal, as measured through skin conductance level (SCL). Other media scholars have investigated the relationship between memory for Web advertisements and heart rate activity using an electrocardiograph (Diao & Sundar, 2004), as well as the association between pace of animation in Web advertising and SCL (Sundar & Kalyanaraman, 2004). In the area of health communication, Turner-McGrievy et al. (2013) found that individuals who received weight-loss information through a podcast experienced greater psychological arousal (as measured through skin conductance) compared with individuals who read text on a Web site. Studies such as these exemplify the many ways that dynamic physiological measures are being integrated into communication research.

Future Directions in Physiological Research

One growing area of physiological research in the field of communication involves neuroimaging procedures to implicate several structures in the brain that process verbal and nonverbal messages. Using the language of neuroimaging research, these are referred to as regions of interest (ROIs), which

are areas of the brain known to be associated with specific functions. Although it is necessary to point out that colleagues are performing outstanding work examining neurological outcomes linked to mass communication (for a review, see Weber, Sherry, & Mathiak, 2009), the following discussion focuses on interpersonal communication.

A large portion of this research focuses on elements of nonverbal communication, including the use of material objects as communicative devices (Tylén, Wallentin, & Roepstorff, 2009), and nonverbal gestures (Lindenberg, Uhlig, Scherfeld, Schlaug, & Seitz, 2012). This line of research also examines activation due to facial expressions (e.g., Sato, Yoshikawa, Kochiyama, & Matsumura, 2004; Wild, Erb, Eyb, Bartels, & Grodd, 2003). For example, Wicker et al. (2003) found increased activation of the *insular cortex* (involved in emotional processing and self-perception) in response to photos of disgusted faces, while multiple studies have found increased activation of the *amygdala* (involved in processing and memory of emotional reactions) in response to emotional faces (Jiang & He, 2006). Other ROIs linked to facial expressions include the *fusiform gyrus* (involved in facial and emotional processing) (Jiang & He, 2006) and the *orbitofrontal cortex* (involved in sensory integration and emotional processing) (Vuilleumier, Armony, Driver, & Dolan, 2001). In a similar vein, Hesse et al. (2013) experimentally examined group differences between high- and low-*alexithymia* (a condition characterized by an unawareness of and inability to identify emotions) participants in terms of activation while watching individuals displaying images of neutral or positive affect. Participants were scanned using functional magnetic resonance imaging (fMRI) and told to attempt to feel what the individuals in the images were feeling. The researchers found several ROIs in which the high-alexithymic group showed significantly lower levels of hemodynamic activity (i.e., blood flow) while viewing images of positive affect than the low-alexithymic group, including in the fusiform gyrus, the hippocampus (which processes visual cues), and the amygdala. Notably, that pattern did not extend to scenes that were emotionally neutral.

Imaging research is beginning to extend to stimuli involving verbal communication, including interactions between participants inside and outside the scanner. Multiple studies have begun to disassociate the ability to understand language from the ability to communicate (for a review, see Willems & Varley, 2010). For example, Willems et al. (2010) asked participants to engage in a task similar to the game "Taboo," whereby the participant inside the scanner played the game with an individual outside the scanner. Certain areas of the brain appeared to be activated because of the communicative manipulation of the game beyond activation due to simple linguistic ability, such as the *medial prefrontal cortex* (involved in social behavior and decision making).

Other studies examine neurological activation in response to vocal stimuli such as verbal expressions of emotions (e.g., Johnstone, van Reekum, Oakes, & Davidson, 2006). Gunther, Beach, Yanasak, and Miller (2009) examined the neurological outcomes of social support by having husbands listen to various topics (e.g., receiving advice on finances and remembering family events) from their wives when in the fMRI scanner. Depending on the importance of the topic (high vs. low), husbands experienced greater activation in ROIs such as the thalamus and the *posterior cingulate* (involved in working memory and emotional processing). They concluded that individuals receiving support in the form of advice are not simply processing positive information but also seeking to understand the motivation of the advice giver. Some innovative studies involve measuring activation in both a speaker and listener of verbal communication. Stephens, Silbert, and Hasson (2010), for example, had one group of participants tell an unrehearsed story when in the fMRI scanner, whereas a second group of participants listened to a recording of the story while in the fMRI scanner. They discovered general levels of coupling activation between speaker and listener during the story, showing shared activation as one way to observe meaning-making occurring between individuals. Overall, this line of research appears to present exciting opportunities for communication scholars who desire to address neurological activation during interpersonal events.

Researchers also explore brain activity using an electroencephalograph (EEG) to obtain dynamic measures of behavior. An EEG detects and records brain waves, allowing researchers to observe brain activity in discrete time units and examine real-time physiological correlates of cognitive and communicative processes and brain activity (see Heisel, 2009, for a review). Researchers place an electroencephalographic amplifier on the head of a participant, using electrodes to look at specific sections of the brain. The amplifier transmits information from the electrodes to a computer, which can record activity in the range of microseconds (Beatty, 2012). For example, Heisel and Beatty (2006) monitored brain activity in individuals who went through a theory-of-mind activity thinking about why a friend might refuse to lend the participant a compact disc. The researchers were able to collect data throughout the exercise, finding differences in levels of activity in two areas of the brain for individuals who went through the theory-of-mind activity compared with individuals who were asked to simply think about their friends (which served as the control activity).

Scholars can also use electroencephalographic research to examine real-time brain activity during interpersonal communication. Beatty and Heisel (2007) had participants come to the lab and walk through repeated planning of an interpersonal scenario (retrieving money from a friend while maintaining the friendship). Each participant had to think through the scenario on three separate occasions. On the subsequent occasions, one group was told that their previous strategy had worked, whereas the other was told that the strategy had failed and their friend still owed them money. The researchers found that levels of brain activity fell from the first round of the exercise to subsequent rounds for individuals who were told that the previous strategy had worked. On the other hand, individuals who were told that the previous strategy had failed increased their brain activity from the first round of the exercise (Beatty & Heisel, 2007). Another study found a correlation between communication apprehension and levels of brain activity while participants were at rest, showing the potential long-term physiological impact of communicative traits (Beatty et al., 2011). In both cases, the EEG gives researchers the ability to look at physiological data during a specific point in time during the exercise.

Conclusions

Research exploring the relationship between physiology and communication behavior continues to grow at a rapid rate. In this chapter, we have focused on two systems investigated in communication research: the neuroendocrine system and the cardiovascular system. Although these two systems served as the basis for this chapter, a multitude of other systems being investigated and worthy of future research include, but are not limited to, the brain and nervous system and the immune system. Although careful planning, substantial research funds, and intricate data collection methods are necessary to conduct physiological research, such studies provide exciting new avenues for investigating communication behavior. These studies offer findings and insights that can both challenge and expand theories of communication and push scholars to consider the complex relationship between communication behavior and physiological response systems.

References

Afifi, T. D., Granger, D. A., Denes, A., Joseph, A., & Aldeis, D. (2011). Parents' communication skills and adolescents' salivary α-amylase and cortisol response patterns. *Communication Monographs, 78,* 273–295. doi:10.1080/03637751.2011.589460

Afifi, T. D., Granger, D. A., Joseph, A., Denes, A., & Aldeis, D. (2013, November 11). The influence of divorce and parents' communication skills on adolescents' and young adults' stress reactivity and recovery. *Communication Research.* doi:10.1177/009 3650213509665

Bailey, R. H., & Bauer, J. H. (1993). A review of common errors in the indirect measurement of blood pressure: Sphygmomanometry. *Archives of Internal Medicine, 153,* 2741–2748. doi:10.1001/archinte.1993.0041 0240045005.

Beatty, M. J. (2012). Some guidelines for electroencephalographic research into social interaction processes. *Communication Research Reports, 29,* 169–174.

Beatty, M. J., & Heisel, A. D. (2007). Spectrum analysis of cortical activity during verbal planning: Physical evidence for the formation of social interaction routines. *Human Communication Research, 33,* 48–63.

Beatty, M. J., Heisel, A. D., Lewis, R. J., Pence, M. E., Reinhart, A., & Tian, Y. (2011). Communication apprehension and resting alpha range asymmetry in the anterior cortex. *Communication Education, 60,* 441–460.

Beatty, M. J., McCroskey, J. C., & Heisel, A. D. (1998). Communication apprehension as temperamental expression: A communibiological paradigm. *Communications Monographs, 65,* 197–219. doi:10 .1080/03637759809376448

Beatty, M. J., McCroskey, J. C., & Pence, M. E. (2009). Communibiological paradigm. In M. J. Beatty, J. C. McCroskey, & K. Floyd (Eds.), Biological dimensions of communication: Perspectives, methods, and research (pp. 3–16). Cresskill, NJ: Hampton.

Beatty, M. J., McCroskey, J. C., & Valencic, K. M. (2001). *The biology of communication: A communibiological perspective.* Cresskill, NJ: Hampton.

Campbell, A. (2010). Oxytocin and human social behavior. *Personality and Social Psychology Review, 14,* 281–285. doi:10.1177/1088868310363594

Caro, C. G. (1978). *The mechanics of the circulation.* Oxford, UK: Oxford University Press.

Carter, C. S. (2003). Developmental consequences of oxytocin. *Physiology & Behavior, 79,* 383–397. doi:10.1016/S0031-9384(03)00151-3

Chatterton, R. T., Jr., Vogelsong, K. M., Lu, Y. C., Ellman, A. B., & Hudgens, G. A. (1996). Salivary alpha-amylase as a measure of endogenous adrenergic activity. *Clinical Physiology, 16,* 433–438. doi:10.1111/j .1475-097X.1996.tb00731.x

Crowley, J. P. (2014). Expressive writing to cope with hate speech: Assessing psychobiological stress recovery and forgiveness promotion for lesbian, gay, bisexual, or queer victims of hate speech. *Human Communication Research, 40,* 238–261. doi:10.1111/hcre.12020

Denes, A. (2012). Pillow talk: Exploring disclosures after sexual activity. *Western Journal of Communication, 76,* 91–108. doi:10.1080/10570314.2011.651253

Denes, A., & Afifi, T. D. (2014). Pillow talk and cognitive decision-making processes: Exploring the influence of orgasm and alcohol on communication after sexual activity. *Communication Monographs, 81,* 333–358. doi:10.1080/03637751.2014.926377

Denton, W. H., Burleson, B. R., Hobbs, B. V., Von Stein, M., & Rodriguez, C. P. (2001). Cardiovascular reactivity and initiate/avoid patterns of marital communication: A test of Gottman's psychophysiologic model of marital interaction. *Journal of Behavioral Medicine, 24,* 401–421. doi:10.1023/A:1012278209577

DeSantis, A., Adam, E., Doane, L., Mineka, S., Zinbarg, R., & Craske, M. (2007). Racial/ethnic differences in cortisol diurnal rhythms in a community sample of adolescents. *Journal of Adolescent Health, 41,* 3–13. doi:10.1016/j.jadohealth.2007.03.006

Diao, F., & Sundar, S. S. (2004). Orienting response and memory for web advertisements: Exploring effects of pop-up window and animation. *Communication Research, 31,* 537–567. doi:10.1177/0093650204267932

Edwards, S., Evans, P., & Clow, A. (2001). Association between time of wakening and diurnal cortisol secretion activity. *Psychoneuroendocrinology, 26,* 613–622. doi:10.1016/S0306-4530(01)00015-4

Emberson, J. R., Whincup, P. H., Walker, M., Thomas, M., & Alberti, K. G. (2002). Biochemical measures in a population-based study: Effect of fasting duration and time of day. *Annals of Clinical Biochemistry, 39,* 493–501. doi:10.1258/000456302320314511

Engler, M. B., & Engler, M. M. (1995). Assessment of the cardiovascular effects of stress. *Journal of Cardiovascular Nursing, 10,* 51–63.

Esch, T., Stefano, G. B., Fricchione, G. L., & Benson, H. (2002). Stress in cardiovascular disease. *Medicine Science Monitor, 8,* 93–101.

Feldman, R., Gordon, I., & Zagoory-Sharon, O. (2011). Maternal and paternal plasma, salivary, and urinary oxytocin and parent–infant synchrony: Considering stress and affiliation components of human bonding. *Developmental Science, 14,* 752–761. doi:0.1111/j. 1467-7687.2010.01021.x

Floyd, K., & Afifi, T. D. (2011). Biological and physiological perspectives on interpersonal communication. In M. Knapp & J. Daly (Eds.), *The handbook of interpersonal communication* (pp. 87–130, 4th ed.). Thousand Oaks, CA: Sage.

Floyd, K., Boren, J. P., Hannawa, A. F., Hesse, C., McEwan, B., & Veksler, A. E. (2009). Kissing in marital and cohabiting relationships: Effects on blood lipids, stress, and relationship satisfaction. *Western Journal of Communication, 70,* 47–63. doi:10.1080/10570310902856071

Floyd, K., & Cole, T. (2009). Communication and biology: The view from evolutionary psychology and psychobiology. In M. J. Beatty, J. C. McCroskey, & K. Floyd (Eds.), *Biological dimensions of communication: Perspectives, methods, and research* (pp. 17–32). Cresskill, NJ: Hampton.

Floyd, K., Hesse, C., & Haynes, M. T. (2007). Human affection exchange: XV. Metabolic and cardiovascular correlates of trait expressed affection. *Communication Quarterly,55,*79–94.doi:10.1080/01463370600998715

Floyd, K., Mikkelson, A. C., Hesse, C., & Pauley, P. M. (2007). Affectionate writing reduces total cholesterol: Two randomized, controlled studies. *Human Communication Research, 33,* 119–142. doi:10.1111/ j.1468-2958.2007.00293.x

Floyd, K., Mikkelson, A. C., Tafoya, M. A., Farinelli, L., La Valley, A. G., Judd, J., . . . Wilson, J. (2007). Human affection exchange: XIII. Affectionate communication accelerates neuroendocrine stress recovery. *Health Communication, 22,* 123–132. doi:10 .1080/10410230701454015

Floyd, K., Pauley, P. M., & Hesse, C. (2010). State and trait affectionate communication buffer adults' stress reactions. *Communication Monographs, 77,* 618–636. doi:10.1080/03637751.2010.498792

Floyd, K., & Riforgiate, S. (2008). Affectionate communication received from spouses predicts stress hormones in healthy adults. *Communication Monographs, 75,* 351–368. doi:0.1080/03637750802512371

Gonzaga, G. C., Turner, R. A., Keltner, D., Campos, B., & Altemus, M. (2006). Romantic love and sexual desire in close relationships. *Emotion, 6,* 163–179. doi:10.1037/1528-3542.6.2.163

Gordis, E. G., Granger, D., Susman, E. J., & Trickett, P. K. (2006). Asymmetry between salivary cortisol and alpha-amylase reactivity to stress: Relation to aggressive behavior in adolescents. *Psychoneuroendocrinology, 31,* 976–987. doi:10.1016/j.psyneuen.2006.05.010

Gordon, I., Zagoory-Sharon, O., Leckman, J. F., & Feldman, R. (2010). Oxytocin, cortisol, and triadic family interactions. *Physiology & Behavior, 101,* 679–684. doi:10.1016/j.physbeh.2010.08.00

Gottman, J. M. (1994). *What predicts divorce? The relationship between marital processes and marital outcomes.* Hillsdale, NJ: Lawrence Erlbaum.

Granger, D. A., Kivlighan, K. T., Fortunato, C., Harmon, A. G., Hibel, L. C., Schwartz, E., & Whembolua, G. (2007). Integration of salivary biomarkers into developmental and behaviorally-oriented research: Problems and solutions for collecting specimens. *Physiological Behavior, 92,* 583–590. doi:10.1016/ j.physbeh.2007.05.004

Gunther, M. L., Beach, S.R.H., Yanasak, N. E., & Miller, L. S. (2009). Deciphering spousal intentions: An fMRI study of couple communication. *Journal of Social and Personal Relationships, 26,* 388–410. doi:10.1177/026540750935055

Heisel, A. D. (2009). An introduction to EEG and its application in communication research. In M. J. Beatty,

J. C. McCroskey, & K. Floyd (Eds.), *Biological dimensions of communication: Perspectives, research, and methods* (pp. 75–94). Cresskill, NJ: Hampton.

Heisel, A. D., & Beatty, M. J. (2006). Are cognitive representations of friends' request refusals implemented in the orbitofrontal and dorsolateral prefrontal cortices? A cognitive neuroscience approach to 'theory of mind' in relationships. *Journal of Social and Personal Relationships, 23,* 249–265.

Hellhammer, D. H., Wust, S., & Kudielka, B. M. (2009). Salivary cortisol as a biomarker in stress research. *Psychoneuroendocrinology, 34,* 163–171. doi:10.1016/j .psyneuen.2008.10.026

Henry, J. P. (1992). Biological basis of the stress response. *Integrative Physiological and Behavioral Science, 27,* 66–83. doi:10.1007/BF02691093

Hesse, C., Floyd, K., Rauscher, E. A., Frye-Cox, N. E., Hegarty, J. P., II, & Peng, H. (2013). Alexithymia and impairment of decoding positive affect: An fMRI study. *Journal of Communication, 63,* 786–806. doi:10.1111/jcom.12039

Hiller, J. (2004). Speculations on the links between feelings, emotions, and sexual behavior: Are vasopressin and oxytocin involved? *Sexual and Relationship Therapy, 19,* 1468–1479. doi:10.1080/14681990412 331297974

Holt-Lunstad, J., Birmingham, W. A., & Light, K. C. (2008). Influence of a "warm touch" support enhancement intervention among married couples on ambulatory blood pressure, oxytocin, alpha amylase, and cortisol. *Psychosomatic Medicine, 70,* 976–985. doi:10.1097/PSY.0b013e318187aef7

Horvat-Gordon, M., Granger, D. A., Schwartz, E. B., Nelson, V. J., & Kivlighan, K. (2005). Oxytocin is not a valid biomarker when measured in saliva by immunoassay. *Physiology & Behavior, 84,* 445–448. doi:10.1016/j.physbeh.2005.01.007

Ivory, J. D., & Kalyanaraman, S. (2007). The effects of technological advancement and violent content in video games on players' feelings of presence, involvement, physiological arousal, and aggression. *Journal of Communication, 57,* 532–555. doi:10 .1111/j.1460-2466.2007.00356.x

Jiang, Y., & He, S. (2006). Cortical responses to invisible faces: Dissociating subsystems for facial-information processing. *Current Biology, 16,* 2023–2029. doi:10.1016/j.cub.2006.08.084

Johnstone, T., van Reekum, C. M., Oakes, T. R., & Davidson, R. J. (2006). The voice of emotion: An fMRI study of neural responses to angry and happy vocal expressions. *Social Cognitive and Affective Neuroscience, 3,* 242–249. doi:10.1093/scan/nsl027

Kiecolt-Glaser, J. K., Glaser, R., Caciopppo, J. T., MacCallum, R. C., Snydersmith, M., Kim, C., & Malarkey, W. B. (1997). Marital conflict in older adults: Endocrinological and immunological correlates. *Psychosomatic Medicine, 59,* 339–349.

Kiecolt-Glaser, J. K., Newton, T., Cacioppo, J. T., MacCallum, R. C., Glaser, R., & Malarkey, W. B.

(1996). Marital conflict and endocrine function: Are men really more physiologically affected than women? *Journal of Consulting and Clinical Psychology, 64,* 324–332. doi:10.1037/0022-006X.64.2.324

Kurup, R. K., & Kurup, P. A. (2003). Hypothalamic digoxin, hemispheric dominance, and neurobiology of love and affection. *International Journal of Neuroscience, 113,* 721–729. doi:10.1080/00207450390200107

Lazarus R. S., & Folkman, S. (1984). *Stress appraisal and coping.* New York: Springer.

Light, K. C., Grewen, K. M., & Amico, J. A. (2005). More frequent partner hugs and higher oxytocin levels are linked to lower blood pressure and heart rate in premenopausal women. *Biological Psychology, 69,* 5–21. doi:10.1016/j.biopsycho.2004.11.002

Lindenberg, R., Uhlig, M., Scherfeld, D., Schlaug, G., & Seitz, R. J. (2012). Communication with emblematic gestures: Shared and distinct neural correlates of expression and reception. *Human Brain Mapping, 33,* 812–823. doi:10.1002/hbm.21258

Lundberg, U., & Frankenhaeuser, M. (1980). Pituitary-adrenal and sympathetic-adrenal correlates of distress and effort. *Journal of Psychosomatic Research, 24,* 125–130. doi:10.1016/0022-3999(80)90033-1

Malarkey, W. B., Kiecolt-Glaser, J. K., & Pearl, D. (1994). Hostile behavior during marital conflict alters pituitary and adrenal hormones. *Psychosomatic Medicine, 56,* 41–51.

McEwen, B. S. (1998). Protective and damaging effects of stress mediators. *New England Journal of Medicine, 338,* 171–179. doi:10.1056/NEJM199801153380307

Meuwly, N., Bodenmann, G., Germann, J., Bradbury, T. N., Ditzen, B., & Heinrichs, M. (2012). Dyadic coping, insecure attachment, and cortisol stress recovery following experimentally induced stress. *Journal of Family Psychology, 26,* 937–947. doi:10.1037/a0030356

Miller, G., Chen, E., & Zhou, E. (2007). If it goes up, must it come down? Chronic stress and the hypothalamic-pituitary-adrenocortical axis in humans. *Psychological Bulletin, 133,* 25–45. doi:10.1037/0033-2909.133.1.25

Minetto, M., Rainoldi, A., Gazoni, M., Terzolo, M., Borrione, P., Termine, A., . . . Paccotti, P. (2005). Differential responses of serum and salivary interleukin-6 to acute strenuous exercise. *European Journal of Applied Physiology, 93,* 679–686. doi:10.1007/s00421-004-1241-z

Morell, M. A., & Apple, R. F. (1990). Affect expression, marital satisfaction, and stress reactivity among premenopausal women during a conflictual marital discussion. *Psychology of Women Quarterly, 14,* 387–402. doi:10.1111/j.1471-6402.1990.tb00027.x

Nater, U. M., & Rohleder, N. (2009). Salivary alpha-amylase as a non-invasive biomarker for the sympathetic nervous system: Current state of research. *Psychoneuroendocrinology, 34,* 386–496. doi:10.1016/j.psyneuen.2009.01.014

Nater, U. M., Rohleder, N., Schultz, W., Ehlert, U., & Kirschbaum, C. (2007). Determinants of the diurnal course of salivary alpha-amylase. *Psychoneuroendocrinology, 32,* 392–401. doi:10.1016/j.psyneuen.2007.02.007

Neumann, I. D. (2008). Brain oxytocin: A key regulator of emotional and social behaviors in both females and males. *Journal of Neuroendocrinology, 20,* 858–865. doi:10.1111/j.1365-2826.2008.01726.x

Priem, J. S., & Solomon, D. H. (2011). Relational uncertainty and cortisol responses to hurtful and supportive messages from a dating partner. *Personal Relationships, 18,* 198–223. doi:10.1111/j.1475-6811.2011.01353.x

Rainey, W. E., Carr, B. R., Sasano, H., Suzuki, T., & Mason, J. I. (2002). Dissecting human adrenal androgen production. *Trends in Endocrinology and Metabolism, 13,* 234–239. doi:10.1016/S1043-2760(02)00609-4

Sato, W., Yoshikawa, S., Kochiyama, T., & Matsumura, M. (2004). The amygdala processes the emotional significance of facial expressions: An fMRI investigation using the interaction between expression and face direction. *NeuroImage, 22,* 1006–1013. doi:10.1016/j.neuroimage.2004.02.030

Scannapieco, F. A., Torres, G., Levine, M. J. (1993). Salivary alpha-amylase: Role in dental plaque and caries formation. *Critical Reviews in Oral Biology and Medicine, 4,* 301–307. doi:10.1107/S0907444995014119

Shirtcliff, E. A., Granger, D., Booth, A., & Johnson, D. (2005). Low salivary cortisol levels and externalizing behavior problems in youth. *Development and Psychopathology, 17,* 167–184. doi:10.1017/S0954579405050091

Smith, T. W., & Uchino, B. N. (2008). Measuring physiological processes in biopsychosocial research: Basic principles amid growing complexity. In L. J. Leucken & L. C. Gallo (Eds.), *Handbook of physiological methods in health psychology* (pp. 11–34). Thousand Oaks, CA: Sage.

Stephens, G. J., Silbert, L. J., & Hasson, U. (2010). Speaker-listener neural coupling underlies successful communication. *Proceedings of the National Academy of Sciences of the United States of America, 107,* 14425–14430. doi:10.1073/pnas.1008662107

Stetler, C. A., & Miller, G. E. (2005). Blunted cortisol responses to awakening in mild to moderate depression: Regulatory influences of sleep patterns and social contacts. *Journal of Abnormal Psychology, 114,* 697–705. doi:10.1037/0021-843X.114.4.697

Strathearn, L., Fonagy, P., Amico, J., & Montague, P. R. (2009). Adult attachment predicts maternal brain and oxytocin response to infant cues. *Neuropsychopharmacology, 34,* 2655–2666. doi:10.1038/npp.2009.103

Sundar, S. S., & Kalyanaraman, S. (2004). Arousal, memory, and impression-formation effects of animation speed in web advertising. *Journal of Advertising, 33,* 7–17. doi:10.1080/00913367.2004.10639152

Taylor, S. (2012). Tend and befriend theory. In P.A.M. Van Lange, A. W. Kruglanski, & E. T. Higgins (Eds.), *Handbook of theories of social psychology* (pp. 32–42). Thousand Oaks, CA: Sage.

Taylor, S. E., Lewis, B. P., Gruenewald, T. L., Gurung, R. A. R., Updegraff, J. A., & Klein, L. C. (2002). Sex differences in biobehavioral responses to threat: Reply to Geary and Flinn (2002). *Psychological Review*, 109, 751–753. doi:10.1037//0033-295X.109.4.751

Turner-McGrievy, G., Kalyanaraman, S., & Campbell, M. K. (2013). Delivering health information via podcast or Web: Media effects on psychosocial and physiological responses. *Health Communication*, 28, 101–109. doi:10.1080/10410236.2011.651709

Tylén, K., Wallentin, M., & Roepstorff, A. (2009). Say it with flowers! An fMRI study of object mediated communication. *Brain and Language*, 108, 159–166. doi:10.1016/j.bandl.2008.07.002

Vuilleumier, P., Armony, J. L., Driver, J., & Dolan, R. J. (2001). Effects of attention and emotion on face processing in the human brain: An event-related fMRI study. *Neuron*, 30, 829–841. doi:10.1016/S0896-6273(01)00328-2

Weber, R., Sherry, J., & Mathiak, K. (2009). The neurophysiological perspective in mass communication research: Theoretical rationale, methods, and applications. In M. J. Beatty, J. C. McCroskey, & K. Floyd (Eds.), *Biological dimensions of communication: Perspectives, research, and methods* (pp. 43–74). Cresskill, NJ: Hampton.

Wicker, B., Keysers, C., Plailly, J., Royet, J. P., Gallese, V., & Rizzolatti, G. (2003). Both of us disgusted in my insula: The common neural basis of seeing and feeling disgust. *Neuron*, 40, 655–664. doi:10.1016/S0896-6273(03)00679-2

Wild, B., Erb, M., Eyb, M., Bartels, M., & Grodd, W. (2003). Why are smiles contagious? An fMRI study of the interaction between perception of facial affect and facial movements. *Psychiatry Research: Neuroimaging*, 123, 17–36. doi:10.1016/S0925-4927(03)00006-

Willems, R. M., de Boer, M., de Ruiter, J. P., Noordzij, M. L., Hagoort, P., & Toni, I. (2010). A cerebral dissociation between linguistic and communicative abilities in the human brain. *Psychological Science*, 21, 8–14. doi:10.1177/0956797609355563

Willems, R. M., & Varley, R. (2010). Neural insights into the relation between language and communication. *Frontiers in Human Neuroscience*, 4, 203–210. doi:10.3389/fnhum.2010.00203

PART 2

Specific Observational Research Systems

5

■

CONCEPTUALIZING AND OPERATIONALIZING NONVERBAL IMMEDIACY

LAURA K. GUERRERO

The Construct of Nonverbal Immediacy

Nonverbal immediacy plays a critical role in how people interpret and evaluate behavior. Early work on nonverbal immediacy was conducted primarily in instructional contexts (Andersen, Andersen, & Jensen, 1979), and that work has continued. Indeed, for decades, nonverbal immediacy has been a central concept studied in relation to instructional communication (Witt, Wheeless, & Allen, 2004). In general, teachers whom students rate as nonverbally immediate are perceived as more effective, and their courses are viewed more favorably. But the importance of immediacy extends beyond instructional contexts; immediacy represents a ubiquitous form of communication within all types of relationships (Andersen, 1985). Nonverbal immediacy helps people develop and maintain close relationships because immediacy communicates caring, involvement, and affection, which enhance feelings of intimacy (Andersen, Guerrero, & Jones, 2006; Guerrero & Wiedmaier, 2013). The lack of nonverbal immediacy can cause relationships to stagnate. People also reduce nonverbal immediacy when they want to end a relationship. Instead, they engage in avoidant behavior, which is the opposite of immediacy behavior (Baxter, 1982; Emmers & Hart, 1996).

Several theories also focus on how people respond to changes in a partner's levels of nonverbal immediacy (see Burgoon, Floyd, & Guerrero, 2010, for a review). Reciprocal nonverbal immediacy promotes relational closeness and intimacy. Responding to a partner's nonimmediate or negative behavior with nonverbal immediacy can restore intimacy. On the other hand, one partner's attempts at increasing intimacy by using nonverbal immediacy can be thwarted if the other partner responds in a nonimmediate fashion (Burgoon et al., 2010).

In this chapter, I focus on ways in which scholars have conceptualized and operationalized nonverbal immediacy. Because nonverbal immediacy is such a fundamental form of nonverbal behavior, it is not surprising that it is conceptualized and operationalized multiple ways. In terms of conceptualization, some scholars view nonverbal immediacy as a construct that encompasses both high levels of involvement and positive affect, whereas other scholars define nonverbal immediacy as a dimension that underlies involvement and is separate from positive affect. In terms of operationalization, researchers measure nonverbal immediacy using scales that tap into perceptions about a person's behavior, as well as ratings from observations of actual immediacy behaviors. Moreover, scholars using observational measures have used both micro measures of specific behaviors (e.g., number of touches, degree of facial animation) and macro measures (e.g., overall degree of immediacy). In this chapter, I review all of these operationalizations in order to provide a comprehensive overview of how nonverbal immediacy has been measured. However, given this volume's focus on observational methods, most attention is given to Guerrero's (1996, 1997, 2005) Nonverbal Involvement Coding System (NICS). Before delving in more depth into the different ways scholars operationalize nonverbal immediacy, various conceptualizations of nonverbal immediacy are discussed.

Conceptualizing Nonverbal Immediacy

The term *immediacy* was first coined by Mehrabian (1967), who defined it as behaviors that "enhance closeness to and nonverbal interaction with another" (p. 203). Mehrabian (1971) argued that people approach and "are drawn toward persons and things they like, evaluate highly, and prefer," whereas people tend to avoid and move away from persons and things "they dislike, evaluate negatively, or do not prefer" (p. 1). Immediacy behaviors reflect this approach tendency by communicating directness, intensity, attentiveness, and liking, as well as increasing sensory stimulation (Mehrabian, 1967, 1981). On the basis of this reasoning, Mehrabian (1971) advanced the immediacy principle, which states that immediacy is a manifestation of internal feelings of liking and positive regard. Mehrabian (1971) identified leaning toward someone, sitting or standing close to someone, touching someone, directly facing someone, and looking into someone's eyes as key immediacy behaviors.

Scholars later expanded upon Mehrabian's (1967, 1971) ideas and added more behaviors to the list of those that qualify as immediate. Andersen (1985) noted that there are four defining features of immediacy behaviors: they increase physical and psychological closeness, signal availability for interaction, heighten sensory stimulation, and communicate liking. On the basis of this definition, many additional immediacy behaviors were identified, including smiling, affirmative head nods that signal agreement, a warm vocal tone, open body positions, and expressive gestures and movement (Andersen et al., 1979; Andersen, 1985; Andersen, Gannon, & Kalchik, 2013). People can also communicate nonimmediacy, or a lack of interest in communicating, by engaging in behaviors such as looking away, sitting or standing apart, speaking in a monotone voice, displaying defensive posture or gestures, and showing little expression, just to name a few such behaviors (Andersen et al., 2013). Finally, as a complement to Mehrabian's (1971) original immediacy principle, which posited that immediacy behavior reflects internal feelings of liking, Richmond and McCroskey (2000) advanced the principle of immediate communication. According to this principle, when people use immediate communication they tend to be liked and evaluated favorably, whereas when people use nonimmediate communication they tend to be disliked and evaluated negatively.

Notice that the aforementioned definitions include the communication of positive affect or liking as a defining feature of immediacy. A related construct, *nonverbal involvement*, includes many of the same behaviors but not those associated primarily with positive affect (Patterson, 1982, 1983). Nonverbal involvement reflects the degree of involvement or engagement between individuals during social interaction without regard for the type of involvement (e.g., positive or negative) that is occurring between people. Involvement behaviors include, but are not limited to, gaze, touch, body orientation, leaning toward someone, facial expressiveness, duration of talk, interruptions, animated gestures, postural openness, vocal animation, and head nods. Coker and Burgoon (1987) found that five components compose involvement: greater immediacy, expressiveness, altercentrism (e.g., being focused on the partner), smooth interaction management, and composure. All of these components can be conceptualized as varying on the basis of the relationship or interaction in which people are involved, as well as the interactants' preferences based on personality and culture (Burgoon & Hale, 1988). The behaviors communicating immediacy were direct body and facial orientation, gaze, forward lean, positive reinforcers (e.g., affirmative head nods), and frequent and animated gesturing.

Some scholars equate immediacy with nonverbal involvement, whereas others see immediacy as a dimension underlying involvement. Edinger and Patterson (1983) noted that although many involvement behaviors are also considered immediacy or intimacy behaviors, involvement is a broader construct than either of these. As they put it, involvement differs from immediacy and intimacy because it is "conceptually distinct from higher order functional constructs. That is, variations in nonverbal involvement may reflect one or more functions, depending on the circumstances and relevant motivation" (p. 32). So rather than communicating liking and positive regard, nonverbal involvement may communicate messages related to dominance, persuasion, or a number of other social functions.

Dillard, Solomon, and Palmer (1999) extended this reasoning by arguing that immediacy primarily reflects the intensity of an interaction rather than a specific type of affect. As Dillard et al. put it, "involvement is best conceived of as a content-free intensifier variable" that is "pertinent to judgments of both affiliation and dominance" as well as liking and disliking (p. 54). Factor analyses supported this contention. They analyzed items from Burgoon and Hale's (1987) Relational Communication Scale (RCS). Earlier analyses had suggested that items representing immediacy and affection factored together (e.g., Coker & Burgoon, 1987). However, in Dillard et al.'s (1999) first-order factor analysis, these items separated into two categories representing immediacy (behaviors showing involvement) and positive affect (behaviors showing warmth and attraction). A second-order factor analysis showed that scales measuring similarity, receptivity, equality, composure, and positive affect loaded together to represent affiliation; the scale measuring dominance loaded on the dominance factor as expected; and scales measuring immediacy and general involvement loaded on both the affiliation and dominance factors. This supports the argument that behaviors that show engagement and involvement can communicate either affiliation or dominance, depending on whether they are communicated alongside positive- or negative-affect cues, respectively.

In line with the idea that involvement and affect are separate dimensions, some scholars view the intersection of high involvement and positive-affect cues as constituting intimacy behavior. When Mehrabian (1967, 1981) and Andersen (1985) conceptualized immediacy behavior as characterized by both involvement and positive affect, they were describing this intersection. However, they labeled this intersection *immediacy*, whereas other scholars, such as Prager (1995, 2000), use the term *positive involvement behavior* to describe behaviors that together communicate both involvement and positive affect. As noted above, Dillard et al. (1999) viewed the intersection of involvement and positive affect as affiliation behaviors, with immediacy cues conceptualized as communicating either affiliation or dominance depending on the affect cues that accompany them. More recently, Andersen et al. (2006) noted that high-involvement behavior coupled with positive-affect cues communicate intimacy and affiliation. In contrast, high-involvement behaviors coupled with negative affect communicate dominance and aggression. Low-involvement behaviors coupled with positive affect communicate social politeness. Finally, low-involvement behaviors coupled with negative affect signal avoidance and withdrawal.

What do these different conceptualizations of immediacy and its sister construct, involvement, indicate? First, scholars who define immediacy in traditional terms, such as Mehrabian (1967, 1981) and Andersen (1985), and those who investigate positive involvement (Prager, 1995, 2000), study very similar constructs, except that the latter acknowledge more explicitly that some cues communicating liking primarily reflect involvement, others primarily reflect positive affect, and still others reflect both. Among scholars focusing on nonverbal involvement as opposed to immediacy, consensus exists that involvement is a broader and more general construct than immediacy that underlies both intimacy (or affiliation) and dominance.

In this chapter, immediacy behaviors are conceptualized as positive involvement behaviors that, as a group, communicate interest and liking, decrease physical and psychological distance between people, and increase sensory stimulation. Involvement is viewed as behavior that indicates engagement in an interaction, regardless of degree of liking or type of affect. Thus, interpersonal interaction can be defined in terms of how involved or uninvolved interactants are, as well as how much positive versus negative affect is exhibited. Nonverbal immediacy behavior is characterized by high involvement and positive affect display. However, these two types of behavior do not necessarily go together. Communicators can also display high involvement with negative affect (such as during a heated argument) or positive affect with low involvement (such as when being socially polite). These distinctions have important implications for measuring nonverbal immediacy in that scholars should not assume that involvement or positive affect alone constitute an immediate interaction.

Operationalizing Nonverbal Immediacy

Nonverbal immediacy has generally been measured one of two ways: by using perceptual-recall measures that involve having participants rate a specific person (e.g., a teacher, a friend) in terms of his or her immediacy behavior or by using observation-anchored measures that involve having observers or coders rate the behavior of others during a live or videotaped interaction. Both perceptual-recall and observation-anchored methods can be divided into those that focus on more macro judgments of behavior (e.g., how much immediacy, involvement, or positive affect is generally displayed) or more micro-level assessments (e.g., how much a person displays specific behaviors, such as touch, eye contact, or smiling). The former focuses more on gestalt judgments of what the observed behavior means, whereas the latter focuses more on the specific behaviors that people display. Although this volume focuses on observational measures and methods, in the case of nonverbal immediacy, perceptual-recall measures provided a basis for creating some of the first observation-anchored measures and are therefore reviewed here.

Perceptual Measures Based on Recollection

These types of perceptual measures have at least five advantages. First, such measures are a relatively easy way to obtain data from a large sample. Second, perceptual measures paint an overall picture of a person's immediacy behavior without necessarily focusing on a limited slice of behavior. Third, these measures are flexible in that they allow people to reference any target as well as to refer to behavior in various contexts. For example, participants can be instructed to rate a friend's nonverbal immediacy behavior in a particular type of social setting. Fourth, perceptual measures allow participants to rate people's private as well as public behavior, which would be difficult (if not impossible) for observers to see. A fifth key advantage of perceptual measures is that they give insight into the participant's perspective, which may be just as important as the actual immediacy behaviors themselves. In other words, if a participant believes that his or her spouse or teacher is highly immediate, this belief may be associated with other perceptions, regardless of how much immediacy behavior the person actually uses.

Of course, this advantage is associated with the possible disadvantage that perceptions do not always correspond with "reality." Indeed, this has been a key criticism of the work on teacher immediacy, with some studies showing little correlation between perceptions of a teacher's nonverbal immediacy behavior and his or her observed display of immediacy behavior (Hess, Smythe, & Communication 451, 2001; Smythe & Hess, 2005). What constitutes "reality" is also unclear. Nonverbal behaviors are often processed automatically, especially when they reflect emotional and motivational states, which is often the case for immediacy cues. Indeed, Buck and Powers (2006, 2013) argued that a substantial amount of nonverbal communication is spontaneous and represents a readout of a sender's internal states. They also contend that receivers automatically pick up on the meaning of these spontaneous cues via preattunements. When nonverbal immediacy is displayed spontaneously and decoded automatically, receivers are unlikely to be able to pinpoint which nonverbal cues caused them to perceive that a sender was immediate. Thus, a receiver's general perception of immediacy and the specific immediacy behaviors that people display (or that receivers perceive them to display) may not always correspond to one another. Moreover, some specific nonverbal immediacy behaviors may not be recalled, because they were processed unconsciously. This is why it is critical that researchers use both macro- and micro-level measures of nonverbal immediacy.

Responses may also be influenced by biases, such as having a tendency to see people's behavior in an overly positive or negative light, wanting to provide responses that seem socially acceptable, or having difficulty recalling a person's behavior accurately. People vary in the extent to which they are accurate in decoding nonverbal behavior (Riggio, 2006). If this extends to nonverbal immediacy, coders who are less accurate or possess different levels of decoding ability may find it difficult to achieve interrater reliability. As this discussion suggests, benefits and drawbacks are associated with using perceptual measures to assess nonverbal immediacy. The perceptual measures that have been used most frequently are reviewed next.

The Behavioral Indicators of Immediacy (BII) scale. This scale, developed by Andersen et al. (1979), assesses perceptions of nonverbal immediacy primarily in instructional contexts, although an alternative version of the scale can be used to assess perceptions of nonverbal immediacy in interpersonal contexts. Thus, two versions of the instrument emerged: the BII scale for instructional contexts entails students rating instructors, whereas the BII scale for interpersonal contexts can refer to any target individual (such as a friend, romantic partner, or new acquaintance). In both versions, items in the BII scale require people to compare a particular person's immediacy behavior with how they perceive other people to act. This feature was criticized by Richmond, Gorham, and McCroskey (1987), who noted that such a measure involves making two judgments: one about a particular person and the other about people in general. Making two judgments is a high-inference task that could dilute the validity of the scale because people may be making different comparisons.

The original version of the BII scale for instructional contexts contained 28 items. However, factor analysis indicated that a 15-item BII scale was more reliable (Andersen et al., 1979). This scale was the most frequently used measure in early studies of nonverbal immediacy (Smythe & Hess, 2005). Sample items from the instructional context scale are "This instructor gestures more while teaching than most other instructors," "This instructor engages in less eye contact with me when teaching than most other instructors" (reverse-coded), "This instructor is more vocally expressive while teaching than most other instructors," and "This instructor smiles less during class than most other instructors" (reverse-coded). Andersen and Andersen (2005) reported that reliability coefficients for this scale have ranged from .74 to .80 across various studies. Also, evidence exists of predictive validity, as scores on the BII scale (instructional context) correlate with more positive attitudes toward course content, more positive affect toward course content and instructors, more behavioral motivation and commitment in courses, and a higher likelihood of taking a similar course in the future (Andersen, 1979; Andersen, Norton, & Nussbaum, 1981; Giglio & Lustig, 1987). Scores on the BII scale (instructional context) are also positively correlated with perceptions that a teacher is credible, similar to students, and able to build solidarity with students, among other attributes (e.g., Allen & Shaw, 1990).

The original BII scale for interpersonal contexts included 22 items but was revised to be a 20-item scale on the basis of the results of a factor analysis. Sample items from the interpersonal context scale are "This person engages in more eye contact with me than most other people," "This person touches me less than most other people usually do" (reverse-coded), "This person smiles more than most other people," and "This person directs his/her body position less toward me than most people usually do" (reverse-coded) (see Andersen et al., 1979, or Andersen & Andersen, 2005, for the full versions of these instruments).

The Generalized Immediacy (GI) scale. Rather than focusing on the specific behaviors that constitute nonverbal immediacy, the GI scale, which was presented by Andersen et al. (1979), assesses an individual's gestalt perceptions of nonverbal immediacy. Thus, the BII scale is more of a micro-level scale, whereas the GI scale is a macro-level scale. The GI scale was based on McCroskey and Richmond's (1996) Generalized Belief Scale, which was not published until later. The GI scale's focus on macro (or gestalt) perceptions is important given Andersen's (1985) contention that people usually process nonverbal immediacy cues holistically. In other words, rather than taking in all of the specific individual nonverbal cues a sender displays, a receiver typically gets an overall impression of immediacy by observing a receiver's behavior more generally. This reasoning is consistent with Buck and Powers's (2006, 2013) argument that much nonverbal communication is spontaneous and processed through the right side of the brain through biologically wired preattunements. Thus, receivers may not recall the specific behaviors a sender used even though they perceived that the sender was immediate. The GI scale captures the gestalt nature of immediacy by including nine semantic differential items that reflect general perceptions of a person's level of immediacy. As with the BII scale, Andersen (1979) advanced two forms of the GI scale, one for instructional contexts and one for interpersonal contexts.

Both versions of the scale begin with a detailed description of the nature of immediacy, including a partial list of nonverbal behaviors that contribute to perceptions of immediacy (e.g., close distances, smiling, eye contact, vocal expressiveness). Then seven-point semantic differential scales are presented in two sets. In the first set, respondents are asked, "In your opinion, the teaching style of your instructor is very immediate" and then asked to respond to this statement using five scales: agree to disagree (reverse-coded), false to true, incorrect to correct, wrong to right, and yes to no (reverse-coded). The second set of items asks respondents to use seven-point semantic differential scales to rate how well each of the following words describes their instructor's teaching style: immediate to not immediate (reverse-coded), cold to warm, unfriendly to friendly, and close to distant (reverse-coded). (See Andersen et al., 1979, or Andersen & Andersen, 2005, for a copy of this measure and the related interpersonal context measure, including scoring instructions.)

Andersen and Andersen (2005) reported that interitem reliability coefficients for the nine-item GI scale ranged from .95 to .98 for the instructional version and from .94 to .97 for the interpersonal version. They also noted that some researchers used only the first five items and that this shorter version of the GI scale produced interitem reliability coefficients ranging from .89 to .96. Richmond, McCroskey, and Johnson (2003) noted that many researchers believed this scale to be superior to the BII scale, partially because it was seen as having stronger face validity because of its focus on general perceptions of immediacy.

The Nonverbal Immediacy Scale (NIS). Initial versions of the NIS were developed by Richmond et al. (1987) and McCroskey, Richmond, Sallinen, Fayer, and Barraclough (1995) to examine immediacy in instructional contexts. The NIS was developed in partial response to shortcomings these researchers identified in the BII scale. One of the most substantial shortcomings involved having people compare a specific teacher's level of nonverbal immediacy to their experiences with other teachers. This is problematic because students very likely had different types of teachers in the past. Students who tended to have less immediate teachers would, by comparison, rate their instructors as higher in immediacy than would students who tended to have more immediate teachers in the past. The NIS corrected for this problem by revising items from the BII scale to reflect more general, noncomparative assessments of nonverbal immediacy. The original

NIS contained 14 items, such as the teacher "gestures while talking to the class," "smiles at the class while talking," and "moves around the classroom while teaching."

In past studies, the NIS had produced reliability estimates ranging from .67 to .89. Thus, Richmond et al. (2003) set out to revise the NIS so that it would be more reliable. This was accomplished in part by adding more items to the scale. Moreover, they developed two versions of the Revised Nonverbal Immediacy Measure (RNIM)—a self-report version (the RNIS-S) and an observer version (the RNIS-O). Each scale contains 26 items that are rated on a scale such that 1 = *never*, 2 = *rarely*, 3 = *occasionally*, 4 = *often*, and 5 = *very often*. Sample items from the self-report scale include "I use my hands and arms to gesture while talking to people," "I use a monotone or dull voice while talking to people," "I sit or stand close to people while talking with them," "I have a bland facial expression when I talk to people," "I lean away from people when I talk to them," and "I smile when I talk to people." As these sample items show, half of the items in NIS reflect immediacy behaviors whereas the other half represent nonimmediacy behaviors and are therefore reverse-coded.

The observer version of the NIS-O contains the same items except that they reference a target person (e.g., "He/she leans away from people when he/she talks to them," "He/she smiles when he/she talks to people"). For example, participants might be directed to rate a romantic partner or specific friend's behavior. These versions of the NIS, as well as the previous versions that focused on immediacy in instructional contexts, are now commonly used to measure perceptions of immediacy (see Richmond et al., 2003, for the complete versions of these scales).

Observation-Anchored Ratings

The perceptual measures discussed above all involve having participants rate a person's immediacy behavior on the basis of recollections of how that person behaves. In contrast, other measures of nonverbal immediacy rely on direct observations of a particular segment of behavior. There are several advantages to this method. Ratings are directly connected to actual behavior and are therefore less subject to problems stemming from inaccurate recollection. These data can also be more precise. In some cases, observers view recorded behaviors several times before making ratings. Given that people display multiple nonverbal behaviors at one time, it can be easy to miss some behaviors if they are only viewed once.

Despite these advantages, limits to data that are obtained through coder ratings can occur. For instance, although such ratings are often precise, they may not reflect what participants see during an actual interaction. Conversational participants are interacting in real time and are focused on a number of different tasks, such as attending to various verbal and nonverbal cues simultaneously while thinking about what to say next. Thus, conversational participants and coders can have very different perspectives about what happened during a given interaction. Conversational participants are also likely to process certain nonverbal behaviors automatically, whereas coders who are told to focus on what behaviors people are displaying are likely to be careful and deliberate when decoding. Both perspectives are valuable. Conversational participants have a unique perspective based on their experience in the interaction, but observers may pick up on behaviors that conversational participants miss. The key to remember is that participants and observers are likely to have different, although complementary, perceptions of the behaviors that occurred. Another issue is that coder ratings can be time-consuming, especially when coders are asked to review interactions and rate a number of different behaviors. Next, some common measures that have been used by coders to rate immediacy behavior are reviewed, with the caveat that some of these scales can also be considered perceptual measures depending on how data were collected.

The Rater's Perception of Immediacy (RI) scale. The first measure created for use by coders was a modified version of the BII scale called the RI scale (Andersen et al., 1979). The scale includes 16 items rated on nine-point semantic differential scales. Sample items include distance from students (far to close), smiles (none to very many), body position (tense to relaxed), and eye contact with students (none to always). Andersen et al. (1979) had coders attend a two-hour training session before observing and rating behavior. Specifically, they presented a lecture on immediacy to the coders followed by a question-and-answer session and then practice exercises. Interrater reliability on the RI has ranged from .70 to .97 (Andersen & Andersen, 2005). Coder ratings using the RI scale correlate highly with students' perceptions of teachers' nonverbal immediacy as measured by the BII scale (Andersen et al., 1979). The complete RI scale can be found in Andersen et al. (1979) and Andersen and Andersen (2005).

The Relational Communication Scale. Burgoon and Hale (1987) created a set of scales that measure seven fundamental themes of relational communication (e.g., intimacy, composure, dominance, formality). Intimacy is measured with scales tapping into immediacy/affection, depth, and receptivity/trust. The immediacy/affection scale is akin to the concept of positive involvement, discussed earlier in this chapter, and is composed of 12 items, including "A was intensely involved in the conversation," "A communicated coldness rather than warmth" (reverse-coded), "A showed enthusiasm while talking with B," and "A acted bored by the conversation" (reverse-coded). Ratings are made on Likert-type scales that indicate the extent of agreement or disagreement on a five- or seven-point scale. (For the complete measure, see Burgoon & Hale, 1987, or Burgoon & Newton, 1991.) Notice that this is a macro-level scale that focuses on making overall judgments of the level of immediacy behavior exhibited rather than focusing on specific behaviors, as the RI scale does. It is assumed that these judgments reflect a gestalt impression that is based on the nonverbal behaviors exhibited.

The immediacy/affection subscale of the RCS has been used in a variety of contexts, including computer-mediated communication (e.g., Campbell & Wright, 2002; Van Der Heide, Schumaker, Peterson, & Jones, 2013), family communication (e.g., Afifi, Huber, & Ohs, 2006), and instructional communication (Guerrero & Miller, 1998; Umphrey, Wickersham, & Sherblom, 2008). Across these studies and others (e.g., Burgoon & Hale, 1987; Burgoon & Newton, 1991; Guerrero, 1996; Mikkelson & Hesse, 2009), interrater reliability estimates for this scale have generally been in the low .70s to mid-.80s, although some have been lower. Interitem reliability coefficients have ranged from .74 to .97. This scale has been used most frequently by observers who rate a target's behavior during a live or videotaped interaction, by participants in the conversation who likewise rate their partners' behavior following an interaction (e.g., Burgoon & Newton, 1991), or by respondents who rate a person's general behavior (e.g., Campbell & Wright, 2002; Mikkelson & Hesse, 2009). In the former two cases, observers or conversational participants rate the immediacy level of the entire interaction on the basis of their observations. (When completed by respondents who rate a person's general behavior, this scale constitutes a perceptual-recall measure.) The scale tends to be most reliable when used by observers to rate behavior.

Although many scholars have treated all of the items in the immediacy/affection subscale as a unidimensional scale, some researchers have either split the items or combined them with other items measuring intimacy. In terms of splitting the items, Dillard et al. (1999) demonstrated that the immediacy/affection scale may actually consist of two subscales that coincide with their conceptualization of involvement and positive affect as separate constructs. As noted previously, in Dillard et al.'s (1999) study, immediacy was measured by items that reference being intensely involved in the conversation, showing enthusiasm, and finding the conversation stimulating, whereas affiliation (or positive affect) is measured by items that reference communicating warmth, interest, attraction, a sense of closeness, and a desire to develop a deeper relationship. In terms of combining items, Ramirez (2007; Ramirez, Zhang, McGrew, & Lin, 2007) and his colleagues have used items from the immediacy/affection, similarity/depth, and receptivity/trust subscales of the RCS to measure the broader construct of intimacy.

The Nonverbal Involvement Coding System. Several scholars have developed coding systems to assess micro-level involvement behaviors, including immediacy. These laid the foundation for Guerrero's (1996, 1997, 2005) Nonverbal Involvement Coding System (NICS). Coker and Burgoon (1987) conducted an experiment investigating how participants changed their behavior when asked to increase or decrease their levels of nonverbal involvement during a second interview. The interviews were videotaped, and then trained coders rated 21 kinesic, proxemic, and vocalic behaviors. Several nonverbal behaviors distinguished among levels of involvement, with forward lean, relaxed laughter, coordinated speech, fewer silences and response latencies, facial animation, and vocal warmth showing higher levels of involvement. Burgoon and Newton (1991) extended this work by determining how 51 nonverbal behaviors associate with the relational messages (e.g., intimacy, dominance, composure) in the Relational Communication Scale. Coders rated behaviors from videotapes of interviews in which a participant increased or decreased nonverbal involvement. They found four behaviors related to nonverbal immediacy: orientation/gaze, lean, facial pleasantness, and gestural animation (see also Coker & Burgoon, 1987).

Guerrero (1996) built on Burgoon and Newton's (1991) work to create an initial version of the NICS for coding nonverbal cues related to involvement. The purpose of her study was to determine if there are attachment-style differences in how people display nonverbal intimacy and involvement. Similar to earlier scholars (e.g., Dillard et al.,

1999), Guerrero considered immediacy and positive affect to be separate constructs that, when combined, constitute positive involvement. In her system, immediacy was composed of proxemic distancing, touch, gaze, lean, and body orientation. Positive affect was measured with a series of semantic differential scales that assessed facial pleasantness, vocal pleasantness, smiling, and relaxed laughter (hardly any/a lot). She also measured expressiveness, altercentrism, social anxiety, and smooth interaction management as part of the broader construct of involvement that also includes immediacy. She tested for attachment-style differences by having people who were high in particular styles engage in videotaped conversations with their romantic partners. Among other findings, participants with dismissive and fearful attachment styles, who are theorized to be uncomfortable with intimacy, were rated as displaying relatively low levels of gaze, facial pleasantness, vocal pleasantness, and nonverbal attentiveness. Those with fearful attachment styles also sat farthest from their partners, were the least fluent, and exhibited the longest response latencies.

Guerrero (1997) used similar scales to examine whether people's nonverbal involvement behavior changes depending on the person with whom they are interacting: a same-sex friend, cross-sex friend, or romantic partner. Participants engaged in three interactions, one with each type of partner. These interactions were videotaped and coded. People were rated as using closer distancing, more touch, more gaze, longer response latencies, and more silence as well as displaying less fluency when talking with their romantic partners. When interacting with friends, people were rated as nodding more frequently and sounding more interested vocally. Finally, same-sex friends displayed the most postural congruence. One important finding from this study was that cues related to nonverbal involvement functioned different ways to distinguish romantic partners from friends. Rather than being consistently higher across all involvement dimensions, romantic partners were higher in some immediacy cues (distancing, touch, gaze) but also showed some cues that may indicate arousal, anxiety, or perhaps thoughtfulness (longer response latencies, silence, and less fluency). This suggests that it is important to measure the various dimensions underlying involvement, including immediacy, separately.

The most updated version of the NICS (Guerrero, 2005) includes measures related to all five involvement dimensions plus affect (see Appendix 5.A). As such, the NICS can be used to measure immediacy and affect, which is consistent with the concept of positive involvement. The NICS can also be used to measure involvement in terms of immediacy, expressiveness, altercentrism, smooth interaction, and composure. The NICS can be used in its entirety, or scholars can choose which subscales are relevant to their research. The measures in the NICS are intended to be used by coders to rate behaviors that have been videotaped. Studies using measures from this system have generally produced interrater reliability estimates in the .80s (e.g., Dillow, Afifi, & Matsunaga, 2012; see Guerrero, 2005, for a summary of reliabilities found in earlier studies). Next, the specific behaviors measured under each of these dimensions—immediacy, expressiveness, altercentrism, smooth interaction management, composure, and affect—are outlined.

Immediacy includes touch, distancing, lean, body orientation, and gaze. Touch is measured by tallying the number of discrete touches, as well as using a stopwatch to calculate the percentage of time a person is touching his or her partner (time touching divided by total interaction time). Before analyzing these data, they should be converted using the square root transformation (for number of touches) and the arcsine transformation (for percentage of time touching), because these data are typically skewed. Proxemic distancing is also measured with two items. One item assesses how far apart the communicators' faces are, and the other assesses how far apart their bodies are. Forward lean is measured by the degree to which a person is leaning forward versus backward (or upright depending on context) and toward or away from the partner. Body orientation is measured in terms of whether a person is facing toward or away from the partner, as well as if he or she is in a face-to-face versus side-by-side position in relation to the partner. Gaze is measured by three items: (a) the extent to which the target participant looks at the other person, with "never" operationalized as zero gaze and "always" conceptualized as constant gaze; (b) how steady versus unsteady the gaze is in terms of whether participants tend to gaze at the partner's face for relatively long segments of time in contrast to looking away frequently; and (c) the level of mutual eye contact in terms of how much they looked into each other's eyes at the same time.

Expressiveness is composed of kinesic and vocalic animation. Kinesic animation includes the amount of facial expressiveness in terms of emotion and interest being displayed; the amount of gesturing, with an emphasis on illustrators, emblems, and expansive gestures; and the overall level of expressive kinesic movement (which can include whole-body movements, such as jumping up in one's seat, gestures, and facial expressions of emotion, but not random or nervous body movement). Vocal animation is also measured with three items: (a) vocal variety in tempo, volume, and pitch, with a monotone voice operationalized as 1 on a scale ranging from 1 to 7; (b) the extent to which the voice is expressive versus inexpressive in terms of conveying moods and emotions; and (c) the degree to which the voice sounds "dull" versus "full of life."

Altercentrism is assessed using both macro- and micro-level measures. At the macro level, general attentiveness and interest is measured with a series of semantic-differential scales that coders use to rate how generally inattentive/attentive, distracted/focused, not alert/alert, bored/interested, and detached/involved a person seems. At the micro-level, coders count the number of times a person nods in a manner that shows agreement, indicates understanding, or suggests that a person is listening. Nods are tallied and then transformed using the square root transformation, because such counts are frequently skewed.

Smooth interaction management is measured by rating fluency, response latencies, and interactional fluency. Fluency is measured by the extent to which a person's speech is free of nonfluencies such as vocalized pauses and within–speaking turn silences, as well as how smooth versus choppy a person's speech sounds, with awkward pauses, hesitancies, slurred speech, stammering, and unclear or nervous vocalizations contributing to choppiness (Guerrero, 2005). Response latencies are measured using a one-item scale that represents how long versus short a participant's response latencies are, with response latencies defined as the amount of time between speaking turns when one person stops speaking and the other starts. Finally, interactional fluency focuses on how "in sync" two individuals are in terms of coordinated turn taking, lack of long or awkward silences, and lack of interruptions and talk-overs.

Composure is operationalized in terms of vocal relaxation, bodily relaxation, and a lack of random movement. Vocal relaxation is determined by how tense/relaxed and anxious/calm a voice sounds. Tense voices are described as sounding tight and somewhat high pitched rather than light. Anxious voices are described as sounding shaking or nervous rather than smooth and confident. Body relaxation is gauged on the basis of how tense/relaxed, closed/open, and rigid/loose the body appears. Tense body positions are exemplified by a stiff, erect positon and tight or clenched limbs. Closed body positions involve taking a defensive stance with arms and legs crossed and the body closed off to take up little space. Rigid body positions are evident when there is a lack of expressive movement that makes a person look stiff rather than relaxed. Finally, lack of random movement is assessed in three ways. First, coders look at the extent to which a person displays random or nervous-looking self- and object adaptors, such as wringing one's hands together or twisting a strand of hair. Second, coders watch for rocking or twisting behaviors, such as swiveling in a chair, rocking back and forth, and shaking one's foot. Finally, coders determine the overall level of random trunk and limb movement, which includes all of the above behaviors as well as other forms of fidgeting.

The last dimension in the NICS is affect. This dimension measures the degree to which people show positive affect by engaging in behaviors that reflect warmth and affiliation rather than behaviors that reflect negative affect and coldness. Three specific behaviors are coded: smiling, general facial pleasantness, and vocal pleasantness. Smiling includes assessments of whether a person was always versus never smiling during an interaction (on the basis of the overall percentage of the time smiling, with 100% equaling always and 0% equaling never), as well as whether he or she smiled a lot versus a little (on the basis of how many times a person seemed to smile in a way that reflects warmth, friendliness, or positive affect). Overall facial pleasantness is assessed by looking at the entire face rather than just the smile. Coders rate the degree to which the face is pleasant versus unpleasant (on the basis of the level of warmth and relaxation displayed by the face) as well as how much the face communicates positive versus negative affect (on the basis of the types of emotions displayed by the face). Vocal pleasantness is rated with three semantic differential items that measure how cold/warm, unpleasant/pleasant, and unfriendly/friendly a voice sounds. Warm voices are described as having a tone that sounds soft and warm, as if someone talking about something highly personal. Pleasant voices are described as clear, expressive, and happy sounding. Friendly voices convey likability and interest.

Recommendations for Using the NICS

Success in using any of the observation-anchored methods is contingent upon providing sufficient coder training. This is especially true when coders are observing and rating behavior from videotaped interactions. Of the various measures reviewed above, the NICS is the most comprehensive and complicated. Therefore, in this section I focus on recommendations for training coders to use this measurement system properly.

It is critical that coders be given exemplars of what constitutes behavior at the high and low ends of each scale within the type of context in which the interaction occurs. For example, in Guerrero's (1996, 1997) study, participants were seated on a couch so that sitting at opposite ends of the couch constituted a far distance and sitting so that bodies were touching constituted a close distance. If participants were seated on chairs or around a table, then different directions should be given on the basis of contextual constraints. Defining the midpoint of the scale is also important. As a case in point, for the items measuring how pleasant (vs. unpleasant) and warm (vs. cold) voices are, the midpoint represents voices that are neutral on the given characteristic (e.g., neither pleasant nor unpleasant).

Initial training is conducted with a pair of coders together so they receive exactly the same instructions. Each pair is assigned to rate a specific group of behaviors. They are then asked to make independent ratings of sample recordings on their own time. These ratings are then compared in a follow-up session so that any major discrepancies can be detected. The investigator will discuss discrepancies and determine why the coders are inconsistent. Often this involves reviewing the tapes together and resetting how both coders see the high, low, and midpoints of a scale. A new sample of interactions (separate from those to be analyzed for the study) is then rated by the two coders to determine if consistency improves. This process is repeated until the experimenter is confident that the two raters are judging behavior similarly on the basis of the criteria given them. It is important to have two people independently code the behaviors so that interrater reliability can be assessed.

Depending on how long the interaction is, investigators might want to break up the coding into smaller time segments. For example, a 10-minute interaction might be broken down into five 2-minute interaction units, with coders making ratings at the end of each 2-minute segment (see Guerrero, 2005, for an example of a coding sheet that includes time intervals). This keeps coders focused, increases accuracy, and can also uncover temporal patterns in the data, such as a general tendency for people to become more relaxed and immediate as an interaction progresses. Coder ratings can be averaged across the various time units, or time can be included as a variable in the study with both average ratings

of specific behaviors and time (as a repeated factor) considered in the analysis.

In addition to unitizing longer interactions by time, the researcher should limit the number of behaviors that coders rate in a pass to two or three specific related behaviors. For example, one pair of coders might judge vocal behaviors, another might code behaviors that can be viewed by looking at the face, and another might code body movements or make general judgments. Appendix 5.A shows how the various behaviors have been grouped together in separate coding sheets for raters. The behaviors shown in each block in Appendix 5.A are coded by the same two coders.

To increase accuracy, coders should be instructed to stop and review the recording whenever they are unsure of their ratings. Nonverbal communication is multimodal, which means that people display a variety of nonverbal cues simultaneously. This makes it difficult to key in on a single behavior. Being able to pause a recording and rewatch sections of an interaction can therefore increase accuracy in terms of what a coder saw. However, researchers should keep in mind that this procedure is different than what occurs in real-life interaction when conversational partners are interacting in real time and cannot replay a video to better interpret their partner's behavior. As discussed previously, there are advantages and disadvantages to measuring nonverbal immediacy using participant versus observer ratings.

For the reasons mentioned previously, it is also advisable to collect data from participants if possible. These can be global measures that simply focus on the overall level of immediacy and positive affect (or affiliation) that participants believe their partner communicated. The Relational Communication Scale (RCS) could be used for these ratings, and participant perceptions on the RCS could be correlated with the various coder ratings to see which specific behaviors (as coded by observers) associate with participant perceptions of immediacy and affiliation. Another recommendation is for coders to also rate immediacy and affiliation in general terms (i.e., again possibly using the RCS) to see how coder ratings of specific behaviors relate to more global measures of immediacy and positive affect. Using these more general macro measures of immediacy and positive affect in conjunction with more micro measures is especially important given that Andersen's (1985, 1999) arguments that nonverbal immediacy behaviors are often processed as a gestalt, with people getting an overall impression of how immediate an interaction is without recalling many of the specific behaviors they unconsciously processed to reach that judgment.

Another important consideration is how the interactions themselves are recorded. Having a system that allows one to put a subject or dyad number in the corner of the interaction is helpful, as is a clock in another corner with a timer running. If coders make their ratings across different time segments, having such a timer on the screen increases accuracy across coders compared with the alternative of having coders use their own stopwatches. Coders should also be instructed to view the interactions on similar devices, such as computer screens that are a standard 15 or 17 inches. It is also preferable to have multiple cameras recording the interaction, with one camera capturing the participants' bodies in a wider screen shot and two other cameras focused separately on each of the individuals' faces (if recording a dyad). Different versions of the interaction are then used for coding various types of nonverbal behaviors. Behaviors such as smiling and eye contact are coded from the face shots, whereas most of the other behaviors are coded from the wide shot.

Finally, it can be helpful to separate visual and vocal behaviors when coding certain involvement cues. For example, when coding vocalics, raters should listen to the voice they are evaluating instead of looking at the screen. Guerrero (1996, 1997) had coders cover the screen with paper before rating vocalics. Similarly, when judging behaviors related to kinesic expressiveness and composure, the volume can be muted. This way, vocalic behaviors do not influence how kinesic behaviors are coded, and vice versa.

Conclusion

Nonverbal immediacy constitutes a central concept in the communication field, as well as in related fields. Given its prominence, it is not surprising that different scholars have variously conceptualized and operationalized nonverbal immediacy. Some scholars view nonverbal immediacy and positive involvement as similar constructs; others see immediacy as a subset of more general involvement behaviors, with immediacy and affect (positive vs. negative) as distinct dimensions underlying involvement. Regardless of the perspective taken, a general consensus exists that behaviors that reflect high levels of involvement and positive affect convey affection and intimacy. Nonverbal immediacy has been measured various ways using perceptual-recall measures and observation-anchored ratings. Some scholars take a macro approach by assessing general perceptions of immediacy or positive involvement. Such approaches are consistent with

Andersen's (1985) contention that immediacy is processed holistically. Others have examined micro behaviors, such as gaze, direct body orientation, close distancing, and smiling, which compose immediacy. A comprehensive approach to measuring immediacy would include both macro and micro ratings. It is important to understand the specific behaviors that people associate with immediacy and involvement but also to realize that gestalt impressions may be what is the most relationally important. Scholars likely will continue to refine how nonverbal immediacy is conceptualized and measured, given the important place that this construct holds in so many different areas of communication research.

References

Afifi, T. D., Huber, F. N., & Ohs, J. (2006). Parents' and adolescents' communication with each other about divorce-related stressors and its impact on their ability to cope positively with the divorce. *Journal of Divorce & Remarriage, 45*, 1–30.

Allen, J. L., & Shaw, D. H. (1990). Teachers' communication behaviors and supervisors' evaluation of instruction in elementary and secondary classrooms. *Communication Education, 39*, 308–322.

Andersen, J. F. (1979). *The relationship between teacher immediacy and teaching effectiveness* (Doctoral dissertation, ProQuest Information & Learning).

Andersen J. F., & Anderson, P. A. (1985). Measurements of perceived nonverbal immediacy. In V. Manusov (Ed.), *Sourcebook of nonverbal measures: Going beyond words*. Mahwah, NJ: Lawrence Erlbaum.

Andersen, J. F., Andersen, P. A., & Jensen, A. D. (1979). The measurement of nonverbal immediacy. *Journal of Applied Communication Research, 7*, 153–180.

Andersen, J. F., Norton, R. W., & Nussbaum, J. F. (1981). Three investigations exploring relationships between perceived teacher communication behaviors and student learning. *Communication Education, 30*, 377–392.

Andersen, P. A. (1999). *Nonverbal communication: Forms and functions*. Mountain View, CA: Academic Press.

Andersen, P. A. (1985). Nonverbal immediacy in interpersonal communication. In A. W. Siegman & S. Feldstein (Eds.), *Multichannel integrations of nonverbal behavior* (pp. 1–36). Hillsdale, NJ: Lawrence Erlbaum.

Andersen, P. A., Gannon, J., & Kalchik, J. (2013). Proxemic and haptic interaction: The closeness continuum. In P. J. Schultz & P. Cobley (Series Eds.) & J. A. Hall & M. Knapp (Vol. Eds.), *Handbooks of communication science, Vol. 2: Nonverbal communication* (pp. 295–329). Berlin, Germany: Walter de Gruyter.

Andersen, P. A., Guerrero, L. K., & Jones, S. M. (2006). Nonverbal behavior in intimate interaction and intimate relationships. In V. Manusov & M. L. Patterson

(Eds.), *Handbook of nonverbal communication* (pp. 259–277). Thousand Oaks, CA: Sage.

Baxter, L. A. (1982). Strategies for ending relationships: Two studies. *Western Journal of Speech Communication, 46*, 223–241.

Buck, R. W., & Powers, S. R. (2006). The biological foundations of social organization: The dynamic emergence of social structure through nonverbal communication. In V. Manusov & M. L. Knapp (Eds.), *The SAGE handbook of nonverbal communication* (pp. 119–138). Thousand Oaks, CA: Sage.

Buck, R. W., & Powers, S. R. (2013). Encoding and display: A developmental-interactionist model of nonverbal sending accuracy. In P. J. Schultz & P. Cobley (Series Eds.) & J. A. Hall & M. L. Knapp (Vol. Eds.), *Handbooks of communication science, Vol. 2: Nonverbal communication* (pp. 403–440). Berlin, Germany: Walter de Gruyter.

Burgoon, J. K., Floyd, K., & Guerrero, L. K. (2010). Nonverbal communication theories of adaptation. In C. Berger, M. E. Roloff, & D. Roskos-Ewoldsen (Eds.), *The new SAGE handbook of communication science* (pp. 93–110). Thousand Oaks, CA: Sage.

Burgoon, J. K., & Hale, J. L. (1987). Validation and measurement of the fundamental themes of relational communication. *Communications Monographs, 54*, 19–41.

Burgoon, J. K., & Hale, J. L. (1988). Nonverbal expectancy violations: Model elaboration and application to immediacy behaviors. *Communication Monographs, 54*, 19–41.

Burgoon, J. K., & Newton, D. A. (1991). Applying a social meaning model to relational message interpretations of conversational involvement: Comparing observer and participant perspectives. *Southern Journal of Communication, 56*, 96–113.

Campbell, K., & Wright, K. B. (2002). On-line support groups: An investigation of relationships among source credibility, dimensions of relational communication, and perceptions of emotional support. *Communication Research Reports, 19*, 183–193.

Coker, D. A., & Burgoon, J. K. (1987). The nature of conversational involvement and nonverbal encoding patterns. *Human Communication Research, 13*, 463–494.

Dillard, J. P., Solomon, D. H., & Palmer, M. T. (1999). Structuring the concept of relational communication. *Communications Monographs, 66*, 49–65.

Dillow, M. R., Afifi, W. A., & Matsunaga, M. (2012). Perceived partner uniqueness and communicative and behavioral transgression outcomes in romantic relationships. *Journal of Social and Personal Relationships, 29*, 28–51.

Edinger, J. A., & Patterson, M. L. (1983). Nonverbal involvement and social control. *Psychological Bulletin, 93*, 30–56.

Emmers, T. M., & Hart, R. D. (1996). Romantic relationship disengagement and coping rituals. *Communication Research Reports, 13*, 8–18.

Giglio, K., & Lustig, M. W. (1987, February). *Teacher immediacy and student expectations as predictors of learning.* Paper presented at the annual meeting of the Western Speech Communication Association, Salt Lake City, UT.

Guerrero, L. K. (1996). Attachment-style differences in intimacy and involvement: A test of the four-category model. *Communications Monographs, 63*, 269–292.

Guerrero, L. K. (1997). Nonverbal involvement across interactions with same-sex friends, opposite-sex friends and romantic partners: Consistency or change? *Journal of Social and Personal Relationships, 14*, 31–58.

Guerrero, L. K. (2005). Observer ratings of nonverbal involvement and immediacy. In V. Manusov (Ed.), *The sourcebook of nonverbal measures: Going beyond words* (pp. 221–235). Mahwah, NJ: Lawrence Erlbaum.

Guerrero, L. K., & Miller, T. A. (1998). Associations between nonverbal behaviors and initial impressions of instructor competence and course content in videotaped distance education courses. *Communication Education, 47*, 30–42.

Guerrero, L. K., & Wiedmaier, B. (2013). Nonverbal intimacy: Affection, positive involvement, and courtship. In P. J. Schultz & P. Cobley (Series Eds.) & J. A. Hall & M. L. Knapp (Vol. Eds.), *Handbooks of communication science, Vol. 2: Nonverbal communication* (pp. 577–612). Berlin, Germany: Walter de Gruyter.

Hess, J. A., Smythe, M. J., & Communication 451. (2001). Is teacher immediacy actually related to student cognitive learning? *Communication Studies, 52*, 197–219.

McCroskey, J. C., & Richmond, V. P. (1996). *Fundamentals of human communication: An interpersonal perspective.* Prospect Heights, IL: Waveland.

McCroskey, J. C., Richmond, V. P., Sallinen, A., Faver, J. M., & Barraclough, R. A. (1995). A cross-cultural and multi-behavioral analysis of the relationship between nonverbal immediacy and teacher evaluation. *Communication Education, 44*, 281–291.

McCroskey, J. C., Sallinen, A., Fayer, J. M., Richmond, V. P., & Barraclough, R. A. (1996). Nonverbal immediacy and cognitive learning: A cross-cultural investigation. *Communication Education, 45*, 200–211.

Mehrabian, A. (1967). Orientation behaviors and nonverbal attitude communication. *Journal of Communication, 16*, 324–332.

Mehrabian, A. (1971). *Silent messages.* Belmont, CA: Wadsworth.

Mehrabian, A. (1981). *Silent messages: Implicit communication of emotions and attitudes* (2nd ed.). Belmont, CA: Wadsworth.

Mikkelson, A. C., & Hesse, C. (2009). Discussions of religion and relational messages: Differences between comfortable and uncomfortable interactions. *Southern Communication Journal, 74*, 40–56.

Patterson, M. L. (1982). A sequential functional model of nonverbal exchange. *Psychological Review, 89*, 231–249.

Patterson, M. L. (1983). *Nonverbal behavior: A functional perspective.* New York: Springer-Verlag.

Prager, K. J. (1995). *The psychology of intimacy*. New York: Guilford.

Prager, K. J. (2000). Intimacy in personal relationships. In C. Hendrick & S. S. Hendrick (Eds.), *Close relationships: A sourcebook* (pp. 229–242). Thousand Oaks, CA: Sage.

Ramirez, A., Jr. (2007). The effect of anticipated future interaction and initial impression valence on relational communication in computer-mediated interaction. *Communication Studies, 58*, 53–70.

Ramirez, A., Jr., Zhang, S., McGrew, C., & Lin, S. F. (2007). Relational communication in computer-mediated interaction revisited: A comparison of participant–observer perspectives. *Communication Monographs, 74*, 492–516.

Richmond, V. P., Gorham, J. S., & McCroskey, J. C. (1987). The relationship between selected immediacy behaviors and cognitive learning. In M. A. McLaughlin (Ed.), *Communication Yearbook 10* (pp. 574–590). Newbury Park, CA: Sage.

Richmond, V. P., & McCroskey, J. C. (2000). The impact of supervisor and subordinate immediacy on relational and organizational outcomes. *Communications Monographs, 67*, 85–95.

Richmond, V. P., McCroskey, J. C., & Johnson, A. D. (2003). Development of the Nonverbal Immediacy Scale (NIS): Measures of self- and other-perceived nonverbal immediacy. *Communication Quarterly, 51*, 504–517.

Riggio, R. E. (2006). Nonverbal skills and abilities. In V. Manusov & M. L. Patterson (Eds.), *The SAGE handbook of nonverbal communication* (pp. 79–95). Thousand Oaks, CA: Sage.

Smythe, M., & Hess, J. A. (2005). Are student self-reports a valid method for measuring teacher nonverbal immediacy? *Communication Education, 54*, 170–179.

Umphrey, L. R., Wickersham, J. A., & Sherblom, J. C. (2008). Student perceptions of the instructor's relational characteristics, the classroom communication experience, and the interaction involvement in face-to-face versus video conference instruction. *Communication Research Reports, 25*, 102–114.

Van Der Heide, B., Schumaker, E. M., Peterson, A. M., & Jones, E. B. (2013). The proteus effect in dyadic communication: Examining the effect of avatar appearance in computer-mediated dyadic interaction. *Communication Research, 40*, 838–860.

Witt, P. L., Wheeless, L. R., & Allen, M. (2004). A meta-analytical review of the relationship between teacher immediacy and student learning. *Communication Monographs, 71*, 184–207.

Appendix 5.A

The Nonverbal Immediacy Coding System

Based on your observation of the target's face, the target:

never looked at the partner	1	2	3	4	5	6	7	always looked at the partner
never smiled	1	2	3	4	5	6	7	always smiled
exhibited unsteady gaze	1	2	3	4	5	6	7	exhibited steady gaze
smiled a little	1	2	3	4	5	6	7	smiled a lot
gave no eye contact	1	2	3	4	5	6	7	gave constant eye contact
was facially unpleasant	1	2	3	4	5	6	7	was facially pleasant
conveyed negative affect	1	2	3	4	5	6	7	conveyed positive affect

Based on your observation of the target's body positioning, the target:

leaned away from the partner	1	2	3	4	5	6	7	leaned toward the partner
faced away from the partner	1	2	3	4	5	6	7	faced toward the partner
sat in a side-by-side position	1	2	3	4	5	6	7	sat in a face-to-face position
leaned back a lot	1	2	3	4	5	6	7	leaned forward a lot

(Continued)

(Continued)

The distance between the bodies was:	far		1	2	3	4	5	6	7	close
The distance between the faces was:	far		1	2	3	4	5	6	7	close

Touch and Nods

Record the # of times (using tally marks) the target nodded her/his head in an affirming manner:
_____

Record the # of times (using tally marks) that touch occurred: _____

What was the total time that the dyad spent touching? (in minutes/seconds): _____

The target's voice:

was monotone	1	2	3	4	5	6	7	contained vocal variety
sounded tense	1	2	3	4	5	6	7	sounded relaxed
sounded cold	1	2	3	4	5	6	7	sounded warm
sounded anxious	1	2	3	4	5	6	7	sounded calm
was inexpressive	1	2	3	4	5	6	7	was animated
sounded unpleasant	1	2	3	4	5	6	7	sounded pleasant
was unfriendly	1	2	3	4	5	6	7	was friendly
was dull	1	2	3	4	5	6	7	was full of life

The target showed:

very little facial expression	1	2	3	4	5	6	7	a lot of facial expression
lots of nervous movement	1	2	3	4	5	6	7	very little nervous movement
frequent rocking or twisting	1	2	3	4	5	6	7	infrequent rocking or twisting
hardly any gesturing	1	2	3	4	5	6	7	a lot of gesturing
hardly any kinesic expression	1	2	3	4	5	6	7	a lot of kinesic expression
a lot of trunk/limb movement	1	2	3	4	5	6	7	very little trunk/limb movement

Based on her/his nonverbal behavior, the target seemed:

anxious	1	2	3	4	5	6	7	calm
inattentive	1	2	3	4	5	6	7	attentive
distracted	1	2	3	4	5	6	7	focused
not alert	1	2	3	4	5	6	7	alert
restless	1	2	3	4	5	6	7	still
flustered	1	2	3	4	5	6	7	composed

bored	1	2	3	4	5	6	7	interested
detached	1	2	3	4	5	6	7	involved

The target's speech was:

filled with nonfluencies	1	2	3	4	5	6	7	very fluent
very choppy	1	2	3	4	5	6	7	very smooth
marked by long response latencies	1	2	3	4	5	6	7	marked by short response latencies

The conversation was characterized by:

a lot of interruptions	1	2	3	4	5	6	7	no interruptions
a lot of awkward silences	1	2	3	4	5	6	7	very few awkward silences
uncoordinated turn-taking	1	2	3	4	5	6	7	coordinated turn-taking

Overall, the target's body position was:

tense	1	2	3	4	5	6	7	relaxed
closed	1	2	3	4	5	6	7	open
rigid	1	2	3	4	5	6	7	loose

6

■

THE RELATIONAL LINKING SYSTEM AND OTHER SYSTEMS FOR STUDYING SELF-PRESENTATION (SELF-DISCLOSURE), ACCEPTANCE-REJECTION, AND CONFIRMATION-DISCONFIRMATION

C. ARTHUR VANLEAR AND LESLEY A. WITHERS

D ance and Larson (1976) pointed out that one of the primary functions of communication is to link people to other people and to their environment. In elaborating "the linking function," they identified two dimensions that are central to the process of people linking together: self-disclosure (self-presentation) and acceptance-rejection (confirmation-disconfirmation) of the other. We propose the following assumptions:

1. *Whenever we communicate, we present self (consciously or unconsciously).* When this self-presentation is explicit, it is called "self-disclosure." Yet whatever we choose to say or do differs from what others may have said or done. Therefore in some way, our communication is always a unique self-presentation, even when it is not strategic or explicit.

2. *Whenever we communicate, we communicate about our relationship* (Watzlawick, Beavin, & Jackson, 1967). In addition to semantic "content," our communication behavior carries a relational level message that indicates how one could interpret the content of the message and that implies a definition of the relationship between communicators.

3. Given the first two assumptions, we hold that when people respond to our communication (self-presentation), their responses can be viewed as confirmation, disconfirmation, acceptance, or rejection of the self as presented. Even when the other person chooses merely to respond directly and relevantly to our contribution in accordance with the implicit rules of conversation (Grice, 1975), that response is a "minimal confirmation" of our existence and presentation of self (Knapp, 1978, 1984; VanLear, 1985).

In this chapter, we review behavioral category systems designed to assess self-presentation or self-disclosure and systems designed to help observe acceptance-rejection or confirmation-disconfirmation of the other person. This discussion is grounded primarily in symbolic interactionism and relational pragmatics (Fisher, 1978; Watzlawick et al., 1967), in addition to Dance and Larsen's (1976) conception of the linking function of human communication. However, a number of theoretical insights from other theoretical perspectives are also included (e.g., Dorian & Cordova, 2004).

We define "self-presentation" as all of the ways in which information about a person's self—his or her identity or self-concept—are revealed through communication behavior. Although there is a rich literature on self-presentation from the dramaturgical perspective (Goffman, 1959) and self-presentation strategies, we focus primarily on the "depth" (Altman & Taylor, 1973) dimension as an expansion of that construct from the self-disclosure literature. Whereas self-concept is a symbolically constructed image of self, aspects of self (traits, motivations, etc.) may not be fully or consciously known to the individual; these are communicated through "habitual responses," "nonverbal leakage," and "spontaneous behaviors" (Buck & VanLear, 2002). Other chapters in this volume focus on "spontaneous" modes of communication (e.g., Hamm, Kohler, Gur, & Verma, this volume). This chapter focuses primarily on category systems that assess the "symbolic" presentation of self, though some systems take "spontaneous" behaviors (biologically wired direct expression of emotions/motivations) into account.

Symbolic messages can take two forms: conventional and analogic. Although the same parts of the brain process both of these types of messages (Buck & VanLear, 2002), the connection between the symbol and the referent is different. For *conventional symbolic communication,* the connection between the symbol and the referent is purely arbitrary and dependent upon the conventions of the language or speech community. However, for *analogic symbolic communication,* the behavior or message is itself a natural analogue or example of the concept being communicated. For example, one can communicate trust by behaving in a trusting manner (e.g., by being vulnerable). In this way, we propose that self-disclosure, especially private-personal disclosure, provides an analogic message of trust that can leave the discloser vulnerable to rejection at a very personal level (Dorian & Cordova, 2004). This is a somewhat different use of the term analogic communication than used by Burgoon et al. (this volume).

First, we distinguish between self-presentation and what we refer to as "other-orientation." Although one of the issues in the literature concerns whether self-disclosure is accepting (and it appears that at least private and personal disclosures are), the Relational Linking System (RLS) treats self-presentation as a separate dimension from "other-orientation." The reason for this two-dimensional approach is that we want to be able to differentiate between the ways in which people present themselves and the ways in which they respond to the self-presentations of others with confirmation, disconfirmation, acceptance, or rejection.

Furthermore, we distinguish between two related concepts involved in other-orientation: *acceptance-rejection* and *confirmation-disconfirmation*. We believe that the need for acceptance by others is fundamental to human beings as social animals (Dance & Larson, 2006; Maslow, 1943). Likewise, interpersonal rejection is typically an intensely painful experience. Acceptance implies a positive evaluation of the other individual's self-presentation, whereas rejection implies a negative evaluation of the self-presentation of the other person. On the other hand, confirmation implies only that the respondent acknowledges the other individual and the validity of his or her self-presentation, whereas disconfirmation implies the relational message "you do not exist" or "you are not who you say you are" (Buber, 1957; Watzlawick et al., 1967). For example, ignoring the other person's comment (when one is expected to respond directly and relevantly; Grice, 1975) or interrupting the other can convey the analogic message "you do not exist" or "you do not matter." Therefore, one can confirm the other by accepting his or her self-presentation as valid but reject the person by indicating a negative evaluation or disdain for that person as presented. Theoretically, rejection and disconfirmation probably have different implications, as they feed back to influence the identity of the discloser or the building of the relational linkage between participants.

Figure 6.1 presents a visual model of the role of these two dimensions (self-presentation and other-orientation) in the evolution of identity. It also presents a view of how, over time, a person's identity can, in part, become formed within and dependent upon a relationship. The model also could be viewed as a visualization of how "working models of self" and "working models of other" evolve in attachment relationships (Bowlby, 1969/1982). The first construct in the model (identity) is an unseen symbolic construction. However, the second two—self-presentation and the reaction to that presentation—manifest visibly in behavior. Not every sender will view a given presentation or disclosure in exactly the same way, nor will every receiver view the same behaviors as equivalent in terms of acceptance and rejection. However, all self-presentation and acceptance or rejection, if it is communicated, must be communicated through behavior. Behavioral category systems identify prototypical ways in which these functions are communicated.

Why Behavioral Measures

It could be argued that *perceptions* of intimacy, vulnerability, and openness are important to both identity and relationship development. It could also be argued that it is the *perception* of acceptance, rejection, confirmation, or disconfirmation that is important in these processes. One might also be able to show that self-reports of perceived intimacy, openness, acceptance, and rejection are more strongly correlated with reported feelings or relational outcomes. The old adage "meanings are in people, not in words" (Richards, 1936) could certainly be

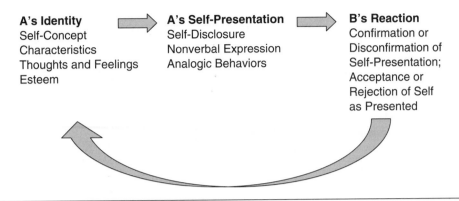

A's Identity
Self-Concept
Characteristics
Thoughts and Feelings
Esteem

A's Self-Presentation
Self-Disclosure
Nonverbal Expression
Analogic Behaviors

B's Reaction
Confirmation or
Disconfirmation of
Self-Presentation;
Acceptance or
Rejection of Self
as Presented

Figure 6.1 Identity development through self-presentation and interpersonal confirmation.

Source: Author.

extended to "meanings are in people, not in behaviors." So why focus on behavioral measures of self-presentation and interpersonal confirmation? First, as indicated above, self can be presented only through behavior, and one can confirm, disconfirm, accept, or reject someone only through communication behaviors. Second, it is of little use to point out, for example, that relationships grow through gradual reciprocal increases in the "depth of disclosure" or degree of "openness" without providing a concrete referent for depth of disclosure or openness. It is of little use to tell people that they need to make people feel accepted and avoid making them feel rejected without offering a guide for the behaviors in which they should engage and those behavioral responses they should avoid. Finally, in any communication encounter, the one thing both senders and receivers share concerns the communication behavior in context. In fact, if it were true that meanings are in people and only in people, then effective communication and understanding would only be the most improbable of accidents. In short, the communication process entails both perception and behavior. Our focus on the behavioral operationalization of confirmation-disconfirmation and self-disclosure is not intended to imply that the perceptual aspect of communication is irrelevant or unimportant.

Behavioral Coding Systems: Confirmation/Disconfirmation

Sieburg's Confirmation Coding Systems

In her 1969 dissertation, Sieburg created the Interpersonal Responsiveness Category System to code observed confirming and disconfirming verbal behaviors into eight categories. Of these eight categories, two were labeled functional responses (content responses and metacommunication), five were labeled dysfunctional responses (involving impervious, tangential, projective, inadequate, and ambiguous communication), and one was an "unclassifiable" category for unclear audio recording (Cissna, 1976). The unit of analysis was the verbal communicative act (both preceded and followed by another person's communicative act; Sieburg, 1969). She did not consider categories mutually exclusive; rather, coders coded each unit to all relevant categories. The reliability of the coding system, as measured by intraclass correlation (.98 and .97) and percentage of agreement ($M = .81$), was considered adequate. To validate the coding system, she compared the interaction of effective and ineffective groups and showed that overall group effectiveness was related to the frequency of functional and dysfunctional responses (Sieburg, 1969).

Building upon her original coding system, Sieburg (1972, 1973) developed a scoring system to differentiate three dimensions of interpersonal confirmation: (1) acknowledgment versus imperviousness, (2) conjunctive response (further divided into either content or emotion) versus disjunctive response, and (3) affiliative response versus disaffiliative response. The affiliative/disaffiliative response explicitly integrated self-disclosure (or lack thereof) as a level of interpersonal confirmation/disconfirmation. Level 1, acknowledgment versus imperviousness, described the basic ways in which we acknowledge (or fail to acknowledge) the other person through the use of nonverbal eye contact, attentiveness, and turn-taking cues and verbally direct responses. The second level, conjunctive responses, were not only direct but also related to the preceding communication, either content or feelings. On the other hand, disjunctive responses were not relevant to the other person's content or emotional state, involving abrupt topic changes, interruptions, evasiveness, denial, or negative evaluation of the other's communication. The third level differentiated between affiliative and disaffiliative responses. Affiliative responses constituted complete, clear, and direct expressions of self, sharing and taking responsibility for one's feelings, and nonverbal cues that reinforced the verbal message. In contrast, disaffiliative responses concealed the self or denied responsibility for one's message (Cissna, 1976).

In 1975, to address questions of discriminant validity raised by Jacobs (1973), Sieburg revised this three-level scoring system into four behavioral clusters. Cluster 1, *indifference*, involved communication that failed to acknowledge the other by ignoring, interrupting, or failing to respond. Cluster 2, *disqualification*, involved unclear, irrelevant, or self-contradictory messages. Cluster 3, *imperviousness*, referred to when one corrected or denied the other's expressed thoughts or feelings, negatively evaluated the other's communication, or told the other how he or she should think or feel. The fourth cluster, *dialogue*, represented confirming communication with clear, direct, relevant, and congruent responses, appropriate turn taking, and attention to the other.

These systems assumed that confirmation is hierarchical in nature; lower level confirmation must occur in order to achieve higher level confirmation. In addition, Sieburg assumed that all communicative acts involve confirmation (or disconfirmation) to some degree. This view differed from that of Dance and Larson (1976), who stated that only some communicative acts (specifically, those that cause an orientational shift) have confirming/disconfirming consequences (Cissna, 1976).

Sieburg partnered with Cissna in 1981 for yet another revision to the system. This version balanced the number of confirming and disconfirming categories. The three categories of disconfirmation remained relatively unchanged: indifferent responses, impervious responses, and disqualifying responses. However, the previous system's one category of confirming communication became three categories: *recognition* of the other's relational attempt; *acknowledgment* of the other with a direct, relevant response; and *endorsement* of the other's feelings as accurate (Cissna & Sieburg, 1981; Smilowitz, 1985).

Smilowitz's Confirming Communication Measure

To analyze confirmation in organizational interactions, Smilowitz (1985) first needed to modify Cissna and Sieburg's (1981) confirmation system to be more useful for interaction analysis. Because each coding decision was based on a verbal (and an audible nonverbal) utterance's relation to the immediately prior utterance, this measure was designed for use in interaction analysis. This measure included five categories of confirmation: maximally disconfirming, disconfirming, other, confirming, and maximally confirming. Maximally disconfirming messages failed to acknowledge the other's existence or right to speak, devalued the other's statement, or involved an abrupt change of topic. Disconfirming messages acknowledged the other person's existence but rejected the other person's value through interruptions, irrelevant statements, ignoring the other's request for an opinion or answer, or not encouraging the other to continue. The other category included messages that cannot be clearly identified as confirming or disconfirming. Confirming messages were direct and relevant responses that acknowledged the other's value or encouraged the other to continue but may have expressed reservations about the other's statement or opinion. Finally, maximally confirming messages acknowledged, accepted, endorsed, and valued both the content and relational dimensions of the other person's message. Reliability was tested with Guetzkow's (1950) method; the researcher's initial codes were later recoded and compared for reliability over time ($\alpha = .94$), and the researcher's codes were compared against three other trained coders' judgments ($\alpha = .89$ to $.93$). Smilowitz found support for the measure's content validity but suggested that future researchers assess the measure's internal validity in a laboratory setting.

Behavioral Coding Systems: Self-Disclosure

Morton's Two-Dimensional Intimacy Scoring System

Morton (1976) created a content analysis coding system to compare the intimacy of self-disclosure within the behavioral interaction of unacquainted and well-acquainted dyads. The system assessed all interactive behavior, verbal and nonverbal, on two dimensions of intimacy: the degree of description (e.g., factual information) and the degree of evaluation (e.g., feeling or opinion). Morton dichotomized these two dimensions into low and high levels of disclosure to create a four-category system: high description/high evaluation, high description/low evaluation, low description/high evaluation, and low description/low evaluation. Trained raters assigned each 10-second interval of interaction to one of the four self-disclosure categories. They also identified the sex of the speaker. In Morton's original study, κ values for trained coders using the Two-Dimensional Intimacy Scoring System averaged .88 overall. Small talk, categorized as low-description/low-evaluation communication, occurred most often, followed by high-description/high-evaluation communication, then high-description/low-evaluation communication. Low-description/high-evaluation communication occurred least frequently. Morton (1978) found evidence of both the face validity and discriminative utility of the Two-Dimensional Intimacy Scoring System. She found that the descriptive dimension of intimacy was positively associated with relational development; that is, spouses reported more descriptive (but not evaluative) intimacy than strangers. Because the system allowed a nuanced measurement of descriptive and affective exchange, Morton suggested that it would be useful for exploring how intimacy and reciprocity vary with relational stages and in the clinical treatment of dysfunctional relationships.

Dindia's (1982) early work on self-disclosure only distinguished between disclosive and nondisclosive statements, with disclosure being defined as any self-reference statement. However, in later work (Dindia, Fitzpatrick, & Kenny, 1997), she distinguished "descriptive self-disclosures" from "evaluative self-disclosure" on the basis of distinctions proposed by Stiles (1978). She also coded the "intimacy" or "depth" of disclosures using Chelune's (1975a, 1975b) five-point scale, which defines intimacy on the basis of the "ego relevance" of the verbal content.

Spencer's Conversational Coding System

In his study of the family context, Spencer (1992) questioned whether conversational self-disclosure can be reliably observed with agreement between conversational partners. To avoid relying on partners' ability to recall the conversation, Spencer recorded the conversation of parent-adolescent dyads and asked them to code their own conversations, circling instances of self-disclosure. He found that when dividing conversations into turn as the unit of analysis, Cohen's κ values were low; only 2 of 24 conversations reached agreement (Cohen's κ) above .40 when tasked with identifying each other's self-disclosures from their audiotaped and transcribed

conversations. When using the speaker turn as the unit of analysis, 10 of the 24 conversations had Cohen's κ values of .40 or better. Spencer acknowledged that agreement was consistently low, stating, "using either unit of analysis, one-third of the dyads failed to show significantly better than chance agreement" (p. 45). Moreover, lag-sequential analysis revealed no evidence of self-disclosure reciprocity. Spencer suggested that coding self-disclosure is complicated by its subjective nature; speakers and receivers may differ in their interpretation of what is considered self-disclosure. He further suggested that self-disclosures could be coded as received or unreceived, and delivered or undelivered, with unreceived and undelivered self-disclosures being considered unsuccessful. Spencer's system, therefore, operates more from the "restrictive subject-privileged mode" or the "experiencer" perspective (Poole & Hewes, this volume) than most other disclosure systems.

VanLear's Relational Linking System (RLS)

VanLear developed the Relational Linking System (RLS) on the basis of Dance and Larson's (1976) discussion of the linking function of communication. VanLear and Coet (1982) borrowed from systems proposed by Sieburg (1972, 1975), Dance and Larson (1976), and Villard and Whipple (1976) in constructing their system for assessing accepting and rejecting behaviors. In their validation study of 11 categories of verbal behavior, participants were asked to indicate the extent to which each category indicated acceptance or rejection of the other person. The study addressed several issues. First, the study sought to confirm that participants viewed behaviors presented in the literature as accepting or rejecting behaviors. As such, the study was conducted in the tradition of the "generalized subject-privileged mode" or "experiencing" perspective (Poole & Hewes, this volume). Second, different scholars held different beliefs about the role of self-disclosure in the linking function. For instance, Dance and Larson viewed disclosure primarily as a stimulus behavior that elicits either acceptance or rejection of self as presented in the disclosure. However, Sieburg viewed disclosure as accepting behavior in its own right. The study sought to determine whether participants viewed self-disclosure itself as accepting, presumably on the basis of the analogic message of trust it conveys. Finally, the study sought to determine the best factor structure or clustering of categories in constructing an observational system for assessing acceptance and rejection.

The results of that study showed that participants perceived that the vast majority of categories suggested by the literature did, in fact, connote acceptance or rejection. Whereas participants did perceive that private-personal disclosures indicated acceptance, they did not necessarily view disclosure at lower levels (i.e., public or semiprivate) as indicating acceptance. Finally, three clear dimensions emerged from the factor analysis of the data: personal acceptance-rejection, disconfirmation, and evaluation of communication content (positive vs. negative). On the basis of these results, a five-category system was proposed: personal acceptance (+P), personal rejection (–P), disconfirmation (–D), positive evaluation of communication content (+C), and negative evaluation of communication content (–C). The system is specifically restricted to verbal communication to be coded using transcripts or audiotape.

On the basis of both theory and preliminary use of VanLear and Coet's (1982) system,[1] VanLear (1985) proposed the Relational Linking System (RLS1). The most notable change was that he presented the RLS1 as a two-dimensional system. The first dimension, Self-Presentation (SP), had four levels/codes: nonsubstantive utterances, public communication, semiprivate presentations, and private-personal presentations, which generally correspond to the levels of self-disclosure/intimacy proposed by Altman and Taylor (1973) and informed by the work of Morton (1976). The second dimension, Other-Orientation (OO), contained six categories: minimal confirmation (added in the RLS1), positive opinion evaluation, personal acceptance, specific differentiation, disconfirmation, and disassociation/personal rejection. Codes for the SP dimension are presented in Box 6.1, and codes for the OO dimension are presented in Box 6.2.

Box 6.1
Dimension 1 (Self-Presentation) of the Relational Linking System, Version 3

1. Nonsubstantive utterances: do not reveal any information about the speaker. They include incomplete or uncodable utterances or nonsubstantive verbal interjections (e.g., "oh" or "uh-hum" when it is not an agreement) and computer-generated statements in online chat.

2. Public comments/small talk: Statements indicate superficial, trivial, or public information about the speaker.

   a. Self-disclosure of demographic information

   b. Public communication/small talk: superficial and/or trivial information discussions of routine day-to-day occurrences and practices, as well as factual verifiable information and often only indirectly present information about the speaker

3. Semiprivate information: disclose information that is neither trivial and superficial nor intimate.

   a. Opinions or judgments on specific issues or topics (neither trivial nor intimate)

   b. Highly unique or original ideas

   c. Unique significant past experiences (neither trivial nor intimate)

   d. Highly unusual or unique (unexpected in that it violates communications rules or rituals)

   e. Agreement or disagreement with the opinion expressed by the other

4. Self-disclosure of private personal information: not easily accessible or verifiable; usually involves vulnerability to risk, often negative information.

a. Information concerning the speaker's core values

b. Information concerning the speaker's central traits

c. Information concerning the speaker's significant life goals

d. Information about the speaker which is risky or embarrassing

Self-Presentation Decision Tree

1st: Is it a private personal disclosure? Yes, code 4. No, continue →

2nd: Is it a semiprivate disclosure? Yes, code 3. No, continue →

3rd: Is it public communication or small talk? Yes, code 2. No, code 1.

Source: Author.

Box 6.2
Dimension 2 (Other-Orientation) of the Relational Linking System, Version 3

0. Nonrelational specific: incomplete, nonintelligible, uncodable, or computer generated.

1. Minimal confirmation: responses indicating only that the other is taken into account or that acknowledge the other's existence.

   a. Direct and relevant responses: acknowledge the other's communicative act and respond to it directly and appropriately

   b. Seeking clarification, attempting to understand other

2. Positive opinion evaluation: positively evaluate or acknowledge the worth of the other's opinions and ideas.

   a. Positive communication content evaluation and agreement

   b. Specific identification ("I feel the same way") identifies with a specific experience, idea, or opinion communicated by the other

   c. Seeking the ideas or opinions of other

3. Personal acceptance: personal acceptance of the other person as a person rather than just specific isolated ideas and opinions.

   a. Positive personal evaluation: attribute some positive (socially desirable) characteristic to the other or attribute credit for desirable occurrences to the other person

   b. Direct expression of commitment

(Continued)

(Continued)

    c. Putting the other first: putting the other person or the relationship ahead of his or her own self-interests

    d. Relationship acknowledgment: acknowledge interdependence or show concern for the relationship between the participants

    e. Positive relational investment: indicating a willingness to invest time, energy, and/or resources to the relationship ("Let me help you with that")

    f. Showing concern ("That's too bad"; "be careful")

    g. General identification ("we have a lot in common")

4. Specific differentiation.

    a. Negative communication content evaluation (disagreement)

    b. Specific differentiation: indicating specific differences ("I'm a Democrat" in response to "I am a Republican")

5. Disconfirmation.

    a. Denial of autonomy (claiming a superior knowledge of the other person's identity, thoughts, or feelings than they have themselves)

    b. Interruptions disregarding other's attempt at talk

    c. Irrelevant responses; disregard for the other's communication when a direct and relevant response is called for

    d. Ignoring: failing to answer a direct question; avoiding appropriate eye contact; attention to something irrelevant to the discussion

6. Disassociation/personal rejection: statements that indicate or contribute to distancing, avoidance, or rejection of the other person, rather than specific isolated ideas or opinions.

    a. Negative personal evaluations (insults/ridicule): also attributing some negative (socially undesirable) characteristic to the other or attribute blame for undesirable situation or occurrences

    b. Discouraging other from participation ("I don't care what you think")

    c. Putting self first ("I have my own problems don't bother me with yours")

    d. Negative relationship investment ("I don't have time to spend with you")

    e. Avoiding commitment ("let's cool it for a while")

    f. General differentiation: indication of incompatibility ("we just don't have the same interest any more")

Other-Orientation Decision Tree

1st: Is it personal acceptance? Yes, code 3. No, →

2nd: Is it personal rejection? Yes, code 6. No, →

3rd: Is it positive opinion evaluation? Yes, code 2. No, →

4th: Is it specific differentiation? Yes, code 4. No, →

5th: Is it disconfirmation? Yes, code 5. No, →

6th: All else code 1 if it is a direct and relevant response to a specific person or persons.

7th: If it is an appropriate statement but does not relate to other specific people, code 0.

Source: Author.

Researchers have used the system to look at variations in the frequencies or proportions of these different behaviors either across different dyads/groups or situations (VanLear, Sheehan, Withers, & Walker, 2005) or over time (VanLear, 1985, 1987, 1991). One novel feature of this system is that either of the dimensions can be used independently, or they can be used together for assessing patterns of interaction. When used as independent dimensions, one can examine reciprocity (or compensation) of self-presentation or reciprocity of aspects of other-orientation, such as reciprocal confirmation or disconfirmation, reciprocal acceptance or rejection, or agreement and disagreement interaction patterns. When researchers use the two dimensions in conjunction, they can assess whether certain levels or kinds of self-presentation call forth or suppress certain kinds of acceptance or rejection in certain relationships or situations.

VanLear (1985) applied this system to the interactions of acquainting dyads as they developed a relationship. Individuals who had never met were paired in same-sex dyads and asked to talk together for half an hour a week for 6 weeks. In addition to the RLS, coders also coded the participants' interactions for relational control using the Relational Communication Coding (Rel/Com) system (Ellis, Fisher, Drecksel, Hock, & Werbel, 1976). VanLear found that whereas lower levels of self-presentation were characterized by more unique trajectories over time, private-personal presentations followed a common trajectory very similar to that predicted by social penetration theory (Altman & Taylor, 1973). During the early stages of the relationships, participants did not engage in much, if any, private-personal disclosure. As the relationships progressed, they began to offer more private-personal disclosure; however, during the last week of interaction, a notable decline occurred in private-personal disclosures. Reciprocity of self-presentation at the same level of intimacy represented the rule rather than the exception, especially at the very beginning and end

of the relationship. However, between the beginning and the end, reciprocity fluctuated in a somewhat cyclical progression. Reciprocity of semiprivate disclosures was the most pronounced of the interaction patterns for self-presentation. The results for the Other-Orientation dimension were disappointing. They did not show a lot of added information beyond that provided by Rel/Com, and OO had less variation than the other dimensions. The vast majority of the acts involved minimal confirmation, indicating that these dyads engaged in little overt acceptance or rejection, and what was present did not change in a systematic or uniform way over time. Finally, unlike the other dimension, it did not provide a substantial amount of sequential structure. However, in examining the data, VanLear suggested that this lack of sequential structure in the OO dimension was a function of the nature of these kinds of interactions. Acquainting dyads in casual conversation simply do not engage in much explicit acceptance or rejection, nor a lot of disconfirmation.

In a study using a very similar design, the Self-Presentation dimension was again coded on the interactions of acquainting dyads over time (VanLear, 1991). That study tested Altman, Vinsel, and Brown's (1981) cyclical model of openness during relationship formation. Using Fourier and cross-spectral analyses of the time series generated by these dyads, VanLear found that (a) there was evidence of cycles of openness of self-presentation over time; (b) cycles were complex, with smaller cycles occurring within conversations nested within larger cycles occurring across conversations; and (c) participants matched and timed their cycles to synchronize with each other. The OO dimension was not included in that study.

VanLear et al. (2005) argued that the process of presenting self and the response of acceptance, confirmation, rejection, or disconfirmation, as presented in Figure 6.1, offered a good model of emotional and esteem support. They applied both dimensions of the RLS to the interactions of online support groups, especially Alcoholics Anonymous (AA) groups, as well as online interest groups. In addition to comparing the interactions of online AA groups with those of other types of online support groups and interest groups, different types of online AA groups were analyzed: informal AA synchronous chats, formal synchronous AA meetings, and asynchronous AA discussion groups. To more adequately assess the interactions of online groups, these researchers made several changes to the RLS. First, residual codes were added to both dimensions to account for computer-generated turns and procedural statements made by moderators. It became apparent that sometimes other-orientation statements were not necessarily referring to the immediately preceding comments but to comments made at prior points in time. This point is particularly true of group interactions, though it can occur in dyadic interaction as well. To account for this, a reference code was included in the category system instructions to coders. Coders first identified to which prior act a given Other-Orientation statement primarily referred, then identified the Self-Presentation code that associated with that statement. This process proved useful not only for more accurately identifying the SP to OO interacts (presentation-response) but also for assessing the reciprocity of self-presentation. Finally, on the basis of the experience with the acquaintance data, the researchers decided that not every act should be coded as providing an other-orientation function. In addition to the computer-generated codes, they omitted from the analyses many "nonsubstantive" incomplete or obscured codes. Likewise, in group interaction or in a bulletin board discussion, although an act may be "direct and relevant" to the discussion overall, it may not necessarily be "minimally confirming" of the immediately prior speaker as we would code it in dyadic interaction. Of the 4,015 turns at talk, about 69% were coded as having a clear other-orientation function.

Both the self-presentation and other-orientation systems tended to chain together in reciprocal interaction patterns, but these tendencies varied across different types of groups. Furthermore, self-presentation behaviors tended to elicit particular other-orientation responses, though the nature of these patterns varied across the different groups. Asynchronous AA groups had the highest proportion of private-personal presentations as well as semiprivate presentations, agreements, and personal acceptance. Sequentially, in these asynchronous groups, private-personal disclosures tended to be followed by personal acceptance other-orientation responses. Reciprocity of private-personal disclosures tended to characterize formal synchronous AA meetings, whereas reciprocity of personal acceptance was most typical of informal chats between alcoholics. Not surprisingly, nonsupport interest groups engaged in more negative other-orientations than the support groups, and negative comments tended to follow opinion disclosures in these nonsupport interest groups more often than in the support groups. This study revealed both behaviors and interaction patterns that characterize online social support in various forms and venues. The study also supported Walther's (1996) analysis of the hyperpersonal nature of asynchronous groups. As Walther predicted, asynchronous groups engaged in more private-personal disclosures. In addition, the study demonstrated the capacity of the RLS to help users discriminate between functionally (support vs. interest) and structurally (format) different groups. The Other-Orientation dimension clearly performed much better on these types of data. Behaviors indicating acceptance were clearly important to the enactment of social support. As one would expect, negative behaviors in the form of disconfirmation and rejection were very rare in the support groups. However, many of the online interest groups included lively debate and conflict that was evidenced by a variety of negative behaviors as well as interaction patterns involving those behaviors.

We focused on studies in which we have been directly involved, as we have used them to develop, modify, and refine the RLS. Other researchers have used the RLS; we would love to hear about the experiences of anyone else who has used the system. The following section reviews many of the specific coding rules and techniques we have used and found useful.

Interaction Patterns and Structure

To date, all studies that have used the Self-Presentation dimension have shown at least first-order Markovity (i.e., that the level of self-presentation enacted by a communicator is related to the level of self-presentation enacted by a responding communicator in the next turn at talk), with some analyses revealing sequential structure at the second-order of Markovity (i.e., that both the initial self-presentation level and the responding self-presentation level are related to the self-presentation level of the third act in the conversational sequence). On the other hand, the Other-Orientation dimension failed to show sequential structure in the acquainting dyadic data; however, it did show sequential structure at both first-order and second-order for some patterns in online groups (see VanLear, this volume, for a more complete explanation of levels of sequential structure). By far the most common patterns above chance on both dimensions were reciprocal interactions, where behaviors elicited responses of the same category type. In the data from acquainting dyads, 54% of conversations displayed clear evidence of public → public reciprocity, and 76% of the conversations showed clear evidence of semiprivate → semiprivate reciprocity. Of the limited number of conversations that contained enough private-personal presentations to estimate sequential structure, 55% showed evidence of reciprocity of private-personal presentations. In the study of online interaction, synchronous online AA groups also tended to display reciprocity of self-presentation, and AA chats showed reciprocity of personal acceptance.

Evidence exists that some types of self-presentation call forth particular other-orientation responses, but these may vary depending upon the type of group. Across a variety of kinds of synchronous interactions, minimal confirmation tends to be the response to public self-presentations. This pattern is probably typical of "small talk." However, somewhat contentious interactions in online interest groups evidenced semiprivate self-presentations evoking negative other-orientation responses. However, support groups often evidenced a pattern of private-personal presentations evoking personal acceptance from the respondent, which is characteristic of the pattern Dorian and Cordova (2004) described as an "intimacy event."

Whereas modest evidence indicated that the other-orientation response influenced the nature of subsequent self-presentations, the effect did not hold when controlling for general reciprocity. Future research should examine whether positive or negative other-orientation behaviors influence the general level of subsequent Self-Presentation disclosures. This effect may or may not show up in an immediate or proximal response as detected in sequential analyses. The following presents some examples of these behaviors and patterns.

Example 1 is from an online AA group chat:

1. LO>I've got 12 days [sober *sic*] . . . and all I've done is obsess over drinking. (4, NA)

2. BW>Don't drink no matter what. (3, 3)

3. LO>I know it's gonna be bad and I know I'm going to hate myself . . . but this little voice goes "so what?" I'm realizing my incredible shyness is gonna get me drunk. I went to a mtg . . . to meet ppl . . . but I left didn't talk to anyone. I spent the whole drive home being pissed at myself and realizing I was gonna be bored all night. I wish I could force myself not to be shy . . . (4, 2)

4. SG>when bored go to page 112 in the Big Book read the 1st 3 words and follow directions. (3, 3)

5. FG>glad you're here LO. KCB! (3, 3)

6. RG>thanks LO, hang in there! Keep coming back!! (3, 3)

7. NJ>thanks LO, I'm shy too, I learned to ask open ended questions. (4, 3)

The first statement is a private-personal disclosure (Self-Presentation 4 [SP4]), as it admits a weakness, but it cannot be coded on Other-Orientation, because it is not in response to a prior behavior. The response in 2 is an opinion and supportive of LO's attempt at abstinence (though very general). LO's statement in 3 is yet another personal disclosure (SP4), as it discloses a personality trait LO feels unhappy about. SG's response in 4 is a suggestion based on opinion (SP3) that is also meant to be supportive of LO's attempt at abstinence. FG's response in 5 is also in response to LO and is a show of support. Because 4, 5, 6, and 7 all have the same reference behavior, this shows the importance of identifying the act that a behavior is responding to in both coding OO and establishing the actual pattern of interaction (reciprocity of SP and SP → OO patterns), especially in group interaction. For example, NJ's statement in 7 is a response to Statement 3, making it a reciprocal disclosure (though not as risky as 3, it is still a personal characteristic) and an attempt to identify with LO at a personal level.

Example 2 is from an online political discussion group:

8. ZM> Israel has THE FULL RIGHT to protect OUR JEWISH country (4, NA)

9. VY> CD, the Palestinians are sending kids out to die. The Palestinians have pledged to wipe out Israel. Israel has a right to protect themselves [*sic*] from such evil. (3, 2)

10. WA> ZM . . . okay, and what kind of army SHOOTS BACK AT CHILDREN WITH BULLETS? You've answered your own question as to who are the assholes here (3, 4)

11. CD> Israel is killing innocent children. (3, 4 as it is a response to VY and ZM)

12. JH> boy you people are hateful today . . . sheesh (3, 6)

ZM has disclosed that he is Israeli, so his disclosure is somewhat personal and related to a central aspect of his identity. Other disclosures are opinions and attitudes. They present self, and by virtue of being controversial, they provide a degree of vulnerability, but they are not very private or personal. Most statements are disagreements (specific differentiation). WA calls Israel "assholes" but not ZM or VY. JH, however, provides a more rejecting statement ("hateful"), though it is directed at the group, not an individual.

Coding Using the RLS

VanLear (1985) developed a detailed coding manual for the Relational Linking System Version 1 (RLS1). VanLear et al. (2005) modified some of those rules, as we referenced in the previous section (RLS Version 2). For the purposes of this chapter, we propose some additional modifications that will incorporate some nonverbal behaviors that allow the new RLS Version 3 to take advantage of the richer set of cues available on video recordings of participant interaction and incorporate information from more recent literature on interpersonal confirmation (e.g., Dorian & Cordova, 2004; Wong, 2014).

Unit. The coding unit for this system is the utterance or a single communicative act by a single participant, regardless of length. The utterance begins when a speaker starts speaking and ends when the other speaker starts speaking. Each utterance receives only one code per dimension, such that each utterance is represented by a code for Self-Presentation and one for Other-Orientation. This unit is practical when examining issues of sequential structure. Also, the decision tree generally allows coders to make reliable decisions when multiple categories could be coded for the same act or turn. However, if different research questions were to suggest that a "thought unit" should be used, the system could be easily adapted to code with that unit.

Likewise, to date, data analyses have focused on the general categories rather than the subcategories. However, we recommend that coders keep track of the subcategories to justify their decisions for training and testing for reliability. Certain research questions might profitably be addressed through analysis of the relative frequencies of certain subcategories for both dimensions. For example, using the subcategories of Self-Presentation's private-personal presentations could allow researchers to distinguish those utterances coded because they are private (risky or negatively valenced) from those that are personal (display highly unique information about

the speaker), as Morton's system does. Likewise, one might sometimes want to distinguish between personal acceptance statements that are positive personal evaluations of the other versus direct expressions of commitment. However, most subcategories do not occur with sufficient frequency in most types of interaction to permit reliable estimates of sequential structure. In fact, in some types of conversations, certain infrequent categories need to be combined in order to permit sequential analyses. For example, when coding conflict interaction, sufficient frequency and diversity of negative behaviors can allow a researcher to maintain the distinction among specific differentiation, disconfirmation, and personal rejection. Yet when coding more cordial types of interaction, these three codes may need to be combined into a single negative orientation code for the purposes of sequential analyses.

Reliability. VanLear (1985, 1987) used six undergraduate coders to code the data. The researcher and coders transcribed the audio-recorded interactions to aid in unitizing reliability, with each turn at talk numbered such that each numbered turn got both a Self-Presentation and an Other-Orientation code. Each coder was extensively trained and checked for reliability before and during coding. Approximately 20% of the data were checked for reliability, with each check involving at least 150 acts. VanLear used Brennan and Prediger's (1981) revision of Cohen's (1960) κ to assess global reliability ($\kappa = .76$ to .85 for SP, $\kappa = .87$ to .94 for OO). In addition to global reliability, specific tests for category-by-category unreliability (Folger, Hewes, & Poole, 1984) were conducted. First, two coders' codes on the same data were used to construct a contingency table with the main diagonal representing agreements. Off-diagonal cells (disagreements) were tested to see if any contained frequencies above that expected by chance. To determine whether unreliability affected sequential structure, Markov tests for homogeneity where conducted across the series of the same data coded by different coders. Both tests failed to find evidence of systematic category-by-category unreliability in the data.

VanLear (1991) used 15 undergraduate coders divided into five teams of 3. After training, each team coded all of the same data such that all data were coded by 3 people. The final data set consisted of the majority decision of the 3 coders, with cases in which there was no majority (<1% of decisions) resolved by discussion and, if necessary, consultation with the researcher. In addition to the reliability of the individual coders, about 20% of the final data were checked for reliability against another team's codes for global reliability ($\kappa = .79$; Brennan & Prediger, 1981). Category-by-category reliability (Poole & Hewes, this volume) was acceptable.

In the VanLear et al. (2005) study, a team of trained graduate students coded the online interaction data on both dimensions of the RLS. In those data, global reliability was $\kappa = .76$ to .96. Again, no evidence of systematic category-by-category unreliability emerged in the final data set.

Dimensional structure and discriminant validity. The original dimensional structure relied on both theory and the results of VanLear and Coet's (1982) study. However, that study did suggest that private-personal disclosures could be viewed as accepting, presumably on the basis of the analogic message of trust they imply. The decision to separate Self-Presentation from Other-Orientation into two dimensions was based primarily on the desire to observe how partners respond to the self-presentations. In fact, some definitions or operationalizations of confirmation, acceptance, or "validation" require that these constructs be considered in reference to prior self-presentations (Linehan, 1997; Shenk & Fruzzetti, 2011). However, the dual function of private-personal presentations raises questions about the distinctiveness of the two dimensions. This issue also recognizes that, in Other-Orientation, both positive and negative communication content evaluations will usually be coded as semiprivate self-presentations because they are also expression of opinions. Of course, many cases of semiprivate self-presentations are neither negative nor positive communication content evaluations of the other. VanLear's (1985) study tested the distinctiveness of the two dimensions. Although the two dimensions were not completely independent, they were not completely redundant. However, the RLS (especially the OO dimension) was not sufficiently distinct from the Rel/Com system. It appears that in these acquainting dyads, being disconfirming or rejecting was inevitably also domineering and being agreeable, and accepting was not sufficiently distinguishable from being deferential as operationalized by the OO dimension and Rel/Com. However, much of this problem reflects the paucity of negative behaviors or even extreme positive behaviors in those data. We have also tested the distinctiveness of the Self-Presentation and Other-Orientation dimensions on the social support and other online interactions from the VanLear et al. (2005) data; those comparisons also find that the OO dimension provides unique information not provided by the SP dimension and vice versa. For example, personal acceptance could either be semiprivate or private personal presentations (above chance). Likewise, disconfirmation did not take place when the disconfirming person was self-presenting at only one particular level. Whereas semiprivate presentations tended not to also be coded minimal confirmations, they could be positive opinion evaluations, personal acceptance, specific differentiations, disconfirmations, or personal rejections (all above chance).

Version 3. The most notable change in Version 3 of the RLS involves the explicit incorporation of some nonverbal information. In prior versions, coders could use nonverbal cues if they felt that such cues clearly changed the meaning of the utterance (e.g., sarcasm). However, no category descriptions included explicit reference to nonverbal cues. Because most prior studies used either audio tapes (VanLear, 1985, 1987, 1991) or computer text transcripts (VanLear et al., 2005), nonverbal cues were limited. Of course, nonverbal cues can emphasize or support, contradict, or replace a verbal message. Prior versions allowed enough flexibility for coders to take into account clear examples of the first two functions, and this usually was made clear during training. "Spontaneous" emotional expressions can provide important information about the relational implications of the verbal message (Buck & VanLear, 2002). The latest version includes several subcategories of exclusively nonverbal cues. However, as with the verbal codes, the interpretation/coding of these cues should always take into account the interactional context. For example, sometimes lack of eye contact can signal disconfirmation, if it is a situation in which people normatively expect such attention. However, other times, other cues in the environment may legitimately call for a person's attention. Future research could combine the RLS with coded nonverbal affiliative/immediacy behaviors (see Guerrero, this volume), or comforting behaviors (Samter and MacGeorge, this volume) to provide a more comprehensive view of acceptance. A complete coding manual for the RLS is available from the authors upon request. The system can be used to examine identity development, relationship development, or supportive and nonsupportive communication.

In summary, we suggest that one useful perspective on how people link themselves together in relationships is by presenting self and reacting to the self-presentation of others. This must take place through the exchange of contingent behavior in social interaction.

References

Altman, I., & Taylor, D. A. (1973). *Social penetration: The development of interpersonal relationships.* New York: Holt, Rinehart.

Altman, I., Vinsel, A., & Brown, B. (1981). Dialectic conceptions in social psychology: An application to social penetration and privacy regulation. In L. Berkowitz (Ed.), *Advances in experimental social psychology* (Vol. 14, pp. 107–160). New York: Academic Press.

Bowlby, J. (1982). *Attachment and loss. Vol. 1: Attachment* (2nd ed.). New York: Basic Books. (Original work published 1969)

Brennan, R. L., & Prediger, D. J. (1981). Coefficient kappa: Some uses, misuses, and alternatives. *Educational and Psychological Measurement, 41,* 687–699.

Buber, M. (1957). Distance and relation. *Psychiatry, 20,* 97–104.

Buck, R., & VanLear, C. A. (2002). Verbal and nonverbal communication: Distinguishing symbolic, spontaneous, and pseudo-spontaneous nonverbal behavior. *Journal of Communication, 52,* 522–541.

Chelune, G. J. (1975a). Self-disclosure: An elaboration of its basic dimensions. *Psychological Reports, 36,* 79–85.

Chelune, G. J. (1975b). *Studies in the behavioral and self-report assessment of self-disclosure* (Unpublished doctoral dissertation). University of Nevada, Reno.

Cissna, K. N. (1976, April). *Interpersonal confirmation: A review of recent theory and research.* Paper presented at the annual meeting of the International Communication Association, Portland, OR.

Cissna, K.N.L., & Sieburg, E. (1981). Patterns of interactional confirmation and disconfirmation. In C. Wilder-Mott & J. H. Weakland (Eds.), *Rigor and imagination: Essays from the legacy of Gregory Bateson* (pp. 253–282). New York: Praeger.

Cohen, J. (1960). A coefficient of agreement for nominal scales. *Educational and Psychological Measurement, 20,* 37–46.

Dance, F.E.X., & Larson, C. E. (1976). *The functions of human communication: A theoretical approach.* New York: Holt, Rinehart.

Dindia, K. (1982). Reciprocity of self-disclosure: A sequential analysis. In M. Burgoon (Ed.). *Communication Yearbook 6* (pp. 506–528). Beverly Hills, CA: Sage.

Dindia, K., Fitzpatrick, M. A., & Kenny, D. E. (1997). Self-disclosure in spouse and stranger interaction: A social relations analysis. *Human Communication Research, 23,* 388–412.

Dorian, M., & Cordova, J. V. (2004). Coding intimacy in couples' interactions. In P. K. Kerig & D. H. Baucom (Eds.), *Couple observational coding systems* (pp. 243–256). Mahwah, NJ: Lawrence Erlbaum.

Ellis, D. G., Fisher, B. A., Drecksel, G. L., Hock, D. D., & Werbel, W. S. (1976). *Rel/Com: A system for analyzing relational communication* (Unpublished coding manual), Department of Communication, University of Utah.

Fisher, B. A. (1978). *Perspectives on human communication.* New York: Macmillan.

Folger, J. P., Hewes, D. E., & Poole, M. S. (1984). Coding social interaction. In B. Dervin & M. Voight (Eds.), *Progress in the communication sciences* (Vol. 4, pp. 115–161). Norwood, NJ: Ablex.

Goffman, E. (1959). *The presentation of self in everyday life.* New York: Anchor.

Grice, H. P. (1975). Logic and conversation. In P. Cole & J. L. Morgan (Eds.), *Syntax and semantics. 3: Speech acts* (pp. 41–58). New York: Academic.

Guetzkow, H. (1950). Unitizing and categorizing problems in coding qualitative data. *Journal of Clinical Psychology, 6,* 47–58.

Jacobs, M. R. (1973). *Levels of confirmation and disconfirmation in interpersonal communication* (Unpublished doctoral dissertation). University of Denver, Denver, CO.

Knapp, M. L. (1978). *Social intercourse: From greeting to goodbye.* Boston: Allyn & Bacon.

Knapp, M. L. (1984). *Interpersonal communication and human relationships.* Boston: Allyn & Bacon.

Linehan, M. M. (1997). Self-verification and drug abusers: Implications for treatment. *Psychological Science, 8,* 181–183.

Maslow, A. H. (1943). A theory of human motivation. *Psychological Review, 50,* 370–396.

Morton, T. L. (1976). *The effects of acquaintance and distance on intimacy and reciprocity* (Unpublished doctoral dissertation). University of Utah, Salt Lake City.

Morton, T. L. (1978). Intimacy and reciprocity of exchange: A comparison of spouses and strangers. *Journal of Personality and Social Psychology, 36,* 72–81.

Richards, I. A. (1936). *The philosophy of rhetoric.* London: Oxford University Press.

Shenk, C. E., & Fruzzetti, A. E. The impact of validating and invalidating responses on emotional reactivity. *Journal of Social and Clinical Psychology, 30,* 163–183.

Sieburg, E. (1969). *Dysfunctional communication and interpersonal responsiveness in small groups* (Unpublished doctoral dissertation). University of Denver, Denver, CO.

Sieburg, E. (1972). *Toward a theory of interpersonal confirmation* (Unpublished manuscript). University of Denver, Denver, CO.

Sieburg, E. (1973). *Interpersonal confirmation: Conceptualization and measurement.* Paper presented at the meeting of the International Communication Association, Montreal, QC, Canada.

Sieburg, E. (1975). *Interpersonal confirmation: A paradigm for conceptualization and measurement.* San Diego, CA: United States International University (ERIC Document ED 098 634).

Smilowitz, M. (1985). *Confirming communication in supervisor/subordinate dyads* (Unpublished doctoral dissertation). University of Utah, Salt Lake City.

Spencer, E. E. (1992). *Self-disclosure in family conversational interaction: Communication between parents and older adolescents* (Unpublished doctoral dissertation). University of Texas at Austin, Austin.

Stiles, W. B. (1978). Verbal response modes and dimensions of interpersonal roles: A method of discourse analysis. *Journal of Personality and Social Psychology, 36*, 693–703.

VanLear, C. A. (1985). *The formation of social relationships: A longitudinal comparison of linear and nonlinear models* (Unpublished doctoral dissertation). University of Utah, Salt Lake City.

VanLear, C. A. (1987). The formation of social relationships: A longitudinal study of social penetration. *Human Communication Research, 13*, 299–322.

VanLear, C. A. (1991). Testing a cyclical model of communicative openness in relationship development: Two longitudinal studies. *Communication Monographs, 58*, 337–361.

VanLear, C. A., & Coet, L. (1982, April). *Accepting and rejecting verbal behaviors in relational communication.* Paper presented at the annual meeting of the Northwest Communication Association, Coeur d'Alene, ID.

VanLear, Sheehan, M., Withers, L. A., & Walker, R. A. (2005). AA online: The enactment of supportive computer mediated communication. *Western Journal of Communication, 69*, 5–26.

Villard, K. L., & Whipple, L. J. (1976). *Beginnings in relational communication.* New York: John Wiley.

Walther, J. (1996). Computer-mediated communication: Impersonal, interpersonal, and hyperpersonal interaction. *Communication Research, 23*, 3–43.

Watzlawick, P., Beavin, J. H., & Jackson, D. D. (1967). *Pragmatics of human communication: A study of interactional patterns, pathologies, and paradoxes.* New York: Norton.

Wong, A. C. (2014). *Reliability and validity of the DBT-VLCS: A measure to code DBT validation levels within and individual therapy session* (Unpublished master's thesis). Rutgers, The State University of New Jersey, New Brunswick.

Endnote

1. VanLear and Coet's system was changed on the basis of experience with the system, the empirical results of the 1982 study, and helpful feedback from the late B. Aubrey Fisher.

7

■

RELATIONAL COMMUNICATION CONTROL

L. EDNA ROGERS AND JENNIFER A. CUMMINGS

Historically, a noted lack of attention has been offered to interaction-based theories in comparison with theories focused on the individual, social structure, and cultural levels of analysis (Wiley, 1988). Likewise, in the development of the communication discipline, early programs of study drew largely from rhetorical and speech-oriented models, with models of interpersonal communication borrowed mainly from psychology. Given these beginnings, it is of little surprise that interaction-focused theories of communication were basically missing, with the more established approaches giving prominence to the study of individual acts, traits, and cognitions. But by the 1970s, an influx of different ways of thinking was emerging that potentially offered alternative perspectives for the study of communication.

With the advent of systems theory and its unfolding impact across the sciences came new modes of thought that presented a worldview not of singular events or unilateral cause but of process and pattern. With an epistemological shift from individual entities to relationships, the importance of the inherent, interconnective quality of communication was clearly highlighted. This alternative view underlies the relational pragmatics perspective, with the conceptual focus centered on the formative communication processes characterizing human relations.

In this chapter, we trace the development of the pragmatic relational communication perspective, beginning with its theoretical foundations in systems theory and cybernetics and including the conceptual structuring of relational control as a primary dimension of interaction. The Relational Communication Control Coding System (RCCCS) is detailed as a reliable means of measuring the temporal qualities of relational control and depicting relational level patterns of communication. Finally, we offer a summary of selected findings from pragmatic relational communication studies of the family.

Theoretical Foundations

The primary features of relational control are embedded within the overarching theoretical foundation of the relational pragmatic communication perspective. In particular, the development of the relational communication control approach for studying relationships rests most directly on the guiding principles of system theory, cybernetics, and the conceptual legacy of Gregory Bateson. In combination, this interrelated set of ideas provided the foundation for an epistemology of form (Ellis, 1981), a way of knowing that places primary importance on the study of interaction patterns. And as Dell (1983) noted, when one shifts attention from singular events to shapes, forms, and relations, events become inseparable from the pattern within which they are embedded, and in this sense, of secondary interest while the emergent pattern becomes primary.

With systemic thinking based on patterns of interrelationship, the organizing principles of systems theory (von Bertalanffy, 1968) focus on the interconnection and integration of the system's components that form the larger systemic whole. The most central defining characteristic of a system is the construct of interdependence. *Interdependence* refers to the reciprocal influence of interacting member parts that creates a system, as well as the embedded levels of systems within larger systems. Each system level represents an integrated whole, and at the same time, it is a part of the higher encompassing system. The intertwined, "part/whole" nature of systems (Koestler, 1978) is such that each system level simultaneously influences, and is influenced by, the higher level, yet each systemic level has properties that are not present in other levels. In other words, different levels of analysis provide different types of information and insight; thus, the analysis at one level does not substitute for another level. Bateson (1972) saw the multileveled structuring of systems as representing an ecology of form, such that by increasingly drawing communicative enactments together in more encompassing systemic patterns, more of the holistic quality of the system comes into view.

Cybernetics, which is derived from the Greek for "steersman" or "pilot," complements systems theory by focusing on the feedback control processes by which systems are continuously regulated through the flow of information occurring within the system (Wiener, 1948). From this perspective, social systems are maintained and modified by the cyclic influences that emerge from and guide the members' communicative behaviors. The cybernetic principles of self-organizing systems reflect the ongoing oscillations of continuity and change in the process of maintaining systemic integration. These fluctuating dynamics reflect the adaptive interplay of the members as they continue to "give off" information about themselves and their relationship through the feedback loops of message exchange.

Both systemic and cybernetic thinking were foundational to Bateson's work. From his earliest writing in 1935, when he first described the concepts of schismogenesis, symmetry, and complementarity, he initiated a set of ideas that laid the groundwork for establishing an interactional, process view of communication. The development of this view necessitated not simply a modification of traditional thought but a fully reformulated line of thought. Bateson criticized the sciences for concentrating far too long on the wrong half of the substance-form dichotomy. He argued that a reversal in thinking was necessary for a "new order of communication" to emerge (Bateson, 1951, p. 209). By focusing on form, this new order placed an emphasis on communication behavior, interactive processes, and multileveled pattern formations. An ongoing dialectic of process and form based on the "patterns that connect" was fundamental to Bateson's "ecological wisdom" which was "knowledge of the larger interactive system" (Bateson, 1972, p. 433). The influence of Bateson's ideas for a process-centered approach is clearly visible in shaping the theoretical and analytical stance of relational communication. Furthermore, his conceptualization of the logical distinctions of levels of message meaning was central to the relational control approach for indexing message behaviors and resulting communication patterns. These distinctions rest on the type of information provided from the perspective of different meta levels.

Bateson (1951) proposed that messages simultaneously "give off" two logically distinct levels of meaning: content and relational. He referred to the informational or content meaning of a message as "report" and to the contextualizing meta level of instructional or relational meaning as "command." Thus, the content-report level of meaning provides representational, digital information that is contextualized by the presentational, analogic form of information of the higher relational-command level of meaning. The content level of information indicates what the message is about, whereas the relational level implies how the message is to be interpreted. In depicting patterns of interaction, message content matters, but it is the relational meaning that is given primary emphasis in coding relational control.

Definition of Relational Communication Control

The conceptual definition of relational control builds on the basic premise of the intrinsic connection between communication and relationship, with each interwoven with the other. Communication is the constitutive process by which relational members reciprocally offer definitions of self in relation to other and simultaneously create the ongoing nature of their relationship. In playing-out these everyday enactments, definitions can be accepted, resisted, or modified, with each of the members actively influencing one another with their lines of action. The focus of relational control is centered on the members' negotiation of message definitions as they co-construct their relationship. In the following exchanges, the husband and wife negotiate their relational definition first using resistance and then acceptance.

Wife: I think I do a good job disciplining the kids, don't you?

Husband: Hardly, they walk all over you.

Wife: I like that we discuss things and make decisions together.

Husband: Yeah, we make a good team.

Of the various dimensions on which to map relationships, control provides a central dimension for describing how relationships are vertically structured, that is, how the members stand vis-à-vis one another on the basis of the relational implications of their messages. _Relational control is defined as the temporal, interactive structuring of the regulative function of message exchange._ The relational control coding system is designed to index the processes of directing, constraining, confirming, or delimiting the interactions of the relational members.

Three types of control are identified according to how a message, in relation to the previous message, defines the relationship. Messages that attempt to direct or assert relational rights are designated as _one-up_ control moves, requests or acceptance of another's relational definition represent _one-down_ moves, and neutralizing, leveling control messages are identified as _one-across_ moves. The combination over time of contiguous control moves provides an unfolding picture of the pattern configurations that describe the relationship. The specifics of applying these procedures are described in full in a later section.

Brief History of the Relational Control Coding System

One obvious challenge in developing the relational control coding system was to provide a set of measurement procedures that were commensurate with the theoretical principals of the relational communication perspective. Thus, an interaction-based, observational approach was necessary for operationalizing the temporal, relational qualities of communication. Fortunately, an Argentine journal article published in Spanish by Sluzki and Beavin (1965) provided an initial, informative basis for indexing relational communication control patterns.

The goal of Sluzki and Beavin's (1965) research was to develop a typology for classifying dyads on the basis of their cumulative frequencies of different types of symmetrical and complementary patterns. Two types of message "positions" described by Haley (1963) were used to indicate the relational definitions constituting these patterns; "one-up" messages defined the speaker in a position of being in charge in the relationship, while "one-down" messages defined the speaker in a position of submission. It was emphasized that single messages

acquire relational meaning only in the context of transactional patterns, with the identification of symmetry and complementarity resting on the similarity or difference of the messages exchanged.

Although the purpose of developing the relational control coding system was to index the ongoing, moment-to-moment interaction process, the procedures outlined for identifying different dyadic types on the basis of their overall, prototypical transactional patterns offered important operational insights. Among these, and most influential in formulating subsequent relational control systems, was Sluzki and Beavin's (1965) proposal that contiguous speech turns be analyzed in terms of how the messages are contextually structured (e.g., affirmations, instructions, negotiations, acceptances) (Ellis, Fisher, Drecksel, Hoch, & Werbel, 1976; Rogers, 1972a) and by their grammatical form (e.g., statements, questions) (Rogers, 1972a). The inclusion of these two types of message identification became a central feature for coding relational control. In Rogers and Farace's (1975) finalized coding scheme, both the grammatical format and response mode code categories were modified and expanded. Another important change in subsequent systems was the addition of a control equalizing, one-across message direction that provided an expanded and clearer specification of message control codes allowing that not all messages are either one-up or one-down, but others assert equality and thus make the system exhaustive.

In the early formation of relational coding schemes, the Relational Communication Coding System (Rel/Com) developed by Ellis et al. (1976) was a major addition to the research procedures for indexing interaction processes. The Rel/Com system consists of five types of message control, with the primary coding distinction based on the degree to which a message, in reference to a previous message, is an attempt to restrict or restrain the behavior options of others. The control categories are identified as Dominance ($\uparrow+$), a strong one-up; Structuring ($\uparrow-$), a weak one-up; Equivalence ($\rightarrow$), a one-across; Deference ($\downarrow-$), a weak one-down; and Submission ($\downarrow+$), a strong one-down. A positive feature of this system is the built-in control intensity distinction. With both the Rel/Com and relational control systems based on the relational pragmatic perspective, they share a common core of foundational similarities but, as well, some noted differences.

The main difference between the two systems rests on the use of different coding strategies. The Rel/Com approach assigns one of the five control codes to each message, while the relational control system codes the relational implications of both the grammatical and response mode of a message. These differences can be seen in a comparative analysis of the two systems by O'Donnell-Trujillo (1981). On the basis of coding the same interactions with each system, he found a fairly low correspondence between the message-by-message code comparisons. However, Ayers and Miura (1981) found a higher level of correspondence on the basis of the coding of complementary patterns.

Relational Communication Control Coding System

The means of operationalizing the tenets of relational communication are systematically embodied in the Relational Communication Control Coding System (RCCCS). In application, the RCCCS is used primarily to assess dyadic interaction data. Typically, conversations are audio- or video-recorded in an environment that is familiar and appropriate to the conversation (e.g., in participants' home for family studies and medical clinics for physician/patient studies). Recorded conversations are transcribed according to the RCCCS coding manual (Rogers, 1972b). Verbal messages, as well as nonverbal gestures and paralinguistic expressions, are transcribed in detail using precise notation of exact words, pauses, tone of voice, interruptions, laughter, facial expressions, incomplete utterances, sighs, and so on. These descriptors aid in discerning meaning when coding. Regardless of turn length, conversations are transcribed at the level of the speech turn. Less substantive utterances such as "uh" and "um" are characterized as backchanneling and are distinguished as a speech turn. Completed transcripts should be reviewed by the researcher and compared with audio- or video-recorded interactions to ensure accuracy and consistency in substance and transcription format.

Coder training is critical for coding consistency and thus the reliability of the coding process. Two or three coders should be trained in the coding system. Initially, coders begin by reading the RCCCS training manual, which establishes coding rules and the prioritization of codes and offers coded examples from actual transcripts. When these procedures are clear, a series of pilot transcripts should be used for coders to practice coding together and independently and to test reliability. Cohen's (1960) κ was used to assess intercoder reliability, but many researchers now use other statistics because of known problems with Cohen's κ (see Poole & Hewes, this volume). In most cases, three training sessions are necessary to reach sufficient coder reliability, but researchers may

need to continue to monitor the coding process, answering questions and clarifying coding rules. To maintain acceptable reliability and to prevent coder drift, it is recommended that a reliability assessment be applied from 10% to 15% of the transcripts in the first and second halves of the coding process. Reliability levels should remain consistent throughout the coding process.

Coding matrices illustrate κ calculations and offer a means for evaluating the distribution of code categories across interactions. Using the RCCCS, reliability can be applied, separately or combined, to the code categories of speaker, message format, and response mode or the overall message control direction. The agreement matrix in Table 7.1 provides an example of RCCCS coded results of independent observers coding individual speech turns. The diagonal axis indicates frequencies of intercoder agreement. The frequency and category of disagreement are shown in codes off the diagonal. Agreement matrices are an informative way to identify coding uniformity and divergence and to check for systematic category-by-category unreliability and can be especially useful during the training process for coders. For example, Table 7.1 suggests that these coders are a little more likely to confuse extension and support than other category pairs. Such systematic disagreement can create bias in results, but when spotted, it can inform researchers about where errors are being made.

Coder reliability is essential to establishing the usability and validity of an observational coding system. Numerous studies spanning several decades have verified consistent and relatively high intercoder reliability across a variety of interactional contexts including marriage (Courtright, Millar, & Rogers-Millar, 1979; Rogers, Castleton, & Lloyd, 1996), family therapy (Friedlander & Heatherington, 1989; Heatherington & Friedlander, 1990), manager-subordinate relations (Courtright, Fairhurst, & Rogers, 1989), and medical settings (McNeilis, Thompson, & O'Hair, 1995; Wigginton Cecil, 1998) among others. The κ reliability estimates across these studies and most others have ranged from .74 to .84.

An appropriate question in assessing validity in observational studies is whether the coding system appropriately identifies (i.e., empirically maps) the theoretical domain under study. The RCCCS is foundationally aligned with Poole, Folger, and Hewes's (1987) "generalized observer" mode of observation, in which interaction is examined theoretically and does not rest on the members' perceptions to establish validity. Capturing what behavior means rather than what persons mean (Scheflen, 1974) is a distinguishing characteristic of the relational approach. The coding system (Rogers & Farace, 1975) has evidenced predictive and construct validity (Ayers & Miura, 1981; Bohn & Bock, 1980), representational validity (Heatherington, 1988), and validity in contexts of therapist-client interaction (Tracey & Miars, 1986), psychotherapy (Beyebach & Escudero, 1997), and family therapy (Gaul, Simon, Friedlander, Heatherington, & Cutler, 1991).

The Coding System

As an interaction coding method, the Relational Communication Control Coding System captures the relational control processes of message exchange. Interaction sequences are analyzed by coding each message in an ongoing conversation according to the regulatory function of the message. Thus, the basic unit of analysis is the message, that is, the unitizing event to be coded. The coding process entails three steps. In the first step, a three-digit code is assigned to each message. The first digit indicates the speaker. In husband-wife interaction, for example, the husband may be indicated by a numeral 1 and the wife by a numeral 2. The second digit identifies the grammatical code. The six grammatical codes are (1) assertion, (2) question, (3) successful talk-over, (4) unsuccessful talk-over, (5) noncomplete, and (6) other. The third digit describes the response mode relevant to the preceding message. Response codes are (1) support, (2) nonsupport,

(3) extension, (4) answer, (5) instruction, (6) order, (7) disconfirmation, (8) topic change, (9) self-instruction, and (0) other. A basic assumption is the mutual exclusivity of the code categories. The following exchange demonstrates the application of the three-digit code for each participant's message.

Wife: What can I do differently to help you understand?   121

Husband: You could explain your reasons beforehand.   214

Table 7.2 offers brief descriptions of format and response mode categories. Box 7.1 indicates the order of coding prioritization of response mode categories when a message serves more than one response function. The coding priority decision is based on a continuum from the most constraining, regulative type of response to less constraining responses. For example, if a message is both an order and nonsupportive, the coding priority indicates that the message be coded as an order.

The second step entails coding each interaction in terms of the relational control direction (see Table 7.3). The three-digit codes in Step 1 translate into one of three possible control directions: one-up, one-down, and one-across messages (Rogers, 1972a). A message that asserts control in defining the relationship or interaction is coded as a one-up (↑) move. One-down maneuvers (↓) accept or acquiesce to the other's definition or

Table 7.1 Agreement/Disagreement Matrix for Intercoding of Response Mode

	Coder B									
Coder A	Support	Nonsupport	Extension	Answer	Instruction	Order	Disconfirmation	Topic Change	Self-Instruction	Other
Support	34	0	4	1	0	0	0	0	0	0
Nonsupport	1	22	0	0	2	1	0	0	0	0
Extension	9	1	46	0	1	0	0	1	1	0
Answer	0	2	0	13	0	0	0	0	0	0
Instruction	0	0	0	0	7	1	0	0	0	0
Order	0	1	0	0	1	4	0	0	0	0
Disconfirmation	0	0	0	0	0	0	2	0	0	0
Topic change	0	0	0	1	0	0	0	4	0	1
Self-instruction	1	0	0	0	1	0	0	0	8	0
Other	0	0	0	0	0	0	0	0	0	2

Source: Author.

Note: Observed agreement = 0.82, chance agreement = .20, κ = .78. See Table 7.2 for definitions of the code categories.

Table 7.2 Basic "Format" and "Response Mode" Categories

Format	Response Mode
Assertion: Any completed referential statement expressed in either the declarative or imperative form.	**Support:** Any message that offers or seeks agreement, rejection, demand, resistance, and/or challenge.
Question: Any message that takes an interrogative form (verb-noun order, rising of voice, etc.).	**Nonsupport:** Any message that implies disagreement, rejection, demand, resistance, and/or challenge.
Talk-over: Any interruption or verbal intervention made while another person is speaking.	**Extension:** Any message that continues the flow or theme of the preceding message.
Talk-overs can be coded as "successful" or "unsuccessful" depending on whether the first speaker relinquishes the floor.	**Answer:** Any message that is a definitive response to a question that has substance and/or commitment.
Noncomplete: Any utterance that is initiated but not completed (without a clear format, or response mode).	**Instruction:** Any regulative message that is a qualified suggestion involving clarification, justification, or explanation.
Other: Any utterance that is indistinguishable or grammatically unclassifiable.	**Order:** Any message that is an unqualified command with little or no explanation, usually in the imperative form.
	Disconfirmation: Any message that ignores or bypasses the request (whether explicit or implicit) of the previous message.
	Topic change: Any message that has little continuity with the previous message but no response continuity was requested.
	Self-instruction: Any message that reflects back on self about what and how self should do and feel.
	Other: Any message that has an unclear, unclassifiable response implication.

Source: Author.

assertion. One-across messages (→) are considered moderating or neutralizing in that they neither assert nor accept bids for control but function as control leveling messages. Ultimately, longer sequences of message control moves form the basis for depicting interaction patterns.

Box 7.1
Coding Priority Table for Response Mode (Digit 3)

1. In an ongoing interaction, first consider whether the message is a response switch.

2. If so, determine if it is a *disconfirmation*.

3. If the message is a response switch but not a disconfirmation, it should be coded as a *topic change*.

4. If the message has regulative function, determine first if it is an *order*.

5. If the message is regulative in function but is not an order, code it as an *instruction* if it indicates what and how other should do or feel.

6. If the message instructs self about what and how self should do or feel, then code the message as *self-instruction*.

7. If the message is none of the above, then determine if it is a *nonsupport* response.

8. Next consider if it is a *support* response.

9. Next consider if the message is an *answer*, with the main function of an answer to provide information.

10. Finally, consider if the message is an *extension*. If there is a coding indecision between whether the message is a nonsupport or a support, it should be coded as an extension.

If a message cannot be categorized as any of the above it is coded as *other*. Any indistinguishable message is coded as other.

Source: Author.

Table 7.3 Control Code Assignment for Message Code Categories

Format	Support	Nonsupport	Extension	Answer	Instruction	Order	Disconfirmation	Topic Change	Self-Instruction	Other
Assertion	↓	↑	→	↑	↑	↑	↑	↑	→	→
Question	↓	↑	↓	↑	↑	↑	↑	↑	↓	↓
Successful talk-over	↓	↑	↑	↑	↑	↑	↑	↑	↑	↑
Unsuccessful talk-over	↓	↑	→	↑	↑	↑	↑	↑	→	→
Noncomplete	↓	↑	→	↑	↑	↑	↑	↑	→	→
Other	↓	↑	→	↑	↑	↑	↑	↑	→	→

Source: Author.

In the third step, control direction codes are combined to form sequential pairs from which transactional patterns can be identified. A transact, or one member's utterance followed by another's response, is indexed in terms of the sequential pairing of the members' one-up, one-down, and one-across movements and represents the minimum unit for capturing relational patterns. Depicted in Table 7.4 are the nine relational control transactional patterns, including two forms of complementarity, four types of transition, and three types of symmetry. Table 7.5 displays the coding and sequential pairing of transacts taken from a conversation between a mother and her adolescent daughter.

Control Measures

The RCCCS makes possible a variety of descriptive measures, such as frequency, proportion, and sequence of the three-digit codes and control direction codes. Among these, a basic set of measures includes domineeringness, dominance, and transactional redundancy. *Domineeringness* represents a monadic measure of individual one-up messages and is determined by the proportion of an individual's one-up messages compared with his or her total number of messages (domineeringness = ↑/total number of maneuvers). *Dominance* is a dyadic measure referring to the number of one-up,

Table 7.4 Relational Control Transact Types

Control Direction of Antecedent Message	Control Direction of Consequent Message		
	One-Up ↑	*One-Down ↓*	*One-Across →*
One-up ↑	↑↑ Competitive symmetry	↑↓ Complementarity	↑→ Transition
One-down ↓	↓↑ Complementarity	↓↓ Submissive symmetry	↓→ Transition
One-across →	→↑ Transition	→↓ Transition	→→ Neutralized symmetry

Source: Author.

Table 7.5 Types of Relational Control Transacts

Mother-Daughter Verbal Interaction	Format	Response Mode	Control Code and Transacts	
M: Okay, um, what else? Do you know what else I could really get mad at if I wanted to?	Question	Extension	↓	
				↓↓
D: What?	Question	Extension	↓	
				↓↑
M: Your bedroom!	Assertion	Answer	↑	
				↑↓
D: Oh, I know. *I'm* mad at my bedroom.	Assertion	Support	↓	
				↓↑
M: And, uh *smacks her on the knee*	Noncomplete	Nonsupport	↑	
				↑↑
D: [But you put all that stuff in there.]	Successful Talk-over	Nonsupport	↑	
				↑↑
M: I know, but still! I don't, I hardly ever get mad at your bedroom.	Assertion	Nonsupport	↑	
				↑↓
D: I know, I know.	Assertion	Support	↓	
				↓↑
M: [And look at Hillary's mom! She . . . if she walked in this house and saw your bedroom, what would she do? Tell us, what would she do?]	Successful Talk-over	Nonsupport	↑	

Source: Author.

or control-asserting, messages made by an individual that are responded to by a one-down, or submissive, message. This is classified as a one-up/one-down ($\uparrow\downarrow$) complementary transact and is referred to as a dominance score. The more one-up messages that are returned with a one-down message, the more dominant that person is considered, at least in that relational context.

Additionally, an overall dominance ratio is obtained by dividing one partner's dominance score by the other partner's dominance score, yielding a comparative measure of dyadic dominance. A dominance ratio close to 1 indicates more equivalency in the members' negotiation of definitional rights, whereas a ratio higher than 1 reveals which dyadic member assumes a more dominant position in the interaction. Similar evaluations for support and nonsupport scores and ratios can also be determined.

The *transactional redundancy* measure represents the amount of rigidity or flexibility exhibited in an overall interaction. The measure rests on the distribution of the observed transacts across the nine transactional control categories given in Table 7.4. The less variation in the use of nine transactional types, the more redundant the interaction, and the more variation in the use of the transactional types, the more flexible the interaction. For example, when each of the nine configurations is equally used in an interaction, this represents a pattern of maximum flexibility. At the other extreme, when only one of the transactional categories is used in the interaction, this represents the maximum degree of redundancy. Transactional redundancy is based on the sum of the absolute deviations from equal, that is, random, use of the nine transactional control categories (Courtright, Millar, & Rogers, 1980).

Patterns of Relational Control

A central goal—and challenge—of process-based research is to identify longer sequentially ordered chains of interaction to more fully depict the communication dynamics that characterize the relationships studied. The RCCCS allows a number of longer interaction sequences to be examined on the basis of the transactional patterns of relational symmetry, complementarity, and transition. Symmetrical sequences are those depicting three or more relationally similar control maneuvers such as competitive symmetry ($\uparrow\uparrow\uparrow$), submissive symmetry ($\downarrow\downarrow\downarrow$), and neutralized symmetry ($\rightarrow\rightarrow\rightarrow$). Occurrences of competitive symmetry, marked by a pattern of active opposition, are of particular interest in relational research for their potential to trigger escalating episodes of competitive symmetry. The

following mother-daughter exchange demonstrates the type of one-up sequence that commonly generates extended conflict episodes:

Mother:	So if you know I'm gonna freak out if your chores aren't done, how come you do it? $\uparrow$
Daughter:	I don't wanna talk about that. $\uparrow$
Mother:	Why? $\uparrow$
Daughter:	Cuz I don't. $\uparrow$
Mother:	It's a problem in our relationship. $\uparrow$
Daughter:	Not for me. $\uparrow$

In contrast, leveling negotiation episodes ($\rightarrow\downarrow\rightarrow\downarrow$ and $\downarrow\rightarrow\downarrow\rightarrow$) are of interest in terms of the neutralizing effect they have been found to have on interactions. The regulative function of this pattern is further illustrated in the following sequence ($\uparrow\uparrow\rightarrow\downarrow\rightarrow\downarrow$), in which the interactors quickly move away from a potential conflict to a neutralizing/accepting sequence.

Wife:	So what do you think we can do better? $\uparrow$
Husband:	We've already been over this. $\uparrow$
Wife:	Well, we talked about making a budget. $\rightarrow$
Husband:	Mm hmm, I'm okay with one we work on together. $\downarrow$
Wife:	And one we can stick to. $\rightarrow$
Husband:	Right, both of us. $\downarrow$

Evaluation of these and similar sequential patterns offers greater insight as to the presence and influence of complex configurations of control maneuvers in the relationship.

Summary of Selected Findings Within the Family Context

Relational communication has been carried out in a number of different relational contexts, but a central line of research has focused on marital and family relationships. A series of relational control studies were based on two randomly selected samples of married couples from different urban areas in the Midwest. The first sample included 45 marital dyads and the second 87 dyads. Two types of data were collected during interviews in each couple's home. First, self-report questionnaires concerning aspects of their relationship were completed by each spouse; second, the interaction data were obtained from the couples' audio-recorded discussions of four family-related topics.

In the initial study, control patterns were found to differ by the couples' level of role discrepancy, an index based on the partners' perceived inequity of who should do what in terms of personal, social, and instrumental aspects of their marital relationship (Rogers, 1972a). In comparison with lower role discrepant couples, dyads with higher role discrepancy were found to use more competitive symmetry and significantly more neutralized symmetry. These couples had higher proportions of one-up messages, lower use of one-down messages, and lower levels of satisfaction with their marriage and their communication with one another. These findings were more pronounced when the wife expressed more one-up messages than the husband. In contrast, one-down/one-across transition patterns, particularly with more husband one-down moves, were significantly more characteristic of couples with low role discrepancy. These couples also expressed more support messages, talked about more topics, had more active turn taking, and relied on fewer silences in their conversations than high role discrepant couples.

A subsequent series of studies (Courtright et al., 1979; Millar, Rogers-Millar, & Courtright, 1979; Rogers-Millar & Millar, 1979) provide an integrated set of findings based on the analysis of the two samples referred to earlier. One of the consistent findings was the inverse relationship between wife domineeringness and marital satisfaction on the part of both spouses. When wives expressed high levels of one-up messages, they gave fewer supportive messages to their husbands and, in turn, received fewer supportive messages from their husbands. However, when husbands were more domineering, they offered more supportive statements to their spouses than did domineering wives. Perhaps this was one of the reasons one-up behaviors on the part of the husband did not engender the level of dissatisfaction as was the case with wife domineeringness. Interestingly, domineering wives expressed relatively low levels of nonsupportive messages to their husbands. Thus, the withholding of support rather than the overt expression of nonsupport appears to represent a somewhat veiled form of conflict avoidance by domineering wives, which may further add to a lack of understanding and the lower satisfaction of these couples.

Conversely, patterns of reciprocal or shared dominance, based on the relatively equal exchange

of one-up/one-down complementarity, were positively related to the couples' mutual satisfaction and understanding of one another's perspective. In contrast, unequal dominance, based on rigid complementarity in which one-up assertions by one partner are more consistently accepted by the other, negatively affected the marital relationship. With this pattern, the more dominant member, although reporting feelings of being understood, had lower levels of understanding his or her partner's view than did the less dominant member. These findings offer further support to the long predicted tie between reciprocal complementarity and relational harmony (Bateson, 1958).

To expand the study of relational communication, the next two studies investigated the dimensions of both relational control and nonverbal affect. The sample for the first study consisted of 20 Spanish couples who sought marital counseling at a clinic in northern Spain (Escudero, Rogers, Gutierrez, & Caceres, 1992). The couples were relatively similar in terms of their demographics and their types of marital problems. They did, however, differ significantly in marital adjustment. On the basis of their scores on the Dyadic Adjustment Scale (DAS; Spanier, 1976), the couples formed three groups: a high-adjustment group ($n = 5$, DAS $M = 116$), a medium-adjustment group ($n = 6$, DAS $M = 102$), and a low-adjustment group ($n = 9$, DAS $M = 63$). In the initial counseling session, each couple discussed one of their typical marital problems. The videotaped discussions resulted in 2,300 messages, which were each coded according to the relational control system and Gottman's (1979) Couples Interaction Scoring System procedures for indexing positive, neutral, and negative nonverbal affect. The affect codes are based on facial expression, voice tone, and body position.

Base-rate comparisons of nonverbal affect found that the mean proportions of positive affect steadily declined across the high-, medium-, and low-adjustment groups from 31% to 16% to 3%, while the negative affect proportions were 15% for the high group, 37% for the medium group, and 55% for the low group. One-up control moves were significantly lower for the high group, while more than half of the messages for the medium- and low-adjustment couples were one-up.

The comparative analysis based on the couples' transacts for both control and affect resulted in distinctive group differences. The high-adjustment couples were characterized by positive and neutral affect reciprocity and one-down/one-across transacts. The median group enacted competitive symmetry and nonverbal negativity. However, these couples also enacted one-across symmetry, one-down/one-across transacts, and positive affect reciprocity. With this offsetting mix, the couples' interactions were somewhat volatile without being overly destructive. In contrast, the low-adjustment couples largely engaged in competitive symmetry and negative affect reciprocity. For this group, Bateson's description of the "tyranny of pattern," which may be too strong to break, seems to apply.

The second study (Escudero, Rogers, & Gutierrez, 1997) provides a more comprehensive investigation of control and affect, on the basis of the combined, concurrent control-affect coding of each message. For this study, two groups of couples, clinic and nonclinic, formed the comparative basis of analysis. The sample of 30 Spanish marital dyads included 18 clinic and 12 nonclinic couples. The clinical couples, who were in the initial stage of counseling, were matched demographically with comparable couples from the same area who had never been in marital counseling. The two groups' dyadic adjustment scores differed significantly, with means of 76 for the clinical group and 110 for the nonclinic group.

The couples' videotaped discussions of their marital problems resulted in a total of 5,389 messages. On the basis of the control-affect message codes, the differences between the two groups of couples were particularly pronounced. Only 4% of the clinical couples' one-up messages were positive in affect (52 of 1,253 one-up messages), with 71% (890) expressed with negative affect. For nonclinical couples, 15% of their one-up messages were positive (135 of 895 one-up messages), 30% were negative, and 55% were neutral in affect. For the clinical group, even 33% of their one-down messages were negative in comparison with 3% by nonclinical couples.

Turning to the heart of the study, the sequential analysis of the interaction data resulted in more specific, significant pattern comparisons. A competitive, one-up/negative affect pattern of symmetry was activated by both couple groups, but the nonclinic couples also enacted two counterbalancing patterns, one-up/neutral affect and one-across/neutral affect symmetry. Another noted difference between the two groups was the number and type of one-across transition sequences activated by the nonclinical couples. From a total of 10 transition patterns, 7 were combinations of one-across and one-down message sequences with all 7 expressed with positive or neutral nonverbal affect. In contrast, of the 5 transition patterns activated in the clinical group, 2 were combinations of one-up and one-across messages, and 3 were negative in affect. These differences are in line

with previous findings of the close association between the one-across/one-down pattern sequences and marital satisfaction.

To examine the potential escalation of the competitive, one-up/negative affect pattern of symmetry activated in both groups of couples, the analytical procedures of Revenstorf, Vogel, Hahlweg, and Schindler (1980) were used. With this method, the unconditional probability of a one-up/negative message was compared (using z scores) with the conditional probability of a one-up/negative message occurring, given previous sequences of two, three, or more one-up/negative messages, until no significance was found. The results of this analysis found the escalating chain of one-up/negative symmetry in the clinical group to be stronger (i.e., higher probabilities), with longer sequences of occurrence than in the nonclinical group. With this type of transaction, the likelihood of moving to a three-message exchange for the clinical couples was .58, compared with .37 for nonclinical couples, and remained high between .52 and .66 until dropping off after a total exchange of eight messages. The nonclinical probability remained lower and ended with a four-message chain. These differences reinforce one of the most telling characteristics of troubled couples of getting trapped in destructive patterns of communication, while the nonclinical couples can more readily move into a different, moderating type of interaction pattern such as the one-across/one-down with positive or neutral affect.

More recently, relational control has been examined in relationships between mothers and adolescent daughters (Cummings, 2011). Following procedures similar to those previously described, 40 mother–adolescent daughter dyads completed questionnaires measuring their relational satisfaction, closeness, and support and were then videotaped at home discussing four relationship-related topics. Conversations were transcribed and coded according to the RCCCS, with an average of 424 transacts per dyad and 16,962 transactions in total. The interaction data were analyzed using Bakeman and Quera's (1995) sequential analysis procedures.

Overall, daughters were more domineering and dominant, while mothers were more submissive. One-up and one-down messages by mothers were typically met with a one-up response from daughters, a pattern that was strongest among lower satisfied pairs. Across relationships, support was more prevalent than nonsupport, and mothers in higher satisfied relationships were particularly supportive. Leveling, or neutralizing, messages prompted leveling responses in both higher and lower satisfied groups. The key finding that distinguished higher from lower satisfied mother-daughter pairs was the tendency for higher satisfaction daughters to respond to one-up messages from their mothers with one-down responses, whereas lower satisfaction daughters more commonly responded with one-up responses.

In addition to RCCCS analysis, this study implemented a qualitative approach in which mother-daughter communication patterns were examined through dyadic discourse analysis and comparison of conversational patterns and responses. Following Fairhurst's (1993) model for qualitative discourse analysis, videotaped conversations and transcripts were reviewed for examples and counterexamples of distinguishing features of behavior, discourse, and pattern and key conversational occurrences. Using RCCCS coded data, sequential graphs of ongoing relational interactions were constructed to systematically identify notable transactional patterns and episodes in the conversation. Conclusions drawn from case comparison examined qualitative distinctions between groups and attempted to depict a range of behaviors and patterns that characterized this set of mother and adolescent daughter interactions in terms of relational control movement. Relevant to the key finding noted above, most mother one-up/daughter one-down exchanges among higher satisfied pairs revealed positive and relationship-affirming content, tone, and effects, while the rarity of the mother one-up/daughter one-down exchange between lower satisfied pairs was indicative of a lesser degree of openness, trust, and positivity.

Conclusions

The central purpose of this chapter was to provide a detailed description of the Relational Communication Control Coding System. The system was designed to put into action the foundational premises of the pragmatic, relational communication perspective to the study of interpersonal relations. Thus, the goal was to develop an interaction-based set of procedures for mapping the temporal processes and patterns of communication that are descriptive of relationships. The coding system rests on the premises that communication is an interactive, formative process, that relationships are co-constructed, and that the relational dimension of control is central for describing how relationships are structured.

On the basis of these principles, the coding system provides a set of methodological procedures appropriate for carrying out process research. The established evidence of the reliability and validity of these observational procedures give credence to the utility of this approach for identifying communication patterns. A noted feature of the coding system is the variety of measures that can be derived from the coded database, such as the message control index of domineeringness but, as well, measures based on the specific grammatical and response codes, such as the proportion of support messages in comparison with nonsupport, and similar indices, for example, of talk-overs or disconfirmation. Depending on the interests of a researcher, this type of information may be a useful extension for describing different aspects of an interaction.

Even though the range of coded messages can be used for analysis, the primary purpose and value of the Relational Communication Control Coding System remains focused on capturing the ongoing formation of relational level patterns of interaction. The coding system, since its development in the early 1970s, has been used in a wide range of relationship studies. On the basis of these research efforts, the coding procedures have been found to be applicable across different types of relationships, different languages, and cultural contexts.

References

Ayers, J., & Miura, S. Y. (1981). Construct and predictive validity of instruments for coding relational control. *Western Journal of Speech Communication, 45,* 159–171.

Bakeman, R., & Quera, V. (1995). *Analyzing interaction: Sequential analysis with SDIS and GSEQ.* New York: Cambridge University Press.

Bateson, G. (1951). Information and codification: A philosophical approach. In J. Ruesch & G. Bateson (Eds.), *Communication: The social matrix of psychiatry* (pp. 168–211). New York: Norton.

Bateson, G. (1958). *Naven.* 2nd ed. Stanford, CA: Stanford University Press.

Bateson, G. (1972). *Steps to an ecology of mind.* New York: Ballantine.

Beyebach, M., & Escudero, V. (1997). Therapeutic interaction and dropout: Measuring relational communication in solution-focused therapy. *Journal of Family Therapy, 19,* 173–212.

Bohn, E., & Bock, D. G. (1980, November). *A study of the predictive validity of the relational control paradigm.* Paper presented at the Speech Communication Association convention, New York.

Cohen, J. (1960). A coefficient of agreement for nominal scales. *Educational and Psychological Measurement, 20,* 37–46.

Courtright, J. A., Fairhurst, G. T., & Rogers, L. E. (1989). Interaction patterns in organic and mechanistic systems. *Academy of Management Journal, 32,* 773–802.

Courtright, J. A., Millar, F. E., & Rogers, L. E. (1980). Message control intensity as a predictor of transactional redundancy. In D. Nimmo (Ed.), *Communication Yearbook 4* (pp. 199–216). New Brunswick, NJ: Transaction.

Courtright, J. A., Millar, F. E., & Rogers-Millar, L. E. (1979). Domineeringness and dominance: Replication and expansion. *Communication Monographs, 46,* 179–192.

Cummings, J. A. (2011). *Relational communication in mother-adolescent daughter interaction* (Unpublished doctoral dissertation). University of Utah, Salt Lake City.

Dell, P. (1983). Researching the family theories of schizophrenia: An exercise in epistemological confusion. In D. Bagarozzi, A. Jurich, & R. Jackson (Eds.), *Marital and family therapy: New perspectives in theory, research and practice* (pp. 236–261). New York: Human Sciences Press.

Ellis, D. (1981). The epistemology of form. In C. Wilder & J. Weakland (Eds.), *Rigor and imagination: Essays from the legacy of Gregory Bateson* (pp. 215–230). New York: Praeger.

Ellis, D. G., Fisher, B. A., Drecksel, G. L., Hoch, D. D., & Werbel, W. S. (1976). *Rel/Com: A system for analyzing relational communication* (Unpublished coding manual), University of Utah, Salt Lake City.

Escudero, V., Rogers, L. E., & Gutierrez, E. (1997). Patterns of relational control and nonverbal affect in clinic and nonclinic couples. *Journal of Personal and Social Relationships, 14,* 5–29.

Escudero, V., Rogers, L. E., Gutierrez, E., & Caceres, J. (1992). *Relational control and nonverbal affect in marital conflict: An exploratory study.* Paper presented at the International Communication Association meetings, Miami, FL.

Fairhurst, G. T. (1993). The leader-member exchange patterns of women leaders in industry: A discourse analysis. *Communication Monographs, 60,* 321–351.

Friedlander, M. L., & Heatherington, L. (1989). Analyzing relational control in family therapy interviews. *Journal of Counseling Psychology, 36,* 139–148.

Gaul, R., Simon, L., Friedlander, M. L., Heatherington, L., & Cutler, C. (1991). Correspondence of family therapists' perceptions with the FRCCCS coding rules for triadic interactions. *Journal of Marital and Family Therapy, 17,* 379–394.

Gottman, J. (1979). *Marital interaction: Experimental investigations.* New York: Academic Press.

Haley, J. (1963). *Strategies of psychotherapy.* New York: Grune & Stratton.

Heatherington, L. (1988). Coding relational control in counseling: Criterion validity. *Journal of Counseling Psychology, 35,* 41–56.

Heatherington, L., & Friedlander, M. L. (1990). Complementarity and symmetry in family therapy communication. *Journal of Counseling Psychology, 37,* 261–286.

Koestler, A. (1978). *Janus: A summing up.* New York: Vintage.

McNeilis, K. S., Thompson, T. L., & O'Hair, H. D. (1995). Implications of relational communication for therapeutic discourse. In G. H. Morris & R. J. Chanaile (Eds.), *The talk of the clinic: Explorations in the analysis of medical and therapeutic discourse* (pp. 291–313). Hillsdale, NJ: Lawrence Erlbaum.

Millar, F. E., Rogers-Millar, L. E., & Courtright, J. (1979). Relational control and dyadic understanding: An exploratory predictive regression model. In D. Nimmo (Ed.), *Communication Yearbook 3* (pp. 213–224). New Brunswick, NJ: Transaction.

O'Donnell-Trujillo, N. (1981). Relational communication: A comparison of coding systems. *Communication Monographs, 48,* 91–105.

Poole, M. S., Folger, J. P., & Hewes, D. E. (1987). Analyzing interpersonal interaction. In M. E. Roloff & G. R. Miller (Eds.), *Interpersonal processes: New directions in communication research* (pp. 220–256). Newbury Park, CA: Sage.

Revenstorf, D., Vogel, B., Wegener, C., Hahlweg, K., & Schindler, L. (1980). Escalation phenomena in interaction sequences: An empirical comparison of distressed and nondistressed couples' behavior. *Analysis and Modification, 2,* 97–116.

Rogers, L. E. (1972a). *Dyadic systems and transactional communication in a family context* (Unpublished doctoral dissertation). Michigan State University, East Lansing.

Rogers, L. E. (1972b). *Relational communication control coding manual* (Unpublished manuscript). Michigan State University, East Lansing.

Rogers, L. E., Castleton, A., & Lloyd, S. (1996). Relational control and physical aggression in satisfying marital relationships. In D. Cahn & S. Lloyd (Eds.), *Family violence: A communication perspective* (pp. 218–239). Thousand Oaks, CA: Sage.

Rogers, L. E., & Farace, R. V. (1975). Analysis of relational communication in dyads: New measurement procedures. *Human Communication Research, 1,* 222–239.

Rogers-Millar, L. E., & Millar, F. E. (1979). Domineeringness and dominance: A transaction view. *Human Communication Research, 5,* 239–246.

Scheflen, A. E. (1974). *How behavior means.* Garden City, NY: Anchor.

Sluzki, C., & Beavin, J. (1965). Simetria y complementaridad: Una definicion operacional y una tipologia de parejas [Symmetry and complementarity: An operational definition and a typology of couples]. *Acta Psiquiatrica y Psicologia de America Latina, 11,* 321–330.

Spanier, G. B. (1976). Measuring dyadic adjustment: New scales for assessing the quality of marriage and similar dyads. *Journal of Marriage and the Family, 38,* 15–28.

Tracey, T. J., & Miars, R. D. (1986). Interpersonal control in psychotherapy: A comparison of two definitions. *Journal of Clinical Psychology, 42,* 585–595.

von Bertalanffy, L. (1968). *General systems theory: Foundations, development, applications.* New York: Braziller.

Wiener, N. (1948). *Cybernetics.* Cambridge, MA: MIT Press.

Wigginton Cecil, D. (1998). Relational control patterns in physician-patient clinical encounters: Continuing the conversation. *Health Communication, 10,* 125–150.

Wiley, N. (1988). The micro-macro problem in social theory. *Sociological Theory, 6,* 254–261.

8

■

CODING COMFORTING BEHAVIOR FOR VERBAL PERSON CENTEREDNESS

WENDY SAMTER AND ERINA L. MACGEORGE

The ability to comfort effectively is a vital communication skill with far-reaching consequences. Recipients of sensitive comforting messages experience greater reductions in emotional distress and improved capacity to cope with their problems than do recipients of less sensitive efforts (Jones & Guerrero, 2001; Jones & Wirtz, 2006). Over time, receiving higher quality comforting in response to stressors can reduce the health impact of emotional distress, promote self-esteem and self-care, and motivate healthy behavior (for a review, see MacGeorge, Feng, & Burleson, 2011). Not surprisingly, given these benefits of effective comfort, individuals who exhibit greater skill at comforting are seen as more sensitive, helpful, and attractive, enjoy greater levels of peer acceptance, and experience less loneliness than their counterparts who are less effective (Burleson & Samter, 1996; Samter & Burleson, 1990; Samter, Burleson, & Basden-Murphy, 1989). Indeed, the provision of comfort constitutes a central expectation and activity in close relationships (Xu & Burleson, 2001), and comforting is a highly rated communication skill in those relationships (Holmstrom, 2009; Samter & Burleson, 2005).

For communication scholars, the most influential way of representing variation in the skillfulness or sophistication of comforting behavior regards the construct of *verbal person centeredness* (VPC). Historically, this construct was referenced as person centeredness, but it has more recently been labeled in ways that acknowledge the focus on verbal rather than nonverbal behavior (Jones & Guerrero, 2001). In constructivist theory, person centeredness concerns

the degree to which messages reflect "an awareness of and adaptation to the subjective, affective, and relational aspects of communicative contexts" (Burleson & Caplan, 1998, p. 249). Person centeredness is not limited to comforting behavior, and indeed has been conceptualized and assessed with regard to a wide range of communicative functions, including persuasion (Clark & Delia, 1979), parental discipline (Applegate, 1980), explanatory discourse (Rowan, 1988), conflict management (Samter & Ely, 1985), and ego support (McCullough & Burleson, 2012). However, when used to describe comforting messages, VPC captures variation in the sensitivity of response to a distressed person's emotional state, perspective, and situation. As detailed in multiple sources over more than three decades (for reviews, see Burleson, 2003; Burleson & MacGeorge, 2002; MacGeorge et al., 2011), comforting messages low in person centeredness deny another person's feelings and perspectives; comforting messages moderate in person centeredness implicitly acknowledge and legitimize another's feelings and perspectives; and comforting messages high in person centeredness explicitly acknowledge, elaborate, and legitimize the other's feelings and perspectives (Applegate, 1980; Burleson, 1982).

As the study of supportive communication has matured, scholars have increasingly recognized that the effective exchange of support is not simply a matter of saying one right thing but of successfully negotiating interactions (MacGeorge et al., 2011). Multiple challenges occur in "capturing" supportive interactions for research purposes, not the least of which is that people's conversations about their problems and feelings are usually regarded as private. However, scholars of supportive communication have become increasingly good at eliciting naturalistic support interactions in the laboratory context (see, e.g., Jones & Wirtz, 2006; MacGeorge, Guntzviller, Hanasono, & Feng, 2013). We anticipate that the increased emphasis on studying communication with interaction data will motivate researchers to obtain access to support interactions in settings where they frequently occur (e.g., advising appointments, support groups, doctors' offices; Limberg & Locher, 2012).

We acknowledge at the outset that most coding for VPC has been conducted on written messages or tape-recorded monologues (see Table 8.1). Nonetheless, such coding has been successfully (and usefully) accomplished with interaction data (Burleson & Samter, 1985; Samter & Burleson, 1984). Given the increasing numbers of scholars examining supportive interaction behaviors, we present the present chapter to assist researchers who want to assess VPC as it occurs in interactions, along with those whose research goals can be met with less naturalistic data. In the following sections, we sketch the historical roots of person centeredness as it relates to the coding of comforting behavior, overview two broad types of research examining person-centered comforting messages, and discuss evidence of validity and reliability in coding to date. We then present guidelines for choosing a unit of analysis, developing a "localized" coding manual, training coders, and coding. We end with a brief discussion of current issues in the study of VPC.

Person Centeredness: A Conceptual History

Originally developed by Delia and his colleagues (Clark & Delia, 1979; Delia & O'Keefe, 1979) as part of the larger theory of constructivism, the concept of VPC emerged from the integration of key elements from several research paradigms including the sociolinguistic theory of Bernstein (1975), the developmental theories of Piaget (1926) and Werner (1957), and the Chicago school of symbolic interactionism (Blumer, 1969; Goffman, 1967; Mead, 1934).

Bernstein (1975) identified two types of linguistic codes, *restricted* and *elaborated*, each of which reflects fundamentally different orientations to the social world rooted in cultural (i.e., socioeconomic) differences. Among restricted-code users, an assumption exists of psychological similarity. Thus, individuals have little need to elaborate on thoughts,

feelings, intentions, and so on, because speech is governed by culturally shared definitions, role expectations, and behavioral norms, that is, by the *positions* individuals occupy. In contrast, an elaborated code reflects a person-centered view of the social world in which other people are seen as psychologically dissimilar and distant. This dissimilarity, in turn, leads to the belief that relationships are based on negotiated and emergent understandings that can be achieved only through the explicit articulation of intentions, motives, lines of reasoning, and so on.

Bernstein's (1975) analysis of sociolinguistic codes contributed several important ideas to the conceptualization of person centeredness. As Burleson (1987) argued, sociolinguistic codes provide a way of conceptualizing major qualitative differences in communication (i.e., position vs. person centered), as well as a detailed understanding "of how such qualitative differences are tied to underlying conceptions of persons, relationships, and the activity of communication" (p. 312). However, unlike Bernstein, who saw the linguistic codes as two exclusive categories of speech, constructivists maintained that the codes were better viewed as poles anchoring a continuum of behavior. They further argued that although Bernstein's analysis illuminated large-scale cultural differences in communication (in this case, defined in terms of socioeconomic strata), it did not explain individual differences in communicative behavior that could be observed among people.

Constructivists turned to cognitive-developmental theories to address individual differences. An important theme within various strains of these theories is that, with development, children move toward increasingly socialized (Piaget, 1926) and autonomous (Werner, 1957) speech that enables them to communicate with people different from themselves. Piaget and Werner maintained that such forms of autonomous speech connect to underlying developments in cognitive structures that allow youngsters to represent and attend to relevant features of people and contexts. Thus, as children develop the capacity to take another person's perspective, they are also increasingly likely to produce messages that adapt to the unique needs and characteristics of the listener. Put differently, with development, a maturing child becomes a more and more "flexible, appropriate, and effective communicator" (Burleson, 1987, p. 313). Thus, with the infusion of ideas from theorists such as Piaget and Werner, person centeredness became viewed as a *developmental accomplishment*, predicted by the sophistication and integration of underlying cognitive structures.

The third key ingredient in the constructivist analysis of person centeredness came from symbolic interactionists. Scholars such as Mead (1934), Goffman (1967), and Blumer (1969) maintained that communication is strategic, contextual, and multifunctional, and each of these features shaped the conceptualization of person centeredness in important ways. For instance, constructivists argued that because communication is undertaken to accomplish a particular instrumental goal (i.e., that it is strategic), person centeredness ought to manifest itself differently according to the particular objective being pursued. In other words, what person centeredness "looks like" when a speaker attempts to alleviate another's emotional distress will differ from what it "looks like" when he or she tries to persuade someone to undertake some action (Clark & Delia, 1977). Constructivists further maintained that if messages are shaped by, among others, cultural, institutional, and performance factors (i.e., that communication is contextual), then only moderate associations should be observed between cognitive development and communicative ability because cognition represents one of many influences on behavior. Finally, the multifunctional character of communication led constructivists to the conclusion that, in addition to reflecting primary instrumental aims, person centeredness should also capture the extent to which secondary goals associated with identity management are pursued by interactants.

With respect to comforting, then, these three historical roots led to the construction of a coding hierarchy in which messages are arrayed within three major divisions reflecting the degree of person centeredness, here conceptualized as *the extent to which the feelings and perspective of a distressed other are acknowledged, elaborated, and legitimized*. Within Major Division 1, comforting messages low in person centeredness deny another person's feelings and perspectives. Such denial can take the form of directly criticizing the other's feelings (Level 1; e.g., "It's silly to feel so bad."), explicitly challenging the legitimacy of those emotions (Level 2; e.g., "It's really not that big of a deal."), or telling the other how he or she should act or feel (Level 3; e.g., "Just try to forget about this and move on."). Comforting messages scored in Major Division 2 are moderate in person centeredness, implicitly acknowledging and legitimizing another's feelings and perspectives. Such acknowledgment can occur via attempts to divert the other person's attention from the distressful situation and associated feelings (Level 4; e.g., "Let's go out for a drink to take your mind off things."), through expressions of understanding

and sympathy (Level 5; e.g., "I'm so sorry this happened to you."), or via the provision of a non-feeling-centered explanation of the situation intended to reduce the partner's distress (Level 6; e.g., "Sounds like a typical guy. Maybe he just needs some time to himself."). Finally, in Major Division 3, messages high in person centeredness explicitly acknowledge, elaborate, and legitimize the other's feelings and perspectives; in other words, these strategies focus on the target's thoughts, feelings, interpretations of, and reactions to the distressful event. Messages scored within Level 7 acknowledge the other's emotional state (e.g., "It hurts so much, though, when you like someone."), while messages coded at Level 8 provide an elaborated acknowledgment and explanation of the target's feelings (e.g., "Well, I would get your thoughts together and go back and talk. Because until you get things real settled between you, there's no way for you to make any plans. I mean I'm just a real advocate for talking things out and getting things out in the open."). Messages coded at Level 9 not only elaborate and legitimize the other's distress, but they also seek to foster an understanding of the hurtful event by encouraging the other to view the situation and its attendant feelings within a broader context (Applegate, 1980; Burleson, 1982). For example, "You put so much into this relationship, and you love him! What a mess. . . . Girl, I am so sorry you are hurting. I am so angry for you too. You know, we are also young. I know that's not what you want to hear. But we are. We have time on our side. There'll be lots of other guys, and someone special who will treat you much, much better. Like you deserve. And you will be strong in yourself because you lived through this" (for additional examples of messages at different levels, see MacGeorge, Gillihan, Samter, & Clark, 2003; MacGeorge & Wilkum, 2012).

Importantly, the integration of sociolinguistic theory, cognitive-developmental theory, and symbolic interactionism did not simply frame the nature and character of person-centered messages but rather suggested that they were structurally and developmentally more sophisticated than position-centered strategies. With respect to comforting messages in particular, Burleson and Samter (1985) explained,

> [strategies] scored within the higher levels of the hierarchy are regarded as structurally and developmentally more sophisticated than those scored at lower levels because the relatively explicit statement, elaboration, and legitimation of the

other's feelings presumably require more advanced cognitive abilities through which the other's perspective can be recognized, internally represented, coordinated with other relevant perspectives, and integrated with the speaker's understanding of the situation. (p. 9)

Stated differently, person-centered comforting strategies represent *formally better* attempts to alleviate another's emotional distress than do position-centered efforts. Moreover, the explicit acknowledgment, validation, and elaboration of another's feelings characteristic of person-centered messages frames an approach to providing comfort that is qualitatively different from that embodied in position-centered strategies. For instance, as Burleson and Samter argued, compared with position-centered messages, person-centered comforting strategies project a greater degree of involvement with the distressed other, adopting a listener-centered (vs. a speaker-centered) orientation; are more evaluatively neutral, describing and explicating feelings (rather than evaluating them); are more feeling centered, focusing on the proximal (as opposed to distal) causes of a distressed state; are more accepting of the distressed other, legitimizing his or her point of view (rather than evaluating it); and contain a cognitively oriented explanation of the feelings being experienced that may help the target obtain some psychological distance from the negative affect. Moreover, Burleson and Goldsmith (1998) argued convincingly that person-centered comforting efforts also foster conversationally induced narratives that help others reappraise a distress-invoking situation (Jones & Wirtz, 2006).

Research on Verbal Person Centeredness: Goals, Methods, and Findings

Scholars have contributed to two major bodies of research that examine verbal person centeredness, one in which VPC is the dependent variable and a second in which VPC is a principle predictor. The first body of research stems from the cognitive-developmental and sociolinguistic roots of constructivist theory and has focused on demonstrating that VPC is predicted by sociocognitive, developmental, and demographic factors such as cognitive complexity, empathy, expressivity, gender, and age (Burleson, 2003; Burleson, Holmstrom, & Gilstrap, 2005). This body of research also includes studies focused on how support providers interpret and respond to variation in characteristics of the support seeker, such as level of distress and physical

attractiveness (Feng, Li, & Li, 2013b; Hale, Tighe, & Mongeau, 1997), and the situation, including responsibility for the problem and time since the distressing event (MacGeorge et al., 2003; MacGeorge & Wilkum, 2012). In this work, comforting behavior is typically elicited in response to hypothetical scenarios, and research participants' written or spoken messages are then classified using a coding system first developed by Applegate (1980) and Burleson (1982) and subsequently elaborated and more broadly disseminated by Samter and Burleson (1984) and Burleson and Samter (1985).

The second body of research derives from the symbolic interactionist component of constructivism and focuses on demonstrating the link between VPC and comforting behavior effectiveness. Consistent with constructivist theory, substantial evidence indicates that VPC predicts the perceived helpfulness, effectiveness, sensitivity, and quality of comforting messages (Burleson, 2003; High & Dillard, 2012), as well as actual effectiveness in the form of affect improvement (Jones, 2004; Jones & Wirtz, 2006). A recent meta-analysis of 23 studies with publication dates between 1985 and 2010 ($N = 4,782$) found an average effect size for VPC of $r = .61$ (High & Dillard, 2012), and indeed no published study exists in which VPC has failed to find a significant, positive effect on measures of effectiveness. The influence of person-centered messages on perceived effectiveness is moderated by several factors, including sex differences, ethnicity, and cognitive complexity (Bodie & Burleson, 2008; Burleson et al., 2009), but these moderating effects are generally small. Importantly, they do not alter the main effect, in which evaluations of high-person-centered (HPC) messages are more positive than those of moderate-person-centered (MPC) messages, which are in turn more positive than evaluations of low-person-centered (LPC) messages. (For example, men tend to evaluate LPC messages more positively than women, but they still evaluate LPC messages less positively than MPC or HPC messages.)

In most investigations within this tradition, participants read scenarios describing a distressed target's situation, and VPC is manipulated within comforting messages or dialogues created by the researchers. Some studies have manipulated VPC using confederates trained to perform messages at varying levels of VPC in response to participants' problem disclosures (Jones & Guerrero, 2001; Jones & Wirtz, 2006). An even smaller group of investigations has tested the effects of VPC for comforting behavior produced in laboratory interaction or posted online. In these studies, comforting behavior has either been given a global rating of person centeredness by trained raters, or it has been coded (Burleson & Samter, 1985; Hersh, 2011; Samter & Burleson, 1984).

As this brief review indicates, VPC has been operationalized in multiple ways, but most typically as researcher-manipulated messages in studies focused on message outcomes and as coded behavior in research focused on message production. Global ratings to assess VPC over the course of an interaction are a relatively recent development that will be discussed later with regard to measurement validity and alternatives (or additions) to coding. For researchers intending to study naturally occurring or naturalistic comforting behavior in interactions, coding is an essential tool for examining VPC. We begin the next section of the chapter with a discussion of existing coding manuals and their application, along with evidence for validity and reliability, and then turn to a discussion of coding,

with specific attention to coding for VPC in natural or naturalistic interaction.

Coding for Person Centeredness

The principal models for coding VPC involve coding manuals developed by Samter and Burleson (1984) and Samter (1989), both of which were based on materials originally created and used by Applegate (1980) and later refined by Burleson (1982). Samter and Burleson developed the initial coding procedure for application to interactions between participants and confederates trained to feign distress about a problem. The later manual was developed to code written responses to hypothetical scenarios. Researchers from many universities studying comforting behavior within a variety of contexts have adopted these procedures with minor alterations (see Table 8.1). The studies provide evidence supporting the validity and reliability of the coding process.

Table 8.1 Publications Based on Data Coded for Verbal Person Centeredness

Authors	Publication Year	Data	Stimulus	Coding Manual or Procedure	Reliability
Angell	1998	Written messages	Scenario (1)	Based on Burleson (1982)	$\kappa = .87$ (4 sublevels only)
Applegate	1980	Spoken messages	Scenario (1)	As stated in article	$r = .85$
Burleson	1983	Written messages	Scenario (4)	Based on Applegate (1980)	$r = .90$
Burleson	1984	Spoken messages (transcribed)	Scenario (4)	Based on Applegate (1980)	$r = .94$
Burleson et al.	1986	Spoken messages (coded from tape recordings)	Scenario (2)	Based on Applegate (1980), Ritter (1979)	$r = .93$ (4 sublevels only)
Burleson and Samter	1996	Written messages	Scenario (1)	Samter (1989)	$\kappa = .83$
Clinton and Hancock	1991	Written messages	Scenario (1)	Based on Burleson (1984)	$r = .94$
Feng et al.	2014	Written messages	Scenario (2)	Based on MacGeorge et al. (2003)	$ICC = .80$
Hale et al.	1997	Written messages	Scenario (4)	Based on Burleson (1984)	$\kappa = .80$
Hersh	2005	Written messages	Posted to online support group	Based on Burleson (1982)	$\kappa = .74$ $r = .90$

(Continued)

Table 8.1 (Continued)

Authors	Publication Year	Data	Stimulus	Coding Manual or Procedure	Reliability
Hoffner and Haefner	1997	Spoken messages (transcribed)	Recalled interaction (1) Scenario (1)	Based on Burleson (1982)	κ = .81 (recall), .79 (scenario)
Burleson et al.	2005	Written messages	Scenarios (5)	Based on Applegate (1980), Burleson (1982)	ICC = .82
MacGeorge and Wilkum	2012	Written messages	Scenario (1)	Adapted from Samter (1989)	κ = .78
MacGeorge et al.	2002, 2003 (same data)	Written messages	Scenarios (6)	Samter (1989)	ICC = .82
MacGeorge et al.	2015	Interaction	Naturalistic interaction	Adapted from Samter (1989)	Krippendorff's α = .79 (initial), .73 (end)
Samter and Burleson	1984	Interaction	Confederate disclosure	Samter (1983)	% agree = 94
Burleson and Samter (same data)	1985 (Study 1)				
Samter	2002	Written messages	Scenarios (3)	Samter (1989)	κ = .83
Tamborini et al.	1993	Interaction	Confederate disclosure	Based on Burleson and Samter (1985)	ICC = .78
Weger and Polcar	2002	Written messages	Scenarios (2)	Based on Burleson (1983)	ICC = .77
Winters and Waltman	1997	Written messages	Scenarios (4)	Based on Applegate (1980), Burleson (1982)	r values ranging from .81 to .99 for different scenarios
Zimmerman and Applegate	1992	Written messages	Scenarios (2)	Based on Applegate (1978), Burleson (1982)	ICC = .84

Source: Author.

Note: ICC = intraclass correlation coefficient.

Validity

Measurement validity is the issue of match between a measurement and the construct it is intended to measure (Levine, 2011). If a coding procedure does not assess variation in the construct of interest, it is invalid and consequently not useful. Because measurement validity has several dimensions, evidence about measurement validity takes a variety of forms. *Content validity* refers to whether the measurement assesses the construct in its complete breadth. In the case of VPC, the descriptions and examples of major and minor levels in both unpublished coding manuals (Feng et al., 2013a; Samter, 1983, 1989) and published versions of coding categories (Feng et al., 2013b; MacGeorge et al., 2003) appear to be a good match to the theory's central distinctions between ways of responding to another person's emotional state (i.e., rejection, implicit acceptance, and explicit validation).

Structural validity refers to the match between the number of constructs a researcher intends to measure and the structure of the measurement instrument. As with all coding schemes, considering structural validity highlights distinctions made in coding and how those distinctions are handled in analyses. Both Applegate's (1980) original coding scheme and Samter's (1983, 1989) coding manuals distinguish three major levels of person centeredness (high, moderate, and low), each divided into three minor levels, for a total of nine distinctions. Researchers examining VPC as a dependent variable have typically coded for nine levels and often report analyses that preserve these distinctions (MacGeorge et al., 2003). However, as previously noted, most researchers examining the effectiveness of VPC (i.e., research treating VPC as a predictor variable) have compared manipulated rather than coded VPC (with the exceptions of Burleson & Samter, 1985; MacGeorge et al., 2015) and conducted their comparisons at the three major levels. High and Dillard (2012) meta-analyzed the three existing studies that compared the perceived effectiveness of VPC across all nine levels and suggested on this basis that messages at Levels 5 and 6 may not be differentiable in impact, and that the same may be true for Levels 8 and 9. However, because of differentiable impact for the remaining minor levels, they also questioned the practice of comparing only three levels in analysis. Clearly, High and Dillard's analysis suggests continued careful attention to the structural validity of coding at nine levels and analyzing at three. Yet, because the nine-level distinction is theoretically grounded, multiple research teams have been successful at coding VPC at nine levels; moreover, because the empirical relationship between distinctions that can be made in coding and the impact of those distinctions has received very little testing, the decision to code at something other than nine levels should be made with caution.

Convergent validity and *divergent validity* refer, respectively, to the degree of match between measures of the same or related constructs and to the degree of mismatch between measures of constructs that should be negatively related or unrelated. The most rigorous assessment of convergent validity for coded VPC would involve showing that another way of assessing verbal person centeredness, such as ratings for person centeredness by trained raters or perceptions of person centeredness by message recipients, was highly correlated with the codes. To our knowledge, these comparisons do not yet exist.

However, Jones and Guerrero (2001) created a five-item scale to assess perceived person centeredness (self-centered vs. other centered, invalidates vs. validates, judges vs. empathizes, disregards vs. acknowledges, and unconcerned vs. concerned). They then trained raters on the person centeredness hierarchy and had them rate (from video recordings) the interaction behavior of confederates who had been trained to deliver messages varying in levels of person centeredness and nonverbal immediacy. Interrater reliability (intraclass r) for perceived person centeredness was .95, and confederates delivering HPC, MPC, and LPC messages received significantly different average ratings of person centeredness in the expected order.

Some important recent evidence of both convergent and divergent validity was provided by Hersh (2011), who coded for VPC in a set of 334 messages posted to an online support group for women with breast cancer. These messages were then analyzed using Pennebaker's Linguistic Inquiry and Word Count (LIWC) software. Consistent with the idea of increased focus on the other and decreased focus on the self at higher levels of person centeredness, a significant increase in the use of *you* and decrease in the use of *I* emerged as coded person centeredness increased. In addition, consistent with coding rejection of negative emotional experience as LPC and validation of that experience as HPC, with minimal attention to emotion in MPC messages, Hersh found that the use of negative emotion words was significantly higher in LPC and HPC messages than in MPC messages. Although studies that manipulate VPC often present HPC messages that are longer than either LPC or MPC messages (High & Dillard, 2012), which creates concerns about confounding between message length and VPC, Hersh's analysis of naturally occurring messages found that LPC and HPC messages were equivalent in length, with MPC messages slightly shorter.

Reliability

The validity of a coding system is a necessary but not sufficient condition for its successful use in research. Evidence must also exist that coding is reliable, meaning that behaviors exhibiting the same qualities will be assigned the same codes with a high degree of consistency across multiple observers making decisions independently (Hruschka et al., 2004). As shown in Table 8.1, a large number of published studies report coding for VPC. These studies report one or more reliability statistics, including percentage of agreement, Pearson's r, Cohen's κ, Krippendorff's α, and the intraclass correlation coefficient (ICC). Although percentage of agreement and Pearson's *r*, used in early work, are no longer regarded as the best evidence for intercoder reliability (see Poole & Hewes, this volume), the remaining work provides consistent evidence that VPC can be coded reliably. For example, six studies reported ICCs, and these ranged from .77 to .84. On the basis of Landis and Koch's benchmarks for ICC, these reliabilities are between "substantial" and "almost perfect."

Coding at Different Levels of Analysis

The level at which one chooses to code involves many considerations, including the question being pursued and the nature of the data gathered to address that question. Historically, the message strategy has been used when coding responses to hypothetical scenarios, while the turn at talk has been used with interaction data. Most recently, MacGeorge et al. (2015) successfully coded support conversations at the level of the entire interaction.

Message Strategy

As noted above, written responses to hypothetical scenarios have typically been unitized at the level of message strategy. In concrete terms, this means looking for the primary line of action or objective accomplished by the entire written response (Samter, 1989) and assigning the most appropriate single code. This process can require excluding from consideration certain kinds of ideas that participants sometimes write but would not actually say in an interaction. These include descriptions of goals or strategies (e.g., "I'd try to make her feel better by being open") and tangible behaviors (e.g., "I'd buy him a drink").

A central challenge involved in coding for message strategy concerns how messages often contain complex mixtures of behavior, including comforting at different levels of VPC and comforting behaviors mixed with other behaviors better classified as something else (e.g., advice, questions, disclosure). This problem can be dealt with by having coders determine the *predominant focus* of the message strategy. As Samter explained in her 1989 manual,

> many of the messages have components that could be coded in any number of levels. However, in the real world people do not respond to the individual components of a message; rather, they respond to the overall effect these components combine to achieve. Because people

experience messages as "wholes," we have chosen to code the predominant focus of [the] strategy. The predominant focus of a message simply reflects the key actions being performed in that strategy.

Turn at Talk

For interaction data, the turn at talk is a natural unit of analysis. However, to code for VPC at this level, it is essential to identify turns that should be regarded as efforts to comfort. Even in laboratory interactions in which participants have been assigned the goal of improving another's emotional state, there are a wide variety of behaviors support providers can use, and many turns will not be devoted to the act of comforting per se. Samter and Burleson (1984) operationalized comforting behavior as "turns in which the participant empathized with the confederate, provided an explanation for another's actions, offered sincere sympathy and support, or suggested a broader perspective from which the confederate could view the situation" (p. 305). In this study, turns were first coded as comforting, acknowledgments (i.e., sought simply to acknowledge the confederate's prior utterance), information seeking (turns in which the participant sought knowledge concerning a fact, circumstance, or feeling), disclosure (participants revealed information, experiences, or feelings of their own or about a known other's past), advice (recommendations for future conduct), or other (content not fitting any of the other categories). Subsequently, turns identified as acts of comforting were coded for person centeredness (for additional detail, see Samter & Burleson, 1984).

Interaction

It is also possible to code for the predominant focus or highest level of VPC present in an entire interaction, or a substantial segment of interaction. For example, when an interaction addresses multiple topics, coding might focus on the level of VPC displayed in the discussion of a particular problem. In what appears to be the first implementation of this approach, MacGeorge et al. (2015) assigned a single code for the VPC displayed in 348 laboratory interactions between friends. In their protocol, descriptions of participants' current problems were elicited prior to interaction, and one was chosen to discuss. Talk unrelated to that problem was not considered when coding. As shown in Table 8.1, MacGeorge et al. reported strong reliability for a team of three coders at both the beginning and end of the coding process.

The central challenge of coding at the level of interaction or interaction segment is the issue of predominant focus. MacGeorge and colleagues reported minor adaptations of Samter and Burleson's coding procedures to accommodate the challenge of coding across long stretches of talk. In particular, their procedures emphasize reliance on what the support provider said (rather than how the recipient responded) and treating explicit talk about negative emotion (either legitimating or rejecting) as especially salient when determining the predominant focus. Additional evidence for the feasibility of interaction-level coding was provided by High (2011), who developed procedures for *rating* entire interactions grounded in the conceptual distinctions between different levels of person centeredness. In his work, trained raters produced highly reliable judgments for 10 different items (e.g., self-centered vs. other-centered, invalidates vs. validates, judges vs. empathizes; all ICCs > .92). These items were then factor-analyzed, resulting in three scales. Although the exact correspondence between these scales and coding for VPC is uncertain, the procedure demonstrates raters' capacity to make reliable judgments about person-centered qualities across longer stretches of interaction.

Developing a Localized Coding Manual

The first step in coding VPC is for the researcher to develop a "localized" coding manual. Although existing descriptions of the person-centered hierarchy and coding manuals (e.g., Samter, 1989; Samter & Burleson, 1984) provide an excellent framework, coding for VPC in any unique data set requires instruction on how to identify variation in VPC given the idiosyncrasies of those data. All coding manuals need to contain many of the same elements, including an explanation of the comforting hierarchy, an overview of the steps to be taken when coding, and examples of the different levels of VPC. However, all of these elements need to be customized to the data set being coded and other elements added that are individual to each data set. We have observed that training is expedited and reliability of coding improved when manuals contain the following content specific to the research project: (a) an orientation to the purpose of the research (minus any details of hypotheses or research questions that would bias coding); (b) a description of the context in which the data were collected, including any methodological details that affect the content or structure of the conversation; (c) examples of each level of VPC that are highly

similar to the ones coders will encounter in the data; and (d) detailed discussion, with examples and decision rules, of any coding challenges that are specific to the data. Appendix 8.A contains an amalgam of the core elements in Samter's 1983 and 1989 coding manuals. To avoid confusion, we have removed references to the specific data sets and their purposes; however, readers should remember that these are important elements that contextualize the coding process.

Creating a localized coding manual thus requires familiarity with one's data before the training or coding processes actually begin. Ideally, primary researchers should not be part of the team that ultimately codes the messages, freeing them to peruse the entire data set for issues and examples without fear of biasing subsequent decisions. (This becomes even more critical if knowledge of the hypotheses or research questions could bias coding.) If personnel limitations require that the primary researcher also code, the data set needs to be large enough to extract messages to use in the coding manual and for practice rounds of coding without unduly depleting the data set. One way of addressing this problem is to collect pilot data that are identical in many relevant respects to the data that will be coded, and use the pilot data for examples in the manual. Alternatively, researchers with similar data sets might share their data as a source of relevant examples.

A hallmark of the localized coding manual are the decision rules that develop in response to the primary researcher's "read" of the data and/or strategies that emerge throughout the training process that pose a challenge to code. It has been our experience that although some decision rules are dependent on the specific character of the data, others seem to cut across studies. For instance, consider the following phrases: "This must be tough for you," "What a terrible loss," and "It's a hard time." Coders often want to treat these phrases as emotion words indicative of strategies in Major Division 3. However, in reality, the phrases actually provide descriptions of the situation. Thus, in prior coding (MacGeorge & Wilkum, 2012), we have used the following rule: "If a message only contains one or more of the phrases 'tough,' 'hard,' 'difficult,' 'terrible,' it would typically be classified as a major division two."

Training Coders

Making nuanced judgments of comforting behavior in consistent ways is not easy and requires a combination of intelligence, precision, rhetorical sensitivity, and perseverance. One criterion we have used to identify promising coders is their level of construct differentiation as assessed by Crockett's (1965) Role Category Questionnaire (RCQ); for procedures, see Burleson and Waltman (1988). This criterion was derived from early constructivist work demonstrating that, compared with individuals with lower levels of cognitive complexity, those with higher levels discriminate more sharply among comforting strategies reflecting various levels of person centeredness (Samter et al., 1989). If, however, it is not possible (or desirable) to select coders on the basis of their RCQ scores, then at the very least, researchers should strive to assemble a large enough coding team so that individuals who lack aptitude (and/or motivation) can be assigned other tasks.

We also advise having coders do some basic reading in constructivist theory, such as Burleson and Waltman's (1988) chapter on cognitive complexity, as well as Burleson's (2007) chapter on constructivism as a general theory of communication skill. If coders have not had reason to think carefully about supportive communication, there are readings that address the topic broadly at a level suited for undergraduates (MacGeorge, 2009; MacGeorge, Feng, Wilkum, & Doherty, 2012) or graduate students (MacGeorge et al., 2011), as well as options that focus more narrowly on comforting for undergraduates (Burleson, 2008) or graduates (Burleson, 2003). If possible, we recommend scheduling time early in the training process to conduct a focused discussion of one or more of these readings, with activities that encourage preparation and engagement (quizzes, exercises). Coders who understand why supportive communication matters, and why distinctions between levels of VPC matter, are more likely to do their work thoughtfully, accurately, and reliably.

Beyond selection and reading, trainers need to familiarize coders with the coding manual and coach them through coding of practice examples. The goal here is to help coders feel comfortable not only with the hierarchy itself but also with rendering judgments on difficult cases. The first objective is most easily accomplished by working through prototypical examples of message strategies representing each level of the hierarchy; the latter aim is best achieved by analyzing difficult cases. Time put into careful development of the localized coding manual and selection of practice examples will pay off at this step of training.

Novice coders sometimes become overwhelmed by the fine-grained discriminations they are being asked to make. We have found it useful to emphasize the sequence for coding: Read the entire message, then identify the major division in which a message belongs, and, finally, place the strategy into its appropriate sublevel within that division. It is also useful for coders to focus on negative emotion words (e.g., *frustrating*, *bummed*, *shocked*, *hurt*) when they occur, because they are more likely to populate messages that are either low or high in person centeredness (for empirical evidence, see Hersh, 2011). With negative emotion words identified, coders can look to the surrounding text to determine how the target's feelings and perspective are being treated.

After initial training is complete, the next step is to have coders work independently and bring their decisions back to the group for discussion. Both correct and incorrect evaluations should be considered in detail. This process can be repeated several times, and researchers can begin calculating intercoder reliability as coding improves. Trainers need to convey the expectation that coders follow procedures carefully and learn from past mistakes. The length of time spent in training will vary depending on the sophistication of the coders (e.g., undergraduates vs. a graduate research team) and the availability they have to devote to the task, but three to four rounds of practice is not unusual, and more may be required. The demands of coding for VPC are typical for systems that involve complex qualitative judgments. Studies examining coding practices in a variety of social science disciplines show that the initial round of content coding typically generates low intercoder reliability and that several rounds of coding are often necessary to achieve adequate levels (Hruschka et al., 2004; Ruggeri, Gizelis, & Dorussen, 2011).

Once acceptable intercoder reliability has been achieved, coders can resolve disagreements in the reliability sample through discussion, and transcripts can be divided between coders for independent work. We suggest that the actual coding of data be completed as quickly as possible while remaining careful and consistent in the application of coding procedures; minimizing the time allotted for coding reduces the chance that individuals will forget their training and slip into idiosyncratic modes of decision making. However, even when the duration of coding is relatively short, researchers should conduct a midway or end-of-coding reliability check to ensure that coding continues to be consistent.

Issues in the Coding of Verbal Person Centeredness

For researchers making choices about coding comforting behavior in their own data, we see three issues to consider with regard to VPC. The first is the utility of coding for VPC versus alternative ways of coding behavior in support interactions. The second involves whether to rate for VPC rather than code it. And the third concerns the issue of cultural variations in person centeredness. We end our chapter with a discussion of these issues.

Alternative Coding Systems

Any supportive behavior can be coded in multiple ways. The choice of a coding system is best decided by the researcher's questions and the data available to answer them, not by popularity or ease of use. Coding for VPC is most appropriate when the research questions have to do with the quality (effectiveness, sensitivity, sophistication, or skill) of comforting (emotional support) behavior. For researchers who need to capture a wide range of support providers' behaviors in support interactions, there are multiple options (e.g., Barbee & Cunningham, 1995; Goldsmith & Dun, 1997; MacGeorge, Graves, Feng, Gillihan, & Burleson, 2004; Verhofstadt, Buysse, & Ickes, 2007). Some of these systems classify behaviors by type or content without asserting a priori distinctions in quality (Goldsmith & Dun, 1997; MacGeorge et al., 2004), whereas others group behaviors into broad categories that are believed and/or empirically verified to differ in their impact on support recipients (Barbee & Cunningham, 1995; Verhofstadt et al., 2007). Some systems also offer ways of classifying support recipients' behaviors (Barbee & Cunningham, 1995; MacGeorge et al., 2013). Jones and colleagues' work provides models for the classification of nonverbal behavior in supportive interactions (Jones & Guerrero, 2001; Jones & Wirtz, 2007).

The alternative coding system most similar to VPC appears to be Fruzzetti's (2001) Validating and Invalidating Behaviors Coding Scale (VIBCS). This system, developed for application to behavior in psychotherapy, identifies degrees of validation in response to others' emotional experience and expression. Validating behaviors convey understanding, legitimization, and acceptance, whereas invalidating responses include those that punish or trivialize the emotional experience (e.g., "I don't understand why you would feel that way," "There's no need to get upset"; Shenk & Fruzzetti, 2011). Behavior that is more validating is associated with greater emotional disclosure and lower levels of emotional dysregulation for the target of the behaviors (Shenk & Fruzzetti, 2011); in addition, families not undergoing psychological treatment are more likely to display validating behaviors (Shenk & Fruzzetti, 2014).

In recent use, trained coders applied the VIBCS to assign a single score (on a scale of 1 to 7) from the entirety of behavior observed during an interaction. Training, described as including "the theoretical background, coding structure, content of each level of validating and invalidating behaviors, decision rules for promoting reliability . . . and consensus coding of specified training sessions" (Shenk & Fruzzetti, 2014, p. 45) required ten 90-minute meetings for a subset of coders to achieve an ICC of .77, with some coders needing additional practice (Shenk & Fruzzetti, 2014). Thus, it appears that coding using the VIBCS requires similar investment from the researcher, for a similar payoff in reliability. We are not aware of any scholars (in either communication or clinical psychology) who have coded data using both the person-centered hierarchy and the VIBCS. Yet given its conceptual similarity and distinctive application, the VIBCS could be a good choice for a validity study.

Coding Versus Rating

Some scholars working with VPC have moved away from coding toward ratings made by trained observers. This practice began with Jones and Guerrero (2001), who measured perceived VPC by having observers respond to semantic differential scales after watching videos of confederates enacting low, medium, or high levels of person centeredness when discussing a participant's problem. We understand the attractiveness of ratings, because coding for person centeredness is not an easy task. However, several reasons lead us to caution against the widespread abandonment of coding efforts. First, studies show not only that individuals discriminate among different levels of the hierarchy but that such discrimination carries with it differential impact on support recipients. For example, in an early study, Burleson and Samter (1985) found that people's judgments of comforting strategies were highly consistent with the constructivist theoretical ordering. Moreover, the overall patterns of rank orderings and sensitivity and effectiveness ratings corresponded exactly with the constructivist hierarchy, with the linear trend component for strategy type explaining over 95% of the between-strategies variance in each of the dependent measures. More recently, High and Dillard's (2012) meta-analysis examining the effects of VPC suggested that the effects of messages at Levels 5 and 6 were not distinguishable from each other and that the same problem existed for messages at Levels 8 and 9. But even these authors did not advocate forgoing the use of the hierarchy.

Our second concern has to do with the fact that few studies have coded comforting occurring in naturalistic or seminaturalistic settings. Yet when we submit real-world interaction to content coding, we increase our understanding of the specific types of communicative behaviors that coincide with each level of person centeredness. Hersh's (2011) work with messages directed at breast cancer patients provides an excellent example of this. By coding transcripts of online support for VPC and submitting them to Pennebaker's LIWC software, Hersh observed that negative emotion words predominate at both the lowest and highest levels of the hierarchy. She also found that LPC and HPC messages were equivalent in length, countering concerns about the number of words in a message strategy and its VPC. It is difficult to see how rating data could have yielded such fine-grained (and important) conclusions. Finally, as noted earlier, we know of no study that has conducted a formal assessment of the degree of association between ratings of person centeredness made by trained observers and actual content coding. Until such information is available, we cannot claim that VPC ratings are an adequate surrogate for the coding of person centeredness.

Cultural Variation in Person Centeredness

Constructivist theory acknowledges that person centeredness takes on slightly different forms according to the particular communicative goal being pursued (i.e., comforting vs. persuading or informing; Burleson, 2007; Clark & Delia, 1977). More recently, scholars have recommended greater attention to the possibility that certain types of message content may function as more person centered for some cultural groups than others. In one study, when presented with standard messages written to reflect each of the nine levels in the comforting hierarchy, African Americans not only rated all messages less favorably than did Caucasians, but they also exhibited less discrimination between messages at the lower and higher ends of the person-centered hierarchy (Samter, Whaley, Mortenson, & Burleson, 1997). However, in a more recent investigation, African Americans evaluated the sensitivity and effectiveness of comforting messages in which concepts such as God, prayer, religion, and faith were woven into LPC, MPC, and HPC messages; in that study, African Americans exhibited the familiar pattern of ratings (Samter, Morse, & Whaley, 2013). That is, "religious" comforting messages embodying various levels of person centeredness produced

differentiated judgments of sensitivity and effectiveness among African Americans. Moreover, African Americans evaluated virtually all levels of "religious" comforting messages as significantly more sensitive and effective than did Caucasians.

These findings suggest not only that religious content is an essential component of comforting for African Americans but that the way person centeredness has been operationalized in researcher-designed comforting messages does a better job of representing variation in Caucasian comforting strategies than African American strategies. Thus, coding for VPC in African American discourse using current manuals might fail to capture religious elements that function as validation (or rejection) of targets' feelings and perspectives for this cultural group. More broadly, this work suggests that person centeredness may be enacted in somewhat different ways across cultural groups and that greater validity will result from coding manuals and procedures that are sensitive to this variation. One way to address this issue is to use what Kreuter and Wray (2003) called "constituent-involving strategies," seeking cultural group members' interpretations of message behavior, especially behavior that is less familiar to researchers. When possible, research teams should include members of the groups whose comforting behavior is being coded.

Conclusion

When used to describe comforting messages, verbal person centeredness captures variation in the sensitivity of response to a distressed person's emotional state, perspective, and situation. VPC has been conceptualized as both a dependent variable (predicted by various sociocognitive, developmental, and demographic factors) and as an independent variable related to the perceived helpfulness, effectiveness, sensitivity, and quality of comforting messages (Burleson, 2003; High & Dillard, 2012) and to actual message effectiveness in the form of affect improvement (Jones & Wirtz, 2006). Studies examining VPC offer strong evidence for the reliability and validity of the nine-level hierarchy used to code for the person-centered quality of comforting messages. General coding procedures are described in existing coding manuals (Samter, 1983, 1989; see Appendix 8.A), but coding is facilitated by the development of localized coding manuals that address nuances of the particular data being examined and articulate pertinent decision rules. As work in the area moves toward analyzing data obtained from support interactions in settings where they actually occur, researchers must remember that person centeredness may be enacted in somewhat different ways across cultural groups and that greater validity will result from coding manuals and procedures that are sensitive to this variation.

References

Applegate, J. L. (1980). Adaptive communication in educational contexts: A study of teachers' communicative strategies. *Communication Education, 29*, 158–170.

Barbee, A. P., & Cunningham, M. R. (1995). An experimental approach to social support communications: Interactive coping in close relationships. In B. R. Burleson (Ed.), *Communication Yearbook 18* (pp. 381–413). Thousand Oaks, CA: Sage.

Bernstein, B. (1975). *Class, codes, and control: Theoretical studies toward a sociology of language.* New York: Shocken.

Blumer, H. (1969). *Symbolic interactionism: Perspective and method.* Englewood Cliffs, NJ: Prentice Hall.

Bodie, G. D., & Burleson, B. R. (2008). Explaining variations in the effects of supportive messages: A dual-process framework. In C. Beck (Ed.), *Communication Yearbook 32* (pp. 354–398). New York: Routledge.

Burleson, B. R. (1982). The development of comforting communication skills in childhood and adolescence. *Child Development, 53*, 1578–1588.

Burleson, B. R. (1987). Cognitive complexity. In J. C. McCroskey & J. A. Daly (Eds.), *Personality and interpersonal communication* (pp. 305–349). Newbury Park, CA: Sage.

Burleson, B. R. (2003). Emotional support skills. In J. O. Greene & B. R. Burleson (Eds.), *Handbook of communication and social interaction skills* (pp. 551–594). Mahwah, NJ: Lawrence Erlbaum.

Burleson, B. R. (2007). Constructivism: A general theory of communication skill. In B. B. Whaley & W. Samter (Eds.), *Explaining communication: Contemporary theories and exemplars* (pp. 105–128). Mahwah, NJ: Lawrence Erlbaum.

Burleson, B. R. (2008). What counts as effective emotional support? Explorations of individual and situational differences. In M. T. Motley (Ed.), *Studies in applied interpersonal communication* (pp. 207–227). Thousand Oaks, CA: Sage.

Burleson, B. R., & Caplan, S. E. (1998). Cognitive complexity. In J. C. McCroskey, J. A. Daly, M. M. Martin, & M. J. Beatty (Eds.), *Communication and personality: Trait perspectives* (pp. 230–286). Cresskill, NJ: Hampton.

Burleson, B. R., & Goldsmith, D. J. (1998). How the comforting process works: Alleviating emotional distress through conversationally induced reappraisals. In P. A. Andersen & L. K. Guerrero (Eds.), *Handbook of communication and emotion: Research, theory,*

applications, and contexts (pp. 245–280). San Diego, CA: Academic Press.

Burleson, B. R., Hanasono, L. K., Bodie, G. D., Holmstrom, A. J., Rack, J. J., Rosier, J. G., & McCullough, J. D. (2009). Explaining gender differences in responses to supportive messages: Two tests of a dual-process approach. *Sex Roles, 61*, 265–280.

Burleson, B. R., Holmstrom, A. J., & Gilstrap, C. M. (2005). "Guys can't say that to guys": Four experiments assessing the normative motivation account for deficiencies in the emotional support provided by men. *Communication Monographs, 72*, 468–501.

Burleson, B. R., & MacGeorge, E. L. (2002). Supportive communication. In M. L. Knapp & J. A. Daly (Eds.), *Handbook of interpersonal communication* (3rd ed., pp. 374–424). Thousand Oaks, CA: Sage.

Burleson, B. R., & Samter, W. (1985). Consistencies in theoretical and naive evaluations of comforting messages. *Communication Monographs, 52*, 103–123.

Burleson, B. R., & Samter, W. (1996). Similarity in the communication skills of young adults: Foundations of attraction, friendship, and relationship satisfaction. *Communication Reports, 9*, 125–139.

Burleson, B. R., & Waltman, M. S. (1988). Cognitive complexity: Using the Role Category Questionnaire measure. In C. H. Tardy (Ed.), *A handbook for the study of human communication: Methods and instruments for observing, measuring, and assessing communication processes* (pp. 1–35). Norwood, NJ: Ablex.

Clark, R. A., & Delia, J. G. (1977). Cognitive complexity, social perspective-taking, and functional persuasive skills in second- to ninth-grade children. *Human Communication Research, 3*, 128–134.

Clark, R. A., & Delia, J. G. (1979). Topoi and rhetorical competence. *Quarterly Journal of Speech, 65*, 187–206.

Crockett, W. H. (1965). Cognitive complexity and impression formation. In B. A. Maher (Ed.), *Progress in experimental personality research* (Vol. 2, pp. 47–90). New York: Academic Press.

Delia, J. G., & O'Keefe, B. J. (1979). Constructivism: The development of communication in children. In E. Wartella (Ed.), *Children communicating: Media and the development of thought, speech, understanding* (pp. 157–186). Beverly Hills, CA: Sage.

Feng, B., Li, S., & Li, N. (2013a). *Coding manual for verbal person centeredness.* Unpublished manuscript, University of California, Davis.

Feng, B., Li, S., & Li, N. (2013b, December 3). Is a profile worth a thousand words? How online support-seeker's profile features may influence the quality of received support messages. *Communication Research.* doi:10.1177/0093650213510942

Fruzzetti, A. E. (2001). *Validating and invalidating behavioral coding scale manual.* Unpublished manuscript, University of Nevada, Reno.

Goffman, E. (1967). *Interaction ritual.* New York: Doubleday.

Goldsmith, D. J., & Dun, S. A. (1997). Sex differences and similarities in the communication of social support.

Journal of Social and Personal Relationships, 14, 317–337.

Hale, J. L., Tighe, M. R., & Mongeau, P. A. (1997). Effects of event type and sex on comforting messages. *Communication Research Reports, 14,* 214–220.

Hersh, A. C. (2011). *Social support online: Testing the effects of highly person-centered messages in breast cancer support groups* (Unpublished doctoral dissertation). University of Pennsylvania.

High, A. C. (2011). *The production and reception of verbal person-centered social support in face-to-face and computer mediated dyadic conversations* (Unpublished doctoral dissertation). Pennsylvania State University, State College, PA.

High, A. C., & Dillard, J. P. (2012). A review and meta-analysis of person-centered messages and social support outcomes. *Communication Studies, 63,* 99–118.

Holmstrom, A. J. (2009). Sex and gender similarities and differences in communication values in same-sex and cross-sex friendships. *Communication Quarterly, 57,* 224–238.

Hruschka, D. J., Schwartz, D., John, D.C.S., Picone-Decaro, E., Jenkins, R. A., & Carey, J. W. (2004). Reliability in coding open-ended data: Lessons learned from HIV behavioral research. *Field Methods, 16,* 307–331.

Jones, S. M. (2004). Putting the person into person-centered and immediate emotional support: Emotional change and perceived helper competence as outcomes of comforting in helping situations. *Communication Research, 31,* 338–360.

Jones, S. M., & Guerrero, L. A. (2001). The effects of nonverbal immediacy and verbal person centeredness in the emotional support process. *Human Communication Research, 27,* 567–596.

Jones, S. M., & Wirtz, J. (2006). How does the comforting process work? An empirical test of an appraisal-based model of comforting. *Human Communication Research, 32,* 217–243.

Jones, S. M., & Wirtz, J. (2007). "Sad monkey see, monkey do": Nonverbal matching in emotional support encounters. *Communication Studies, 58,* 71–86.

Kreuter, M. W., & Wray, R. J. (2003). Tailored and targeted health communication: Strategies for enhancing information relevance. *American Journal of Health Behavior,* 27(Suppl. 3), S227–S232.

Levine, T. R. (2011). Quantitative social science methods of inquiry. In M. L. Knapp & J. A. Daly (Eds.), *The SAGE handbook of interpersonal communication* (pp. 25–57). Thousand Oaks, CA: Sage.

Limberg, H., & Locher, M. A. (Eds.). (2012). *Advice in discourse.* Amsterdam, the Netherlands: John Benjamins.

MacGeorge, E. L. (2009). Social support. In W. Eadie (Ed.), *21st century communication: A reference handbook* (Vol. 1, pp. 283–291). Thousand Oaks, CA: Sage.

MacGeorge, E. L., Branch, S., Yakova, L., Lindley, C., Pastor, R., Cummings, R., & Robinson, J. (2013).

Coding advice recipients' immediate responses. Unpublished manuscript, Brian Lamb School of Communication, Purdue University.

MacGeorge, E. L., Feng, B., & Burleson, B. R. (2011). Supportive communication. In M. L. Knapp & J. A. Daly (Eds.), *The SAGE handbook of interpersonal communication* (4th ed., pp. 317–354). Thousand Oaks, CA: Sage.

MacGeorge, E. L., Feng, B., Wilkum, K. C., & Doherty, E. F. (2012). Supportive communication: A positive response to negative life events. In T. J. Socha & M. J. Pitts (Eds.), *The positive side of interpersonal communication* (pp. 211–228). New York: Peter Lang.

MacGeorge, E. L., Gillihan, S. J., Samter, W., & Clark, R. A. (2003). Skill deficit or differential motivation? Accounting for sex differences in the provision of emotional support. *Communication Research, 30,* 272–303.

MacGeorge, E. L., Graves, A. R., Feng, B., Gillihan, S. J., & Burleson, B. R. (2004). The myth of gender cultures: Similarities outweigh differences in men's and women's provision of and responses to supportive communication. *Sex Roles, 50,* 143–175.

MacGeorge, E. L., Guntzviller, L. M., Bailey, L., Brisini, K., Salmon, S., Severen, K., . . . Cummings, R. (2015, May). *The influence of emotional support quality on advice evaluation and outcomes.* Paper presented at the annual convention of the International Communication Association, San Juan, PR.

MacGeorge, E. L., Guntzviller, L. M., Hanasono, L. K., & Feng, B. (2013, November 12). Testing advice response theory in interactions with friends. *Communication Research.* doi:10.1177/0093650213510938

MacGeorge, E. L., & Wilkum, K. C. (2012). Predicting comforting quality in the context of miscarriage. *Communication Reports, 25,* 62–74.

McCullough, J. D., & Burleson, B. R. (2012). Celebratory support: Messages that enhance the effects of positive experience. In T. J. Socha & M. J. Pitts (Eds.), *The positive side of interpersonal communication* (pp. 229–248). New York: Peter Lang.

Mead, G. H. (1934). *Mind, self, and society.* Chicago: University of Chicago Press.

Piaget, J. (1926). *The language and thought of the child.* London: Routledge & Kegan Paul.

Rowan, K. E. (1988). A contemporary theory of explanatory writing. *Written Communication, 5,* 23–56.

Ruggeri, A., Gizelis, T.-I., & Dorussen, H. (2011). Events data as Bismarck's sausages? Intercoder reliability, coders' selection, and data quality. *International Interactions, 37,* 340–361.

Samter, W. (1983). *Effects of cognitive and motivational variables on comforting behavior in a quasi-natural context* (Unpublished master's thesis). Purdue University, West Lafayette, IN.

Samter, W. (1989). *Communication skills predictive of interpersonal acceptance in a group living situation: A sociometric study* (Unpublished doctoral dissertation). Purdue University, West Lafayette, IN.

Samter, W., & Burleson, B. R. (1984). Cognitive and motivational influences on spontaneous comforting behavior. *Human Communication Research, 11*, 231–260.

Samter, W., & Burleson, B. R. (1990). Evaluations of communication skills as predictors of peer acceptance in a group living situation. *Communication Studies, 41*, 311–326.

Samter, W., & Burleson, B. R. (2005). The role of communication in same-sex friendships: A comparison among African Americans, Asian Americans, and European Americans. *Communication Quarterly, 53*, 265–283.

Samter, W., Burleson, B. R., & Basden-Murphy, L. (1989). Behavioral complexity is in the eye of the beholder: Effects of cognitive complexity and message complexity on impressions of the source of comforting messages. *Human Communication Research, 15*, 612–629.

Samter, W., & Ely, T. (1985). *Children's conflict management strategies: Assessments of individual and situational differences.* Paper presented at the Central States Speech Association Convention, Indianapolis, IN.

Samter, W., Morse, C. R., & Whaley, B. B. (2013). Do we need to put God into emotional support? A comparison of Caucasians' and African-Americans' evaluations of religious versus non-religious comforting messages. *Journal of Intercultural Communication Research, 42*, 172–191.

Samter, W., Whaley, B. B., Mortenson, S. R., & Burleson, B. R. (1997). Ethnicity and emotional support in same-sex friendship: A comparison of Asian-Americans, African-Americans, and Euro-Americans. *Personal Relationships, 4*, 413–430.

Shenk, C. E., & Fruzzetti, A. E. (2011). The impact of validating and invalidating responses on emotional reactivity. *Journal of Social and Clinical Psychology, 30*, 163–183.

Shenk, C. E., & Fruzzetti, A. E. (2014). Parental validating and invalidating responses and adolescent psychological functioning: An observational study. *The Family Journal, 22*, 43–48.

Verhofstadt, L. L., Buysse, A., & Ickes, W. (2007). Social support in couples: An examination of gender differences using self-report and observational methods. *Sex Roles, 57*, 267–282.

Werner, H. (1957). The concept of development from a comparative and organismic point of view. In D. B. Harris (Ed.), *The concept of development* (pp. 125–146). Minneapolis: University of Minnesota Press.

Xu, Y., & Burleson, B. R. (2001). Effects of sex, culture, and support type on perceptions of spousal social support: An assessment of the "support gap" hypothesis in early marriage. *Human Communication Research, 27*, 535–566.

Appendix 8.A

Comforting Coding Manual

Coding Comforting
Messages: An Introduction

The purpose of this manual is to describe a system for coding an individual's level of *comforting* skill. In this system, skillfulness is defined in terms of the extent to which a comforting strategy acknowledges, elaborates, and legitimizes the feelings and perspective of a distressed other. Individuals who construct messages that acknowledge, elaborate, and legitimize the other's feelings and perspective are viewed as having a greater degree of comforting skill than individuals who construct messages that do not acknowledge, elaborate, and legitimize the distressed other's feelings and perspective. A system for coding comforting skill in this manner is presented below. Prior to the explanation of this system, the manual discusses some of the more important features of comforting messages. Next, the nine-level hierarchy for coding comforting messages is presented. Finally, procedures for using the hierarchy when coding transcripts are outlined.

The Nature of Comforting Messages and the Situations Used to Elicit Them

A Definition of Comforting

In the current project, comforting strategies are defined as verbal messages aimed at alleviating the negative feelings that arise from everyday hurts and disappointments. This definition has several implications for the study of comforting behavior.

One implication of this definition is limiting comforting to an activity directed at managing the *psychological* states of others. Although material and physical problems can contribute to emotional distress, this particular definition focuses on the kind of comforting that manages feelings. Second, in centering on distress arising from everyday events, comforting is viewed as an activity that deals with *moderate* feelings of sadness and disappointment. The behavioral strategies used to cope with more extreme forms of depression stemming from such extraordinary events as the loss of a spouse or parent are not addressed. Finally, this definition narrows the study of comforting to the *verbal* strategies through which people attempt to make others feel better. Certainly, empathy and support can be conveyed through a variety of nonverbal channels; however, the current project is concerned with the verbal means through which an individual seeks to comfort another.

The Hierarchy for Coding Comforting Messages

An Overview of the Hierarchy

The system for coding comforting messages consists of three major divisions reflecting the extent to which the perspective of a distressed other is recognized. At Major Division 1, there is clear denial of individual perspective; at Major Division 2, there is implicit recognition of individual perspective; and at Major Division 3, there is explicit recognition and elaboration of individual perspective.

Each of these major divisions is further partitioned into "sublevels" according to the extent to which the feelings of the distressed other are acknowledged, elaborated, and legitimized. In general, messages at the lowest levels of the hierarchy do not acknowledge, elaborate, or legitimize the other's feelings. For example, messages scored at Major Division 1, Level 1, condemn the feelings of the distressed other. Messages scored at Level 2 challenge the legitimacy of the other's feelings. And messages scored at Level 3 ignore the feelings of the distressed other.

In contrast, messages coded at all levels of Major Division 2 implicitly acknowledge, elaborate, and legitimize the other's feelings. In these strategies, the speaker performs actions that demonstrate his or her awareness of the hurt and confusion present in the situation. Thus, messages scored at Major Division 2, Level 4, attempt to divert the other's attention away from the situation and the feelings present there. Messages coded at Level 5, acknowledge the other's feelings but do not attempt to help him or her cope with them. Level 6 messages provide a non-feeling-centered explanation of the situation intended to reduce the other's distress.

Messages coded in the highest levels of the hierarchy clearly and explicitly acknowledge, elaborate, and legitimize the feelings of the distressed other. These messages focus on the target's thoughts, feelings, interpretations of, and reactions to, the distressful event. For example, messages coded at Level 7 explicitly acknowledge the other's feelings but do not provide an elaborated explanation of these feelings. Messages coded at Level 8 provide an elaborated acknowledgment and explanation of the other's feelings. Finally, messages coded at Level 9 not only elaborate and legitimize the other's distress but also seek to foster an understanding of the event by leading the other to take a different perspective on the situation.

Why high-level messages are more "skillful." After reading through the explanation of the system, you can probably think of several reasons why strategies scored at the higher levels of the hierarchy are viewed as more skillful than strategies scored at the lower levels of the hierarchy. For one thing, when compared with low-level messages, higher level comforting strategies tend to be more *accepting* of the distressed other and his or her point of view. Such acceptance may play an important role in skillful comforting, because emotional distress often stems from some sort of rejection (e.g., of one's self, one's ideas, one's talents). Higher level messages also tend to be mor*e evaluatively neutral.* Whereas lower level messages typically contain judgments of the feelings and people associated with a distressful situation, messages scored at the highest levels of the hierarchy usually describe the actions, emotions, and persons connected with the event. Blaming or attacking the target for being upset is less likely to make him or her feel better than discussing or working through the distress. Finally, higher level messages often contain a *cognitively oriented explanation* of the feelings involved in the distressful situation. Such explanation may provide the other with insights he or she would otherwise miss because of the intensity and confusion that typically characterize emotional distress.

To summarize, high-level comforting strategies are viewed as more skillful ways of alleviating distress because they acknowledge, elaborate, and legitimize another's feelings. Explicitly recognizing another's feelings implies that the speaker accepts the distressed other, maintains evaluative neutrality, and can offer some new understanding of the event.

The Hierarchy

As you read through the hierarchy, you will notice that many comforting messages contain elements of strategies that reflect different levels in the system. In other words, many of the messages have components that could be coded at any number of levels. However, in the real world, people do not respond to the individual components of a message; rather, they respond to the overall effect these components combine to achieve. Because people experience messages as "wholes," we have chosen to code the predominant focus of comforting strategies. The predominant focus of a message simply reflects the key actions being performed in that strategy. Thus, instead of looking for messages that are "pure" in type, look for the predominant focus of the components as they function together within the strategy.

0. No Response

Speaker does not say anything.

I. Denial of Individual Perspective

Turns, messages, or interactions in which the subject condemns or ignores the specific feelings that exist in the situation for the confederate. This denial may be either explicit or implicit.

1. Speaker condemns the feelings of the other.

   For example, "It's really stupid to feel so bad. You're an adult now and should realize that these things happen."

2. Speaker challenges the legitimacy of the other's feelings.

   a. Speaker explicitly asserts that the other's feelings or actions are unwarranted, unfair, or unreasonable (but does not directly criticize or condemn these feelings or actions).

   For example, "No guy is worth getting so worked up about."

   b. Speaker asserts or implies that some action of the other is responsible for producing the present situation.

   For example, "You knew going into it that being in a long-distance relationship was going to be tough, so I don't understand why you're so worked up about this."

   For example, "Maybe you needed to put a little more effort into the relationship and spend less time working on school stuff."

Coding note: The distinction between 1 and 2 is determined by how explicitly the target's feelings or perspective are rejected. To be coded as a 1, a message must explicitly (i.e., directly, overtly) condemn what the target feels or thinks. Messages coded as 2 need only implicitly condemn the feelings or perspective.

3. Speaker ignores the other's feelings.

   a. Speaker makes an evaluative claim that functions to deny the other's feelings or imply that these feelings are somehow unwarranted or illegitimate.

   For example, "It's not the end of the world."

   For example, "I'm not sure about the breakup being a complete surprise."

   b. Speaker cites a general rule, principle, or axiom that, in effect, serves to derogate the other's feelings.

   For example, "It's not unusual for these things to happen."

   For example, "Things always happen for a reason."

   For example, "When God shuts one door, He opens another."

   c. Speaker asserts how the other should feel and/or act in the situation.

   For example, "That's one of those things you really can't regret getting into."

   For example, "With finals and everything, I'd worry about studying."

   For example, "You'll get over it."

   For example, "You should go and get totally wasted."

   d. Speaker advocates an immediate modification in the other's feeling state (usually in the form of a behavioral directive).

   For example, "Just forget about him, you, the whole thing. Just stop thinking about it."

   For example, "I'd just forget about him and find somebody else."

   For example "I'd start going out with somebody else and I'm sure he'd know."

   e. Speaker denigrates the object or source of the other's feelings.

   For example, "I wouldn't look at you, I'd look at him because he was scared to tell you, you know? What kind of. He must have been a real jerk at the end, you know?"

   For example, "Sounds like a real turkey!"

II. Implicit Recognition of Individual Perspective

Turns, messages, or interactions in which the subject provides some implicit acceptance of and/or positive response to the feelings of the other, but does not explicitly mention, elaborate, or legitimize those.

4. Speaker attempts to reframe the situation in a positive way by diverting the other's attention from the distressing situation and the feelings arising from that situation, or attempts to "smooth over" the situation.

a. Speaker attempts to redirect the other's attention from the situation and the feelings present there.

For example, "C'mon, let's go to the movies or shopping or out to eat or something. You know you always feel better when we do that."

For example, "Let's go out this weekend and go dancing. I'll invite some people from my classes. It will be great!"

b. Speaker attempts to "smooth over" the situation and the feelings present there. These attempts must aim at getting the other to focus on some "happy" or "positive" event in a time other than the here and now.

For example, "God, there are so many guys on campus. You're so cute and fun! They'd all be dying to ask you out once they know you're, you're ready."

(Although the above statement is similar to those presented in Level 3, it contains an implicit acknowledgment of the other's feelings. The subject clearly understands that the confederate is experiencing emotional distress and that she will not be ready to see other men until at least some of this distress has been alleviated.)

For example, "Maybe he'll change his mind."

For example, "He's gonna realize he can't live without you and you guys will get back together."

c. Speaker offers some sort of compensation for the other's distressed feelings.

For example, "Even though he doesn't love you anymore, I do."

(In the above example, the speaker offers some aspect of herself as a way of compensating the other for the distressed feelings.)

For example, "Try not to think you're a failure—you have so much going for you. You're it, man."

(In this case, the speaker offers a generic form of compensation by suggesting that the friend has a lot going for him despite the breakup situation.)

d. Speaker suggests a method of repairing the situation.

e.g., "Well, maybe you could go talk to him about the situation."

(This example is similar to the behavioral directives scored in Level 3. However, in this instance, the speaker does not tell the distressed other how she should or should not act. Rather, the speaker is suggesting a possible way to remedy the situation; in other words, the speaker is suggesting a method of repair. When suggestions or advice are not given in the imperative form, they are to be coded higher than the simple behavioral directives that appear in Level 3.)

5. Speaker acknowledges the other's feelings but does not attempt to help the other understand why those feelings are being experienced or how to cope with them.

a. Speaker expresses regret or offers an apology.

For example, "I bet. Oh gosh. I'm sorry to hear that."

b. Speaker asks questions that suggest he or she acknowledges the other's interpretation of the situation.

For example, "Well, did you have any inkling? Do you think it would help to talk to him? Do you want to make an appointment with counseling services?"

c. Speaker provides a description of the situation that implicitly acknowledges the other's point of view and feelings.

For example, "Mm-hmm. I know what you mean exactly. It's hard"

For example, "It's alright. I know sometimes you just have to talk to anyone you can talk to."

For example, "I mean I don't see how you could do that to somebody."

(This might be mistakenly classified as Level 6, but it does not actually "explain" the situation. Instead, it indicates the speaker's recognition that the target has been harmed and is thus best coded as Level 5.)

For example, "It's a tough situation. But you're not crawling back to him. You're just gonna want to know why."

Coding note: Most offers to talk should be classified as Level 5 because they implicitly acknowledge the target's feelings and perspective (i.e., if something weren't wrong, there would be no need for talking). However, if a message recommends or offers talking about something other than the current problem (e.g., "Let's go have some coffee and a good gossip"), this is Level 4 (compensation). Additionally, if a message recommends or offers talk specifically about the person's feelings (e.g., "I'll be your shoulder to cry on"), it should be considered for classification as a Major Division 3.

6. Speaker provides a non-feeling-centered explanation of the situation to reduce the other's distressed emotional state.

   a. Speaker suggests certain circumstances intended to mitigate the other's interpretation of the situation and her feelings.

   For example, ". . . but it sounds like maybe he just wants to. See, maybe he thinks. Oh your parents always say, like I know mine do, they say, 'Oh the college years are the best years of your life. And you should get out and not get tied down right away for awhile.' So see, maybe he, maybe he just is thinking like that, you know?"

   For example, "Maybe he just needs some time to himself, you know?"

   For example, "And maybe he'll come out and tell you that he really just wants to, it's just other things."

(Because of the statement "he just wants to," this message might be considered a Level 4 strategy, seeking to divert attention from or smooth over the situation. Yet this portion of the subject's utterance is incomplete. The statement "it's just other things" then becomes the predominant focus of the utterance. This statement embodies a Level 6 strategy, through which the subject suggests circumstances intended to mitigate the other's interpretation of the situation.)

   b. Speaker invokes a general principle designed to "explain away" the other's feelings.

   For example, "Sounds like guys."

   For example, "Guys are so much trouble."

   For example, "It's nerve wracking when they don't say much."

Coding note: Don't confuse general principles to be coded as Level 6 with the denigration of the object or source of feelings that can occur in Level 3 (see 3c). As shown above, general principles coded as Level 6 can "put down" classes of people (e.g., guys), but do

not target the specific object or source of feelings (e.g., the boyfriend).

III. Explicit Recognition and
Elaboration of Individual Perspective

Messages, turns, or interactions in which the subject explicitly acknowledges, elaborates, and legitimizes the feelings of the other. These strategies may include attempts to provide a general understanding of the situation. Coping strategies may be suggested in conjunction with an explication of the other's feelings.

7. Speaker explicitly recognizes and acknowledges the other's feelings but does not provide an elaborated explanation of these feelings.

   a. Speaker explicitly acknowledges the other's feelings and attempts to reassure and comfort the other, but does not discuss the source of the feelings or the nature of the situation.

   For example, "I know you feel bad about all this. But just remember, I still love you and no matter what happens, you'll always be my friend."

   For example, "JoEllen, you did all you could and it didn't work and it's gonna hurt for a while. I still love you and you've got so much going for you."

   b. Speaker provides an explicit acknowledgment of the other's feelings coupled with a non-feeling-centered explanation of the situation.

   For example, "How upsetting! I couldn't rest until I found out why. It doesn't change anything, but at least you'd be satisfied. And you'd know why he acted that way."

   For example, "Boy, I know this is really hard to cope with. But guys are really weird sometimes."

8. Speaker provides an elaborated acknowledgment and explanation of the other's feelings.

   a. Speaker provides legitimizing reasons why the experienced feelings are felt in this situation.

   For example, "You might, you know, you might feel bad after you talk to him. It might hurt then if you talk to him. And if you don't have another chance, you might regret it later on."

For example, "Well, I would get your thoughts together and go back and talk. I mean, it's no wonder that you're all upset. Until you get things real settled between you, there's no way for you to make any plans, and that's not fair to you. I mean I'm just a real advocate for talking things out and getting things out in the open. And if he can't be open enough with you, then, you know, if he can't do that then I would say, 'Then I'm going to have to go on.'"

b. Speaker elaborates the feelings of the other and makes truncated efforts to have the other put her feelings in context by getting the other to take the perspective of the speaker or some other person.

For example, "Gosh, I really know it hurts now. The same thing happened to me and I really understand how rotten it makes you feel. But believe me, in a few months, you'll be over it. Time's the most important thing."

For example, "It hurts so much, too, though. I mean when you really like somebody."

(Although this statement appears similar to those presented in Level 5, it provides an explicit identification and legitimization of the other's feelings, along with a brief indication of why the feelings arose in the situation.)

9. Speaker helps the other gain a perspective on her own feelings and attempts to help the other see these feelings in relation to a broader context or the feelings of others in similar situations.

For example, "Omigosh. I would be devastated. How are you even holding up? If you talk to him maybe there is a chance that this is just a misunderstanding. Maybe he's a senior and he's leaving. And that's why he's scared, you know? And that's why he's trying to break it up. Sometimes guys do that."

For example, "You put so much into this relationship, and you love him! What a mess. . . . Girl, I am so sorry you are hurting. I am so angry for you too. You know, we are also young. I know that's not what you want to hear. But we are. We have time on our side. There'll be lots of other guys, and someone special who will treat you much, much better. Like you deserve. And you will be strong in yourself because you lived through this."

Coding Note: Emotion Words and Major Divisions

To aid in the distinction between Major Division 2 (Levels 4 to 6) and Major Division 3 (Levels 7 to 9), it is important to look for explicit, legitimating references to the target's negative emotional state or perspective. These are usually signaled by negative emotion words.

Common negative emotion words in interactions dealing with loss are *sad/sadness, pain/painful, grief/grieving, hurt/hurting/hurtful, upset/upsetting*, and *cry/crying*, but many other emotions may be discussed when interactions are focused on other kinds of problems (e.g., *anxious, worried, afraid, scared, angry, frustrated, mad, irritated, guilty, ashamed*). Emotions are also commonly referenced in statements like "You must feel so X." In general, you should avoid classifying a message, turn, or interaction in Major Division 3 unless it contains one or more emotion terms *and* explicitly legitimates the experience of that emotion.

In general, statements that a situation has negative characteristics (e.g., is *tough, hard*, or *difficult* for the target) should be regarded as implicitly acknowledging emotion rather than explicitly legitimizing it. Thus, a message, turn, or interaction containing such phrases (without additional legitimization of negative emotion) would typically be classified as Major Division 2 rather than Major Division 3.

If the speaker claims sympathetic or empathic experience of a negative emotion, such as "I feel terrible for you," this is *implicit* rather than *explicit* acknowledgment of the target's emotion and should be coded at Major Division 2, not Major Division 3. "I don't know how you feel" or similar claims should also be coded at Major Division 2, not Major Division 3.

Some messages contain explicit references to the other's *positive* emotional states, or to actions that assume a positive emotional state. Positive emotion words and phrases include (but are not limited to) feeling good, feeling better, doing better, looking up, and moving on. In general, references to positive emotions should not be treated as indicators of a Major Division 3 message, because they do not legitimate the negative emotions generated by the problem. Positive emotion terms could appear in any major division.

Procedures for Coding Comforting Messages

Having presented the comforting hierarchy, we can now outline the steps you should follow when coding transcripts. Because the data will already be unitized, you will know whether any given response contains more than one message strategy. If more than one strategy is present, repeat the following process for each individual message in the response.

Step 1

Read the entire message. Decide in what *major division* the message belongs.

Step 2

After the major division has been identified, place the message into its *appropriate sublevel* within that division.

Practice Examples

Try to code the following comforting messages using the procedures presented above. Read the entire message. First decide in what major division the message belongs, then place it into its appropriate sublevel within that division.

Example 1

"It wasn't that you are a bad person or anything that he broke up with you; you were just, I mean, there were probably lots of reasons that were all his stuff. Guy stuff, you know? Don't be down, we're gonna get you through this."

Major division coding. At the end of Example 1, the speaker tries to comfort the other by suggesting that the breakup is nothing to be down about. In telling the other not to be down, the speaker ignores how the other *actually* feels and, instead, suggests how she *should* feel. In isolation from the rest of the message, these components would be coded in Major Division 1, Level 3. Remember, however, that we are not interested in coding the individual components of a message strategy; rather, we are interested in capturing the overall effect or predominant focus of these components as they function together within the message. Prior to the last two sentences, the speaker focuses more on the feelings and perspective of the distressed other. In suggesting a possible explanation for the breakup, she demonstrates an implicit recognition of her friend's feelings; in other words, the speaker would not offer possible explanations of the event if she did not implicitly recognize that the other was distressed. Thus, although Example 1 contains an element of a Level 3 strategy, the key action performed by the speaker is to offer an explanation

of the situation. Because the explanation reflects an implicit recognition of the other's feelings and perspective, the strategy belongs in one of the levels of Major Division 2.

Sublevel coding. In pointing out a possible explanation, the speaker suggests a set of circumstances intended to mitigate her friend's distress. These circumstances present the distressed other with a framework for interpreting the situation and the feelings surrounding it. Given these characteristics, the entire message would be coded as a Level 6 strategy.

Example 2

"It's not the end of the world. I mean, I think nothing's gonna make you feel a whole lot better probably, but you just have to remember that this one thing isn't gonna be the end of your life. There are lots of other guys out there. I'm sorry about the way things worked out."

Major division coding. In isolation from the rest of the strategy, the speaker's statement "I'm sorry about the way things worked out" could be coded as a Level 5 apology. However, such implicit recognition and legitimation of the other's feelings is not present throughout the rest of the message. In fact, by suggesting that the breakup is "not the end of the world," the speaker implies that her friend's depression is unwarranted. The speaker also suggests that "this one thing isn't gonna be the end of [the other's] life" and that "there are lots of other guys out there." These suggestions not only minimize the significance of the breakup but in so doing also minimize the other's distress. Thus, although Example 2 contains an element of a Level 5 strategy, it is the speaker's explicit denial of feelings (as opposed to his or her initial recognition and legitimation) that emerges as the key action in the message. Strategies that clearly deny the feelings and perspective of a distressed other are coded in Major Division 1.

Sublevel coding. In the example, the speaker makes two evaluative claims that function to deny or ignore her friend's distressed emotional state. By saying that "there are lots of other guys out there" and that the loss of this particular one is "not the end of the world," the speaker minimizes the distress and, therefore, ignores her friend's feelings. Within the hierarchy, comforting strategies that explicitly ignore another's feelings are coded in Level 3.

Example 3

"I know you're really upset about the breakup and I'm sorry. I, I know how frustrating it can be to lose someone, especially if you've been going out for a while. Plus, it was like a big surprise. It hurts, but you can't let yourself drown in that. You just have to keep going."

Major division coding. In this example, the speaker pays a great deal of attention to her friend's distress. She also cites legitimizing reasons why these feelings are present in the situation. Such explicit recognition and elaboration of the other's feelings and perspective suggests that the strategy belongs in one of the levels under Major Division 3.

Sublevel coding. The message provides explanation for the other's feelings and consequently should be coded higher than Level 7. However, it does not attempt to get the other to see the situation either from a general social perspective or from the more specific perspective of any of the individuals involved in the situation. In the absence of any attempt to get the friend to take another perspective, the strategy cannot be coded at the highest level of the hierarchy. Thus, this message belongs in Level 8.

Aside from demonstrating the steps to follow when coding text, the above examples also illustrate the fact that one comforting strategy may contain elements of messages that reflect different levels in the hierarchy. Remember, however, that we are not interested in coding the individual sentences or components that make up a message strategy. Rather, we are interested in capturing the overall effect these components combine to achieve. *When a single strategy is composed of elements that reflect different levels in the hierarchy, it is your job to determine the overall effect these elements combine to achieve.* In other words, you must focus on the key actions being performed in the message.

Thus, coding will sometimes require you to make an important interpretive decision: to identify which level of the hierarchy *best reflects* the predominant focus of the message.

To better understand this task, try to identify the key actions being performed in the following messages.

Example 4

"I know that you're sad, but sounds like you just have to forget about him. He sounds like he was a jerk anyway. There are lots of other fish in the sea."

Explanation. By acknowledging the other's sadness, the speaker explicitly recognizes the other's feelings. Thus, there is an element of Level 7 in the above response. However, the speaker's next statements minimize the other's distress by suggesting that she may be wallowing in the sadness and that the boyfriend is a jerk and not worth the feelings. When viewed in relation to the entire message, then, the initial acknowledgment is overshadowed by the criticism that follows. Because the key action of the message is to ignore the other's feelings, Example 4 would be coded as Level 3.

Conclusion

To summarize, the process of coding comforting messages involves two basic steps. First, you must decide in which of the three major divisions a message belongs. After identifying the appropriate division, you can then place the message into its proper level within that division.

At each step, remember that it is the predominant focus of a message that should be coded, not its individual components. Thus, it is your responsibility to choose the level of the hierarchy that best reflects the *key actions* being performed.

9

■

MICROANALYSIS OF FACE-TO-FACE DIALOGUE

An Inductive Approach

JANET BAVELAS, JENNIFER GERWING,
SARA HEALING, AND CHRISTINE TOMORI

Microanalysis of face-to-face dialogue (MFD) began in the 1980s with a project on the curious phenomenon of *motor mimicry*, in which an observer responds in a way that would be appropriate to the situation of the person he or she is observing; for example, wincing when someone else is injured. Since Adam Smith (1759/2002, p. 12) described an example of motor mimicry, it had remained "a riddle in social psychology" (Allport, 1968, p. 30). Most theorists treated motor mimicry as an involuntary empathic reflex. However, in the course of 17 pilot studies aimed at capturing motor mimicry on video (Bavelas, Black, Lemery, MacInnis, & Mullett, 1986), we began to notice that it was more likely to happen when the other person would see it, which would not be true for a reflex.

Finally, on our 18th try (Bavelas, Black, Lemery, & Mullett, 1986), we discovered that motor mimicry was both extremely quick and highly social. This experiment was a carefully controlled 4-second sequence in which the participant was a passive observer. During the first 2 seconds, two experimenters were setting up equipment when one of them apparently dropped a heavy monitor on his obviously bandaged finger, then reacted by gasping and cringing in pain. His actions in the next 2 seconds created two experimental conditions: The experimenter either turned to face the participant, glanced at her, then made full eye contact (the experimental condition), or he turned away from her, toward the other experimenter, and interacted

with him (the control condition). In the eye-contact condition, the participants started to display motor mimicry within an average of 1.04 seconds, and they continued with a kaleidoscope of mimetic expressions for a few more seconds; see Example 1 (in Figure 9.1). Without eye contact, participants either did not react at all or started a mimetic reaction and quickly stopped.

We began to appreciate that this rapid and precise sensitivity to the other person might be true of most communication in face-to-face dialogue (as our predecessors in the Natural History of an Interview project had proposed; Leeds-Hurwitz, 1987). However, this experiment was obviously not a dialogue. Because our ultimate interest was dialogue itself, we began to develop a method for the second-by-second analysis of face-to-face dialogues, for example, with speakers telling their own close-call stories rather than an experimenter enacting an injury. Example 2 (in Figure 9.2) illustrates an addressee's motor mimicry while the speaker was telling his close-call story about an accident in the wilderness (see Bavelas, Coates, & Johnson, 2000).

What Is Microanalysis of Face-to-Face Dialogue?

The method that has evolved from that initial discovery is microanalysis of face-to-face dialogue, the detailed and replicable examination of any aspect of

129

Figure 9.1 Motor mimicry timed to eye contact. Example 1, the observer's motor mimicry in an experiment. She was watching as the experimenter directly across from her (inset in the upper right quadrant) apparently dropped a heavy monitor on his finger. Frame 2 shows the experimental condition in which he glanced at her, then made direct eye contact (Frame 3). In the other condition, the experimenter enacted the same injury but then turned away, toward the other experimenter.

Source: Bavelas, Black, Lemery, and Mullett (1986).

Figure 9.2 Motor mimicry in dialogue. Example 2, the addressee's motor mimicry while listening to a close-call story. The addressee (inset at the upper left) was seated directly across from the speaker. In Frame 1, the speaker had come to the key point of his story, namely, when he suddenly slipped and fell into a fast-running river. The addressee's reaction quickly followed, in Frame 2.

observable communicative behavior as it occurs, moment by moment, in a face-to-face dialogue. Unlike many other methods for studying interaction behavior, MFD is not a coding procedure devoted to a particular variable or set of variables. Instead, it is an *open-ended, inductive method* for identifying and analyzing any behavioral, observable phenomenon within its theoretical scope. In this respect, MFD is similar to other meta-methods, such as conversation analysis, interactional sociolinguistics, action-implicative discourse analysis, critical discourse analysis, and discursive psychology (see Tracy, 1995, for a comparison of the other five approaches). Each of these meta-methods offers a theoretical and methodological framework for capturing any phenomenon a researcher finds interesting within its broad framework of assumptions.

To illustrate the wide applicability of MFD, Appendix 9.A describes the dozens of different analyses members of our research group developed for 24 projects on topics as diverse as conversational (co-speech) hand and facial gestures, ironic humor, dyadic decision making, generic versus specific listener responses, gaze patterns, positive versus negative topical content in psychotherapy sessions, collaboration in face-to-face versus computer-mediated communication, figurative language, early responsiveness of an infant with autism, patient-centered information in oncology consultations, formulations in psychotherapy sessions, and direct quotations. This chapter describes the theoretical and methodological choices (summarized in Box 9.1) that define and have shaped MFD.

Box 9.1
Characteristics of Microanalysis of Face-to-Face Dialogue

Theoretical

Discovering phenomena inductively, through observing the data

vs. taking topics from the literature

Integrating spoken language with conversational hand gestures, facial gestures, and gaze

vs. separating verbal and nonverbal communication

Collaborative model—dialogue as joint action; focus on the interactional function of acts

vs. studying isolated acts of an individual or alternating monologues

Observable, functional perspective on interaction

vs. inferences or attributions about cognition, motivation, emotion, etc.

Requirements

Spontaneous[a] face-to-face dialogue

vs. interaction with a confederate or the experimenter

Video recording (preferably with all interlocutors on camera)

vs. audio recording or transcript

Analysis linked to video (preferably annotation of digitized video)

vs. annotation on a transcript or in a separate document

Analysis of moment-by-moment details, often in fractions of seconds

vs. paraphrasing, summarizing, or rating

Analysis takes into account the accumulating conversational context

vs. decontextualized utterances

Options

Location can be in a lab experiment or field observation

vs. either exclusively experimental or exclusively "naturalistic"

Research design can be experimental, quasi-experimental, or no experimental design

vs. either limited to experiments or excluding experiments

(Continued)

(Continued)

Overlapping Phases of Analysis

The analyst can identify the phenomenon inductively, then verify by cross-validation

    vs. standardized ratings or a priori analysis rules

The analyst develops a detailed operational definition with extensive examples and rules

    vs. providing only broad conceptual definitions

Two or more independent analysts work to achieve high interanalyst agreement

    vs. one expert decides what is correct

Summary of data can be qualitative or quantitative

    vs. either always quantified or never quantified

Source: Author.

a. The term *spontaneous* is used with a different technical meaning in other chapters in this book.

An Inductive Approach

In research, to *induce* is "to infer from particulars" rather than using a priori or preexisting principles. For example, although Sherlock Holmes is usually described as "deductive," he consistently formed his hypotheses inductively by observing the particulars closely and making inferences from them rather than by relying on what he had been told about the situation.

Being inductive does not mean having a blank mind; one always starts with interests and curiosities within an explicit or implicit theoretical framework. Being inductive means building theory up from the particulars of observed data. Inductive discovery is valued in many scientific fields, from Francis Bacon (1620/1911) to Nobel Prize winners such as Sir Peter Medawar (1979), Barbara McClintock (in Keller, 1983), and Rita Levi-Montalcini (1988).

An inductive approach is rarely reflected in the text of published articles because their function is to report results efficiently within the context of existing theory and literature rather than tracing the chronological development of projects with inductive origins. Although some methods texts and research courses mention inductive methods, a great deal of what students learn to do leads them away from beginning inductively. Box 9.2 summarizes the guidelines from an essay on inductive research (Bavelas, 1987), with suggestions on how to nurture a new idea as well as how to avoid losing it.

The inductive phase precedes and supports—but does not replace—the later, deductive phase of critical assessment and hypothesis testing. When we have used MFD for formal hypothesis testing, our hypotheses often came from repeated viewing and analysis of video-recorded dialogues. Appendix 9.A notes the studies that started inductively, that is, where the phenomenon itself (or the approach to it) came from observing data rather than reading the literature. Although the relevant established literature can provide some necessary background, it is close observation that directs the researcher's attention to patterns of behaviors that could be fruitful for systematic analysis. Decisions about what could be of particular interest (and why) arise in the relationship between curiosity and direct observation.

Starting inductively has advantages. First, face-to-face dialogue is so intricate and complex that innumerable findings still await discovery. As an alternative to seeking gaps in the literature that might need filling, observing dialogues directly can expand the literature and even take it in new directions. Second, building a theory from data creates a secure empirical base and acts as a restraint on overgeneralization. There is a risk that "grand theories" may achieve their scope more by the encompassing language of the theory than by the data that support it. Third, exploring hunches to find new phenomena is scary but also exciting. Testing these hunches by watching and listening to a dialogue can be far more motivating than using a "top-down"

Box 9.2
Some Guidelines for the Inductive Phase of Research

First, you notice something that intrigues you . . .

1. Don't dismiss it (e.g., concluding it's just "chance" or misperception).

2. Don't go find a category to put it in (e.g., naming it with a technical term from the literature or an expert).

3. Don't belittle it (e.g., seeing it too narrowly or literally).

4. Don't be practical or critical (e.g., worrying about all of the problems that lie ahead).

5. Don't panic (e.g., rushing into a study too soon).

All of those will kill your intuition for sure. Instead you should proceed slowly:

1. Do get more examples: Collect observed examples; no verbal labels yet. Call them instances of "X."

2. Do start developing a schema or class. Consider what these examples might have in common.

3. Do articulate by analogues. Think in metaphors ("It is as if . . ."), not technical language.

4. Do unearth the model. Be an archeologist, uncovering what is there.

5. Finally, do start pilot work. Arrange to see more of X.

Now it is safe to start putting X into words, preferably a full phrase, describing its function, not just a single term.

Source: Adapted from Bavelas (1987), where these steps are described more fully.

---

approach that starts with someone else's theory. Finally, the focus on the micro-details of dialogue pays off—one sees a new phenomenon directly and can show it to other researchers, who can then see it as well. The "new" phenomenon was always there; we just had to notice it.

Theoretical Framework

All observation is selective, and the decisions that shape any analysis inevitably reflect the analyst's theoretical assumptions (e.g., Ochs, 1979). MFD rests on two theoretical assumptions about face-to-face dialogue (described in more detail below) that have been the focus of our long-term program of research. First, because interlocutors in face-to-face dialogue can see and hear each other, they use both visible and audible communicative resources, which are tightly integrated with each other. Second, because interlocutors are engaged in social interaction, their actions must be understood as coordinated and mutually influential.

Integrated Audible and Visible Acts

One major theoretical assumption of MFD is that face-to-face dialogue consists of highly integrated combinations of audible communicative acts (words and prosody) with a defined set of visible co-speech acts. Birdwhistell (1970) proposed that communication consisted of "a structural system of significant symbols (from all of the sensorily based modalities) which permit ordered human interaction" (p. 95), and subsequent scholars have used terms such as *ensembles* (Kendon, 2004), *composites* (Clark, 1996), and *integrated messages* (Bavelas & Chovil, 2000, 2006) to describe these multimodal acts. This position contrasts with some other approaches that, implicitly or explicitly, treat all nonverbal behaviors as either redundant with speech or as conveying an entirely different kind of information.

Bavelas and Chovil (2006) specified *conversational hand gestures*, *conversational* (nonemotional) *facial gestures*, and *mutual gaze* as the visible co-speech acts that contribute to meaning in face-to-face dialogue because they are tightly synchronized with speech in both timing and meaning. Conversational hand gestures are rapid and precise enough to be timed within fractions of seconds of the words they are related to (e.g., Kendon, 1980; McNeill, 1992; Nobe, 2000) as well as adapting to disfluencies (Seyfeddinipur, 2006). Chovil (1989, 1991/1992) found that conversational facial displays are timed to a single word or even syllable. The meaning of a hand or facial gesture is also synchronized with the words it accompanies, conveying information that supplements or even complements (i.e., is not redundant with) these words. Hand and facial gestures can contribute both semantic content and pragmatic information about the ongoing interaction. Gestures are "visible utterances" (Kendon, 2004), and the majority of facial actions in dialogues are not about emotion (Fridlund, Ekman, & Oster, 1987, p. 160). (See Bavelas, Gerwing, & Healing, 2014b, for a review of research on conversational hand and facial gestures.) Patterns of mutual gaze are also precisely timed and tend to serve interactive functions, especially marking speaking and listening roles (Argyle & Cook, 1976; Duncan & Fiske, 1977; Kendon, 1967).

MFD includes these co-occurring audible and visible communicative acts as an integrated whole and interprets them in relationship to their immediate conversational context. Three examples will illustrate conversational hand gestures, facial gestures, and gaze, as well as providing an introduction to the micro level of our analysis, which is often frame by frame.

Example 3: A Conversational Hand Gesture

Two students were being video-recorded as part of a psychology study. They began by getting acquainted, and one of them explained how he came to be in this study:

Speaker: "I, uh, I'm taking a couple of, uh, Psyc courses—'Drugs and Behavior'—<u>so that's how they got my name</u>."

Addressee: "So that's how they got yours, huh."

The underlining indicates where the speaker gestured a writing motion, as if filling out the volunteer form handed out in all psychology courses (in his case, Drugs and Behavior), which led to his being called for this study. Figure 9.3 shows frame shots of this sequence. The speaker's hands were clasped loosely in his lap, then in the 1.37 seconds it took to say "so that's how they got my name," he raised his right hand, mimed a writing motion, and returned his hand to its original position. The writing motion itself was 0.36 seconds and was

Figure 9.3 Complementary function of a hand gesture. Example 3, the speaker uses a nonredundant hand gesture. The speaker and addressee were sitting directly across from each other. Frame 1 shows the split-screen configuration with both of them; Frames 2 and 3 show only the speaker's side. His writing motion in Frame 2 conveyed essential information that was not in his words, that is, that he had filled out a volunteer form.

timed precisely with the words "how they got." Notice that his words did not mention filling out the form, so without the gesture, "that's how" would be unclear. This is an example of a nonredundant gesture, which provides relevant information that the accompanying speech does not convey. In face-to-face dialogues (vs. on the phone), nonredundant gestures are significantly more frequent, and speakers convey less of the essential information in their speech (e.g., Gerwing & Allison, 2011).

Example 4: Two Functions
of Conversational Facial Gestures

The speaker had watched scenes from the movie *Shrek 2* and was now recounting them to the addressee. At one point, she described a scene in which Shrek was talking to Donkey about Puss in Boots:

"And Shrek's like, 'How can we not take him, he's so— look at him, he's so cute. Ohhh. How many cats can wear boots?' And then [pause, 0.77 seconds], I guess they take him [pause, 0.67 seconds] and that's the end."

During the first three underlined phrases, the speaker was not only quoting Shrek but was also *portraying* him with her head and face by looking down (as Shrek had looked down at the tiny cat) and pursing her lips as she spoke in a singsong voice. The second frame in Figure 9.4 shows one of these portrayals. Then, during the two underlined pauses, her facial gestures served a different function. Both of these were *facial shrugs* (Chovil, 1989, 1991/1992): She looked away from the addressee, flashed her eyebrows, and quickly pulled

one corner of her closed mouth down and then back to level (e.g., the third frame in Figure 9.4). Like a shoulder shrug, a facial shrug indicates uncertainty or dismissal. Listening to an audio recording would leave the two pauses open to interpretation, whereas the video shows that she was indicating to the addressee that she had nothing more to say. (See Chovil, 2005, for further methodological details.)

Example 5: A Conversational Function of Gaze

The speaker was telling a close-call story in which the heat from a reading lamp on her headboard set her pillow on fire as she slept. She had already explained where the lamp was and how hot it was. Now she began to foreshadow the close call:

I guess it was on for—I don't know how long it was on for.

Figure 9.5 shows the gaze pattern for this sequence. Notice that in Frame 1, the speaker is looking down, and the addressee is holding her previous expression (two fingers near her mouth). In Frame 2, as she said the words underlined above, the speaker looked up and came into full eye contact with the addressee, who immediately raised her eyebrows noticeably, creating a wide-eyed and somewhat alarmed facial gesture, which she held for 1 second, still saying nothing. Bavelas, Coates, and Johnson (2002) showed that these brief moments of mutual gaze during the speaker's turn have a very high probability of eliciting a new response from the addressee.

The above examples illustrate that a theory of integrated audible and visible co-speech acts has clear

Figure 9.4 Two complementary functions of facial gestures. Example 4, two nonredundant facial gestures. Both conveyed information that was not in the speaker's words. (The addressee, who was sitting directly across from the speaker, is inset in the circle in the upper right corner.) The speaker was describing a scene from the movie *Shrek 2*, and in Frame 2, she enacted Shrek talking about the cat while looking down at him, with pursed lips and a doting expression. Immediately after, in Frame 3, she paused, made a quick facial shrug, and provided no additional details.

"I don't know"   "how long it was on for"

Figure 9.5 Complementary function of gaze. Example 5, the speaker's gaze elicits an addressee response. (The speaker and addressee were sitting directly across from each other and recorded in a vertically split screen.) The speaker had been describing the reading lamp on her headboard, which was ultimately the cause of her close call. In Frame 1, she was looking down and away. Then in Frame 2, she looked directly at the addressee, who immediately raised her eyebrows sharply.

methodological implications: Analyzing an audio recording or a transcript of a face-to-face dialogue will exclude meaningful information that is likely to affect the interpretation of the words themselves.

Dialogue as Joint Action

Our other major theoretical assumption owes a great deal to the collaborative theory of Clark and his colleagues (e.g., Clark, 1992, 1996). This theory casts dialogue as coordinated joint action between speaker and addressee rather than as autonomous actions by individuals. Experiments by Clark and Wilkes-Gibbs (1986), Isaacs and Clark (1987), Schober and Clark (1989), and Bavelas et al. (2000, 2002) have shown that a collaborative model predicts what happens in dialogue better than an autonomous model does.

The above dialogue examples all illustrated this moment-by-moment coordination:

- In Example 2 (Figure 9.2), the addressee's wince and "Ooooh" were not his individual emotional reactions; they were perfectly timed to fit a particular moment in the speaker's narrative.
- In Example 3, the speaker's gesture drew on their shared knowledge. Notice that the addressee collaborated by confirming that he had indeed understood, using the speaker's exact words, including the demonstrative pronoun referring to the gesture ("*that*'s how they got").

- In Example 4, the facial shrug was important information for the addressee. It accounted for the speaker's momentary pause and also qualified what she said next as inexact but good enough.
- In Example 5, the speaker's gaze elicited the addressee's response (looking alarmed), which in turn showed the speaker that the addressee was following her story closely without interrupting it.

An Observable, Functional
Perspective on Interaction

Studying dialogue as collaborative interaction limits both theory and data to the analysis of each act's *function* in the dialogue, that is, the moment-by-moment effect of what the interlocutors display to each other, as the dialogue unfolds. A particular project may focus only on the speaker or the addressee, but our collaborative approach directs the focus outward to what the action is doing in the dialogue rather than inward to what it might mean about that individual. MFD explicitly avoids inferences about unobservable mental processes (e.g., an individual's cognition, intention, motivation, emotion, attitude, ability, or personality) and instead focuses on how an act responds to what happened before or leads to what happens next. We propose that careful documentation of what is observable in dialogue should precede speculation about possible mental or neurophysiological explanations.

Data Requirements: What Is Essential and What Is Not

As a practical matter, it is possible to embark on the study of observable behaviors only with suitable data and technology. Fortunately, the minimum requirements (outlined in this section) are neither onerous nor expensive.

Spontaneous Face-to-Face Dialogue

Because MFD was developed for the analysis of face-to-face dialogues, this method requires spontaneous dialogues in which participants can see and interact with each other. Most obviously, the data must be social behavior in a dialogue, not the increasingly common use of self-reports or responses to stimuli on a computer (Baumeister, Vohs, & Funder, 2007; Patterson, 2008; Patterson, Giles, & Teske, 2011). Other settings, such as telephone or mediated dialogues, are not inherently less interesting or informative, but one cannot assume without evidence that they will generalize to face-to-face dialogues. Indeed, their value may be the contrast they provide to a face-to-face dialogue (e.g., Bavelas, Gerwing, Sutton, & Prevost, 2008; Bavelas, Gerwing, & Healing, 2014a; Phillips, 2007).

A defining feature of face-to-face dialogue is the participants' reciprocal ability to act and react spontaneously. In Clark's (1996, p. 10) terms, a true dialogue requires extemporaneity, self-determination, and self-expression. Even though dialogues in experiments typically have a particular focus or task that directs the topic of their conversation (e.g., getting acquainted, telling a story, giving directions), ensuring spontaneous interaction within that task is still essential. Social psychology experiments frequently seek to trade off spontaneity for experimental control by using a confederate or experimenter as one of the participants. However, Kuhlen and Brennan (2013) have raised serious questions about actually achieving experimental control with confederates. There is also evidence that the results with confederates or experimenters may differ from the results with free dialogues (Bavelas & Healing, 2013; Brown-Schmidt & Tanenhaus, 2008; Lockridge & Brennan, 2002). Ethical considerations, such as in medical interactions, often mandate analog or simulated dialogues, but these also raise questions about control and generalizability to free dialogues (e.g., de la Croix & Skelton, 2009; Clever et al., 2011). Fortunately, more and more lab experiments on language and communication are using free dialogues, which demonstrates that shifting the unit of analysis from the individual to the dyad does not compromise experimental control.

Video Recording of Both (or All) Participants

In face-to-face dialogues, the participants can see and hear each other (Clark, 1996, p. 9), and video recording is the only method that preserves the participants' integrated audible and visible communicative acts. Working with an audio recording or a transcript of a face-to-face dialogue implicitly assumes that visible behaviors are either redundant with speech, are irrelevant, or are a separate "channel" conveying information that is unrelated to the co-occurring speech (e.g., emotional or relationship information). Yet some visible acts, such as nodding, are directly equivalent to verbal alternatives such as "yeah," and omitting them creates an apparently less responsive addressee. Similarly, as illustrated in Examples 3 to 5, leaving visible co-speech acts unrecorded will often lead to erroneous or ambiguous interpretations of the speech itself. Even some basic assumptions may no longer apply. For example, observing how the addressees in Examples 2 and 5 provided overlapping but noninterruptive facial reactions to their speaker makes it hard to maintain an individual's speaking turn as the basic unit of dialogue.

A less obvious reason for video recordings is that these capture an often overlooked feature of copresence, namely, the physical and social context that the participants share, including how they use objects and refer to what is mutually visible. When listening to an audio recording or reading a transcript, it is easy to forget whether the participants were in a medical office, a living room, a bar, or a psychology experiment, much less how they used that environment as part of their dialogue.

Studying face-to-face dialogue requires that both (or all) participants be on video at all times. In the lab or a setting in which seating can be assigned, a precisely planned side view with a single camera will capture two participants. Two or more cameras and a special effects generator can create a variety of split-screen configurations, but a well-placed mirror can also create a split-screen image with one camera (Bavelas, Black, Lemery, MacInnis, et al., 1986, pp. 107–108). Luff and Heath (2012) provided an excellent discussion of the possibilities for field studies. Getting both participants on screen is more than a technical issue; it also reveals how theory can shape method even at the data collection stage. For example, switching the camera back and forth to record only the person who is speaking at the time imposes a theory that treats dialogue as alternating monologues.

Analysis of such recordings preserves the autonomous model, as there is no record of the listener's visible behaviors, let alone their effect on the speaker. For example, in a classic study, Goodwin (1981) challenged those who interpreted speakers' frequent sentence fragments in spontaneous dialogue as evidence of "the apparent disorderliness of natural speech." By video-recording both participants, Goodwin showed that speakers broke off midsentence when their addressees were not looking at them and then restarted when they had established mutual gaze—an orderly collaborative pattern. A camera view that focuses only on the speaker makes it difficult if not impossible to document such collaboration.

Any Setting, Any Design

Assuming that the aforementioned requirements are feasible, any setting and any research design will work. Face-to-face dialogue is the pervasive form of language use (e.g., Goodwin, 1981, p. 12; Goodwin, 1990, p. 1; Levinson, 1983, p. 284; van Dijk, 1985, p. 2) and is remarkably adaptive to the particular contexts in which it occurs. Given this diversity of contexts, no single setting has a claim to being the "real world," and none can be dismissed as "artificial." We do primarily lab experiments but have also studied oncology consultations (Healing, 2013), hospital interactions (Gerwing & Dalby, 2014), psychotherapy sessions (Korman, Bavelas, & De Jong, 2013; Phillips, 1998, 1999; Tomori, 2004; Tomori & Bavelas, 2007; Smock Jordan, Froerer, & Bavelas, 2013), and home videos of infants (Gerwing, 2008).

As for research design (e.g., a randomized controlled experiment, a quasi-experiment, a field study, or pure observation), the choice will primarily affect the interpretation of results, that is, internal versus external validity. It is probably more accurate and fruitful to combine curiosity about others' data in different settings with more modest generalizations about our own.

Using Video Annotation
Rather Than a Transcript

For many years, our research group used a variety of low-tech methods, mostly looking at analogue video and recording our decisions on paper. The current variety of video annotation software systems offer distinct advantages, but researchers should approach these systems with specific questions: First, if the cost of the software and support is covered by a site license at the researcher's institution, what happens if the researcher moves elsewhere? Or if the institution decides to let the license expire? The researcher's previous or ongoing data analysis using this system

could be lost or made unavailable. Second, does the software accommodate a novel analysis system, or does it impose fixed coding criteria? Does it allow the researcher to work inductively, being responsive to the data and adapting to what it is revealing? Annotation software should support both the inductive phase and the final, formal, or deductive phase.

Our research group has settled on ELAN software for annotating digitized video (http://tla.mpi.nl/tools/tla-tools/elan/; Wittenburg, Brugman, Russel, Klassman, & Sloetjes, 2006). ELAN is open-source, free software developed and maintained at the Max Planck Institute for Psycholinguistics in the Netherlands. ELAN is a highly flexible and intuitive tool for the analysis of most digitized formats and has several valuable functions. As shown in the screen shot in Figure 9.6, the analyst can play and move around the video at a variety of speeds, including fractions of seconds. Even more important, dragging the mouse along the time line (creating the blue column) selects any section of dialogue for repeated or frame-by-frame viewing, as well as preserving it. Selection is the core of MFD, because it reveals details of sequences that are often not obvious in a first or real-time viewing. ELAN is not only the microscope that takes the analyst into the world of these details, it is a method for preserving them.

Figure 9.6 shows the tiers (rows) below the video where the researcher can annotate multiple, even overlapping behaviors. For example, the speaker's actions can be noted on one tier, and overlapping addressee contributions can be annotated on another tier. The researcher can add as many tiers as needed and label them as he or she wishes; there are no imposed units, features, or variables. Figure 9.6 includes a simple illustration, showing how ELAN captured the information needed for Example 3 (i.e., the exact timing of the speaker's gesture to his words). First, the analyst had to locate where his entire hand movement occurred, from the moment he raised his hand to when he put it back on his lap. Using ELAN with the sound off, the analyst located those two points by moving backward and forward repeatedly, then selected that segment and saved it on the top tier, which she named "full gesture phase." She could then listen to this selection repeatedly to be able to record the precise speech accompanying the movement into this tier. More repeated viewing located exactly where the meaningful part of the gesture began and ended, as well as the exact words it accompanied. This smaller selection was saved on the second tier, using the technical term *gesture stroke*. These two tiers could later be used to record all of the gesture-word combinations in this dialogue as part of a fuller study of the precise synchronization of gestures to words.

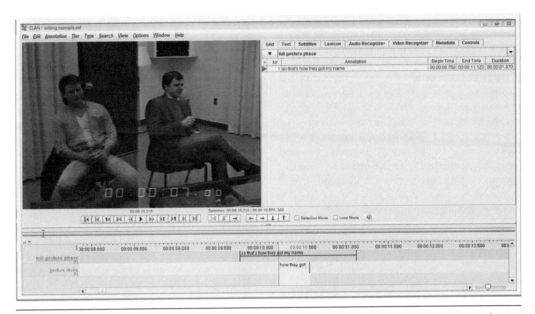

Figure 9.6 Screenshot of ELAN software in use. The ELAN screen includes the digitized video, action buttons, and tiers for annotation. The action buttons directly below the video include play (or pause) and frame-by-frame forward or backward. The buttons to their right are for playing a selected excerpt. The tiers below illustrate the selection and annotation used to analyze Example 3. The upper right quadrant includes a choice ("Grid") to view all annotations on a given tier.

For MFD, the essential feature of ELAN is that it links the words, prosody, and visible acts just as they occurred in the dialogue. Relying on a separate written transcript of the video recording may lead to analyzing the transcript rather than the dialogue. Although it is quicker to read a transcript than to look at a video, one's memory of the visible and prosodic features is fallible. Even notations of these features on the transcript are still only the transcriber's version of the data. ELAN displays what the interlocutors actually did.

The Scale of Microanalysis

As illustrated in Examples 1 to 5, "micro" in our method means attending to the observable moment-by-moment details of dialogue, often at the level of fractions of seconds. The goal is to discover the precision with which the participants create and manage their dialogue. Therefore, the primary raw data for microanalysis are these details, not the analyst's paraphrase, summary, or linguistic gloss. The latter are processed versions of what happened, usually at a theoretical or conceptual level.

Although the focus of MFD is the specific behavior or behavioral process that is of interest in a particular project, it is essential to situate each instance in a nested set of contexts. These include the *setting* of the

dialogue in the broadest sense (e.g., a medical consultation, a psychology experiment, or home videos of infants), who the *interlocutors* are (e.g., physician and patient, strangers meeting for the first time, infant siblings), the *purpose* of their dialogue (e.g., diagnosing the patient's illness, getting acquainted, playing with new toys), the *accumulated dialogue* so far (e.g., the topics covered, who has said or done what), and finally the *micro-moment* in which a particular instance happens. As the dialogue proceeds, the participants inevitably draw on and create shared understandings, which shape their subsequent actions and meanings. For example, when information is new to the dialogue, the participants tend to use full noun phrases and to articulate the information clearly. Later, when that information becomes "given," participants often replace nouns with pronouns or other shorthand references and even speak less clearly (Fowler, 1988). In a larger sense, what either person says builds on the dialogue they have created together so far.

Overlapping Phases of an Inductive Microanalysis

Many researchers approach video-recorded dialogues with their own particular curiosity, like a detective seeking to uncover specific information.

The curiosity might be about how a particular kind of communicative act (e.g., hesitation, metaphor, disagreement) functions in dialogue or about how a particular interactive process unfolds during dialogue (e.g., cooperating on a task, constructing the solution to a problem). The path that starts with curiosity goes through definition and analysis, until it reaches its goal of satisfying the curiosity and explaining it to the wider world. Be aware that this path is rarely as straightforward as can be presented here; the phases will overlap and often involve backtracking. In this section we illustrate several stages on the path for Healing's (2013) master's thesis on oncology consultations.

On Being Inductive

In the study of face-to-face dialogue, being inductive means developing an analysis from the observable details of interlocutors' communicative behaviors, rather than relying solely on previous work or existing theory. Being inductive does not mean avoiding any theoretical framework; ideally, the researcher thinks globally and acts locally. As noted at the outset, MFD includes a global framework that suits our interests; focusing on local details within this framework can lead to innovation. Being inductive does not mean abandoning one's training in rigorous research methods for a carefree romp through the data. Nor does it mean passively waiting for inspiration to strike. It means adopting the equally demanding mental discipline of patience, of initially postponing those rigorous, hypercritical research methods that will be necessary later, in order to engage with the data intensively and freely at the beginning.

Healing (2013) explicated and documented (http://dspace.library.uvic.ca/bitstream/handle/1828/4835/Healing_Sara_MSc_2013.pdf?sequence=7&isAllowed=y) the inductive process that led to her analysis of the information patients contributed during their oncology consultations. As part of a larger project at a cancer agency, Healing had the opportunity to sit in on oncology consultations when the physician and patient agreed. She soon became interested in shared decision making: The oncologists contributed essential information relevant to treatment options, but Healing was curious about the patients' unique contributions about their own situations (e.g., what a particular patient valued or feared). She proposed that a truly shared decision process should, at a minimum, include contributions from the patient that were relevant to the decision. Healing found that the literature on patient-centered communication focused on how health care professionals should talk to patients but not on what an individual patient can contribute to the dialogue. She was confident that she could find the answer inductively, through close examination of video-recorded consultations. After the necessary ethical and logistical steps, she was able to video-record eight full oncology consultations.

In these consultations, Healing's (2013) raw data consisted of everything each patient said, so she began by creating an ELAN tier with an entry each time a patient said something: 1,585 utterances. Then she immersed herself in a subset of about 30% of her data until she began to be able to articulate patterns in what patients were contributing, mainly by making notes on the *function* of what the patient said. This was a time-consuming, trial-and-error process, but it brought the patient's contributions out of the background and began to reveal their variety.

The first major distinction that emerged was between two different functions: Naturally, many utterances contributed *biomedical information* about the patients' cancer, treatment, or other procedures (e.g., telling the physician what tests they were taking). Other utterances functioned to introduce *patient-centered information*, which she defined as *information that contributed this particular patient's unique position or point of view*. Patient-centered information included, for example, factors affecting this individual's choice of treatment:

- "We were kinda *hoping*, in September, to go on a cruise" [i.e., it would be better to have treatment concentrated in a shorter time].
- "So, yeah, um, and a, I like to, ah I *don't expect* to be a rocket scientist so I *want* a brain that will function for everyday activities. I *like* to do photography and, a, I *like* being involved, you know, in art things and whatnot."
- "Um, I pretty well came here with a *totally open mind* [about treatment options]."

Other topics were the patient's limitations or resources:

- "I seem to ah, if, if ah drugs have a downside, or, or a counter-effect thing I seem to get them. The, the Statin drugs *are really a problem for me*."
- "And since *I've got so many buddies who've been through systems and everything*, ah yeah, *very good* support system."

Patients also talked about their hopes and fears:

- "If I make it into my eighties, kickin' and screamin' *then that's good.*"
- "That's probably the thing that *scares* me the most ah, is incontinence."
- "[When the other doctor said] that the chances of survival are 80%, I said, *'well gee, I'll take the 80%'* [slight laugh]."
- "If, if I'm, if things are so bad—*I'd just as soon take a potion and exit.*"

Healing's immersion in the data identified two more functions of client's utterances: *small talk*, which contributed information not directly related to the illness or the treatment, and *generic listening responses* (e.g., "yeah" or "mm hmm" when these simply showed that the patient was listening and following what the physician was saying). However, like the biomedical information, these were not the focus of her research. Instead, she defined and identified these three functions in order to provide contrasts that sharpened the definition of her primary interest in patient-centered information.

Developing an Operational Definition

Once the researcher's immersion in the data has led to an intuitive recognition of the phenomenon, it is time to start thinking about how to articulate it for other researchers, that is, to develop an operational definition. An operational definition connects the researcher's broad, usually abstract definition of the phenomenon with specifics about how to recognize the phenomenon in a dialogue. Formally, an operational definition is a set of rules and procedures (ideally with many examples) that permit others to locate instances such as those the researcher has intuitively uncovered (e.g., Healing, 2013, pp. 27–38). A fully explicit operational definition serves to share knowledge with other researchers, to permit others to check on the researcher's conclusions, and to encourage replication. As a bonus, the process of becoming very explicit inevitably leads to a deeper understanding of the topic itself.

Creating a logical sequence of decisions. A typical analysis requires more than one decision about the same section of data. Most often, the first task is simply to *locate* all instances of the phenomenon (e.g., all patient utterances). The second decision is to *characterize* each of these instances according to the operational definition (e.g., as small talk, a generic listener response, biomedical information, or patient-centered information). Locating and characterizing phenomena at the same time conflates decisions that should be separate and makes disagreements between analysts difficult to interpret. For example, if one of the analysts overlooked a patient utterance, but the other one analyzed it, they would inevitably (and spuriously) disagree about what its function was. The best procedure is to complete one level of decisions, assess agreement, and resolve any disagreements before proceeding to the next level.

Sometimes the analysis requires several contingent decisions; that is, one decision determines what the choices will be for the next decision. Constructing a formal *decision tree* that describes these branching decisions is a useful addition to an operational definition because it ensures that each analyst follows the same logical decision processes. Appendix 9.B includes decision trees from three different projects, including Healing (2013). In each example, the easiest decisions come first; these usually locate instances that clearly do or do not fit the operational definition. In Healing's data, utterances that were small talk or generic listener responses were easy to recognize, so identifying them and removing them from further consideration left the analyst free to focus on the more difficult distinctions between biomedical and patient-centered information.

Interanalyst Agreement and Cross-Validation

Two criticisms or concerns often arise about inductive research. The first is that the findings could be idiosyncratic to this researcher and no one else could see them. The answer is *high interanalyst agreement* using the operational definitions. On the basis of approximately 15% of the data that were not part of the inductive data set, Healing (2013) demonstrated 90% agreement (205 of 228 decisions) with an independent analyst. The second concern is that the finding might fit only the specific data set it came from and would not hold in other relevant data. The answer is *cross-validation* with new data. If the analysis fit only the specific data set it came from, then it would not apply to new data, leading to numerous cases that were "not analyzable" or "other." Healing's cross-validation included the reliability data set plus the remainder of the data (which she analyzed herself). Over 96% of these 1,135 utterances fit one of the four functions she defined in her analysis. Her analysis was ready for use in new research projects or for teaching physicians to recognize patient-centered information.

Concluding Thoughts

In this chapter we have described and illustrated microanalysis of face-to-face dialogue, which is an open-ended, inductive method for the detailed and replicable examination of any aspect of observable communicative behavior in its immediate context. We have been explicit about the theoretical framework of this approach as well as the data it fits and as explicit as possible about the process of doing research inductively.

Some nontechnical advice may be helpful as well. First, it is essential to recognize that the inductive phase is a distinct initial phase of a process that eventually leads to the more familiar, formal procedures (e.g., design and hypothesis testing). However, in the early phase, it is often difficult to put aside those formal criteria, simply out of fear. After all, methods textbooks and courses often overwhelm students with all of the possible errors and misinterpretations lying in wait for a researcher (e.g., alternative explanations, Type I error). If internalized, this kind of criticism is crippling during the early phases (e.g., Bavelas, 1987). A clear recognition that those formal issues will come later can allay the fear, leaving the researcher free to follow his or her intuition and passion in the early phases.

A second question arises because MFD (as some other similar approaches) is so time-consuming. More than one colleague has suggested that a "quick and dirty" analysis would be just as good. Curiously, no one suggests faster alternatives in other sciences, such as neuroscience, deep-space astronomy, and higher mathematics, in which painstaking and time-intensive analysis is the norm. Some phenomena are simply not visible except at a micro level. For example, Gerwing's (2008; https://dspace.library.uvic.ca//handle/1828/1226) data were home videos of infant triplets, one of whom was later diagnosed with autism. Several professionals had watched these videos in real time, and none had identified which infant would later be diagnosed. Gerwing created an intensive microanalysis of each infant's immediate response to any interactional overture by a parent (see Appendices 9.A and 9.B) and applied it twice with "blind" analysts. The analysis not only differentiated between the infant with autism and his typically developing siblings, it also documented when the differences from his siblings appeared and in which kinds of interactions. In our experience, the seconds and fractions of seconds of a face-to-face dialogue often contain interactional patterns and processes discoverable only with a "slow but clean" microanalysis.

References

Allport, G. W. (1968). The historical background of modern social psychology. In G. Lindzey & E. Aronson (Eds.), *The handbook of social psychology* (2nd ed.). Menlo Park, CA: Addison-Wesley.

Argyle, M., & Cook, M. (1976). *Gaze and mutual gaze.* Cambridge, UK: Cambridge University Press.

Bacon, F. (1911). *Novum organum* (J. Devey, Ed.). New York: Collier. (Original work published 1620). Retrieved from http://archive.org/details/novumorganum00bacouoft/

Baumeister, R. F., Vohs, K. D., & Funder, D. C. (2007). Psychology as the science of self-reports and finger movements: Whatever happened to actual behavior? *Perspectives on Psychological Science, 2,* 396–403.

Bavelas, J. B. (1987). Permitting creativity in science. In D. N. Jackson & J. P. Rushton (Eds.), *Scientific excellence: Origins and assessment* (pp. 307–327). Beverly Hills, CA: Sage.

Bavelas, J. B., Black, A., Lemery, C. R., MacInnis, S., & Mullett, J. (1986). Experimental methods for studying "elementary motor mimicry." *Journal of Nonverbal Behavior, 10,* 102–119.

Bavelas, J. B., Black, A., Lemery, C. R., & Mullett, J. (1986). "I show how you feel": Motor mimicry as a communicative act. *Journal of Personality and Social Psychology, 50,* 322–329.

Bavelas, J. B., & Chovil, N. (2000). Visible acts of meaning: An integrated message model of language use in face-to-face dialogue. *Journal of Language and Social Psychology, 19,* 163–194.

Bavelas, J. B., & Chovil, N. (2006). Hand gestures and facial displays as part of language use in face-to-face dialogue. In V. Manusov & M. Patterson (Eds.), *Handbook of nonverbal communication* (pp. 97–115). Thousand Oaks, CA: Sage.

Bavelas, J. B., Chovil, N., Coates, L., and Roe, L. (1995). Gestures specialized for dialogue. *Personality and Social Psychology Bulletin, 21,* 394–405.

Bavelas, J. B., Chovil, N., Lawrie, D. A., & Wade, A. (1992). Interactive gestures. *Discourse Processes, 15,* 469–489.

Bavelas, J. B., Coates, L., & Johnson, T. (2000). Listeners as co-narrators. *Journal of Personality and Social Psychology, 79,* 941–952.

Bavelas, J. B., Coates, L., & Johnson, T. (2002). Listener responses as a collaborative process: The role of gaze. *Journal of Communication, 52,* 566–580.

Bavelas, J., Gerwing, J., Allison, M., & Sutton, C. (2011). Dyadic evidence for grounding with abstract deictic gestures. In G. Stam & M. Ishino (Eds.), *Integrating gestures: The interdisciplinary nature of gesture* (pp. 49–60). Amsterdam, the Netherlands: John Benjamins.

Bavelas, J. B., Gerwing, J., & Healing, S. (2014a). Effect of dialogue on demonstrations: Direct quotations, facial portrayals, hand gestures, and figurative references. *Discourse Processes, 51,* 619–655.

Bavelas, J. B., Gerwing, J., & Healing, S. (2014b). Hand gestures and facial displays in conversational interaction. In T. Holtgraves (Ed.), *Oxford handbook of language and social psychology* (pp. 111–130). New York: Oxford University Press.

Bavelas, J. B., Gerwing, J., & Healing, S. (2014c). Including facial gestures in gesture-speech ensembles. In M. Seyfeddinipur & M. Gullberg (Eds.), *From gesture in conversation to visible action as utterance: Essays in honor of Adam Kendon* (pp. 15–33). Amsterdam, the Netherlands: John Benjamins.

Bavelas, J. B., Gerwing, J., Sutton, C., & Prevost, D. (2008). Gesturing on the telephone: Independent effects of dialogue and visibility. *Journal of Memory and Language, 58*, 495–520.

Bavelas, J. B., & Healing, S. (2013). Reconciling the effects of mutual visibility on gesturing: A review. *Gesture, 13*, 63–92.

Birdwhistell, R. (1970). *Kinesics and context: Essays on body motion communication*. Philadelphia: University of Pennsylvania Press.

Brown-Schmidt, S., & Tanenhaus, M. K. (2008). Real-time investigation of referential domains in unscripted conversations: A targeted language game approach. *Journal of Cognitive Science, 32*, 643–684.

Chovil, N. (1989). *Communicative functions of facial displays in conversation* (Unpublished doctoral dissertation). University of Victoria, Victoria, BC, Canada.

Chovil, N. (1991). Social determinants of facial displays. *Journal of Nonverbal Behavior, 15*, 141–153.

Chovil, N. (1991/1992). Discourse-oriented facial displays in conversation. *Research on Language and Social Interaction, 25*, 163–194.

Chovil, N. (2005). Measuring conversational facial displays. In V. Manusov (Ed.), *The sourcebook of nonverbal measures: Going beyond words* (pp. 173–188). Hillsdale, NJ: Lawrence Erlbaum.

Clark, H. H. (1992). *Arenas of language use*. Chicago: University of Chicago Press & Center for the Study of Language and Information.

Clark, H. H. (1996). *Using language*. Cambridge, UK: Cambridge University Press.

Clark, H. H., & Wilkes-Gibbs, D. (1986). Referring as a collaborative process. *Cognition, 22*, 1–39.

Clever, S. L., Dudas, R. A., Solomon, B. S., Yeh, H. C., Levine, D., Bertram, A., . . . Cofrancesco, J., Jr. (2011). Medical student and faculty perceptions of volunteer outpatients versus simulated patients in communication skills training. *Academic Medicine, 86*, 1437–1442.

Coates, L. J. (1991). *A collaborative theory of inversion: Irony in dialogue* (Unpublished master's thesis). Department of Psychology, University of Victoria, Victoria, BC, Canada.

de la Croix, A., & Skelton, J. (2009). The reality of role play: Interruptions and amount of talk in simulated consultations. *Medical Education, 43*, 695–703.

Duncan, S., Jr., & Fiske, D. W. (1977). *Face-to-face interaction*. Hillsdale, NJ: Lawrence Erlbaum.

Fowler, C. A. (1988). Differential shortening of repeated content words produced in various communicative contexts. *Language and Speech, 31*, 307–319.

Fridlund, A. J., Ekman, P., & Oster, H. (1987). Facial expressions of emotion: Review of literature, 1970-1983. In A. W. Siegman & S. Feldstein (Eds.), *Nonverbal behavior and communication* (2nd ed., pp. 143–224). Hillsdale, NJ: Lawrence Erlbaum.

Gerwing, J. (2008). *Quantifying infant social responsiveness: Microanalysis of home videos of a set of triplets for early indications of autism* (Unpublished doctoral dissertation). University of Victoria, Victoria, BC, Canada. Retrieved from https://dspace .library.uvic.ca//handle/1828/1226

Gerwing, J., & Allison, M. (2009). The relationship between verbal and gestural contributions in conversation: A comparison of three methods. *Gesture, 9*, 313–336.

Gerwing, J., & Allison, M. (2011). The flexible semantic integration of gestures and words: Comparing face-to-face and telephone dialogues. *Gesture, 11*, 308–329.

Gerwing, J., & Dalby, A. M. (2014). Gestures convey content: An exploration of the semantic functions of physicians' gestures. *Patient Education and Counseling, 96*, 308–314.

Goodwin, C. (1981). *Conversational organization: Interaction between speakers and hearers*. New York: Academic Press.

Goodwin, M. H. (1990). *He-said-she-said: Talk as social organization among Black children*. Bloomington: Indiana University Press.

Healing, S. (2013). *Development of a method of analysis for identifying an individual patient's perspective in video-recorded oncology consultations* (Unpublished master's thesis). University of Victoria, Victoria, BC, Canada. Retrieved from https://dspace.library .uvic.ca/bitstream/handle/1828/4835/Healing_Sara_ MSc_2013.pdf?sequence=7&isAllowed=y

Isaacs, E. A., & Clark, H. H. (1987). Experts in conversation between experts and novices. *Journal of Experimental Psychology: General, 116*, 26–37.

Johnson, T. (1995). *Decision-making as a social process* (Unpublished master's thesis). Department of Psychology, University of Victoria, Victoria, BC, Canada.

Keller, E. F. (1983). *A feeling for the organism: The life and work of Barbara McClintock*. San Francisco, CA: W. H. Freeman.

Kendon, A. (1967). Some functions of gaze-direction in social interaction. *Acta Psychologica, 26*, 22–63.

Kendon, A. (1980). Gesticulation and speech: Two aspects of the process of utterance. In M. R. Key (Ed.), *The relationship of verbal and nonverbal communication* (pp. 207–227). The Hague, the Netherlands: Mouton.

Kendon, A. (2004). *Gesture: Visible action as utterance*. Cambridge, UK: Cambridge University Press.

Korman, H., Bavelas, J. B., & De Jong, P. (2013). Microanalysis of formulations in solution-focused brief therapy, cognitive behavioral therapy, and motivational interviewing. *Journal of Systemic Therapies, 32*, 32–46.

Kuhlen, A. K., & Brennan, S. E. (2013). Language in dialogue: When confederates might be hazardous to your data. *Psychonomic Bulletin and Review, 20*, 54–72.

Leeds-Hurwitz, W. (1987). The social history of The Natural History of an Interview: A multidisciplinary investigation of social communication. *Research on Language and Social Interaction, 20*, 1–51.

Levi-Montalcini, R. (1988). *In praise of imperfection: My life and work* (L. Attardi, Trans.). New York: Basic Books.

Levinson, S. C. (1983). *Pragmatics*. Cambridge, UK: Cambridge University Press.

Lockridge, C. B., & Brennan, S. E. (2002). Addressees' needs influence speakers' early syntactic choices. *Psychonomic Bulletin & Review, 9*, 550–557.

Luff, P., & Heath, C. (2012). Some "technical challenges" of video analysis: Social actions, objects, material realities and the problems of perspective. *Qualitative Research, 12*, 255–279.

McNeill, D. (1992). *Hand and mind: What gestures reveal about thought*. Chicago: University of Chicago Press.

Medawar, P. B. (1979). *Advice to a young scientist.* New York: Harper & Row.

Nobe, S. (2000). Where do most spontaneous representational gestures actually occur with respect to speech? In D. McNeill (Ed.), *Language and gesture* (pp.186–198). Cambridge, UK: Cambridge University Press.

Ochs, E. (1979). Transcription as theory. In E. Ochs & B. B. Schiefflen (Eds.), *Developmental pragmatics.* New York: Academic Press.

Patterson, M. L. (2008). Back to social behavior: Mining the mundane. *Basic and Applied Social Psychology, 30*, 93–101.

Patterson, M. L., Giles, H., & Teske, M. (2001). The decline of behavioral research? Examining language and communication journals. *Journal of Language and Social Psychology, 30*, 326–340.

Phillips, B. (1998). *Formulation and reformulation in mediation and therapy* (Unpublished master's thesis). Department of Psychology, University of Victoria, Victoria, BC, Canada.

Phillips, B. (1999). Reformulating dispute narratives through active listening. *Mediation Quarterly, 17*, 161–180.

Phillips, B. (2007). *A comparison of autonomous and collaborative models in computer-mediated communication*

(Unpublished doctoral dissertation). Department of Psychology, University of Victoria, Victoria, BC, Canada.

Pinch, D. (1995). *Spontaneous irony in post-stroke individuals* (Unpublished doctoral dissertation). University of Victoria, Victoria, BC, Canada.

Schindler, E. (1996). *Smiling: Beyond happiness* (Unpublished honor's thesis). Department of Psychology, University of Victoria, Victoria, BC, Canada.

Schober, M. F., & Clark, H. H. (1989). Understanding by addressees and overhearers. *Cognitive Psychology, 21*, 211–232.

Seyfeddinipur, M. (2006). *Disfluency: Interrupting speech and gesture* (Unpublished doctoral dissertation). Max Planck Institute, Nijmegen, the Netherlands.

Smith, Adam. (2002). *Adam Smith: The theory of moral sentiments. Cambridge texts in the history of philosophy.* Cambridge, UK: Cambridge University Press. Retrieved March 10, 2014, from http://www.myilibrary.com?ID=42924 (Original work published 1759)

Smock Jordan, S., Froerer, A., & Bavelas, J. B. (2013). Microanalysis of positive and negative content in solution-focused brief therapy and cognitive behavioral therapy expert sessions. *Journal of Systemic Therapies, 32*, 47–60.

Tomori, C. (2004). *Microanalysis of communication in psychotherapy: Are they doing what they say they are doing?* (Unpublished honors thesis). Department of Psychology, University of Victoria, Victoria, BC, Canada.

Tomori, C., & Bavelas, J. B. (2007). Using microanalysis of communication to compare solution-focused and client-centered therapies. *Journal of Family Psychotherapy, 18*, 25–43.

Tracy, K. (1995). Action-implicative discourse analysis. *Journal of Language and Social Psychology, 14*, 195–215.

van Dijk, T. A. (1985). Introduction: Dialogue as discourse and interaction. In T. A. van Dijk (Ed.), *Handbook of discourse analysis, Vol. 3: Discourse and dialogue* (pp. 1–11). London: Academic Press.

Wittenburg, P., Brugman, H., Russel, A., Klassman, A., & Sloetjes, H. (2006). ELAN: A professional framework for multimodality research. In *Proceedings of LREC 2006, Fifth International Conference on Language Resources and Evaluation, Genoa.*

Woods, J. (2005). *New vs. given information: Do gestures dance to the same tune as words?* (Unpublished honor's thesis). Department of Psychology, University of Victoria, Victoria, BC, Canada.

Appendix 9.A

Studies by Our Research Group Using Microanalysis of Face-to-Face Dialogue

Year	Study	Inductive Origin?	Analysis	Interanalyst Agreement for Each Analysis
1989; 1991/1992	Chovil (doctoral dissertation; journal article)	Yes	What kinds of conversational facial displays occur in dialogue? (This was the first systematic study of nonemotional facial actions.)	
			a. Whether a *conversational facial display* occurred	a. 90%
			b. Deciding on the general function of the display (*syntactic, semantic,* or *nonlinguistic*)	b. 96%
			c. Deciding on the specific function of the display (e.g., *question marker, portrayal, adaptor*)	c. 87%
			Note: The analysis did not include smiles.	
1989; 1991	Chovil (doctoral dissertation; journal article)	Yes	Does visibility or being in a dialogue affect the frequency of addressees' facial motor mimicry?	
			a. Number of *motor mimicry displays* per listener	a. $r = .94$
1991	Coates (master's thesis)	Yes	How do participants collaborate on irony in dialogue?	
			a. Identifying inversions (*instances of ironic humor*)	a. 92%
			b. General meaning of an utterance: *mock vs. serious*	b. 100%
			c. Specific meaning of an utterance (14 categories, including *serious excitement/mock excitement, serious insult/mock insult, serious/mock horror,* etc.)	c. 88%
			d. Identifying the four phases of an inversion sequence (*implicit agreement, delivery of inversion, displaying understanding,* and *closure*)	d. 96%
1992	Bavelas, Chovil, Lawrie, & Wade (journal article)	Yes	What is the nature of hand gestures that are not depicting topical content? (See decision tree in Appendix 9.B.) Experiment 1.	
			Locating *topical vs. interactive gestures*	

(Continued)

145

(Continued)

Year	Study	Inductive Origin?	Analysis	Interanalyst Agreement for Each Analysis
			a. Training data	a. All five analysts ≥90%
			b. One speaker in a dyad	b. Median pairwise = 90% (range = 75% to 100%)
			c. One speaker who was alone	c. Median pairwise = 88% (range = 71% to 94%)
			Experiment 2	
			d. Locating *topical* vs. *interactive gestures*	d. Median pairwise = 86% (range = 83% to 95%)
			e. *Degree of redundancy of gesture with words* in its phonemic clause (0 to 3)	e. Two analysts, two checks: $r = .93, .95$
1995	Bavelas, Chovil, Coates, & Roe (journal article)	No	Do interactive gestures occur more in dialogue than in alternating monologues, and do they elicit predictable responses from addressees? Study 1:	
			a. Locating *topical* vs. *interactive gestures*	a. Four analysts: pairwise agreements ≥ 90%
			Study 2: Identifying *addressee's first* response after an interactive gesture:	
			b. Six possible responses; e.g., *confirming* (nod, "mhm"), *specific content, hesitation*	b. Three analysts: overall pairwise agreement = 83%
1995	Johnson (master's thesis)	Yes	How do dyads make decisions about ambiguous stimuli?	
			a. Dividing utterances into units with *only one function*	a. 87%
			b. Identifying the *specific function* of each unit, i.e., *hypothesis, individual fact,* or *social fact*	b. 90%
1995	Pinch (doctoral dissertation)	No	Does neurological status (right, left, or no hemispheric damage) affect spontaneous irony in dialogue?	
			a. Identifying each utterance as *ironic* or *not ironic*	a. 90%
			b. Locating *ironic utterances only*	b. 78%

146

Year	Study	Inductive Origin?	Analysis	Interanalyst Agreement for Each Analysis
1996	Schindler (honor's thesis)	Yes	Do situations that are not happy (e.g., when arguing or guessing wrong) elicit smiles? a. Locating *smiles* during not-happy situations within five different tasks	a. 85% over all tasks (range = 82% to 100%)
2000	Bavelas, Coates, & Johnson (journal article)	Yes	What is the nature of the responses addressees make when they are listening to a close-call story? Experiment 1: a. Deciding whether to divide a contiguous listener response or not b. Distinguishing between *generic* and *specific* listening responses (e.g., "mhm") and *specific* listener responses (e.g., wincing) c. Global rating of the quality of the *story plot* d. Global rating of the *quality of the story telling* e. Number of negative features of the story ending (e.g., *appropriate, abrupt, choppy, or overjustified*) Experiment 2: f. Distinguishing between *generic* and *specific listener responses* g. Number of negative features of the story ending (e.g., *appropriate, abrupt, choppy, or overjustified*) Note: The analysis excluded smiles when they occurred alone.	a. >90% b. 95% c. Intraclass r (7 raters) = .69 d. Intraclass r (3 raters) = .83 e. Two analysts vs. a third analyst, r = .76 f. 99.6% g. Two analysts vs. a third analyst, r = .69
2002	Bavelas, Coates, & Johnson (journal article)	Yes	What predicts the placement of the listener responses found in Bavelas et al. (2000)? a. Identifying periods of *mutual gaze* b. Timing the *onset and offset of mutual gaze*	a. Two dyads: 100% b. First dyad: 84% within 0.1 second Second dyad: 87% within 0.2 seconds

(Continued)

Year	Study	Inductive Origin?	Analysis	Interanalyst Agreement for Each Analysis
2005	Woods (honor's thesis)	No	Do hand gestures show a given-new effect, becoming abbreviated over repeated trials with the same partner? a. Whether the speaker *gestured* during a given trial b. Whether the gesture was *analyzable* c. The *duration* of each gesture	a. 100% b. 96% c. $r = .995$
2004; 2007	Tomori (honor's thesis); Tomori & Bavelas (journal article)	No	Do experts in two different approaches to psychotherapy differ in how they talk with clients? a. Whether the therapist's utterance was a *formulation*, a *question, both,* or *neither* b. Whether the content of a formulation or question was *positive, negative, both,* or *neither*	Separately for each of the four therapists: a. 80%, 86%, 95%, and 95% b. 85%, 86%, 90%, and 100%
2007	Phillips (doctoral dissertation)	Yes	Experiment 2: How do face-to-face dialogues differ from online chats or bulletin-board formats? a. Identifying a single, discrete *idea unit* (topic) b. Identifying *topically related idea units* c. Separating idea units into *statements, replies, questions,* and *answers* These combined to measure: • Development of ideas: the proportion of replies to each other's statements • Coherence: proportion of replies that were not adjacent to the original statement and proportion of answers that were not adjacent to the question d. Number of *audible listener responses* (used to measure the density of listener responses: the ratio of listener responses to words spoken)	a. 90% b. 87% c. 88% d. First two analysts: 96%; third analyst: 95%

Year	Study	Inductive Origin?	Analysis	Interanalyst Agreement for Each Analysis
2008	Bavelas, Gerwing, Sutton, & Prevost (journal article)	Yes	Does being in a dialogue or monologue or being visible to the addressee (or not) affect the rate or kind of hand gestures?	
			a. Whether each hand movement was *gesturing*	a. 92%
			b. Whether each period of *gesturing should be divided* (i.e., locating individual gestures)	b. 78%
			c. Total number of gestures per speaker	c. $r = .98$
			d. *Bias check*: each speaker's rate of gesturing by naive and nonnaive analysts	d. $r = .89$
			e. Whether the function of each gesture was *topical, interactive, or picture oriented*	e. 92%; 93%; $\kappa = .70$
			f. Total number of *topic gestures per speaker*	f. $r = .996$
			g. Total number of *interactive gestures per speaker*	g. $r = .87$
			h. Total number of *picture-oriented gestures per speaker*	h. $r = .93$
			i. *Size of each gesture* (scale of 1 to 5)	i. $r = .92$
			j. Average size of gesture per speaker	j. $r = .97$
			k. Whether there was a *verbal deictic* with each topic gesture	k. 97%
			l. Proportion of *topic gestures with verbal deictics per speaker*	l. $r = .98$
			m. Whether each topic gesture for two specific features was *redundant with the words that accompanied the gesture vs. conveying additional information*	m. First feature: 84%; second feature: 83%
			n. Proportion of each speaker's *topic gestures that were redundant with words*	n. First feature: $r = .92$; second feature: $r = .71$ ($r = .95$ without the highest and lowest outliers)

(Continued)

Year	Study	Inductive Origin?	Analysis	Interanalyst Agreement for Each Analysis
2008	Gerwing (doctoral dissertation)	Yes	Using home videos, was an infant who was later diagnosed with autism less socially responsive to his parents' social overtures than his two triplet siblings were? Study 1 (on sample of home videos) a. Is each *infant on screen* (second by second)? b. *Is a parent directing an overture (i.e., a social action) toward one infant* (yes or no, second by second)? c. Is a parent directing an overture toward one infant (not based on time, which is potentially inflated, but on *episodes of social actions*)? d. *Should the overture be divided* (based on *source, function, or modality*)? e. Did the infant make an *observable response to the overture*? Study 2 (on the home videos not included in Study 1) (See sample decision tree in Appendix 9.B.) a. Is *a parent directing an overture* (i.e., a social action) toward one infant who is onscreen (yes or no, second by second)? b. Same as above, calculated by *change from overture to not overture* (i.e., event by event) c. Who was the agent of the overture (*mother, father, both*)? d. Should the overture be divided, based on source, function, or modality? e. What was the function of the overture: *attention-seeking, directing, helping, greeting, playful, conversational, rewarding, narrative,* or *instrumental*	a. All three infants = 98%; infant A = 96%; B = 98%; C = 98% b. All three infants = 96%; infant A = 97%; B = 94%; C = 97% c. All three infants = 81% d. Source = 100%; function = 98%; modality = 89% e. All three infants = 85% a. 97% b. 84% c. 100% d. 85% e. 85%

Year	Study	Inductive Origin?	Analysis	Interanalyst Agreement for Each Analysis
			f. Was the *agent of the overture on screen?*	f. 99%
			g. Were the *agent's hands and face on screen?*	g. 99%
			h. Was the *infant's response to the social overture analyzable* (both visible and sufficient time)?	h. 93%
			i. Did *infant's behavior change after the social overture?*	i. 93%
			j. Did *infant's new behavior match what the social overture had projected?*	j. 96%
			k. Was the *infant's response to the nonsocial overture analyzable* (visible and sufficient time)?	k. 100%
			l. Did infant *cooperate with the nonsocial overture?*	l. 100%
			m. Before the overture, was the infant *attending the agent, otherwise engaged, or potentially available?*	m. 84%
2009	Gerwing & Allison (journal article)	No	What are the differences between three methods for analyzing the relationship of hand gestures to words?	
			a. Distinguishing between *periods of gesturing, holding a gesture, and not gesturing*	a. 87%
			b. Whether the *gesture was about their task* (creating a floor plan) or not	b. 91%
			c. Whether the *gesture was about an identifiable room* in the floor plan or not	c. 80%
			d. Whether the *words in each speech-gesture combination included a deictic expression* (e.g., "this" or "here") or not	d. 96%
			e. Whether the *gesture depicted a room vs. an object within a room*	e. 94%
			f. Whether the *gesture or words conveyed information about each of four semantic features*	f. 95%
			g. Whether the *information in the words and the gesture was general vs. specific*	g. 90%

(Continued)

(Continued)

Year	Study	Inductive Origin?	Analysis	Interanalyst Agreement for Each Analysis
2011	Bavelas, Gerwing, Allison, & Sutton (book chapter)	Yes	Do addressees understand gestures that are not redundant with speech, as shown by completed grounding sequences? a. Locating gestures depicting an identifiable room in the floor plan b. Whether each gesture was redundant with words or not c. Whether the addressee's response to a nonredundant gesture was explicit vs. implicit d. Whether the addressee's explicit response was positive vs. negative (e.g., indicated understanding vs. asked for clarification) e. Whether the addressee's implicit response was positive vs. moot f. Whether the speaker/gesturer's acknowledgment was explicit, implicit, or other	a. Range = 80% to 97% b. 97% c. 89% d. 96% e. 91% f. 87%
2011	Gerwing & Allison (journal article)	No	Do speakers shift semantic information between words and hand gestures as a function of visibility? a. Whether the speaker's words conveyed information in each of five categories b. Whether the speaker's gestures conveyed information in each of the five categories	a. 92% b. 86%
2013	Healing (master's thesis)	Yes	In oncology consultations, do patients contribute information about their individual perspective (i.e., patient-centered information) as well as biomedical information? a. Whether a patient utterance contributed small talk, a generic listening response, biomedical information, or patient-centered information (See decision tree in Appendix 9.B.)	a. 90%

Year	Study	Inductive Origin?	Analysis	Interanalyst Agreement for Each Analysis
2013	Korman, Bavelas, & De Jong (journal article)	Yes	What are the ways in which therapists' formulations change what their clients have said?	
			a. Whether each speaking turn by a therapist included a *formulation or not*	a. 90%
			b. Locating the *exact words in the utterance that were the formulation*	b. 96%
			c. Identifying each word in the client's previous utterances that was *preserved exactly, preserved deictically, or omitted* in the formulation	c. 90%
			d. Identifying words in the formulation that *preserved the client's words in altered form* (e.g., a paraphrase); words that were not in what the client said (i.e., *added by the therapist*); and *discourse markers* (e.g., "So you mean . . .")	d. 89%
2013	Smock Jordan, Froerer, & Bavelas (journal article)	No	Do therapists differ in their use of positive vs. negative topical content as a function of their model of therapy?	
			a. Whether each *therapist utterance* contained *positive content, negative content, both, or neither*	a. For the six therapists, 75% to 88%; median = 85%
			Does the positive vs. negative topical content of the therapist affect the next client utterance?	
			b. Whether each *client utterance* contained *positive content, negative content, both, or neither*	b. For the six clients, 69% to 87%, median = 80%
2014b	Bavelas, Gerwing, & Healing (journal article)	No	Does being in a dialogue (vs. a monologue) increase the rate of demonstrations, independently of the effect of visibility?	
			a. Identifying the speakers' *exact words that accompanied a facial portrayal* of a character in the movie they were retelling	a. 91%

(Continued)

(Continued)

Year	Study	Inductive Origin?	Analysis	Interanalyst Agreement for Each Analysis
			b. Identifying events in the movie in which the speaker *quoted* a character in the movie	b. 97%
			c. Identifying the *exact words in each quotation*	c. 99%
			d. Locating speakers' hand gestures	d. 94%
			e. Deciding whether to divide periods of *continuous gesturing*	e. 93%
			f. Locating speakers' *nouns or noun phrases referring to any of nine features in the picture they were describing*	f. 94%
			g. Deciding whether each reference was *literal vs. figurative*	g. 98%
2014c	Bavelas, Gerwing, & Healing (book chapter)	No	Do participants shift information into visible means (i.e., facial as well as hand gestures) when having a face-to-face dialogue vs. on the phone?	
			a. Deciding whether speakers contributed information about each of three semantic features using *visible vs. audible means*	a. 93%
2014	Gerwing & Dalby (journal article)	Yes	Do physicians use semantic gestures when speaking with patients during conversations about treatment plans?	
			a. Decide whether physicians' *hand movements are gestures.*	a. 100%
			b. Decide whether physicians' gestures have *semantic, beat,* or *interactive functions*	b. 91% (Cohen's κ = .82)

154

Appendix 9.B

Examples of Decision Trees

Decision Tree from Healing (2013)

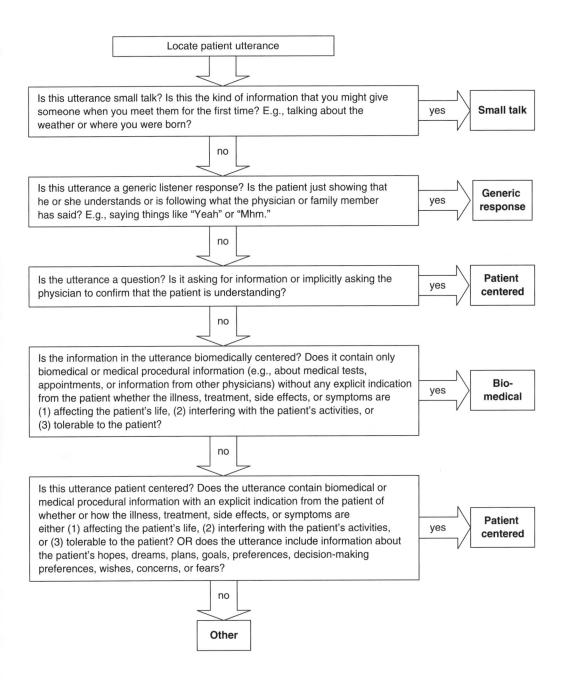

Decision Tree from Gerwing (2008)

Summary of response analysis (please use in conjunction with detailed rules):

1. In the video clip, select the time from a couple of seconds before overture onset up to the actual time of onset (i.e., not including overture). Watch a few times.

2. Note baby's behavior during this section on your sheet.

3. Now watch again but allow selection to play past overture onset into the overture, *but not past onset of next overture.*

4. Now use this decision tree:

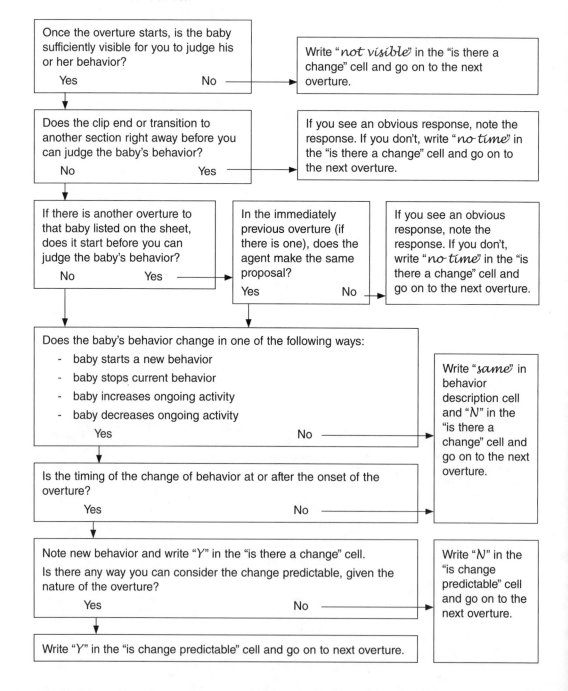

Decision Tree from Bavelas et al. (1992)

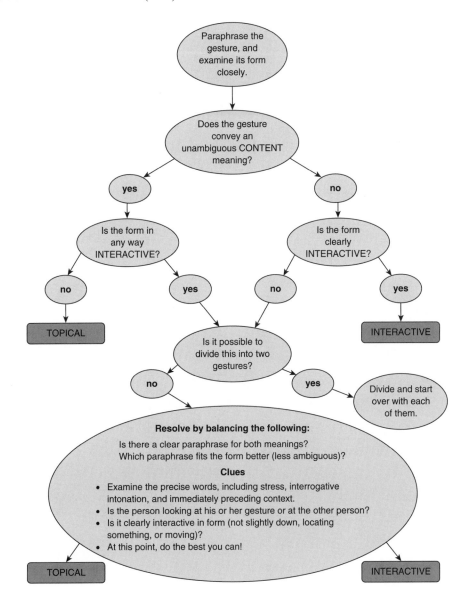

10

THE CONVERSATIONAL ARGUMENT
CODING SCHEME

DAVID R. SEIBOLD AND HARRY W. WEGER, JR.

Introduction

The Conversational Argument Coding Scheme (CACS) provides a content analytic method for studying conversational argument in communicative interactions. It has been used for more than three decades, and Canary and Seibold (2010) documented that researchers have variously used the CACS to investigate conversational argument in close relationships (Weger & Canary, 2010), marital problem solving (Canary, Brossmann, Sillars, & LoVette, 1987), interpersonal conflicts (Johnson & Averbeck, 2010; Semic & Canary, 1997, 2003), deliberations in face-to-face as well as computer-mediated group (CMG) discussions (see summary in Seibold & Meyers, 2007), jury decision making (Burnett & Badzinski, 2000; Meyers, Seibold, & Kang, 2010), political discussions on TV (Brossmann & Canary, 1990), mediation (Trego, Canary, Alberts, & Mooney, 2010), and ethnopolitical intergroup conflicts (Ellis & Maoz, 2002, 2007). In addition, some of the scholars cited here and others have revised the CACS in attempts to improve it (Canary & Seibold, 2010), including adding categories, establishing unitizing rules, creating a multistage coding process (Canary, 1992; Meyers & Brashers, 2010), and weighting categories (Seibold & Lemus, 2005; Seibold, Lemus, & Kang, 2010).

The CACS emerged from these revisions as a useful and flexible instrument for analyzing many aspects of argument. As Meyers and Seibold (2012) noted, scholars find the following to be among the uses of the CACS: depiction of specific features of conversational argument in interpersonal and group interactions, identification of argument structures in those interactions, and insights into patterns and sequences of argument between and among people. Identifying features, distributions, structures, patterns, and sequences of argument in communication enables investigators to view the development of interaction processes and to test theory-driven predictions about conversational argument antecedents, processes, and effects. In some instances, use of the CACS illuminates unexpected interaction functions or outcomes (e.g., Meyers & Seibold, 2012; "process statements").

In the remainder of this chapter, we define conversational (interpersonal and group) argument and distinguish it from related concepts; review the theoretical perspectives that have been informed by the development and use of the CACS; offer a brief history of this coding scheme; describe categories in the CACS, beginning with its earliest version and including modifications by interpersonal argument researchers and separate revisions by group argument scholars; address unit-of-analysis issues, unitizing rules, coding procedures, and reliability; and summarize major findings in interpersonal and group argument studies using the CACS.

Definition of Argument and Relevant Concepts

Interpersonal and group argument research that has informed the development of the CACS combines three areas of study in communication:

159

(a) argumentation (e.g., reasoning and logic, formal proof, quality of evidence), (b) conversational argument (i.e., argument as discursive and interactive), and (c) interpersonal and group influence (e.g., offering and defending reasons, processes, message valences). The conception of *interpersonal and group argument* emerging at this confluence is a discourse process that reveals people's agreement (i.e., persons coordinating and supporting others' points) as well as disagreement (i.e., stating and defending reasons for verbal claims to resolve interpersonal issues or collective decisions) (Seibold, in press).

Theoretical Bases for the CACS

As described in Canary and Seibold's (2010) review, the CACS was grounded in at least four theoretical perspectives or traditions: rhetoric and argument (Perelman & Olbrechts-Tyteca, 1969), logic and argument (Toulmin, 1958), pragmatic conversational argument (Jackson & Jacobs, 1980; Jacobs & Jackson, 1981), and structuration theory (Giddens, 1979; Seibold, McPhee, & Poole, 1980; Seibold, McPhee, Poole, Tanita, & Canary, 1981).

Findings generated with use of the CACS also have aided in the development of the *theory of minimally rational argument* (MRA; Canary, Brossmann, Brossmann, & Weger, 1995) and *structuration argument theory* (SAT; for a summary, see Seibold & Meyers, 2007). These two theories have dominated the use and modifications of the CACS.

Theory of Minimally Rational Argument

First introduced in Canary et al. (1995), five axioms compose the bases of the MRA (Canary & Weger, 2014; Weger & Canary, 2010).

Axiom 1: Individuals engage in minimally rational argument.

According to Cherniak (1981, 1986), people can at best achieve minimally rational thinking, which involves people's sometimes linking their desires to their beliefs. Minimal rationality is more effective than irrationality and more realistic than idealized logic.

Axiom 2: Conversational argument is convergence-seeking discourse.

Axiom 3: Conversational argument involves multiple cognitive and emotional processes.

For instance, Cherniak indicated that the tendency to rely on heuristics (i.e., mindless, mental shortcuts) illustrates people's lack of idealized logic.

Axiom 4: Conversational arguments both constitute and are constituted by the relationship as a system.

This axiom reflects an important SAT feature that remains from the prepublication phase of the CACS.

Axiom 5: Conversational argument as a research enterprise requires a coding system to observe minimally rational arguments when and how they occur.

This last axiom underscores how people can use the CACS for theory development.

Cherniak's (1981, 1986) theory of minimal rationality deals with belief-desire sets, that is, how cognitions might lead directly to desired outcomes. A limiting feature of Cherniak's theory is that he does not connect an individual's beliefs with his or her communicative behavior, which then might lead to desired outcomes. Canary and Weger expanded on Cherniak's minimal rationality theory by suggesting that beliefs subjectively linked to desires must manifest themselves *socially* in conversational argument. This expansion helps one focus theoretical and analytical attention on how people use arguments to seek convergence through introducing and developing ideas in at least minimally rational ways.

Structuration theory remains a common foundational basis for the CACS and, as reviewed earlier, underlies Axiom 4 of the MRA (i.e., patterns of interpersonal argumentation both constitute and are constituted by the relationship as a system). Relationships reflect partners' understandings of the emergent rules and resources available for seeking convergence, and they are constituted by the application of those rules and resources during interaction. Accordingly, sequences and structures of arguments form the foundation for partners' understandings and interpretations of both the ongoing stream of the current conversation, and the rules, resources, perceptions, and constraints that influence how people present ideas. The MRA predicts that variation in sequences and structures of arguments reflects partners' beliefs about the relationship and the partner. Thus, the CACS serves as a theoretically derived coding system designed to allow researchers to detect small and large patterns of argument development during dyadic, group, or any other sort of interaction.

Structuration Argument Theory

SAT has evolved across more than 30 years (Seibold et al., 1981; Seibold, Lemus, & Kang, 2010). Group argument represents a *structured* and a *structuring* practice among interacting members. SAT proposes that group argument occurs in the context of members' interpersonal influence attempts, and it is communication at the group level, not simply individual reasoning; enabled and constrained by social norms, not only logical rules; produced by group members advancing arguable statements that may be disagreeable to other members but are developed in convergence-seeking discourse in which people test and refine proposals, alternatives are evaluated, and ideas are eliminated; and functions to move group members toward a group decision (Seibold & Meyers, 2007).

As Seibold and Meyers further explained, argument organizes interaction in groups through three mechanisms. First, members' micro-interactional acts appropriate rules and resources for the production of argument (e.g., conversational conventions regarding disagreement-expression and disagreement-repair, canons of logic, and social norms for facilitating agreement); second, members' broader communication patterns exist (e.g., tag-teaming with others); and third, simultaneous structuring occurs across three modalities (as schemes for interpretation, as facilities enabling the exercise of power, and as norms for acceptable reasoning and interaction).

Origins of the CACS: A Brief History

Informed by sociologist Anthony Giddens's (1976, 1979) structuration theory, Seibold, McPhee, and Poole (1980) proposed that group decision-making structures are produced and reproduced in members' streams of interaction. Embedded in the communication-influence-outcome perspective of Seibold and colleagues was a conception of influence in group communication in terms of three message levels: *valence*, or the expressed positivity or negativity of any message relative to a proposed decision; *argument*, involving reason using and reason giving represented in a message sequence that supports or opposes an option; and *strategy*, which aggregates tactics embedded in a message about a decision option. Canary and Seibold (2010) reviewed the research lines, theories, and debates that encouraged Seibold's interest in exploring argument during group deliberations from a structuration theory perspective.

An independent program focused on interpersonal conversational argument paralleled the program that focuses on group decision discussions (Canary & Seibold, 2010). Working with another early collaborator, Canary, Seibold, and Tanita (later Ratledge and then Tanita-Ratledge) brought several theoretical perspectives to bear on the study of conversational argument in only group deliberations at first, a focus that endured in Dave Seibold's work with Renee Meyers (Seibold & Meyers, 2007), and subsequently expanded during the past three decades in research by Dan Canary and his colleagues, especially Harry Weger, on interpersonal argument research across a range of interpersonal contexts. During the early 1980s, Canary, Tanita, and Seibold addressed how one could trace group argument empirically via extant conceptualizations of argument. They drew on three prominent yet quite different perspectives to view argument. In a preliminary qualitative analysis of a group's deliberation, Canary and colleagues developed three coding procedures on the basis of the approaches to argument of Toulmin (1958), Perelman and Olbrechts-Tyteca (1969), and Jacobs and Jackson (1981; Jackson & Jacobs, 1980).

As predicted by SAT, argument acts generated as claims initially were later reproduced as claims, although interactants also used them as proposals. It was also simple to trace arguments using the scheme derived from Toulmin's corpus and to use it to identify areas of disagreement. Specifically, the scheme based on Toulmin was excellent for distinguishing segments of discourse as arguments (e.g., minimal argument conditions of claim, data, and warrant). The techniques following from Perelman and Olbrechts-Tyteca did not detect an orderly sequence of argument development (or resolution) but did reveal the unfolding of argument (starting points, argument techniques, and amplification toward convergence). The adjacency pair analysis motivated by the studies of Jackson and Jacobs highlighted structural markers of disagreement and underscored the tendency for some members to finish others' arguments. Taken together, the three theories revealed that arguments during group interactions could be identified across the deliberation.

Description of the CACS Categories

Development of the Initial Version of CACS

A primary aim of Canary, Ratledge, and Seibold (1982) was to adopt the strongest aspects of these three perspectives and to integrate them in a single scheme. The resultant CACS relied on a definition of argument deriving from Perelman and Olbrechts-Tyteca (1969) as *convergence-seeking discourse*: communicative attempts to reach or to demonstrate accord with the minds and/or behaviors of another person (or, importantly, a third party witnessing the interaction). *Arguables*, or components of the over-time conversation that revealed a single argument or a number of arguments in the conventional sense (i.e., a statement that supports another proposition) then could be identified. The coding categories benefited most from Toulmin's (1958) theorizing concerning the organization of argument in general and by Jackson and Jacobs's (1980) theorizing about micro-level features of argument. (See Table 1 in Canary & Seibold, 2010, for the initial CACS from 1982.)

The core features of argument traditionally involve *Potential Arguables* (*Assertions* and *Propositions*) and their development (*Elaborations*, *Amplifications*, and *Justifications*). Other types of statements occur in arguing. First, people frequently disagree with entire claims or with subparts of them. Such disagreements and challenges were labeled *Arguable Promptors*. Specifically, persons may *Object* to what they view as the (lack of) truth of a statement, or they may state a *Challenge* such as a problem or question that others must address in order to reach convergence. Second, some verbal acts restrict the nature and/or breadth of people's arguments. Canary et al. (1982) identified these as "Delimiting Arguables" or *Delimitors*. Drawing on the terms used by Jacobs and Jackson (1981), Delimitors include *Frames*, or communicative acts that offer a context or qualification of a point; *Forestall/Secure*, or acts that people use to secure common ground on a topic and thus to forestall refutation; and *Forestall/Remove*, when people attempt to obviate discussion about topics and thus to forestall refutation.

Finally, additional categories in the CACS flowed from Canary et al.'s (1982) study. The category *Non-Arguments* resulted from the observation that some statements were irrelevant to the primary arguable (e.g., off-topic acts and incomplete messages). The implied structure of a prototypical argument was apparent: Arguments started with an assertion or a proposition, followed by elaborations or responses, then amplifications, and ultimately justifications. Promptors and Delimitors were viewed as intervening, even interfering, with argument development. Four rules for coding turns also were created.

Alterations in the CACS With a Focus on Interpersonal Interaction

Amplifications and justifications were combined in the rubric *Reason-Giving Arguables* in Canary, Brossmann, and Seibold (1987), the first

publication in which the CACS was reported. Consistent with Toulmin (1958), explicit reason giving (vs. implicit reason using) occurs in statements that link previous statements to the argument by showing the logic used. Hence, justifications and amplifications functions in a similar way (e.g., to support an assertion or a proposal). Canary et al. (1987) also proposed, "for future use agreements are separated from other assertions" (p. 34).

In a study of argument behavior on *Nightline*, a late-night news program, agreement and acknowledgment were added within a new category called *Convergence Markers* (Brossmann & Canary, 1990). The researchers also reorganized Canary et al.'s (1982) major categories: (a) *Convergence Markers* (CM) (agreement and acknowledgment); (b) *Arguables* (AR) (potential arguables involving assertions and propositions, reason-using arguables involving elaborations and responses, and reason-giving arguables involving amplifications and justifications); (c) *Promptors* (PO) (composed of objections and challenges); (d) *Delimitors* (LM) (continued as frames, forestall/secure, and forestall/remove); and (e) *Non-Arguables* (NA) (messages lacking a clear argument-relevant function or turn finished at another place in the interaction). The CACS was greatly enhanced through these developments in the categories, and subsequent investigations of specific argument types were possible as a result.

For example, research revealed that participants used *responses* primarily to defend their positions rather than to seek convergence (Weger & Canary, 1991). Accordingly, Weger and Canary moved responses to the *Promptor* category. Also, on the basis of the function of each arguable as well as empirical data, Canary, Weger, and Stafford (1991) found four higher ordered principal categories and distinguished the *Starting Points* (SP) of argument from the *Developing Points* (DP) of argument. Important to this research, they also proposed new definitions of some argument codes. *Starting Points* included assertions and propositions (and replaced the category of potential arguables), and *Developing Points* included elaborations, amplifications, and justifications (i.e., higher order support statements). Scholars associated with the Canary and Weger group or doing research in that tradition have consistently used the Canary et al. (1982, 1991) version of the CACS. Canary (1992) revised the coding manual, including examples, unitizing rules, and a hierarchical coding set of decision rules for coding. (This manual is available from Dan Canary at dan.canary@utah.edu.) The revised manual includes instructions with examples and decision rules for unitizing and coding. Box 10.1 depicts this revised version of the CACS that has been used until now by Canary, Weger, and colleagues.

Box 10.1
Revised Version of the Conversational Argument Coding System (CACS)

Starting Points (SP)

ASRT:	Assertions. Statements of belief or opinion.
PROP:	Propositions. Statements that call for discussion or action.

Developing Points (DP)

ELAB:	Elaborations. Statements that support other statements by providing evidence or clarification.
AMPL:	Amplification. Explicit inferential statements.
JUST:	Justifications. Statements that offer norms, values, or rules of logic to support the validity of other statements.

Convergence Markers (CM)

AGMT:	Agreements. Statements that show agreement.
ACKN:	Acknowledgments. Messages indicating recognition and/or understanding, but not agreement to, another's point.

Promptors (PO)

OBJC:	Objections. Statements that deny the truth or accuracy of another statement.
CHAL:	Challenges. Messages that present problems, questions, or reservations that must be addressed to reach agreement.
RESP:	Responses. Statements that support other statements that have been explicitly refuted.

Delimitors (LM)

FRAM:	Frames. Statements that provide a context and/or qualification for another statement.
F/SE:	Forestall/Secure. Attempts to forestall discussion by securing common ground.
F/RE:	Forestall/Remove. Attempts to forestall discussion by preventing conversation on a point.

Non-Argument

NARG:	Non-Arguments. Behaviors with no argumentative function.
*:	An asterisk plus a turn number indicates that the thought is completed elsewhere.

Source: Canary et al. (1991). The initial CACS copyright was by the Southern Speech Communication Association (Canary et al., 1987).

Alterations to the CACS With a Focus on Group Interaction

As Meyers and Brashers (2010) described at length, new categories were added to the CACS during the mid-1980s, with an evolving conception of group argument rooted in structuration theory (Giddens, 1984; Meyers, 1987; Poole, Seibold, & McPhee, 1985, 1986). Although convergence-production constituted a central facet of the structurational conception of group argument, indicators of convergence-production were limited to two categories in the original scheme (Canary et al., 1982; Seibold, Canary, & Tanita-Ratledge, 1983). Both the interpersonal and group researchers concurred that *Reinforcers* (statements of agreement that serve to reinforce or extend argument) needed to be included in the original CACS. Two forms of this category were added: (a) simple agreement and (b) agreement [+ another statement] (Meyers, 1987). Regarding the importance of the first category, Ratledge (1986) noted that half of the *Assertions* in her dissertation were expressions of agreement or support. The second category highlighted agreement that was extended by an additional arguable. This emendation to the scheme was theoretically consistent with structuration theory and empirically heuristic.

Later in the 1980s, three additional modifications were made to the CACS by the researchers focused on group argument. *Objection* [+ statement] was added to distinguish between simple expressions of disagreement and extended disagreement. A *Qualifiers* category—message acts that qualify arguables by indicating a subjective or personal frame of reference—was added to the *Delimitor* section to capture argument-related messages that were becoming apparent in group members' deliberations. Third, the *Non-Argument* category now included (a) *Process*, (b) *Unrelated*, and (c) *Incomplete*. These three subcategories offered a more precise view of the function of Non-Arguments in facilitating or constraining group argument. These codes also proved especially helpful in a later investigation of argument in a jury deliberation trial, in which *Process* messages were often integrated into the discourse (Huber, Johnson, Hill, Meyers, & Seibold, 2007).

The resultant 18-category CACS was used by group argument researchers for a time in the late 1980s. However, the (plus) categories for Agreement and for Objection, respectively, later were subsumed within the unitizing process so that these types of statements considered as one of two distinct codable units (i.e., as Agreement or Acknowledgment and as Objections or Challenges). Furthermore, Qualifier statements later were integrated back into the Frames category. See Box 10.2 for the coding scheme used in investigations of group argument since the late 1980s.

Box 10.2
Conversational Argument Coding Scheme (CACS) Used in Group Argument Studies Since the 1980s (From Meyers & Bashers, 2010)

I. ARGUABLES

   A. Generative Mechanisms

   1. <u>Assertions</u>: Statements of fact or opinion.

   2. <u>Propositions</u>: Statements that call for support, action, or conference on an argument-related statement.

   B. Reasoning Activities

   1. <u>Elaborations</u>: Statements that support other statements by providing evidence, reasons, or other support.

   2. <u>Responses</u>: Statements that defend arguables met with disagreement.

   3. <u>Amplifications</u>: Statements that explain or expound upon other statements in order to establish the relevance of the argument through inference.

   4. <u>Justifications</u>: Statements that offer validity of previous or upcoming statements by citing a rule of logic (provide a standard whereby arguments are weighed).

II. CONVERGENCE-SEEKING ACTIVITIES

1. <u>Agreement</u>: Statements that express agreement with another statement.

2. **Agreement**+: Statements which express agreement with another statement and then go on to state an arguable (assertion, proposition, elaboration, response, amplification, justification), Promptor, Delimitor, or Non-Argument.

III. DISAGREEMENT-RELEVANT INTRUSIONS

1. <u>Objections</u>: Statements that deny the truth or accuracy of any arguable.

2. **Objection**+: Statements which disagree with another statement and then go on to state another arguable, Promptor, Delimitor, or Non-Argument.

3. <u>Challenges</u>: Statements that offer problems or questions that must be solved if agreement is to be secured on an arguable.

IV. DELIMITORS

1. **Qualifiers**: Statements that qualify arguables by indicating the subjective frame of reference of the arguable (in my opinion, that's my point of view, in your opinion, that's as I see it)

2. <u>Frames</u>: Statements that provide a context for upcoming arguables. These statements sketch a hypothetical or real-life context/drama that has some similarity to the situation being discussed by the group. These statements "set the scene" for upcoming arguables.

3. <u>Forestall/Secure</u>: Statements that attempt to forestall refutation by securing common ground.

4. <u>Forestall/Remove</u>: Statements that attempt to forestall refutation by removing possible objections.

V. NON-ARGUMENTS

1. <u>Process</u>: Non-Argument-related statements that orient the group to its task or specify the process the group should follow.

2. <u>Unrelated</u>: Statements unrelated to the group's argument or process (tangents, side issues, self-talk, etc.).

3. <u>Incompletes</u>: Statements that do not contain a complete, clear idea due to interruption or a person discontinuing a statement.

Source: Author.

Note: Bold categories (8, 10, and 12) reflect codes that were added in the 1980s but later removed.

CACS Units of Analysis,
Unitizing Rules, and Coding Procedures

As Meyers and Brashers (2010) explained, argument units originally were treated as turns reflected in complete sentences or incomplete but discrete message acts (Canary et al., 1982; Seibold et al., 1983); later they were treated as thought units (Canary et al., 1987; Meyers, 1987). In general, Hatfield and Weider-Hatfield (1978) defined a thought unit as "the minimum meaningful utterance having a beginning and an end" (p. 46). Specific operational definitions depend on a list of coding rules that explicate the researcher's procedure for identifying thought units in a particular study. To refine the unitizing process, Meyers (1987) developed a set of rules for coding thought units

(Hatfield & Weider-Hatfield, 1978; Murray, 1956). A "thought unit" was defined as any statement that contained a subject (explicit or clearly implied) and predicate/verb (explicit or clearly implied) and/or could function independently as a complete thought (including terms of address, acknowledgments, functioning independent clauses, nonrestrictive dependent clauses, etc.). This unitizing rule has been used consistently in conversational argument studies in the small group literature since then. The researchers working on dyadic argumentation maintained a slightly more traditional, and less structured, definition of a thought turn, consisting of any independent thought that could be represented as independent clauses, dependent clauses, individual words, or vocalized indicators of agreement or disagreement (e.g., "uh-huh" or "huh-uh") (Canary, 1992).

By the early 1990s, as Meyers and Brashers (2010) noted, the large number of categories and the complexity of the scheme were creating coding challenges. Cohen's κ reliability was .72, which is acceptable (Nunnally, 1978), and reliabilities were good across categories (e.g., Brossmann & Canary, 1990). With categories included into five broader categories, reliability increased to .79 (Brossmann & Canary, 1990), which certainly is acceptable. However, coders appeared to be underusing the full range of categories. For example, Meyers, Seibold, and Brashers (1991) discovered that coders relied excessively on Assertions, Elaborations, and Agreements rather than higher level arguables or Promptors because they could not connect statements coded to utterances much earlier or later in the transcript. Consequently, Meyers and Brashers (1995) developed their multistage coding model that involved parsing the interaction data first and then coding those in successive iterations.

Multistage coding model. In brief (see full discussion in Meyers & Bashers, 2010), the multistage procedure first involves three levels of *parceling* the data so a more coherent picture of group argument is available to the coders than is apparent from examining all interactions in a transcript at once. Non-Argument statements first are sorted from the argument statements. At the second level, all coders separate argument statements relative to the final group decision alternative they recommend and support. The third level of data partitioning involves distinguishing lines of argument. Coders then classify each argument unit in the group discussion. Each message is highlighted (often with different colors) in terms of the topical line of argument in which it is embedded. The color highlighting allows coders to trace the development of argument throughout a group's discussion. This process also reveals topics shifts and clarifies whether arguments represent new starting points (arguables in the group system) or are extensions of arguments offered earlier in the discussion.

After the data are parceled to reveal the structure and organization of the group's or dyad's arguments more clearly, six *successive coding iterations* ensue. These steps can be very helpful for enabling coders to make accurate judgments concerning the components of arguments, which typically are quite complex because of the lengthy duration of decision-making sessions and the number of participants contributing to those arguments over time. First, coders assign messages to one of the four global-level CACS categories in Box 10.2: Arguables (Starting Points and Developing Points in the interpersonal system), Convergence Markers, Promptors, or Delimitors (coding of the Non-Arguments occurred in the earlier parceling stage). Second, coders using the group argument version of the CACS categorize each Arguable into one of the six subcategories: Assertion, Proposition, Elaboration, Response, Amplification, or Justification. In the interpersonal version of the CACS, Starting Points are categorized as Assertions or Propositions, and Developing Points are categorized into Elaboration, Amplification, or Justification. Third, coders categorize Convergence Marker statements as Agreements or Acknowledgments. Fourth, Promptors are (re)coded as Objections or Challenges. Fifth, Delimitors are further coded as Frames, Forestall-Secure, or Forestall-Remove. Finally, coders can recode Non-Arguments as Process, Unrelated Statements, or Incompletes. Thus, at each step in this multistage coding process, and often in separate sessions, coders focus on different aspects of group argument. Their tasks are thereby made more manageable, and with each reading of the transcript, they become more familiar with the full group discussion. In sum, the modifications to the CACS by group argument researchers included addition of categories, establishment of unitizing rules, and development of a multistage coding model with initial parceling of data and iterative coding.

In the following example, we show how these iterations unfold when coding a portion of data. Notice that we have already segmented the messages into thought turns and have numbered the turns consecutively. The illustration is drawn from data gathered by Canary, and the example begins 30 turns into the couple's discussion. In Turn 30, the husband begins a new discussion by making a statement that identifies a difference between his own attitude and the wife's attitude toward spending time in casinos. At this point, coders do not decide which type of starting point to assign to the message. In Turn 31, the wife neither agrees nor disagrees, nor does she offer any sort of support for the husband's statement, and she does not start a new discussion. This turn is best thought of as a Delimitor, because the message is relevant to understanding the argument stream being developed by contextualizing the message in the preceding turn. So it is not a Non-Argument, but it does not function to move the discussion in any particular direction. The husband's disagreement with the wife's message is coded as a Promptor in Turn 32. Turn 33 is coded a convergence marker, as the wife clearly expresses agreement. Here it is important to note that "no" actually signals agreement, as it refers to what her husband says she does not do (i.e., "you don't spend that much"). In Turns 34.1 and 34.2, the husband develops the disagreement he expressed in Turn 32. Finally, in Turn 35, the wife advances the husband's developing point in Turn 34.2 by adding some detail to his message. Identifying the major code categories first reduces individual subtype code selection from 13 or 18

choices to 2 to 4 choices depending on the category. This procedure improves coder agreement.

Table 10.2 provides an example of data that have undergone Steps 2 through 6 of the coding procedure, with CACS subtypes identified. The starting point in Turn 30 is coded first, in which the man offers a statement rather than posing a question, so the assertion code is selected. Next, the developing points are seen in Turns 34.1 and 34.2. The husband supports the Promptor in Turn 32 by offering additional detail and explanation rather than making an explicit inference or offering a norm or rule, which leads the coder to select elaboration as the subtype. In the next iteration, convergence markers in Turns 33 and 35 convey agreement with the proceeding turns by the husband. In Turn 33, the wife essentially confirms the husband's contention that she does not spend much money, and in Turn 35, she verifies his perception of the amount of money she spends at the casino. The coder therefore selects the agreement code for each message. Promptors are coded next. The husband's message in Turn 32 is counted as an objection because it denies the wife's observation that his assertion in Turn 30 concerns money.

Table 10.1 Coding Iteration: Step 1

Turn	Speaker	Message	Code
30	M	Okay, Jan likes to go to the casinos and I <u>don't</u>.	Starting Point
31	F	(Laughs) It's funny because that involves money doesn't it?	Delimitor
32	M	Well, no, not really because you don't spend that much.	Promptor
33	F	No, I don't.	Convergence Marker
34.1	M	You play the small machines,	Developing Point
34.2	M	and you probably don't spend over ten or twenty dollars.	Developing Point
35	F	I usually go with twenty.	Convergence Marker

Source: Author.

Table 10.2 Coding Iteration: Steps 2 Through 6

Turn	Speaker	Message	Code Subtype
30	M	Okay, Jan likes to go to the casinos and I <u>don't</u>.	Assertion
31	F	(Laughs) It's funny because that involves money doesn't it?	Frame
32	M	Well, no, not really because you don't spend that much.	Objection
33	F	No, I don't.	Agreement
34.1	M	You play the small machines,	Elaboration
34.2	M	and you probably don't spend over ten or twenty dollars.	Elaboration
35	F	I usually go with twenty.	Agreement (34.2)

Source: Author.

Finally, the wife's message in Turn 31 offers context for the husband's message in Turn 30, so the frame subtype in the Delimitor category is selected.

Sequences and Structures

Although several studies have profitably analyzed single codes as the unit of analysis (e.g., Semic & Canary, 1997; Steward, Setlock, & Fussel, 2004), the identification of argument sequences and structures allows researchers to track patterns of argument development. Sequences are chains of adjacent behaviors (Rausch, 1965), also called "first-ordered sequences," "lag 1 sequences," and the "interact" (Messman & Canary, 1998). Observing sequences of CACS-coded behaviors enables a systematic examination of patterns of argument development in relationships. Four types of sequences are identified in Canary et al. (1991). *Developing sequences* consist of the development of a person's idea (a starting point or a developing point) with an elaboration, justification, or amplification. *Converging sequences* represent one statement providing agreement with, or acknowledging understanding of, another statement. *Diverging sequences* reflect disagreement and consist of a Promptor (objection, challenge, or response) combining with another Promptor or developing point. Finally, *rudimentary sequences* reveal a lack of idea development and are seen in starting points (assertions or propositions) followed by other starting points or messages that limit or frame the discussion rather than developing the initial idea. Researchers can identify sequences using lag sequential analysis to find pairs of CACS-coded messages that regularly occur together (see VanLear, this volume).

Argument structures usually represent longer chains of development than act-to-act sequences, although a structure can exist in a single interact. To date, four general types of argument structures have been empirically uncovered (Canary et al., 1987). *Simple* argument structures involve the development of a single statement, usually an assertion or proposition, with one or more statements of support. *Compound* structures exist as one of three subtypes: (a) *embedded structures* that involve one line of argument embedded within another, (b) *parallel arguments* that advance multiple points with the same structure, or (c) *extended arguments* created through complex chains of development. *Joint* argument structures are produced by more than one individual to develop a single line of argument. Finally, *eroded* arguments simply fall apart because of interruptions, topic shifts, or participant failure to complete a thought.

Unlike sequences, which can be identified statistically by searching for specific act-to-act behaviors, structures must be identified by coders. Structures vary in their length, making them more time consuming to use in analyzing data. The multistage coding system can be used to identify structures as the original codes by first identifying lines of argument. Coders then label points of argument on the basis of the particular structure the line of argument exhibits. For example, a line of argument in which a single starting point can be developed through elaboration, amplification, or justification, that is, a Starting Point followed by a Developing Point, would be categorized as a "simple" argument structure.

Important Findings Using the CACS

Interpersonal Argument Research Using the CACS

Research examining interpersonal interactions largely involves samples of romantically involved and friendship dyads, although one study reported later examines interactions between strangers. CACS data serve as both predictor and criterion variables in these studies. Although several studies rely on individual CACS codes, research associated with the theory of minimally rational argument more often uses argument sequences (and sometimes structures) as a way to trace patterns of idea development in conversation.

Factors that predict conversational argument behavior. Several studies using the CACS have looked at relationship characteristics, demographics, personality traits, and contextual features that predict the types of argument moves people make in dyadic interaction. In one study, Canary et al. (1991) examined argument sequences and their associations with control mutuality in romantic dyads. Consistent with predictions, Canary et al. found that couples who agree on how to share control in their relationships produce more developing and converging sequences and fewer diverging sequences. However, couples with unilateral control orientations (i.e., they seek and keep control over decisions) produced more diverging sequences.

In a cross-cultural study, Steward et al. (2004) found that Chinese students (speaking English) produced more developing points compared with their American counterparts, who produced more assertions and acknowledgments. Overall, twice as many Chinese as American students' thought turns were disagreement relevant (i.e., Promptors). A study of trait verbal aggressiveness and argumentativeness found no simple association between conversational argument behavior and measures of trait verbal aggressiveness or argumentativeness (Semic & Canary, 1997). However, dyads in which both friends were high in argumentativeness developed more arguments (i.e., production of elaborations, amplifications, justifications, or responses) than did dyads that were either dissimilar or similarly low in argumentativeness. Interestingly, friends who both scored high in trait verbal aggressiveness produced fewer developed arguments than dissimilar or similarly low dyads. Finally, a study of sex differences derived from a dual-culture theory of sex differences did not find sex differences in the production of argumentative interaction in romantic couples' conversations (Weger & Canary, 1991).

Importantly, context can influence argument interactions. For example, Johnson, Brown, and Wittenberg (2005) examined arguments between friends about either a public issue (e.g., abortion, death penalty, the environment) or a personal issue (e.g., showing consideration, roommate problems, broken plans). Dyads arguing over public issues produced more challenges than dyads arguing about personal issues, whereas personal issue topics produced more acknowledgments than public issue topics. No differences in starting or developing points were found. Another study examining contextual influences compared argument behavior in face-to-face interactions with arguments through instant messaging technology (Steward et al., 2004). Arguments using instant messaging entailed more divergence (challenges, objections, and responses), more assertions, and more developing points than did face-to-face arguments. Interestingly, Steward et al. found that the use of convergence markers was not associated with individuals' attitude changes about the topic, suggesting that conversational convergence does not necessarily represent attitude convergence.

Predicting partner and relationship perceptions. Studies by interpersonal scholars provide evidence that perceptions of partner competence and communication satisfaction associate positively with sequences and structures of conversational argument (Canary & Weger, 1993, 2009; Canary et al., 1991, 1995; Semic & Canary, 2003). These positive associations reflect convergence (i.e., converging sequences and joint structures) and the development of ideas (i.e., developing sequences and complex structures). These studies also indicate that divergent sequences and eroded structures reduce perceptions of competence and communication satisfaction. For example, eroded and undeveloped argument

structures associate negatively with perceptions of partner appropriateness, effectiveness, reasonableness (Canary et al., 1995, Study 1). Likewise, well-developed and complex argument structures positively associate with perceptions of a speaker's reasonableness, effectiveness, and task attractiveness (Canary et al., 1995, Study 2).

Consistent with research on partner perception, well-developed and jointly produced structures associate positively with relationship satisfaction, whereas undeveloped and diverging sequences correlate strongly, and negatively, with satisfaction in marital and dating relationships (Canary et al., 1991; Canary & Sillars, 1992). One of the most interesting implications of these findings concerns how these argument sequences occur in act-to-act lags or across speaking turns that most probably evade participants' conscious perceptions and recollections (Sillars, Roberts, Leonard, & Dun, 2000). Accordingly, sequences of argument in these dyads denote patterns that reflect the quality and possibly the long-term stability of relationships. For example, conversations typified by minimal rationality characterize a relationship in which partners cooperate in finding ways to satisfy each person's needs and desires.

Group Argument Research Using the CACS

Empirical investigations of group argument have used the CACS in descriptive analyses of argument acts and structures as well as statistical predictions of decision choices. Face-to-face groups of students and jurors, subgroups, and computer-mediated groups have been investigated.

Argument structures, strategies, and contextual differences. As noted earlier, analysis of people seeking group consensus revealed four argument *structures* (Canary et al., 1987) Simple arguments reflected a clear argument pattern of assertion, elaboration, and amplification and were the most frequently observed group argument structures. Compound arguments involved combinations of arguments that resulted in extended arguments, embedded arguments, and parallel arguments. Dissembling was the key feature of eroded arguments. Some members used others' positions to create agreement or convergent argument. In a separate study, assertions, elaborations, and agreement were prominent during group argument; group members rarely moved beyond claims and the data adduced to support them (Meyers, Seibold, & Brashers, 1991).

Interestingly, the number of arguments, their development, and the degree of disagreement in groups appear to be greater in CMGs of students working on collaborative tasks with meaningful rewards (see reasons offered in Seibold, in press). Furthermore, in one study, the interaction-structuring features of the group support system influenced group argument by encouraging a sequential process leading to clarification and development of ideas, developing a group memory of issues throughout discussion, and encouraging critical discussion (Brashers, Adkins, & Meyers, 1994).

Group members' collaborative production of arguments, through adding acts to others' acts—that is, offering one another preferred pair parts (Seibold et al., 1981)—is a *strategy* by members who share similar positions (Brashers & Meyers, 1989). Beyond this "tag-team argument," three other strategies were discussed by Meyers and Seibold (1990). "Repetitive agreement and consistent support" lead to networks of influence that link members with outcomes. "Extended elaborations" enable others to link themselves with the ensuing decision proposal. "Questioning and testing" push members' argument into more complex reasoning and prompt members to analyze interpretations against new evidence.

Other group argument forms and functions are apparent in a jury. For example, generative mechanisms, reasoning activities, and convergence seeking (from categories in the version of the CACS in Box 10.2) were prominent early in deliberations during the penalty phase of a murder trial, yet there were few Promptors and Delimitors (Meyers et al., 2010). Arguments became more complex as jurors became aware of others' positions and justifications. The arguments reflected acts that provide a context (e.g., Frames) for arguables and that forestall or remove grounds for refutation. This required understanding others' positions and their arguments, which may be why they surfaced later in the jury's deliberations.

Majority and minority subgroups (i.e., the relative number of members supporting a decision proposal) produce different argument patterns (Gebhardt & Meyers, 1995). Meyers, Brashers, and Hanner (2000) found that majority subgroups were less likely to disagree and were more likely to use convergence statements (and tag-team argument). Winning majorities used disagreements and frames for arguments, and less than losing minority subgroups used disagreements and frames. Minority subgroups used more disagreement messages to defend their positions against a unified majority.

Argument and group outcomes. Some of the studies mentioned used the CACS not simply to analyze argument interactions in groups but to assay the relationship between argument processes and group outcomes. For example, compared with dissensus groups, groups reaching consensus create greater proportions of argument structures in their discussions (and fewer undeveloped Arguables) (Canary et al., 1987). Convergent argument structures also were more frequent in consensus groups. In addition to the difference in positive and negative reactions to decision proposals, Lemus, Seibold, Flanagin, and Metzger (2004) also reported that the number of responses in support of or against a decision proposal predicted decision outcomes.

The more developed the group argument, the greater the likelihood that it will predict decision options. For example, the number of members in support of a proposal (relative to those in opposition), and the degree of development of the arguments in support of a proposal, predicted people's support for decisions in CMGs (Lemus et al., 2004). In other studies (Lemus & Seibold, 2008, 2009), when the development of argument structures in support of a decision proposal was greater than the development of the structures against it, CMG members more likely endorsed the former. Conversely, when the development of argument structures in opposition was greater than the development of the argument structures in support of the decision proposal, CMG members were less apt to endorse it. Finally, using the CACS to create alternative indexes of argument quality (Seibold & Lemus, 2005), Lemus and Seibold (2008) found that argument *development* (i.e., arguments developed through disagreement-repair and convergence-production) predicted decision choices better than did argument *strength/force* (in which the argument components are presumed to have psychological impact).

Conclusion

The Conversational Argument Coding System has been used to a useful extent and effect for 30 years by both interpersonal and small group communication researchers. The system is theoretically derived, and although it has undergone several changes over time, the essential features of the system remain intact. Iterative coding processes, created independently by interpersonal and small group researchers, help make the CACS a reliable system for coding argument in interaction. Research on interpersonal as well as small group interaction demonstrates both the criterion- and predictor-related validity of the system. Future use of the CACS naturally relies on researchers' vision, creativity, and ability to explain why conversational argument functions as it does in various contexts.

References

Brashers, D. E., Adkins, M., & Meyers, R. A. (1994). Argumentation in computer-mediated decision making. In L. Frey (Ed.), *Communication in context: Studies of naturalistic groups* (pp. 262–283). Hillsdale, NJ: Lawrence Erlbaum.

Brashers, D., & Meyers, R. A. (1989). Tag-team argument and group decision-making: A preliminary investigation. In B. Gronbeck (Ed.), *Spheres of argument: Proceedings of the Sixth SCA/AFA Conference on Argumentation* (pp. 542–550). Annandale, VA: Speech Communication Association.

Brossmann, B. G., & Canary, D. J. (1990). An observational analysis of argument structures: The case of *Nightline. Argumentation*, *4*, 199–212.

Burnett, A., & Badzinski, D. M. (2000). An exploratory study of argument in the jury decision-making process. *Communication Quarterly*, *48*, 380–396.

Canary, D. J. (1992). *Manual for coding conversational arguments*. Unpublished manuscript, Department of Speech Communication, Pennsylvania State University, University Park.

Canary, D. J., Brossmann, J., Brossmann, B. G., & Weger, H., Jr. (1995). Toward a theory of minimally rational argument: Analyses of episode-specific effects of argument structures. *Communication Monographs*, *62*, 183–212.

Canary, D. J., Brossmann, B. G., & Seibold, D. R. (1987). Argument structures in decision-making groups. *Southern Speech Communication Journal*, *53*, 18–37.

Canary, D. J., Brossmann, B. G., Sillars, A. L., & LoVette, S. (1987). Married couples' argument structures and sequences: A comparison of satisfied and dissatisfied dyads. In J. W. Wenzel (Ed.), Argu*ment and critical practices: Proceedings of the Fifth SCA/AFA Conference on Argumentation* (pp. 475–484). Annandale, VA: Speech Communication Association.

Canary, D. J., Ratledge, N. T., & Seibold, D. R. (1982, November). *Argument and group decision-making: Development of a coding scheme*. Paper presented at the annual meeting of the Speech Communication Association, Louisville, KY.

Canary, D., & Seibold, D. R. (2010). Origins and development of the Conversational Argument Coding Scheme. *Communication Methods and Measures*, *4*, 7–26.

Canary, D. J., & Sillars, A. L. (1992). Argument in satisfied and dissatisfied married couples. In W. Benoit, D. Hample, & P. J. Benoit (Eds.), *Readings in argumentation* (pp. 737–764). Amsterdam, the Netherlands: Foris.

Canary, D. J., & Weger, H., Jr., (1993). Competence assessments of interpersonal argument structures: An observational analysis. In R. E. McKerrow (Ed.), *Argument and the postmodern challenge: Proceedings of the Eighth SCA/AFA Conference on Argumentation* (pp. 252–259). Annandale: Speech Communication Association.

Canary, D. J., & Weger, H., Jr. (2009). An observational analysis of conversational argument sequences and assessments of communication quality: A minimally rational perspective. In S. Jacobs (Ed.), *Concerning argument: Selected papers from the Fifteenth Biennial Conference on Argumentation* (pp. 95–109). Washington, DC: National Communication Association.

Canary, D. J., & Weger, H., Jr. (2014, February). *A theory of minimally rational argument*. Paper presented at the annual meeting of the Western States Communication Association, Anaheim, CA.

Canary, D. J., Weger, H., Jr., & Stafford, L. (1991). Couples argument sequences and their associations with relational characteristics. *Western Journal of Speech Communication*, *55*, 159–179.

Cherniak, C. (1981). Feasible inferences. *Philosophy of Science*, *48*, 248–268.

Cherniak, C. (1986). *Minimal rationality*. Cambridge, MA: MIT Press.

Ellis, D. G., & Maoz, I. (2002). Cross-cultural argument interactions between Israeli-Jews and Palestinians. *Journal of Applied Communication Research*, *30*, 181–194.

Ellis, D. G., & Maoz, I. (2007). Online argument between Israeli Jews and Palestinians. *Human Communication Research*, *33*, 291–309.

Gebhardt, L. J., & Meyers, R. A. (1995). Subgroup influence in decision-making groups: Examining consistency from a communication perspective. *Small Group Research*, *26*, 147–168.

Giddens, A (1976). *New rules of sociological method*. New York: Basic Books.

Giddens, A (1979). *Central problems in social theory: Action, structure, and contradiction in social analysis*. Berkeley: University of California Press.

Giddens, A. (1984). *The constitution of society: Outline of the theory of structuration*. Berkeley: University of California Press.

Hatfield, J. D., & Weider-Hatfield, D. (1978). The comparative utility of three types of behavioral units for interaction analysis. *Communication Monographs*, *45*, 44–50.

Huber, J., Johnson, M., Hill, R., Meyers, R. A., & Seibold, D. R. (2007, November). *Examining the argument process in jury decision making*. Paper presented to the Group Communication Division, National Communication Association, Chicago.

Jackson, S., & Jacobs, S. (1980). Structure of conversational argument: Pragmatic cases for the enthymeme. *Quarterly Journal of Speech*, *66*, 251–265.

Jacobs, S., & Jackson, S. (1981). Argument as a natural category: The routine grounds for arguing in conversation. *Western Journal of Speech Communication*, *45*, 111–117.

Johnson, A. J., & Averbeck, J. M. (2010). Using the conversational argument coding scheme to examine interpersonal conflict: Insights and challenges. *Communication Methods and Measures*, *4*, 114–132.

Johnson, A. J., Brown, K., & Wittenberg, E. M. (2005). Type of argument and argument composition. In C. A. Willard (Ed.), *Critical problems in argumentation* (pp. 577–586). Washington, DC: National Communication Association.

Lemus, D. R., & Seibold, D. R. (2008). Argument development versus argument strength: The predictive potential of argument quality in computer-mediated group deliberations. In T. Suzuki, T. Kato, & A. Kubota (Eds.), *Proceedings of the 3rd Tokyo Conference on Argumentation: Argumentation, the law and justice* (pp. 166–174). Tokyo, Japan: JDA.

Lemus, D. R., & Seibold, D. R. (2009). Argument structures and decision outcomes in computer-mediated groups. In S. Jacobs (Ed.), *Concerning argument: Selected papers from the Fifteenth Biennial Conference on Argumentation* (pp. 478–486). Washington, DC: National Communication Association.

Lemus, D. R., Seibold, D. R., Flanagin, A. J., & Metzger, M. J. (2004). Argument in computer-mediated groups. *Journal of Communication*, *54*, 302–320.

Messman, S. J., & Canary, D. J. (1998). Conflict patterns. In W. R. Cupach & B. H. Spitzberg (Eds.), *The dark-side of personal relationships*. Mahwah, NJ: Lawrence Erlbaum.

Meyers, R. A. (1987). Argument and group decision-making: An interactional test of persuasive arguments theory and an alternative structurational perspective (Doctoral dissertation, University of Illinois, 1987). *Dissertation Abstracts International*, *49*, 12.

Meyers, R. A., & Brashers, D. E. (1995). Multi-stage versus single-stage coding of small group argument: A preliminary comparative assessment. In S. Jackson (Ed.), *Argumentation and values: Proceedings of the Ninth SCA/AFA Conference on Argumentation* (pp. 93–100). Annandale, VA: Speech Communication Association.

Meyers, R. A., & Brashers, D. E. (2010). Extending the conversational argument coding scheme: Argument categories, units, and coding procedures. *Communication Methods and Measures*, *4*, 27–45.

Meyers, R. A., Brashers, D. E., & Hanner, J. (2000). Majority/minority influence: Identifying argumentative patterns and predicting argument-outcomes links. *Journal of Communication*, *50*, 3–30.

Meyers, R. A., & Seibold, D. R. (2012). Coding group interaction. In A. B. Hollingshead & M. S. Poole (Eds.), *Research methods for studying groups and teams: A guide to approaches, tools, and technologies* (pp. 329–357). New York: Taylor & Francis/Routledge.

Meyers, R. A., & Seibold, D. R., & Brashers, D. (1991). Argument in initial group decision-making discussions: Refinement of a coding scheme and a descriptive quantitative analysis. *Western Journal of Speech Communication*, *55*, 47–68.

Meyers, R. A., Seibold, D. R., & Kang, P. (2010). Examining the argument process in naturally occurring jury deliberations. *Small Group Research*, *41*, 452–473.

Murray, E. J. (1956). A content-analysis method for studying psychotherapy. *Psychological Monographs*, *70*, (13, Whole No. 420).

Nunnally, J. C. (1978). *Psychometric theory* (2nd ed.). New York: McGraw-Hill.

Perelman, C. H., & Olbrechts-Tyteca, L. (1969). *The new rhetoric: A treatise on argumentation* (J. Wilkinson & P. Weaver, Trans.). Notre Dame, IN: University of Notre Dame Press.

Poole, M. S., Seibold, D. R., & McPhee, R. D. (1985). Group decision-making as a structurational process. *Quarterly Journal of Speech*, *71*, 74–102.

Poole, M. S., Seibold, D. R., & McPhee, R. D. (1986). A structurational approach to theory development in group research. In R. Y. Hirokawa & M. S. Poole (Eds.), *Communication and group decision-making* (pp. 237–264). Beverly Hills, CA: Sage.

Ratledge, N.E.T. (1986). *Theoretical and methodological integrity of a structurational scheme for coding argument in decision-making groups* (Unpublished doctoral dissertation). University of Southern California, Los Angeles.

Rausch, H. L. (1965). Interaction sequences. *Journal of Personality and Social Psychology*, *2*, 487–499.

Seibold, D. R. (in press). Group argument structure. In C. R. Berger & M. E. Roloff (Eds.), *International encyclopedia of interpersonal communication*. Hoboken, NJ: Wiley-Blackwell.

Seibold, D. R., Canary, D. J., & Tanita-Ratledge, N. (1983, November). *Argument and group decision-making: Interim report on a structurational research program*. Paper presented at the annual meeting of the Speech Communication Association, Washington, DC.

Seibold, D. R., & Lemus, D. R. (2005). Argument quality in group deliberation: A structurational approach and quality of argument index. In C. A. Willard (Ed.), *Critical problems in argumentation* (pp. 203–215). Washington, DC: National Communication Association.

Seibold, D. R., Lemus, D. R., & Kang, P. (2010). Extending the conversational argument coding scheme in studies of argument quality in group deliberations. *Communication Methods and Measures*, *4*, 46–64.

Seibold, D. R., McPhee, R. D., & Poole, M. S. (1980, April). *New prospects for research in small group communication*. Paper presented at the annual meeting of the Central States Speech Association, Chicago.

Seibold, D. R., McPhee, R. D., Poole, M. S., Tanita, N. E., & Canary, D. J. (1981). Argument, group influence, and decision outcomes. In C. Ziegelmueller & J. Rhodes (Eds.), *Dimensions of argument: Proceedings of the Second SCA/AFA Summer Conference on Argumentation* (pp. 663–692). Annandale, VA: Speech Communication Association.

Seibold, D. R., & Meyers, R. A. (2007). Group argument: A structuration perspective and research program. *Small Group Research*, *38*, 312–336.

Semic, B. A., & Canary, D. J. (1997). Trait argumentativeness, verbal aggressiveness, and minimally rational argument: An observational analysis of friendship discussions. *Communication Quarterly*, *45*, 355–378.

Semic, B. A., & Canary, D. J. (2003). *An investigation of the association among friends' argument sequences, perceptions of communicative competence, and communication satisfaction.* Paper presented at the annual conference of the International Communication Association, San Diego, CA.

Sillars, A., Roberts, L. J., Leonard, K. E., & Dun, T. (2000). Cognition during marital conflict: The relationship of thought and talk. *Journal of Social and Personal Relationships*, *17*, 479–502.

Steward, C. O., Setlock, L. D., & Fussel, S. R. (2004). Conversational argumentation in decision making: Chinese and U.S. participants in face-to-face and instant-messaging interactions. *Discourse Processes*, *44*, 113–139.

Toulmin, S. E. (1958). *The uses of argument.* Cambridge, UK: The University Press.

Trego, A., Canary, D. J., Alberts, J. K., & Mooney, C. (2010). Mediators' facilitative versus controlling argument strategies and tactics: A qualitative analysis using the conversational argument coding scheme. *Communication Methods and Measures*, *4*, 147–167.

Weger, H., Jr., & Canary, D. J. (1991). A closer look at argument behavior in dyads. In D. W. Parson (Ed.), *Argument in controversy: Proceedings of the Seventh SCA/AFA Conference on argumentation* (pp. 211–216). Annandale, VA: Speech Communication Association.

Weger, H., Jr., & Canary, D. J. (2010). Conversational argument in close relationships: A case for studying argument sequences. *Communication Methods and Measures*, *4*, 65–87.

11

AUTOMATED VIDEO-BASED ANALYSIS OF FACIAL EXPRESSIONS IN SCHIZOPHRENIA

JIHUN HAMM, CHRISTIAN G. KOHLER, RUBEN C. GUR, AND RAGINI VERMA

Abnormality in facial expression has been often used to evaluate emotional impairment in neuropsychiatric patients. In particular, inappropriate and flattened facial affect are well-known characteristic symptoms of schizophrenia (Andreasen, 1984a; Bleuler, 1911; Gelber et al. 2004; Gur et al. 2006; Kohler, Gur, Swanson, Petty, & Gur, 1998; Shtasel, Gur, Gallacher, Heimberg, & Gur, 1992; Walker, Grimes, Davis, & Smith, 1993). Several clinical measures have been used to evaluate these symptoms (Andreasen, 1984a, 1984b; Kring, Kerr, Smith, & Neale, 1993; Kring & Sloan, 2007). In these assessments, an expert rater codes the facial expressions of a subject using a clinical rating scale such as the Scale for the Assessment of Negative Symptoms (SANS; Andreasen, 1984a) or ratings of positive or negative valence or prototypical categories such as happiness, sadness, anger, fear, disgust, and surprise, which are recognized across cultures in facial expressions (Eibl-Eibesfeldt, 1970; Ekman & Friesen, 1975; Izard, 1994). However, affective impairment from neuropsychiatric conditions often results in (a) ambiguous facial expressions that are combinations of emotions and (b) subtle expressions that have low intensity or small change, as demonstrated in Figure 11.1. Consequently, such expressions are difficult to categorize as one of the prototypical emotions by an observer.

Ekman and Friesen (1978a, 1978b) proposed the Facial Action Coding System (FACS), which is based on facial muscle movements and can characterize facial actions that constitute an expression irrespective of emotion. FACS encodes the movement of specific facial muscle groups called action units (AUs), which reflect distinct momentary changes in facial appearance. In FACS, a human rater can encode facial actions without necessarily inferring the emotional state of a subject, and therefore one can encode ambiguous and subtle facial expressions that are not clearly categorized into one of the universal emotions.

The sensitivity of FACS to subtle expression differences was demonstrated in studies showing its capability to distinguish genuine and fake smiles (Del Giudice & Colle, 2007), characteristics of painful expressions (Prkachin & Mercer, 1989; Craig, Hyde, & Patrick, 1991; Prkachin, 1992; Rocha, Prkachin, Beaumont, Hardy, & Zumbo, 2003; Larochette, Chambers, & Craig, 2006; Lints-Martindale, Hadjistavropoulos, Barber, & Gibson, 2007), and depression (Reed, Sayette, & Cohn, 2007). FACS was also used to study how prototypical emotions are expressed as unique combinations of facial muscles in healthy people (Ekman & Friesen, 1978a; Gosselin, Kirouac, & Dor, 1995; Kohler et al., 2004), and to examine evoked and posed facial expressions in schizophrenia patients and controls (Kohler et al., 2008a, 2008b), which revealed substantial differences in the configuration and frequency of AUs in five universal emotions.

Notwithstanding the advantages of FACS for systematic analysis of facial expressions, it has a major limitation. FACS rating requires extensive training and is time-consuming and subjective and thus prone to rater bias. This limitation makes large-sample studies challenging. An automated computerized scoring system, whose aim is to produce FACS scores objectively and fast, is a promising

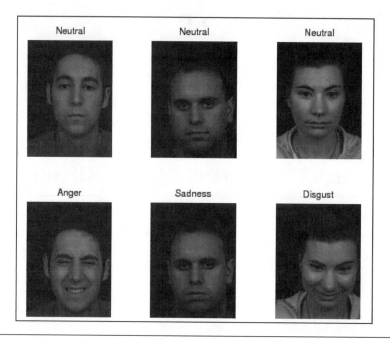

Figure 11.1 Examples of ambiguous (left), subtle (middle), and inappropriate (right) facial expressions. The left subject is showing an ambiguous expression, where the upper facial region is showing anger or disgust emotions while the lower facial region is showing a degree of happiness. The middle subject is exhibiting a subtle expression that is barely perceived as sadness by an observer. Additionally, the right subject is displaying an inappropriate expression of happiness when the person is experiencing a disgust emotion. To accurately describe these ambiguous and/or subtle expressions, we use the Facial Action Coding System to delineate the movements of individual facial muscle groups.

Source: Author.

alternative. Our group has proposed various approaches in the past to automate the measurements of facial expressions (Alvino et al., 2007; Verma et al., 2005; Wang et al., 2008). Verma et al. (2005) and Alvino et al. (2007) quantified regional volumetric difference functions to measure high-dimensional face deformation. These measures were used to classify facial expressions and produce clinical scores that showed correlations with video SANS ratings. However, these methods required human operators to manually define regional boundaries and landmarks in face images, which is not suitable for large sample studies. Wang et al. (2008) proposed a fully automatic method of analyzing facial expressions in videos by quantifying the probabilistic likelihoods of happiness, sadness, anger, fear, and neutral for each video frame. Case studies with videos of healthy controls and patients with schizophrenia and Asperger's syndrome were reported. However, the method had limited applicability in cases of ambiguous or subtle expressions, as exemplified in Figure 11.1, because it used only four universal emotions.

In the section "Automated Facial Action Coding System," we present a state-of-the-art automated FACS system we developed to analyze dynamic changes of facial actions in videos of neuropsychiatric patients (Hamm, Kohler, Gur, & Verma, 2011). In contrast to previous computerized methods, the new method (a) analyzes dynamical expression changes through videos instead of still images, (b) measures individual and combined facial muscle movements through AUs instead of a few prototypical expressions, and (c) performs automatically without requiring interventions from an operator. These advantages facilitate a high-throughput analysis of large-sample studies on emotional impairment in neuropsychiatric disorders.

We initially applied the automated FACS method to videos from eight representative neuropsychiatric patients and controls as illustrative examples to demonstrate its potential applicability to subsequent clinical studies. Qualitative analysis of the videos provides detailed information on the dynamics of the facial muscle movements for each subject, which can aid diagnosis of patients. From the videos, we also computed the frequencies of single and combined AUs for quantitative analysis of differences in facial expressions. We used those frequencies to derive measures of flatness and inappropriateness of facial expressions. Flat and inappropriate affect are defining characteristics of abnormalities in facial expression observed in schizophrenia, and these measures can serve to quantify these clinical characteristics of neuropsychiatric disorders.

The major advantages offered by automated FACS is its objectivity compared with rater-based ratings, which categorize a facial expression into positive or negative or five or six prototypical emotions. However, FACS alone does not clarify to role of altered individual facial muscle movements on global expressivity and respective differences in schizophrenia. We address this problem in the section "Information-Theoretic Facial Expression Analysis," which is based on Hamm, Pinkham, Gur, Verma, and Kohler (2014). In that section, we present novel measures of facial expressivity, based on individual muscle movements that are derived from information theory (Shannon, 1948), and apply these measures to matched groups of schizophrenia and control subjects. Information theory originated in the 1950s from the field of applied mathematics to analyze the capacity of communication channels. The method has provided powerful tools to analyze human performance measures in psychological experiments (Garner, 1962) and a framework for understanding emotional communication (Dittman, 1972). Information theory has also been successfully used in biomedical investigations, such as processing capacity of neural coding (Borst & Theunissen, 1999), complexity in electrocardiographic sequences (Costa, Goldberger, & Peng, 2005), and electroencephalography in Alzheimer's disease (Jeong, Gore, & Peterson, 2001) and schizophrenia (Na, Jin, Kim, & Ham, 2002).

We test the sensitivity of the information-theoretic measures in characterizing and quantifying affective expression deficits in schizophrenia in "Information-Theoretic Facial Expression Analysis" and examine their relationship with observer-based ratings of inappropriate and flattened emotion expressions. We apply two-dimensional measures of facial expressivity that can be computed objectively from videos of facial expressions without requiring observer-based ratings: (a) *ambiguity* of facial expressions within a single emotion and (b) *distinctiveness* of facial expressions between separate emotions. These measures correspond to the two most important information-theoretic quantities of (a) *conditional entropy* and (b) *mutual information.*

Briefly, ambiguity is the amount of uncertainty in a person's facial muscle patterns during the expression of a single emotion as contrasted with consistency of the pattern. A person whose facial muscle pattern is ambiguous, that is, only brief or continuously varying during emotion expression, will be less effective in communicating his or her intended emotion to another person. Distinctiveness is the capacity of a person to express different emotions succinctly through facial muscles. A person who is unable to produce distinct facial patterns for different emotions will also be less effective in communicating a specific emotion. We anticipated that ambiguity and distinctiveness can be applied to large data sets of dynamic expressions and that they can capture aspects of expressivity deficits that would improve our understanding of emotional expression abilities in persons with schizophrenia. In addition, although representing different theoretical constructs, we examined whether information-theoretic measures correlate with observer-based ratings such as inappropriate and flattened affect.

This chapter has two main sections. In "Automated Facial Action Coding System," we describe the details of our automated FACS system and the methods of qualitative and quantitative analysis, and we present the results of the experiments. In "Information-Theoretic Facial Expression Analysis," we introduce the new measures of ambiguity and flatness and present experimental results with discussions.

Automated Facial Action Coding System

In this section, we describe the details of our automated FACS system and methods of qualitative and quantitative analysis, and we present the results of the experiments.

Subjects and Procedures

We collected videos of healthy controls and persons with schizophrenia for a neuropsychiatric study of emotions under an institutional review board–approved protocol at the University of Pennsylvania. After describing the study to the subjects, we obtained written informed consent, including consent to publish pictures. There were 28 outpatients with *Diagnostic and Statistical Manual of Mental Disorders*, Fourth Edition, diagnoses of schizophrenia and 26 healthy controls balanced in gender, race, age, and parents' education. All patients were clinically stable, without hospitalization for at least 3 months prior to research assessment, and had been maintained on their present medications for the past month. Presence of significant acute extrapyramidal symptoms as evidenced by scores of 1 or higher on at least two of the rigidity or tremor items (Items 2, 3, 4, 5, and 9) was exclusionary. Likewise, presence of significant tardive extrapyramidal symptoms as evidenced by scores of 2 or higher on Items 1 to 4 (facial and oral movements) was exclusionary. All patients were treated with second-generation antipsychotics that were converted to dosages equivalent to olanzapine; two patients were also treated with first-generation antipsychotics that were converted to dosages equivalent to chlorpromazine. All medication dosages were stable for the month prior to testing, and no patient was treated with anticholinergic medications. Pertinent demographic and clinical information is summarized in Table 11.1.

Although the results presented in "Information-Theoretic Facial Expression Analysis" used all subjects for analysis, the results in the present section

used only four healthy controls and four patients with schizophrenia who were initially recruited for a pilot study by Hamm et al. (2011). In these eight subjects, each group was balanced in gender (two male and two female subjects) and race (two Caucasians and two African Americans). A summary of the eight subjects and their videos is given in Table 11.2.

To test emotion expression ability, we followed the emotion elicitation procedure previously described (Gur et al., 2002) and adapted for use in schizophrenia (Kohler et al., 2008b). Videos were obtained for neutral expressions and for five universal emotions (happiness, sadness, anger, fear, and disgust). Before recording, participants were asked to describe biographical emotional situations, when each emotion was experienced in mild, moderate, and high intensities, and these situations were summarized as vignettes. Subsequently, subjects were

Table 11.1 Participant Demographics ($n = 56$)

Group	Age (y), M ± SD (RNG)	Sex	Race	Daily Dosage (mg), M ± SD	SANS Flat, M ± SD (RNG)	SANS Inappropriate, M ± SD (RNG)	Extrapyramidal Symptoms
Patients ($n = 28$)	32.3 ± 9.0 (20–47)	14 Male 14 Female	9 Cc 16 AfAm 3 others	13.6 ± 7.6 (OLZ) 225 ± 247 (CPZ)	0.8 ± 1.2 (0–4)	1.0 ± 1.2 (0–4)	None
Controls ($n = 26$)	33.0 ± 8.6 (20–48)	16 Male 10 Female	8 Cc 15 AfAm 3 others	NA	NA	NA	NA

Source: Author.

Note: AfAm = African American; Cc = Caucasian; CPZ = chlorpromazine; NA = not applicable; OLZ = olanzapine; RNG = Range; SANS = Scale for the Assessment of Negative Symptoms.

Table 11.2 Summary of Eight Subjects and Their Videos

Subject	Gender	Race	Qualitative Description of the Videos
Control 1	Male	Caucasian	Mildly expressive, smooth expressions
Control 2	Male	African American	Mildly expressive, lack of defined distinction between emotions
Control 3	Female	Caucasian	Expressive, smooth expressions
Control 4	Female	African American	Very expressive, abrupt expressions
Patient 1	Male	Caucasian	Very flat, intermittent expressions
Patient 2	Male	African American	Flat, intermittent expressions
Patient 3	Female	Caucasian	Mildly expressive, very inappropriate
Patient 4	Female	African American	Very flat, mildly inappropriate

Source: Author.

seated in a brightly lit room where recordings took place, and emotional vignettes were recounted to participants in a narrative manner using exact wording derived from the vignettes. The spontaneous facial expressions of the subjects were recorded as videos. Before and between the five emotion sessions, the subjects were asked to relax and return to a neutral state. The duration of each session was about 2 minutes (110 ± 54 seconds).

Methods

In the first stage of the automated FACS system, we detect facial regions and track facial landmarks defined on the contours of the eyebrows, eyes, nose, lips, and so on, in videos. For each frame of the video, an approximate region of a face is detected by the Viola-Jones face detector (Viola & Jones, 2001). The detector is known to work robustly for large intersubject variations and illumination changes. Within the face region, we search the exact location of facial landmarks using a deformable face model. Among the various types of deformable face models, we use active shape modeling (ASM; Cootes, Taylor, Cooper, & Graham, 1995), for several reasons. ASM is arguably the simplest and fastest method among deformable models, which fits our

need to track a large number of frames in multiple videos. Furthermore, ASM is also known to generalize well to new subjects because of its simplicity (Gross, Matthews, & Baker, 2005). We train ASM with 159 manually collected landmark locations from a subset of still images that are also used for training AU classifiers. The typical number of landmarks in publicly available databases ranges between 30 and 80. We use 159 landmarks to accurately detect fine movements of facial components (Figure 11.2). ASM performs better with more landmarks in the model (Stegmann, Ersbol, & Larsen, 2003). When we track landmarks from videos, a face is often occluded by hand or leaves the camera view angle. Such frames are discarded from the analysis automatically. The estimated locations of landmarks for all frames in a video can be further improved by using a temporal model, as in Wang et al. (2008). We use a Kalman filter, which combines the observed landmark locations (these are inherently noisy) with the predicted landmark's locations from a temporal model (Wikle & Berliner, 2007). Sample video tracking results are shown in Figure 11.2. Because the movement of landmarks is also caused by head pose change unrelated to facial expression, it is important to extract the relevant features only as explained in the following paragraphs.

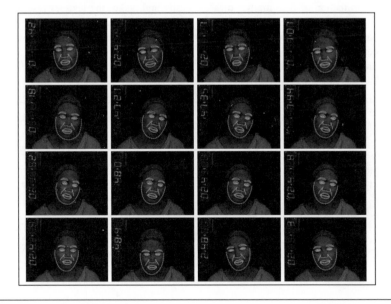

Figure 11.2 Sample tracking result. On each face, dots indicate the locations of 159 landmarks, and lines indicate different facial components. Note that the accuracy of tracked landmarks is crucial for videos of spontaneously evoked emotions (disgust in this example), because the movement of landmarks due to facial expression is very small compared with the overall movement of the head.

Source: Author.

We use the detected landmark locations to extract two types of features for AU detection: *geometric* and *texture*. Previous facial expression recognition systems typically used either geometric or texture features, not both. We use both features because they convey complementary information. For example, certain AUs can be detected directly from geometric changes: Inner Brow Raiser and Outer Brow Raiser (AU1 and AU2) cause displacements of the eyebrows, even when the associated texture changes (increased horizontal wrinkles in the forehead) are not visible. However, when Inner Brow Raiser (AU1) is jointly present with Brow Lowerer (AU4), the geometric displacement of eyebrows is less obvious. In that case, texture changes (increased vertical wrinkles between eyebrows) provide complementary evidence of the presence of AU4.

We extract the two features separately and combine them in the classification stage. To define geometric features, we create a landmark template from the training data by Procrustes analysis (Mardia & Dryden, 1998). Starting with the averaged landmark locations as a template, we align landmarks from all training faces to the template and update the template by averaging the aligned landmarks. This procedure is repeated for a few iterations. From the landmark template, we create a template mesh by Delaunay triangulation, which yields 159 vertices and 436 edges. Deformation of face meshes measured by compression and expansion of the edges reflects facial muscle contraction and relaxation.

To extract geometric features of a test face, we first align the face to the template by similarity transformations to suppress within-subject head pose variations and intersubject geometric differences. Next, we use differences of edge lengths between each face and a neutral face of the same person, formed into a 436-dimensional vector of geometric features, thereby further emphasizing the change due to facial expressions and suppressing irrelevant changes. Figure 11.3 demonstrates the procedure for extracting geometric features.

To extract texture features, we compute a Gabor wavelet response, which has been used widely for face analysis (Pantic & Bartlett, 2007). We use Gabor filter banks with nine different spatial frequencies from 1/2 to 1/32 in units of $pixel^{-1}$ and eight different orientations from 0° to 180° with a 22.5° step (Figure 11.4).

Before applying the filters, each face image is aligned to a template face using its landmarks and resized to about 100 to 120 pixels. The magnitudes of the filters form a 72-dimensional feature at each pixel of the image. In Bartlett et al. (2006), the Gabor responses from the whole image were used as features, whose dimensionality is huge (165,888). In Valstar and Pantic (2006), 20 regions of interest (ROIs) affected by specific AUs were selected. We also use ROIs to reduce the dimensionality, but we took the approach further: Gabor responses in each ROI are pooled by 72-dimensional histograms. This reduces the dimensionality of the features dramatically and makes the features robust to local deformations of faces and errors in the detected landmarks locations. Furthermore, AU classifiers can be trained in much shorter time. The ROIs we use are shown in Figure 11.5.

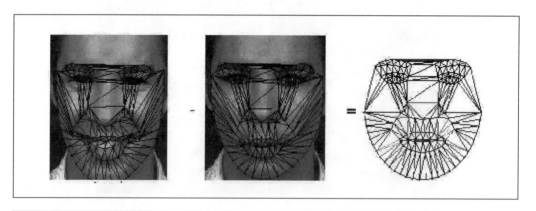

Figure 11.3 Geometric features for action unit classification. Deformation of the face mesh (left) relative to the mesh at a neutral state (middle) is computed and normalized to a subject-independent template mesh (right).The edges on the template mesh indicate compression and expansion of the edges, respectively.

Source: Author.

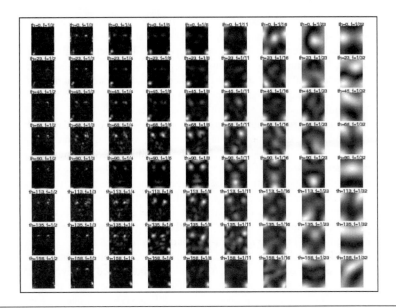

Figure 11.4 Examples of Gabor features of multiple spatial frequencies and orientations from a face image. Convolution of an image with Gabor wavelets yields high magnitudes around the structures such as facial contour, eyes, and mouth (shown as white blobs in the above images) because of frequency and orientation selectivity of the wavelets. By taking the difference of Gabor features between an emotional face and a neutral face, we can measure the change of facial texture due to facial expressions. Spatial frequency ranges from 1/2 to 1/32 in units of pixel^{-1}, and orientation ranges from 0° to 180° with a 22.5° step.

Source: Author.

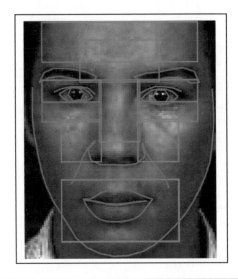

Figure 11.5 Regions of interest (ROIs) for extracting texture features for action unit classification. In each ROI (rectangle), a histogram of Gabor features is computed for multiple spatial frequencies and orientations.

Source: Author.

Similar to geometric features, texture features also have unwanted within-subject and intersubject variations. For example, a person can have permanent wrinkles in the forehead, which, for a different person, appear only when the eyebrows are raised and therefore interfere with the correct detection of eyebrow movements. By taking the difference of Gabor response histograms between each face and a neutral face of the same person, we measure the relative change of textures. This approach accounts for newly (dis)appearing wrinkles as well as deepening of the permanent wrinkles, instead of the simple presence or absence of wrinkles.

We adopt a classification approach from machine learning to predict the presence or the absence of AUs. A classifier is a general-purpose algorithm that takes features as input and produces a binary decision as output. In our case, we feed geometric and textural features from a face to a classifier, and the classifier makes a decision as to whether a certain AU is present in the given face. Three necessary steps of a classification approach include (a) data collection, (b) classifier training, and (c) classifier validation, as we describe below.

A classifier "learns" patterns between input features and output decisions from training data, which consist of examples of face images and their associated FACS ratings, from human raters in this case. Our group has been collecting still face images of the universal facial expressions. These include expressions in mild, moderate, and high intensities, in multiple emotions, and in both posed (subjects were asked to express emotions) and evoked (subjects spontaneously expressed emotions) conditions from various demographic groups (Kohler et al., 2004, 2008a, 2008b). Note that the rules of FACS are not affected by these conditions, because it describes only the presence of facial muscle movements. These face images are FACS-rated by experts in our groups. There are three initial raters, who achieved FACS reliability from the Ekman lab in San Francisco. All subsequent FACS raters had to meet interrater reliability of >0.6, stratified by emotional valence for the presence and absence of all AUs rated on a sample of 128 happy, sad, angry, and fearful expressions. Two raters, one FACS certified and one FACS reliable, coded the presence and absence of AUs in 3,419 face images. Instances in which ratings differed between the two raters are resolved by visual analysis requiring agreement on absence and presence by both raters. Faces are presented in random order to the raters, along with neutral images of the same person to serve as a baseline face. Among the AUs rated, Lip Tightener (AU23) and Lip Pressor (AU24), which both narrow the appearance of lips, and Lips Part (AU25) and Jaw Drop (AU26), which constitute mouth opening, are collapsed, because they represent differing degrees of the same muscle movement.

We select Gentle AdaBoost classifiers (Friedman, Hastie, & Tibshirani, 1998) from among a few possible choices of classifiers used in the literature. AdaBoost classifiers have several properties that make them preferable to other classifiers for the problem at hand. First, AdaBoost selects only a subset of features, which is desirable for handling high-dimensional data. Second, the classifier can adapt to inhomogeneous features (geometric and texture features) that might have very different distributions. Third, it produces a continuous value of confidence along with its binary decisions through a natural probabilistic interpretation of the algorithm as a logistic regression. We train AdaBoost classifiers following Friedman et al. (1998). A total of 15 classifiers are trained to detect each of the 15 AUs independently, using the training data of face images and their associated FACS ratings from human raters.

Although the manual FACS ratings included Nasolabial Deepener (AU11), Cheek Pucker (AU13), Dimpler (AU14), and Lower Lip Depressor (AU16), we do not train classifiers for these AUs, because the number of positive samples of these AUs in our database was too small to train a classifier reliably.

Before we use the classifiers, we verify the accuracy of the automated FACS ratings against the human FACS ratings by two-fold cross-validation as follows. We divide the training data into two sets. Subsequently, we train the classifiers with one set using both face images and human ratings and collect the classifier outputs on the other set using face images only. Then we compare the predicted ratings with the human ratings on the other set. In particular, we divide the training data into posed and evoked conditions to validate that the classifiers are unaffected by these conditions. Table 11.3 summarizes the agreement rates between automated and manual FACS ratings for 15 AUs representing the most common AUs used for facial expressions. Overall, we achieve an average agreement of 95.9%. The high agreement validates the accuracy of the proposed automated FACS.

We use the AU classifiers to qualitatively and quantitatively analyze the dynamic facial expression changes in videos. This includes (a) creation of temporal AU profiles, (b) computation of single and combined AU frequencies, and (c) automated measurements of affective flatness and inappropriateness. The AUs are detected for each and every frame of a video for the whole course of the video, which results in creating temporal AU profiles of the video. Originally, a classifier outputs binary decision (i.e., presence or absence of an AU), but it also produces the confidence of the decision (i.e., the posterior likelihood of the AU's being present) as continuous values in the range of 0 to 1. We use the binary decisions for quantitative analysis and the continuous values for qualitative analysis. When we apply the classifiers to a video, we can create continuous temporal profiles of AUs, which will show the intensity, duration, and timing of simultaneous facial muscle actions in a video.

Various types of measures can be derived from the AU profiles for quantitative analysis of facial expressions. In Kohler et al. (2008a, 2008b), the frequencies of single AUs were analyzed to study group differences between healthy people and schizophrenia patients. AUs are manually rated for a few still images per subject. Our proposed method enables automatic collection of AUs and

Table 11.3 Agreement Rates of Automated and Manual FACS Ratings for 15 AUs

AU	Description	Rate (%)
AU1	Inner Brow Raiser	95.8
AU2	Outer Brow Raiser	97.8
AU4	Brow Lowerer	91.0
AU5	Upper Lid Raiser	96.9
AU6	Cheek Raiser	93.0
AU7	Lid Tightener	87.0
AU9	Nose Wrinkler	97.5
AU10	Upper Lip Raiser	99.3
AU12	Lip Corner Puller	97.1
AU15	Lip Corner Depressor	99.2
AU17	Chin Raiser	96.5
AU18	Lip Puckerer	98.6
AU20	Lip Stretcher	97.7
AU23	Lip Tightener	96.9
AU25	Lips Part	95.7

Source: Author.

Note: AU = action unit; FACS = Facial Action Coding System.

computation of single AU frequencies for the whole video. We compute the following:

Frequency of single AUs = Number of frames in which an AU is present/Total number of frames,

and

Frequency of AU combinations = Number of frames in which an AU combination (e.g., AU1 + AU4) is present/Total number of frames.

The AU combination measures the simultaneous activation of multiple action units in facial expression, which is more realistic than isolated movements of single action units and therefore provides more accurate information than single AU frequencies.

In the analysis of facial expressions, flatness and inappropriateness of expressions can serve as basic clinical measures for severity of affect expression in neuropsychiatric disorders. For example, in the SANS (Andreasen, 1984a), a psychiatric expert interviews the patients and manually rates the flatness and the inappropriateness of the patient's affect. However, the scales are subjective, require extensive

expertise and training, and can vary across raters. By using AU frequencies from the automated FACS method, we can define objective measures of flatness and inappropriateness as follows:

Flatness measure = Number of neutral frames in which no AU is present/Total number of frames,

and

Inappropriateness measure = Number of "inappropriate" frames/Total number of frames.

To define "inappropriate" frames, we used the statistical study of Kohler et al. (2004), who analyzed which AUs are involved in expressing the universal emotions of happiness, sadness, anger, and fear. Specifically, they identified AUs that are uniquely present or absent in each emotion. AUs that are uniquely present in a certain emotion were called "qualifying" AUs of the emotion, and AUs that are uniquely absent were called "disqualifying" AUs of the emotion, as shown in Table 11.4. On this basis, we define an image frame from an intended emotion as inappropriate if it contains one or more disqualifying AUs of that emotion or one or more qualifying AUs of the other emotions. This decision rule is applied to all frames in a video to derive the inappropriateness measure automatically.

Results

We apply the AU classifiers to the videos of evoked emotions, which record the spontaneous responses of the subjects to the recounting of their own experiences. This results in continuous temporal profiles of AU likelihoods over the course of the videos.

We compare temporal AU profiles of the subjects for five emotions and show examples that best demonstrate the characteristics of the two groups in Figures 11.6 to 11.9. The profiles in Figure 11.6 represent a healthy control, who exhibits gradual and smooth

Table 11.4 Qualifying and Disqualifying Action Units in Four Emotions (Summarized From Kohler et al., 2004)

Emotion	Qualifying AUs	Disqualifying AUs
Happiness	AU6, AU12	AU4, AU20
Sadness	AU17	AU25
Anger	AU9, AU16	AU1
Fear	AU2	AU7, AU10

Note: AU = action unit.

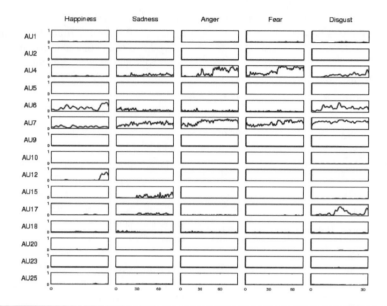

Figure 11.6 Temporal action unit (AU) profiles of Control 3 for five emotion sessions. For each AU, the graph indicates the likelihood (between 0 and 1) of the presence of the AU, for the duration of five video (in seconds). The subject exhibits gradual and smooth increase of AU likelihoods over time.

Source: Author.

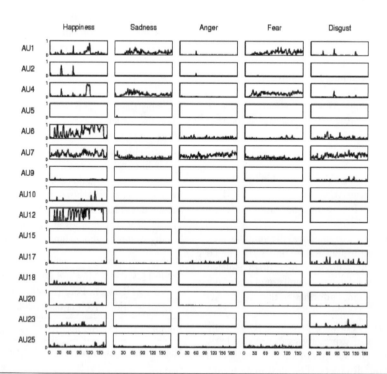

Figure 11.7 Temporal action unit (AU) profiles of Control 4 for five emotion sessions. The subject exhibits facial actions in most of the AUs. There are bursts of facial actions in happiness and disgust, while there are more gradual actions in other emotions.

Source: Author.

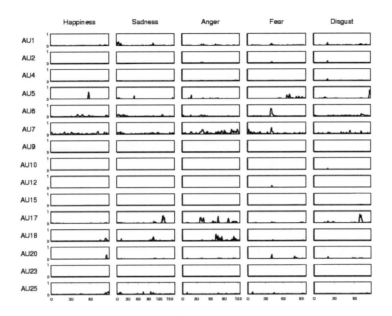

Figure 11.8 Temporal action unit (AU) profiles of Patient 1 for five emotion sessions. The subject exhibits little facial action but for a few abrupt peaks of individual AUs such as AU5, AU6, AU7, AU17, and AU18.

Source: Author.

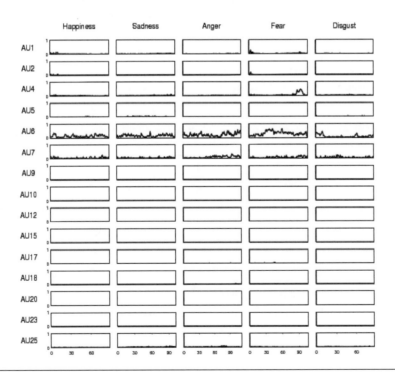

Figure 11.9 Temporal action unit (AU) profiles of Patient 4 for five emotion sessions. The subject exhibits almost no facial action except for AU4, AU6, and AU7.

Source: Author.

increase of AU likelihoods and relatively distinct patterns between emotions in terms of the magnitude of common AUs such as Inner Brow Raiser (AU1), Brow Lowerer (AU4), Cheek Raiser (AU6), Lid Tightener (AU7), Lip Corner Puller (AU12), Chin Raiser (AU17), and Lip Puckerer (AU18). The profiles in Figure 11.7 represent another healthy control, who displays a very expressive face. Different emotions show distinctive dynamics. For example, happiness and disgust have several bursts of facial actions, whereas other emotions are more gradual. The profiles in Figure 11.8 represent a patient who shows flattened facial action (i.e., mostly a neutral expression) throughout the session, with a few abrupt peaks of individual AUs such as Upper Lid Raiser (AU5), Cheek Raiser (AU6), Lid Tightener (AU7), Chin Raiser (AU17), and Lip Puckerer (AU18). The profiles in Figure 11.9 represent another patient, which are even flatter than the first patient, except for weak underlying actions of Check Raiser (AU6), Lid Tightener (AU7), and a peak of Brow Lowerer (AU4) in fear. The temporal profiles of other subjects not shown in these figures exhibit intermediate characteristics; that is, they are less expressive than the two control examples but not as flat as the two patient examples. Additional figures are reported in Hamm et al. (2011), and we refer the reader to that article for descriptions of the temporal profiles for each emotion.

We compute the single and combined AU frequencies measured from the videos of the eight subjects. We show frequencies from one control and one patient in Tables 11.5 and 11.6 as illustrative examples. In single and combined AU frequencies, there are common AUs, such as Cheek Raiser (AU6) and Lid Tightener (AU7), that appear frequently across emotions and subjects. However there are many other AUs whose frequencies are different across emotions and subjects. On the basis of the AU frequencies of all eight subjects, we consequently derive the measures of *flatness* and *inappropriateness* to get more intuitive summary parameters of the AU frequencies. Table 11.7 summarizes the automated measures for each subject and emotion, except for the inappropriateness of disgust emotion, which is not defined in Kohler et al. (2004). The table also shows the flatness and inappropriate measures averaged over all emotions.

According to the automated measurement, Controls 3, 2, and 4 are very expressive (flatness = 0.0051, 0.0552, and 0.1320), while Patients 1, 2, and 4 are very flat (flatness = 0.8336, 0.5731, and 0.5288). Control 1 and Patient 3 are in the medium range (flatness = 0.3848 and 0.3076). Inappropriateness of expression is high for Patients 4 and 3 (inappropriateness = 0.6725, 0.3398, and 0.3150) and moderate for Patient 1 and Controls 1 to 4 (inappropriateness = 0.2579, 0.2506, 0.2502, 0.1464, and 0.0539). The degree of flatness and inappropriateness of expressions varies across emotions, which will be investigated in a future study with a larger population.

Discussion

We have presented a state-of-the-art method for an automated Facial Action Coding System for

Table 11.5 Frequencies of Single AUs From the Videos of One Control and One Patient in Different Emotions

	Happiness		Sadness		Anger		Fear		Disgust	
Control 1	AU7	1.000	AU7	0.269	AU7	0.905	AU7	0.176	AU7	0.476
	AU2	0.286	AU4	0.154	AU4	0.381	AU4	0.059	AU6	0.381
	AU6	0.214			AU6	0.381	AU1	0.039		
	AU25	0.143					AU2	0.020		
Patient 1	AU7	0.068	AU1	0.049	AU7	0.194	AU7	0.082	AU17	0.071
	AU5	0.045	AU17	0.049	AU17	0.097	AU5	0.041	AU5	0.024
	AU18	0.023	AU18	0.024	AU18	0.097	AU6	0.041		
	AU20	0.023	AU7	0.012	AU5	0.016	AU20	0.020		
	AU25	0.023								

Source: Author.

Note: The frequency of a single action unit (AU) is defined as the ratio between the number of frames in which the AU is present and the total number of frames.

Table 11.6 Frequencies of AU Combinations From the Videos of One Control and One Patient in Different Emotions

	Happiness		Sadness		Anger		Fear		Disgust	
Control 1	7	0.357	Neutral	0.731	6 + 7	0.333	Neutral	0.765	Neutral	0.333
	2 + 7	0.286	4 + 7	0.154	4 +7	0.333	7	0.137	7	0.286
	6 + 7	0.214	7	0.115	7	0.190	4 + 7	0.039	6	0.190
	7 + 25	0.143			Neutral	0.095	4	0.020	6 + 7	0.190
					4 + 6 + 7	0.048	1	0.020		
							1 + 2	0.020		
Patient 1	Neutral	0.818	Neutral	0.890	Neutral	0.677	Neutral	0.878	Neutral	0.905
	7	0.068	17	0.049	7	0.129	7	0.041	17	0.071
	5	0.045	1	0.024	18	0.065	5	0.041	5	0.024
	25	0.023	18	0.012	7 + 17	0.048	6 + 7	0.020		
	20	0.023	1 + 18	0.012	17	0.032	6 + 7 + 20	0.020		
	18	0.023	1 + 7	0.012	17 + 18	0.016				
					7 + 18	0.016				
					5	0.016				

Source: Author.

Note: The combined action unit (AU) frequency is defined similar to the single AU frequency.

Table 11.7 Measures of Flatness and Inappropriateness Computed From the Automated Analysis of All Eight Subjects

	Happiness		Sadness		Anger		Fear		Disgust		Average	
Subject	Flat	Inapp	Flat	Inapp	Flat	Inapp	Flat	Inapp	Flat	Inapp	Flat	Inapp
Contrl 1	0.0000	0.1739	0.7308	0.0000	0.0952	0.2286	0.7647	0.6000	0.7647	—	0.3848	0.2506
Contrl 2	0.0526	0.0000	0.0000	0.1356	0.0312	0.0857	0.1642	0.7794	0.1642	—	0.0552	0.2502
Contrl 3	0.0000	0.0000	0.0256	0.0714	0.0000	0.0000	0.5143	0.0000	0.0000	—	0.0051	0.1464
Contrl 4	0.0119	0.0470	0.2841	0.0000	0.1224	0.0444	0.1125	0.1240	0.1125	—	0.1320	0.0539
Patient 1	0.8182	0.1250	0.8902	0.0000	0.6774	0.2400	0.8776	0.6667	0.8776	—	0.8336	0.2579
Patient 2	0.5833	0.2286	0.3784	0.1562	0.7805	0.2500	0.5517	0.6250	0.5517	—	0.5731	0.3150
Patient 3	0.4545	0.1190	0.1864	0.0517	0.1869	0.3885	0.7101	0.8000	0.7101	—	0.3076	0.3398
Patient 4	0.7209	0.0000	0.6078	1.0000	0.3036	0.8222	0.1509	0.8679	0.1509	—	0.5288	0.6725

Source: Author.

Note: Controls 3, 2, and 4 are very expressive (low flatness), while Patients 1, 2, and 4 are very flat. Control 1 and Patient 3 are in the medium range. Patients 4 and 3 are highly inappropriate, while Patient 1 and Controls 1 to 4 are moderately inappropriate. Contrl = Control; Flat = flatness; Inapp = inappropriateness.

neuropsychiatric research. By measuring the movements of facial action units, our method can objectively describe subtle and ambiguous facial expressions such as in Figure 11.1, which is difficult for previous methods that use only prototypical emotions to describe facial expressions. Therefore the proposed system, which uses a combination of responses from different AUs, is more suitable for studying neuropsychiatric patients, whose facial expressions are often subtle or ambiguous. Although there are other automated AU detectors, they are trained on extreme expressions and are hence unsuitable for use in a pathology that manifests as subtle deficits in facial affect expression.

We piloted the applicability of our system in neuropsychiatric research by analyzing videos of four healthy controls and four patients with schizophrenia balanced in gender and race. We expect that the temporal profiles of AUs computed from videos of evoked emotions (Figures 11.6 to 11.9) can provide clinicians an informative visual summary of the dynamics of facial action. They show which AU or combination of AUs is present in the expressions of an intended emotion from a subject and quantify both intensity and duration.

Figures 11.6 to 11.9 visualize dynamical characteristics of facial actions of each subject for five emotions at a glance. Overall, these figures revealed that the facial actions of the patients were more flattened compared with those of the controls. In a healthy control (Figure 11.6), there was a gradual buildup of emotions that manifested as relatively smooth increases of multiple AUs. Such a change in profile is expected from the experimental design: The contents of the vignettes progressed from mild to moderate to extreme intensity of emotions. For another control (Figure 11.7), there were several bursts and underlying activities of multiple AUs. In contrast, patients showed fewer facial actions (Figures 11.8 and 11.9) and a lack of a gradual increase of AU intensities (Figures 11.8 and 11.9). Also, the AU peaks were isolated in time and across AUs (Figure 11.8). Such sudden movements of facial muscles may be symptomatic of the emotional impairment. These findings lay the basis for a future study to verify the different facial action dynamics patterns in patients with schizophrenia and other neuropsychiatric populations.

The AU profiles from the pilot study were also analyzed quantitatively. From the temporal profiles, we computed the frequency of AUs in each emotion and subject, independently for each AU (Table 11.5), and jointly for AU combinations (Table 11.6). AU combinations measure the simultaneous activation of multiple facial muscles, which will shed light on the role of synchronized facial muscle movement in facial expressions of healthy controls and patients. This synchrony cannot be answered by studying single AU frequencies alone. The quantitative measures will allow us to statistically study the differences in facial action patterns between emotions and in multiple demographic or diagnostic groups. Such measures have been used in previous clinical studies (Kohler et al., 2004, 2008a, 2008b) but were limited to a small number of still images instead of videos because of the impractically large degree of effort in rating all individual frames manually. Last, we derived the automated measures of flatness and inappropriateness for each subject and emotion. Table 11.7 shows that the healthy control has both low flatness and low inappropriateness measures, whereas patients exhibited higher flatness and higher inappropriateness in general. However, there are intersubject variations; for example, Control 1 showed lower inappropriateness but slightly higher flatness than Patient 3. These automated measures of flatness and inappropriateness also agreed with the flatness and inappropriateness from visual examination of the videos (Table 11.2). The correlation between the automated and the observer-based measurements will be further verified in a future study with a larger sample size. Compared with qualitative analysis, the flatness and inappropriateness measures provide detailed automated numerical information without an intervention of human observers. This highlights the potential of the proposed method to automatically and objectively measure clinical variables of interest, such as flatness and inappropriateness, which can aid in diagnosis of affect expression deficits in neuropsychiatric disorders.

Information-Theoretic Facial Expression Analysis

In the previous section, we presented an automated FACS method, whose major advantage is its objectivity compared with rater-based ratings that categorize a facial expression as positive or negative or into a few prototypical emotions. Although the measured AU patterns are quantitatively and qualitatively different between patient and control groups, the high dimensionality of the AU measurement makes it difficult to interpret the patterns intuitively. To provide summarizing measures of the AU activities, we introduce *ambiguity* and *flatness* as two-dimensional measures based on information-theoretic analysis of AUs. In this section, we define these measures and present experimental results with discussions.

Subjects and Procedures

We use the same subject pool and experiment procedures as those in the previous section, except for the fact that all subjects in the pool are used for analysis.

Methods

We use the automated FACS developed in the previous section to collect the temporal profiles of 15 AUs. From the distribution of 15-dimensional continuous variables for each video, we compute information-theoretic measures of expressivity for each subject. Specifically, we measure *ambiguity* of facial expression patterns within each emotion and *distinctiveness* of facial expression patterns between emotions. These two measures correspond to conditional entropy and mutual information, which are the fundamental variables of information theory (Shannon, 1948). Interpretations of the two information-theoretic measures depend on the experiments being conducted, and ambiguity and distinctiveness are specific interpretations of our experimental results with the spontaneous expression of emotions. In psychology, the two measures have been called equivocation and information transmission, respectively, in the context of absolute judgment tasks (Garner & Hake, 1951).

Computation of ambiguity and distinctiveness requires estimation of differential entropy from facial muscles. Differential entropy is the amount of uncertainty in continuous probabilistic distributions from which we derive mutual information and conditional entropy. Let x denote the (discrete) emotional state of an individual and y denote the (continuous and multivariate) facial muscle activity. Differential entropy is then defined by $H(p(y)) = E[-\log p(y)] = -\int_d p(y) \log p(y) dy$. Unlike discrete entropy, differential entropy is a relative measure and can have negative values; a univariate Gaussian distribution with $\sigma = (2\pi e)^{-1/2}$ has zero differential entropy, and Gaussian distributions with narrower or wider peaks have negative or positive entropy, respectively. Because we do not know $p(y)$ a priori, the differential entropy must be estimated from samples, much like estimation of mean and variance. Several estimation methods have been proposed, including adaptive partitioning, kernel density estimation, and nearest neighbor estimation (see Beirlant, Dudewicz, Gyoerfi, and Meulen, 1997, for a review). We use a k-nearest neighbor estimator of entropy (Kozachenko & Leonenko, 1987; Goria, Leonenko, Mergel, & Novi Inverardi, 2005; Mnatsakanov, Misra, Li, & Harner, 2008):

$$H(p(y)) \approx \frac{d}{n} \sum_i^n \log \rho + v_d - \psi(k) + \log n.$$

The $v_d = \pi^{d/2}/\Gamma(d/2+1)$ is the volue of a d-dimensional unit sphere, where Γ is the gamma function $\Gamma(z) = \int_0^\infty t^{z-1} e^{-t} dt$, and $\psi(z)$ is the digamma function

$\psi(z) = \Gamma(z)'/\Gamma(z)$. The only free parameter of nearest neighbor estimate is the size of the neighbors k, for which we used the heuristic rule (Goria et al., 2005): $k = \text{round}(n^{1/2} + 0.5)$, where n is the number of samples. For numerical stability, we also add a negligible amount (10^{-8}) of random noise to the data while computing entropy.

In our experiments, the conditional entropy is defined as

$$H(y \mid x) = \sum_{x = x_i} p(x_i) H(y \mid x_i)$$
$$= \sum_{x = x_i} p(x_i) \int -p(y \mid x_i) \log(p(y \mid x_i)) dy,$$

which is the average entropy of facial expression per emotion computed from facial muscle activity y in the video of each emotion x with equal priors for each emotion ($p[x] = 1/5$). We refer to this conditional entropy as *ambiguity* in the following context: When an individual's facial expression is consistent within each emotion, the conditional entropy is low, and when the expression is varying and ambiguous within each emotion, the conditional entropy is high.

The mutual information $I(x,y)$ can be computed from $I(x;y) = H(y) - H(y|x)$. Mutual information between discrete and continuous variables, as in our case, is also known as Jensen-Shannon divergence (Lin, 1991; Endres & Schindelin, 2003) and is nonnegative and bounded. By reformulating $I(x;y)$ as the average KL divergence (Kullback & Leibler, 1951) between conditional $p(y|x)$ and marginal $p(y)$ distributions

$$I(x; y) = KL(p(x, y) \| p(x)p(y))$$
$$= \sum_x p(x) \int p(y \mid x) \log \frac{p(y \mid x)}{p(y)} dy$$
$$= \sum_x p(x) KL(p(y \mid x) \| p(y)),$$

we notice that mutual information measures the average distance of emotion-specific facial expression pattern ($p[x|y]$) from the patterns of all emotions combined ($p[x]$); hence our choice of the term *distinctiveness* for mutual information.

In this chapter, we report the ambiguity and the distinctiveness as z scores ($[x - m]/s$) instead of their raw values for easier interpretation, where the mean and the standard deviation are computed using all subjects and conditions. We do this because these values are unitless and dependent on the experimental setting and therefore meaningful only in a relative sense. For example, if we use six basic emotions, including surprise, instead of five, the absolute values of ambiguity and distinctiveness will change.

However, the difference of values in diagnostic groups or conditions still measures the relative amount of the ambiguity and distinctiveness of facial expressions and provides meaningful information. Note that the standardization of raw values using z scores does not affect the subsequent statistical analysis. Lastly, the ambiguity and the distinctiveness are computed across all emotions, not for individual emotions. Although it is possible to analyze ambiguity for each emotion, pooling the values across emotions results in more reliable measures.

To verify that the information-theoretic measures agree with an observer's interpretation of ambiguity and distinctiveness from videos, the following criteria for manual scores from 0 to 4 are defined, and each video is rated by an observer blind to the diagnosis of subjects. For ambiguity, which is rated for videos of each emotion, 0 means very consistent (with only a single facial expression pattern in the single video of an emotion) and 4 means very ambiguous (with more than four different facial expression patterns in the video of an emotion). Scores 1 to 3 correspond to intermediate levels of ambiguity (with one, two, and three major facial expression patterns in a video, respectively). For distinctiveness, which is rated across videos of five emotions of a single subject, 0 means the five emotional videos are totally indistinguishable in representing the target emotions, and 4 means all five videos are distinctive and representative of the target emotions. Scores 1 to 3 correspond to intermediate levels of distinctiveness (with 1, 2, and 3 videos of distinctive emotions, respectively).

To compare information measures with previous observer-based ratings, flatness and inappropriateness of facial expression from the Scale for the Assessment of Negative Symptoms are adapted to video-based ratings (Alvino et al., 2007). Two raters scored each video with separate scores for flat and inappropriate affect, ranging from 0 (none) to 4 (extremely flat or inappropriate). SANS raters knew the intended emotions of the videos but not the diagnoses of subjects. Video-based SANS was based on a 5-point rating scale, similar to observer-based SANS. Ratings that differed by 2 or more points were reviewed for consensus, and average ratings were used as final ratings.

The following data analysis is performed to demonstrate the applicability and validity of the measures of ambiguity and distinctiveness. Group-based comparisons for ambiguity and distinctiveness of expressions involved two-way analysis of variance (ANOVA) of ambiguity and distinctiveness separately, using sex and diagnosis as grouping factors. We also measure the effect size of diagnosis by Cohen's d ($[m_1 - m_2]/\{0.5[s_1^2 + s_2^2]\}^{1/2}$). Validation of computerized measures of ambiguity and distinctiveness against observer-based measures is performed by Pearson correlations, where higher values mean better agreement between the computerized and observer-based measures. For observer-based ratings of inappropriateness and flatness of expressions, we perform separate two-way ANOVAs using sex and diagnosis as grouping factors. We also measure the effect size of diagnosis by Cohen's d. For the purposes of interpretability and comparison with alternative measures of symptom severity, we perform multiple regression analysis to study the explanatory power of the computerized measures of ambiguity and distinctiveness for observer-based ratings of inappropriate and flat affects, in which computerized measures are used as independent variables, and each of the observer-based ratings is used as a dependent variable. We perform multiple regression also in the other direction, in which observer-based ratings are used as independent variables and each of the computerized measures is used as a dependent variable.

Results

Ambiguity of expression, averaged across emotions, shows a strong effect of diagnosis ($F = 12$, $df = 1, 53, p = .0012$) but no effect of sex ($F < 0.001$, $df = 1, 53, p = .99$) nor interaction ($F = 0.78, df = 1, 53$, $p = 0.38$) by two-way ANOVA. Patients show higher ambiguity (0.41 ± 1.0) than controls (-0.44 ± 0.79), with a large effect size of 0.93 (Cohen's d). Likewise, distinctiveness of expression shows a strong effect of diagnosis ($F = 8.3, df = 1, 53, p = .0057$) but no effect of sex ($F = .056, df = 1, 53, p = 0.81$) nor interaction ($F = 0.26, df = 1, 53, p = .61$) by two-way ANOVA. Patients show lower distinctiveness (-0.37 ± 0.88) than controls (0.40 ± 0.98), with a large effect size of Cohen's $d = 0.83$.

The characteristics of ambiguity and distinctiveness measures are demonstrated with sample videos of subjects in Figures 11.10 to 11.13, which illustrate the expressions of subjects with ratings for low ambiguity and high distinctiveness, in contrast to subjects with ratings for low ambiguity and low distinctiveness, high ambiguity and low distinctiveness, and high ambiguity and high distinctiveness.

The computerized measures of ambiguity and distinctiveness are well correlated with the observer's scores of ambiguity ($r = .71, p < 0.01$) and distinctiveness ($r = .60, p < .01$). These correlations support the notion of agreement between the

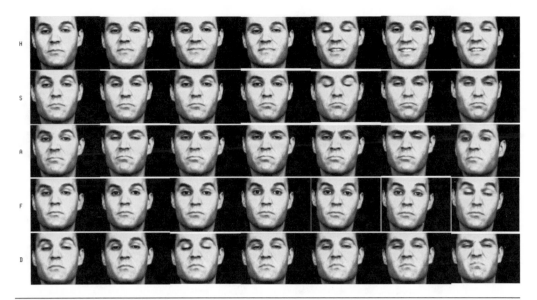

Figure 11.10 Sample videos of a subject with low ambiguity and high distinctiveness. Each row shows sample images evenly chosen from a video of one emotion. Facial expressions of low ambiguity and high distinctiveness are consistent within each emotion and also different between emotions, which makes each emotion well recognizable.

Source: Author.

Note: A = anger; D = disgust; F = fear; H = happiness; S = sadness.

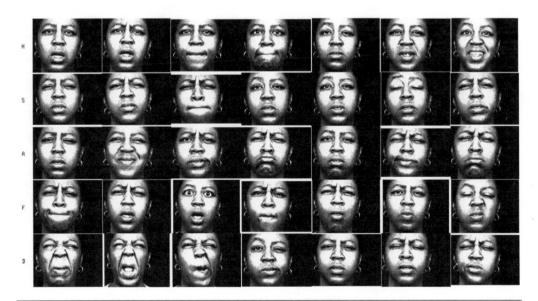

Figure 11.11 Sample videos of a subject with high ambiguity and low distinctiveness. High ambiguity and low distinctiveness appear as inappropriate facial expressions, because of the lack of consistent patterns within each emotion and the overlap of patterns across emotions.

Source: Author.

Note: A = anger; D = disgust; F = fear; H = happiness; S = sadness.

Figure 11.12 Sample videos of a subject with high ambiguity and high distinctiveness. High ambiguity and high distinctiveness also appear as inappropriate facial expressions because of the lack of consistent patterns within each emotion.

Source: Author.

Note: A = anger; D = disgust; F = fear; H = happiness; S = sadness.

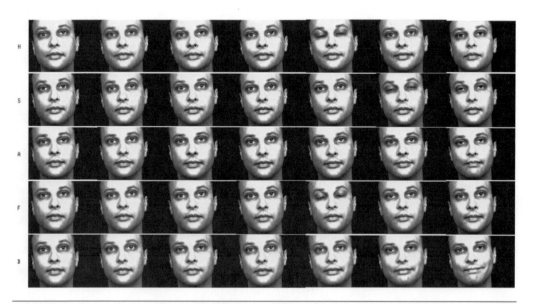

Figure 11.13 Sample videos of a subject with low ambiguity and low distinctiveness. Facial expressions of low ambiguity and low distinctiveness present themselves as muted or flat expressions throughout all emotions.

Source: Author.

Note: A = anger; D = disgust; F = fear; H = happiness; S = sadness.

computerized measures from information theory and the observer-rated measures from visual examination of the videos.

For video-based expert SANS ratings, flatness of expression shows a moderate effect of diagnosis ($F = 4.6$, $df = 1,53$, $p = .038$) but no effect of sex ($F = 3.9$, $df = 1, 53$, $p = .055$) nor interaction ($F = 0.19$, $df = 1, 53$, $p = .66$) by two-way ANOVA. Patients are more flat (2.0 ± 0.93) than controls (1.5 ± 0.91), with a medium effect size of 0.57. The inappropriateness of expression shows a strong effect of diagnosis ($F = 9.6$, $df = 1, 53$, $p = .0033$) but no effect of sex ($F = 0.99$, $df = 1, 53$, $p = .33$) nor interaction ($F = 0.0047$, $df = 1, 53$, $p = .95$) by two-way ANOVA. Patients are rated higher on inappropriate affect (1.1 ± 0.65) than controls (0.63 ± 0.37), with a large effect size of 0.92.

We examine the relationships between information-theoretic measures of ambiguity and distinctiveness and observer-based measures of inappropriate and flattened facial expressions of emotions. Regression of ambiguity on observer-based measures is moderately predictive ($R^2 = .13$, $F = 3.4$, $p = .040$), and the coefficients from flatness and inappropriateness are $-.14$ ($p = .30$) and $.50$ ($p = .032$), respectively. Regression of distinctiveness on observer-based measures is highly predictive ($R^2 = .19$, $F = 5.8$, $p = .0056$), and the coefficients from flatness and inappropriateness are $-.32$ ($p = .027$) and $-.65$ ($p = .0063$), respectively. Regression of flatness on computerized measures is moderately predictive ($R^2 = .15$, $F = 4.3$, $p = .019$), and the coefficients from ambiguity and distinctiveness are $-.33$ ($p = .025$) and $-.34$ ($p = .013$), respectively. Last, regression of inappropriateness on computerized measures is moderately predictive ($R^2 = .15$, $F = 4.3$, $p = .018$), and the coefficients from ambiguity and distinctiveness are $.14$ ($p = .11$) and -0.14 ($p = .11$), respectively.

Discussion

Impaired abilities of facial expression of emotions are common dysfunctions in schizophrenia that are associated with worse quality of life and poorer outcome (Gur et al., 2006; Ho, Nopoulos, Flaum, Arndt, & Andreasen, 1998). Clinical assessment of emotion expression abilities is typically obtained using observer-based rating scales administered during interviews that are not standardized to elicit emotion expressions and with limited potential to compare data across different studies and populations. More advanced observer-based measurements of facial expressions have been challenged by the complexity inherent in rating regional and global

changes in dynamic facial expressions, and their applications have been limited mainly to research. Nevertheless, these investigations using standardized observer-based ratings and electromyography have underscored that persons with schizophrenia exhibit altered expressions of volitional and of more fleeting spontaneous facial emotions that do not necessarily reflect their internal emotional state. Another challenge of measuring emotion expressions has been the importance to obtain emotion expressions that are genuine and naturalistic and not obscured by the artifice of the testing setting and methodology or influenced by rater fatigue. This is where automated computerized measurement offers an advantage over other methods to investigate dynamic expressions.

Our group has developed computerized assessment of emotion expression abilities that allows objective measurement of facial expressions that are obtained in a standardized setting (Alvino et al., 2007; Hamm et al., 2011; Verma et al., 2005; Wang et al., 2008). As an extension to these efforts, we have applied computerized assessments of facial expressivity to patients with schizophrenia and healthy controls to examine whether the novel methodology can elucidate differences in facial expression of emotions. Computerized information-theoretic measures focus on differences in ambiguity, which represents the measure of variability within the expression of a single emotion, and distinctiveness, which represents the measure of how distinctive facial expressions are for a particular emotion in comparison with other emotions. The computerized approach was validated by observer-based ratings of ambiguity and distinctiveness. In addition, when computerized measures were predicted by observer-based ratings, ambiguity was positively related with inappropriateness, and distinctiveness was negatively related with both flatness and inappropriateness. Conversely, when observer-based ratings were predicted by computerized measures, flatness was negatively related with both ambiguity and distinctiveness, while inappropriateness was not significantly related with either measure alone, although it was significantly predicted by overall ambiguity and distinctiveness. As illustrated in Figures 11.10 to 11.13, computerized measures of ambiguity and distinctiveness were associated with facial expressions that, in the combination of low ambiguity and high distinctiveness (Figure 11.10), were well recognizable within each emotion and also different between emotions. High ambiguity with either low (Figure 11.11) or high (Figure 11.12) distinctiveness values appeared as inappropriate expressions that were either similar or differed between emotions. The computerized measures also indicate flatness, as when facial expressions are not variable within an emotion (low ambiguity) and also indistinguishable between emotions (low distinctiveness) (Figure 11.13). These results suggest that the information-theoretic measures of emotion expressions are related to the observer-based ratings, and computerized measures may provide quantifiable information on different causes of observed inappropriate affect. Specifically, inappropriateness of expression may result from ambiguous and inconsistent facial expressions in each emotion regardless of distinctiveness across emotions. Flat affect, on the other hand, was related mainly to emotion expressions being indistinct across emotions.

Conclusion

In this chapter, we have presented our automated FACS and new dimensional measures on the basis of information theory. This combination of automated FACS and information-theoretic analysis offers several methodological advantages over currently available observer-based rating scales and FACS-based rating instruments. For example, our method is more objective and repeatable for any number of subjects; at the same time, it is less labor intensive and time-consuming. It is more objective than FACES, because the method does not involve observer judgment of emotions expressed, and it is less labor and time intensive than FACS and FACES because it is fully automated, similar to electromyography, without the inconvenience of physically placing electrodes on participants' faces.

Although we have demonstrated the feasibility and applicability of these measures with patients with schizophrenia and healthy controls, we can potentially apply the analysis to a larger sample that can better reflect the range of individual differences in the respective populations. A major limitation of our approach is that no computerized determination was made regarding emotional valence, and such qualitative information could have enhanced the results on the basis of information-theoretic measures of expressivity. Another limitation of the present study is that the induction procedure within the laboratory, although standardized, may lack ecological validity. A more naturalistic setting would include filming participants while they recount their own experiences. Unfortunately, given the present state of this methodology, facial movements on account of speech would generate too much noise for our algorithms to overcome.

In conclusion, our method offers an automated means for quantifying individual differences in emotional expressivity, similar to what has been accomplished in the area of emotion recognition. This capability opens new venues for delineating emotional expressivity in healthy people and across clinical populations. As for investigations in healthy population, the automated procedure is well suited to examining both age- and gender-related changes in emotion expression abilities. Potential clinical applications may include repeated monitoring of facial expressions to investigate effects of disease progression and more general treatment effects or to measure targeted efforts to remediate emotion expression abilities. Automated comparisons need not be limited to select clinical populations, and they may allow effective comparisons of emotion expressivity across different psychiatric disorders.

References

Alvino, C., Kohler, C., Barrett, F., Gur, R., Gur, R., & Verma, R. (2007). Computerized measurement of facial expression of emotions in schizophrenia. *Journal of Neuroscience Methods*, *163*, 350–361.

Andreasen, N. (1984a). *The Scale for the Assessment of Negative Symptoms (SANS)*. Iowa City: University of Iowa.

Andreasen, N. (1984b). *The Scale for the Assessment of Positive Symptoms (SAPS)*. Iowa City: University of Iowa.

Bartlett, M. S., Littlewort, G., Frank, M. G., Lainscsek, C., Fasel, I. R., & Movellan, J. R. (2006). Automatic recognition of facial actions in spontaneous expressions. *Journal of Multimedia*, *1*, 22–35.

Beirlant, J., Dudewicz, E. J., Gyoerfi, L., & Meulen, E. C. (1997). Nonparametric entropy estimation: An overview. *International Journal of Mathematical and Statistical Sciences*, *6*, 17–39.

Bleuler, E. (1911). Dementia praecox, oder die Gruppe der Schizophrenien. In G. Aschaffenburg (Ed.), *Handbuch der Psychiatrie*. Leipzig, Germany.

Borst, A., & Theunissen, F. (1999). Information theory and neural coding. *Nature Neuroscience*, *2*, 947–958.

Cootes, T. F., Taylor, C. J., Cooper, D. H., & Graham, J. (1995). Active shape models—Their training and application. *Computer Vision and Image Understanding*, *61*, 38–59.

Costa, M., Goldberger, A. L., & Peng, C. K. (2005). Multiscale entropy analysis of biological signals. *Physics Review E: Statistical, Nonlinear, and Soft Matter Physics*, *71*, 021906.

Craig, K., Hyde, S., & Patrick, J. (1991). Genuine, suppressed and faked facial behavior during exacerbation of chronic low back pain. *Pain, 46*, 161–71.

Del Giudice, M., & Colle, L. (2007). Differences between children and adults in the recognition of enjoyment smiles. *Developmental Psychology, 43*, 796–803.

Dittman, A. T. (1972). *Interpersonal messages of emotion.* New York: Springer.

Eibl-Eibesfeldt, I. (1970). *Ethology, the biology of behavior.* New York: Holt, Rinehart.

Ekman, P., & Friesen, W. (1975). *Unmasking the face.* Englewood Cliffs, NJ: Prentice Hall.

Ekman, P., & Friesen, W. (1978a). *Facial Action Coding System: Investigator's guide.* Palo Alto, CA: Consulting Psychologists Press.

Ekman, P., & Friesen, W. (1978b). *Manual of the Facial Action Coding System (FACS).* Palo Alto, CA: Consulting Psychologists Press.

Endres, D. M., & Schindelin, J. E. (2003). A new metric for probability distributions. *IEEE Transactions on Information Theory, 49*, 1858–1860.

Friedman, J., Hastie, T., & Tibshirani, R. (1998). Additive logistic regression: A statistical view of boosting. *Annals of Statistics, 28*, 2000.

Garner, W. R. (1962). *Uncertainty and structure as psychological concepts.* New York: John Wiley.

Garner, W. R., & Hake, H. W. (1951). The amount of information in absolute judgments. *Psychological Review, 58*, 446–459.

Gelber, E., Kohler, C., Bilker, W., Gur, R., Brensinger, C., Siegel, S., & Gur, R. (2004). Symptom and demographic profiles in first-episode schizophrenia. *Schizophrenia Research, 67*, 185–194.

Goria, M. N., Leonenko, N. N., Mergel, V. V., & Novi Inverardi, P. L. (2005). A new class of random vector entropy estimators and its applications in testing statistical hypotheses. *Journal of Nonparametric Statistics, 17*, 277–297.

Gosselin, P., Kirouac, G., & Dor, F. (1995). *Components and recognition of facial expression in the communication of emotion by actors.* Oxford, UK: Oxford University Press.

Gross, R., Matthews, I., & Baker, S. (2005). Generic vs. person specific active appearance models. *Image and Vision Computing, 23*, 1080–1093.

Gur, R., Kohler, C., Ragland, J. D., Siegel, S. J., Lesko, K., Bilker, W., & Gur, R. (2006). Flat affect in schizophrenia: Relation to emotion processing and neurocognitive measures. *Schizophrenia Bulletin, 32*, 279–287.

Gur, R., Sara, R., Hagendoorn, M., Marom, O., Hughett, P., Macy, L., . . . Gur, R. (2002). A method for obtaining 3-dimensional facial expressions and its standardization for use in neurocognitive studies. *Journal of Neuroscience Methods, 115*, 137–143.

Hamm, J., Kohler, C. G., Gur, R. C., & Verma, R. (2011). Automated facial action coding system for dynamic analysis of facial expressions in neuropsychiatric disorders. *Journal of Neuroscience Methods, 200*, 237–256.

Hamm, J., Pinkham, A., Gur, R. C., Verma, R., & Kohler, C. G. (2014). Dimensional information-theoretic measurement of facial emotion expressions in schizophrenia. *Schizophrenia Research and Treatment, 2014*, Article ID 243907. Retrieved August 2, 2015, from http://www.hindawi.com/journals/schizort/2014/243907/

Ho, B. C., Nopoulos, P., Flaum, M., Arndt, S., & Andreasen, N. C. (1998). Two-year outcome in first-episode schizophrenia: predictive value of symptoms for quality of life. *American Journal of Psychiatry, 155*, 1196–1201.

Izard, C., 1994. Innate and universal facial expressions: Evidence from developmental and cross-cultural research. *Psychological Bulletin, 115*, 288–299.

Jeong, J., Gore, J. C., & Peterson, B. S. (2001). Mutual information analysis of the EEG in patients with Alzheimer's disease. *Clinical Neurophysiology, 112*, 827–835.

Kohler, C., Gur, R., Swanson, C., Petty, R., & Gur, R. (1998). Depression in schizophrenia: I. Association with neuropsychological deficits. *Biological Psychiatry, 43*, 165–172.

Kohler, C., Turner, T., Stolar, N., Bilker, W., Brensinger, C., Gur, R., & Gur, R. (2004). Differences in facial expressions of four universal emotions. *Psychiatry Research, 128*, 235–244.

Kohler, C. G., Martin, E. A., Milonova, M., Wang, P., Verma, R., Brensinger, C., . . . Gur, R. C. (2008a). Dynamic evoked facial expressions of emotions in schizophrenia. *Schizophrenia Research, 105*, 30–39.

Kohler, C. G., Martin, E. A., Stolar, N., Barrett, F. S., Verma, R., Brensinger, C., . . . Gur, R. C. (2008b). Static posed and evoked facial expressions of emotions in schizophrenia. *Schizophrenia Research, 105*, 49–60.

Kozachenko, L. F., & Leonenko, N. N. (1987). Sample estimate of the entropy of a random vector. *Problemy Peredachi Informatsii, 23*, 916.

Kring, A., Kerr, S., Smith, D., & Neale, J. (1993). Flat affect in schizophrenia does not reflect diminished subjective experience of emotion. *Journal of Abnormal Psychology, 102*, 507–517.

Kring, A., & Sloan, D. (2007). The Facial Expression Coding System (FACES): Development, validation, and utility. *Psychological Assessment, 19*, 210–224.

Kullback, S., & Leibler, R. A., (1951). On information and sufficiency. *Annals of Mathematical Statistics, 22*, 79–86.

Larochette, A., Chambers, C., & Craig, K. (2006). Genuine, suppressed and faked facial expressions of pain in children. *Pain, 126*, 64–71.

Lin, J. (1991). Divergence measures based on the Shannon entropy. *IEEE Transactions on Information Theory, 37*, 145–151.

Lints-Martindale, A., Hadjistavropoulos, T., Barber, B., & Gibson, S. (2007). A psychophysical investigation of the Facial Action Coding System as an index of pain variability among older adults with and without Alzheimer's disease. *Pain Medicine, 8*, 678–689.

Mardia, K. V., & Dryden, I. L. (1998). *Statistical shape analysis*. Chichester, UK: Wiley.

Mnatsakanov, R. M., Misra, N., Li, Sh., & Harner, E. J. (2008). *K*-nearest neighbor estimators of entropy. *Mathematical Methods of Statistics, 17,* 261–277.

Na, S. H., Jin, S. H., Kim, S. Y., & Ham, B. J. (2002). EEG in schizophrenic patients: Mutual information analysis. *Clinical Neurophysiology, 113,* 1954–1960.

Pantic, M., & Bartlett, M. (2007). *Machine analysis of facial expressions*. Vienna, Austria: I-Tech Education and Publishing.

Prkachin, K. (1992). The consistency of facial expressions of pain: A comparison across modalities. *Pain, 58,* 297–306.

Prkachin, K., & Mercer, S. (1989). Pain expression in patients with shoulder pathology: Validity, properties and relationship to sickness impact. *Pain, 39,* 257–265.

Reed, L., Sayette, M., & Cohn, J. (2007). Impact of depression on response to comedy: A dynamic facial coding analysis. *Journal of Abnormal Psychology, 116,* 804–809.

Rocha, E., Prkachin, K., Beaumont, S., Hardy, C., & Zumbo, B. (2003). Pain reactivity and somatization in kindergarten-age children. *Journal of Pediatric Psychology, 28,* 47–57.

Shannon, C. E. (1948). A mathematical theory of communication. *Bell System Technical Journal, 27,* 623–656.

Shtasel, D., Gur, R., Gallacher, F., Heimberg, C., & Gur, R. (1992). Gender differences in the clinical expression of schizophrenia. *Schizophrenia Research, 7,* 225–231.

Stegmann, M., Ersbol, B., & Larsen, R. (2003). FAME—A flexible appearance modeling environment. *IEEE Transactions on Medical Imaging, 22,* 1319–1431.

Valstar, M., & Pantic, M. (2006). Fully automatic facial action unit detection and temporal analysis. *Proceedings of the 2006 IEEE Conference on Computer Vision and Pattern Recognition*, p. 149.

Verma, R., Davatzikos, C., Loughead, J., Indersmitten, T., Hu, R., Kohler, C., . . . Gur, R. (2005). Quantification of facial expressions using high-dimensional shape transformations. *Journal of Neuroscience Methods, 141,* 61–73.

Viola, P., & Jones, M. (2001). Rapid object detection using a boosted cascade of simple features. *Proceedings of the 2001 IEEE Conference on Computer Vision and Pattern Recognition*, pp. 511–518.

Walker, E., Grimes, K., Davis, D., & Smith, A. (1993). Childhood precursors of schizophrenia: Facial expressions of emotion. *American Journal of Psychiatry, 150,* 1654–1660.

Wang, P., Barrett, F., Martin, E., Milonova, M., Gur, R. E., Gur, R. C., . . . Verma, R. (2008). Automated video-based facial expression analysis of neuropsychiatric disorders. *Journal of Neuroscience Methods, 168,* 224–238.

Wikle, C., & Berliner, L. (2007). A Bayesian tutorial for data assimilation. *Physica D, 230,* 1–16.

PART 3

General Issues Regarding Methods and
Measures of Observational Research

12

CODING OBSERVED INTERACTION

ALAN L. SILLARS AND NICKOLA C. OVERALL

In this chapter, we discuss practical and conceptual issues when coding observed communication. At first glance, the process can seem straightforward: One selects a coding system, trains coders to use the manual, and checks reliability. However, coding requires more than mechanically applying categories or ratings to message units. Coding is a form of message interpretation, analogous to what happens in all communication (Folger, Hewes, & Poole, 1984). Coders, like participants in communication, apply interpretive rules to discourse and nonverbal behavior in order to discern meaning, either conventional meaning or meaning specific to observer or participant goals. In observational coding, as in everyday communication, standardized coding rules promote shared meaning (i.e., reliability) but do not remove all ambiguity (Sillars & Vangelisti, 2006). Coders must improvise when interpreting novel or ambiguous examples, drawing on their own experience and anticipating how others would view the same message. Coding is also an exercise in selective perception. Because messages are multifunctional (Sillars & Vangelisti, 2006) and have different levels of meaning (e.g., content vs. relational), the same interaction can be coded many ways that do not inherently compete. Coding methods selectively highlight functions of communication (e.g., persuasion or support), levels of analysis (e.g., molar vs. molecular), intended meanings (e.g., observer vs. participant), structural properties (e.g., base rates vs. sequential structure), and so forth. Thus, many alternative ways of coding exist that may be appropriate (or not), depending on one's purpose and perspective.

Our experience with observational coding stems mostly from research on couple and family conflict.

We draw on this experience to ground discussion of general issues in coding. Conflict is one of the most researched aspects of family communication (Sillars & Canary, 2013) and an area with a long tradition of observational work. Whereas another chapter provides a review (see D. Canary, this volume), we cite conflict coding methods selectively to illustrate issues, options, and trade-offs when conducting any form of interaction analysis.

Conceptual Foundations of Observational Coding

Observational coding typically involves coders' independently categorizing or rating the verbal and nonverbal content of a recorded interaction according to specified protocols and coding schemes. Coding yields a systematic record of ongoing communication, albeit a selective one structured by researcher assumptions and theories. As Krippendorff (2004) stressed, inference is inherent to content analysis of communication, because the outward (physical) features of messages have no meaning of their own; messages acquire "content" only when people engage them conceptually. Even automated coding performed by computers rests on theories of programmers about how humans read and respond to messages (Krippendorff, 2004). Coding supplies content by filtering, segmenting, and highlighting aspects of communication that have meaning relative to one's purpose and conceptual framework. Of necessity, the process highlights certain features while disregarding many others. Moreover, *interaction analysis* (i.e., content analysis of free-flowing conversation) is especially selective. The verbal, vocal, and kinetic activities people carry out while speaking and listening are so complex and information dense per unit of time that formal analysis cannot presume to yield more than partial understanding (Street & Cappella, 1985, p. 4).

Given the interpretive and selective nature of coding, trade-offs occur when deciding to adopt a coding system, adapt one, or invent one's own. Well-studied aspects of communication, including most topics in this book, have already spawned multiple systems. It is clearly more efficient to use an existing system than to begin from the ground up. The proliferation of coding schemes also complicates synthesis of results, leading some authors to even call for a moratorium on the development of new methods (Kerig, 2001). On the other hand, adopting a coding scheme means buying into particular assumptions about what message features are important and what they signify. Thus, well-established coding options are not all purpose. Bakeman and Gottman (1997) commented that borrowing a coding scheme can feel like "wearing someone else's underwear" (p. 15), because coding represents a theoretical act originating within the confines of a particular research program.

Research on couple conflict illustrates connections between coding methods and researcher perspectives. Box 12.1 reports categories from familiar coding schemes for couple conflict, including the Marital Interaction Coding System (MICS-IV), Kategoriensystem für Partnerschaftliche Interaktion (KPI), Couples Interaction Scoring System (CISS), and Verbal Tactics Coding Scheme (VTCS). Box 12.2 reports similar codes from two rating systems: the Conflict Rating System (CRS) and Communication Strategies Coding Scheme (CSCS). (Categorical codes and ratings are discussed further under "Forms of Coding.") Collectively, the systems share much in common. Systems used to code couple conflict tend to reflect two broad dimensions: valence and directness (see Overall, Fletcher, Simpson, & Sibley, 2009; Sillars & Canary, 2013). The valence dimension is explicit in systems that collapse into positive-negative supracategories (KPI, CRS, CSCS); however, all of the coding systems have been used to operationalize positive-negative communication. Directness is reflected in engagement versus avoidance of conflict (e.g., the demand and withdraw subscales of the CRS), along with direct and indirect influence attempts (as in the CSCS). The coding systems in Boxes 12.1 and 12.2 are also similar in what they omit. That is, they foreground relational aspects of conflict at the expense of other potentially important processes, for example, bargaining tactics (Putnam & Jones, 1982) and argument structure (see Seibold & Weger, this volume). Thus, the coding schemes are well suited to research on valence and directness of conflict communication but disregard many other potentially important features.

Box 12.1
Categorical Coding Systems for Couple Conflict

Marital Interaction Coding System (Heyman, Weiss, & Eddy, 1995)

Blame (criticize, mind-read negative, putdown, turnoff)

Description (problem description, internal and external)

Dysphoric Affect

Facilitation (assent, disengage, humor, mind-read positive, positive touch, paraphrase/reflect, question, smile/laugh)

Invalidation (disagree, disapprove, deny responsibility, excuse, noncomply)

Irrelevant (unintelligible talk)

Propose Change (compromise, negative and positive solution)

Validation (agree, approve, accept responsibility, comply)

Withdrawal

Kategoriensystem für Partnerschaftliche Interaktion (Hahlweg, 2004)

Positive Verbal

Self-Disclosure (expression of feelings, wishes, attitudes, or behavior)

Positive Solution (constructive proposal, compromise suggestions)

Acceptance of the Other (paraphrase, open question, positive feedback, understanding, agreement)

Neutral Verbal

Problem Description (neutral description, neutral questions)

Meta Communication (clarifying requests, related to topic)

Rest (inaudible or does not fit other categories)

Listening

Negative Verbal

Criticize (devaluation of partner, specific criticism)

Negative Solution (destructive solution, demand for omission)

Justification (excuse own behavior, deny responsibility)

Disagreement (direct disagreement, yes-but, short disagreement, blocking off)

Couples Interaction Scoring System (Gottman, 1979)

Content Codes

Problem Information or Feelings About a Problem

Mindreading

Proposing a Solution

Communication Talk

Agreement

Disagreement

Summarizing Other

Summarizing Self

Nonverbal Behavior

Positive (face, voice, and body cues such as smiling, warm voice, touching)

Negative (face, voice, and body cues such as frown, cold voice, inattention)

Neutral (absence of positive or negative nonverbal cues)

(Continued)

(Continued)

Verbal Tactics Coding Scheme (Sillars, 1986)

Denial and Equivocation (direct or implicit denial, evasive replies)

Topic Management (topic shifts, topic avoidance)

Noncommittal Remarks (noncommittal statements and questions, abstract or procedural remarks)

Irreverent Remarks (friendly joking)

Analytic Remarks (descriptive, disclosive, or qualifying statements; soliciting disclosure or criticism)

Confrontative Remarks (personal criticism, rejection, hostile imperatives, hostile jokes, or questions, presumptive attribution, denial of responsibility)

Conciliatory Remarks (supportive remarks, concessions, acceptance of responsibility)

Source: Author.

Box 12.2
Rating Systems for Couple Conflict

Conflict Rating System (Heavey, Lane, & Christensen, 1993)

Demand Subscale

Discussion (tries to discuss a problem, is engaged and emotionally involved)

Blames (blames, accuses, or criticizes; uses sarcasm or character assassination)

Pressures for Change (requests, demands, nags, or otherwise pressures)

Withdraw Subscale

Avoidance (hesitating, changing topics, diverting attention, or delaying discussion)

Withdraws (withdraws, becomes silent, refuses to discuss topic, looks away, disengages)

Positive Subscale

Negotiates (suggests solutions and compromises)

Backchannels (shows listening through positive minimal responses)

Validates Partner (indicates verbal understanding or acceptance of partner's feelings)

Positive Affect (expresses caring, concern, humor, or appreciation)

Communicates Clearly (expresses self in a way that is easy to understand)

Negative Subscale

Expresses Critical Feelings (verbally expresses hurt, anger, or sadness directed at partner)

Interrupts

Dominates Discussion (dominates, tries to take control of the discussion)

Negative Affect (verbal or nonverbal anger, frustration, hostility, hurt, or sadness)

Communication Strategies Coding Scheme (Overall, Fletcher, Simpson, & Sibley, 2009)

Negative-Direct

Coercion (derogate partner, indicate negative consequences for partner, display negative affect, accuse and blame partner)

Autocracy (insist or demand, talk from a position of authority, invalidate partner's point of view, take a domineering and/or nonnegotiative stance)

Negative-Indirect

Manipulation (attempt to make partner feel guilty, appeal to partner's love and concern)

Supplication (use emotional expression of hurt, debase self and/or present self as needing help, emphasize negative consequences for self)

Positive-Direct

Rational Reasoning (use and seek accurate information, use logic and rational reasoning, explain behavior or point of view in a way the partner would find reasonable)

Positive-Indirect

Soft Positive (soften persuasion attempts, encourage partner to explain point of view and express feelings, acknowledge and validate partner's views, be charming and express positive affect)

Source: Author.

Despite broad similarities, the coding schemes in Boxes 12.1 and 12.2 also reflect important differences that stem from research goals and observational contexts. Some coding schemes originating in clinical psychology, such as the MICS, KPI, and CISS, were designed to isolate communication skill deficits of unhappy couples as a basis for couple therapy. Early studies in this tradition conceptualized communication according to social learning principles, as contingent patterns of positive and negative behavioral reinforcement (Birchler, Weiss, & Vincent, 1975; Gottman, 1982). Thus, codes are organized and aggregated into positive and negative forms of communication, partly on the basis of how messages are presumed to affect marital outcomes. Although this division serves a purpose for behaviorally oriented therapists, others might find the approach limiting. In their dialectical critique of the satisfaction literature, Erbert and Duck (1997) chafed at the notion that interaction characteristics discriminating adjusted-maladjusted relationships can be dichotomized as positive or negative communication. In their view, the positive-negative duality reinforces an idealized view of relationships as either happy or conflicted and obscures ways that interactions may be simultaneously positive and negative.

In contrast to clinically based research, Sillars developed the VTCS with the assumption that dyadic interaction styles may have variable associations with outcomes, depending on relationship context (see Sillars & Wilmot, 1994).[1] Similarly, Overall, Fletcher, Simpson, and Sibley (2009) developed the CSCS to move past assumptions that "positive" and "negative" messages inherently benefit or harm relationships by distinguishing between direct (e.g., *coercion*) and indirect (e.g., *manipulation*) influence strategies. Research using the CSCS and VTCS provides evidence that seemingly "negative" acts can sometimes help couples directly tackle relationship problems (McNulty & Russell, 2010; Overall et al., 2009).

The treatment of avoidance also differs across conflict coding schemes. Early generation coding systems in psychology (e.g., MICS, CISS; Box 12.1) primarily featured direct forms of conflict engagement (although *withdrawal* was added as a category in the fourth revision of the MICS). This reflects the main observational method, the *problem-solving paradigm*, whereby couples interact in a lab under instruction to discuss and resolve an acknowledged problem (Gottman, 1994, pp. 18–19). Although the problem-solving paradigm remains a dominant approach, later generation systems (e.g., the CRS[2]; Box 12.2) focus more on withdrawal from interaction. In contrast to research using the problem-solving paradigm, the VTCS (Box 12.1) was developed from research that allowed greater latitude for conflict avoidance and neutrality; for example, couples were instructed to discuss *potential* conflicts "until they had nothing further to say" (e.g., Sillars, Pike, Jones, & Murphy, 1984). Consequently, the VTCS distinguishes nonengagement tactics more than do other coding schemes.

Despite these contrasts, all coding systems in Boxes 12.1 and 12.2 rely on structured observation, at home or in a lab, whereby researchers prompt couples to discuss relationship issues. No doubt, naturalistic observation of conflict would reveal other forms of avoidance, such as leaving the scene, retreating to electronic devices (Heyman, Lorber, Eddy, & West, 2014), or interspersing confrontation with attention to daily tasks (Sillars & Wilmot, 1994). Observational context also affects the dimensions of communication readily observed. For example, the coding schemes in Boxes 12.1 and 12.2 contain more "negative" codes than "positive" or constructive ones. Heyman (2001) noted, "Whereas it is relatively easy to get unhappy couples to argue on command, behaviors that promote the various forms of love . . . are much more challenging to witness in the laboratory" (p. 7).

In sum, coding schemes connect to researcher assumptions, goals, and observational methods. No coding scheme can suffice for all purposes, and most require significant adaptation when there is a shift from the original context in which methods were developed.

Forms of Coding

Coding may take a variety of forms, including categorical codes, checklists, and ratings. Each approach invokes conceptual and practical trade-offs.

Discrete Coding Systems

Categorical codes. In the classic sense, coding involves classifying message units into mutually exclusive and exhaustive categories (Krippendorff, 2004). Categorical coding schemes are sometimes referred to as *micro* codes, because they code communication at the level of individual messages, whereas *macro* codes (e.g., ratings) describe longer segments of interaction (Lindahl, 2001). The CISS, KPI, MICS, and VTCS (Box 12.1) illustrate categorical coding schemes. These systems first identify a unit of observation (such as the speaking turn or thought unit[3]) and then exhaustively code these units into a fixed set of categories. Subcategories might be nested under broader categories in order to yield a more detailed description at the level of subcategories, while providing sufficient observations for quantitative analyses after collapsing codes (e.g., *blame* in the MICS-IV is a combination of *criticize*, *mindread*, *putdown*, and *turn-off*).

The primary advantages of categorical codes are their descriptiveness and flexibility. Although not nearly as fine grained as qualitative conversation analysis (CA; Robinson, 2011), categorical coding yields a more detailed record than do other forms of quantitative interaction analysis.[4] Categorical coding is also conducive to statistical analysis of sequential structure, which examines whether specific codes elicit an immediate response (VanLear, this volume). In relationship conflict, important sequences include the probability that negative codes are reciprocated by the partner (negative reciprocity) or that demand is followed by withdrawal. The categorical coding systems in Box 12.1 were developed in a period marked by influential calls to focus on the temporal organization of interaction as a way to operationalize systems thinking about relationships (e.g., Gottman, 1979; Watzlawick, Beavin, & Jackson, 1967). Categorical codes also offer flexibility in subsequent aggregation, assuming that the initial round of coding identifies more than a few categories. When detailed codes are aggregated into broad categories, the research can document how specific codes contribute to summary scores. Unfortunately, this step is often omitted when researchers report aggregate codes.

The time and expense of categorical coding pose a clear trade-off. For instance, trained coders need 1½ to 2 hours to analyze a 10-minute interaction using the MICS (Heyman, 2004) and even longer periods using the CISS (Notarius, Markman, & Gottman, 1983). Detailed coding of interactions requires, at minimum, an audio (and sometimes video) record, and is usually assisted by written transcripts. In addition to the time and expense of transcription, the interaction record must be *unitized*, which requires separate coder training and reliability assessment if the unit of analysis involves significant coder judgment (as with thought units). Coding itself can require difficult decisions about how to assign borderline examples to similar categories, which fatigue coders and contribute to poor reliability. Thus, as Heyman et al. (2014) noted, microanalytic coding carries a poor cost-benefit trade-off when a large number of initial categories are later aggregated into just a few (e.g., positive vs. negative communication).

One way to make coding more efficient is to apply coding schemes selectively, using only the categories of greatest relevance. For example, McNulty and Russell (2010) limited their use of the VTCS (Box 12.1) to negative (i.e., *confrontative*) codes, as their purpose was to assess longitudinal impacts of negative messages on marital satisfaction. Others have developed "rapid" coding systems, such as the Rapid Couples Interaction Scoring System (RCISS; Krokoff, Gottman, & Hass, 1989) and Rapid Marital Interaction Coding System (RMICS; Heyman, 2004), which mimic the CISS and MICS (Box 12.1) but dispense with detailed subcategories. These rapid coding systems make restrictive assumptions about what aspects of interaction are of interest (again focusing primarily on positive vs. negative communication), which can represent an advantage or limitation depending on one's point of view.

Mutually exclusive and exhaustive coding schemes pose conceptual as well as practical challenges. Mutual exclusivity requires the assignment of a single code per unit, although, in theory, messages perform multiple functions simultaneously (Jacobs, 2002; Robinson, 2011). For example, friendly joking during conflict might show affection at the same time that it conveys tacit criticism. Thus, coders must judge the *primary* function of a message relative to the purpose of the coding system. To assist coders, categorical coding sometimes invokes rules of precedence that assign a coding unit to one particular category when it potentially fits multiple categories. For example, the MICS-IV and VTCS (Box 12.1) assign priority to codes seen as more important or as offering clearer interpretation.

Folger et al. (1984) advised against strict adherence to mutual exclusivity and suggested that validity concerns can require one to code each unit into multiple categories or along more than one dimension. However, one can readily see practical limitations to such advice. Allowing multiple codes increases the complexity of coding and subsequent analysis: One must determine when and how to assign multiple codes without compromising reliability, how to collate variable codes per unit, and how to analyze sequential structure if there are multiple antecedent and consequent acts. Instead of multiple codes, another way to address multifunctionality is to use more than one coding system. For example, the CISS has separate codes for verbal content and nonverbal affect. Of course, this approach also multiplies the time and expense of coding.

The conventional requirement of exhaustiveness raises a different conceptual issue. To ensure exhaustiveness, categorical systems routinely include a default category, such as *uncodable*, *other*, or *neutral*, that provides designations for units that are not otherwise classified by the system. Krippendorff (2011) advised against overly broad application of the default category, as this suggests that the coding system is logically incomplete and yields unusable information. An overly broad default category also provides coders with an easy way of avoiding difficult decisions that can be a source of unreliability (Krippendorff, 2011). On the other hand, coding every unit risks overinterpreting messages that lack clear meaning on the dimensions coded. An alternative involves *sieve* coding (Guetzkow, 1950), whereby researchers designate only certain units for coding on the basis of their research aims (Folger et al., 1984). McNulty and Russell's (2010) selective coding of negative messages illustrates this strategy, as does coding of question sequences in physician-patient interviews (Robinson, 2011).

Checklists. When using checklists, coders identify all categories that apply to the coding unit in binary fashion (i.e., each code is either present or absent). Checklist coding methods are especially common in observational studies of parent-child interaction (e.g., Roggman, Cook, Innocenti, Norman, & Christiansen, 2013). The RCISS illustrates the use of a checklist system for coding couple conflict (Krokoff et al., 1989). Checklists might apply to short units, such as speaking turns (as in the RCISS), longer time-based intervals (e.g., Vivian,

Langhinrichsen-Rohling, & Heyman, 2004), or entire interactions. In contrast to categorical systems, checklist codes are not mutually exclusive and are not necessarily exhaustive. For example, one could code for verbal confrontation without discerning any relevant forms in a given interaction. Checklists thereby simplify coding relative to categorical systems because coders do not have to fit each unit into one and only one category. This makes it practical in some cases to conduct coding "live" during naturalistic observation or to code recorded interactions without transcripts. However, the relative efficiency of checklists can partly rest on application of a relaxed reliability standard, in which reliability is assessed in terms of summary scores (e.g., overall positivity or negativity) rather than unit-by-unit coder agreement (e.g., Krokoff et al., 1989).

Rating Systems

Rating systems involve coders rating the degree to which people display targeted communicative acts. As with the rapid versions of the categorical systems described above (RMICS and RCISS), rating systems typically focus on higher order categories that categorical micro-codes are often combined into. Rather than distinguishing a large list of distinct acts, coders consider a range of relevant acts to determine the presence of broadly defined dimensions, such as positive, negative, and avoidance (Gill, Christensen, & Fincham, 1999; Julien, Markman, & Lindahl, 1989). Researchers using this approach recognize that theoretically relevant dimensions often represent clusters of interrelated acts. These clusters of interrelated acts might not all be exhibited or enacted to the same degree by a particular person. Whereas categorical codes indicate whether a code happens or not, ratings often integrate information on frequency, intensity, and duration to index the magnitude of the targeted act (Margolin et al., 1998).

A good example of a rating system is the Conflict Rating System (CRS; see Box 12.2), which was designed to assess demand-withdraw patterns in couple conflict. Observers watch the entire interaction and rate the degree to which each partner exhibited each dimension (e.g., *discussion, blames, pressures for change*) during the interaction (1 = *none*, 9 = *a lot*). Coders are instructed to consider the frequency, intensity, and duration of the verbal and nonverbal behaviors relevant to each dimension and to make a judgment of magnitude relative to other individuals in similar interactions. Christensen, Heavey, and colleagues decided to use global ratings

to focus on interaction patterns that can manifest in a variety of ways and to assess the intensity rather than frequency of such patterns (Sevier et al., 2004). The resulting ratings distinguish between mild and severe forms of demand-withdraw that may or may not occur at the same frequency. For example, mild but frequent hesitation to discuss topics would produce a lower "withdraws" rating (see codes in Box 12.2) than extreme disengagement and silence that occurred for a shorter time. Balancing frequency with intensity in ratings of magnitude is important because instances of extreme disengagement at pivotal moments in the interaction are likely to have a more pronounced impact on problem resolution and subsequent relationship outcomes (see Sevier et al., 2004).

A central benefit of rating systems is that they reduce the time and expense required to obtain analyzable data while producing similar results as categorical codes (Gill et al., 1999; Julien et al., 1989). Gill et al. (1999) coded couples' conflict interactions using the VTCS (Box 12.1), a categorical code system, and the revised CRS to contrast the utility of each system. The VTCS required more training for coders to reliably distinguish specific codes (about 15 hours) and additional hours to transcribe, unitize, and code interactions. In contrast, the CRS assumes that coders are already equipped with a general understanding of coding constructs and thus require only a short training period to fine-tune this existing knowledge (about 8 hours). Rating entire interactions (vs. speaking turns) directly from video recordings (vs. transcripts and video for the VTCS) took less than an hour per couple. After combining VTCS discrete codes into similar dimensions as the CRS, the scores derived from each coding system were associated. The systems also predicted concurrent and longitudinal satisfaction in similar ways. The one difference, however, was that global ratings of avoidance in the CRS appeared to capture a broader array of communicative acts than those assessed by the VTCS, which could enhance predictive utility but might also reduce understanding of the meaning and impact of specific acts.

Although ratings are an efficient approach to coding, this can be partially offset by the need for multiple raters per interaction to ensure adequate reliability. For example, Gill et al. (1989) had eight raters (four per spouse) analyze each interaction, with reliability based on combined ratings (the Spearman-Brown formula). A single coder applied the VTCS, except for 20% of interactions that were double-coded to check reliability (κ).

Critically, rating systems allow messages to own multiple functions. As described above, in most categorical code systems, observers need to assign one code to each unit, which can involve tough decisions regarding the principal function of the unit. In rating systems, communication can be indexed as a blend of different acts, with the final ratings capturing the relative weight of applicable categories. For example, the CSCS (Box 12.2) organizes ratings into higher order categories that reflect the valence and directness of communication strategies. Partners' communication across the interaction or within a specific speaking turn can be a blend of all four types. For example, a person might try to reason with his or her partner (positive-direct) while also threatening negative consequences if his or her solution is not adopted (negative-direct). The resulting ratings represent the relative magnitude of each type, such as high levels of positive-direct (5 out of 7) and relatively mild negative-direct (3 out of 7) or vice versa. By assessing the relative presence of different strategies, this approach does not truncate assessment to the primary strategy only but still maintains the ability to hone which aspects of communication are most predictive of outcomes. For example, accounting for the associations across direct strategies, Overall et al. (2009) found that both positive-direct and negative-direct strategies were independently associated with greater problem resolution over time. Rating the magnitude of all strategies also avoids the difficulty of trying to classify polysemous (i.e., multiple-meaning) messages into discrete codes.

Rating systems also contain important drawbacks. Global ratings lack detail regarding the specific acts present and therefore which acts might have the strongest explanatory power. Rating systems also lack information about time and sequential contingencies across partners, such as the likelihood that demand prompts withdraw. Although the CRS ratings of one partner's demand and the other partner's withdraw can be combined to create demand-withdraw composites, such an index does not reveal whether withdraw was contingent on (i.e., was influenced by) the partner's demand (Sevier, et al., 2004).

Alternatively, the presence of specific sequences can be rated, such as the degree to which a parent demands and child withdraws across an interaction (e.g., Caughlin & Ramey, 2005). This approach does not constrain assessment of sequences to each turn or unit of analysis (as does sequential analyses). Such lack of constraint proves useful if important interaction patterns occur across wider time spans and, more important, if the time course of dyadic patterns or the length of interaction varies across the sample. In addition, rather than rating the entire interaction, the interaction can be divided into shorter time intervals, rating systems applied to each interval, and then time-series analyses used to test contingency-based predictions. For example, Overall, Simpson, and Struthers (2013) used the CSCS to rate interactions every 30 seconds to test whether positive-indirect strategies by one partner were associated with reductions in withdrawal in the next 30-second interval.

The most important limitation of rating systems might be that they rely heavily on coders' interpretation of the communication exhibited, even more than typical categorical systems. By coding more global categories, rating systems focus on what the researcher believes is theoretically relevant. This helps ensure that the design tests research questions of interest and is valuable when the wider context of the interaction alters the meaning of the same specific act, such as whether advice on how to tackle a problem represents reasoning or autocracy (CSCS; Box 12.2). However, focusing on broader categories asks coders to make inferences about the meaning of observed communication and then aggregate these inferences with frequency and intensity to generate a holistic rating (Margolin et al., 1998). Both the CRS and the CSCS (Box 12.2) adopt a "cultural informant" approach (Gottman & Levenson, 1986), which assumes that coders possess a deep understanding of social interactions, make such interpretations in their day-to-day lives, and thus can reliably decode the meaning of communication. Nonetheless, relying on coders' interpretations inevitably provides more room for idiosyncratic views to bias ratings. In contrast, the descriptiveness of many categorical codes reduces the level of inference required, which may reduce coder bias. Next, we discuss coder inference and bias in more detail.

The Role of Inference in Communication Coding

Sources and Levels of Inference

Although inference is inherent to observational coding (Krippendorff, 2004), it is not always clear what kinds of inferences are carried by communication codes (Folger et al., 1984). Much of the time, observational codes are simply called "communication behaviors," suggesting that codes reference outward features of communication only (i.e., what people "actually" do). Although actual behavior is the starting point for observational research, coding schemes typically do not describe behavior so much as produce structured inferences about functional properties of communication (e.g., messages as forms of affection, social support, or conflict avoidance).

As Stone, Tai-Seale, Stults, Luiz, and Frankel (2012) observed, inferences made by coders can be ambiguous in ways that are not obvious from the usual description of coding procedures. These authors coded illness-related emotions expressed by patients and empathic responses by physicians, phenomena that have parallels in the way couples express and respond to emotionally laden disclosures during conflict. Although they used a previously validated coding system, Stone et al. (2012) found that patient verbal expression of emotion was ambiguous in unanticipated ways. For example, emotion words and other cues were often "fuzzy" and varied from one patient to another; moreover, discussion of illness appeared emotionally laden to coders even in the absence of emotion cues recognized by the coding system.

Coding systems differ in how they resolve such ambiguities. On one hand, a system might restrict attention to readily observable emotion cues, as in automated analysis of affect on the basis of word valence (Baek, Cappella, & Bindman, 2011), facial expressions (Cohn & Sayette, 2010), or acoustic features of speech (Black et al., 2013). Alternatively, coders might identify emotions from context, on the basis of their own implicit cultural knowledge and experience.

The different approaches reflect a distinction between *manifest* (physical or surface) versus *latent* (symbolic) content analysis (e.g., Holsti, 1969). Most obviously, manifest content includes nonverbal behaviors recorded without assistance by human coders or inference about sender intent. Whereas inferences about message intent are essential to interpretation of verbal communication (Jacobs, 2002), Buck and VanLear (2002) argued that many nonverbal behaviors are emitted and apprehended spontaneously (i.e., unintentionally and automatically) on the basis of biologically programed response patterns. Coding of *spontaneous* communication still involves inference, insofar as it rests on theoretical assertions about which manifest cues are important to observe and what functions they serve. Nonetheless, coding of physical cues (e.g., movement of facial muscles) does not require inference about conventional or personal meaning, as does coding of verbal communication or symbolic forms of nonverbal expression.[5] Between strictly manifest and latent content lie forms of coding that involve low-level inferences about speaker intent that are performed easily by any competent language user (e.g., whether a question is rhetorical).

However, most interaction coding is more inferential: the codes identify abstract relational events (e.g., confrontation) and associated acts (e.g., criticism). Here again, considerable variation occurs in the discretion afforded to coders. Some systems constrain coder inferences through extensive rules and training, whereas others (such as the rating systems noted earlier) treat coders as cultural informants and allow them greater latitude to fill in meaning.

In addition to the inferences conveyed by coders, a second level of inference occurs when researchers aggregate codes into summary measures. For example, most categorical coding systems confine coder judgments to moderate inferences (e.g., whether an utterance represents acceptance or denial of responsibility) but aggregate on the basis of researcher theories connecting specific codes to summary constructs (e.g., overall positivity or negativity).[6] Notably, coding methods do not always collapse codes in the same way. For example, avoidance and withdrawal are treated as communicative negativity in some systems (RCISS, RMICS) but not others (CRS, VTCS), and problem description may be construed as positivity (RCISS) or neutrality (RMICS). Moreover, researchers often modify constructs ad hoc when collapsing codes. Heyman (2001) noted that researchers have "mixed and matched" codes from the MICS to such an extent that virtually no studies evaluate identical constructs.

Locus of Meaning

Another general principle of message interpretation is that the same overt signals can mean something different to participant versus observer (Surra & Ridley, 1991) or to multiple observers with different frames of reference. Coding methods also assess meaning from varying perspectives. Poole, Folger, and Hewes (1987) identified four such perspectives (see also Poole & Hewes, this volume). *Generalized observer* meanings are those available to any uninvolved onlooker to an interaction (e.g., a vocalized pause), whereas *restricted observer* meanings are derived from application of a specialized interpretive scheme by outsiders (e.g., conversational coherence). *Generalized subject* meanings are available to any member of a cultural or subcultural group (e.g., topic shifts), whereas *restricted subject* meanings are accessible only to relationship insiders (e.g., inside jokes or conflict triggers).

In what domain does most communication coding reside? The perspective of the generalized observer is well represented in interaction research but limited to features that can be assessed through manifest content. Restricted subject meaning is not assessable via observer coding, at least as practiced in quantitative interaction research. Instead, most interaction research spans the boundary of restricted observer and generalized subject meaning. For example, all of the coding schemes in Box 12.1 use specialized interpretive rules applied by trained observers, which suggests restricted observer meaning. However, the systems also rely on coders to use their own cultural knowledge to fill in where coding rules are incomplete; for example, when discriminating friendly from hostile joking or criticism from neutral description on the basis of context.

Herein lies the central dilemma of interaction coding. A primary reason for doing interaction coding is to provide an "objective" (i.e., standardized, outsider) perspective on communication that avoids the biases of self-report data and provides a contrast to participant meaning. However, because it is not always possible to codify interaction constructs in terms of manifest content or clearly identifiable stimulus features, coding methods ultimately rely on intuitive judgments by observers to interpret meaning. An advantage of human coders over automated coding is that coders can use their own cultural knowledge to make sense of implicit features of communication. A limitation is that coders can interject their own knowledge in ways that threaten reliability and validity.

Coder Bias

To the extent that observational methods rely on coders to fill in meaning from cultural knowledge, the methods assume that coders represent cultural or subcultural groups in which these meanings reside. Coding methods also assume that coders can apply cultural knowledge to the specific context under investigation. Coders are usually undergraduate or graduate college students. Students can represent broader cultural meanings when these meanings are widely shared. This should be the case with low-level inferences about speech acts but not necessarily so with abstract relational events. Moreover, student coders often fail to represent the cultural and socioeconomic mix of the sample, which potentially affects interpretation of the acts coded. The relative homogeneity, and therefore interpretation, across student coders might also mean that potentially distinct interpretations are not revealed by reliability checks. Their life and relationship experiences can also mean that student coders are ill equipped with contextual knowledge central to the domain of investigation,

such as examining communication during the transition to parenthood, within parent-child dynamics, or in distressed samples, such as people suffering from depression, coping with chronic illness, or facing high levels of violence.

Indeed, as Margolin et al. (1998) noted, life experience, gender, and ethnicity can all affect coder judgments. Male coders have a greater propensity than women to view adult behavior as angry and resentful (Davidson et al., 1996) and to see aggressive behavior in children's interactions (Pellegrini et al., 2011). Gender stereotypes are also likely to affect the way women and men are coded, including the inferred intent behind similar behaviors (e.g., silence as sullen guilt induction vs. withdrawal). Similarly, stereotypes of ethnic and cultural groups can bias coding (Bente, Senokozlieva, Pennig, Al-Issa, & Fischer, 2008). Cultural differences can also affect coder inferences because of the way targeted constructs manifest across cultural groups. For example, cultural differences in the appropriateness of direct conflict (Sillars & Canary, 2013) could mean that interactions that appear contentious or avoidant to observers are not experienced in the same way by cultural insiders.

Coders' own relationship experiences are also likely to affect how they evaluate and infer meaning from other people's communication. The relationship field is replete with examples of individual and contextual factors that shape how relationship events are construed and responded to, such as attachment insecurity, relational standards, or levels of relationship satisfaction. Examining families within diagnostic contexts, such as discussing areas of conflict or supporting each other, will undoubtedly activate associated expectations, preferences, and perceptual sets that affect the way interactions are perceived. People are also highly motivated to maintain positive evaluations of their own relationships, and one way this is managed is by downplaying the positivity of other relationships (e.g., Rusbult, Van Lange, Wildschut, Yovetich, & Verette, 2000). This bias might produce a tendency to perceive others' communication as less constructive or loving than is justified (Gagné & Lydon, 2004). Finally, coders might generate their own understanding of the goals of the research (Harris & Lahey, 1982). By extension, individual coders possess their own conceptions about what constitutes "good" or "bad" communication. Coders' application of these tendencies can potentially undermine the assessment intended by the researcher.

What can be done to counteract coder bias? Margolin et al. (1998) recommended ensuring that coding teams are diverse in gender, culture, and general background, including replacing or combining student coders with coders sourced from the wider community. However, achieving representativeness among coders in relation to the target population may not be practical, and it can lead to other problems, such as the coding schedule's being applied in unintended ways and increasing training time. Nonetheless, coder bias is a significant issue. The potential for bias does not render observational coding invalid or useless; however, we do think it necessary to assess results of coding in light of the limitations of human judgment and the perspectives and dispositions coders bring to the task. Moreover, researchers should take every step to minimize coder bias by structuring, limiting, and monitoring coder inference during the coding process.

Managing the Coding Process

Ultimately, coding procedures are designed to coordinate inferences while maintaining the integrity of coding constructs, which equates to the topics of reliability and validity. Whereas a subsequent chapter provides a comprehensive discussion of reliability and validity (Poole & Hewes, this volume), we highlight how reliability and validity are affected by coding procedures and coder characteristics. Reliability and validity are analogous to the problem of intersubjectivity that is the crux of symbolic communication. To coordinate inferences, coders must apply coding rules consistently and fill in meaning by adopting the perspective of others who operate within a particular (generalized or restricted) meaning domain. The success of this enterprise is affected by characteristics of the coding scheme, coding procedures, and coders.

With respect to the coding scheme, more inferential codes are potentially subject to greater bias, as noted above. More inferential codes also tend to be, but are not inevitably, less reliable. As Krippendorff (2004, p. 20) noted, coders can sometimes read between the lines with remarkable consistency. On the other hand, Stone et al. (2012) ultimately limited their coding of emotional expression to the most explicit examples after attempts to code indirect emotional expression proved unreliable. Similar compromises are built into most coding schemes. Researchers often omit subtle and variable features of communication for reliability reasons, no matter how theoretically heuristic these features might be. The complexity of a coding system also affects intercoder reliability. Heyman et al. (2014) advised that coders generally cannot maintain adequate agreement when there are a large number of subtle codes. However, exceptions exist (e.g., Cegala, McClure, Marinelli, & Post, 2000; Sillars et al., 1984).

Procedures can reduce the burden on coders when categorizing or rating a large number of constructs or difficult to judge constructs. For example, in the CSCS, interactions are coded for one category at a time to ensure that coders focus on the particular influence strategy targeted during that wave. Coding in waves reduces cognitive demand; although coders still need to distinguish between multiple strategies, they only need to assess the strategy they are rating in that wave. Applying rating systems to small time intervals, rather than rating multiple dimensions across entire interactions, has the same benefits and may enable coders to more effectively rate and distinguish between multiple codes. These procedures might also reduce the degree to which coders' subjective evaluations can infiltrate the coding process. Furthermore, additional coding waves can minimize the degree to which the tone of the interaction influences coding. For example, using a separate team of coders to index broad dimensions, such as general valence or problem resolution, can provide a way of ensuring that more specific codes are not "infected" by coders general sense of the interaction.

Although more complex coding systems are not inherently less reliable or subject to bias, they might require more detailed coding manuals, greater rule specification, and more extensive training. A coding manual extends the coding scheme by specifying and illustrating coding rules in detail. A more complete coding manual simplifies coding by anticipating and resolving areas of confusion. Inexperienced coders may expect the coding manual to remove all ambiguity; that is, they assume that there is always a "correct" code under the coding rules. Inevitably, however, examples emerge that the author(s) of the coding manual had not anticipated. Furthermore, even familiar examples can become ambiguous because of a shift in context. In such cases, some unreliability is preferable to perfect reliability achieved through arbitrary decision rules that sacrifice validity. Ideally, observers should code clear examples with a very high degree of consistency and make ambiguous judgments with reasonable (at least above chance) reliability while retaining the spirit of coding distinctions.

The coding manual alone cannot always convey subtle distinctions and ambiguities that must be understood to code reliably. Much of this information is transmitted during the training phase. Even systems that rely on coders' existing culturally relevant knowledge need to organize that knowledge into the constructs and language of the coding system and ensure that coders apply that knowledge in the same way. Coder training typically occurs in a stacked fashion. Coders first get familiar with the manual, and then examples of specific codes and difficult distinctions are used to enhance understanding. For rating systems, examples of levels (e.g., low, medium, high) should also be presented to anchor coders' ratings of relative magnitude. Practice sessions are then conducted, which are used to check coder application, isolate areas of confusion, and build coder confidence. Extensive discussion throughout this process can help identify and clarify any problematic areas and to revise coding rules if needed. Low reliability in this phase provides important information about needed refinements and can assist the researcher in clarifying distinctions, both procedurally and theoretically (see Poole & Hewes, this volume).

The amount of coder training and practice needed is relative to the demands of the coding system. Some codes can be applied reliably by observers after only minimal training. Lorber (2006) had minimally trained raters assess *overreactive discipline* of mothers after receiving a 10-minute introduction to coding. Compared with "gold standard" raters, who participated in weekly training and practice sessions over 8 weeks, minimally trained raters were less reliable, but primarily in terms of mean ratings. Rank order was relatively consistent between coders ($r = .61$). Furthermore, minimally trained raters had good concurrent validity with raters who underwent gold-standard training ($r = .72$). These results suggest that minimal training may suffice for assessing relative (vs. absolute) scores for interaction, which is often all that is needed to test hypotheses. However, minimal training is most likely to suffice if coding is confined to surface features of communication (e.g., overreactive discipline was partly defined in terms of yelling, pushing, pulling) and simple constructs that tap shared meanings and experiences among coders (e.g., similar experiences of student coders with parental overreaction).

If two or more coders are reliable, this does not necessarily mean that they applied the coding scheme in the same way any other set of coders would or as the researcher intends. For example, under pressure to improve reliability, coders may independently or collectively improvise ad hoc rules that simplify judgments but transform the meaning of codes (Harris & Lahey, 1982). As much as possible, ad hoc rules should be self-consciously identified and, if appropriate, formalized and incorporated into the coding manual. In that way, one can

assess whether coder improvisations maintain the integrity of conceptual distinctions. A common temptation is to fashion an ad hoc default category (i.e., "when in doubt, assign code X") for ambiguous examples. This tendency makes the code less descriptive and offers a potential source of spurious observation, especially when coders apply ad hoc rules inconsistently (e.g., ambiguous examples are interpreted as verbal aggression when the interaction "feels" tense but are seen as neutral communication otherwise).

Coder training typically should not stop after coding has begun. Instead, regular meetings with coding teams provide the opportunity for continual discussion and reflection regarding areas of uncertainty. Reliability problems and discrepancies in codes should be carefully examined as a team to reiterate or refine coding categories and rules. In this way, and throughout the coding process, the researcher explicitly and implicitly clarifies the coding terms. Frequent meetings with discussion of discrepancies help counteract against coders drifting from the coding system. The more interactions that are viewed and coded, the more opportunity coders have to generate their own rules and for idiosyncratic biases to creep into coders' understanding and application of the coding system. Thus, continuous monitoring of reliability and frequent discrepancy discussions are essential to maintaining reliability.

Furthermore, when coders are aware that their ratings are checked, they are more likely to stay on task (Harris & Lahey, 1982). Regular checks also provide the chance to consider the presence of coder biases. Discussing bias openly can help coders recognize the filters they bring to the coding process and, in turn, may reduce the impact coder bias has on the resulting data. However, regular meetings and joint coding also has the potential to produce new rules and definitions, or to create "consensual drift" away from the original meaning of particular categories, as coders' discussions generate shared implicit rules for evaluating interactions (Harris & Lahey, 1982). This drift from the original coding manual may result, as described above, in greater reliability across coders but codes that do not represent the theoretical construct as originally conceptualized. Guidance by a principal assessor to keep coders true to the coding system and to record systematic alterations or formal clarifications may be crucial to prevent this from occurring. However, the assessor must also be reflexive enough to enable coders to query and challenge in order to prevent coders from simply mimicking the investigator's view. Investigators also should ensure they do not label, discuss, or interpret codes in ways that convey the central hypotheses to coders, thereby compromising coder neutrality (Harris & Lahey, 1982). Another way to check consensual drift, and reduce the variability that might occur as coders become more accurate across the sample, is to recode the first 10% to 20% of interactions.

Along with characteristics of the coding system and coding process, characteristics of coders affect reliability and validity. The sources of coder bias noted above highlight that coder demographics can affect the results of coding. Moreover, reliability tends to reflect the similarity of coders in terms of their cultural, educational, and professional background, as well as experience with texts (Krippendorff, 2004, p. 128). College students are the default choice as coders, both for convenience and familiarity with coding constructs. Many of the coding schemes used in clinical psychology and family studies (see Kerig & Lindahl, 2001) require coders with advanced, specialized education (reflecting a restricted observer perspective). However, researchers using systems that rely on lay concepts (generalized subject meaning) could prefer coders without specialized training, because they are less prone to overinterpret interactions. As with decisions regarding the type of coding system used, coders should also be selected according to the aims of the research, the coding being conducted, and the nature of the sample assessed.

Conclusion: Coordinating Perspectives on Communication

Observational coding of communication represents a form of message interpretation that parallels everyday communication but with a formal structure for interpretation and self-reflexive attention to the reliability and validity of inference. As we have noted, most communication coding represents a standardized observer perspective, which combines elements of restricted (theory-driven) and generalized (culturally derived) observer meaning. Observational coding provides an "objective" perspective in the sense that observations are not tainted by involvement in the communication episode and are replicable across observers. A key motivation for doing observational coding is to provide a more objective assessment of communication than participants' own self-reports typically provide. Participant accounts of communication are subject to many known biases, and we often assume that people may not know, or cannot accurately assess, the acts they and others enact during interactions.

Nonetheless, as we have discussed, coding constitutes an inferential act that often reflects bias. Whereas participant perspectives are biased by involvement in communication and other limitations of informal observation, observers are biased by their own goals and experiences. Observers also lack access to insider context that informs meaning for participants, such as relationship history and culture. Thus, we caution against treating observational coding as an unfiltered behavioral description and the only valid or true representation of actual communication. Kerig (2001) summed this point nicely:

> People behave in ways that are discrepant from their self-perceptions, and only direct observation can capture their behavior independently of their appraisals of it. . . . However, saying that the observer has a unique viewpoint does not mean that it necessarily is the most valid one. Observational methods are no more purely "objective" than any other tool in the researcher's toolbox. Underlying every coding category lie choices, and every choice . . . is informed by the investigator's conceptual framework. (p. 2)

In sum, the coding methods we considered in this chapter offer an important way in which social interaction can be assessed. Nonetheless, the value and utility of the outsider perspective must be considered in light of the ways coding methods are applied and, in turn, the degree to which coding procedures rely on or reduce coder inference and bias. We see observational methods as a valuable addition to insider perspectives rather than a superior assessment of communication. Some interaction constructs are best assessed by insider perspectives. Participants' subjective emotional experiences, internal dialogue, and communication intentions are difficult (and perhaps impossible) to discern accurately because insiders' shared histories and understandings influence the meaning of communicative acts (restricted subject meaning). Moreover, regardless of the veracity of people's reports, subjective experiences and perceptions have a powerful impact on people's relationship evaluations and ultimately the courses of their relationships. The most complete approach, therefore, is to assess both insider and outsider perspectives in order to examine how both participants' subjective perceptions and the observable patterns that stimulate and result from participant sense-making shape relationships and the people in them.

References

Baek, Y. M., Cappella, J. N., & Bindman, A. (2011). Automating content analysis of open-ended responses: Wordscores and affective intonation. *Communication Methods and Measures, 5*, 275–296.

Bakeman, R., & Gottman, J. M. (1997). *Observing interaction: An introduction to sequential analysis* (2nd ed.). New York: Cambridge University Press.

Bente, G., Senokozlieva, M., Pennig, S., Al-Issa, A., & Fischer, O. (2008). Deciphering the secret code: A new methodology for the cross-cultural analysis of nonverbal behavior. *Behavior Research Methods, 40*, 269–277.

Birchler, G. R., Weiss, R. L., & Vincent, J. P. (1975). Multimethod analysis of social reinforcement exchange between maritally distressed and nondistressed spouse and stranger dyads. *Journal of Personality and Social Psychology, 31*, 349–360.

Black, M. P., Katsamanis, A., Baucom, B. R., Lee, C., Lammert, A. C., Christensen, A., . . . Naravanan, S. S. (2013). Toward automating a human behavioral coding system for married couples' interactions using speech acoustic features. *Speech Communication, 55*, 1–21.

Buck, R., & VanLear, C. A. (2002). Verbal and nonverbal communication: Distinguishing symbolic, spontaneous, and pseudo-spontaneous nonverbal behavior. *Journal of Communication, 52*, 522–541.

Caughlin, J. P., & Ramey, M. E. (2005). The demand/withdraw pattern of communication in parent-adolescent dyads. *Personal Relationships, 12*, 339–355.

Cegala, D. J., McClure, L., Marinelli, T. M., & Post, D. M. (2000). The effects of communication skills training on patients' participation during medical interviews. *Patient Education and Counseling, 41*, 209–222.

Cohn, J. F., & Sayette, M. A. (2010). Spontaneous facial expression in a small group can be automatically measured: An initial demonstration. *Behavior Research Methods, 42*, 1079–1086.

Davidson, D., MacGregor, M. W., MacLean, D. R., McDermott, N., Farquharson, J., & Chaplin, W. F. (1996). Coder gender and potential for hostility ratings. *Health Psychology, 15*, 198–302.

Erbert, L. A., & Duck, S. W. (1997). Rethinking satisfaction in personal relationships from a dialectical perspective. In R. J. Sternberg & M. Hojjat (Eds.), *Satisfaction in close relationships* (pp. 190–217). New York: Guilford.

Folger, J. P., Hewes, D. E., & Poole, M. S. (1984). Coding social interaction. In. B. Dervin & M. Voight (Eds.), *Progress in communication sciences* (Vol. 4, pp. 115–161). Norwood, NJ: Ablex.

Gagné, F. M., & Lydon, J. E. (2004). Bias and accuracy in close relationships: An integrative review. *Personality and Social Psychology Review, 8*, 322–338.

Gill, D. S., Christensen, A., & Fincham, F. D. (1999). Predicting marital satisfaction from behavior: Do all roads really lead to Rome? *Personal Relationships, 6*, 369–387.

Gottman, J. M. (1979). *Marital interactions: Experimental investigations.* New York: Academic Press.

Gottman, J. M. (1982). Temporal form: Toward a new language for describing relationships. *Journal of Marriage and the Family, 44*, 943–962.

Gottman, J. M. (1994). *What predicts divorce? The relationship between marital processes and marital outcomes.* Hillsdale, NJ: Lawrence Erlbaum.

Gottman, J. M., & Levenson, R. W. (1986). Assessing the role of emotion in marriage. *Behavioral Assessment, 8*, 31–48.

Guetzkow, H. (1950). Unitizing and categorizing problems in coding qualitative data. *Journal of Clinical Psychology, 6*, 47–58.

Hahlweg, K. (2004). Kategoriensystem für Partnerschaftliche Interaktion (KPI): Interactional coding system (ICS). In P. K. Kerig & D. H. Baucom (Eds.), *Couple observational coding systems* (pp. 122–142). Mahwah, NJ: Lawrence Erlbaum.

Harris, F. C., & Lahey, B. B. (1982). Recording system bias in direct observational methodology. *Clinical Psychology Review, 2*, 539–556.

Heavey, C. L., Layne, C., & Christensen, A. (1993). Gender and conflict structure in marital interaction: A replication and extension. *Journal of Consulting and Clinical Psychology, 61*, 16–27.

Heyman, R. E. (2001). Observation of couple conflicts: Clinical assessment applications, stubborn truths, and shaky foundations. *Psychological Assessment, 13*, 5–35.

Heyman, R. E. (2004). Rapid Marital Interaction Coding System (RMICS). In P. K. Kerig & D. H. Baucom (Eds.), *Couple observational coding systems* (pp. 67–93). Mahwah, NJ: Lawrence Erlbaum.

Heyman, R. E. Lorber, M. F., Eddy, J. M., & West, T. V. (2014). Behavioral observation and coding. In H. T. Reis & C. M. Judd (Eds.), *Handbook of research methods in social and personality psychology* (2nd ed., pp. 343–370). New York: Cambridge University Press.

Heyman, R. E., Weiss, R. L., & Eddy, J. M. (1995). Marital Interaction Coding System: Revision and empirical evaluation. *Behaviour Research and Therapy, 33*, 737–746.

Holsti, O. R. (1969). *Content analysis for the social sciences and humanities.* Reading, MA: Addison-Wesley.

Jacobs, S. (2002). Language and interpersonal communication. In M. L. Knapp & J. A. Daly (Eds.), *Handbook of interpersonal communication* (3rd ed., pp. 213–239). Thousand Oaks, CA: Sage.

Julien, D., Markman, J. J., & Lindahl, K. M. (1989). A comparison of global and a microanalytic coding system: Implication for future trends in studying interactions. *Behavioral Assessment, 11*, 81–100.

Kerig, P. K. (2001). Introduction and overview: Conceptual issues in family observational research. In P. K. Kerig & K. M. Lindahl (Eds.), *Family observational coding systems: Resources for systemic research* (pp. 1–22). Mahwah, NJ: Lawrence Erlbaum.

Kerig, P. K., & Lindahl, K. M. (Eds.) (2001). *Family observational coding systems: Resources for systemic research*. Mahwah, NJ: Lawrence Erlbaum.

Krippendorff, K. (2004). *Content analysis: An introduction to its methodology* (2nd ed.). Thousand Oaks, CA: Sage.

Krippendorff, K. (2011). Agreement and information in the reliability of coding. *Communication Methods and Measures, 5*, 93–112.

Krokoff, L. J., Gottman, J. M., & Hass, S. D. (1989). Validation of a global rapid couples interaction scoring system. *Behavioral Assessment, 11*, 65–79.

Lindahl, K. M. (2001). Methodological issues in family observational research. In P. K. Kerig & K. M. Lindahl (Eds.), *Family observational coding systems: Resources for systemic research* (pp. 23–32). Mahwah, NJ: Lawrence Erlbaum.

Lorber, M. F. (2006). Can minimally trained observers provide valid global ratings? *Journal of Family Psychology, 20*, 335–338.

Margolin, G., Oliver, P. H., Gordis, E. B., O'Hearn, H. G., Medina, A., Ghosh, C. M., & Morland, L. (1998). The nuts and bolts of behavioral observation of marital and family interaction. *Clinical Child and Family Psychology Review, 1*, 195–213.

McNulty, J. K., & Russell, V. M. (2010). When "negative" behaviors are positive: A contextual analysis of the long-term effects of problem-solving behaviors on changes in relationship satisfaction. *Journal of Personality and Social Psychology, 98*, 587–604.

Notarius, C. I, Markman, H. J., & Gottman, J. M. (1983). Couples Interaction Scoring System: Clinical applications. In E. E. Filsinger (Ed.), *Marriage and family assessment* (p. 117–151). Beverly Hills, CA: Sage.

Overall, N. C., Fletcher, G.J.O., Simpson, J. A., & Sibley, C. G. (2009). Regulating partners in intimate relationships: The costs and benefits of different communication strategies. *Journal of Personality and Social Psychology, 96*, 620–639.

Overall, N. C., Simpson, J. A., & Struthers, H. (2013). Buffering attachment-related avoidance: Softening emotional and behavioral defenses during conflict discussions. *Journal of Personality and Social Psychology, 105*, 854–871.

Pellegrini, A. D., Bohn-Gettler, C. M., Dupuis, D., Hickey, M., Roseth, C., & Solberg, D. (2011). An empirical examination of sex differences in scoring preschool children's aggression. *Journal of Experimental Child Psychology, 109*, 232–238.

Poole, M. S., Folger, J. P., & Hewes, D. E. (l987). Methods of interaction analysis. In G. R. Miller & M. Roloff (Eds.), *Interpersonal processes: New directions in communication research* (pp. 220–256). Beverly Hills, CA: Sage.

Putnam, L. L., & Jones, T. S. (1982). Reciprocity in negotiations: An analysis of bargaining interaction. *Communication Monographs, 49*, 171–191.

Robinson, J. D. (2011). Conversation analysis and health communication. In T. L. Thompson, A., R. Parrott, &

J. F. Nussbaum (Eds.), *The Routledge handbook of health communication* (2nd ed., pp. 501–518). New York: Routledge.

Roggman, L. A., Cook, G. A., Innocenti, M. S., Norman, V. J., & Christiansen, K. (2013). Parenting Interactions With Children: Checklist of Observations Linked to Outcomes (PICCOLO) in diverse ethnic groups. *Infant Mental Health Journal, 34*, 290–306.

Rusbult, C. E., Van Lange, P.A.M., Wildschut, T., Yovetich, N. A., & Verette, J. (2000). Perceived superiority in close relationships: Why it exists and persists. *Journal of Personality and Social Psychology, 79*, 521–545.

Sevier, M., Simpson, L. E., & Christensen, A. (2004). Observational coding of demand-withdraw interactions in couples. In P. K. Kerig & D. H. Baucom (Eds.), *Couple observational coding systems* (pp. 159–172). Mahwah, NJ: Lawrence Erlbaum.

Sillars, A., & Canary, D. J. (2013). Conflict and relational quality in families. In A. L. Vangelisti (Ed.), *Routledge handbook of family communication* (2nd ed., pp. 338–357). New York: Routledge.

Sillars, A. L. (1986). *Procedures for coding interpersonal conflict: The Verbal Tactics Coding Scheme (VTCS)*. Unpublished coding manual, University of Montana, Missoula.

Sillars, A. L., Pike, G. R., Jones, T. S., & Murphy, M. A. (1984). Communication and understanding in marriage. *Human Communication Research, 3*, 317–350.

Sillars, A., & Vangelisti, A. L. (2006). Communication: Basic properties and their relevance to relationship research. In A. L. Vangelisti & D. Perlman (Eds.), *The Cambridge handbook of personal relationships* (pp. 331–351). New York: Cambridge University Press.

Sillars, A. L., & Wilmot, W. W. (1994). Communication strategies in conflict and mediation. In J. Wiemann & J. A. Daly (Eds.), *Strategic interpersonal communication* (pp. 163–190). Hillsdale, NJ: Lawrence Erlbaum.

Stone, A. L., Tai-Seale, M., Stults, C. D., Luiz, J. M., & Frankel, R. M. (2012). Three types of ambiguity in coding empathic interactions in primary care visits: Implications for research and practice. *Patient Education and Counseling, 89*, 63–68.

Street, R. L., & Cappella, J. N. (1985). Sequence and pattern in communicative behavior: A model and commentary. In R. L. Street, Jr., & J. N. Cappella (Eds.), *Sequence and pattern in communicative behavior* (pp. 243–276). London: Edward Arnold.

Surra, C. A., & Ridley, C. A. (1991). Multiple perspectives on interaction: Participants, peers, and observers. In B. Montgomery & S. Duck (Eds.), *Studying interpersonal interaction* (pp. 35–55). New York: Guilford.

Vivian, D., Langhinrichsen-Rohling, J., & Heymay, R. E. (2004). The thematic coding of dyadic interactions: Observing the context of couple conflict. In P. K. Kerig & D. H. Baucom (Eds.), *Couple observational coding systems* (pp. 273–288). Mahwah, NJ: Lawrence Erlbaum.

Watzlawick, P., Beavin, J., & Jackson, D. D. (1967). *Pragmatics of human communication: A study of interactional patterns, pathologies, and paradoxes.* New York: Norton.

Endnotes

1. The original version of the VTCS collapsed into three macro-categories (i.e., *integrative*, *distributive*, and *avoidance*) but was revised to reflect more descriptive macro-categories that avoid a priori assumptions about which messages serve positive or negative functions.

2. An even more recent system that evolved from the CRS, the Couples Interaction Rating System, has summary scores for demand and withdrawal but lacks the positive and negative scales of the CRS (see Sevier, Simpson, & Christensen, 2004).

3. A thought unit is a segment of speech that expresses a single, unified thought.

4. Although CA and interaction analysis are separate research traditions with very different methods and assumptions, Robinson (2011) argued that the two approaches can form a symbiotic relationship. In an observational study of physician-patient interviews, CA insights gleaned from close analysis of individual interactions have informed development of traditional coding schemes, thereby contributing to validity. Traditional coding methods have helped demonstrate that CA informed distinctions matter by documenting their statistical association with outcomes (Robinson, 2011).

5. In practice, it can be nearly impossible to discern the difference between spontaneous communication and intentional manipulation of the same signals (i.e., *pseudospontaneous* communication; Buck & VanLear, 2002). Regardless of their true origins, nonverbal signals may be interpreted at the level of manifest content or symbolic meaning.

6. The same may be said for coding of relational control (see Rogers & Cummings, this volume), which begins with low-level inferences about the grammatical and pragmatic form of utterances but aggregates specific codes into patterns of dominance and domineeringness.

13

RELIABILITY AND VALIDITY IN THE MEASUREMENT OF SOCIAL INTERACTION

MARSHALL SCOTT POOLE AND DEAN E. HEWES

Measurement constitutes the foundation of the scientific enterprise.[1] No theory can be tested without it; no statistical method can yield useful results without it. Quality of measurement, however, is a complex subject. The most common touchstone for rigorous measurement in the social and behavioral sciences is the variety of different "-metrics": psychometrics, sociometrics, econometrics, scientometrics, et cetera. These make us aware of the importance of establishing quality of measurement but also of the different criteria that must be applied across different contexts and objects of study. This is also the case in the measurement of social interaction. Although psychometric theory can still provide useful guidance, the requirements for good measurement are distinctive in the study of social interaction. Establishing the reliability and validity of measures of social interaction is more complex both conceptually and methodologically than for scales for experimental and survey variables or measures of personality.

The uniqueness of validity in the realm of social interaction stems from the fact that meaning is intimately tangled up with our ability to understand social interaction. In many cases, the investigator is interested primarily in identifying observer-defined characteristics of interaction, such as who interrupts whom, the number of times parties express agreement, characteristics of argument, and nonverbal cues. These characteristics seem to be independent of the meaning of the interaction to participants, constructs that can simply be coded by a trained and systematic observer, or perhaps even automatically by a text analysis program. In other cases, the investigator is directly interested in the meaning of the interaction to participants. In studies of interpersonal conflict, for example, whether a comment is insulting or the degree to which a party's reaction is avoidance depends on how the initiator and recipient understand the meaning of the comment. In such cases, the quality of measurement depends on whether the interaction analysis system generates data that reflects the meanings participants assign to the interaction episode and to specific acts.

Complications arise in this simple distinction, however. Every social scientific theory is, at least to some extent, derived from and embedded in its social milieu. The theorist is not a Martian but a product of and participant in the social world the theory describes and explains. So theoretical constructs have a dual nature; they have specialized and delimited definitions, but they also come loaded with everyday meaning. This dual nature creates a difficulty for scholars who want to argue that they alone have determined the meaning of their constructs and that their constructs are independent of commonsense understandings. It also poses a dilemma for scholars who claim that their theoretical constructs correspond to meaningful distinctions made by those being studied. In the end, we would argue that the status of constructs—whether they are largely artificial creations or reflect social meanings—is an empirical question as well as a conceptual one. If a scholar wants to make a claim about the status of the constructs his or her interaction analysis system embodies, this claim should be backed by evidence. Evidence for the quality of

217

data produced by interaction analysis systems is bound up with the type of claim being made.

With this in mind, we base our discussion on four premises. First, without establishing both the reliability and validity of measures of social interaction, we can have little confidence in the conclusions drawn from studies using these measures. This does not mean that these conclusions are implausible, but their plausibility awaits evidence of reliability and validity. Second, establishing reliability and validity is a process, not just an outcome. Lack of adequate reliability and validity in the early stages of development of an interaction analysis system should result in an empirical and, more important, a conceptual reevaluation of the construct(s) in question. This may result in a reworking of the system and continued rounds of testing. This reevaluation should occur with each new use of the interaction analysis system, because transfer to different contexts and types of interaction may well result in a need to adapt the system if it is to maintain its reliability and validity. Third, we accept the premise from psychometric theory that reliability constitutes a necessary prerequisite for validity, although reliability does not imply validity. Typically, published studies of social interaction are anchored only on the reliability of rating systems or coding schemes. It remains important to generate evidence for the validity of the interaction analysis system beyond reliability assessment.

Fourth, the interpretation of communication variables can vary with the perspective being applied to them. The meaning of messages, or a sequence of messages, differs depending on whose meaning is of interest. Although these meanings might well be consensual within an audience composed of people of the same culture or language community, interpretations may differ for particular speakers or listeners within a relationship or culture, between cultures or language communities, or because of specialized meanings imposed by theory irrespective of human conventions. We will distinguish three different modes of observation that represent different types of claims that can be made concerning the meaning of data generated by interaction analysis systems. Assessment of validity for each of the modes of observation requires different types of evidence.

In what follows we apply these four premises, first to a discussion of the reliability of two measures of social interaction, coding schemes and rating scales. Following this, we discuss the validity of both types of measurement. Before turning to these two topics, we first consider some examples.

Illustrative Examples

In this section, we present some examples that illustrate the range of interaction analysis systems this chapter covers. Three general classes of interaction analysis systems are considered: rating systems, systems that code manifest units to measure higher level constructs, and coding schemes.

An important feature of these systems is that each relies to some degree on the judgment of coders or raters. Potter and Levine-Donnerstein (1999) developed a useful set of distinctions related to the amount of judgment that must be applied in content analysis. *Manifest content* is "that which is on the surface and easily observable, such as the appearance of a particular word in a written text, the gender of a character in a film, or certain behaviors (blinking eyes, scratching head)" (p. 259). Coders must exercise relatively limited judgment in the case of manifest content, simply recognizing whether a feature is or is not there.

Latent content refers to the "meaning underlying the elements on the surface of a message" (Potter & Levine-Donnerstein, 1999, p. 259) and requires a greater degree of judgment. Potter and Levine-Donnerstein (1999) distinguished two types of latent content. *Pattern content* refers to meaning that can be tapped through the identification of patterns of cues that are more or less objectively evident. For example, a system used by Johnston and White (1994) to code political commercials identified the dress of female candidates (formal suit, dress, casual) on the basis of specific features (jacket, skirt, scarf, pants, sweater, etc.) that defined type of outfit. In this case, coders are asked to recognize a pattern formed by a set of manifest features that, together, constitute a particular meaningful ensemble. *Projective content* refers to socially shared meanings that must be identified by accessing coders' "pre-existing schema" (Potter & Levine-Donnerstein, 1999, p. 259). Johnston and White generated projective content in coding the rhetorical style of the female candidates (exhortative, bureaucratic emotional, etc.). Potter and Levine-Donnerstein explained the difference in coding procedures: "The rules for coding dress could be more concrete and inclusive than the rules for rhetorical style, which were more suggestive and relied on coders' experience to make distinctions among the styles" (p. 260).

The degree of subjective judgment or interpretive latitude an interaction analysis system involves is an important design parameter for interaction analysis systems. Potter and Levine-Donnerstein

(1999) discussed the three types of content as though they provide more or less fixed categories into which types of content can be placed definitively. There is, however, reason to believe that the same constructs may be coded with varying degrees of interpretive latitude. Rhetorical style, for example, is often assessed through critical analysis and judgment, and if this is the approach we take, it is best thought of as projective content. On the basis of more extensive analysis, however, scholars might more precisely specify patterns that identify styles, as Hart (1984) did when he developed the DICTION text-analysis program (http://www.dictionsoftware.com), transforming style into pattern content. Indeed, DICTION bases classification into patterned styles on word counts, which are manifest content. This example implies that as interaction analysis systems develop and the discourse being coded is better understood, the amount of subjective judgment involved decreases. However, things could go the other way: A construct originally thought to be manifest or patterned content might be "problematized" and recognized to have important and unspecifiable cultural meanings and hence be reframed as projective content. Dress, for example, might be reconceptualized as "fashion," pattern content transforming into projective content.

Although no single "proper" bucket exists into which a construct can a priori be consigned, Potter and Levine-Donnerstein's (1999) analysis provides a useful description of the types of judgments involved in interaction analysis and content analysis. As these examples show, there are a variety of ways in which workable interaction analysis systems can be constructed. Some fall into a single category of their classification, and others combine categories.

Scales for Rating Human Interaction

One class of interaction analysis systems asks observers to rate interaction on scales similar to those used in psychometric or survey instruments. Scales are meant to provide descriptions of interaction along general dimensions and are designed to be used by raters with relatively little training. Leathers (1971) developed the Feedback Rating Instrument, a nine-item instrument designed to measure characteristics of feedback statements given in response to claims or assertions made in group interaction. The instrument was developed on the basis of inductive content analysis of 30 group discussions, guided by theories of interpersonal and group interaction. Dimensions for rating feedback

statements include *deliberateness* (carefully reasoned and systematic vs. automatic and unthinking), *relevancy* (extent to which the statement relates the feedback to the stimulus statement), *atomization* (degree to which the statement is incomplete, fragmented, or disjointed), and *fidelity* (extent to which the statement asks for clarification, definition, or expansion of the stimulus statement). Leathers attempted to elucidate a pattern of cues for each dimension of the instrument, targeting this as a pattern content coding system. Another instrument, the Interaction Behavior Measure (McCroskey & Wright, 1971), is composed of 12 items that factored into six dimensions (Orientation, Tension, Flexibility, Relevance, Interest, and Verbosity) and was used to code individual statements in group discussion. This instrument left a good deal of latitude to raters, yielding projective content ratings.

Rating scales have also been applied to larger units of interaction, such as entire discussions or episodes of teamwork. Gouran, Brown, and Henry (1978) developed a set of nine scales for rating behavior in group discussions that were designed to tap task-oriented behavior, socioemotional behavior, and procedural behavior. Items included whether the behavior of the group was goal directed or not goal directed, whether participation was unevenly distributed or evenly distributed, and whether functions of leadership were poorly served or well served. The group is the basic unit of analysis in this case, though some items pertained to individuals in the group. Students from the same population as the discussants rated 35-minute discussions using the scales, which elicited projective judgments. Likewise, Marks, Mathieu, and Zaccaro (2001) developed a series of behaviorally anchored rating scales for teamwork on the basis of a taxonomy of team processes. These scales assess dimensions such as goal specification, strategy formulation and planning, and systems monitoring and give raters descriptions of patterns of behaviors corresponding to low, adequate, and high levels on these dimensions to anchor their ratings.

Measurement Based on Manifest Units

A second approach to the measurement of human interaction relies on the identification of higher order units, such as an emotion, from manifest units that can be systematically and (more or less) objectively coded, such as the words a person uses. One example of this approach is the Linguistic Inquiry and Word Count (LIWC) system developed by Pennebaker, Chung, Ireland, Gonzales, and

Booth (2007). Building on the tradition of the General Inquirer (Stone, Dunphy, Smith, & Ogilvie, 1966), the LIWC system uses word counts to gauge constructs such as emotion (positive affect, anxiety, anger), cognitive processes (insight, causation), and current concerns (work, achievement, leisure) from transcribed text passages. It generated indices for these constructs and numerous other properties of the distribution of words in documents. To operationalize its constructs, the LIWC system uses dictionaries of words corresponding to each category, and the rate of occurrence of words is a measure of the degree to which the construct is manifest in the passage. For example, to measure the amount of anger in a passage, the words in the passage are counted and compared with the dictionary for anger, which comprised 184 words; the number of times these words occurred in the passage would be a raw measure of anger expressed in the passage (and by implication of the emotional state of the person or group generating the passage). Manifest units (words) are thus used to operationalize more complex higher level units such as emotion and cognitive activity. The higher order units represent latent content, but the projective interpretations were performed not by the coder (a computer) but by those who constructed the dictionaries that associated words with higher level units. The LIWC system was constructed by Pennebaker et al. in several steps: (a) They compiled the dictionaries for constructs starting with words used in rating scales for constructs, dictionaries, and thesauri; (b) they decided whether a word belonged in a category and also sorted words into categories; (c) they tested the system on a broad set of passages of various types and removed any words that occurred only occasionally; and (d) they continually updated the system on the basis of ongoing analysis.

Another example of the use of manifest units to measure characteristics of higher level interaction is the Facial Action Coding System (FACS), developed by Ekman and Friesen (1978). Based on a system developed by Hjortsjö (1969), the FACS codes basic "action units" (i.e., relaxation or tension in specific facial muscles, head movements, eye movements, and gross behaviors such as sniffing or chewing). The intensity of these 87 action units can be coded on the basis of direct observation of the face and head and provide a physical description of facial expression that applies to multiple cultures and multiple species. Higher order characteristics, such as emotional expressions, can be identified on the basis of patterns based on combinations or sequences of action units. For example, anger is indicated by a combination of four action units:

"brow lowerer," "upper lid raiser," "lid tightener," and "lip tightener." The FACS has been widely used in studies of emotion and deception. One challenge is the extensive and intensive training coders must undergo to gain facility in its application. This challenge is being addressed by automated systems such as those described by Hamm et al. in this volume.

Manifest units have also been used to inductively derive higher level characteristics of content. "Topic modeling" (e.g., McCallum, 2002; Quinn, Monroe, Colaresi, Crespin, & Radev, 2010) uses unsupervised machine learning to identify meaningful clusters of terms that indicate classifications for textual content. These and similar methods are promising approaches to develop automated interaction and content analysis methods that eliminate the need for human coding. One major limitation of these approaches is that they require much larger corpuses of text for training than is typical of human interaction episodes.

Coding Schemes

The most common means of measuring interaction is through assigning units of interaction to meaningful categories using interaction coding systems. A good example of this approach is the Conversational Analysis Coding System (Canary & Seibold, 2010: Seibold & Weger, this volume), adapted to groups in the Group Argument Coding System (Seibold & Meyers, 2007). The unit of analysis for this system is the thought turn or utterance. The thought turn is important to conversational argument because people can communicate a thought with a single utterance (e.g., the word *no*) or independent clauses. The utterance can capture "each stretch of talk that can be interpreted as an independent clause, nonrestrictive dependent clause, term of address, acknowledgement, or element of a compound predicate" (Stiles, 1978, p. 32). After a dyadic or group discussion has been divided into units, each unit is assigned to one of six primary categories: starting points, developing points, convergence seeking, divergence, delimiters, and nonarguables (see Seibold & Weger, this volume for a more detailed explanation). There are several finer subcategories within each primary category (e.g., starting points include assertions and propositions for behavior). Seibold and Meyers conducted coding in a multistage process: "(a) argument versus nonargument determination; (b) lines of argument based on decision alternatives supported; (c) coding between five macrolevel categories; and (d) coding microlevel subcategories within each primary category" (p. 318). Canary (1992) provided an alternative, multistage process in the CACS coding manual.

The Group Working Relationships Coding System (GWRCS; Poole, 1983; Poole & Dobosh, 2010; available at http://www.ideals.illinois.edu/handle/2142/14539) codes patterns of interaction among group members during short segments (30 to 45 seconds) of group discussion rather than single acts or utterances by individuals (see Box 13.1). It thus is designed to measure the tenor of a group interaction as a whole rather as opposed to individual behavior. The rationale for this is that relationships can be understood only by focusing on interchanges among members. The GWRCS identifies seven distinct patterns of interaction. Four of these—focused work, critical work, opposition, and relational integration—are primary forms of interaction that indicate the working climate of a group at a given period of time. Three patterns—open discussion, tabling, and capitulation—are secondary forms of interaction that occur only in response to an opposition and represent modes of dealing with the opposition. This coding scheme has been used to study conflict and confrontation in jury deliberations and group decision making.

Box 13.1
Group Working Relationship Coding System

1. *Focused work* refers to periods when members are primarily task focused, and so there is no disagreement.

2. *Critical work* refers to periods when members disagree with one another, but the disagreements are centered on ideas, and opposing sides are delineated.

3. *Opposition* refers to periods in which disagreements are expressed through the formation of opposing sides; the existence of a conflict or disagreement is openly acknowledged.

4. *Open discussion* refers to a mode of resolution of opposition that involves mutual engagement of parties in problem-solving discussions, negotiation, or compromise.

5. *Tabling* refers to a mode of resolution of opposition in which the subject is dropped.

6. *Capitulation* refers to a mode of resolution of opposition in which one side gives into the other, either because it is convinced of the correctness of the other side or because it is forced to do so.

7. *Relational integration* refers to periods when the group is not task focused; these often exhibit tangents, joking, and positive socioemotional interaction.

Source: Author.

It is noteworthy that this system, and most interaction coding systems, comprise sets of mutually exclusive and exhaustive categories that span some domain of interest appearing in social interaction. To be mutually exclusive means that all events of interest to the coding scheme can be categorized using the category scheme. To be mutually exclusive, any event of interest in social interaction must be able to be placed into one and only one category. If events can be coded into more than one category, dependencies among categories create a methodological problem, because many statistics (e.g., reliability coefficients, general linear model statistics, factor analysis, sequential models) assume independence of observations (Hewes, in press). Events that can be categorized in more than one category can be included only if additional categories are added that are "multifunctional"; that is, they contain categories that fuse two or more of the original set (Hewes, 1985). For example, if a single statement is both a move to establish a person's control or power and a suggested course of action, it has two functions:

(a) a bid for relational control and (b) a proposal for organizing subsequent interaction. If both functions are part of the same coding scheme but occur simultaneously in the same event, we should create a new category that combines them (bid for relational control/organizing) to capture this event while maintaining the requirement for mutually exclusive categories (Hewes, 1985; Hewes, Planalp, & Streibel, 1980). By creating this multifunctional category, we are acknowledging the possibility that a simple attempt to establish any kind of relational control (talking over another person, dominating the floor) is different from a person's proposing a group agenda to pursue some shared goal while attempting to assert personal control

These six examples will be touchstones in the remainder of this chapter. No one best way captures interpersonal or group interaction. Rather, this depends on the aim of the researcher and the theoretical framework involved.

Estimating the Reliability of Measures of Social Interaction

Reproducibility of measurements is the hallmark of science. Without it we have no patterns to explain. Determining the reproducibility of measures of social interaction is relatively easy to accomplish in ratings and more difficult in coding schemes.

Reliability of Coding Systems

The reliability of coding schemes is not merely a warrant for claims of the scientific status of a piece of research. It also plays a critical role in the development and revision of the coding schemes themselves. To develop acceptable levels of reliability, we must answer three questions: Can we identify consistently each communication event to be coded subsequently? Can we label those units consistently on the basis of some coding scheme? Have we removed systematic sources of bias from our estimates of reliability?

There are at least 11 distinct indices we could use to assess reliability, including such commonly used indices as percentage of agreement, Krippendorff's index, and Scott's (1955) π. These are covered in depth by Zhao, Liu, and Deng (2013) and in Krippendorff's (2013) response, both of which we recommend to all readers interested in coding social interaction. However, our approach differs from theirs in two ways. First, rather than reviewing the disparity of indices, we begin with only one (percentage of agreement) and unfold the special-purpose indices from this case. Second, we focus on the role of reliability in category scheme development rather than as a final reported index in a study, although *sets* of our reliability indices will play a critical role in the final report of any study.

The first step, seldom used in most studies of social interaction, is to establish *unitizing reliability* for every category of the coding system and rating system (Folger, Hewes, & Poole, 1984; Meyers & Seibold, 2012). This means that, ignoring the content of ratings or coding systems, there is agreement among coders as to which events are being coded. This can be done in two ways. One is to have two or more coders parse the transcript by bracketing each event to be coded as they see it. If the remarks are based on turns-at-talk reliability (who is speaking), estimates are relatively easy to derive because the turns mark the events. The major problem in this case is in coding turns as with talk overs. If the remarks can occur within turns, reliable coding is more difficult, because there are no external markers of the unit of events. Another unit of analysis is the thought turn, or demarcating each thought—no matter how brief—into coding units (e.g., Weger & Canary, 2010).

Unitizing reliability is estimated by taking the number of total judgments in which events are coded consistently across coders divided by the total number of events recorded by all coders regardless of agreement. It is critical for this estimate to approximate 1.00, because all other estimates of reliability are based on the assumption that units have been defined reliably. It is important to use unitizing reliability during the development of coding procedures and revise category definitions as necessary. When revising the definitions of either categories or events to be coded, it is necessary to use an independent set of texts or coders or both when reassessing unitizing reliability so that observations are independent.

Once we have established unitizing reliability, we can assess the reliability of the category scheme as a whole, or *coding scheme reliability*. As noted, a number of reliability coefficients have been developed (see Zhao et al., 2013, for a listing of possible coefficients). In its most basic form, reliability is calculated by dividing the number of events coded similarly across categories by both coders divided by the total number of events coded (giving it a range of 0.00 to 1.00). This statistic is widely used either directly or by using it as a computational element in other indices. In this simple form, the reliability index does not take into account the natural distribution of acts across categories; acts falling into some categories may be more common in the discourse being coded than in others.

Unfortunately, problems occur with relying only on overall reliability of coding systems. This is because assessments of coding scheme reliability can miss important differences in reliability of individual categories. The percentage agreements for each category considered alone are arguably more useful than the reliability across the whole scheme, because they may uncover weaknesses in particular categories that are missed by estimated reliability across all categories combined. Reliability assessment opens the opportunity to refine those categories and to identify systematic bias in coding. For instance, the definitions of individual or sets of categories may need to reworked so that coders can better agree on coded events. This is signified by low category-by-category reliability for one or more categories, even when the reliability for the whole scheme aggregated across all categories is adequate. Conversely, weak overall coding scheme reliability may obscure the fact that agreement for some categories is high, which indicates that these categories do not require tinkering. If coding scheme and category-by-category reliabilities are high, by convention 0.70 or higher, refinement of categories or retraining of coders may not be a problem. If not revisions are required to have an adequate coding scheme.

To measure potential problems resulting from low category-by-category or low overall coding scheme reliability, it is useful to create a "confusion matrix," as in Figure 13.1. A confusion matrix is simply a table in which one coder's categorizations are the rows and the other's the columns, resulting in a cross-classification of the classifications made by each. Thus, we can see how frequently the two coders agreed or disagreed on the coding of the full set of events. Large off-diagonal elements indicate categories that tend to be confused or confounded with each other. Figure 13.1 exemplifies a confusion matrix and contains a concrete illustration plus instructions of how to assess several reliability problems.

It is also important to consider the issue of random error in estimates of coding scheme and category-by-category reliabilities, because they give a "baseline" against which to assess potential biases in coding. Our tests for reliability are not only estimates of reliability per se, as they are often portrayed in discussions of indices of reliability (Zhao et al., 2013), they also can serve as diagnostic tools to assess potential problems in percentage

		Coder 2		
		a	b	c
Coder 1	a	60	0	0
		A	B	C
	b	3	20	4
		D	E	F
	c	20	0	40
		G	H	I

Figure 13.1 A confusion matrix of observed frequencies for coded interaction data from two coders over a specified time period.[a,b,c,d]

Source: Authors.

a. The "specified period of time" designates that the confusion matrix might or might not be created using data from the entire conversation. Alternatives might be over some fraction of the interaction or some segment identified as being coherent because of the content of the interaction, for instance, "phases." Generating confusions for multiple segments separately is useful if there is concern about changing levels of reliability over time.

b. The left-hand side of the table contains data from Coder 1 for each category (**a**, **b**, and **c**). Coder 2's data and categories are described across the top of the table.

c. Each cell contains two pieces of information. The first is the cell frequency. The second is a capital letter identifying each cell (*A*, *B*, etc.).

d. *Coding scheme reliability* is computed by summing the frequencies for cells **A**, **E**, and **I** divided by the sum of the frequencies for all cells (**A** through **I**), that is, 120/147 = 0.82. *Category-by-category reliabilities* are computed by dividing the frequency for each category by the total for the row. The reliability of category **a** is derived from the frequency for cell **A** divided by the sum of the frequencies for **A**, **B**, and **C**, that is, 60/60 = 1.00. Note that this reliability is computed from the standpoint of Coder 1. There is a separate reliability for Category **a** from the standpoint of Coder 2. This is given by the frequency of **A** divided by the sum of the frequencies of the cells **A**, **D**, and **G**, that is, 60/83 = 0.72. This differs from the first reliability estimate for Category **a**, because Coder 2 confuses more of his or her Category **a**'s with the other categories (**b** and **c**) for Coder 1 (23) than Coder 1 does with Coder 2 (0). Reliability for Category **b** is created by dividing the frequency for cell **E** by the sum of frequencies for cells **D**, **E**, and **F**, that is, 20/27 = 0.74. Note that this is the reliability from the perspective of Coder 1. From the standpoint of Coder 2, the reliability is 20/20 (1.00). For Category **c**, the reliability from the standpoint of Coder 1 is 40/60 (0.67).

agreement estimates. The first of these diagnostics for biases focuses on sources of potential error in coding scheme reliability. A good estimate of the effect of random error on coding scheme reliability estimates is based on comparison of coding scheme reliability in comparison with agreement that would be expected by chance. For example, if each of two categories has 50% of the observations, then coding scheme reliability across categories could be as high as 0.50 by chance alone. In other words, as much as 50% of the events coded as being agreed upon by all coders may be due to randomness alone. In this case, a percentage agreement figure of 0.80 is only 30% above chance. In cases of different distributions of marginal frequencies and/or numbers of categories, coding scheme reliability may also be inflated by chance. One need only think of the confusion matrix as any table that one could analyze using a χ^2 statistic. The expected frequency for each cell in the table is the frequency expected by chance. If we subtract the totals of those frequencies due to chance from the frequencies of agreement and sum all categories and then divide the resulting frequency by the total frequency of agreement, the result is an estimate of reliability corrected for chance for each category. Note, however, that just because an estimate of coding scheme reliability may be inflated because of chance does not mean that it is inflated. It means that if such a bias exists, the maximum possible amount of that inflation is characterized by our index of bias.

A number of reliability indices (Scott's π, Cohen's κ, Fleiss's K, and Krippendorff's α) correct for expected frequencies of acts in the sample being coded for reliability assessment (Krippendorff, 2004, 2013). One limitation of these indices is that the actual population proportions of acts are usually not known or easily obtainable. Scott's π and Cohen's κ apply only for two coders, while Fleiss's K and Krippendorff's α apply for multiple coders. Scott's π, Cohen's κ, and Fleiss's K apply only for nominal coding categories, whereas Krippendorff's α applies for all types of data, from binary through ratio level. Because most coding systems define categories at the nominal level, this is not, however, a severe limitation.

Comparable indices of random biases in category-by-category reliabilities are computed analogously. In this case, the expected frequency for randomness is given by the total frequency of category occurrence for each category for a given coder divided by the number of categories. This is subtracted from the category agreement for each category and divided by the total frequency of category events

for each coder. The result is, again, an estimate of maximum *potential*, category-by-category reliabilities corrected for chance biases. Separate estimates can be calculated for these potential biases from the perspective of each coder, just as separate estimates exist for category-by-category reliabilities without such a correction.

Reliability for Ratings

The most common approach to assessing inter-rater reliability is the intraclass correlation. A Pearson correlation can be used if there are only two coders, but with multiple raters, the intraclass correlation coefficient (ICC) is required (Shrout & Fleiss, 1979).

The ICC essentially provides an analysis of variance (ANOVA) in which the factors are the raters and the units being rated are acts, segments of interaction, or even entire interaction episodes. Properties of the raters and units determine which type of ANOVA is appropriate. The relevant properties of the raters are (a) whether the same raters rate every unit or not, (b) whether the entire population of raters is being used or just a sample of raters, and (c) whether the absolute agreement of ratings is important compared with consistency among raters without exact agreement on the rating. In some cases, there are so many units to rate that all raters do not rate every unit; for example, a design might involve four raters and 210 meetings and have each rater judge 70 meetings, with overlaps among raters. In this instance, it is not possible to separate the effects of rater error from the effects of the units rated (e.g., some meetings may cover many more topics than others and thus be more difficult to rate). In this case ICC(1), derived from a one-way random ANOVA, is appropriate. Because it does not separate the two types of error, ICC(1) has the lowest value of the three varieties of ICC.

If each rater rates all units, and only a sample of raters is used, ICC(2), derived from a two-way random ANOVA, is appropriate. This index allows the effects of raters to be separated from those of the units being rated. An additional consideration in using ICC(2) is whether ratings will be individual measures or whether they will be averaged together to combine raters' responses into a single index. If a single rater will be used and the ICC is being computed simply to verify the reliability of ratings, then ICC(2,1) is the appropriate index. But if k raters are averaged, then ICC(2,k) is the appropriate statistic. Typically ICC(2,1) is smaller than ICC(2,k). A final consideration is whether exact agreement on ratings is needed or the ratings only need to be consistent but not agree exactly (e.g., Rater A gives four units ratings of 3, 4, 2, and 4, while Rater B gives them 4, 5, 3, and 5, always one unit higher than Rater A). Calculation of the ICC is adjusted depending on which is required.

If the entire population of raters is used, then ICC(3), based on a two-way mixed ANOVA, is appropriate. Although most rating systems will use samples of raters, when members are asked to rate interactions in their own relationships, families, or groups, and all members of the social group in question are rating all units, then the entire population can be regarded as raters. ICC(3) will typically be larger than ICC(1) or ICC(2) because of more valid estimates and control of error. All of these variations on ICC can be calculated using the reliability option in SPSS, and they are also available in SAS and R.

Validity Assessment

Basic Principles

In educational and psychological testing, validity is defined as the extent to which a test accurately measures what it purports to measure. "Validity refers to the degree to which evidence and theory support the interpretations of test scores entailed by proposed uses of tests" (American Educational Research Association, American Psychological Association, & National Council on Measurement in Education, 1999). The validity of measures of social interaction, correspondingly, can be defined as the extent to which a coding or rating system accurately yields the type of information it is designed to obtain. Exactly what constitutes validity and how validity is assessed depend on the purpose of the coding or rating system, which in turn delimits the types of claims the researcher can make about interaction (Folger et al., 1984; Poole, Folger, & Hewes, 1987).

In their classic discussion of the construction of coding systems, Lazarsfeld and Barton (1969) noted that the purpose of content and interaction analysis systems is to allow the researcher to recode a complex phenomenon systematically and rationally into a simpler set of attributes. Recoding inevitably involves reduction of the complexity of a phenomenon, as when sentences worded differently but with similar meanings are assigned to the same category. According to Lazarsfeld and Barton, a coding system is valid if this reduction meets two conditions: (a) the set of classificatory dimensions or categories must capture the phenomenon adequately for the

purposes of the researcher, and (b) the coding system must not distort important dimensions of the phenomenon. A valid coding or rating system should capture accurately those aspects of interaction the system is designed to code. The meaning of *accurately* differs, however, depending on the purpose for which the coding system is designed and used.

One common purpose of interaction coding or rating systems is to measure constructs defined by the researcher's theory or conceptual scheme. In this *observer-privileged* mode of observation, the researcher characterizes interaction "from the outside," without reference to participants' perspectives or meanings; Poole and colleagues (Poole & Folger, 1981b; Poole et al., 1987) termed this the *experienced* mode of observation. For example, to identify how people develop their ideas in conversation, Canary's (1992) system for coding conversational argument relies on theoretical terms (e.g., "convergent arguables"). The LIWC system uses word counts to identify emotional states such as anger and personal concerns such as a focus on work as defined by the authors of the system and a few other social scientists who helped with scale development. In this case, the emphasis is on operationalization of theoretical constructs meaningful to the researcher; whether participants in the interaction understand the constructs is not relevant for assessing validity.

A second purpose for coding and rating systems is to identify or to measure how participants interpret interaction. This *subject-privileged* mode of observation attempts to approximate the results of participants' interpretive processes. There are two distinct ways to approach subject-privileged coding. In the *generalized subject-privileged* mode, researchers seek to develop a system that identifies the shared meaning utterances have for members of a culture or community; Poole and colleagues (Poole et al., 1987; Poole & Folger, 1981b, 2009) termed this the *experiencing* mode of observation. Sillars, Roberts, Leonard, and Dun (2000), for example, had individuals recall their thoughts as they watched a video of their conflict interactions with their spouses. Sillars et al. then correlated these recollections with their coded conflict behaviors. Another approach is the *restrictive subject-privileged* mode, in which the goal is to capture the idiosyncratic meanings of utterances for people in a particular relationship; Poole and colleagues (Poole et al., 1987; Poole & Folger, 1981b, 2009) termed this the *experiencer* mode of observation. Labov and Fanshel (1977) used this mode of observation in their book *Therapeutic Discourse*, which explores the particular linguistic structures of therapy for pairs of patients and therapists. For purposes of simplicity, we drop the *privileged* denotation for both subject modes, using the labels *generalized subject* and *restrictive subject* henceforth.

Each of the three modes of observation just described warrants different claims about interaction. An observer-privileged system can support only claims related to the theory that underlies the system. It cannot warrant claims about the meaning of the interaction to participants. Similarly, data generated using a generalized subject system cannot warrant claims about the meanings of interaction to a specific set of interactors; instead it can only support claims about the intersubjective meaning of the interaction, that is, of typifications used by the community being studied (Schutz & Luckmann, 1974).

Scholars who develop observer-privileged coding and rating systems often draw on their own experiences with the community of language users being studied and on prior research on that community. Bales's Interaction Process Analysis (IPA; Bales, 1950), for example, relies on a long tradition of American pragmatist thought that focuses on problem solving as a way of knowing, on sociological studies of groups, and on deep experience with the types of groups the IPA was designed for. Hence, it is tempting to assume that the categorizations or ratings reflect at least the common understandings of the groups being studied. This is, however, to confuse the construction of an interaction analysis system with its validation. Personality measures and other psychometric instruments are also constructed using knowledge of the subjects they will be applied to. Still, an acknowledged requirement remains for formal validation of these instruments subsequent to and independent of their development. The IPA system is based on a theory of problem solving as a set of task and socioemotional activities (orientation, evaluation, control, tension release, shows solidarity, etc.) that was developed by Bales and does not necessarily reflect the understandings of group process of the members themselves. Additional evidence must be offered that the IPA validly reflects interpretations of participants before claims about subject interpretations are warranted.

The same strictures apply in the case of reuse or adaptation of existing interaction analysis systems. Just as they would review and weigh the evidence for the validity of a psychometric measure, scholars should carefully consider evidence for the validity of the system vis-à-vis the three modes of observation. If no formal validity study supporting either subject mode has been conducted, and if no evidence exists for generalized or restricted subject

validity in studies in which the system has been applied, one should only presume observer-privileged status for the system. It is all too easy for "interpretive creep" to occur, in which a coding system that captures only observer-privileged meaning is presumed to reflect subjective meanings as well. For scholars who want to make claims about generalized or restricted subject interpretations, the safest route when applying an interaction analysis system in a new setting or with a different language community is to test its validity for these modes of observation.

This also holds true for interaction analysis systems that have been modified or adapted. It is commonplace to combine, add, or modify categories or scales in interaction analysis systems. When this is done, just as with a psychometric instrument, it is necessary to reassess both the reliability and the validity of the coding system for the three modes of observation.

Methods for Validation

Whichever of the three modes of observation a researcher aspires to, claims about the meaning of classifications must be supported by evidence for their validity. Each mode of observation requires different types of evidence and, hence, different validity study designs.

Validation for the observer-privileged mode. In this mode of observation, validity concerns the degree to which the dimensions or categories of the interaction analysis system measure the theoretical construct(s) they are intended to measure. This definition closely parallels the concept of validity as it is used in psychological and educational testing that was cited at the beginning of this section. Cronbach and Meehl (1955) distinguished three types of evidence for validity of educational and psychological measures: content validity, criterion-oriented validity, and construct validity. Although subsequent discussion, systematized by Messick (1995), argued for additional types of validity evidence, the three distinguished by Cronbach and Meehl map the terrain of interaction analysis validity thoroughly.

Content validity depends on two judgments: (a) Does the interaction analysis system reflect theoretical constructs accurately and capture all the ways in which the constructs may occur in interaction? and (2) Is the interaction analysis system clearly defined and logically consistent? These questions are relevant during the construction of the interaction analysis system (Folger et al., 1984;

Lazarsfeld & Barton, 1968; Neuendorff, 2002). They can also be addressed after the interaction analysis system has been constructed, ideally in a separate validity assessment, but also on the basis of experience applying the system in research.

In developing the Feedback Rating Instrument, for example, Leathers identified 20 possible dimensions of feedback responses and developed explicit definitions for each. He then had two sets of judges apply these dimensions to samples of 100 feedback statements and retained the 9 dimensions that were readily identifiable as applicable to 90% or more of the statements by all judges. Leathers also found that judges could differentiate the 9 dimensions across the samples of feedback statements. The Conversational Argument Coding System (Canary, 1992; Canary & Seibold, 2010; Seibold & Weger, this volume) has been modified several times over the years, in some cases to reflect new distinctions in argument that emerged from research and in other cases to make the process of coding more systematic and straightforward. Both types of modifications may improve the content validity of a system, the first through more accurate reflection of argumentation constructs and the second through making the system clearer and more logically consistent.

Pennebaker et al. (2007) described a number of steps taken to enhance content validity of the LIWC system. The dictionaries for various constructs were originally compiled by drawing words from psychometric scales, thesauri, and dictionary definitions. Second, three judges rated the word lists, indicating whether each word should or should not be included in a category, and also suggested additional words for the lists. Two rounds of ratings were conducted to refine the categories, and words were added or deleted if two of the three judges agreed that they should be. In a third step, the LIWC system was used to analyze texts comprising 8 million words, and any categories that were used at very low rates were deleted. Some additional categories and word lists were added as well. Since its original construction in 1997, the LIWC system has been updated on the basis of analyses of hundreds of thousands of text files, following the three steps just described.

Whereas Pennebaker et al. (2007) used dictionaries to operationalize their constructs, Quinn et al. (2010) reported an inductive method for generating topics in text using unsupervised machine learning; this technique is increasingly common and will no doubt be used in interaction analysis as well in cases in which extensive transcriptions exist. Their method derived 42 issue clusters from texts of U.S. Senate bills. They assessed content validity substantively by scanning the word lists associated with each topic cluster for plausibility and quantitatively by conducting cluster analysis of the topics and assessing whether those that clustered had related meanings. This represents an interesting combination of qualitative and quantitative approaches.

Content validity can also be enhanced by deriving the system through empirical analysis of the discourse under study. Many interaction analysis systems have been developed using this bottom-up approach, which is systematized in the grounded theory coding process (Bryant & Charmaz, 2007; Charmaz, 2006; Strauss & Corbin, 1998). Content validity can also be "built into" a system using statistical and text-analytic methods, as illustrated by the Group Working Relationships Coding System (Poole, 1983). Poole coded 10 decision-making sessions using Bales's (1950) Interaction Process Analysis and Fisher's (1970) Decision Proposal Coding System, and then he derived clusters of codes that co-occurred in short segments of decision-making interaction. Assuming these clusters represented commonly occurring group activities, Poole used them to construct "a descriptive system directly tied to specific patterns of group activity" (p. 208). The categories of the GWRCS were derived from analysis of these patterns, and rules were subsequently written that defined the categories and the classification process. Some of these rules drew on coding procedures described in Bales's and Fisher's systems.

Criterion-oriented validity depends on whether constructs coded or measured using the interaction analysis system correlate with criterion variables that the system is used to predict. The criterion variables are assumed to be accurately and validly measured. The LIWC system, for example, explicitly measures psychological constructs such as anxiety, anger, or inhibition, for which validated measures exist that can serve as criterion variables. Pennebaker et al. (2007) reported a study in which they had college students write essays about their early college experiences. One group was asked to write about "their deepest thoughts and feelings" and another about any event of their choosing in an unemotional way. Judges assessed the essays on emotion and social processes, and their ratings were correlated with LIWC counts on these dimensions. Correlations were moderate to high, suggesting that the LIWC scores reflected the criterion variables. Gottschalk (1997) described a number of criterion-oriented validity studies on the Gottschalk-Gleser method, the precursor of the LIWC system. Most interaction coding or rating systems, however, are designed to capture constructs that do not have criteria, so this type of validity has limited utility.

Construct validity is a more useful form of evidence for the validity of an interaction analysis system. Cronbach and Meehl (1955) provided the following rationale and method for construct validation:

> A construct derives its meaning from the theory in which it occurs. The theory can be expressed as a network of propositions and associations among variables. When some of the statements in the network lead to predicted relations among observables, the measure corresponding to the constructs in question may be validated by ascertaining whether it relates to these observables as the theory specifies. The construct may be related to the observable directly or through intermediate statements in the network. If the construct in question (as tapped by the measure) shows the relationships to the other observables that are predicted by the theoretical network, this is positive evidence for validity of the measure. If the predicted relation fails to occur, the fault may lie either in the proposed interpretation of the measure or in the theoretical network. If the network is altered, the measure must be revalidated with a new set of data. If the researcher is confident of the theoretical network, then the measure is valid. (p. 300)

To assess the construct validity of an interaction analysis system, a researcher would first identify a number of input and output variables that relate to constructs captured by the system. If the relationships that are predicted do in fact hold, then there is evidence for the construct validity of the system. If we follow the canons of psychometric methods, construct validity should be assessed through one or more validation studies; in practice, however, construct validity of an interaction analysis system is more often assessed through survey of results of studies in which it has been used.

Formal construct validity studies typically specify hypotheses that make "obvious" predictions and also demonstrate the value of the interaction or content analysis system. Often these predictions involve outcomes. Gouran et al. (1978) had 147 undergraduate students rate three different discussions on the scales described previously; they also had the students rate the quality of the discussions. They found substantial relationships, suggesting that the dimensions in their measure correlated with outcomes, as would be expected. Ting-Toomey (1983) validated the Intimate Negotiation Coding

System by assessing the degree to which its three major classes of acts—integrative, descriptive, and disintegrative—related to reported marital satisfaction of the coded couples. Inui, Carter, Kukull, and Haigh (1982) regressed counts of acts coded with Bales's Interaction Process Analysis, Roter's Medical Interaction Process Analysis, and Stiles's Verbal Response Modes Coding System on patient knowledge, satisfaction, and compliance after a medical consultation. On the basis of their results, they judged the Bales and Roter systems superior to the Verbal Response Modes Coding System.

A second strategy for formal construct validation is to assess differential validity by applying the system to different groups of subjects that should exhibit differences on the constructs in the system. The Group Working Relationships Coding System could be validated, for example, by comparing the codings of all male groups with those of all female groups. A difference would be expected, because we know from other research that interaction patterns in these two types of groups are considerably different. Poole (1983) assessed the validity of the constructs underlying the GWRCS by testing whether the temporal patterns of coded interaction showed intergroup differences for a set of 10 group decision sessions that had previously been shown to differ in their developmental patterns.

A third strategy is an analogue of convergent validity in psychometrics: Identify parallel variables from a different measurement "realm" and test for relationships with constructs in the system. Poole (1983) assessed the degree of similarity between the levels of GWRCS constructs for 1-minute segments of decision-making discussion and minute-by-minute verbal summaries of the discussion prepared by the independent researcher. He found that 10 of 13 constructs had more than 85% correspondence with verbal descriptions, and the other three had 75% or greater correspondence. Ekman, Friesen, and Tomkins (1971) compared classifications of photographs of faces on the basis of an early version of the FACS for six emotions with judges' evaluation of those emotions, finding high levels of agreement on four of the six emotions. Quinn et al. (2010) validated an inductively derived topic model of U.S. Senate speeches by correlating the topics of speeches with external events just preceding or co-occurring with the speeches. They reasoned that the topics of speeches should relate to current events if their model was accurate.

Despite a fairly intensive search, we found very few formal validation studies of interaction and content analysis systems. Much more common are assessments of validity based on research studies that found significant relationships among constructs in the system and other variables. Seibold and Meyers (2007), for example, provided an extensive summary of findings using the Group Argument Coding Scheme as used in the group context, with the implications for its construct validity. Pennebaker et al. (2007) provided validation studies for the LIWC system. This is an acceptable way to argue for the construct validity of an interaction or content analysis system, provided we acknowledge two caveats. First, in many studies there are nonsignificant, as well as significant, relationships, and the balance between these—not just the ones that support the validity claim—should be taken into account in judging the construct validity of the system. Second, we should also acknowledge the "file drawer effect" noted in meta-analysis, in which studies showing mostly nonsignificant or across-the-board nonsignificant effects are not published or even publicly reported. Assessment of construct validity on the basis of substantive studies using an interaction or content analysis system would do well to take a cue from meta-analysis and undertake systematic assessment of all results.

In evaluating construct validity of coding systems, it is also important to consider how the data are transformed into "variable" format. In most of the studies reviewed in this chapter, researchers simply defined a variable as the total number of times a given act occurred during a discussion. Although this is a viable way to derive interaction variables, other options should be considered. One is to use what Gouran termed *distributional structure* by deriving profiles using the total number of acts (or proportions of acts) for all categories. In this case it is the relative prevalence of the entire set of acts that relates to other variables. This option is useful when the researcher wants to take the relationships among categories into account. For example, in a discussion between married partners coded with Ting-Toomey's Intimate Negotiation Coding System, a discussion with high levels of disintegrative and low levels of integrative behavior would seem likely to be qualitatively different from one with high levels of both disintegrative and integrative behavior. A second option is to take longitudinal patterns in the interaction into account by identifying short-term *sequential structure* or longer term *phasic patterns* in single or multiple acts (Poole, 1983). Short-term sequences can be operationalized using pairs or triples of consecutive acts as variables rather than individual acts. Longer term sequences can be operationalized by developing typologies of sequences (e.g., Poole & Roth, 1989). In the study that was the foundation for the GWRCS,

Poole (1983) identified three different types of longitudinal patterns of conflict management interaction and found that member perceptions of the decision sessions on a postmeeting questionnaire differed systematically across the three types.

The format of the interaction data should ideally be justified for theoretical reasons. If the theory focuses on single categories or dimensions of interaction, then totals or average ratings are appropriate; if it focuses on profiles or relative amounts of acts, on sequential structure, or on longer term patterns, then more complex formats should be used in the validation.

Validation for the generalized subject-privileged mode. When the researcher wants to justify claims about the meaning of the interaction to participants on the basis of an interaction analysis system, it is necessary to provide evidence that its classifications or ratings are consistent with the interpretations of the participants. Poole and Folger (1981b) called this *representational validity* and argued that it is established through showing that "the theoretical domain specified by the researcher and the category [or rating] system which operationalizes it are, in fact, meaningful vis-à-vis the socially defined interaction situation" (p. 487). As with content and construct validity, several different types of evidence may be advanced for representational validity.

One test for representational validity establishes the degree of correspondence between observer and participant codings or ratings of interaction. In a good example of this approach, Gouran and Whitehead (1971) had four four-person groups engage in discussions that were recorded. Each discussion was then played back one statement at a time, and the group that participated in it and one of the other groups rated the statements on scales measuring orientation and provocativeness. The ratings had high reliability, and correlations were substantial, suggesting overlap in the interpretations of observers and participants. If the observers and participants are from the same culture or language community, correlation between participant and observer ratings suggests that speaker and hearer perspectives overlap, and interrater reliability supports the assumption that these ratings reflect intersubjective or shared meaning.

One limitation of this approach is that it assumes that *orientation* (defined as "an attempt on the part of its maker to move a group toward its goal") and *provocativeness* (defined as reflecting "a desire or willingness on the part of its maker to have another person make an overt response to it") are elements of the interpretive schemes of both participants and observers. It is, however, possible that these dimensions are not meaningful to participants; the researchers may have imposed their own dimensions onto participants, and participants were able to understand them well enough to adopt the researchers' frame of reference and make consistent ratings. A second limitation of this design is that it can assess the representational validity only of rating scales. It is not feasible to apply this method to interaction coding systems, which are based on systematic classification procedures and usually require considerable training.

Wish, D'Andrade, and Goodnow (1980) developed an approach for comparing observer and participant perspectives with data generated by interaction coding. They had subjects from the same population as participants rate twenty 1- to 2-minute videotaped scenes of dyadic interaction on 18 bipolar semantic differential scales (e.g., very cooperative to very competitive). They also coded the interactions with a speech act coding system they developed as well as with Bales's Interaction Process Analysis system. To allow comparison of the ratings and codings, they first computed the total amount of each type of act in each of the scenes as indicators of the nature of interaction and used a multidimensional scaling technique (MDPREF) to derive common factors. The resulting five-factor solution provided a representation of dimensions underlying the coding systems. The second step repeated the MDPREF analysis on the ratings of each scene, yielding a four-factor solution. The four factors of this solution—upward-downward, positive-negative, forward-backward, and arousal—strongly resembled dimensions commonly obtained in factor analyses of sets of semantic differential scales used to rate interpersonal behavior and interaction (Bales & Cohen, 1979; Foa, 1961) and stimuli such as nations (Osgood, Suci, & Tannenbaum, 1957).

The analytical method used to derive the factors, MDPREF, generated coordinates for each of the 20 scenes in the multidimensional spaces of codings and ratings, yielding two data sets that could be correlated to assess correspondence between the ratings and the codings. The results indicated meaningful relationships between the ratings and codings, with more than 25% of the variance explained for each dimension. Wish et al. concluded that there was a correspondence between the two realms of measurement, providing evidence for the representational validity of the coding systems. Other studies that took a similar approach are those of Bales and Cohen (1979) and Stiles (1980).

As with Gouran and Whitehead's (1971) study, a limitation of this design is that it elicits subjects'

perspectives on the interaction using scales determined by the researchers. There is a good deal of evidence that three basic evaluative dimensions (positive-negative, active-passive, instrumental-socioemotional) underlie responses to interpersonal relationships and other types of objects as well (Bales & Cohen, 1979; Foa, 1961; Osgood et al., 1957; Rosenberg, 1976; Triandis, Vassiliou, & Nassiakou, 1968). Most of this evidence, however, has been gathered by having subjects rate objects on scales that are then factor-analyzed, yielding three and sometimes four dimensions. Hence methods effects cannot be ruled out.

Poole and Folger (1981a) sought to avoid this problem with a design that did not use a priori categories. They elicited subjects' perceptions of seven utterance passages from a dyadic discussion using the method of paired comparisons: They asked members of a common language community to indicate the degree of similarity of all possible pairs of 11 passages. They then used individual differences multidimensional scaling (INDSCAL) to derive a semantic space. The same passages were coded with three coding systems, Bales's (1950) Interaction Process Analysis system, Fisher's (1970) Decision Proposal Coding System, and Mabry's (1975) Pattern Variable Coding System. Distances between coded passages were computed using a string-matching algorithm, and the data were also analyzed using INDSCAL. The subject space had four dimensions, and there were some differences in the weights subjects attached to the four dimensions, suggesting differences among raters. The spaces for all three coding systems also were four dimensional. The subjects' semantic and coding system spaces were then compared using regression. The results showed clear and substantial relationships for all three systems, with the IPA and Decision Proposal Coding System exhibiting somewhat stronger match than the Pattern Variable Coding System.

This approach has the advantage of not presuming to know the dimensions underlying s interpretations of interaction. Its major disadvantage is fatigue due to having to judge the similarity of large numbers of pairs of passages or statements (55 judgments for 11 passages in Poole & Folger's study). This limits the number of passages or statements that can be used, lowering the statistical power of the comparison of the subject and coding spaces.

Representational validity is an important type of evidence supporting claims about the intersubjective meaning of interaction to participants. As we noted previously, content validity also speaks to this issue when there is evidence that participants were consulted or studied during the development of the interaction analysis system. In addition, it is also important to establish the construct validity of interaction analysis systems operating in the generalized subject-privileged mode: A system that corresponds to intersubjective meaning but does not relate to any theoretical constructs is not particularly useful.

Validation for the specific subject-privileged mode. In this case, the researcher wants to capture the meaning of interaction to a specific individual, dyad, or group. In each case, meaning is particularized to the individual or relationship and also to the specific context in which the interaction occurs. For example, a researcher may be interested in "secret code words" used by a couple in a romantic relationship. In this case, validity stems primarily from how the system is constructed and from specific evidence that "triangulates" with the ratings or codings to show that they capture meaning specific to the unit under study. Fanshel and Moss (1972) offered an excellent example of a valid system for capturing the meanings of interactions for a troubled couple. Ethnographic or deep qualitative analysis studies are also appropriate to capture this level of meaning. Developing a particularized interaction analysis system for this mode of analysis may be "overkill," because it can only be used once.

The study by Poole and Folger (1981a) reviewed in the previous section offers a way to get at specific adaptations of intersubjective interpretive schemes by individuals. As previously noted, INDSCAL generates individual weights for each dimension of the common solution. This allows researchers to determine how specific subjects interpretive schemes relate to the more general shared semantic space. In their study, several subjects weighted all four dimensions high, some only had substantial weights on three dimensions, and some on only two. This suggests that participants either used the common semantic space differently or had their own idiosyncratic interpretive schemes that mapped into the common space in different ways. Other multidimensional scaling techniques allow even finer grained differences, such as differences in the relationships between dimensions in the semantic space. Again, the disadvantage is that gathering data for this type of analysis is very fatiguing.

Conclusion

The reliability and validity of interaction analysis systems are necessary conditions for substantive studies of social interaction. As this chapter shows,

assessment of reliability and evaluation of validity present complex processes with multiple facets. The important role of reliability indices and validity assessment as summative properties of measurement instruments may obscure their significant role in the development of interaction analysis systems. As this chapter makes clear, the reliability and validity of complex, meaning-laden interaction analysis systems depends in part on how they are constructed and refined on the basis of iterative reliability and validity assessments.

Reliability is often thought of as a single coefficient that applies to an entire interaction analysis system, analogous to the reliability of a psychometric test. Just as the reliability of individual items in a test must be assured, however, so too must category-by-category or scale-by-scale reliability of interaction analysis measures. Indeed, the use of sequential structure models such as Markov chains in interaction analysis makes category reliability even more important than in the case of scale items, because they model temporal relationships among categories, and differential category reliability can introduce severe biases.

The validity of interaction analysis systems depends strongly on the purposes for which they are used and the claims researchers want to make about the data they generate. If researchers want to operationalize specialized constructs meaningful only to them, then an analogue of construct validity is sufficient. If they want to capture the meaning of the interaction to participants, however, then representational validity must be established as well. Achieving representational validity sets a high bar, because it involves mapping the meanings participants share, and there are not well-established canons for doing so. Its difficulty notwithstanding, evidence that an interaction analysis system generates data meaningful to subjects is a prerequisite for any claims about how participants interpret or "see" interaction.

References

American Educational Research Association, American Psychological Association, & National Council on Measurement in Education. (1999). *Standards for educational and psychological testing.* Washington, DC: American Educational Research Association.

Bales, R. F. (1950). *Interaction Process Analysis: A method for the study of small groups.* Cambridge, MA: Addison-Wesley.

Bales, R. F., & Cohen, S. (1979). *SYMLOG: A system for multilevel observation of groups.* New York: Free Press.

Bryant, A., & Charmaz, K. (Eds.) (2007). *The SAGE handbook of grounded theory*. Thousand Oaks, CA: Sage.

Canary, D. J. (1992). *The conversational argument coding manual*. Unpublished manuscript.

Canary, D. J., & Seibold, D. R. (2010). Origins and development of the Conversational Argument Coding Scheme. *Communication Methods and Measures, 4,* 7–26.

Charmaz, K. (2006). *Constructing grounded theory: A practical guide through qualitative analysis*. London: Sage Ltd.

Cronbach, L. J., & Meehl, P. E. (1955). Construct validity in psychological tests. *Psychological Bulletin, 52,* 281–302.

Ekman, P., & Friesen, W. V. (1978). *Manual for the Facial Action Coding System*. Palo Alto, CA: Consulting Psychologists Press.

Ekman, P., Friesen, W. V., & Tomkins, S. S. (1971). Facial affect scoring technique: A first validity study. *Semiotica, 3,* 37–58.

Fanshel, D., & Moss, F. D. (1972). *Playback: A marriage in jeopardy examined*. Chicago: University of Chicago Press.

Fisher, B. A (1970). Decision emergence: Phases in group decision-making. *Speech Monographs, 37,* 53–66.

Foa, U. G., (1961). Convergences in the analysis of the structure of interpersonal behavior. *Psychological Review, 68,* 341–353.

Folger, J. P., Hewes, D. E., & Poole, M. S. (1984). Coding social interaction. In B. Dervin & M. Voight (Eds.), *Progress in communication sciences* (Vol. 5, pp. 115–161). Norwood, NJ: Ablex.

Gottschalk, L. A. (1997). The unobtrusive measurement of psychological states and traits. In C. E. Roberts (Ed.), *Text analysis for the social sciences* (pp. 117–130). Mahwah, NJ: Lawrence Erlbaum.

Gouran, D. S., Brown, C., & Henry, D. R. (1978). Behavioral correlates of perceptions of quality in decision-making discussions. *Communication Monographs, 45,* 51–63.

Gouran, D., & Whitehead, J. (1971). An investigation of ratings of discussion statements by participants and observers. *Central States Speech Journal, 21,* 263–268.

Hart, R. P. (1984). *Verbal style and the presidency: A computer-based analysis*. New York: Academic Press.

Hewes, D. E. (1985). Systematic biases in coded social interaction data. *Human Communication Research, 11,* 554–574.

Hewes, D. E. (in press). Studying the role of time and order in interpersonal communication: Methods, models and statistics. In C. Berger & M. Roloff (Eds.), *The international encyclopedia of interpersonal communication*. Thousand Oaks, CA: Sage.

Hewes, D. E., Planalp, S. K., & Streibel, M. (1980). Analyzing social interaction: Some excruciating models and exhilarating results. In D. Nimmo (Ed.), *Communication Yearbook 4* (pp. 123–144). New Brunswick, NJ: Transaction.

Hjortsjö, C-H. (1969). *Man's face and mimic language*. Lund, Sweden: Studen Litteratur.

Inui, T. S., Carter, W. B., Kukull, W. A., & Haigh, V. H. (1982). Outcome-based doctor-patient interaction analysis: I. Comparison of techniques. *Medical Care, 20,* 535–549.

Johnston, A., & White, A. B. (1994). Communication styles and female candidates: A study of political advertising during the 1986 state elections. *Journalism Quarterly, 71,* 321–329.

Krippendorff, K. (2004). Reliability in content analysis: Some common misconceptions and recommendations. *Human Communication Research, 30,* 411–433.

Krippendorff, K. (2013). A dissenting view on so-called paradoxes of reliability coefficients. In C. Salmon (Ed.) *Communication Yearbook 36* (pp. 481–499). New York: Routledge.

Labov, W., & Fanshel, D. (1977). *Therapeutic discourse: Psychotherapy as conversation*. New York: Academic Press.

Lazarsfeld, P. F., & Barton, A. H. (1969). Qualitative measurement: A codification of techniques unique to the social sciences. In L. I. Krimmerman (Ed.), *The nature and scope of social science* (pp. 514–549). New York: Appleton-Century-Crofts.

Leathers, D. G. (1971). The feedback rating instrument: A new means of evaluating discussion. *Central States Speech Journal, 22,* 32–42.

Mabry, E. A. (1975). An instrument for assessing content themes in group interaction. *Communication Monographs, 42,* 291–297.

Marks, M., Mathieu, J. E., & Zaccaro, S. J. (2001). A temporally based framework and taxonomy of team processes. *Academy of Management Review, 26,* 356–376.

McCallum, A. (2002). *MALLET: A machine learning for language toolkit*. Available at http://mallet.cs.umass.edu

McCroskey, J. C., & Wright, D. W. (1971). The development of an instrument for measuring interaction behavior in small groups. *Speech Monographs, 38,* 335–340.

Messick, S. (1995). Validation of inferences from persons' responses and performances as scientific inquiry into score meaning. *American Psychologist, 9,* 741–749.

Meyers, R., & Seibold, D. (2012). Coding interaction data. In A. Hollingshead & M. Poole (Eds.), *Research methods for studying groups and teams: A guide to approaches, tools, and technologies* (pp. 329–357). New York: Routledge.

Neuendorff, K. A. (2002). *The content analysis guidebook*. Thousand Oaks, CA: Sage.

Osgood, C., Suci, G. J., & Tannenbaum, P. (1957). *The measurement of meaning*. Urbana: University of Illinois Press.

Pennebaker, J. W., Chung, C. K., Ireland, M., Gonzales, A., & Booth, R. J. (2007). *The development and psychometric properties of LIWC2007*. Austin, TX: LIWC.net.

Poole, M. S. (1983). Decision development in small groups II: A study of multiple sequences in decision-making. *Communication Monographs*, *50*, 206–232.

Poole, M. S., & Dobosh, M. (2010). Exploring conflict management processes in jury deliberations through interaction analysis. *Small Group Research*, *41*, 408–426.

Poole, M. S., & Folger, J. P. (1981a). A method for establishing the representational validity of interaction coding systems: Do we see what they see? *Human Communication Research*, *8*, 26–42.

Poole, M. S., & Folger, J. P. (1981b). Modes of observation and the validity of interaction coding systems. *Small Group Research*, *17*, 477–494.

Poole, M. S., & Folger, J. P. (2009). Modes of observation and the validation of interaction analysis systems. In K. Krippendorff & M. A. Bock (Eds.), *The content analysis reader* (pp. 367–375). Thousand Oaks, CA: Sage.

Poole, M. S., Folger, J. P., & Hewes, D. E. (1987). Methods of interaction analysis. In G. R. Miller & M. Roloff (Eds.), *Explorations in interpersonal communication* (2nd ed., pp. 220–256). Beverly Hills, CA: Sage.

Poole, M. S., & Roth, J. (1989). Decision development in small groups IV: A typology of decision paths. *Human Communication Research*, *15*, 323–356.

Potter, W. J., & Levine-Donnerstein, D. (1999). Rethinking validity and reliability in content analysis. *Journal of Applied Communication Research*, *27*, 258–284.

Quinn, K. M., Monroe, B. L., Colaresi, M., Crespin, M. H., & Radev, D. R. (2010). How to analyze political attention with minimal assumptions and costs. *American Journal of Political Science*, *54*, 209–228.

Rosenberg, S. (1976). New approaches to the analysis of personal constructs in person perception. In A. W. Landfield (Ed.), *Nebraska Symposium on Motivation* (pp. 179–242). Lincoln: University of Nebraska Press.

Schutz, A., & Luckmann, T. (1974). *Structures of the life-world*. London: Heinemann.

Scott, W. A. (1955). Reliability of content analysis: The case of nominal scale coding. *Public Opinion Quarterly*, *19*, 321–325.

Seibold, D. R., & Meyers, R. (2007). Group argument: A structuration perspective and research program. *Small Group Research*, *38*, 312–336.

Shrout, P., & Fleiss, J. (1979). Intraclass correlations: Uses in assessing rater reliability. *Psychological Bulletin*, *86*, 420–428.

Sillars, A., Roberts, L. J., Leonard, K. E., & Dun, T. (2000). Cognition during marital conflict: The relationship of thought and talk. *Journal of Social and Personal Relationships*, *17*, 479–502.

Stiles, W. B. (1980). Comparison of dimensions derived from rating versus coding of dialogue. *Journal of Personality and Social Psychology*, *38*, 359–374.

Stone, P. J., Dunphy, D. C., Smith, M. S., & Ogilvie, D. M. (Eds.). (1966). *The General Inquirer: A computer approach to content analysis*. Cambridge, MA: MIT Press.

Strauss, A., & Corbin, J. (1998). *Basics of qualitative research* (2nd ed.). Thousand Oaks, CA: Sage.

Ting-Toomey, S. (1983). Coding conversation between intimates: A validation study of the Intimate Negotiation Coding System (INCS). *Communication Quarterly*, *31*, 68–77.

Triandis, H. , Vassiliou, C., & Nassiakou, N. (1968). Three cross-cultural studies of subjective culture. *Journal of Personality and Social Psychology*, *8*(Monogr. Suppl.), 1–42.

Weger, H., Jr., & Canary, D. J. (2010). How people develop ideas with each other: Analyses of argument sequences in close relationships. *Communication Methods and Measures*, *4*, 65–87.

Wish, M., D'Andrade, R. G., & Goodnow, J. E. (1980). Dimensions of interpersonal communication: Correspondences between structures for speech acts and bipolar scales. *Journal of Personality and Social Psychology*, *39*, 848–860.

Zhao, X., Liu, J. S., & Deng, K. (2013). Assumptions behind intercoder reliability indices. In C. Salmon (Ed.), *Communication Yearbook 36* (pp. 419–480). New York: Routledge.

Endnote

1. Preparation of this chapter has been supported by CDI Program Grant BCS 0941268 from the National Science Foundation. Any opinions expressed herein are those of the authors and not of the National Science Foundation.

14

MODELING AND ANALYZING BEHAVIORS AND THE DYNAMICS OF BEHAVIORAL INTERACTION

C. ARTHUR VANLEAR

At least one of the reasons why there are not more quantitative studies of behavioral interaction present in our journals is that the analysis and modeling of such interaction data often require the use of statistical methods not frequently taught as a normal part of our graduate course curriculum, or that methods be used in unique ways. The process of reducing behavioral observations of interaction to valid indices is covered in detail in other chapters in this volume (e.g., Sillars & Overall; Poole & Hewes). However, once the observations have been recorded as a set or series of codes or scores, they must be analyzed to answer research questions, test hypotheses, or evaluate the adequacy of a model of behavioral interaction. There are several things that make the analysis and modeling of behavioral data uniquely challenging. First, distributions of behavioral data do not always meet the assumptions of traditional statistical tests. Also, the interaction behaviors of individuals are "nested within" dyads or groups, such that they are neither independently sampled nor statistically independent from the behavioral measures of other members of their dyad or group. Finally, the codes or scores representing qualities or values of interaction behaviors are situated or sequenced in time, and this temporal location is often essential to the "meaning," function, or importance of the data. As such, behavioral interaction data are typically organized and conceptualized as a "time series" and, therefore, require special treatment in data analyses. This chapter summarizes some variable analytic approaches to analyzing and modeling behavioral interaction data.

Whereas some behavioral observations may naturally be represented by continuous scores (e.g., volume of speech), most behavioral observations are initially recorded as a series of nominal (e.g., smiles, doesn't smile) or sometimes ordinal (e.g., level of self-disclosure: public, semiprivate, private-personal; levels of supportive verbal behaviors) codes (Burgoon, Dunbar, & Elkins, this volume; Sillars & Overall, this volume).

The nature of the "temporal unit of analysis" is also an important consideration in organizing and analyzing the data. Initially this is established at the time of coding and measurement, but it is sometimes modified for analysis purposes. Data can be coded and recorded in either "clock time" or "event time" (VanLear & Watt, 1996). Clock time establishes a temporal window in which behaviors are coded. For example, a person could be coded as either smiling or not smiling every half second. One could then record the frequency of smiles in every 2-second window such that a person's score would range from 0 to 4 for every window, thus converting a nominal measure into a ratio measure (see the example discussed later in this chapter).

Often, however, researchers code data in event time (e.g., words, "thought units," illocutionary acts, turns at talk), and time is therefore ordinal, and the data remain represented as a sequential series of nominal or ordinal discrete codes. Given that the data codes are discrete and that one cannot assume that there are equal intervals between codes, we must often use different statistical techniques to analyze and model the data.

Statistical Analysis of Behavioral Data as a Distribution of Behaviors

Although researchers can most profitably analyze interaction behavior as a temporal sequence or time series, researchers also often analyze the overall frequency or proportion of behaviors for each person, dyad, or group. The summaries can take the form of frequencies of categories (overall or per unit of time), the proportions or percentages of categories, "type-token" ratios (e.g., frequency of smiles/frequency of frowns; frequency of third-person pronouns/total number of pronouns), or the median code of an ordinal category system.

Frequencies and Proportions

Researchers often use frequencies as a ratio measure of the strength or pervasiveness of a particular type of behavior. One obvious problem with the use of frequencies is that the overall number of coded units might vary considerably across different people, dyads, groups, or conversations. This is likely if "turn at talk," "acts," or "thought units" are the coded units of analysis. One way to solve this problem is by using frequencies per unit of time or converting frequencies to proportions. If the number of units is not standardized across people, dyads, or groups, then the sheer loquacity or amount of behavior of the people involved may produce a potential confound when analyzing the frequencies of specific categories of behaviors. For example, dyads that are more engaged in the topic of interaction may generate more codable behaviors. In short, some control for variations in the number of total coded behaviors is desirable if we are to use frequency of acts as a measure of the strength or pervasiveness of a given behavior for an individual, dyad, or group. The simplest solution is to convert frequencies into percentages or proportions of the total number of coded units.

If the category system is mutually exclusive and exhaustive, then there is a built-in dependency between the frequencies or proportions of the categories such that the more of one category, the fewer that are in others, and researchers should consider this when analyzing the data. This dependency is lessened if the designer of the system achieves exhaustiveness through the use of a large "residual" category that researchers ignore during analysis. Otherwise, the analyst must remember that the results of the analyses of a given category are redundant to the analyses of the other categories when taken together.

The next problem is that neither frequencies nor proportions typically distribute normally, and this violates the assumptions of most standard statistical techniques such as analysis of variance (ANOVA) and regression. This is particularly true for categories with very low frequencies or small proportions. Of course, some statistical techniques (e.g., logistic regression, log-linear analysis) handle these kinds of data automatically through their design or by presuming different sampling distributions, but when researchers use frequencies or proportions of behaviors per person, dyad, or group as variables in traditional analytical procedures, they must transform the data to make the analysis appropriate. One way researchers deal with this is to apply logarithmic transformations (either the natural log or base 10) to frequencies, except for the frequencies of relatively rare behaviors, for which they may use a square-root transformation. When the behavior is dichotomous, the researcher uses the "logit," or logarithm of the odds ($\ln[p/1 - p]$) (Pampel, 2000) or a Bernoulli distribution.

When researchers use proportions, they often transform the data using an arcsine transformation.[1] Typically, the least frequent behavioral categories are the most skewed, and the arcsine transformation is useful for these proportions. However, many scholars have argued that the use of logistic regression is superior to the use of arcsine transformation (Wilson et al., 2013) and this is now the preferred approach. Therefore, if researchers use some statistical techniques, such as logistic regression, they do not need to manually transform their data.

Sequential Analysis of Nominal-Level Data Using Event Time

Pierce (1976) defined interpersonal communication as "the sequencing of messages into conversations and the sequencing of conversations into relationships" (p. 17). One paradigm for analysis of behavioral interaction data involves coding each person's turn or act into a nominal category such that the data from the conversation are a sequence of nominal codes by separate speakers or communicators. Fisher and Hawes (1971) identified the "interact"—two contiguous sequential acts by separate communicators—as the fundamental unit of interpersonal communication. To keep things simple, we first assume only a dyad with each member's turn at talk or act being the coding unit, coded into a nominal-level category system. For example, if Speaker A's behavior during his turn at talk can be coded as a "one-up" behavior (↑) on a system designed to tap relational control (see Rogers & Cummings, this volume), and Speaker B's immediate response can be coded as a "one-up" behavior (↑) on the same category system, then the action-response "interact" is an example of "competitive symmetry" (↑↑), which theorists often consider as a representation of the relationship at that moment in time. However, if the category system classifies B's response to A's ↑ act as a "one-down" (↓) because it is deferring or submissive, then the exchange is an example of a "complementary interact" (↑↓) and represents a very different picture of the relationship at that moment in time. Of course, B's response is followed by a response by A, coded on the same category system, and the whole three-act sequence identifies a "double interact" (Fisher & Hawes, 1971), and so on. Systems theorists consider such a double interact a "feedback loop," as the third act is an adjustment to the response (second act) to the initial act in the series. Of course, each subsequent act simultaneously initiates a new sequence, is a response to the prior act, and so on. Even a short conversation is a sequence of actions by various participants in which the actions of each participant have some, at least minimal, connection to the actions of those preceding him or her.

One way we can represent the "strength" of an interact is by its conditional probability, (i.e., "transition probability"). Given that Speaker A's antecedent act is coded as, say, ↑, the probability that Speaker B's subsequent response is a ↑ behavior as well is the transition probability. On the other hand, given A's initial ↑ behavior, the probability that B's response is a ↓ behavior could represent the strength of the complementary interact.[2] If researchers use these "transition probabilities" individually as the values of various interacts, given that they are proportions, they can transform them in the same way that the proportions of individual frequencies are. The problem with this approach, by itself, is that the more frequent a behavioral type is overall, the more likely it is that it will be the next act in the sequence, regardless of whether its occurrence, as a response, is contingent upon the type of behavior that preceded it. The idea of the Interact Systems Model (ISM) is that the nature of A's behavior calls forth a particular type of response from B, such that the nature of the subsequent response is contingent upon the nature of the act that elicited it (Fisher & Hawes, 1971). Or, in terms of information theory, knowledge of A's behavior

at Time $t-1$ reduces our uncertainty about the nature of B's behavior at Time t.

By definition, a fundamental characteristic of interpersonal communication is "mutual influence" or "mutual adaptation" (Cappella, 1980, 1996): A influences B, and B influences A. If this is the case, then the nature of A's behavior, as identified by the category system, will have some relationship to B's responses. Likewise, if the interaction involves true *mutual* adaptation, then the nature of B's behavior will have some relationship to A's subsequent response.

We can characterize most studies of interaction behavior and patterns as one of two kinds of models: The ISM (Fisher & Hawes, 1971) or the Human Systems Model (HSM) (Hewes, 1979). The ISM holds that in emergent systems, relational properties characterize social/relational systems. These properties are patterns of mutual adaptation that emerge or evolve through interaction; are not predictable from the initial characteristics, dispositions, or roles of the individuals involved; but are identified by the patterns of interaction (interacts, double interacts, etc.) that manifest over the course of interaction (Fisher & Hawes, 1971). As such, the behaviors (actions and reactions), not people, are the components of the social/relational system, because behavior is the only thing people have to contribute to the system and create a connection with others. The HSM, however, holds that people are the components of the system and that their roles and individual differences are an important part of what creates the patterns of interaction (interacts, double interacts, etc.), as well as other variables within the system.

Researchers operating from an HSM perspective are far more likely to measure nonbehavioral variables such as self-reports or perceptions of relational partners and are more concerned with the frequencies or proportions of individual behaviors, as discussed in the prior section, than are ISM researchers. Finally, though they may identify patterns of behaviors such as types of interacts and double interacts, they also keep track of who is performing both the antecedent and the consequent behaviors in the interaction sequence: A's response to B is part of a different pattern than B's response to A. Given these differences, the analysis of interaction tends to be more complex when operating from an HSM perspective. Both ISM and HSM researchers have used many of the following techniques. Lag sequential analysis and Markov-chain analysis are two methods analysts traditionally use to model interaction sequences composed of nominal categories sequenced in event time.

Revised Lag Sequential Analysis

Sackett (1979) developed lag sequential analysis and John Gottman (e.g., Gottman & Bakeman, 1997; Gottman, Markman, & Notarius, 1977) and others (e.g., Dindia, 1982, 1986) extensively applied it for examining the sequential structure of interpersonal interactions. However, other scholars have criticized the original paradigm and statistics and proposed alternative, more appropriate methods of lag sequential analysis (Allison & Liker, 1982; Kellerman, 1988; Morley, 1987). I touch only briefly on the original methods but focus on the newer variations. Generally, lag sequential analysis assumes that behaviors are coded into a dichotomous category system (e.g., 1 or 0 for self-discloses or doesn't self-disclose or smiles vs. doesn't smile).

Sackett (1979) proposed a binomial z statistic designed to indicate the extent to which a particular kind of behavior by Person X at Time $t - 1$ (X_{t-1}) predicts a particular kind of behavior in response by Person Y at Time t (Y_t); the resultant z ($Z_{Yt|Xt-1}$) is the lag 1 effect. More generally, one can also calculate the effect of X's behavior at any Time $t - k$ on Y's behavior at any lag k as $Z_{Yt|Xt-k}$, where the data are sequential behaviors in an interaction between Person X and Person Y with n time points.

Several scholars have criticized the original lag sequential paradigm. First, Allison and Liker (1982) pointed out that Sackett's use of a binomial z was the incorrect statistic, because it assumes that the probabilities are the true probabilities in the population. Of course, in virtually all applications, the probabilities are empirically derived estimates, and therefore the standard error is estimated differently. Allison and Liker provided the correct statistic as[3]:

$$Z_{Y|X} = P_{Y|X} - P_Y \sqrt{([P_Y(1 - P_Y)}$$
$$(1 - P_X)] / [(n - k)P_X]). \quad (1)$$

where P_{Yx} is the proportion for the conditional probability for Person Y engaging in a particular type of behavior (coded 1), given that Person X engaged in the behavior (coded 1) k lags earlier. P_Y is the proportion of times that Y's behavior is coded 1, and P_X is the proportion of times that X's behavior is coded 1, while n is the total number of acts or behaviors in the sequence. The value of Z is positive if X's behavior (coded 1) makes Y more likely to respond with a behavior coded 1. This statistic is always larger than Sackett's z. Its absolute value is equivalent to the square root of the Pearson chi-square for the test of independence between X_{t-k} and Y_t:

$$Z_{YiX} = \sqrt{\chi^2_{YiX.}} \quad (2)$$

The problems with the original approach to lag sequential analysis do not end with the substitution of the correct z statistic. Gottman et al. (1977) used z as a score representing the strength of the sequential dependency of one person's behavior on another. This is problematic in that either z is highly dependent upon the number of acts in the sequence (n). Different dyads may generate different numbers of codable behaviors in the same time period if events are being coded. Likewise, given that the acts are not independently sampled, to treat Z as inferential is problematic. Allison and Liker (1982) suggested a logit-linear approach. They proposed the following effect size measure:

$$\beta = \text{logit}[\Pr(Y_t = 1|X_{t-k} = 1)]$$
$$- \text{logit}[\Pr(Y_t = 1|X_{t-k} = 0)]. \quad (3)$$

They also proposed a test of difference in the degree of sequential dependency between two groups:

$$Z_{AL2} = (\beta_1 - \beta_2)/[\sqrt{(\Sigma 1/f_i)}]. \quad (4)$$

Morley (1987) suggested that Allison and Liker's Z can be transformed into a Φ coefficient, which is equivalent to Pearson's r:

$$r_\Phi = \sqrt{[(Z_{AL})^2/(N - 1)]} = \sqrt{[\chi^2/(N - 1)]}. \quad (5)$$

A positive Z value means that the antecedent behavior calls forth the subsequent behavior at lag k more often than if the response was independent from the prior behavior. A negative sign suggests that the antecedent behavior suppresses the likelihood of that particular response. The researcher can transform the r_Φ using Fisher's Z_F to make the data more closely approximate a normal distribution. In Morley's approach, the analyst calculates a set of Z_F scores for each dyad and then in essence conducts a meta-analysis treating each dyad or group as a study or uses the Z_F scores as values in conventional statistical analyses as causal or criterion variables (for examples, see VanLear, 1987; VanLear, Sheehan, Withers, & Walker, 2005; VanLear & Zietlow, 1990).

In practice, Gottman did not take into account the autocorrelation of the behaviors of dyadic participants, and this is also one of the criticisms Allison and Liker (1982) and Morley (1987) leveled against him. There are a couple of ways one can control for autocorrelation in a revised form of lag sequential analysis. Allison and Liker extended their logit-linear model to account for the effects of

Y_{t-k} when considering the effect of X_t on Y_{t+1}. As Morley pointed out, Allison and Liker's approach to autocorrelation is similar in practice to a Markov-chain approach (see the next section). Morley suggested that the autodependency of X's behavior can easily be calculated in the same way as cross-dependency with $Z_{Xt|Xt-k}$. Once analysts convert the Z to a Φ (correlation coefficient), they can partial out the effects of autocorrelation of Person Y's own behavior at various lags from the lagged effect of Person X's effect on Person Y's behavior by the use of a partial correlation (partial Φ) (Morley, 1987). Researchers can use the same logic to control for the effects of intervening behaviors by either party at higher-order lags. For example, we can represent the partial Φ for the effect of X_{t-2} on X_t while controlling for the effect of X_{t-1} as $\Phi_{2(0.1)}$, where $\Phi_{2(0)}$ is the Φ for X_{t-2} predicting X_t (the lag 2 effect) and $\Phi_{2(1)}$ is the relationship between X_{t-1} and X_t.

Gottman et al. (1977) used the original lag sequential analysis to compare distressed and non-distressed married couples. He argued that these results show longer, more pronounced sequences of negative/negative reciprocity of affect in the conflict communication of distressed couples. In addition, Gottman often did not do formal tests of difference between groups, and this may have resulted in erroneous conclusions (Allison & Liker, 1982; Morley, 1987). Several scholars have applied the revised lag sequential analyses proposed by Morley. Dindia (1986) examined the issue of antecedents and consequences of silence. Escudero, Rogers, & Gutierrez (1997) used these procedures to examine patterns of relational control and nonverbal affect in clinical and nonclinical marital couples. VanLear et al. (2005) examined the differences in interaction patterns in different types of online support groups.

Revised lag sequential techniques have several limitations. One of the most obvious is that they are best suited for dealing with dichotomous category systems. Researchers often perform lag sequential analyses on behavioral sequences coded into systems with more than two codes (e.g., a, b, and c), when they treat each behavior and response as "a" or "~a," "b or ~b," "c or ~c," and so on. However, when the categories are mutually exclusive and exhaustive, such tests are not independent of each other. Markov chain and log-linear analyses can handle data coded into multiple categories. Some scholars (Fisher & Drecksel, 1983; Kellerman, 1988; VanLear, 1987; VanLear et al., 2005) combined Markov chain statistics with lag sequential Z scores to analyze sequences of nondichotomously coded behaviors. Here the logic is

similar to traditional approaches to multiple regression or ANOVA, in which if the results of global tests of effects are significant, specific effects are tested to reveal what is responsible for the general effect. Researchers use Markov (or log-linear) tests to establish the general structural characteristics of the data set, and then they use the lag sequential Z scores and r_Φ coefficients to create a picture of the specific interaction patterns within the constraints of the general model.

An Example of Sequential
Dyadic Interaction Analysis[4]

We created the data in this example to simulate dyadic interaction coded as dichotomous categories in which there is reciprocity at varying degrees at the first-order. Ten simulated conversations generated sequential codes of 50 "turns at talk," such that each successive code alternates between speakers. We began by having the sequences representing varying levels of reciprocity from high to moderate (0,0 and 1,1 interacts) and then added a systematically increasing number of random codes to the sequence to simulate systematic decreasing reciprocity (10%, 20%, 30%, 40%, 50%, 60%, and 70% error). This was repeated 10 times. We therefore have 70 sequences of 50 "turns" with 10 sequences for each level of reciprocity.

Table 14.1 presents the SPSS cross-tabulation results for lag 1 and 2 at the level of reciprocity (20% random error) for one of the hypothetical dyads using an ISM approach (i.e., speakers not distinguished). The standardized residual is equivalent to Sackett's (1979) Z_S.[5] The adjusted residual (3.4) is equivalent to Allison and Liker's Z_{AL}. Applying Equation 5, the Φ coefficient is .49 ($r_\Phi = \sqrt{3.4^2/N - 1}$) and in these results is positive for reciprocal interacts and negative for compensatory interacts as reflected in the signs of the Z scores. Reciprocity is clearly indicated such that if one speaker enacts a 0, that tends to elicit a 0 from the partner, and 1's elicit 1's. The lag 2 effect indicates that if a speaker enacts a 0, after his or her partner's response, that speaker tends to enact another 0 in his or her next turn. Whereas this could be considered autocorrelation (pooled across both speakers), it does not take into account the effect of the partner's intervening response. A partial phi ($\Phi_{2[0.1]}$) would be $\Phi_{2(0.1)}$ = $(.296 - .49^2)/\sqrt{1 - 49^2} \times \sqrt{1 - 49^2} = .056/.5774 = .097$, which is not much of an effect. This indicates that the tendency for a speaker to continue to enact the same behavior as in his or her prior turn can be explained by the speaker's tendency to reciprocate his or her partner's immediate past behavior, which was likely a reciprocation of the speaker's own original action.

Table 14.1 Example ISM Lag 1 and Lag 2 Results for One Dyad 20% Random, Revised Lag Sequential Analysis

		SPSS Crosstab		
a. ISM Model Without Speaker Identification, Lag 1		*ACTLag0*	*Total*	
ACTLag-1		0	1	
0	Count	7	4	11
	% within ACL010	63.6%	36.4%	100.0%
	Residual	4.3	−4.3	
	Std. residual[a]	2.6	−1.5	
	Adjusted residual[b]	3.4	−3.4	
1	Count	5	33	38
	% within ACL010	13.2%	86.8%	100.0%
	Residual	−4.3	4.3	
	Std. residual[a]	−1.4	.8	
	Adjusted residual[b]	−3.4	3.4	
	Count	12	37	49
	% within ACL0	24.5%	75.5%	100.0%
χ^2 first-order	11.754**	$df = 1$	$r_\phi = .49**$	

b. ISM Model Without Speaker Identification, Lag 2		*ACTLag0*	*Total*	
ACTLag-2		0	1	
0	Count	5	5	10
	% within ACL010	50.0%	50.0%	100.0%
	Residual	2.5	−2.5	
	Std. residual[a]	1.6	−.9	
	Adjusted residual[b]	2.1	−2.1	
1	Count	7	31	38
	% within ACL010	18.4%	81.6%	100.0%
	Residual	−2.5	2.5	
	Std. residual[a]	−.8	.5	
	Adjusted residual[b]	−2.1	2.1	
	Count	12	36	48
	% within ACL0	25.0%	75.0%	100.0%
χ^2 second-order	4.211*	$df = 1$	$r_\phi = .296*$	

Note: ISM = Interact Systems Model.

[a]Standardized residual = Sackett *Z*.

[b]Adjusted residual = Allison and Liker *Z*.

*$p < .05$. **$p < .01$.

Table 14.2 presents the cross-tabulation results for the same data for lag 1 reciprocity broken down by speaker or communicator position (the HSM approach). The results indicate that both Speaker A and Speaker B tend to reciprocate each other's behavior, though there may be a nonsignificantly greater tendency for A to reciprocate B's behavior than for B to reciprocate A's behavior.

Table 14.2 Example HSM Lag 1 Results One Dyad 20% Random, Revised Lag Sequential Analysis

		SPSS Crosstab		
a. Speaker A Antecedent, B Subsequent		*ACTLag0*	*Speaker B*	*Total*
Speaker A Lag 1		0	1	
0	Count	3	1	4
	% w/in ACT20L0	75.0%	25.0%	100.0%
	Residual	1.8	−1.8	
	Std. residual[a]	1.7	−1.1	
	Adjusted residual[b]	2.2	−2.2	
1	Count	4	16	20
	% w/in ACT20L0	20.0%	80.0%	100.0%
	Residual	−1.8	1.8	
	Std. residual[a]	−.8	.5	
	Adjusted residual[b]	−2.2	2.2	
	Count	7	17	24
	% w/in ACT20L-1	29.2%	70.8%	100.0%
χ^2 independence	4.881	*df* = 1	r_Φ = .451	*p* = .027

b. Speaker B Antecedent, A Subsequent		*ActLag+0*		*Total*
Speaker B Lag 1		0	1	
0	Count	4	3	7
	% within ACT20L0	57.1%	42.9%	100.0%
	Residual	2.6	−2.6	
	Std. residual[a]	2.2	−1.1	
	Adjusted residual[b]	2.9	−2.9	
1	Count	1	17	18
	% within ACT20L0	5.6%	94.4%	100.0%
	Residual	−2.6	2.6	
	Std. residual[a]	−1.4	.7	
	Adjusted residual[b]	−2.9	2.9	
	Count	5	20	25
	% w/in ACT20L-1	20.0%	80.0%	100.0%
χ^2 independence	8.383	*df* = 1	r_Φ = .579	*p* = .0004

Note: HSM = Human Systems Model

[a]Standardized residual = Sackett *Z*.

[b]Adjusted residual = Allison and Liker *Z*.

Figure 14.1 graphs the average Allison and Liker and Sackett *Z* scores for lag 1 (reciprocity), lag 2, maintenance of a speaker's original behavior, and lag 3, continued reciprocity of the original act, at the seven levels of reciprocity/error for the whole data set.

The average Φ for lag 1 at 10% error was r_Φ = .565, and the average lag 2 Φ for 10% error was r_Φ = .269. The average Φ for lag 1 at 20% error was r_Φ = .518, and the average lag 1 Φ for 70% error was r_Φ = .171. Figure 14.2 graphs the Φ coefficients at lags 1, 2, and 3 as well as the partial Φ

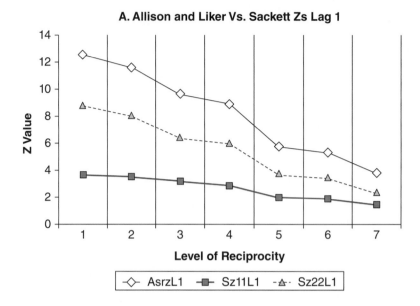

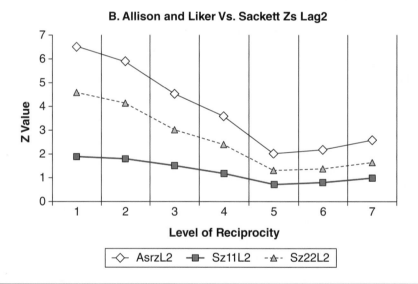

Figure 14.1 Comparison of Allison and Liker Z scores with Sackett Z scores at lags 1 and 2 for various degrees of reciprocity.

Source: Author.

coefficients for lag 2 controlling for lag 1 and for lag 3 controlling for lags 1 and 2. The correlation between the simulated reciprocity rate and the lag 1 Φ coefficients is .685, and it is .442 for the lag 2 Φ coefficients, but only .180 for lag 3, indicating that the simulation was successful and detected by the analysis. Figure 14.1 shows not only that Allison and Liker's Z is consistently higher than Sackett's Z but that the difference is more pronounced the greater the sequential connection between the antecedent and consequent actions. Figure 14.2 indicates that even though the Φ coefficients for lag 1 are substantial for the higher levels of reciprocity (up to 60% error) and the lag 2 effect persists up to at least 40% error, when we control for the effects of intervening lags through the partial Φ coefficient, we see that only the immediate preceding behavior has much effect. The higher-order lag effects are only indirect because of the transmission of the effects of earlier acts through the immediately preceding act. This is not an unusual result in real data. However, when researchers report only the bivariate lags at higher-orders, it may appear that behaviors continue to have a direct effect for a long period of time. Of course, this is not to say that the persistence of the effect of a behavior through indirect effects is not important. If these were real data, the aggregate effects would need to be interpreted with care given that a meta-analysis of the effects at higher levels of reciprocity (lower levels of error) are somewhat heterogeneous, reflecting the fact that the simulated data were constructed to represent varying degrees of reciprocity from the start (e.g., meta-analysis of homogeneity within the 20% error dyads $\chi^2 = 20.96$, $df = 9$, $p < .01$). If we build in a moderator variable by dividing the data for the 20% error groups into two subgroups to represent, say, friends (average $r_\Phi = .36$) versus acquaintances (average $r_\Phi = .59$) and use meta-analysis to test for homogeneity within the subgroups, we find that each subgroup is homogeneous within itself (friends, $\chi^2 = 9.00$, $df = 4$, $p = .06$; acquaintances, $\chi^2 = 1.74$, $df = 4$, $p = .78$), but there is a significant difference between the two subgroups ($z = 3.37$, $p < .001$). However, a test of homogeneity for the data with 50% error ($\chi^2 = 6.93$, $df = 9$, $p > .05$), 60% ($\chi^2 = 13.35$, $df = 9$, $p > .05$), 60% ($\chi^2 = 13.35$, $df = 9$, $p > .05$), and 70% ($\chi^2 = 3.68$, $df = 9$, $p = .05$) random codes failed to reject homogeneity. It is not surprising

that as more randomness is built in, homogeneity increases as everything gets closer to random.

Markov Chain Analysis

Markov chain analysis was introduced into communication by Hewes (1975) and extensively applied to the analysis of behavioral interaction by the late B. Aubrey Fisher (Ellis & Fisher, 1975; Fisher & Drecksel 1983) and others (Cappella, 1980). Markov chain models are finite stochastic models that analyze processes consisting of transitions of a system from one state (e.g., type of behavior) with a probability of occurrence to another state (type of behavior) over time. In a simple Markov model, we let ^{t+0}V stand for a vector of the initial distribution of state probabilities (probabilities of different types of behavior). Given that the categories of behavior are mutually exclusive and exhaustive, the elements sum to 1.0 ($\Sigma p_i = 1.0$). We then identify M, the transition matrix, which is composed of the "transition probabilities" (p_{ij}), or the probability of being in state j (observing behavior j) at Time $t + 1$, given that the state of the system at Time t was i. Therefore,

$$^{t+1}V = {}^{t+0}V(M), \tag{6}$$

provided that three testable conditions hold: a first-order process, stationarity of transition probabilities

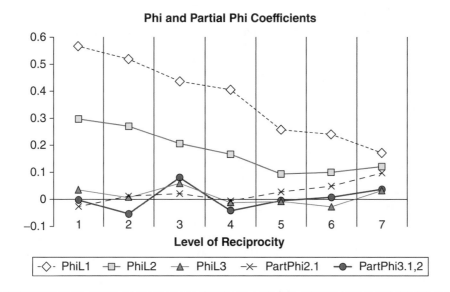

Phi and Partial Phi Coefficients

Level of Reciprocity

-◇- PhiL1   -□- PhiL2   -▲- PhiL3   -✕- PartPhi2.1   -●- PartPhi3.1,2

Figure 14.2 Phi coefficients at lag 1, 2, and 3 with partial Φ coefficients.

Source: Author.

over time, and homogeneity of transition probabilities across cases.

The first assumption is that the interaction process is structured at the first-order: that the state of the system at Time $t + 1$ is contingent upon the state of the system at Time t, but the state of the system at Time $t + 2$ is contingent upon the state of the system only at $t + 1$, but not at Time t, and so on. The usual test of this assumption is the maximum likelihood χ^2, though some have used the familiar Pearson χ^2 test of independence to test a first-order process against sequential independence. Tests of higher-order processes have been devised (Anderson & Goodman, 1957) or can be carried out using log-linear modeling (Bishop, Fienberg, & Holland, 2007).

The second condition of the simple Markov chain is that the elements of M (the transition probabilities) be constant across time. In practice, a researcher may test the transition matrix in the first half of a conversation against the transition matrix in the second half (or thirds, etc.), or one conversation compared with a later interaction. A maximum likelihood χ^2 test of this assumption is given by Anderson and Goodman (1957), but it too can be tested using log-linear modeling.

The third condition is that the transition probabilities that constitute M are homogeneous across cases (e.g., different dyads or groups in a sample). Different dyads or groups exhibit the same contingencies or sequential structure. The original test was provided by Kullback, Kupperman, & Ku (1962), but again this assumption can be tested using log-linear modeling, though the logic of the tests is different and the log-linear models are slightly less sensitive to variations in interaction structure across dyads, but they can differentiate between a second-order lagged effect and a second-order Markov process, as well as heterogeneity in the distribution of act types (VanLear, 1988). Programs that apply the original Markov tests are not as readily available as are log-linear modeling programs, so I focus on those for testing Markov assumptions. Including a code for person, or dyad, in the log-linear model allows one to separate within-group (or within-person) variation from between-group (or between-person) variations.

If L0 and L1 represent the antecedent and subsequent act, L2 represents the third act in the sequence, and Dy represents the dyad identification, then in log-linear notation a [L0*L1, L1*L2, Dy] model is a first-order homogeneous model with first-order interactions (relationship) between adjacent acts. A [L0*L1, L1*L2, L1*Dy, L2*Dy] model allows differences in the distributions of acts across dyads, but the interaction structure does not vary across

dyads. A [L0*L1, L1*L2, L0*L2, Dy] model represents a lag 1 and lag 2 model, and a [L0*L1*L2, Dy] model represents a second-order Markov model, or a double-interact structure, in which knowledge of the joint occurrences of L0 and L1 (the L0*L1 interact) is necessary to predict the third act (L2) in the sequence. If speaker codes are included (i.e., an HSM analysis) and a speaker cannot follow himself or herself, and is present in only one dyad or group, then the nested nature of such data creates cells that are logically null, and these must be replaced with "structural zeros" before analysis. This can become very complex, especially if the researcher tries to test too many assumptions simultaneously. To maintain simplicity, when looking for variation in interaction patterns across speakers, researchers might still want to test for homogeneity across speakers on a dyad-by-dyad or group-by-group basis. For simplicity, our example analyses will use an ISM approach without designation of speaker within dyads given that no systematic variation was built into the simulated data.

If we apply a log-linear model representing a first-order Markov process to our simulated data, it reveals a similar picture of the level of sequential structure, as do the revised lag sequential procedures using Morley's approach. That is, the data are structured as a first-order sequential process, with the effects on later lags being accounted for by the immediately preceding act. However, the log-linear models did not detect significant heterogeneity in the interaction structure across dyads within the same reciprocity group as the meta-analysis did. Table 14.3 gives the results of the simultaneous tests for order of sequential structure and homogeneity for the 10 dyads with 20% random codes and the 10 dyads with added 70% error. Both tests show significant improvement in model fit from the model of independence (Tables 14.3a and 14.3c, respectively) to the model representing a first-order lag/Markov process (Models 3b and 3d, respectively [20% random: $\Delta\chi^2 = 242.708$, $df = 2$, $p < .001$; 70% random: $\Delta\chi^2 = 24.994$, $df = 3$, $p < .005$]) showing significant sequential structure. The model for the first-order process for the 20% error group (Table 14.3b) is clearly nonsignificant, indicating that there is no significant difference between the expected values on the basis of the model and the observed values in the data, which in turn means that there is no two-way interaction between the dyad variable and either the frequency of coded acts or a three-way interaction between dyad * antecedent * subsequent act, [Dy*L0*L1], necessary to explain the data. In other words, the interaction structure (as well as the frequency of act types) is homogeneous across dyads with 20% random codes. However, the model in Table 14.3d shows a significant difference between the expected values on the basis of the model and the observed values in the data. The model in Table 14.3e shows that it is the heterogeneity of act types across dyads that is necessary to explain the data, but not differences in the structure of interaction patterns across dyads, which differs somewhat from the meta-analyses of lag 1 effects in the prior section.

If all three Markov assumptions are met, then Equation 6 can be generalized to

$$^{t+n}V = {}^tV(M^n). \tag{7}$$

We can predict the probabilities of being in any state at any time if we have knowledge of the initial state probabilities, M, and the assumptions are met. Raush (1972) detailed several types of interaction sequences that fit these assumptions. In a "regular chain," it is possible to go from one state to every other state given sufficient time. In a "cyclical chain," partners cycle among a set of states at periodic intervals. In an "absorbing chain," the system moves inexorably toward a given state or set of states.

In practice, real data will usually violate at least one of the three assumptions. Such "violations" of these assumptions merely point to the need for more complex models. For example, a second-order Markov model would indicate that knowledge of the joint probabilities at Time t and Time $t + 1$ increases our ability to predict behavior at Time $t + 2$. In ISM terms, the data would be structured at the level of the double interact such that knowledge of the nature of the type of interact would help predict the third act in the sequence. In HSM terms, knowledge of both Person A's initial behavior and B's response to A are necessary to reduce uncertainty about A's response to B's response. Once the appropriate level of structure is established through Markov or log-linear analyses, the revised lag sequential analyses are sometimes used to examine the specifics of which types of behaviors tend to chain together. If log-linear models are used to test the assumptions, then the λ values could also be used to identify specific patterns of interaction. Though the original application of lag sequential analysis often produced long sequences of lagged dependencies at higher-ordered lags, when the effects of intervening lags are partialed out using either Morley's procedures or Markov tests of order, interaction data are rarely structured beyond a second-order process.

Ellis and Fisher (1975) used evidence that transition probabilities changed over time to argue for

Table 14.3 Log-Linear Test for Order and Homogeneity

A. 20%; [Dy+L0+L1+L2]	Value	df	Sig	$\Delta\chi^2$	Δdf	Sig
Likelihood ratio	311.967	67	.00			
Pearson χ^2	451.047	67	.00			
B. 20%; [Dy+L0*L1+L1*L2]	Value	df	Sig	$A \rightarrow B$		
Likelihood ratio	69.259	65	.34	242.708	2	$p < .001$
Pearson χ^2	60.993	65	.62			
C. 70%; [Dy+L0+L1+L2]	Value	df	Sig			
Likelihood ratio	115.299	67	.00			
Pearson χ^2	138.056	67	.00			
D. 70%; [Dy+L0*L1+L1*L2]	Value	df	Sig	$C \rightarrow D$		
Likelihood ratio	90.305	65	.02	24.994	2	$p < .005$
Pearson χ^2	87.625	65	0.03			
E. 70%; [Dy*L0+Dy*L1+Dy*L2+L0*L1+L1*L2]	Value	df	Sig	$D \rightarrow E$		
Likelihood ratio	35.409	38	.59	54.896	27	$p < .005$
Pearson χ^2	32.464	38	.72			

phases of conflict in group decision making such that different phases of group process are characterized by different types of interaction processes. In other cases, variations in interaction patterns over time displayed an apparent cyclical process or rises and falls in symmetry and reciprocity (Fisher & Drecksel, 1983; VanLear, 1987).

When homogeneity is rejected, it indicates that interaction patterns vary across dyads or groups. When this occurs, the question becomes what makes these patterns of interaction different and/or what are the consequences of these differences in interaction patterns. For example, VanLear et al. (2005) found that different types of online groups generated different types of interaction patterns. VanLear and Zietlow (1990) found an interaction effect between type of marriage and interaction patterns of relational control in predicting marital satisfaction. It is also possible to test the homogeneity of the transitions from Speaker A's behavior to Speaker B's behavior against the transitions from Speaker B's behavior to Speaker A's behavior. VanLear (1985) applied such a homogeneity test to the relational control interaction patterns of acquaintances and found no differences across partners, indicating that neither partner dominated the other despite the pervasive complementary interaction patterns ($\uparrow\downarrow$; $\uparrow\downarrow$; see Rogers & Cummings, this volume).

The use of revised lag sequential analysis implies stationarity of lagged effects over time and homogeneity of the lagged effects across similar dyads or groups. As previously noted, these Markov tests are sometimes used in conjunction with lag sequential z scores. Both lag sequential and Markov methods also assume that each category of behavior is sufficiently frequent to yield reliable estimates of sequential structure. Some categories of behavior (e.g., extreme negative behaviors, extreme domineering behaviors, or highly private and personal disclosures) may not generate enough instances of the behavior to allow a reliable estimate of sequential structure in certain types of interactions. The rule of thumb we typically use is that the expected value of a given pattern's frequency must be at least five to warrant a sequential estimate. To allow sequential analysis of such categories of behavior, researchers sometimes combine them with the most similar other categories (e.g., extreme negative behaviors combined with all negative behaviors, extreme domineering behaviors combined with all domineering behaviors). However, the fact that these behaviors are rare may mean that their mere occurrence has important implications for the interaction. Therefore, such rare codes may need to be identified at least for the nonsequential analyses.

Both lag sequential and Markov analyses assume nominal level data and event time. Hewes (1979; Hewes, Planalp, & Streibel, 1980) suggested a "semi-Markov" model that allows researchers to build in the duration and latency of the behavioral codes in "clock time."

Modeling Continuous Behavioral Data in Clock Time

The methods for sequential analysis reviewed to this point assume that the behavioral data are coded into nominal categories, and time is typically treated as "event time," though these methods can also be used to analyze categorical data sequenced in clock time. Sometimes behavioral interaction data are measured on a continuous (interval or ratio) metric in clock time.

To illustrate the techniques that follow, we will use a data set collected by Powers and Rauh (2006) and coded and analyzed using time-series data by Kotz, Renfro (Powers), and Cistulli (2006). The data in this example are from ten 10-minute conversations (configured as 10 dyads).[6] All interactions took place over mediated video conferencing. In 5 of the interactions, a 1-second delay was introduced into the signal, whereas there was no delay in the other 5 interactions, and this is identified as a between-dyad variable in the current analyses. In addition to the person ID, a fake person-level variable was added to permit a three-level analysis in HLM 7 (Raudenbush et al., 2011), given that we did not have an actual person-level variable with sufficient variance and distribution to permit analysis. The videos of each person were coded for smiling on the basis of the Facial Action Coding System (see Hamm et al., this volume). Every half second was coded for smiling (1) or not smiling (0) for each person. The tapes were then segmented into two-second intervals, with the number of half seconds of smiling during that period representing the smiling score, ranging from 0 to 4. We therefore have two contemporaneous time series (one for each person) of about 300 data points for each dyad representing smiling throughout the conversation. The central issue is whether the dyads exhibit reciprocity of smiling and whether that reciprocity or synchrony is moderated by the tape delay.

ARIMA

A classic model used to analyze such conversational behavior is the autoregressive, integrative, moving average (ARIMA) model. ARIMA modeling was first presented by Box and Jenkins (1976) and applied to the analysis of behavioral interaction by Cappella (1996). Summaries of ARIMA in communication can be found in Cappella (1996), Gottman (1981), Yanovitzky and VanLear (2008), and VanLear (in press).

The acronym ARIMA identifies three kinds of serial dependency in a time series. The logic behind ARIMA is to first identify the type of serial dependency in each time series—diagnosis. Next, the serial dependency is removed from the data through a process called "prewhitening," until the series is a "white noise process." Finally, the relationships between two contemporaneous, prewhitened time series can be analyzed.

Univariate ARIMA: diagnosis. Diagnosis involves identifying the form(s) of serial dependency in the data. First, the data are usually graphed against time. This will often reveal trends or cycles within the series. Next, autocorrelation functions (ACFs) (or the correlation of a variable with itself at k lags in time) are calculated. Then the partial Autocorrelation Functions (PACFs) (or the partial correlation of a variable with itself at various lags k, when controlling for the intervening effects of prior lags). These three pieces of information are used to diagnose the most likely type of serial dependency. An *integrated* process ($I_{[i]}$) is a cumulative pattern and represents a trend, either linear or curvilinear, in the series. A first-order process would be a linear trend, a second-order process might look like a quadratic trend, and so on. An autoregressive (AR) process is one in which values of a variable at Time t are regressed upon the values of that variable at Time $t - a$. The order of the $AR_{(a)}$ process is the lag a. An AR process shows an exponentially decreasing pattern of ACFs as the number of lags increase. The PACFs will show spikes, and the number of spikes in PACFs correspond to the order of the AR process.

A moving average ($MA_{[m]}$) process predicts values of the variable from the weighted average of past errors of prediction in the series X (error that cannot be predicted by the AR process). This occurs when the effects of random shocks on the values of X_{t-m} persist for some number of lags m in the series. For an MA process, the PACFs will show an exponential decrease with each successively higher-order lag, while the ACFs will show significant peaks corresponding to the order of the $MA_{(m)}$ process.

The most appropriate general ARIMA model is represented as $ARIMA_{(a,i,m)}$, where the subscripts a, i, and m correspond to the order of the AR (a), I (i), and MA (m) processes respectively. Whereas combinations of many different order processes of different types may be possible in a series, most series are represented by one or two types of dependency at first or second-order.

Figure 14.3 presents the ACFs and PACFs for the aggregated smiling data for the nondelay conversations. These graphs display a picture that closely resembles an AR1 model, which explains almost 43% of the variation in the data, though a negligible lag 2 effect (−.080) exists in the PACF graph. When each individual series is graphed for ACFs and PACFs, they show that the AR1 process generally explains the serial dependency in each of the 10 conversations (Kotz et al., 2006).

Prewhitening. If the pattern of serial dependency is best described as an integrated process (e.g., a trend), then it can be removed by differencing. A linear trend or a first-order integrative process is represented as $ARIMA_{(0,1,0)}$. It would be removed by first-order differencing, or subtracting the immediate prior value of a series ($t - 1$) from the value at Time t. A quadratic trend, or second-order integrative process ($ARIMA_{[0,2,0]}$) could be removed by also subtracting the value two lags prior ($t - 2$) from the value at Time t, and so on.[7]

If the serial dependency is an AR process, like the example above, it can be removed by regressing the values at Time t on the values at Time $t - k$ and retaining the residuals as the new time series. So an $ARIMA_{(1,0,0)}$ process would be prewhitened by regressing the values of the series on the immediately preceding values using a maximum likelihood regression (Box & Jenkins, 1976) and saving the residual values, which should then be a white noise process.

If the serial dependency is an MA process, it is estimated by a nonlinear likelihood procedure (Box & Jenkins, 1976). The order m represents the number of time lags the effects of random shocks persist in a series.

Once a pattern of serial dependency has been removed from the series, ACFs and PACFs are again run on the residual series to confirm that no significant or substantial serial dependence still exists, and the series is now a white noise process. In practice, diagnosis, removal, and retesting are parts of an iterative process that may go through several possibilities until the best model is identified (the most parsimonious that yields a white noise process). However, overcorrection can increase serial dependency in the series. When there are cyclical or seasonal processes operating over time, researchers could use seasonal ARIMA modeling. However, we favor the

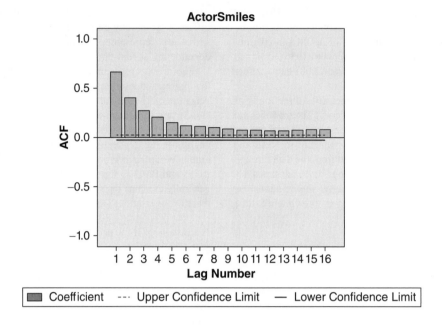

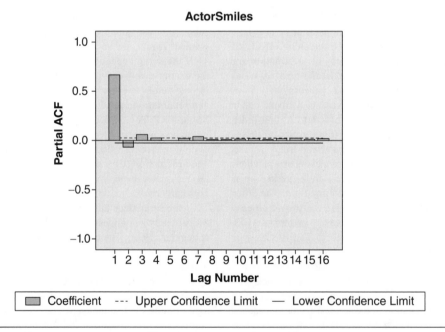

Figure 14.3 Autocorrelation functions (ACFs) and partial ACFs on aggregate smiling data.

Source: Author.

use of frequency domain time series (Gottman, 1981; Watt & VanLear, 1996; Yanovitzky & VanLear, 2008) as a more efficient method when cyclical processes are detected.

Figure 14.4 presents the ACFs and PACFs of the residual series after the AR1 has been removed.

Whereas the lag 1 and 2 effect is slightly above the confidence interval, the size of the effect (.052, −.086 respectively) is small. Likewise, when this pattern (AR1) is extracted from these data of each of the individual conversations, the series generally display white noise processes (Kotz et al., 2006).

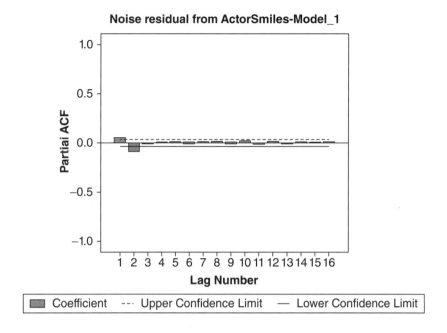

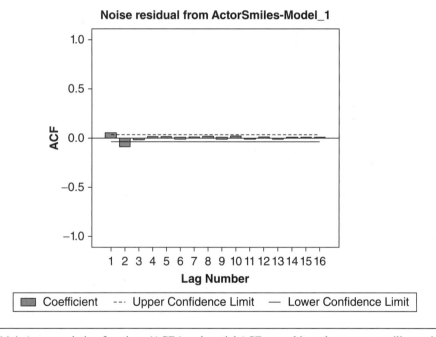

Figure 14.4 Autocorrelation functions (ACFs) and partial ACFs on whitened aggregate smiling series.

Source: Author.

Bivariate ARIMA modeling. In communication research using ARIMA, we typically want to examine the relationship between two contemporaneous time series. In interaction research, the two series are most often the series representing the behaviors of the conversational partners. For example, does Person A's smiling predict Person B's smiling and vice versa; does Person A's vocal volume predict Person B's vocal volume? Of course, a researcher could also look at the relationship between the series representing two different behaviors by the same communicator. For example, does A's smiling predict A's time holding the floor, or heart rate?

In the case in which we look at the relationship between A's and B's behavior over time, the researcher would identify the pattern of serial dependency in each series, remove it, and save the residual series. The two prewhitened series are then submitted to cross-correlation analyses. This technique calculates cross-correlation functions (CCFs) between the two series in which the series of Person A's behavior is correlated with the series of Person B's behavior at various lags. The CCFs can be used to examine whether Person A's behavior at Time t, $t - 1$, $t - 2$, or $t - k$ predicts Person B's behavior at Time t. Likewise, the CCFs can show whether Person B's behavior at Time t, $t - 1$, $t - 2$, or $t - k$ predicts Person A's behavior at Time t. Symmetrical patterns of mutual influence may represent reciprocity, whereas clear asymmetrical patterns may indicate behavioral dominance whereby one person influences the other, but not vice versa.

ARIMA has a set of assumptions that are analogous to the assumptions of Markov chain analysis. It is assumed that the series is stationary (or can be made stationary by transformation) in level, variance (homoscedasticity), and process. As shown earlier, the series can be made stationary in level by differencing or fitting the appropriate trend. If the series is not stationary in variance, it is not homoscedastic, and it often may be made homoscedastic through a log transformation (Gottman, 1981). Finally, the values of the ACFs, PACFs, and CCFs must be stationary across time, meaning that they must be the same across different segments of the conversation or across different conversations of the same dyad.

As with the other analyses, ARIMA is basically an *individual* time-series method, meaning that it is not designed to analyze multiple time series from many different cases (dyads or groups). When applying ARIMA to aggregated data, one is assuming that the pattern of serial dependency and the CCFs are homogeneous across cases. If each dyad or group is independently analyzed and prewhitened, then the CCFs can be tested for homogeneity using meta-analysis. If they are not homogeneous, then the Fisher z transformations of the CCFs can be used as scores for tests of difference between groups or in regression analyses to explain the variations or for the variations to explain interaction outcomes. Such an approach is obviously very time intensive, requiring a whole set of time-series analyses for each case. A possible alternative would

be to randomly select a subsample of dyads, individually analyze each dyad, and test them for homogeneity. If the subsample were homogeneous, then all of the dyads in the larger sample could be aggregated to form a single time series. However, this approach would assume that the series from each dyad had the same starting point and that the dyads are "distinguishable" such that members of the dyad can be separated by role or some variable meaningful to the analysis (e.g., husband/wife, male/female, boss/subordinate, parent/child).

A meta-analysis of CCFs across the example dyads smiling data failed to find clear evidence of lagged effects (average lag 1 $r = .164$). However, the simultaneous CCF (average $r = .30$) is significant and meaningful. A test of the difference between the control (average $r = .37$) and delay (average $r = .21$) condition failed to find a significant difference ($p > .05$).

Some researchers have also used frequency-domain time-series analyses to model behavioral interactions in dyads (Buder, 1996; VanLear, 1991; Warner, 1996) such as Fourier, spectral, and cross-spectral analyses. We view these techniques as particularly appropriate when there is the expectation of seasonal or other cyclical processes present in dyadic interaction. Several sources are available for an introduction to these methods in communication data (VanLear, in press; VanLear & Watt, 1996; Yanovitzky & VanLear, 2008). However, further treatment of these methods is beyond the scope of this chapter.

Multilevel Modeling of Behavioral Interactions

The advantage of individual time series in which each behavior or time period is the unit of analysis is that they can identify and analyze very complex temporal patterns and processes. However, as discussed above, they are not built to efficiently handle variations in such patterns over a large number of cases (e.g., individuals, dyads, or groups). When one has repeated-measures data across a large number of cases, researchers are more often turning to multilevel modeling (MLM), also called hierarchical linear modeling to more efficiently analyze their data. MLM is a technique built to handle "nested data," such that each unit of analysis is nested within a larger unit. Interaction behavior is "doubly nested," such that behaviors are nested within people, and people are nested within dyads or groups. MLM can analyze both within-case and between-case variance, and unlike ARIMA, it can efficiently handle missing data and does not require that observations be equally spaced in time, though it can treat time as continuous rather than simply ordinal. MLM can now handle cases in which the dependent variable (behavior) is continuous, ordinal, dichotomous, or multicategorical using a variety of distributions. As such, it offers an alternative to the sequential analyses, as well as to ARIMA when there are many dyads or groups being analyzed. A complete introduction to MLM is beyond the scope of this chapter, but we will provide a brief sketch of its application to modeling behavioral interaction data. For issues such as appropriate "centering" of variables and the application of specific programs, researchers should consult a source exclusively concerned with MLM, especially its application to longitudinal or time-series data (e.g., Luke, 2004; Raudenbush & Bryk, 2002; Henry & Slater, 2008; Singer & Willett, 2003).

There are two ways to handle the doubly nested nature of interaction data. First, if the dyad is "distinguishable" (e.g., husband/wife), then the behaviors of each party can be treated as separate variables organized by role within the dyadic units. In this case, only a two-level MLM needs to be used. Of course, when dyads, not individuals, are units, the number of "cases" is halved. The other approach would be to use a three-level MLM with the behaviors of individuals and time as the Level 1 variables, individuals and their characteristics as the Level 2 variables, and dyad (or group) and their characteristics as Level 3 variables.

Modelling Interactions of
Distinguishable Dyads With MLM

We first describe a two-level MLM growth model for a distinguishable dyad with time and the behaviors of husband and wife as the Level 1 variables and dyad (and dyadic characteristics) as the Level 2 variables. We will use Husband's Behavior at Time t for Case/Dyad j (HB_{tj}), along with time (the point in the conversation, T) to predict Wife's Behavior (WB_{tj}) at Time t in Dyad j. We then add the lagged effects of HB at $t-1$ $HBL1_{t-1j}$ to predict WB_{tj} at Time t. Because hierarchical linear modeling or HLM (Raudenbush et al., 2011) and most MLM programs require that one build the model by specifying the equations, we present the equations associated with each model we discuss. We wait to present actual data until we get to the more complex case of the three-level model for indistinguishable dyads.

To test whether there is a need for MLM because of a significant nesting effect, we can calculate the intraclass correlation coefficient (ICC) using MLM.

This is simply the proportion of between-case (Level 2) variance of the total variance (within + between, or Level 1 + Level 2). We can obtain this using MLM by fitting the "null model":

$$\text{Level 1: } WB_{tj} = \beta_{0j} + \varepsilon_{tj}, \tag{8a}$$

$$\text{Level 2: } \beta_{0j} = \gamma_{00} + \mu_{0j}, \tag{8b}$$

where β_{0j} is the mean for Dyad j (based on the average of wife's behavior for Dyad j), and γ_{00} is the average of WB across cases/dyads and is the only "fixed effect" in the model. The μ_{0j} term indicates the extent to which dyads vary around γ_{00}. This system can be written as a single mixed-effects model:

$$WB_{tj} = \gamma_{00} + \mu_{0j} + \varepsilon_{tj}. \tag{8c}$$

The error can be separated as the between-case variability between cases/dyads (μ_{0j}) and the variability within cases/dyads (ε_{tj}). The ICC is then

$$\text{ICC} = \mu_{0j}/(\mu_{0j} + \varepsilon_{tj}). \tag{9}$$

Significant or meaningful between-case variability or ICC would indicate the need for MLM because of the effects of the nested data and the violation of the assumptions of traditional tests.

Given the need for an MLM or similar approach, we first start with the simple linear growth model (Singer & Willett, 2003) for WB_{tj} (wife's behavior at Time t for Case/Dyad j) with the addition of the husband's contemporaneous behavior (HB) into the Level 1 equation:

$$\text{Level 1: } WB_{tj} = \beta_{0j} + \beta_{1j}(T_{tj}) + \beta_{2j}(HB_{tj}) + \varepsilon_{tj}, \tag{10a}$$

$$\text{Level 2: } \beta_{0j} = \gamma_{00} + \mu_{0j}, \tag{10b}$$

$$\beta_{1j} = \gamma_{10} + \mu_{1j}, \tag{10c}$$

$$\beta_{2j} = \gamma_{20} + \mu_{2j}, \tag{10d}$$

where β_{0j} is the intercept for Dyad j (based on the average of wife's behavior for Dyad j), β_{1j} is the slope (effect) for the linear change over time for Case/Dyad j, and β_{2j} is the slope for husband's behavior. T_{tj} is the temporal variable representing time in the conversation (typically centered at zero). This model represents the linear growth model. The three Level 1 parameters are predicted by Level 2 effects. Specifically, γ_{00} is the average of WB across cases at the intercept (the beginning of the interaction) and μ_{0j} is the extent to which individual cases vary at the intercept. γ_{10} is the average linear rate of change (slope) in WB in the population, and μ_{1j} is the extent to which individual cases vary in their rate of change (slopes). β_{2j} is predicted by the means of husband's behavior (γ_{20}) and the variation of HB around the mean (μ_{2j}) or the error in predicting HB_j from the mean. If μ_{2j} is significant and meaningful, then it indicates that the effects of HB differ across dyads. This opens the door for the inclusion of a Level 2 explanatory variable (moderator) to explain that variation or a lack of homogeneity in the effects of HB.

We can substitute the Level 2 equations into the Level 1 equation to get

$$WB_{tj} = (\gamma_{00} + \mu_{0j}) + (\gamma_{10} + \mu_{1j})$$
$$(T_{tj}) + (\gamma_{20} + \mu_{2j})(HB_{tj}) + \varepsilon_{tj} \qquad (10e)$$

or

$$WB_{tj} = [\gamma_{00} + \gamma_{10}(T_{tj}) + \gamma_{20}(HB_{tj})] +$$
$$[\mu_{0j} + \mu_{1j}(T_{tj}) + \mu_{2j}(HB_{tj}) + \varepsilon_{tj}], \qquad (10f)$$

where the terms in the first set of brackets in Equation 10f are the "fixed effects," and the terms in the second set of brackets are the "random effects." Of course, the quadratic or even cubic effects of time could be included in an MLM model much like this.

It is a rather straightforward extension to the 10th set of equations to include the Husband's Behavior at lag −1 (HBL1; Husband's Behavior in the time immediately preceding WB_{tj})[10] as a separate time varying predictor variable:

$$\text{Level 1: } WB_{tj} = \beta_{0j} + \beta_{1j}(T_{tj}) + \beta_{2j}(HB_{tj}) +$$
$$\beta_{3j}(HBL1_{tj}) + \varepsilon_{tj}, \qquad (11)$$

simply adding the Level 2 equation $\beta_{3j} = \gamma_{30} + \mu_{3j}$ to the other Level 2 equations listed previously.

The preceding models deal with the problems of the nested nature of time-series data by separating within-dyad (Level 1) from between-dyad (Level 2) variation and representing the linear (T_{tj}) effect of time. However, simply separating within-dyad from between-dyad variance assumes that the correlated errors are basically equal across all within-dyad observations. Our description of ARIMA models showed that with time-series data, this is often not the case. In stochastic time series, adjacent observations are usually more highly correlated within cases than observations more distally spaced in time. The presence of the T_{tj} variable is analogous to the "integrative" component of the ARIMA model, but behavioral data often (but not always) are better

captured by an AR process than a linear (or curvilinear) trend. We can use MLM to represent a model in which serial dependency is best assessed by an AR1 process rather than an I_1 process. Let WBAR1$_{tj}$ represent the AR effect of Wife j's behavior at the time point immediately preceding WB_{tj}.

$$\text{Level 1: } WB_{tj} = \beta_{0j} + \beta_{1j}(WBAR1_{tj}) + \beta_{2j}(HB_{tj})$$
$$+ \beta_{3j}(HBL1_{tj}) + \varepsilon_{tj}, \qquad (12a)$$

$$\text{Level 2: } \beta_{0j} = \gamma_{00} + \mu_{0j}, \qquad (12b)$$

$$\beta_{1j} = \gamma_{10} + \mu_{1j}, \qquad (12c)$$

$$\beta_{2j} = \gamma_{20} + \mu_{2j}, \qquad (12d)$$

$$\beta_{3j} = \gamma_{30} + \mu_{3j}. \qquad (12e)$$

This time, β_{1j} represents the first-order AR effect of Wife j's immediately preceding behavior, γ_{10} is the mean of the prior behaviors across all wives, and μ_{1j} is the departure of Wife j's behavior from that mean.

It is also possible to add a Level 2 variable as a predictor of both the intercept and slopes of the Level 1 variables. For example, the length of the relationship (RL) might affect both the intercept and the effects of husband's behavior (HB and HBL1). In this model, we assume that there is no linear (or other) effect of time (T_{tj}), so we drop that variable. Then,

$$\text{Level 1: } WB_{tj} = \beta_{0j} + \beta_{1j}(HB_{tj}) +$$
$$\beta_{2j}(HBL1_{tj}) + \varepsilon_{tj}, \qquad (13a)$$

$$\text{Level 2: } \beta_{0j} = \gamma_{00} + \gamma_{01}(RL)_j + \mu_{0j}, \qquad (13b)$$

$$\beta_{1j} = \gamma_{10} + \gamma_{11}(RL)_j + \mu_{1j}, \qquad (13c)$$

$$\beta_{2j} = \gamma_{20} + \gamma_{20}(RL)_j + \beta_{2j}. \qquad (13d)$$

Because we dropped time (T), the referents for the subscript numbers differ from the prior equations.

Modeling Interactions of Indistinguishable Dyads With MLM

To model the interactions of indistinguishable dyads, in which no dyadic role (husband/wife, boss/subordinate) or variable (male/female) allows us to consistently differentiate between the two members of the dyad, we use the strategy of the Actor/Partner Interdependence Model (APIM; Cook & Kenny, 2005). In this model, each behavioral period of each person is a Level 1 unit. Both members of the dyad (Person A and Person B) are designated as "actors," and both are designated as "partners." If we are willing to stay with an ISM model in which the behaviors of individuals and their individual differences are not partitioned from their dyad, then we can model these dyads' interactions in much the same way as we did previously with the distinguishable dyads, using only two-level MLM (see the later example using the simulated data). Here the designation of actor and partner simply replace the designation of husband and wife as used in the above examples, if the person-level information does not significantly or substantially improve model fit over the between-dyad information or knowing the dyad does not provide information above knowing the person.

However, if we wish to partition the effects of individuals from the dyads in which they are interacting, this will necessitate three-level MLM, because behaviors (Level 1) are nested within individuals (Level 2), which are in turn nested within dyads or groups (Level 3). The data are configured as presented in Table 14.4. We use the smiling data as our example. The natural log of these data did not provide a clearly superior

approximation of a normal distribution, so the original metric is retained.

We begin with a basic model in which we specify no Level 2 or Level 3 variables apart from the designation of individuals and dyads and without a time or autocorrelation predictor at Level 1. (In practice, some programs, such as HLM 7, require the identification of at least one Level 2 and one Level 3 variable in addition to the identification of people and dyads, though these variables need not be included in the actual models tested; as long as they are identified, the following model can still be tested.) At Level 1, we use the "actor" smiling behavior variable (AS_{tij}) as the behavioral dependent variable at Time t for Actor i in Dyad j and only the mean as a predictor:

Level 1: $AS_{tij} = \pi_{0ij} + \varepsilon_{tij}$ (within person),   (14a)

Level 2: $\pi_{0ij} = \beta_{00j} + r_{0ij}$ (within dyad, between person),   (14b)

Level 3: $\beta_{00j} = \gamma_{000} + \mu_{00j}$ (between dyad/group),   (14c)

Table 14.4 APIM Person-Period Data Configuration With Lag 1 Effects for Three-Level HLM

ID	Dyad	Person	Lev2var	Delay	Time	AS	ASAR1	PS	PSLag-1
1	1	1	1	1	0	1		1	
2	1	1	1	1	1	4	1	4	1
3	1	1	1	1	2	4	4	4	4
4	1	1	1	1	3	3.5	4	4	4
:	:	:	:	:	:	:	:	:	:
327	1	2	3	1	0	1		1	
328	1	2	3	1	1	4	1	4	1
329	1	2	3	1	2	4	4	4	4
:	:	:	:	:	:	:	:	:	:
653	2	3	2	1	0	2		1.5	
654	2	3	2	1	1	4	2	4	1.5
655	2	3	2	1	2	4	4	4	4
656	2	3	2	1	3	3	4	3	4
:	:	:	:	:	:	:	:	:	:
:	:	:	:	:	:	:	:	:	:
3155	6	11	1	0	0	0		2	
3156	6	11	1	0	1	1.5	0	3	2
3157	6	11	1	0	2	3	1.5	0.5	3
:	:	:	:	:	:	:	:	:	:
$n = 6{,}266$	10	20	4	0	333	4	0	2	0

where π_{0ij} is the intercept for Person i's behavior when identified as "actor" in Dyad j (based on the average of i's behavior). The error of prediction of an actor's smiles at Time t not explained by the mean of that actor's smiling at that time is ε_{tij}. β_{00j} is the intercept based on the mean of Dyad j's smiling, and r_{0ij} allows that the ability of those means to predict individual means may vary within dyads. Finally, γ_{000} represents the grand mean, and μ_{00j} allows that dyads vary around the grand mean. Whereas the effect of the one fixed effect representing the mean is clearly significant (coefficient = 1.080, $t = 8.841$, $df = 9$, $p < .001$), the sizes of the variances of the random effects indicate that there is room for explanatory variables (Var[e_{tij}] = 2.058, Var[e_{tij}/total] = 92%; Var[r_{0ij}] = .061, $\chi^2 = 105.856$, $df = 10$, $p < .001$, Var[r_{0ij}/total] = 2.7%; Var[μ_{00j}] = .115, $\chi^2 = 44.240$, $df = 9$, $p < .001$, Var[μ_{00j}/total] = 5.2%). So, the vast majority of the variance to be explained is at Level 1 (over time), the second most is at Level 3 (between dyad), and the least is at Level 2 (within dyad, between people). Although the Level 2 variance is significant, it is probably small enough to justify an ISM (vs. HSM) model, similar to the prior section, but we will illustrate how to include a personal-level (Level 2) variable. The deviance for this basic model is 22,288.033, with four parameters estimated.

Most frequently when using MLM to model longitudinal or time-series data, the next move would be to estimate a linear growth model (Henry & Slater, 2008; Singer & Willett, 2003).[8] However, as we have already indicated, interaction data more often display an AR pattern, and we will therefore first estimate an AR1 model by inclusion of the lagged effect of the Actor's Smiling in the prior time period (ASAR1$_{tij}$) as a Level 1 predictor. (Of course, our decision is also influenced by the fact that the ARIMA analyses showed that an AR1, not an integrative process, was the best model for these data.)

$$\text{Level 1: AS}_{tij} = \pi_{0ij} + \pi_{1ij}(\text{ASAR1}_{1ij}) + \varepsilon_{tij}, \quad (15a)$$

$$\text{Level 2: } \pi_{0ij} = \beta_{00j} + r_{0ij}, \quad (15b)$$

$$\pi_{1ij} = \beta_{10j} + r_{1ij}, \quad (15c)$$

$$\text{Level 3: } \beta_{00j} = \gamma_{000} + \mu_{00j}, \quad (15d)$$

$$\beta_{10j} = \gamma_{100} + \mu_{10j}. \quad (15e)$$

The results show a significant decrease in the deviance statistic (19,011, parameters = 9) from the base model (Δ deviance = 22,288 $-$ 19,011 = 3,277, Δ parameters = 5). The fixed-effect coefficient associated with the slope of ASAR1 was .637, which is

significant ($t = 26.077$, $df = 9$, $p < .001$). This is consistent with the finding of a first-order autocorrelation effect in the ARIMA analyses. This model allows the slopes of the AR effects to vary across people and dyads, but the results indicate that the ASAR1 slope (effect) does not vary between dyadic partners (r_{1ij}: $SD = .035$, variance = .001, $df = 10$, $\chi^2 = 17.477$, $p = .06$), but the slope does vary across dyads (μ_{10j}: $SD = .066$, variance = .004, $df = 9$, $\chi^2 = 36.883$, $p < .001$), indicating room for a between-dyad (Level 3) variable to explain this variation.

We might next test the effect of partner's smiling behavior (PS$_{tij}$) as the simultaneous behavior of the "partner," as a Level 1 predictor. To save space, we will also add to the model the behavior of the partner at one prior lag (PSlag-1$_{tij}$) as another Level 1 predictor.

$$\text{Level 1: AS}_{tjk} = \pi_{0ij} + \pi_{1ij}(\text{ASAR1}_{1ij}) + \pi_{2ij}(\text{PS}_{1ij})$$
$$+ \pi_{3ij}(\text{PSlag-1}_{1ij}) + \varepsilon_{tij}, \quad (16a)$$

$$\text{Level 2: } \pi_{0ij} = \beta_{00j} + r_{0ij}, \quad (16b)$$

$$\pi_{1ij} = \beta_{10j} + r_{1ij}, \quad (16c)$$

$$\pi_{2ij} = \beta_{20j} + r_{2ij}, \quad (16d)$$

$$\pi_{3ij} = \beta_{30j} + r_{3ij}, \quad (16e)$$

$$\text{Level 3: } \beta_{00j} = \gamma_{000} + \mu_{00j}, \quad (16f)$$

$$\beta_{10j} = \gamma_{100} + \mu_{10j}, \quad (16g)$$

$$\beta_{20j} = \gamma_{200} + \mu_{20j}, \quad (16h)$$

$$\beta_{30j} = \gamma_{300} + \mu_{30j}, \quad (16i)$$

where π_{0ij} is the intercept for Person i's behavior when identified as "actor" in Dyad j (based on the average of i's behavior). π_{2ij} is the slope or effect of partner's smiling behavior during the same point in time (PS$_{1ij}$). π_{3ij} is the slope or effect of partner's smiling behavior in the 2 seconds prior to the actor's smiling at Time t. The error of prediction of an actor's smiles at Time t is not explained by the mean of that actor's smiling and his or her partner's smiling at that time is ε_{tij}. β_{00j} is the intercept based on the average of Dyad j's behavior, and by including r_{0ij}, we allow that the intercepts may vary across dyads, whereas r_{1ij} is the variation in the effects (slopes) of partner's behavior across dyads. Finally, γ_{000} is based on the grand mean across individuals and dyads.

The results show that there is a significant effect for partner's simultaneous smiling (PS$_{1ij}$ coefficient = .306, $df = 9$, $t = 6.407$, $p < .001$), but the lagged effect of the partner's prior smiling is not significant (PSlag-1$_{1ij}$ coefficient = $-.055$, $t = -2.010$, $df = 9$, $p = .075$). All random effects (variances) are significant except for the Level 3 intercept (μ_{00j}: $p > .50$), indicating that the extent to which individual actors vary around the grand mean does not vary by dyad.[9] The deviance for the model is 18,264, with 25 parameters estimated. The fact that the other random effects are significant indicates that there is plenty of room for explanatory Level 2 and Level 3 variables to act as moderators of partner's smiling.

With that in mind, we next present a model with a Level 2 predictor representing an individual difference across people. For the purposes of this example, we created a fake person-level continuous predictor (Lev2Var_{ij}), which should not have a significant effect. Given that the lagged effect of partner's smiling had no significant effect, we have dropped it from the model to simplify the analysis. (Of course, one could choose to leave it in, as the person-level moderator may be responsible for the lack of significance.) For illustration, we have also chosen to leave out some of the Level 3 random effects.

$$\text{Level 1: AS}_{tjk} = \pi_{0ij} + \pi_{1ij}(\text{ASAR1}_{1ij}) + \beta_{2ij}(\text{PS}_{1ij}) + \varepsilon_{tij}, \tag{17a}$$

$$\text{Level 2: } \pi_{0ij} = \beta_{00j} + \beta_{01j}(\text{Lev2Var}_{ij}) + r_{0ij}, \tag{17b}$$

$$\pi_{1ij} = \beta_{10j} + \beta_{11j}(\text{Lev2Var}_{ij}) + r_{1ij}, \tag{17c}$$

$$\pi_{2ij} = \beta_{20j} + \beta_{21j}(\text{Lev2Var}_{ij}) + r_{2ij}, \tag{17d}$$

$$\text{Level 3: } \beta_{00j} = \gamma_{000}, \tag{17e}$$

$$\beta_{01j} = \gamma_{010}, \tag{17f}$$

$$\beta_{10j} = \gamma_{100} + \mu_{10j}, \tag{17g}$$

$$\beta_{11j} = \gamma_{110}, \tag{17h}$$

$$\beta_{20j} = \gamma_{200} + \mu_{20j}, \tag{17i}$$

$$\beta_{21j} = \gamma_{210} + \mu_{30j}. \tag{17j}$$

In this model, the Lev2Var variable is allowed to predict both the intercept and the slopes of all the Level 1 variables. As we might expect, this Level 2 variable does not have any significant contribution to the intercept or to the slopes of either the lagged effect of the actor's own smiling or the simultaneous effect of the partner's smiling ($p > .05$), given that it was not a real variable or constructed to show a relationship, and the within-dyad variance is minimal anyway.

Finally, we fit a model in which a Level 3 dyadic predictor is built into the model. The Level 3 dummy-coded predictor is a time delay ([Delay] grand mean centered) that was built into half of the conversations. Table 14.5 presents these results in a

manner similar to the HLM 7 output. The Level 1 model is the same as the prior model.

$$\text{Level 1: AS}_{tjk} = \pi_{0ij} + \pi_{1ij}(\text{ASAR1}_{1ij}) + \pi_{2ij}(\text{PS}_{1ij}) + \varepsilon_{tij}, \tag{18a}$$

$$\text{Level 2: } \pi_{0ij} = \beta_{00j} + r_{0ij}, \tag{18b}$$

$$\pi_{1ij} = \beta_{10j} + r_{1ij}, \tag{18c}$$

$$\pi_{2ij} = \beta_{20j} + r_{2ij}, \tag{18d}$$

$$\text{Level 3: } \beta_{00j} = \gamma_{000}, \tag{18e}$$

$$\beta_{10j} = \gamma_{100} + \gamma_{101}(\text{Delay}_j) + \mu_{10j}, \tag{18f}$$

$$\beta_{20j} = \gamma_{200} + \gamma_{201}(\text{Delay}_j) + \mu_{20j}, \tag{18g}$$

$$\text{Mixed Model: ACTORSMI}_{tij} = \gamma_{000} + \gamma_{100} \times \text{PS}_{tij} + \gamma_{101} \times \text{PS}_{tij} \times \text{Delay}_j + \gamma_{200} \times \text{ASAR1}_{tij} + \gamma_{201} \times \text{ASAR1}_{tij} \times \text{Delay}_j + r_{0ij} + r_{1ij} \times \text{PS}_{tij} + r_{2ij} \times \text{ASAR1}_{tij} + \mu_{10j} \times \text{PS}_{tij} + \mu_{20j} \times \text{ASAR1}_{tij} + e_{tij}. \tag{18h}$$

In this model, only one Level 3 random effect is not included, as there was little variance around the grand mean intercept in the prior models, so none was included here. We also have omitted the effect of Delay on β_{00j}, because the prior models showed that little variance was left to be explained.

Table 14.5 shows that, as before, the AR effect of the actor's prior smiling is strongly significant (coefficient = .516, $t = 19.375$, $df = 8$, $p < .001$), as is the effect of the partner's simultaneous smiling (coefficient = .280, $t = 7.500$, $df = 8$, $p < .001$). However, the Delay does not appear to moderate either of these effects, as the effects on the slope of ASAR1 (coefficient = .071, $t = -1.353$, $df = 8$, $p = .213$) and on the slope of PS (coefficient = .091, $t = 1.268$, $df = 8$, $p = .241$) are both nonsignificant. Furthermore, the random effects associated with both ASAR1 and PS remain significant and therefore indicate that there is significant variance in both ASAR1 and PS that remains to be explained by other Level 2 and Level 3 predictors. These results are consistent with the meta-analysis of ARIMA analyses conducted by Kotz et al. (2006) on these data.

Although it is possible to include both Level 2 (individual) and Level 3 (dyadic/group) predictors together simultaneously, the limited degrees of freedom typically restrict the number of random effects that can be included in such models. With the limited number of dyads in the example data set, we have chosen not to include that example analysis.

MLM With Nominal Data

The principles of MLM do not apply only to cases in which the dependent variable is interval

Table 14.5 HLM 7 Output for Three-Level Model Predicting AS_{tjk} From ASAR1, PS, Level 1, and Delay Level 3

Final estimation of fixed effects

Fixed Effect	Coefficient	Standard Error	t Ratio	Approx. df	p Value
For INTRCPT1, π_0					
For INTRCPT2, β_{00}					
INTRCPT3, γ_{000}	1.085219	0.040508	26.790	19	<.001
For ACTSMLAG slope, π_1					
For INTRCPT2, β_{10}					
INTRCPT3, γ_{100}	0.515997	0.026633	19.375	8	<.001
CONV01, γ_{101}	−0.071354	0.052727	−1.353	8	.213
For PARTNERS slope, π_2					
For INTRCPT2, β_{20}					
INTRCPT3, γ_{200}	0.279861	0.037316	7.500	8	<.001
CONV01, γ_{201}	0.090709	0.071551	1.268	8	.241

Final estimation of Level 1 and Level 2 variance components

Random Effect	SD	Variance Component	df	χ^2	p Value
INTRCPT1, r_0	0.17046	0.02906	19	176.84868	<.001
ACTSMLAG slope, r_1	0.03828	0.00147	10	23.09454	.011
PARTNERS slope, r_2	0.05228	0.00273	10	35.13969	<.001
Level 1, e	1.04048	1.08259			

Final estimation of Level 3 variance components

Random Effect	SD	Variance Component	df	χ^2	p Value
ACTSMLAG/INTRCPT2, u_{10}	0.07266	0.00528	8	41.37796	<.001
PARTNERS/INTRCPT2, u_{20}	0.10705	0.01146	8	93.10427	<.001

Statistics for the current model

Deviance = 18,306.047471

Number of estimated parameters = 15

level. MLM can handle either dichotomous or multiple categorical data. We will use the simulated dyadic data to illustrate. The simulated dyadic interactions used to demonstrate the lag sequential and Markov analyses were constructed with no intended individual differences within dyads and, therefore, a two-level analysis representing an ISM is appropriate.[11] Given that the data are dichotomous (zeroes and ones) a Bernoulli distribution was adopted. Because of the limited amount of space, I will present only a brief summary of the model and results. The model tested is as follows:

$$\text{Level 1: Prob(ACTION}_{ti} = 1|\pi_j) = \phi_{ti}, \quad (19a)$$

$$\log[\phi_{tj}/(1 - \phi_{ti})] = \eta_{tj}, \quad (19b)$$

$$\eta_{tj} = \pi_{0j} + \pi_{1j} \times (\text{ACTIONL1}_{tj}), \quad (19c)$$

$$\text{Level 2: } \pi_{0j} = \beta_{00} + \beta_{01} \times (\text{Reciprocity}_j) + r_{0j}, \quad (19d)$$

$$\pi_{1j} = \beta_{10} + \beta_{11} \times (\text{Reciprocity}_j) + r_{1j}. \quad (19e)$$

where Action_{tj} is the code for the subsequent act for Dyad j (the criterion variable) at Time t, ActionL1 is the code for the antecedent act by the other speaker in Dyad j, and Reciprocity$_i$ (really the inverse of reciprocity rate) is the level of reciprocity for Dyad j built into the data for each dyad by the addition of systematically increasing levels of random error to a preestablished high to moderate level of reciprocity.

The results are consistent with the prior analyses in showing a significant lag 1 effect (β_{10} coefficient = 1.648, t = 20.622, df = 68, p < .001), which is moderated by the built-in systematic variation in the amount of error resulting in a systematic decrease in the amount of reciprocity (β_{11} coefficient = −.065, t = −8.165, df = 68, p < .001). However, MLM found that the variance of the error terms (r_{0j} and r_{1j}) were small and nonsignificant, suggesting that these effects are homogeneous, with no further need for other moderator variables at Level 2 to explain either the intercept (code frequency) or the level of lag 1 effect. Hence, the tests for homogeneity in the meta-analyses of the lag sequential results appear a little more sensitive to variations in interaction structure than the MLM analyses. However, if we add the lag 2 effect (not shown in above equation), the MLM analysis does show a significant, yet somewhat modest, effect. This shows greater sensitivity than the partial Φ coefficients of the lag sequential analyses.

Modeling Group Interaction

The application of the prior models to group interaction is rather straightforward, as people are nested within groups instead of dyads. Individual roles (e.g., mother, father, son, daughter) can be included as Level 2 factors. In fact, because there are more people nested within groups, there are more degrees of freedom for estimating individual difference variables. Space limitations preclude the application of specific examples on actual data.

A special model we could profitably apply to group interaction data is the Social Relations Model (SRM) (Kenny & La Voie, 1984; Warner, Kenny, & Stoto, 1979). The SRM is basically an extension of the APIM and uses some of the same terminology, but with a different operationalization. Although the SRM has been used to examine perception and personality, it has also been applied to the study of social interaction (Dindia, Fitzpatrick, & Kenny, 1997; Warner et al., 1979). In this application of the SRM, a person's behavior (or response to another's behavior) can be seen as a function of three effects: the "actor effect," "partner effect," and "relationship effect." In this application, the actor effect is the consistency with which a person performs a

particular behavior regardless of who he or she is interacting with or the occasion of interaction. The partner effect is the consistency with which a person elicits a particular behavior from others across partners or situations. Finally, the relationship effect is the unique adjustment that a particular actor makes to a particular partner, which remains stable across multiple occasions.

Dindia et al. (1997) used the SRM to analyze self-disclosures in the dyadic interactions between spouses and strangers in a round-robin design in which each person interacted not only with his or her own spouse but with the spouses of others participating in the study. In this way, they could assess a person's self-disclosure as a function of the consistency of that person's self-disclosure across partners (actor effect), his or her partner's ability to elicit self-disclosure from a variety of partners (partner effect), and the uniqueness of a person's self-disclosure in a particular dyad (relationship effect) that is not predicted by his or her own actor effect or partner's partner effect.

Whereas the use of the SRM to analyze dyadic interaction requires a round-robin or blocked round-robin design, a researcher can exploit the nature of group interactions in which each group member interacts with each other member multiple times to simulate a round-robin analysis.

For example, let the consistency of a person's smiling behavior no matter who is talking (as coded every half second, summed within every 2-second window, then averaged for each turn of a group member) be that person's actor effect. The tendency of a person to receive smiles from all other group members while that person is talking is his or her partner effect. The relationship effect is the tendency for particular speakers to receive smiles from particular group members or, put another way, the tendency of particular group members to smile while a particular member is speaking, over and above (statistically controlling for) the smiler's actor effect and the recipient's partner effect.

In addition to being able to decompose the variance into actor, partner, and relationship effects, the SRM allows the calculation of "reciprocity effects." For example, if Person A's tendency to make unique adjustments in smiling when interacting with B is related to Person B's tendency to make unique adjustments in smiling when interacting with A, then this is reciprocity. Whereas these reciprocity effects are calculated in a different way than in the sequential analyses we have examined, meta-analysis has shown that the estimates of the reciprocity of affect that the two methods produce are surprisingly similar (VanLear, Hamilton, Veksler, & Hull, 2012).

Conclusion

There are a number of ways in which behavioral data can be modeled and analyzed. This chapter has focused primarily on how to model the effect of one person's behavior on that of another person in a dyad or group, as this is the basis of mutual adaptation during interaction. Other methods exist for analyzing and modeling behavioral data (see Davis, this volume), and there is no single best approach. The method selected should be based on the purposes of the analysis and the strengths of that particular method. Whereas some scholars may consider some of the older approaches reviewed here (e.g., lag sequential analysis) passé, I believe that they still have some utility, provided they are appropriately used with an understanding of their assumptions and limitations. ARIMA analyses allow the detection of complex variations in patterns over time. Fourier and spectral analyses are quite useful for uncovering cyclical periodicities in behavioral data (VanLear, 1991). As we have seen, MLM is particularly well suited when one has conversational data constructed as time series across a number of dyads or groups.

References

Allison, P. D., & Liker, J. K. (1982). Analyzing sequential categorical data: A comment on Gottman. *Psychological Bulletin, 91*, 393–403.

Anderson, T. W., & Goodman, L. A. (1957). Statistical inference about Markov chains. *Annals of Mathematical Statistics, 28*, 89–110.

Bakeman, R., & Gottman, J. M. (1997). *Observing interaction: An introduction to sequential analysis* (2nd ed.). Cambridge, UK: Cambridge University Press.

Bishop, Y. M., Fienberg, S. E., & Holland, P. W. (2007). *Discrete multivariate analysis: Theory and practice.* New York: Springer.

Box, G., & Jenkins, G. (1970). *Time series analysis: Forecasting and control.* San Francisco, CA: Holden-Day.

Buder, E. H. (1996). Dynamics of speech processes in dyadic interaction. In J. H. Watt & C. A. VanLear (Eds.), *Dynamic patterns in communication processes* (pp. 301–326). Thousand Oaks, CA: Sage.

Cappella, J. N. (1980). Talk and silence sequences in informal conversations II. *Human Communication Research, 6*, 130–145.

Cappella, J. N. (1996). Interaction consequences of adaptation. In J. H. Watt & C. A. VanLear (Eds.), *Dynamic patterns in communication processes* (pp. 382–386). Thousand Oaks, CA: Sage.

Cook, W. L., & Kenny, D. A. (2005). The Actor-Partner Interdependence Model: A model of bidirectional effects in developmental studies. *International Journal of Behavioral Development, 29*, 101–109.

Dindia, K. (1982). Reciprocity of self-disclosure: A sequential analysis. In M. Burgoon (Ed.), *Communication Yearbook 6* (pp. 506–530). Beverly Hills, CA: Sage.

Dindia, K. (1986). Antecedents and consequents of silence: A replication using revised lag sequential analysis. *Human Communication Research, 13*, 108–125.

Dindia, K., Fitzpatrick, M. A., & Kenny, D. A. (1997). Self-disclosure in spouse and stranger dyads: A social relations analysis. *Human Communication Research, 23*, 388–412.

Ellis, D. G., & Fisher, B. A. (1975). Phases of conflict in small group development: A Markov analysis. *Human Communication Research, 1*, 195–212.

Escudero, V., Rogers, L. E., & Gutierrez, E. (1997). Patterns of relational control and nonverbal affect in clinic and nonclinic couples. *Journal of Personal and Social Relationships, 14*, 5–29.

Fisher, B. A., & Drecksel, G. L. (1983). A cyclical model of developing relationships: A study of relational control. *Communication Monographs, 50*, 66–78.

Fisher, B. A., & Hawes, L. C. (1971). An interact systems model: Generating a grounded theory of small group decision making. *Quarterly Journal of Speech, 58*, 444–453.

Gottman, J. M. (1981). *Time-series analysis: A comprehensive introduction for social scientists.* Cambridge, UK: Cambridge University Press.

Gottman, J. M., & Bakeman, R. (1979). The sequential analysis of observational data. In M. E. Lamb, S. J. Suomi, & G. R. Stephenson (Eds.), *Social interaction analysis: Methodological issues* (pp. 185–206). Madison: University of Wisconsin Press.

Gottman, J. M., Markman, H., & Notarius, C. (1977). The topography of marital conflict: A sequential analysis of verbal and nonverbal behavior. *Journal of Marriage and Family, 39*, 461–477.

Henry, K. L., & Slater, M. D. (2008). Assessing change and intraindividual variation: Longitudinal multilevel and structural equation modeling. In A. F. Hayes, M. D. Slater, & L. B. Snyder (Eds.), *The SAGE sourcebook of advanced data analysis methods for communication research* (pp. 55–87). Thousand Oaks, CA: Sage.

Hewes, D. E. (1975). Finite stochastic modeling of communication processes: An introduction and some basic readings. *Human Communication Research, 1*, 271–283.

Hewes, D. E. (1979). The sequential analysis of social interaction. *Quarterly Journal of Speech, 65*, 56–73.

Hewes, D. E., Planalp, S., & Streibel, M. (1980). Analyzing social interaction: Some excruciating models and exhilarating results. In D. Nimmo (Ed.), *Communication Yearbook 4* (pp. 123–141). New Brunswick, NJ: Transaction.

Kellerman, K. (1988, May). *The limits of lag sequential analysis in description of patterns of dependency: Incomplete, unbounded, and inaccurate descriptions of dependence.* Paper presented at the annual meeting of the International Communication Association, New Orleans, LA.

Kenny, D. A., & La Voie, L. (1984). The social relations model. In L. Berkowitz (Ed.), *Advances in experimental social psychology* (Vol. 18, pp. 142–182). Orlando, FL: Academic Press.

Kotz, J., Renfro (Powers), S., & Cistulli, M. (2006, November). *The effect of audio-video signal delay on interpersonal synchrony of gaze and smile: A frequency domain and time domain time-series analysis.* Paper presented at the 92nd Annual Convention of the National Communication Association, San Antonio, TX.

Kullback, S., Kupperman, M., & Ku, H. H. (1962). Tests for contingency tables and Markov chains. *Technometrics, 4*, 573–608.

Luke, D. A. (2004). *Multilevel modeling.* Thousand Oaks, CA: Sage.

Morley, D. D. (1987). Revised lag sequential analysis. In M. McLaughlin (Ed.), *Communication Yearbook 10* (pp. 172–182). Beverly Hills, CA: Sage.

Pampel, F. C. (2000). *Logistic regression: A primer.* Thousand Oaks, CA: Sage.

Pierce, W. B. (1976). The coordinated management of meaning: A rules-based theory of interpersonal communication. In G. R. Miller (Ed.), *Explorations in interpersonal communication* (pp. 17–36). Beverly Hills, CA: Sage.

Powers, S. R., & Rauh, C. (2006, November). *The effect of feedback delay on the experience and communication of emotions: A dyadic analysis.* Paper presented at the 92nd Annual Convention of the National Communication Association, San Antonio, TX.

Raudenbush, S. W., & Bryk, A. S. (2002). *Hierarchical linear models: Applications and data analysis methods* (2nd ed.). Thousand Oaks, CA: Sage.

Raudenbush, S. W., Bryk, A. S., Cheong, A. S., Fai, Y. F., Congdon, R. T., & du Toit, M. (2011). *HLM 7: Hierarchical linear and nonlinear modeling.* Lincolnwood, IL: Scientific Software International.

Raush, H. L. (1972). Process and change—A Markov model for interaction. *Family Process, 11*, 275–298.

Sackett, G. P. (1979). The lag sequential analysis of contingency and cyclicity in behavioral interaction research. In J. Osofsky (Ed.), *Handbook of infant development.* New York: John Wiley.

Singer, J. D., & Willett, J. B. (2003). *Applied longitudinal data analysis: Modeling change and event occurrence.* Oxford, UK: Oxford University Press.

VanLear, C. A. (1985). *The formation of social relationships: A longitudinal comparison of linear and nonlinear models* (Unpublished doctoral dissertation). University of Utah, Salt Lake City.

VanLear, C. A. (1987). The formation of social relationships: A longitudinal study of social penetration. *Human Communication Research, 13*, 299–322.

VanLear, C. A. (1988, May). *If I had a hammer: The uses and misuses of log linear analysis in modeling social interaction data.* Paper presented at the annual meeting of the International Communication Association, New Orleans, LA.

VanLear, C. A. (1991). Testing a cyclical model of communicative openness in relationship development: Two longitudinal studies. *Communication Monographs, 58*, 337–361.

VanLear, C. A. (in press). Time series analysis: ARIMA and spectral analysis. In C. R. Berger & M. E. Roloff (Eds.), *International encyclopedia of interpersonal communication.* Hoboken, NJ: John Wiley.

VanLear, C. A., Hamilton, M., Veksler, A., & Hull, K. (2012, July). *The relational quid pro quo: A meta-analysis of reciprocity of affect and reciprocal liking in personal and social relationships.* Paper presented at the annual meeting of the International Association of Relationship Researchers, Chicago.

VanLear, C. A., Sheehan, M., Withers, L., & Walker, R. (2005). AA online: The enactment of supportive computer mediated communication. *Western Journal of Communication, 69*, 5–26.

VanLear, C. A., & Watt, J. H. (1996). A partial map to a wide territory. In J. H. Watt & C. A. VanLear (Eds.), *Dynamic patterns in communication processes* (pp. 3–34). Thousand Oaks, CA: Sage.

VanLear, C. A., & Zietlow, P. H. (1990). Toward a contingency approach to marital interaction: An empirical integration of three approaches. *Communication Monographs, 57*, 202–218.

Warner, R. M. (1996). Coordinated cycles in behavior and physiology during face-to-face social interaction. In J. H. Watt & C. A. VanLear (Eds.), *Dynamic patterns in communication processes* (pp. 327–352). Thousand Oaks: Sage.

Warner, R., Kenny, D. A., & Stoto, M. (1979). A new round robin analysis of variance for social interaction data. *Journal of Personality and Social Psychology, 37*, 1742–1757.

Watt, J. H. (1994). Detection and modeling of time-sequenced processes. In A. Lang (Ed.), *Measuring psychological responses to media.* Hillsdale, NJ: Lawrence Erlbaum.

Watt, J. H., & VanLear, C. A. (Eds.). (1996). *Dynamic patterns in communication processes.* Thousand Oaks, CA: Sage.

Wilson, E., Underwood, M., Puckrin, O., Letto, K., Doyle, R., Caravan, H., . . . Bassett, K. (2013). *The arcsine transformation: Has the time come for retirement?* Retrieved August 8, 2015, from http://www.mun.ca/biology/dschneider/b7932/B7932Final10Dec2010.pdf

Yanovitzky, I., & VanLear, C. A. (2008). Time series analysis: Traditional and contemporary approaches. In A. F. Hayes, M. D. Slater, & L. B. Snyder (Eds.) *The SAGE sourcebook of advanced data analysis methods for communication research* (pp. 89–124). Thousand Oaks, CA: Sage.

Endnotes

1. A complete discussion of transformations is beyond the scope of this chapter. One cannot apply log transformations to zeroes or negative values, so if any zeroes are present in the data, one adds a constant of +1 before transformation. A constant of .5 is usually added before the square-root transformation.

2. As we will see, transition probabilities form the basis of Markov chain analysis. Rogers and Cummings (this volume) offer similar proportional measures of the strength of certain kinds of interacts in their measures of dominance.

3. Allison and Liker's Z is equivalent to the "adjusted standardized residual" in the cross-tabs analysis in SPSS.

4. I would like to thank Amna Al-Abri and Yi Wang for helping create and structure these simulated data. They also helped with the lag sequential analyses. We are currently conducting a more extensive comparison of these methods.

5. Because of the way Sackett calculated the standard deviation, there is a different value for 1,1 reciprocity than for 2,2 reciprocity even in a dichotomous system. However, the value for Allison and Liker's (1982) z is the same for 1,1 and 2,2 reciprocity when the system is dichotomous.

6. We would like to thank Christian Rauh and Stacy Renfro Powers for the data used in these examples and Jeff Kotz and Mark Cistulli for unitizing and coding those data. The data have been somewhat reconfigured to make them appropriate for this analysis. As a result, the between-dyad variable may not be the most appropriate estimate of that effect but should be a good example of how to conduct these analyses.

7. Watt (1994) argued that differencing distorts the parameter estimates of the series. He suggested that trends be removed by fitting the appropriate polynomial or curve function and extracting the residuals.

8. We did run a linear growth model on these data, and the effect of the linear trend of time was nonsignificant (coefficient = $-.0002$, $t = -0.846$, $p = .40$). More important, delay did not moderate either the intercept ($p = .66$) or the slope ($p = .26$) of the linear trend in the multilevel growth model. This indicates that the AR1 (the first-order AR process) is the best control for serial dependency in these data.

9. The reason some of these variance estimates are now significant in this model when they were not previously is probably that with the addition of PS, some of the unexplained variance is now explained, so the denominator in the test statistic is smaller.

10. HBL1 (as well as other lagged effects) is given the subscript tj instead of t-1j in the MLM equations because they are generally created before the analysis and entered as if they were occurring simultaneously. Therefore, this is the way they would be identified in the computer model and on output.

11. Three-level MLM conducted on these data confirm that the variance due to individual differences within dyads is negligible and nonsignificant ($p > .05$).

15

MODELING BEHAVIORAL INTERACTION
AS A NONLINEAR DYNAMICAL SYSTEM

Cross-Recurrence Quantification Analysis

TEHRAN J. DAVIS

S tudents of human behavior confront a difficult problem: the behavior of any one individual is the complicated result of myriad evolving psychological, physiological, and historical factors. Indeed, this acknowledgment has led many a great thinker to conclude that a scientific enterprise focused on human behavior is dubious at best. The problem becomes compounded when we consider that many of our daily actions are in fact *interactions*. We chat, we dance, we work together, we compete in sport— these sorts of social interactions reside at the very core of what it is to be human. If the study of one person's behavior is difficult, then surely investigating the joining of ideas and actions between two people, and all of the multilevel and mutually influencing interactions this entails, seems most challenging (lest we even speak of triadic or quadratic interactions and even larger collectives).

Yet the study of human behavior, including sociality, language, and communication, is a thriving scientific enterprise. Research within these domains has historically focused on observed discrete or aggregate outcomes as a proxy for the underlying dynamics of the behavior of interest. For example, reaction times may act as indices for covert cognitive processes; self-reports may be used to measure degrees of motivation, state, or affiliation; and researchers use performance measures to infer agreement between individuals. More sophisticated techniques might enable research on associations between or among these observed outcomes. Of course, here much is owed to important developments in statistical modeling during the past century that allowed researchers to infer associations and make reasonable predictions of gross behavioral phenomena from a relatively small number of variables. Although remarkably successful, in many respects these approaches often sidestep the issue raised at the outset by reducing the time-dependent complexity of behavior down to counts and means. And whereas a tacit acceptance exists that the nuances of any behavior far outstrip such measures, research is often constrained by the tools at its disposal.[1] As one of my graduate school professors would often remark, "Many influences, many interactions, constantly changing and evolving at multiple time scales . . . of course it is that way! But how in the hell are you going to study it?"

Fortunately for the enterprising behavioral scientist, there are tools to help. The present chapter introduces one of these tools, cross-recurrence quantification analysis (CRQA), which has proved over the past decade to be especially useful in modeling the deterministic characteristics of interactions between pairs of actors. Although CRQA has existed in some form for nearly two decades (Zbilut, Giuliani, & Webber, 1998), a major barrier has been the relative inaccessibility or difficulty in using the specialized programs required for analysis. However, the recent development of widely available toolboxes and open-source program packages has made the application of CRQA much more accessible to new investigators.[2] My goal here is to provide an introductory outline of the key concepts related to this modeling technique, as well as an overview of the procedures involved in analyzing dyadic interactions, interspersed with examples highlighting its use in domains that may be of interest to the reader. Given limitations in space, I do not develop the mathematical underpinnings of these techniques, but rather I focus on building intuitions. For interested readers, Marwan, Romano, Thiel, and Kurths (2007) and Shockley (2005) provide more comprehensive treatments.

An All Too Brief Introduction to Dynamical and Complex Systems

Although behavioral scientists prioritize outcomes of human interaction, the "structures of process" that organize activity are just as important (Juarrero, 1999, p. 124). To this end, recent trends in research have focused on the time-course evolution of human interaction. This includes a growing subset of researchers who have approached this problem using methods and techniques borrowed from dynamical systems theory. A thorough description of dynamical systems theory remains far beyond the scope of this chapter; however, for the present purposes, several key characteristics of dynamical systems need to be mentioned.

Formally defined, a dynamical system involves a state, a time series, and a rule that specifies how the state evolves with time. Dynamical systems theory promises that provided a known state and a known rule, one may reasonably model the behavior of a system at any point of its evolution in time. Beginning with Poincaré's (1892/1893/1899/1993) now classic monographs on celestial mechanics, mathematicians and physicists have applied dynamical systems approaches to model the behavior of a wide array of physical systems, ranging from simple mass springs, to electronic circuits, to the motions of heavenly bodies. Crucially, key theoretical and computational advancements in the 20th century allowed the modeling of *nonlinear dynamical systems*, those whose outputs are not directly reducible to the linear addition of their input components. The behavior of a nonlinear system is not equal to the sum of its parts but instead *emerges from the interactions* of its components. Research has shown that the modeling of many physical, chemical, and biological processes requires an understanding of the underlying multiplicative and

nonlinear processes that are at play. Even the most "simple" living systems exhibit dynamics that are best described as nonlinear, nonstationary, and high dimensional (Zbilut, Thomasson, & Webber, 2002); that is, living systems are *complex*.

Saying that human behaviors and interactions are complex in the same manner perhaps reflects an exercise in the obvious. Indeed, a recurrent theme in the present volume is that the joined behavior of dyads cannot be easily reduced to the separate, simple (i.e., linear) analysis of individuals. Developing relatively accessible methods of modeling behavior to match these intuitions has proved far more challenging. When considering more traditional methods, two considerable problems surface. First, the behavior of many naturally occurring complex systems is governed by a large number of interdependent variables, many of which may be nonobvious, unknown, and, perhaps most daunting, inaccessible to the investigator. Undoubtedly, approaching this problem by focusing on the identification and measure of each of the individual components of a system will prove untenable. Additionally, any faithful model will likely violate the basic assumptions of stationarity and linearity that are central to many statistical methods for modeling behavior. With this in mind, techniques designed to assess complex systems, such as CRQA, are not bound by assumptions about the distributions of measures or stationarity within the time series.

Phase Space Reconstruction

As suggested above, attempting to investigate a system as complex as human interaction by isolating its individual components is wrought with difficulty. If one instead emphasizes the *interactions between components* (Van Orden, Holden, & Turvey, 2003), modeling complex behavior becomes a more manageable problem. Although the number of components may indeed be large, varied, and almost impossible to index, the interactions between them are often lawfully constrained and exhibit certain regularities (Riley, Richardson, Shockley, & Ramenzoni, 2011). The goal of dynamical systems approaches is to uncover the rules that govern the evolution of a given system by describing its *attractors*, or states the system tends toward or revisits over time. Takens's (1981) mathematical theorem suggests that these regularities might be exploited to reconstruct the global behavior of a complex system, even when many of its individual components are not fully known. That is, as a result of the tight mutual coupling between components, a time series of any single measure might in fact be richly informative about the dynamics of the entire system and can be used to create a "reconstructed" time series that reflects this global dynamic. This process, known as *phase space reconstruction*, often constitutes the first step in the analysis of complex systems.

As should be readily apparent, this approach presents advantages for researchers investigating human behavior and interaction, where few components are available for direct measure or known a priori. That said, in order to provide an illustration of phase space reconstruction, we may borrow the example of a relatively simpler system about which we have more detailed knowledge. The famous Lorenz attractor (Lorenz, 1963) is a model of fluid convection that may be described by three coupled first-order differential equations corresponding to two temperature measures and a velocity measure:

$$\dot{x} = \sigma(y - x),$$

$$\dot{y} = x(\rho - z) - y,$$

and

$$\dot{z} = xy - \beta z.$$

This chaotic attractor exhibits hallmarks of a dynamic, nonlinear system: the time-dependent changes in its state are governed by the mutual, multiplicative (feedback) influences of x, y, and z. Figure 15.1a shows the phase portrait of the Lorenz system, a graphical representation of its time-course evolution along these three dimensions. Takens' delay embedding theorem holds that the phase space (the set of all possible states a system can enter) of a complex system may be reconstructed (Abarbanel, 1996) by using the time series of only a single variable and matching it against time-delayed (τ) copies of itself, where the original series starts at $x(t)$, the second $x(t + \tau)$, the third $x(t + 2\tau)$, and so forth, $x(t + N\tau)$. Each time-delayed series acts as a surrogate for an unmeasured (or unknown) dimension of the system. In the case of the Lorenz system, this would be accomplished by taking a time series of any of the three variables, for example x (Figure 15.1b), and lagging it against itself twice to create surrogates for y and z (Figure 15.1c). The resulting "reconstructed" phase space trajectory has a topography that is akin to the original system (Figure 15.1d), allowing a reasonable approximation of its dynamics.

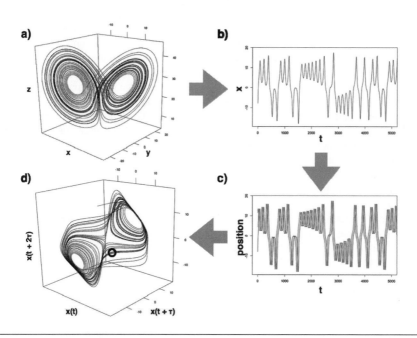

Figure 15.1 (a) The original phase space of the Lorenz attractor. (b) The corresponding values of x during the first 5,000 points in the time series. (c) The original time series x is lagged against it twice and used to (d) reconstruct the trajectory of the attractor. Note that although not identical, the reconstructed phase space has a topography similar to the original. The circle depicts a chosen radius for recurrent points.

Source: Author.

The selection of an appropriate time *delay* and number of surrogates, or *embedding dimensions*, is not arbitrary. For example, the usefulness of a surrogate time series depends on the amount of new information it reveals about the system. If the delay is too short, each surrogate time series is too highly correlated to the original time series and provides little additional information. However, if the delay is too long, the events in the time series become essentially independent of one another, and too little information can be gained from their comparison. At the same time, if the number of embedding dimensions used for phase space reconstruction is too high, one risks introducing spurious noise; a number that is too low might leave the system's dynamics underdetermined (e.g., attempting to model the Lorenz system with only two variables).

Obviously, the tuning of the optimal parameters represents a delicate process. Several methods exist for deriving the appropriate parameters for phase space reconstruction (Cao, 1997; Shockley, 2005). Perhaps the most common approach begins with the identification of an optimal value for the delay parameter (τ) using the first minimum of the *average mutual information* (Fraser & Swinney, 1986). Figure 15.2a shows a plot of the average mutual information (AMI) as a function of delay using the x time series from our Lorenz example, where the first minimum is found at $\tau = 37$. Once an appropriate delay parameter has been selected, we may proceed to the selection of the appropriate embedding dimension. This involves the identification of *false nearest neighbors* (FNNs) within the reconstructed phase space. FNNs are points that appear to be close to one another (as defined by a selected radial distance) in the reconstructed phase space but are in fact much farther apart in the original phase space. For example, the relative distance between real-world objects in the foreground and background in a three-dimensional environment is often distorted or lost entirely when projected onto a two-dimensional photograph. When deciding on an appropriate embedding dimension, one should start with a preselected minimum and increase the embedding dimension until the percentage of FNNs approximates zero or reaches some asymptotic minimum (see Figure 15.2b). Note that the goal here is not necessarily to determine how many dimensions the system has in reality but instead to model the dynamics of the system while minimizing distortion (Shockley, 2005).

Recurrence and Recurrence Plots

If two time series have been collected, we may project both reconstructed trajectories into the same phase space. Cross-recurrence analysis begins with this shared phase space. Although this space may represent a manifold of all possible behavioral states, as mentioned above, most natural systems have preferred states they revisit: stretches of repeating patterns, or *recurrences*. Of course, the same can be said for human behavior, including our daily routines (revisiting tasks and locations), our language (repeating syntax and words), and our physiological rhythms (circadian and hormonal cycles). The Lorenz model provides a visual example of a system that continuously revisits its states over time, resulting in its famous "butterfly" or "figure 8" shape. Importantly, even in its reconstructed phase portrait, we can see these recurrent characteristics. When considering two separate trajectories, such as the time-series measures of two people, we may instead look for patterns of *cross-recurrences*. Cross-recurrence may be interpreted as patterns of *covisitation* between the time series, observing how one time series is revisiting states previously occupied by the other.

Formally, cross-recurrence is determined by noting for each time index along one trajectory the points in the other trajectory that are within a predefined radius (e.g., Figure 15.1d, circle). In the simplest case, this radius is a constant Euclidean distance in the phase space (though this value can be rescaled in other manners; see Marwan et al., 2007). When deciding on an appropriate radius, one must consider the resulting density of cross-recurrent points, or *recurrence rate* (RR), expressed as a ratio of all observed points in the phase space. An r too large may result in a disproportionally large number of points in the phase space being considered cross-recurrent (as an extreme, all of them); an r too low and the criteria for recurrence may be too conservative to yield any meaningful measures. In both cases, researchers gain little information about the interaction between the two systems. A general rule of thumb is to select a radius such that the percentage of recurrent points to all points in the time series is 1% to 5% (Schinkel, Dimigen, & Marwan, 2008). It is often the case that for continuous data, such as limb movement, this radius normally is some value larger than zero (i.e., the second time series does not need to visit the exact same location as the first to be considered cross-recurrent, but instead needs only to closely approximate that space). However, depending on what the researcher is observing, having a radius greater than zero may make little sense. For example, although it may be easy to conceive of the distance between limbs in space, it may not be terribly meaningful to talk about degrees of "distance"

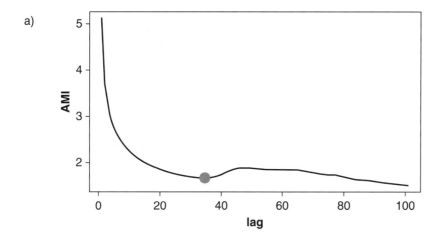

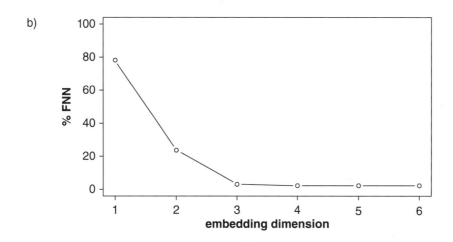

Figure 15.2 (a) Average mutual information (AMI) function of the original time series x of the Lorenz attractor. The gray circle indicates the first minimum at Lag 37. Using this value as a delay, (b) the percentage of false nearest neighbors (FNNs) was computed as a function of embedding dimension. On the basis of these outputs, the optimal parameters for phase space construction in the Lorenz example are $m = 3$ and $\tau = 37$. Note that AMI and percentage FNNs were calculated using the tseriesChaos (http://cran.r-project.org/web/packages/tseriesChaos/) package in R.

Source: Author.

between words (how might one measure the closeness between *dog* and *cat* relative to *dog* and *dock*?). Therefore, nominal (Dale & Warlaumont, 2011) and other kinds of discrete data are usually approached by setting the radius to some value approximating zero (e.g., when considering a conversation, a specific utterance must be repeated exactly for it to be considered recurrent; see Dale & Spivey, 2006).

Before continuing, let us briefly turn to a tangible example. Many basic human interactions involve the mutual handling or passing of objects. Whereas we often pass a cup or hand a tool to another with little concerted effort or thought, these tasks do in fact involve a high degree of coordination in motor movement and control. A very simple description of this problem involves not only the coordination of hand movements between actors (the focus of the interaction) but also the coordination of muscles, joints, limbs, and posture within and across actors that provides a foundation for the task at hand. To investigate the interpersonal coordinative processes involved in this sort of task, researchers have asked coactors to perform a continuous task (with a sufficiently long time series) with similar demands. For example, several studies have investigated the interpersonal coordination of hand and torso movements between two people who were asked to hold objects (e.g., pointers) in alignment with one another for an extended period of time (Athreya, Riley, & Davis, 2014; Ramenzoni, Davis, Riley, Shockley, & Baker, 2011; Ramenzoni, Riley, Shockley, & Baker, 2012). Whereas such a task obviously requires a high degree of coordination between the hand movements of the coactors, less obvious forms of postural coordination may emerge. In the present example, we focus on postural data obtained while coactors performed a similar alignment task (Nguyen, Baranowski-Pinto, & Davis, in press). In this case, two standing actors controlled computer-generated circles of various sizes (one larger than the other) that were projected onto a screen placed between them (see Figure 15.3). The movement of the circles was mapped to a motion capture sensor each participant held in his or her dominant hand. Additional measures of postural movement were collected by another motion sensor attached to each person's waist. Figure 15.3 (top) shows the normed torso trajectories of two coactors during this task. Applying the techniques outlined above, both original time series (Figure 15.3a) may be used to construct embedded time series in a shared phase space.

When dealing with two separate original time series, it is commonly the case that the optimal embedding parameters for the higher dimensional system are applied to both. This ensures that both time series are appropriately unfolded (see Figure 15.3 for an example).

Visualizing the characteristics of the reconstructed phase space is difficult when it has more than three dimensions. To this end, Eckmann, Kamphorst, and Ruelle (1987) developed a method for visualizing the recurrence of a system in a two-dimensional plot. Researchers note cross-recurrent points between the embedded time series in an $N \times M$ matrix, where N is the length of Person A's time series and M is the length of Person B's time series. Note that whereas the two time series are often the same length (as they are usually measured simultaneously under identical experimental conditions), they need not be. A line of identity (LOI) starting at point (1,1) and ending at point (N,M) can be visualized on the plot indicating points at which both time series are synchronous. Cross-recurrent points are marked at the intersections in this matrix. For example, imagine Person A visits a particular state at $t = 10$, while Person B enters an approximate state at $t = 25$. This would result in an index at (10,25) in our matrix. The resulting figure, known as a cross-recurrence plot (CRP), provides a visual representation of the deterministic processes within the systems under observation.

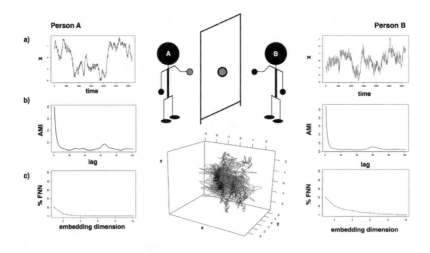

Figure 15.3 (Center) Depiction of the alignment task and original phase portrait of coactors' torso trajectories. (a) Time series of torso movements in the mediolateral (x) plane for Person A and Person B. The (b) average mutual information (AMI) and (c) percentage false nearest neighbors (FNNs) were computed separately for each time series. Because the resulting values were not identical, the values for the higher dimensional series were used. In this case, phase space was reconstructed using $m = 9$ and $\tau = 25$.

Source: Author.

Returning to our manual coalignment task, Figure 15.4a contains CRPs obtained from the medial-lateral torso movements of a single pair of participants in three separate trials. Even to the untrained eye, it should be obvious that the top and center plots are quite distinct from the plot at the bottom. As might be guessed, each plot was taken from a different experimental condition. The first two plots capture trials in which each member of the pair performed the task standing with his or her feet shoulder width apart, while in the bottom-most plot, each person stood in a tandem (heel-to-toe) stance that increased the relative difficulty of maintaining balance. One can distinguish the top and center plots by which partner controlled the larger circle. In this instance, this corresponded to differences in *role*: the person with the smaller circle had to keep his or her circle in the bounds of his or her partner's circle (in this case Person A at the top and Person B in the middle). If we were to focus only on overall performance, we might say that participants performed the task equally well in all three conditions: the performance scores indexing the percentage of time spent in alignments are nearly identical (92%, 95%, and 90%). However, looking at the CRPs, the underlying dynamics that supported the pair's performance obviously were quite distinct.

This raises several key questions: What influence does the relative role of each partner have on the temporal organization of postural coordination between actors? What changes occur in this temporal structure when posture is compromised? At a glance, insights into each of these questions can be inferred from visual inspection of the CRP. For example, patterns of adjacent recurrent points provide evidence for determinism (DET) and periodicity between the two trajectories. Diagonal lines running parallel to the line of identity occur when segments of the two trajectories evolve parallel to one another in the same region of the phase space, while the length of these lines is a measure of the duration of sustained covisitation. Vertical or horizontal lines in the CRP indicate

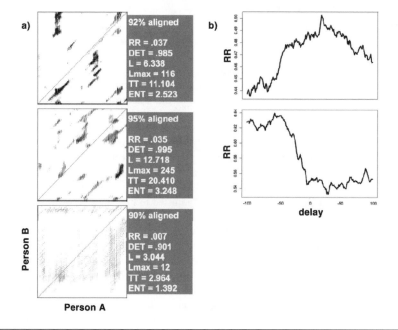

Figure 15.4 (a) Cross-recurrence plots (CRPs) and corresponding Cross-Recurrence Quantification Analysis values of interpersonal torso coordination in the mediolateral plane. Each CRP is 2,100 points squared. Solid diagonal lines bisecting the CRPs were added to represent the line of identity (LOI). (b) Diagonal recurrence rate (RR) as a function of delay corresponding to top and middle CRPs. Because the data were sampled at 100 Hz, the delays pictured represent ±1 second. Note that the top CRP corresponds to the time-series data presented in Figure 15.3.

Source: Author.

Note: DET = determinism; ENT = Shannon entropy; L = meanline (mean length of diagonal line segments); Lmax = maxline (length of the longest diagonal line in the plot); TT = trapping time (average length of vertical lines).

stationary states in which the systems persist in the same region for extended periods of time. Changes in the density of recurrent points across the CRP indicate drift or trends in the time series, whereas isolated recurrent points indicate states in the interaction that are rare and transient. As one might expect, highly coordinated and deterministic interactions tend to exhibit more structure in the CRP (long periods of diagonal and vertical lines) with fewer isolated points. For stochastic systems the opposite is true.

Cross-Recurrence Quantification Analysis

A more rigorous description of the CRP may be provided by extension of a method developed by Webber and Zbilut (1994) that begins with quantifying the instances of recurrent points. From here, CRQA proceeds to compute several measures that are based on the topography of the CRP, focusing on the number of contiguous recurrent points and densities in the diagonal and vertical line structures that form. Although many measures can be calculated in this analysis (see Marwan et al., 2007, for an extensive list), focusing on a few key measures offers interesting insights into the interactions between agents.

We have already introduced one measure, the recurrence rate (RR), a global measure of the density of recurrent points in the reconstructed phase space. We express RR in the CRP as the ratio of recurrent points to the total number of points in the plot. Researchers often view the global RR as an index of the degree of coordination (Athreya et al., 2014, Ramenzoni et al., 2011; Shockley, Santana, & Fowler, 2003; Tolston, Shockley, Riley, & Richardson, 2014; Varlet, Marin, Lagarde, & Bardy, 2011) or cognitive alignment (Richardson & Dale, 2005; Richardson, Dale, & Kirkham, 2007) between coactors. For example, Richardson et al. (2007) observed that interlocutors who were given similar briefings about a work of art exhibited higher RR of eye gaze positions when later looking at and conversing about said painting compared with participants with different briefings. This suggests that the coupling of eye movements corresponds to an aligned common ground (Clark, 1996). Consistent with a recent emphasis on embodied cognition (Clark, 2008), this alignment often appears across multiple channels (motor, linguistic) and modalities (Louwerse, Dale, Bard, & Jeuniaux, 2012; Tolston et al., 2014). It might come as little surprise, then, that many of these measures correspond to other measures of shared understanding (e.g., tests of comprehension; Richardson & Dale, 2005) between interlocutors.

Moreover, the diagonal-wise RR (the density of recurrent points along the diagonals parallel to the line of identity) provides a measure corresponding to cross-correlation lag analysis (Dale, Warlamount, & Richardson, 2011; Marwan et al., 2007; VanLear, this volume). Recalling that the LOI represents instances when the two embedded time series join in temporal synchrony, recurrent points above the LOI represent instances when Person B is visiting a state previously occupied by Person A, and vice versa for points below the LOI. The orthogonal distance from the LOI corresponds to the time lag at which the recurrent point occurs. Figure 15.4b shows the corresponding diagonal-wise RR as a function of delay for the top and middle CRPs for our present example. In contemporary research, this simple measure can identify instances of conversational dominance, as when, for example, parents lead conversations with children (Dale & Spivey, 2006; Warlaumont, Richards, Gilkerson, & Oller, 2014). In this case, decreases in the amount of overall lag often accompany typical development (i.e., children become more active initiators in the conversation as they grow older) but are not seen to the same degree in children (Warlaumont et al., 2014) or adults (Reuzel et al., 2013) with social or cognitive disorders.

Importantly, CRQA provides additional measures that quantify the patterns of coevolution of the two systems by looking for the structure of recurrent points in the CRP. The fraction of recurrent points that form diagonal lines provides an index of the predictability or determinism (DET) of the shared trajectories. Minimally, a line references two contiguous recurrent points, but for a more conservative criterion, this minimum can be adjusted to higher values. Meanline (L), the mean length of diagonal line segments, and Maxline (Lmax), the length of the longest diagonal line in the plot, provide measures of periodicity and stability in the interaction. Calculations from the vertical line segments of the CRP include laminarity (LAM)—the fraction of recurrent points forming vertical lines—and trapping time (TT), the average length of vertical lines. These measures index instances when the system remains at a specific state. Together, these line-based measures have been interpreted as capturing the rigidity, adaptability, and flexibility of a system.

For example, Gorman, Cooke, Amazeen, and Fouse (2012) observed that newly formed teams of workers are less rigid in the structure of their discrete (turn-taking) verbal exchanges (i.e., lower communication DET as measured by auto-recurrence) than those who have worked together for longer periods of time, at the same time performing at the level of or better than their more familiar counterparts. Here, adaptive flexibility in discourse was key in promoting more efficient and productive outcomes. Similar changes in conversational dynamics occur between parents and children. Measuring the lengths of both the child's and parent's respective utterances, Cox and van Dijk (2013) observed decreases in the rigidity (indicated by decreases in TT and LAM) of shared grammatical forms as the child developed from 1.5 to 2.5 years of age.

Returning to our present alignment task, Figure 15.4a presents the aforementioned CRQA measures alongside the example CRPs. I also included the Shannon entropy (ENT), a measure of the distribution of lengths of the diagonal lines that indexes the complexity of the interaction; as well as trend, which indexes the degree of its overall stationarity. Here, differences in CRQA measures indicate changes in the postural organization between individuals. Recall that for each case presented in Figure 15.4, participants' performance was nearly identical. However, distinctions between the two uppermost CRPs and the bottom CRP suggest that how the pairs went about completing the alignment task clearly differed. Briefly, overall coordination between coactors' torsos was greater (RR), was more stable (Lmax), and exhibited longer and more frequent periods of coevolution (DET and L) and stationarity (TT) when participants were in a stable stance compared with when faced with a challenge to postural stability. That overall performance was not impaired invites further questions related to a compensatory, synergistic relationship between postural coordination and other components (e.g., coordination at the hands, interpersonal coordination between hand and torso; Ramenzoni et al., 2011). At the same time, differences in the topography of recurrent points between the top and middle plots suggest that the leader-follower dynamic between coactors changed with assigned roles. More specifically, the person controlling the larger circle appears to lead the interaction (top, Person A; middle, Person B).

In addition, epoching can help determine how CRQA outputs change over time. Here, the original time series may be subdivided into overlapping windows of a set length, and CRQA is performed on each of these windows. This technique provides snapshots of how the system is evolving. For example, for some metastable, deterministic systems, DET remains invariant over time despite large fluctuations in RR (Webber & Zbilut, 1994). Dramatic changes in the DET/RR ratio can be interpreted as indicating points of transition at which the system is moving from one steady state (behavior) to another. Similar interpretations have been gained from changes in ENT (Stephen, Dixon, & Isenhower, 2009).

In experimental designs, where appropriate, the output CRQA values can be submitted to statistical analyses (e.g., analysis of variance, mixed models) to uncover systematic differences in experimental conditions. Often these methods use surrogate time series as a control to demonstrate that the observed measures of interpersonal coordination are not incidental. Often-used surrogates include creating virtual partners (e.g., comparing the time series of two participants who both performed the task but were members of different experimental dyads) or creating a randomized shuffle of the original time series. The former maintains the temporal dynamics of the time series but (depending on the task) destroys the interaction dynamics between coactors; the latter completely destroys any temporal structure of values in the time series while preserving their distribution.

Conclusions

The use of nonlinear methods in behavioral research has grown exponentially in the past decade, including CRQA, which is useful in most cases when one wants to assess the time-dependent coordination of two interacting systems. Although in this chapter I have briefly highlighted examples related to simple motor control and conversation, it should be emphasized that this technique has been used to investigate patterns of coordination for wide range of psychological and social phenomena, including dance (Washburn et al., 2014), team problem solving (Shockley, Baker, Richardson, & Fowler, 2007; Shockley et al., 2003; Strang, Funke, Russell, Dukes, & Middendorf, 2014), shared community rituals (Konvalinka et al., 2011), song recognition (Serrà, Serra, & Andrzejak, 2009), and semiotics (Orsucci et al., 2006) (for a comprehensive review, see Fusaroli, Konvalinka, & Wallot, 2014). Compared with other methods of analysis, CRQA is well equipped to handle the kinds of time-series data that those studying human behavior routinely encounter, data that are often noisy and exhibit significant nonstationarity (Strang et al., 2014). For research in these arenas, CRQA offers a wonderful complement to more traditional, aggregate measures, allowing investigators to characterize the dynamics of the processes unfolding during interpersonal coordination as well as their outcomes.

References

Abarbanel, H.D.I. (1996). *Analysis of observed chaotic data*. New York: Springer-Verlag.

Athreya, D. N., Riley, M. A., & Davis, T. J. (2014). Visual influences on postural and manual interpersonal coordination during a joint precision task. *Experimental Brain Research, 232*, 2741–2751.

Cao, L. (1997). Practical method for determining the minimum embedding dimension of a scalar time series. *Physica D, 110*, 43–50.

Clark, A. (2008). *Supersizing the mind: Embodiment, action, and cognitive extension*. Oxford, UK: Oxford University Press.

Clark, H. H. (1996). *Using language*. Cambridge, UK: Cambridge University Press.

Coco, M. I., & Dale, R. (2014). Cross-recurrence quantification analysis of categorical and continuous time series: An R package. *Frontiers in Psychology, 5*.

Cox, R.F.A., & van Dijk, M. (2013). Microdevelopment in parent-child conversations: From global changes to flexibility. *Ecological Psychology, 25*, 304–315.

Dale, R., & Spivey, M. J. (2006). Unraveling the dyad: Using recurrence analysis to explore patterns of syntactic coordination between children and caregivers in conversation. *Language Learning, 56*, 391–430.

Dale, R., & Warlaumont, A. S. (2011). Nominal cross recurrence as a generalized lag sequential analysis for behavioral streams. *Chaos, 21*, 1153–1161.

Eckmann, J. P., Kamphorst, S. O., & Ruelle, D. (1987). Recurrence plots of dynamical systems. *Europhysics Letters, 4*, 973–977.

Fraser, A. M., & Swinney, H. L. (1986). Independent coordinates for strange attractors from mutual information. *Physical Review A, 33*, 1134.

Fusaroli, R., Konvalinka, I., & Wallot, S. (2014). Analyzing social interactions: The promises and challenges of using cross recurrence quantification analysis. *Springer Proceedings in Mathematics & Statistics, 103*, 137–155.

Gorman, J. C., Cooke, N. J., Amazeen, P. G., & Fouse, S. (2012). Measuring patterns in team interaction sequences using a discrete recurrence approach. *Human Factors, 54*, 503–517.

Juarrero, A. (1999). *Dynamics in action*. Cambridge, MA: MIT Press.

Konvalinka, I., Xygalatas, D., Bulbulia, J., Schjodt, U., Jegindø, E. M., Wallot, S., . . . Roepstorff, A. (2011). Synchronized arousal between performers and related spectators in a fire-walking ritual. *Proceedings of the National Academy of Sciences of the United States of America, 108*, 8514–8519.

Lorenz, E. N. (1963). Deterministic nonperiodic flow. *Journal of the Atmospheric Sciences, 20*, 130–141.

Louwerse, M. M., Dale, R., Bard, E. G., & Jeuniaux, P. (2012). Behavior matching in multimodal communication is synchronized. *Cognitive Science, 36*, 1404–1426.

Marwan, N., Romano, M. C., Thiel, M., & Kurths, J. (2007). Recurrence plots for the analysis of complex systems. *Physics Reports, 438*, 237–329.

Nguyen, M., Baranowski-Pinto, G., & Davis, T. J. (2015). The influence of individual postural demands on role in interpersonal coordination. In J. Weast-Knapp, M. Malone, & D. Abney (Eds.), *Studies in Perception & Action XIII*. London: Taylor & Francis.

Orsucci, F., Giuliani, A., Webber, C., Jr., Zbilut, J., Fonagy, P., & Mazza, M. (2006). Combinatorics and synchronization in natural semiotics. *Physica A: Statistical Mechanics and Its Applications, 361*, 665–676.

Poincaré, H. J. (1993). *Les méthodes nouvelles de la mécanique céleste, Vols. 1–3* (D. Goroff, Ed.). New York: American Institute of Physics. (Original work published 1892, 1893, and 1899)

Ramenzoni, V. C., Davis, T., Riley, M. A., Shockley, K., & Baker, A. A. (2011). Joint action in a cooperative precision task: Nested processes of intrapersonal and interpersonal coordination. *Experimental Brain Research, 211*, 447–457.

Ramenzoni, V. C., Riley, M. A., Shockley, K., & Baker, A. A. (2012). Interpersonal and intrapersonal coordinative modes for joint and single task performance. *Human Movement Science, 31*, 1253–1267.

Reuzel, E., Embregts, P.J.C.M., Bosman, A.M.T., Van Nieuwenhuijzen, M., & Jahoda, A. (2013). Interactional patterns between staff and clients with borderline to mild intellectual disabilities. *Journal of Intellectual Disability Research, 5*, 53–66.

Richardson, D. C., & Dale, R. (2005). Looking to understand: The coupling between speakers' and listeners' eye movements and its relationship to discourse comprehension. *Cognitive Science, 29*, 1045–1060.

Richardson, D. C., Dale, R., & Kirkham, N. Z. (2007). The art of conversation is coordination: Common ground and the coupling of eye movements during dialogue. *Psychological Science, 18*, 407–413.

Riley, M. A., Richardson, M. J., Shockley, K., & Ramenzoni, V. C. (2011). Interpersonal synergies. *Frontiers in Psychology, 2*.

Schinkel, S., Dimigen, O., & Marwan, N. (2008). Selection of recurrence threshold for signal detection. *European Physical Journal—Special Topics, 164*, 45–53.

Serrà, J., Serra, X., & Andrzejak, R. G. (2009). Cross recurrence quantification for cover song identification. *New Journal of Physics, 11*, 093017.

Shockley, K. (2005). Cross recurrence quantification of interpersonal postural activity. In M. A. Riley & G. C. Van Orden (Eds.), *Tutorials in contemporary nonlinear methods for the behavioral sciences: Proceedings of the National Science Foundation Workshop on Nonlinear Methods in Psychology* (pp. 142–177). Washington, DC: National Science Foundation.

Shockley, K., Baker, A. A., Richardson, M. J., & Fowler, C. A. (2007). Articulatory constraints on interpersonal postural coordination. *Journal of Experimental Psychology: Human Perception and Performance, 33*, 201–208.

Shockley, K., Santana, M. V., & Fowler, C. A. (2003). Mutual interpersonal postural constraints are involved in cooperative conversation. *Journal of Experimental Psychology: Human Perception and Performance, 29*, 326–332.

Stephen, D. G., Dixon, J. A., & Isenhower, R. W. (2009). Dynamics of representational change: Entropy, action, and cognition. *Journal of Experimental Psychology: Human Perception and Performance, 35*, 1811–1832.

Strang, A. J., Funke, G. J., Russell, S. M., Dukes, A. W., & Middendorf, M. S. (2014). Physio-behavioral coupling in a cooperative team task: Contributors and relations. *Journal of Experimental Psychology: Human Perception and Performance, 40*, 145–158.

Takens, F. (1981). Detecting strange attractors in turbulence. In D. Rand & L.-S. Young (Eds.), *Lecture notes in mathematics* (Vol. 898, pp. 366–381). Berlin, Germany: Springer.

Tolston, M. T., Shockley, K., Riley, M. A., & Richardson, M. J. (2014). Movement constraints on interpersonal coordination and communication. *Journal of Experimental Psychology: Human Perception and Performance, 40*, 1891–1902.

Van Orden, G. C., Holden, J. G., & Turvey, M. T. (2003). Self-organization of cognitive performance. *Journal of Experimental Psychology: General, 132*, 331–350.

Varlet, M., Marin, L., Lagarde, J., & Bardy, B. G. (2011). Social postural coordination. *Journal of Experimental Psychology: Human Perception and Performance, 37*, 473–483.

Warlaumont, A. S., Richards, J. A., Gilkerson, J., & Oller, D. K. (2014). A social feedback loop for speech development and its reduction in autism. *Psychological Science, 25*, 1314–1324.

Washburn, A., DeMarco, M., de Vries, S., Ariyabuddhiphongs, K., Schmidt, R. C., Richardson, M. J., & Riley, M. A. (2014). Dancers entrain more effectively than nondancers to another actor's movements. *Frontiers in Human Neuroscience, 8*, 800.

Webber, C. L., & Zbilut, J. P. (1994). Dynamical assessment of physiological systems and states using recurrence plot strategies. *Journal of Applied Physiology, 76*, 965–973.

Zbilut, J. P., Giuliani, A., & Webber, C. L., Jr. (1998). Detecting deterministic signals in exceptionally noisy environments using cross-recurrence quantification. *Physics Letters A, 246*, 122–128.

Zbilut, J. P., Thomasson, N., & Webber, C. (2002). Recurrence quantification analysis as a tool for nonlinear exploration of nonstationary cardiac signals. *Medical Engineering and Physics, 24*, 53–60.

Endnotes

1. Please make no mistake, the present chapter is not intended as a critique of this framework. One cannot deny its relative success and importance in the rise of behavioral science in the 20th century. Rather, there is a growing appreciation that in order to improve our understanding of human interactions, new tools that include the temporal dimension of behavior are also warranted.

2. Interested readers are invited to visit http://www.recurrence-plot.tk/programmes.php for an extensive list of currently available tools. Unless otherwise noted, the examples here use Marwan's CRP toolbox (http://tocsy.pik-potsdam.de/CRPtoolbox/), a freely available command-line toolkit. For those inclined to R (http://cran.r-project.org) Coco and Dale (2014) recently developed a wonderful package that incorporates many of the methods mentioned in this chapter.

INDEX

ABOUT THE EDITORS

C. Arthur VanLear earned his PhD from the University of Utah. He is an Associate Professor in the Department of Communication at The University of Connecticut. He has published a number of scholarly articles and sat on the editorial boards of major communication journals, as well as interdisciplinary journals dealing with personal relationships. His co-authored article won the B. Aubrey Fisher Outstanding Article Award in 2005. He has authored or co-authored a number of book chapters in interpersonal communication, social and personal relationships, and research methods. He is the co-editor (with James Watt) of *Dynamic Patterns in Communication Processes* (Sage, 1996). His research interests have focused on relational communication (e.g., relationship formation, marital and family communication, and support in the addiction recovery process, and self-fulfilling prophecies) and both methodological and theoretical issues involved in dynamic modeling of interpersonal processes including behavioral interaction analysis and longitudinal and time-series analyses of communication.

Daniel J. Canary (PhD, University of Southern California, 1983) is an adjunct professor at the University of Utah. He has formerly taught at Penn State University, Arizona State University, Ohio University, California State University Fullerton, and elsewhere. A current member of several editorial boards, Professor Canary's research interests revolve around the symbiotic association between interpersonal communication and personal relationships. With over 10 books and 75 articles and book chapters, his particular research interests include relational maintenance strategies, interpersonal conflict management, and conversational argument. Dan is a former president of the Western States Communication Association and the International Network on Personal Relationships.

ABOUT THE CONTRIBUTORS

Tamara D. Afifi is a Professor in the Department of Communication Studies at the University of Iowa. Her research focuses on communication patterns that foster risk and resiliency in families and other interpersonal relationships, with particular emphasis on: (1) information regulation and (2) how people communicate when they are stressed and the impact of these communication patterns on personal and relational health. Her research examines how environmental factors interact with family members' communication patterns (e.g., conflict, stressful disclosures, social support, avoidance, verbal rumination, communal coping) to affect stress, adaptation, growth, and physical/mental/relational health. Professor Afifi is the editor elect for *Communication Monographs*. She has also received numerous research awards, including the Young Scholar Award from the International Communication Association in 2006, the Brommel Award for a distinguished career of research in family communication from the National Communication Association (NCA) in 2011, and three distinguished article awards from the NCA.

Janet Beavin Bavelas was educated at Stanford (A.B., Psychology; A.M., Communication Research; PhD, Psychology) and has spent her academic career at the University of Victoria, where she is currently an active Emeritus Professor of Psychology. She has co-authored *Pragmatics of Human Communication* (1967) and *Equivocal Communication* (1990) as well as over 90 journal articles or book chapters. Bavelas and her research team conduct experiments on the unique features of face-to-face dialogue, specifically, the integration of words and co-speech acts (hand and facial gestures, gaze) and the moment-by-moment collaboration between speakers and addressee. Microanalysis of face-to-face dialogue (MFD) developed out of this program of research. More recently, the team have been applying this method and their findings to dialogues outside the lab: in psychotherapy, medicine, parent-infant interaction, and computer-mediated interaction. (see http://web.uvic.ca/psyc/bavelas/) Academic honors include Fellowships in the Royal Society of Canada, the International Communication Association, and the Canadian Psychological Association.

Judee K. Burgoon is Professor of Communication, Family Studies and Human Development at the University of Arizona, where she is Director of Research for the Center for the Management of Information and Site Director for the Center for Identification Technology Research, a National Science Foundation Industry/University Cooperative Research Center. She has authored or edited 14 books and monographs and over 300 published articles, chapters, and reviews related to nonverbal and verbal communication, interpersonal deception, and computer-mediated communication. Her current program of research centers on developing tools and methods for automated detection of deception and has been funded by the National Science Foundation, Department of Defense, and Department of Homeland Security, among others.

Heather E. Canary (PhD, Arizona State University) is Associate Professor, Department of Communication, University of Utah. Her primary research focus is communication across lay and professional groups, particularly processes of knowledge construction and decision-making among family members and health care professionals. Dr. Canary conducts studies in family and organizational contexts involving health, disability, and policy implementation. She has published articles in *The American Journal of Public Health, Communication Theory,* and *Management Communication Quarterly,* among other scholarly journals. Dr. Canary co-authored the book *Family Conflict* and co-edited the book *Communication and*

Organizational Knowledge: Contemporary Issues for Theory and Practice. She has chapters in several edited volumes, including the *Handbook of Communication Science* and *The SAGE Encyclopedia of Health Communication.*

Jennifer A. Cummings is an Assistant Professor (Lecturer) in the Department of Management at the David Eccles School of Business at the University of Utah. She received a Ph.D. in Communication from the University of Utah in the Department of Communication. Her research interests include relational communication, interpersonal and family communication, mother/daughter relationships, health communication, and organizational communication. She currently teaches communication in the undergraduate and MBA programs. She is also a certified conflict mediator and communication consultant.

Tehran J. Davis is an Assistant Professor of Psychology at the University of Connecticut and faculty member at the Center for the Ecological Study of Perception and Action (CESPA). He received his Ph. D. from the University of Cincinnati in 2012. His main research interests lie in ecological and dynamical systems approaches to the selection, control, and coordination of action, including applications to joint action and interpersonal coordination within multi-agent systems.

Amanda Denes, PhD, is an Assistant Professor in the Department of Communication at the University of Connecticut. She received her PhD in Communication from the University of California, Santa Barbara, with an emphasis in Feminist Studies. Her primary area of specialization is interpersonal communication, with emphases in disclosure, sexuality, and identity. Much of her work looks at the association between communication in interpersonal relationships and people's physiological, psychological, and relational health. In particular, she is interested in why individuals disclose information about themselves to others, how they disclose that information, and the effects of such disclosures on individuals and their relationships.

Norah E. Dunbar is a Professor of Communication at University of California Santa Barbara. She teaches courses in nonverbal and interpersonal communication, communication theory, and deception detection. She was the Principal Investigator of a $5.4 million contract from the Intelligence Advanced Research Projects Activity in 2011-2013 and has had her research funded by the National Science Foundation, the Central Intelligence Agency, and the

Center for Identification Technology Research. She has published over 35 peer-reviewed journal articles and book chapters and has presented over 60 papers at national and international conferences. Her research has appeared in journals such as *Communication Research, Communication Monographs*, and *Journal of Computer-Mediated Communication* as well as interdisciplinary journals such as *Journal of Management Information Systems* and *Computers in Human Behavior*. She has served on the editorial board of six disciplinary journals and is the Chair of the Nonverbal Division of the National Communication Association.

Aaron C. Elkins is a Postdoctoral Researcher in the MIS department at the University of Arizona. Aaron was previously a Research Fellow at the Intelligent Behaviour Understanding Group at Imperial College London and the National Center for Border Security and Immigration, a Department of Homeland Security Center of Excellence. Aaron conducts laboratory and field experiments that investigate how the voice, face, body, and language reveal emotion, deception, and cognition for human-computer interaction applications. He also researches how decision makers will actually use and are affected by these artificial intelligence-based technologies.

Jennifer Gerwing (PhD, Psychology, University of Victoria, Canada) uses microanalysis in both lab experiments and applied settings. Her experiments focus on the effects of face-to-face dialogue on hand and facial gestures, especially in relation to speech. She applies microanalysis in clinical settings, including her present position as a senior researcher at the Health Services Research Center at Akershus University Hospital in Oslo, Norway. Jennifer's main interest is multimodality, specifically the semantic role that hand and facial gestures play in clinical interactions and how these modalities integrate with speech to convey essential information. She is currently studying videotaped clinical interactions that involve a language barrier between patient and health care provider. She has also studied interactional coordination, both in home videos of triplets, one of whom was later diagnosed with autism, and also in medical emergency telephone dialogues. Jennifer collaborates with researchers in Canada, the US, the UK, and Norway.

Laura K. Guerrero is a Professor in the Hugh Downs School of Human Communication at Arizona State University. Her research focuses on relational, nonverbal, and emotional communication, with an emphasis on how communication affects relationships in positive and negative ways. She has studied how people communicate intimacy and forgiveness as ways to keep relationships healthy. She has also looked at how people communicate in situations where they are jealous, hurt, or angry. She has published over 100 articles and chapters on these topics, as well as several books, including *Close Encounters: Communication in Relationships* (Guerrero, Andersen & Afifi, 2014), *Nonverbal Communication in Close Relationships* (Guerrero & Floyd, 2006), *Nonverbal Communication* (Burgoon, Guerrero, & Floyd, 2010), *The Nonverbal Communication Reader* (Guerrero & Hecht, 2008), and *The Handbook of Communication and Emotion* (Andersen & Guerrero, 1998).

Ruben C. Gur received his BA in Psychology and Philosophy from the Hebrew University of Jerusalem, Israel, in 1970 and his MA and PhD in Psychology (Clinical) from Michigan State University in 1971 and 1973, respectively. He did Postdoctoral training with E.R. Hilgard at Stanford University and came to Penn as Assistant Professor in 1974. His research has been in the study of brain and behavior in healthy people and patients with brain disorders, with a special emphasis on exploiting neuroimaging as experimental probes. His work has documented sex differences, aging effects, and abnormalities in regional brain function associated with schizophrenia, affective disorders, stroke, epilepsy, movement disorders, and dementia. His work has been supported by grants from the NIMH, NIH, NIA, NINDS, NSF, DOD, private foundations (Spencer, MacArthur, EJLB, Brain and Behavior Research Foundation), and industry (Pfizer, AstraZeneca, Lilly, Merck).

Jihan Hamm is a Research Scientist at the Department of Computer Science and Engineering, the Ohio State University. He received his PhD from the University of Pennsylvania in 2008, with a focus on dimensionality reduction for machine learning. He was a postdoctoral researcher at the Penn medical school working on machine learning applications in medical data analysis, including computational morphological analysis of medical images and analysis of facial expression for affect disorders.

He has a best paper award from medical imaging (MedIA-MICCAI, 2010), and was also a finalist for MICCAI Young Scientist Publication Impact Award (2013). His recent research is focused on machine learning problems in big data analysis.

Sara Healing obtained her degrees in the Department of Psychology at the University of Victoria (Canada). Her honours thesis was an experiment on the effects of two different lines of questioning about the same task and was subsequently published in a psychotherapy journal. For her M.Sc. thesis, she developed a microanalysis that identified the unique information an individual patient can contribute to oncology consultations. Her primary research interests are using microanalysis to study face-to-face dialogue, and she has collaborated in 18 such studies, including both basic research in lab experiments and applications of the method in various applied settings, especially medical and psychotherapy dialogues. Her publications include experiments on hand and facial gestures in psycholinguistics journals, bad-news delivery in a medical journal, and a chapter in a language and social interaction handbook. As part of Victoria Microanalysis Associates, she teaches international professional workshops on microanalysis and communication research.

Colin Hesse, Assistant Professor, joined the Department of Speech Communication at Oregon State University in September 2013. Colin completed his PhD at Arizona State University in 2009. His research focuses on the links between interpersonal communication and both psychological and physiological health. Specific communication processes of interest include the communication of affection, alexithymia, and family communication.

Dean E. Hewes is a Professor of Communication Studies at the University of Minnesota, Minneapolis. He specialized in group communication, interpersonal communication, the cognitive bases of communication, and process analysis techniques. His publications have appeared in such outlets as *Communication Monographs, Human Communication Research, Quarterly Journal of Speech, Communication Research,* and the *Journal of Communication,* as well as chapters in numerous edited books.

Christian G. Kohler, MD, is associate professor of psychiatry and neurology at the Hospital of the University of Pennsylvania, PA. Dr. Kohler received his medical degree from Innsbruck University in Austria and underwent specialty training at Wright State University and the University of Cincinnati in Ohio, and the University of Pennsylvania, where he is medical director of the neuropsychiatry section. Over the past 20 years, Dr. Kohler has investigated emotion processing in persons with schizophrenia, in particular emotion recognition and emotion expression. His research has been supported through grants from the National Institutes of Mental Health and private foundations.

Erina L. MacGeorge (PhD, University of Illinois) is associate professor in communication arts and sciences at the Pennsylvania State University. She studies how communication influences problem-solving, decision-making, and coping, with a focus on advice and support in interactions between friends, and with regard to health issues that include miscarriage, bipolar disorder, and breast cancer. Her work has been funded by the National Science Foundation.

Nickola C. Overall is an Associate Professor of Social Psychology at the University of Auckland, New Zealand. Nickola's research interests focus on identifying the factors that determine the relative success of different communication strategies used when relationship partners are trying to resolve conflict or support each other. Nickola also examines how depression, attachment insecurities, and sexist attitudes effect relationship functioning, and the relationship and family processes that exacerbate or overcome these difficulties. Nickola's primary methodological aim is to assess people's relationship perceptions and behavior as it matters in real-life. To achieve this, Nickola combines various methodologies, including behavioral observation, social interaction, and daily diaries, and longitudinal designs to track individual and relationship progress over time. Nickola has published over 60 empirical research articles and book chapters, and she is currently Associate Editor for *Social Psychological and Personality Science*.

Marshall Scott Poole (Ph.D University of Wisconsin-Madison) is David L. Swanson Professor of Communication, Senior Research Scientist at the National Center for Supercomputing Applications, and Director of the Institute for Computing in the Humanities, Arts, and Social Sciences at the University of Illinois Urbana-Champaign. His research interests include group and organizational communication, information systems, collaboration technologies, organizational innovation, and theory construction. He has authored or edited 11 books and over 150 articles, book chapters, and proceedings publications.

L. Edna Rogers (PhD, Michigan State University) is a professor of Communication at the University of Utah. Her research focuses on the interaction processes of interpersonal relationships with a special emphasis on marital and family communication systems. She is a past president of the International Communication Association and, across her career, a recipient of multiple teaching and research awards.

Wendy Samter serves as Dean of the College of Arts and Sciences at Bryant University. In that role, she is responsible for eight academic departments, fifteen undergraduate majors, and three graduate programs. As a scholar of interpersonal communication, Dr. Samter's research focuses on communication skills predictive of relational success across the lifespan. In particular, her work examines how individual differences in social cognition, beliefs about the role communication skills play in relationships, and skill performance influence a person's ability to initiate and maintain successful interpersonal relationships. Dr. Samter has also explored how definitions and enactments of relevant communication skills vary as a function of age, ethnicity, relationship type, and context. She has published widely with books and articles, served as journal editor, and received numerous awards for her teaching.

David R. Seibold is a professor of technology management (and an affiliate professor of communication) at the University of California, Santa Barbara. Author of more than 150 scholarly publications in communication, psychology, and management, his research examines argument, influence, and group decision making; communication and temporality; and innovation and organizational change. A former editor of the *Journal of Applied Communication Research* and recipient of numerous career awards and recognitions for individual papers, he is a Distinguished Scholar in the National Communication Association and a Fellow of the International Communication Association.

Alan L. Sillars teaches classes related to interpersonal communication, conflict processes, and family relationships at the University of Montana. He is best known for his research on conflict and interpersonal perception in close relationships and families, which includes a number of observational studies. Sillars is the former Editor of *Communication Monographs* and twice received the Franklin H. Knower Award from the National Communication Association (USA) for the best article published on interpersonal communication. He also received the Bernard J. Brommel Award for outstanding scholarship in family communication and the Mark L. Knapp Award honoring career contributions to the study of interpersonal communication.

Christine Tomori's degrees are from the University of Victoria (Canada). Her honours thesis, which was later published, used microanalysis to compare the communication patterns of therapists using two different approaches. Her MSc thesis developed the

Patient-centred assessment of symptoms and activities (P-CASA), based on the individual patient's priorities rather than a standard list of symptoms. As part of Victoria Microanalysis Associates, Tomori has developed and taught international professional workshops on microanalysis and contemporary communication research for practitioners. including psychotherapists, coaches, and physicians. She has a particular interest and expertise in solution-focused brief therapy and coaching. She is currently the principal of Tomori Solutions, Ltd., a consulting company that provides research, project management, and professional development within the fields of health care administration and communicative processes in applied settings (workplace, health, social services). Current clients are: BC Ministry of Health, Vancouver Coastal Health Authority, and the Victoria Division of Family Practice.

Ragini Verma is an Associate Professor in Section of Biomedical Image Analysis (SBIA) and the Center for Biomedical Image Computing and Analytics, Department of Radiology at University of Pennsylvania. She has masters in mathematics and computer applications followed by a PhD in computer vision and mathematics, from IIT Delhi (India). She did a postdoc at INRIA, Rhone-Alpes, with the MOVI project (currently LEARS and PERCEPTION) on computer vision, followed by a post doc in medical imaging at SBIA, prior to taking up her current position. Ragini's research interest spans the area of diffusion imaging, structural and functional connectomics, and facial expression analysis. She is actively involved in several clinical studies in schizophrenia, autism, and brain tumors as well as projects in animal imaging, and imaging studies of sex differences.

Harry Weger, Jr. (PhD, University of Arizona) is an Associate Professor in the Nicholson School of Communication at the University of Central Florida in Orlando. His research using the Conversational Argument Coding Scheme goes back to his graduate school days where his thesis advisor was Dan Canary. Besides his work on interpersonal argument, his research covers topics including nonverbal communication, argumentation in televised political debates, argumentation theory, cross-sex friendship, compliance gaining in customer service encounters, and identity confirmation in personal relationships. Dr. Weger's research appears in a variety of journals such as *Communication Monographs, Communication Methods and Measures, Journal of Hospitality Marketing, Social Psychology, Argumentation,* and *Journal of Social and Personal Relationships.*

Lesley A. Withers, PhD, is the Interim Associate Dean for the College of Communication and Fine Arts and a Professor of Communication at Central Michigan University. Her research interests are in the "dark side" of interpersonal communication (embarrassment, communication apprehension, aversive online behavior) and collaboration in virtual worlds (online social support; issues of identity, presence, pedagogical potential in Second Life®). Her research has been published in the *Journal of Applied Communication Research, the Western Journal of Communication,* and *Personality and Individual Differences* and she has presented at regional, national, and international conferences. Dr. Withers and her co-authors received the 2005 B. Aubrey Fisher Outstanding Article Award from the Western States Communication Association for their article, "*AA online: The enactment of computer mediated social support.*" She's been interviewed about online anger and sharing secrets by CNN.com and about obscene gestures by National Public Radio.